Special Edition

Using

Using
MICROSOFT®
FrontPage 98
Second Edition

W9-AOC-971

que®

Special Edition

Using

Using
MICROSOFT®
FrontPage 98
Second Edition

Dennis Jones, Neil Randall

Special Edition Using Microsoft™ FrontPage 98

Library of Congress Catalog No.: 97-68704

ISBN: 0-7897-1343-8

99 98   6 5 4 3

Interpretation of the printing code: the rightmost double-digit number is the year of the book's printing; the rightmost single-digit number, the number of the book's printing. For example, a printing code of 97-1 shows that the first printing of the book occurred in 1997.

Screen reproductions in this book were created with Collage Plus from Inner Media, Inc., Hollis, NH.

Contents at a Glance

VI | Using the FrontPage 98 SDK

VII | Integrating Microsoft FrontPage 98 and Microsoft Office

VIII | Using Other Servers with FrontPage 98

IX | Advanced Database Connectivity

X | Appendixes

Table of Contents

IV | Integrating Active Content into Your Web

17   Using ActiveX Controls   343

18   Scripting with VBScript   369

V | Building and Managing a Web

X | Appendixes

Credits

PRESIDENT
Roland Elgey

SENIOR VICE PRESIDENT/PUBLISHING
Don Fowley

GENERAL MANAGER
Joe Muldoon

MANAGER OF PUBLISHING OPERATIONS
Linda H. Buehler

PUBLISHING MANAGER
Tim Ryan

EDITORIAL SERVICES DIRECTOR
Carla Hall

MANAGING EDITOR
Patrick Kanouse

ACQUISITIONS MANAGER
Cheryl D. Willoughby

ACQUISITIONS EDITORS
Jeff Taylor
Philip Wescott

PRODUCT DIRECTORS
Ben Milstead
Jácquelyn Mosley Eley

PRODUCTION EDITOR
Jim Bowie

EDITOR
Judy Ohm

COORDINATOR OF EDITORIAL SERVICES
Maureen A. McDaniel

WEBMASTER
Thomas H. Bennett

PRODUCT MARKETING MANAGER
Kourtnaye Sturgeon

ASSISTANT PRODUCT MARKETING MANAGER
Gretchen Schlesinger

TECHNICAL EDITORS
Rick Darnell
Patricio S. Incé

SOFTWARE SPECIALIST
Adam Swetnam

SOFTWARE RELATIONS COORDINATOR
Susan D. Gallagher

SOFTWARE COORDINATOR
Andrea Duvall

EDITORIAL ASSISTANTS
Jennifer L. Chisholm
Wendy Layton

BOOK DESIGNERS
Ruth Harvey
Kim Scott

COVER DESIGNER
Sandra Schroeder

PRODUCTION TEAM
Maribeth Echard
Trey Frank
Julie Geeting
Laura A. Knox

INDEXER
Craig Small

Composed in *Century Old Style* and *ITC Franklin Gothic* by Que Corporation.

About the Authors

Dennis Jones is a freelance technical writer, software trainer, creative writing teacher, and novelist. He lives near Ottawa, Canada.

Neil Randall is the author or coauthor of several Internet books, including Special Edition Using Microsoft FrontPage 97 (Que). He writes the bi-weekly PC Tech Tutor column for PC Magazine, and contributes regularly to the Internet and Operating Systems columns for that magazine as well. He has also published in many other magazines, including Windows, CD-ROM Today, The Net, and Internet World. As a professor of English at the University of Waterloo (Canada), he teaches and researches multimedia design and professional communication at the undergraduate and graduate levels. He can be reached at **nrandall@watarts.uwaterloo.ca**.

Ryan Sutter has been a computer nut since he got his first Commodore VIC20 in 1982. He specializes in Internet/intranet development and currently works for Bloomington, Minnesota based Performark, Inc., doing such. He also runs a small media company called Nuclear Gopher Productions, located on the Web at **http://www.nucleargopher.com**. When he isn't busy with either of those things, he writes freelance, listens to jazz, plays basketball and spends most of his free time with his wife, son, cat and fish (respectively: Tabithah, Sydney, Parker and Hera).

Robert Niles is a systems administrator and Web programmer for InCommand Inc., a company located in Yakima, Washington that specializes in Internet and intranet applications. Robert loves all things Internet and has been online since 1983. He specializes in the UNIX environment, Perl, and SQL. Previously, he was a coauthor of QUE's *CGI by Example* and *Special Edition Using CGI*. Robert lives in Selah, Washington with his wife, Kimberly; his son, Michael; and his daughter, Shaela. You can find him on the Web at **http://www.selah.net/cgi.html** or via email at **rniles@selah.net**.

Scott Warner is a private consultant in the computer and publishing arenas. He has written and contributed to numerous computer books including: *Platinum Edition Using Office 97, Special Edition Using Office 97, Easy Windows NT Workstation 4.0, 10 Minute Guide to Microsoft Exchange 5.0, Special Edition Using SQL Server*, and *Special Edition Using PowerBuilder*. He graduated from Purdue University in Computer Information Systems, worked in computer and publishing positions, and currently lives in Arizona. Visit his Web site at **www.infinet-is.com/~warner**.

Sue Charlesworth has 14 years experience in PC software development, holding various roles from tester to programmer to team leader responsible for developing quality assurance standards and high-performance test teams. She has a master's degree in international management. Over the years, she has found that her most enjoyable work involves writing and helping others as a knowledge resource. This has led to recent work in HTML Web page development and multimedia courseware authoring. Sue currently works for United Airlines, programming mutimedia lessons for pilot ground school.

Acknowledgments

I'd like to thank the Que editorial staff, particularly Jeff Taylor and Jim Bowie, for helping to make the writing of this edition of the book an almost painless experience. I'd also like to thank my coauthor Neil Randall for his help in unravelling some of the more arcane mysteries of FrontPage 98.—Dennis Jones

We'd Like to Hear from You!

Que Corporation has a long-standing reputation for high-quality books and products. To ensure your continued satisfaction, we also understand the importance of customer service and support.

Tech Support

If you need assistance with the information in this book or with a CD/disk accompanying the book, please access Macmillan Computer Publishing's online Knowledge Base at **http://www.superlibrary.com/general/support**.

Also be sure to visit Que's Web resource center for all the latest information, enhancements, errata, downloads, and more. It's located at **http://www.quecorp.com/**.

Orders, Catalogs, and Customer Service

To order other Que or Macmillan Computer Publishing books, catalogs, or products, please contact our Customer Service Department at **800/428-5331** or fax us at **800/835-3202** (International Fax: 317/228-4400). Or visit our online bookstore at **http://www.mcp.com/**.

Comments and Suggestions

We want you to let us know what you like or dislike most about this book or other Que products. Your comments will help us to continue publishing the best books available on computer topics in today's market.

Tim Ryan
Executive Editor
201 West 103rd Street
Indianapolis, Indiana 46290 USA
E-mail: **tryan@mcp.com**

Please be sure to include the book's title and author as well as your name and phone or fax number. We will carefully review your comments and share them with the author. Please note that due to the high volume of mail we receive, we may not be able to reply to every message.

Thank you for choosing Que!

Introduction

Microsoft FrontPage 98 is the most recent version of the popular all-in-one Web design tool kit. It's the third major release of the product, and the second since Microsoft acquired it from Vermeer Technologies in 1995. This is obviously good news because the last thing you want, when you shell out hard-earned money for a software package, is to discover that the company doesn't intend to support or upgrade it. Microsoft's upgrades to FrontPage 97 and now FrontPage 98, in fairly rapid succession, clearly demonstrate that they intend to stick with it. That's comforting, not to mention important.

Since late 1995, FrontPage has evolved into one of the most significant pieces of software in the Web's brief history because it was the first package to allow users to not only design Web pages (lots of packages handle that task), but also create, publish, and manage entire sites. Anyone buying FrontPage needed only an Internet connection to host a Web site—a high-speed, 24-hour connection was best, but not required—and that site could include such features as fill-in forms and other elements that formerly required a knowledge of programming. FrontPage, in effect, lets anyone create sophisticated Web sites—or, glitzy, bouncy, and tacky ones if that's what they prefer.

Until very recently, setting up a Web site required not only an Internet connection, but some pretty specialized knowledge about how Webs are built and maintained, and the ability to create the pages of the Web site by using a language called Hypertext Markup Language (HTML). Not everyone who wanted a Web site had that knowledge and ability, or the time or desire to acquire them.

This is where FrontPage comes in. FrontPage is an integrated site development environment and includes a Web creation and maintenance package called FrontPage Explorer, a WYSIWYG (what-you-see-is-what-you-get) Web page editor called FrontPage Editor, and a fully functioning Personal Web Server that turns a PC into a Web host machine. With FrontPage, you can create a complete Web site on your PC and link your PC to the World Wide Web and the Internet. You don't even have to know HTML because FrontPage Editor works like a word processor. You make your page look the way you want it, and the software puts the HTML code together for you. It also gives you the ability to put together Web pages that include elements that formerly demanded a knowledge of programming.

From the moment it was first released by its original producers, Vermeer Technologies, FrontPage 1.0 garnered an unusual degree of critical praise. Everyone who wrote about it had great things to say about it, and as it made its way into circulation, its users quickly agreed. The package was so well received that software giant, Microsoft, realizing that its Internet efforts lacked a Web design package, bought out the entire company for $130 million. Vermeer Technologies was now on its way to Redmond, Washington, to join Bill Gates and company.

For version 1.1, Microsoft revised the FrontPage interface, but touched up the program itself in only minor ways. What the company did do, however, was to make the beta versions of the package available as free downloads from its Web site. Users were able to work with the full product for a limited period of time, and over 400,000 took the company up on its offer. On release, the package sold well, and work had already begun on a much pumped-up version 2.0.

At the same time, Microsoft placed FrontPage within the Microsoft Office family of applications, thereby announcing to the world that it was intended for anyone in business who wanted to build a Web site. Even though it was not planned as part of the Microsoft Office suite itself (Word, Excel, PowerPoint, and Access) but rather a member of the family to be purchased separately, FrontPage was no longer a specialty product, but part of the Office mainstream. As a member of the Office family, FrontPage had to adopt Office's numbering system, so when the upcoming main product was named Office 97, FrontPage 2.0 became FrontPage 97.

The challenge for the FrontPage 97 design team was to keep up with the explosive growth of technologies that has come to the World Wide Web over the past year. Version 1.1 lets you produce reasonably advanced pages, but the advancements went only as far as the inclusion of frames, tables, and programmable forms. What the package didn't include were those features that professional designers now demand: Java, JavaScript, VBScript (Visual Basic Script), ActiveX, Netscape plug-ins, and perhaps most importantly, database integration. You could include these things in your FrontPage documents, but you first had to write the code elsewhere and then copy it into FrontPage. That was okay, but not very helpful.

FrontPage 97 went a long way toward filling those holes. You could now design JavaScripts and VBScripts right inside special FP dialog boxes. You couldn't do any actual designing of Java applets or Netscape plug-ins, but you could import them with their own specialized dialog boxes. Linking to databases began with a newly designed wizard and support for ActiveX was exemplary, with the imported ActiveX controls displayed in the FP documents as they would appear on the Web. The result was a much more complete package, and one that gave you nearly everything you can do with Web pages. A few things remain unsupported—style sheets and the newest Netscape extensions stood out here—but these were browser-specific (rather than standard) at that point, anyway.

Microsoft FrontPage 97 showed very well the package's power of letting users create all but the most technologically advanced Web sites as well as Microsoft's commitment to both the product and the Web design area itself. A wide range of computer magazines rated it at or very near the top of the growing category of Web design software, and almost universally at the top of the smaller, but related, category of software for Web design and management. Importantly, it also became a favorite among professional and amateur Web site designers.

But as good as it was, FrontPage 97 wasn't perfect. Important tasks such as the creation of navigation buttons, the alteration of the dimensions of table cells, and the manipulation of graphic images either took too long to perform, or (worse) weren't included in the product at all. No support existed for the new W3C Organization standard known as Cascading Style Sheets (CSS), for example, and frames—another extremely popular feature—were difficult to work with and unintuitive to create. It wouldn't be so bad if these things were obscure Web design add-ons, but they weren't. They were growing in popularity and, therefore, importance.

Microsoft FrontPage 98 has been designed to address these and many other issues, including some of the difficulties with usability encountered by the product's growing number of users. The result is a product that manages the difficult task of providing both a more complete set of features and an easier learning curve. Sophisticated Web sites are now within the grasp of an increasing number of users.

Once again, the challenge for the FrontPage design team was to make an already strong product stronger, and to keep up with the Web's newest innovations. To that end, FrontPage 98 contains many enhancements to FrontPage Editor, and a few important ones to FrontPage Explorer. FrontPage Editor now contains an extremely rich tables manipulation toolkit that allows you to customize tables (a highly important layout tool). In addition, frames are now WYSIWYG-supported, and Cascading Style Sheets are built throughout the product. New and better templates help your site get produced faster, and image manipulation tools allow you to work directly with graphics. Dynamic HTML makes its appearance with FrontPage 98 with many special effects now possible.

FrontPage Explorer contains an entirely new Navigation View where you can easily create new pages and restructure your entire site with simple drag-and-drop actions. All the views are now contained in an interface resembling Microsoft Outlook (part of Office 97), and switching among views is simpler. Also available through Explorer is the Channel Definition Wizard that lets you publish your Web site according to the Channel Definition Format standard for *push* systems. Essentially, push systems allow users to subscribe to your Web site, and they automatically receive your Web pages at specified intervals. You no longer have to wait for users to visit your site; you can simply send it out to them.

Microsoft FrontPage 98 is, in many respects, the first truly mature version of this acclaimed package. Novice users can get started more quickly, intermediate users can develop and maintain sophisticated sites more easily, and advanced users need fewer external tools to produce the sites. Room for enhancements remain, but at this stage there's every reason to suspect that FrontPage will continue to draw its share of accolades, awards, and editor's choice assignations.

Microsoft FrontPage 98 is a powerful suite of software, and *Special Edition Using Microsoft FrontPage 98* gives you all the information you need to use its power to your best advantage. ■

How to Use This Book

The book has been written to do four things:

- Make it easy for you to use FrontPage Explorer to create, maintain, and develop your Web site with a maximum of efficiency and a minimum of difficulty.

- Show you how to use FrontPage Editor to design, create, and maintain Web pages that people will both enjoy and find useful.

- Give you the technical elements of Web design beyond FrontPage 97, including the coding and details necessary for HTML, Java, scripting, and database integration.

- Help you understand the technicalities of the World Wide Web and the Internet, and how you can best design your site to take advantage of the present, and possibly the future, technology.

Given this, what's the best way for you to approach the book?

You may already be knowledgeable about Web-site design and construction. If so, you may want to skim the first chapters of this book and concentrate on the sections that deal with FrontPage Editor because that's the tool you'll likely spend most of your time using. Later, when you're using FrontPage in earnest, you'll find that FrontPage Explorer (covered in detail in Part V, "Building and Managing a Web") has many features that will make your life as a Webmaster a lot easier.

If you're new to site setup but know a lot about HTML, work on FrontPage Explorer first. Knowing how FrontPage Explorer handles Web construction helps you when you start to create pages with FrontPage Editor. (With the Editor, you'll be in for a treat—you may never have to worry about tags again.)

Finally, if you're already an experienced Webmaster, first browse Parts I, II, and V to learn how to use FrontPage 98 and how it can make your job easier and then use the Table of Contents to identify areas of immediate interest to you. Be sure to check out the advanced features of FrontPage 98 as well as the chapters devoted to technical coding and the appendixes (which you can keep beside you as you design your site).

Eventually, though, you'll want to delve into all of the material on FrontPage Editor, FrontPage Explorer, and the Personal Web Server because together they provide a seamless, powerful environment that can handle all but the most exotic of your site construction needs.

How This Book Is Organized

Special Edition Using Microsoft FrontPage 98 covers all the features and functions of the integrated environment. It has ten major parts, each of which is summarized briefly in the following.

The organizing principle is to introduce you to the FrontPage suite and demonstrate the features of the WYSIWYG FrontPage Editor. Chapters cover Web elements specific to the two major browsers, Microsoft Internet Explorer and Netscape Navigator, and you are introduced to the powerful new Image Composer software included with FrontPage 98. An entire section discusses the details of providing active content in your sites, such as Java, ActiveX, scripting, database integration, and VRML.

With all the Web coding issues taken care of, the book shifts to Web site management and creation. Included here is a major section on all the features of FrontPage Explorer, the powerful heart of the FrontPage 98 package, including wizards and templates, Web management and security, and FrontPage's capabilities for building and maintaining intranets. For advanced Webmasters, FrontPage 98's Software Development Kit (SDK) is covered in detail, with information about creating your own templates, wizards, and interface elements.

The next two parts cover FrontPage 98's integration with Microsoft Office, both Office 95 and the upcoming Office 97, and using FrontPage with other popular Web servers. The book next details methods of integration with databases, an increasingly important component of advanced Web design. Finally, comprehensive appendixes cover HTML, Java, JavaScript, VBScript, and VRML.

Part I: Understanding the FrontPage Integrated Environment

Chapter 1, "Getting Started," introduces the various parts of the integrated environment and explains how to install FrontPage.

Chapter 2, "Looking Over Microsoft FrontPage 98," outlines each part of the FrontPage 98 package in greater detail, including FrontPage Explorer, FrontPage Editor, and the Microsoft Personal Web Server.

Chapter 3, "Essential Tools for Webmasters," orients you to some of FrontPage 98's advanced capabilities. These include the powerful FrontPage Components and the new and equally powerful Image Composer graphics program. Also covered are FrontPage 98's built-in tools for linking to databases and incorporating ActiveX, Java, JavaScript, and VBScript, as well as the ways in which FrontPage 98 integrates with Microsoft Office 95 and 97.

Part II: Creating Your Web Pages with FrontPage Editor

Chapter 4, "Introducing FrontPage Editor," brings you up to speed on page creation, saving, and retrieval, using either FrontPage Editor and FrontPage Explorer in concert, or FrontPage Editor as a stand-alone application. It also shows you the ways to adapt the editor display to your preferences.

Chapter 5, "Developing the Basic Page: Text, Lists, and Hyperlinks," gives you the basics of good page design, the fundamentals of HTML structure, and three fundamental elements of a Web page—text, lists, and hyperlinks.

Chapter 6, "Enhancing Pages with Themes, Graphics, and Multimedia," offers detailed instruction on images and image layout, colors and backgrounds, graphical hyperlinks, and imagemaps.

Chapter 7, "Using Dynamic HTML, Active Elements, Shared Borders, and Navigation Bars," deals with several advanced but easy-to-implement HTML features, designed to ease navigation of your site and to give it a great deal of pizzazz.

Chapter 8, "Creating Tables," explores FrontPage 98's easy-to-use but sophisticated system for creating and editing one of the Webmaster's most important tools, HTML tables.

Chapter 9, "Enhancing Web Sites with FrontPage Frames," teaches you about designing for a *framed* site, about using frames with links and images, and how to create framed environments with FrontPage Editor's frame templates.

Chapter 10, "Creating Pages with FrontPage Editor Templates," steps you through FrontPage's supplied templates, which speed up the creation of pages such as bibliographies, glossaries, directories, and publicity instruments (for example, press releases).

Chapter 11, "Using FrontPage Components, Forms, and Interactive Page Templates," explains what FrontPage Components are and how to use them. You also learn all about forms, about getting information from people who visit your site, about forms security, and about the FrontPage templates that help you make your pages interactive.

Chapter 12, "Using Style Sheets with Pages and Web Sites," introduces the HTML feature known as Cascading Style Sheets, an extremely important feature that gives you the ability to offer rich and consistent layout across your site.

Part III: Creating and Adapting Graphics with Image Composer

Part III examines the wealth of features in Microsoft Image Composer, the graphics program included with the FrontPage 98 package.

Chapter 13, "Getting Started with Image Composer," introduces the various elements of the new graphics package.

Chapter 14, "Working with Sprites," demonstrates the way in which the program revolves around the concept of the graphical "sprite."

Chapter 15, "Using Effects for Maximum Impact," outlines the wide variety of tools available in Image Composer for producing special graphical effects.

Chapter 16, "Tailoring Your Images for FrontPage Documents," examines the techniques for making your Image Composer creations suitable for import into an effective FrontPage Web document.

Part IV: Integrating Active Content into Your Web

Part IV introduces you to FrontPage 98's expanded capabilities for including a variety of active content in your Web designs.

Chapter 17, "Using ActiveX Controls," shows how to implement FrontPage 98's close integration with ActiveX programmable controls to give your sites even more features.

Chapter 18, "Scripting with VBScript," examines the sophisticated features in FrontPage 98 that let you import existing scripts or create them from scratch.

Chapter 19, "Scripting with JavaScript," demonstrates the techniques and procedures for writing applets by using the JavaScript language.

Chapter 20, "Inserting Java Applets and Browser Plug-Ins," shows the procedures for including Java applets and applications, as well as files designed for Web plug-ins, in your FrontPage documents.

Chapter 21, "VRML and Java," explains the details behind writing code for Java applications and 3-D Virtual Reality Modeling Language components.

Part V: Building and Managing a Web

Part V examines the features of FrontPage Explorer, the program in the FrontPage suite that lets you create, maintain, and manage entire sites.

Chapter 22, "Building a Web," covers Web creation in detail and introduces the FrontPage wizards that help you set up specialized types of Webs.

Chapter 23, "FrontPage's Web Templates and Wizards," steps you through using wizards and templates to set up normal and empty Webs and to create the more complex Discussion Webs, Customer Support Webs, Project Webs, and Personal Webs.

Chapter 24, "Working with an Existing Web," deals with FrontPage Explorer's different views of a Web, along with the features offered by its menus, and demonstrates how to import existing directories into FrontPage to create a Web.

Chapter 25, "Configuring Your Web," shows you how to administer a Web by setting Web parameters, permissions, passwords, and proxy servers and by configuring editors.

Chapter 26, "Managing a Web," covers managing hardware, software, and people and using the To Do List to keep your site maintenance up-to-date, and demonstrates how to use FrontPage 98's advanced maintenance features such as global spell, global search and replace, and hyperlink updating.

Chapter 27, "Serving Your Web to the World with the Microsoft Personal Web Server," examines what's involved in using server software to make your Web public.

Chapter 28, "Defining Your Web as a Channel," takes you through the Channel Definition Wizard, by which you establish your site as a channel to which your visitors can subscribe and receive updated pages on their desktop.

Chapter 29, "Using Microsoft Personal Web Server and FrontPage Personal Web Server," explores the details of the the powerful Windows 95 Web server known as Microsoft Personal Web Server, and of the older and less powerful FrontPage Personal Web Server. Both are included with the FrontPage 98 package.

Chapter 30, "Setting Up an Intranet with FrontPage," shows how to use FrontPage 98 to establish an intranet for your organization.

Part VI: Using the FrontPage 98 SDK

Part VI introduces you to the FrontPage Software Developer's Kit, a powerful document that shows you how to fully customize FrontPage.

Chapter 31, "Extending and Customizing FrontPage with the SDK," examines the features of the SDK and demonstrates how to create custom menus.

Chapter 32, "Creating Templates," details the procedures in the SDK for developing your own templates.

Chapter 33, "Creating Wizards," outlines the SDK's procedures for designing specialty wizards and FrontPage Components.

Part VII: Integrating Microsoft FrontPage 98 and Microsoft Office

Part VII provides an examination of the increasing degree of integration between FrontPage 98 and Microsoft Office, especially the new Office 97.

Chapter 34, "FrontPage 98 and Office 97," looks at the ways in which FrontPage 98 and Microsoft Office 97 work hand in hand to let you create advanced Web sites.

Chapter 35, "Using the Internet Assistant for PowerPoint 95," demonstrates how to use Microsoft's Internet Assistant add-on for Microsoft PowerPoint, the popular graphics presentation program included with Microsoft Office

Chapter 36, "Using the Internet Assistants for Excel 95 and Word 95," shows how to use Microsoft Internet Assistant for both Word and Excel, as well as how to use them together for text and table integration.

Chapter 37, "Using the Internet Assistants for Schedule+ and Access," demonstrates how to use the HTML assistants for the remaining components of Microsoft Office.

Part VIII: Using Other Servers with FrontPage 98

Part VIII demonstrates the issues involved with publishing sites created with FrontPage on Web servers beyond the Personal Web Server.

Chapter 38, "Using FrontPage with Microsoft Internet Information Server," looks at the details of the highly regarded IIS and the details behind using FrontPage 98 with this server.

Chapter 39, "Using NonMicrosoft Servers," shows how to publish FrontPage documents to servers running O'Reilly WebSite, Netscape FastTrack, and other popular Web server software.

Part IX: Advanced Database Connectivity
Part IX gives you the details behind building database connectivity into your Web sites, beyond the capabilities of FrontPage 98 itself.

Chapter 40, "Custom Database Query Scripts," looks at the details of producing scripts to request information from large databases maintained by your organization.

Part X: Appendixes
Part X, the appendixes, offers references for coding HTML documents and their components.

Appendix A, "FrontPage on the Net"

Appendix B, "HTML 4.0 Quick Reference"

Appendix C, "VBScript Command Reference"

Appendix D, "JavaScript Command Reference"

Appendix E, "What's on the CD-ROM"

Special Features in the Book

Que has a long track record of providing the most comprehensive resource books for users and developers of computer hardware and software. This volume includes many features to make your learning faster and more efficient.

Chapter Roadmaps
Each chapter begins with a roadmap, which is a bulleted list of the chapter's key topics. With each topic is a brief description of what's covered. This helps you understand where you're going before you start.

Tips
Tips help you use the software more effectively or to maneuver you around problems or limitations.

 TIP To avoid typing a long URL, you can use Edit, Copy to copy the URL from your browser's Location box and paste it by pressing Ctrl+V.

Notes
Notes provide information that is generally useful but not specifically needed for what you're doing at the moment. Some are similar to extended tips.

N O T E FrontPage Editor makes it convenient to move among pages. It keeps a history list of the pages you've displayed, and you can choose Tools, Forward or Tools, Back to get around. ▨

Cautions

These tell you to beware of a dangerous act or situation. In some cases, ignoring a caution could cause you very significant problems, so don't disregard them!

> **CAUTION**
>
> Once you've changed the Quality setting and saved the image, you can't change that setting again, even if you delete the image and reinsert it from the saved page. If you're experimenting, be sure to keep a backup!

Troubleshooting

Even the best designed software has dark corners you'd rather not find yourself in. Troubleshooting information gives you a flashlight to dispel the darkness, in the form of advice about how to solve a problem or avoid it in the first place. They're in Q&A form.

TROUBLESHOOTING

I want to use an image as a bookmark, and I can't find a way to do it. Is there one? No, there isn't. This is because an HTML page doesn't actually contain the image data but rather a *pointer* to the file where the image is stored. HTML doesn't let you define such a pointer as a named anchor, which is what a bookmark actually is. To get around this, use some text near the image (the caption, if there is one) as the bookmark.

Book Cross-References

In a package as tightly integrated as FrontPage 98, many operations are related to features that appear elsewhere in the book. Book cross-references, like the one next to this paragraph, direct you to the related material.

▶ **See** "Wizards, What They Are and How They Work," **p. xxx**

On the Web

These sections serve the same purpose as book cross-references but direct you to an Internet resource by giving you its URL.

ON THE WEB

http://www.europe.ibm.com/go/uk/about.html Visit the IBM Europe page site for an office directory example.

Hotkeys

Hotkeys are indicated by an underlined letter, just as they appear in FrontPage's menus and dialog boxes. For example, the hotkey to open the Insert menu is <u>I</u>. To use it, press the Alt key and then press I. The Insert menu appears.

Shortcut Key Combinations

Shortcut key combinations in this book are shown as the key names joined with plus signs (+). For example, Ctrl+N means: "Hold down the Ctrl key and, while holding it down, press the N key." This combination opens a new page in FrontPage Editor.

Menu Commands

Everywhere in this book, you'll see instructions such as:

>   Choose Edit, Bookmark.

This means "Open the Edit menu and select Bookmark." This particular example opens the Bookmark dialog box.

The instruction "Mark the Set Color check box" means you can either click in the check box to put a check in it or press the C key, which does the same thing.

What's on the CD-ROM?

Because Microsoft FrontPage 98 is so new, no third-party add-ons have appeared as this book was being written. However, you may want to explore other Web page authoring tools and utilities in conjunction with using FrontPage 98. The CD-ROM includes browsers, HTML editors (for both Windows 3.1 and Windows 95), graphics programs, Winsock FTP clients, and specialty software for audio, video, forms creation, search engine interfacing, as well as some helpful graphics and sound files.

Web Site Support

For updates to this book, please check our Web site at www.mcp.com/info. Type in the ISBN for this book (0-7897-1343-8) and you'll receive access to additional material.

Understanding the FrontPage Integrated Environment

Getting Started

Welcome to *Special Edition Using Microsoft FrontPage 98*. FrontPage 98 is the most recent version of the popular and increasingly powerful software package, and like previous versions, is designed to make your site creation and management both easier and more complete. This chapter introduces you to the hardware and this book, near the end, tells you how to install the program and get it running. ■

What FrontPage 98 is all about

Why Web designers and managers feel they've found a piece of paradise, and why you should consider it for yourself if you intend to be one or the other.

How this book will help you learn FrontPage 98

The structure of *Special Edition Using Microsoft FrontPage 98* makes it easy to learn the ins and outs of the software package itself.

Where FrontPage 98 came from

A short history of the FrontPage package, and a good lesson in making oodles of money by developing Internet technologies.

The parts of FrontPage 98

What are the various parts of the FrontPage 98 package? What do they all do? How do they fit together?

Installing FrontPage 98 and the Bonus Pack programs

You've bought it, you want to use it, and you need to get it installed.

What FrontPage 98 Is All About

Microsoft FrontPage 98 lets you plan, design, implement, develop, administer, and update World Wide Web and intranet sites. Not just Web *pages*, which any number of excellent programs let you do (although even here FrontPage 98 offers many competitive advantages), but entire Web or intranet *sites*, collections of publicly or privately available linked pages. The program is so complete that, once you've acquired it, there's literally nothing between you and putting your site up live on the Web or on your company's network.

FrontPage 98 Components

FrontPage 98 contains the three major components including FrontPage Explorer, FrontPage Editor, and Microsoft Personal Web Server.

FrontPage Explorer　FrontPage Explorer helps you create Web sites from scratch and gives you wizards and templates to take you from no site at all to a site with a solid basis in only a few minutes. If you already have a Web site, Explorer can import the site, give you a visual view of it, and allow you to develop it further. Explorer lets you organize and create hierarchies at your site to make it as logical as possible to navigate.

FrontPage Editor　FrontPage Editor allows you to create individual pages from scratch, or to edit those you've created earlier. The editing environment is WYSIWYG (What You See Is What You Get), which means that authoring FrontPage documents is similar in many respects to producing word processor documents. From Editor, you can format documents, add graphics and multimedia, and enliven your Web site with the latest in HTML (Hypertext Markup Language) technology, without the need to know programming.

Microsoft Personal Web Server　Microsoft Personal Web Server (MS-PWS) gives you the technology you need to mount your site on a publicly available server and publish it on the Internet or your company's network. MS-PWS installs only on the Windows 95 and Macintosh platforms.

Additional Components

In addition, FrontPage 98 ships with an additional group of programs, including Microsoft Image Composer, Web Publishing Wizard, and FrontPage Personal Web Server. These programs will make your life as a Webmaster easier and more complete.

Microsoft Image Composer　Microsoft Image Composer gives you the tools you need to design and develop graphics specially suited for use on the Web, whether or not you're an accomplished graphic artist.

Included with Image Composer is Microsoft GIF Animator, a tool to help you create animated, cartoon-like images for Web pages.

Web Publishing Wizard　Web Publishing Wizard helps you place your Webs on computers with powerful Web server software, even if those servers do not support FrontPage 98's special "server extensions."

N O T E FrontPage server extensions are programs that allow nonMicrosoft Web servers to perform FrontPage-specific functions, including authoring FrontPage Webs and administering FrontPage Webs. ▣

FrontPage Personal Web Server FrontPage Personal Web Server, which debuted in the very first FrontPage release, is included with FrontPage 98 but is no longer officially supported by Microsoft. It has been supplanted by MS-PWS, and is included on the CD-ROM solely for the sake of full compatibility with Webs created with previous FrontPage editions.

Put all these components together, and you have what amounts to a comprehensive Web site publishing environment. To make your Web site complete, you'll want to mount it on a computer that's connected to the Internet over a fast connection 24 hours a day, but even with a lowly modem, you can serve up a part-time site to get started.

What's New in FrontPage 98

FrontPage 1.1 was an immediate hit on its release in mid-1996, but it lacked some very important features. FrontPage 97, released in late 1996, represented a major enhancement to the package, partly because of added programs, new features, and a general interface improvement. FrontPage 98 improves the interface still further, and adds support for the wide variety of major changes to Web design capabilities that have taken place over the course of 1997. In many ways, FrontPage 98 represents the first truly mature release of the product, and Microsoft's commitment to it points to a very strong future for its users.

Here's what's new in FrontPage 98:

Navigation View	This new view in FrontPage Explorer lets you add new pages and move existing pages to create the organizational structure you want for your Web. Navigation view combines with Hyperlink view to offer another important means of site management. This view also allows you to print a map of the Web site for further study and enhancement.
Themes	FrontPage themes are design templates that extend across all documents in a Web site. Each theme offers consistent backgrounds, fonts, bullets, lines, and buttons. FrontPage 98 ships with 50 themes.

Table Editing

Editing HTML tables is immensely improved from FrontPage 97. Users have full control over the layout and the structure of the table's columns and rows. Commands have been added to distribute rows and columns evenly for a consistent appearance, and the tables toolbar includes a pencil to draw tables manually, plus an eraser to let users get rid of individual cell or row divisions.

Frame Editing

Creating frames is a fully WYSIWYG function in FrontPage 98, allowing users to produce framesets that appear in the FrontPage Editor exactly as they'll appear in browsers.

Image Editing

Image editing tools are now part of FrontPage Editor. These tools, which are designed primarily with scanned images in mind, let users add washout effects to images, as well as perform such actions as cropping, rotating, and beveling. Images can also be resized to save download time.

Automatic Navigation Bars

Users can easily create navigation bars to help visitors find their way through the site. The text on the bars can now be changed after the bars are in place, for greater flexibility in design.

Fancy Bullets

Instead of standard HTML bullets, users can specify graphic images that will constitute the bullets for a page or an entire site.

Hover Buttons

Hover buttons are buttons consisting of Java applets created without programming that animate or change color or shape when the site visitor passes the mouse pointer over them. Animation editing is built into this extremely useful feature.

Banner Ad Manager	Users can now create banners that automatically load a series of graphic images at specific intervals. Several transition effects can be specified as well.
Text Overlays on Images	This useful and much needed feature lets users add text to graphics, thereby allowing names, labels, and any other textual element.
HTML Editing	It's no longer necessary for users to shell out to an external editor to type their own HTML code. FrontPage 98 contains a WYSIWYG HTML editor and displays HTML code much more efficiently.
Form Results as E-Mail	One of the most requested features for the new product, this option lets users specify an e-mail address to which the contents of fill-in forms are to be sent.
Support for CSS	Cascading Style Sheets allow Web authors to create a unified layout for groups of pages or entire sites. FrontPage 98 offers full support for CSS, and this includes a Style button in many areas of the interface.
Channel Definition Format Support	Push technology is frequently acknowledged as the coming trend in Web publishing. FrontPage 98 lets users develop their sites as channels to which visitors can subscribe. These channels support Microsoft's CDF format, and are useful primarily for visitors using Microsoft Internet Explorer 4.0 or higher.
Support for Dynamic HTML	Dynamic HTML extends standard HTML in many ways, primarily to allow changes in Web pages to occur on the visitor's computer without the need to request page updates from the server. FrontPage 98 offers support for text effects, form field navigation, expanding and collapsing outlines, and page transitions, all without the need for user programming.

Making the Best Use of This Book

Special Edition Using Microsoft FrontPage 98 is designed as a tool to help you get the most out of the FrontPage 98 package. The first thing that has to be said (and as authors we shudder to say it) is that you don't have to read the whole book and you don't have to read it from start to finish. It's split up into sections that help you play off your existing strengths and your existing knowledge of Web-building packages.

If you're already familiar with Web page editors (HTML editors), for instance, you might want to skim through Part II, "Creating Your Web Pages with FrontPage Editor," then load the program and experiment with it for a while. After that, you should hunker down with this book and work through Part V, "Building and Managing a Web," which deals primarily with FrontPage Explorer, and create and view several full Webs as you go along. Part V also covers FrontPage's included Web servers, the server administration tools, and configuration issues, so these will also be of interest to you in your quest for perfect Web development and management.

On the other hand, if you're a beginning Web builder, working through the book part by part is the best approach. As you discover new features and capabilities, experiment with them until you're comfortable using them and then continue to learn new skills and new tasks. Don't worry if you don't know CGI from CIA; FrontPage performs some of the more difficult Web programming tasks for you. The point is that FrontPage 98 works as a beginner's package as well as a veteran's package, and this book caters to both groups (and those in between).

Where FrontPage Came From

Microsoft Corporation is brilliant in one regard: recognizing excellent technology and then adapting it to its own needs. The Windows environment itself provides an example of this, with most of its features coming from Apple's Macintosh environment, which in turn saw its origins in a mouse-based graphical user interface developed by Xerox's Palo Alto Research Center (Xerox PARC). Microsoft Excel took the best features of the DOS-based Lotus 1-2-3 (itself a successful clone of the older Visicalc), and made them dance in Windows.

Such is the case with FrontPage. The program was introduced in mid-1995 by Vermeer Technologies of Cambridge, Massachusetts, and it was immediately lauded by reviewers in computer magazines. Microsoft obviously read these reviews and agreed, because on January 16, 1996, the company bought not only FrontPage, but Vermeer Technologies itself, for a reported $130 million. On April 8, 1996, Microsoft announced that the finished program would be available for $149 (way down from Vermeer's original $695), and even less for owners of Microsoft Office. As a member of the immensely popular Microsoft Office suite, FrontPage stands a chance of becoming the most widespread complete Web-creation system ever made.

But, FrontPage really came from the Web itself because the entire purpose of the World Wide Web is to offer a multimedia interface for the global distribution of linked documents. FrontPage lets you create for precisely this interface, and it lets you easily distribute your own information in a graphically well-designed format. FrontPage makes easy the formerly difficult and complex task of merging the creation of Web documents with the publishing of those documents on the Internet, and therein lies its most important strength. The Web was initially supposed to be a medium in which practically anyone could publish, and FrontPage offers that possibility once more.

The Parts of FrontPage 98

FrontPage consists of several parts, all of which fit together to make a complete Web site publishing package. The integration of the programs is covered in the next chapter; the following short descriptions serve only as a means for getting you started thinking about the package's many possibilities.

FrontPage Explorer

The heart of the entire FrontPage package, Explorer is designed to let you see the Web you have created. Explorer provides several views of your Web. The Hyperlinks View lets you see the hierarchical relationships and links among pages and resembles the outline view in a word processor. It also gives you a clear graphical picture of how pages in your Web are linked together, and also how they link to Web documents outside your Web. Navigation View gives you another look at the hierarchy of your Web, but goes a major step further by letting you order and reorder the site to make navigation logical and easy to follow. Navigation View acts essentially as a whiteboard, letting you work on the Web's organization and change it or add to it as often as you wish.

The other views are more specialized. Here's a quick rundown:

- Folders View gives you a look at your Web from the standpoint of folders and files, much the same as the view in Windows Explorer itself.
- All Files View offers a similar look at the Web, but this time with the files and their associations as the focus.
- Hyperlinks Status View shows you which hyperlinks are working properly and which must be altered or updated.
- Tasks View gives you a list of tasks that must be completed on your Web, and lets you assign specific tasks to specific contributors (excellent for intranet development).
- Finally, Themes View offers graphical themes that you can select as common across all pages in the Web.

Together, these views let you see how your Web is constructed and, in the process, help you determine what else needs to be done to perfect that Web.

Perhaps even more importantly, Explorer lets you create Webs from scratch. You can build Webs that are entirely empty, into which you must insert all your documents from scratch, or Explorer's wizards and templates will build entire Webs for you and set them in place. Once your Webs exist, your task is to customize them and add to them, but having something to start with—which is precisely what the wizards and templates offer—always makes the overall task easier.

Finally, Explorer lets you set options for your Webs to help you manage them. You can determine who will have access to the Web sites at various levels—everyone from administrators to Web authors and even end users. If you want to restrict access to your Webs to people within your own company, you can do so. If you want users to register before entering your site, you can do that as well. If you want coworkers to be able to author pages in the Web but not change the administrative options, it's as easy as a few entries in a dialog box.

FrontPage Editor

There's no lack of good programs out there that let you author Web documents. Typically, they're called HTML editors because Web pages are written primarily in *Hypertext Markup Language* (HTML), but in the case of Microsoft FrontPage (and, certainly an increasing number of others), you really don't have to know HTML to generate first-rate pages. Like your word processor, which doesn't show you the formatting codes unless you specifically ask to see them, FrontPage Editor operates on the principle that you want to see the results of your work rather than the codes and tags necessary for the implementation of those results. In other words, FrontPage Editor is a WYSIWYG program, and while it's not the first WYSIWYG Web editor to hit the market, it's possibly the most complete.

FrontPage Editor easily supports HTML features such as tables, forms, and frames and offers advanced features such as database linkages, scripting, dynamic HTML, cascading style sheets, and fast inclusion of ActiveX controls and Java applets. It permits you to set the color and formatting of the pages through a series of dialog boxes, thereby making it easier to standardize the way your Web looks to others. In the case of forms, frames, database linkages, and scripts, it goes a step further and offers wizards to help you build and include these relatively complex elements. It also goes another step further, offering automation tools called FrontPage Components (they used to be called Web bots, but large companies usually default to much more boring names).

If you've ever tried to get a form on your Web to actually do anything, you know how difficult it can be. Designing a form itself is relatively easy; programming the scripts to allow it to interact with the server so that clicking the Submit button sends the data somewhere useful is another matter entirely. FrontPage's Components remove much of this difficulty, and they also remove the need to learn the interface scripting process known as CGI (Common Gateway Interface). You can't do all complex CGI-like interactions with these Components, but FrontPage makes it possible for even Web-authoring novices to offer full interaction in their Web sites.

However, simply authoring Web pages isn't enough for FrontPage. Instead, the package integrates Editor and Explorer to make Web planning and Web authoring a seamless activity, and it ups the ante even further by giving you the means to put your site on the World Wide Web itself. That's the role of the Personal Web Server.

Microsoft Personal Web Server

If you want to host your own Web site, you need some Web *server* software. This software, when installed on a computer that's connected to the Internet, makes your Web site accessible to users on the World Wide Web. To be effective, a Web server machine should be connected to the Internet 24 hours per day at a much higher speed than even the fastest modem allows. You still need server software even if you just want to test your Webs to make sure they work. The difference is that a full-time public Web needs more powerful and robust server software than the local, private Web.

If you're working on a Windows NT machine, server software is included as part of the operating system. NT Workstation users have Peer Web Services, while NT Server users have Internet Information Server (one of the most powerful server packages available on any platform). Windows 95 doesn't ship with server software, so FrontPage 98 includes the Microsoft Personal Web Server (MS-PWS) on the FrontPage 98 CD-ROM. This software isn't as powerful as the Internet Information Server, but it's capable of hosting a test Web site, either locally or publicly. FrontPage 98 also includes the FrontPage Personal Web Server (FP-PWS), but it's not as capable and is included only for full compatibility with earlier versions of FrontPage.

(Of course, by now you'll be seeing a pattern in Microsoft's naming schemes. Not only do we have FrontPage *Explorer* offering confusion with Windows *Explorer* and Internet *Explorer*, we also have *three* PWS's to sort out: the Microsoft PWS, the FrontPage PWS, and the NT Workstation Peer Web Services (PWS).)

Server Extensions

The most important concession made by the FrontPage package is that people will want to use its Web creation tools but not necessarily its included server. In fact, there's no way a professional Web server site would be willing to change from its well-established server software, so the only way to make FrontPage widely useful was to include support for existing servers. FrontPage does this through *server extensions*, which install files and directories into the existing server software to let the server work with all of FrontPage's features.

Getting data from forms is only one example (albeit an important one) of what the server extensions accomplish. As explained earlier, FrontPage takes the programming sting out of making forms return the data that users provide. But, because FrontPage does this in a non-standard way (for example, it doesn't use CGI scripts), something has to tell the server software what the FrontPage form is trying to do. That something, in fact, is the server extension. Essentially, the server extensions add functionality to the server software to allow it to work with FrontPage as well as with the software it already supports.

FrontPage offers server extensions for many of the most popular servers. Some of these are included on the CD-ROM, while others are downloadable from the FrontPage Web site at **http://www.microsoft.com./frontpage/**.

Microsoft Image Composer

Whether you're a graphics professional or, like the vast majority of people, pretty much artistically challenged, Microsoft Image Composer will suit many of your needs. The principle behind this program isn't to create graphics from scratch (although you can do this), but rather to edit graphics files to suit the way you want them to look on your Web site. You can merge multiple *sprites* (individual images) into one single complex image, then alter each of the component sprites or the entire image by applying a huge assortment of special effects. You can add text, change color patterns, and perform a wide range of other edits as well. You can also save your finished image as a Web-standard JPEG or GIF file for incorporation into your FrontPage document.

Installing FrontPage 98

As of this writing, FrontPage 98 was available for Windows 95 and Windows NT only. An earlier version of FrontPage was available for the Macintosh, but whether that version would be updated to FrontPage 98 remained unclear. And, as with so many other things in the Microsoft world, Windows 3.x users have been abandoned. Even if these versions were developed, however, you can rest assured that the 32-bit Windows version will remain the primary development environment. Examples you see throughout this book are from the Windows version (the 95 and NT versions are the same), including this section on installation.

If you've downloaded a beta version of the program, it arrives as a series of executable, self-extracting files. Run the main file and then look for the setup program in the same directory. Run setup and the installation will be more or less automated.

If you have the CD-ROM, put it in the CD-ROM drive and close the door. The Installation screen should appear (Figure 1.1). If it doesn't, go into Windows Explorer, click your CD-ROM drive, and launch the setup program.

FIG. 1.1
The installation window give you one-click access to the installation routines for the three programs.

You have three installation choices here: FrontPage 98 itself, Microsoft Image Composer, or Microsoft Internet Explorer. To get started, click the program you want to install. If you're a Windows 95 user and you click to install FrontPage 98, the installation program will check to see if you have the Microsoft Personal Web Server installed. If not, it will offer to install it first. If you do so, it will ask you to restart your machine (a technical necessity, but an annoying one), and then will return you to the installation window.

Once the installation process begins, you must choose a typical installation or custom installation. Typical installation includes giving you everything you need to start producing and publishing Webs. Custom installation includes the older FrontPage Personal Web Server (again, don't confuse it with MS-PWS), as well as additional clip art (if you have room on your hard disk, go for it) and the FrontPage Server Extensions SDK (software development kit). If you need to do detailed work with servers, install this; if not, don't bother.

Like all programs, FrontPage offers to install itself into a default directory, which you can change if you want. It also creates a separate directory for each of the MS-PWS and the FrontPage PWS (if you install them), but you get a choice only with the latter. FrontPage will automatically recognize your server software and install the appropriate server extensions, unless you're using a less well-known server package, in which case you must install extensions (if they exist) through the Server Administrator.

When the installation is finished, you'll be asked if you want to start FrontPage Explorer. Since you'll want to spend the next few weeks of your life learning how to use the full suite of capabilities in this package, say yes and get started. When FrontPage Explorer has started, choose File, New Web and start your Web creation career (if you want, jump straight to Chapter 22, "Building a Web," to get going).

Installing Microsoft Image Composer and Microsoft Internet Explorer

To install either of these packages, click their icons on the installation screen. Be sure to install Internet Explorer if your version number is older than 3.02, or you won't be able to make full use of FrontPage's capabilities. In fact, upgrade to IE 4.0 as quickly as possible because some FrontPage features only work with its advanced capabilities.

For Image Composer, you'll have to decide how many multimedia files you want to include with the installation. Keep careful watch of the disk space you're using. A full installation of Image Composer consumes nearly 400 *megabytes* of disk space! Most of this, however, is image files, which you can choose not to install.

From Here...

At this point, you have FrontPage 98 up and running. Obviously, that's only the very beginning. FrontPage is a rich program, and as with all rich programs, mastering it takes time and effort. Your introduction to the package continues in the next chapter, and then it's on to the actual production of Web sites and pages in Parts II and III. From here, you can look forward to the following:

■ Chapter 2, "Looking Over Microsoft FrontPage 98," takes you through the ways in which the programs interact.

■ Part II, "Creating Your Web Pages with FrontPage Editor," is where you'll discover the WYSIWYG power and features of the package's HTML editor.

■ Part V, "Building and Managing a Web," works through the details of Web site creation and management in FrontPage Explorer.

Looking Over Microsoft FrontPage 98

FrontPage 98 is an integrated package, combining the powerful HTML page creation features of FrontPage Editor, the sophisticated site management system of FrontPage Explorer, and a capable and strongly featured HTTP (Web) server. If you need to publish your Web on a remote server, FrontPage also ships with *extensions* that allow most popular servers to work with its advanced features.

With these elements comes a set of FrontPage Components and Active Elements. These features relieve you of writing CGI scripts for interactive processes. Also included are systems for editing images, creating scripts, inserting Java applets and ActiveX controls, and establishing your Web as a channel for use in Internet Explorer 4 and Windows 98. Using these tools, you can establish your own Webs, create extremely sophisticated pages for them, and offer your Web site to millions of viewers and readers. ■

Starting a new Web with FrontPage Explorer

Choose from a number of Web templates and wizards to get a brand-new Web, ripe for expansion.

Designing a Web page with FrontPage Editor

FrontPage Explorer is your Web manager, but the Editor is where you'll expend most of your creative energies in a robust, full-featured, near-WYSIWYG environment.

Presenting your Web site to the world, with the Personal Web Server

Get a glimpse of the Personal Web Server, which turns your PC into a real, fully functional Web server.

Explorer, Editor, and the Server Extensions: Working Together

Before getting started in designing your first-class Web sites, it's useful to consider how the four primary parts of the FrontPage package—Explorer, Editor, Server, and server extensions —function together.

> **N O T E**   Whereas Windows 95 refers to *folders*, and MS-DOS and earlier versions of Windows refer to *directories*, FrontPage uses the two names pretty much interchangeably. In this book, *folder* and *directory* mean the same thing, and they're given the name used by each particular portion of FrontPage itself. ▉

FrontPage Editor lets you create HTML documents, otherwise known as World Wide Web pages. It's a WYSIWYG system, which means that, for the most part, what you see in the Explorer windows is what you'll see in your Web browser when you retrieve that page. Authoring Web pages in FrontPage Editor is relatively easy and extremely pleasing, because as you create the page, you see almost exactly what it's going to look like to the people who visit your Web sites.

Despite the importance of FrontPage Editor, the true core of Microsoft FrontPage is FrontPage Explorer. Explorer lets you create Webs, delete Webs, import files into Webs, and manage your Web sites at all levels. Explorer gives you a graphical view of your Webs, letting you see how the various pages are linked together, and it offers tools to update links as they change with the growth of the Web. It also gives you tools that allow you to control access to your site and other tools that give you global control over replacing data, establishing design *themes*, and publishing your Web as a channel. With Editor, you author and edit *pages*, but with Explorer, you build and manage *Webs*.

The relationship between these two main tools is a rich one. On a simple functional level, you can double-click a document icon in Explorer and that page opens for editing inside Editor. More significantly, though, Editor offers powerful items known as Components and Active Elements, and these tie in directly with Explorer. Components and Active Elements spare you the difficulty and drudgery of programming your World Wide Web pages. They let you do such things as create forms that produce usable data, establish counters that display the number of visitors to your site, and display information fields that update whenever the page is loaded. In order to work, Components and Active Elements are tied both to FrontPage Explorer, which establishes them within your Web, and the FrontPage server extensions, which let them work with the HTTP server software on which you publish your Web.

That brings us to the third and fourth major features of FrontPage: servers and server extensions. Web sites can be accessed by visitors only if they're *served* by HTTP *server* software. Through server extensions, FrontPage Explorer works hand in hand with special software that tells the server how to respond to pages produced by FrontPage. This is necessary because FrontPage's Components and Active Elements, along with a few other features, aren't part of the growing HTTP standard. They exist exclusively in sites created with FrontPage. HTTP server software doesn't know how to handle these features, and without the server extensions, these features would be useless. FrontPage 98 offers server extensions for the most popular server software on UNIX, Windows NT, and Windows 95 platforms.

If you don't have a server on which to mount your Web, the FrontPage 98 CD-ROM includes two Web server packages for use with Windows 95. The Microsoft Personal Web Server is powerful enough to serve small, live Webs, while the FrontPage Personal Web Server is useful primarily as a test server only (i.e., not across the Internet).

Part

I

___

Ch

2

All of these features are covered in this book. What's important to keep in mind for now is that the three major parts of FrontPage operate hand in hand. You can use Editor without Explorer, but many of Editor's most important features won't work. Similarly, you can use Explorer with a different editor, but the entire WebBot system won't exist for you, and without the server extensions, you can't use either with any useful effect.

Using Explorer to Start Your Web

If you haven't created your first FrontPage Web already, you're probably itching to find out what it's actually like to do so, so let's begin. This will be just a quick run-through to get you used to Explorer's behavior; you'll learn about Web creation in far more detail in the next few chapters.

Go to the Win95/NT Start button, go to Programs, and select Microsoft FrontPage. After the inevitable pause for loading, you'll see the Explorer screen overlaid with the Getting Started dialog box. Close this dialog box by clicking Cancel.

Choose File, New, FrontPage Web from the Explorer menu bar. You immediately see a dialog box with a list of Web templates and wizards. This New FrontPage Web dialog box is shown in Figure 2.1.

Several choices are available from this dialog box. You can import a Web you've created with other tools, or you can create one of the Webs in the next list. This dialog box also lets you name your Web and establish its location on a Web server.

These are the possible Webs you can create:

- The One Page Web, available with the top option button on the dialog box, creates a Web with a single blank page, which will be the Web site's home page.

- The Corporate Presence Wizard walks you through the process of creating an organization-style Web.

- The Customer Support Web provides you with a framework for developing customer support services.

- The Discussion Web is excellent for setting up a discussion site, but creating one from scratch is very time-consuming.

- The Empty Web is just that—it creates a Web structure without even one page in it. You use this if you've already prepared a home page and need an empty Web in which to install it.

FIG. 2.1

The New FrontPage Web dialog box lets you select a Web template, name your Web, and place it on a server.

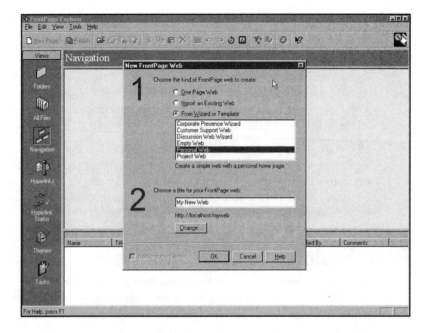

■ The Personal Web sets up a single home page for you, with a selection of possible hyperlink destinations you can delete or customize.

■ The Project Web establishes a Web you can use to manage and track a project.

▶ **See** Chapter 23, "FrontPage's Web Templates and Wizards," **p. 535** where these Webs are covered in much more detail.

For your test run, select Personal Web by clicking it in the small viewing pane. Move the cursor to the title field beside the large numeral 2, highlight "My New Web," and type whatever title you want your Personal Web to have (your name is a reasonable idea).

Next, click the Change button. Here is where you tell FrontPage the server location for your Web, including the directory location on that server. For now, we'll assume that you've installed either the Microsoft Personal Web Server (MS-PWS) or the FrontPage Personal Web Server (FP-PWS) during the installation procedure, or, if you're working on an NT machine, that you've already installed either Peer Web Services (NT Workstation) or Internet Information Server (IIS).

We'll make this Web a local Web, which means assigning it to the server on the local machine. Type **http://127.0.0.0/myWeb** in the location field of the Change Location dialog box. This places the new Web on your local server; 127.0.0.0 is the Internet Protocol (IP) address for the location called "localhost." The final part of the location, "/myWeb" denotes the folder that will be created on the server to store this particular Web.

N O T E The name of your Web must obey the naming conventions of the server—FrontPage Web names can't, for example, include spaces. Also, the name is case sensitive. To the server, "MyWeb" is not the same as "myWeb." Keep this in mind when you're trying to access your Web site through your Internet Service Provider. ■

Click OK to return to the New FrontPage Web dialog box, double check to see that everything's as you selected or typed it, and click OK. FrontPage Explorer now starts generating the Web. If FrontPage asks you for the username and password for the Web administrator, type in the username and password you established when you installed FrontPage and click OK. In a few minutes, Explorer finishes creating the Web and opens it for you in the Explorer workspace. At the same time, it automatically starts the Personal Web Server.

And that, believe it or not, is all there is to it! You have a brand-new Web ready for expansion.

Explorer gives you several views of your Web that you can access by clicking in the Views bar of the Explorer workspace (see Figure 2.2). The Navigation View, which appears by default, shows the hierarchical structure of the Web, and lets you add pages quickly and link them to existing pages. The Hyperlink view, by comparison, shows an outline-like hierarchy in the left pane, and a graphical view of the Web in the right pane. The right pane shows icons for each page, image, or World Wide Web URL, with lines showing the links among them.

▶ **See** Chapter 24, "Working with an Existing Web," **p. 557**, for details on updating and managing Webs that are already in place.

▶ **See** Chapter 26, "Managing a Web," **p. 595**, for information about FrontPage Explorer's Web management capabilities.

Part

I

Ch

2

FIG. 2.2

On the left side of the FrontPage Explorer workspace (here showing the Hyperlink View), are the buttons for accessing the various views.

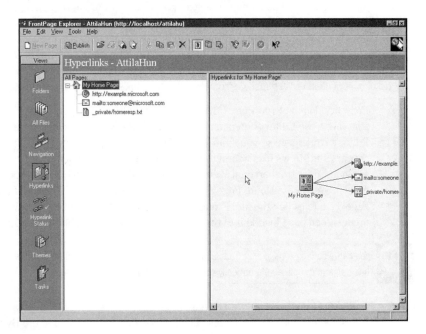

Another view available in FrontPage Explorer is the Folder view. This shows a view of your Web much like the directory and file appearance of Windows Explorer, and functions in much the same way. In the Folder view, you have file-level control of your Web, something you'll want as your Web grows more complex. The All Files view gives you easy access to all files that are linked in your Web, no matter what folder they might be stored in.

You can switch between these views by choosing the appropriate view in the View menu or by clicking the appropriate View button in Explorer's Views bars. These views are extremely useful for managing your Web's structure and for moving pages into FrontPage Editor for editing.

Using FrontPage Editor to Create Your Pages

Although FrontPage Explorer is the manager for your Web, the Editor is where you'll expend most of your creative energies. FrontPage Editor is a very robust, full-featured Web page editor with numerous extensions beyond the HTML 3.2 and 4.0 standards. It is a primarily WYSIWYG environment, and whereas a growing number of other HTML editors are also WYSIWYG, FrontPage Editor competes very well with them. You can do more than just edit—you can follow links from one page to another even while editing them, which in effect turns FrontPage Editor into a minibrowser; and you can load pages from remote Web sites into the Editor to study the HTML code that makes such pages work.

FrontPage Editor resembles a word processor in many ways. You can open several pages at the same time and switch between them; cut, copy, and paste page elements; do spell checks; and format character appearance and size. FrontPage Editor also supports tables, just as Word and WordPerfect do, and with FrontPage 98, the table formatting options are rich enough to allow for advanced page layout capabilities (which is what tables are primarily used for in Web creation). Insertion of graphics also resembles word processor methods, and like today's word processors, FrontPage 98 contains built-in image manipulation tools. As for hyperlinking, that most crucial of Web tasks, FrontPage Editor makes it fast, easy, and thorough.

For a first look at FrontPage Editor, start it up by choosing Tools, Show FrontPage Editor. After a moment, the Editor screen appears. Now get the home page of your new Web into FrontPage Editor's workspace so you can view it. Choose File, Open from Web. The Open File dialog box appears and shows files within the Web that are currently opened in FrontPage Explorer (you are looking for the Personal Web, which you just created). The only Web page showing in the current Web is the Home Page, with the file name DEFAULT.HTM and the title "My Home Page." Double-click the file. FrontPage Editor opens (it might take a few seconds) with the predesigned page loaded into the workspace. Your screen should look like Figure 2.3.

 TIP You can also drag a page icon from Explorer's Navigator, Hyperlinks, or Summary view to the Editor's title bar, and the page automatically opens in the Editor.

From here, you begin the full development of your page, adding images, text, hyperlinks, tables, imagemaps, forms, tables of contents—the list goes on and on. By the end of this book, you'll be knowledgeable about them all.

FIG. 2.3

The Personal Web's home page, loaded and ready for editing.

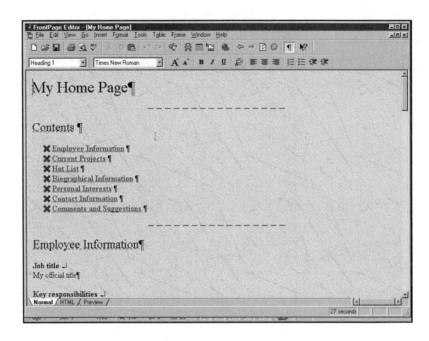

Try out a few items to show how easy FrontPage Editor is to use with these steps:

1. Highlight the large title, "My Home Page." and click the centering icon on the toolbar.

2. Double-click the word "My" and delete it by pressing the Delete key or by right-clicking and selecting Cut. Click the cursor (actually an insertion point) to the right of the line and type "of *Your Name*." (for example, "of Scarlett O'Hara"). The heading now reads, "Home Page of *Your Name*."

3. Put the cursor on the dotted horizontal line below the link named Comments and Suggestions and press Enter to add a graphic to the page. The horizontal line moves down and the cursor is on the left side of the screen. Select Clipart from the Insert menu and click the Web Navigators category in the left pane. Scroll until you find the gray button with the red arrow in the middle, click it, and click Insert. Figure 2.4 shows this button in place, on the left side of the FrontPage document.

4. Double-click FrontPage to see how it treats the images. You'll see the Image Properties dialog box with several options. Experiment to see what happens with each choice.

5. Add a table by placing the cursor where you want the table to be located. Click Table/Insert Table and select 3 Rows and 5 Columns. Select Center Alignment, a Border size of 3, and specify the Width as 75 in Percent. Click OK and the table appears, ready for data.

6. Experiment with everything you want on your page, even if you don't intend to keep any of it. Try a marquee (Insert/Marquee), then a Hyperlink (Insert/Hyperlink). Continue until your page is cluttered with all sorts of options. Save the page to the Web by choosing File/Save.

FIG. 2.4

FrontPage 98 ships with a good selection of graphic images, clip art, and multimedia inserts.

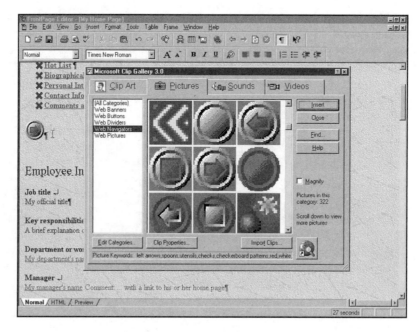

7. See what your page looks like as HTML code by clicking the HTML tab at the bottom of the screen. Click the Preview tab to see how it will look on the Web. In this latter case, the file automatically saves to the Web and the page displays in FrontPage Editor itself. If you want more control over the preview, select File/Preview in Browser. If you do so, you'll see the dialog box shown in Figure 2.5 and you can choose whatever browser you have installed and the resolution at which you wish to view your page. Select a resolution different from the one you're currently running, click Preview, and watch what happens.

▶ **See** Chapter 5, "Developing the Basic Page: Text, Lists, and Hyperlinks," **p. 71**.

FIG. 2.5

You can preview your Web in any browser you have installed and at any screen resolution.

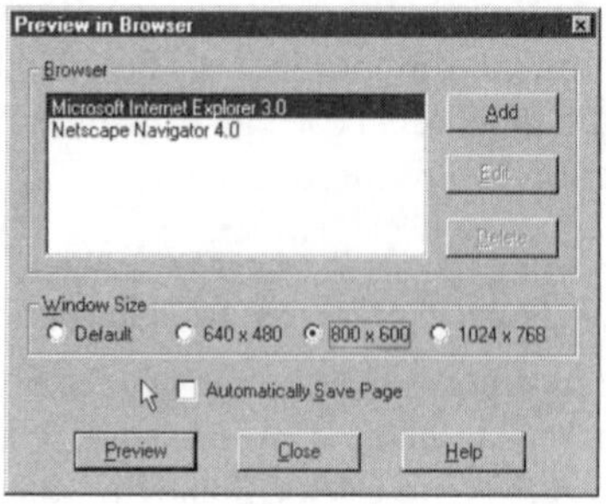

Using the Microsoft Personal Web Server to Offer Your Web to the World

You'll learn much more about this in Part V, "Building and Managing a Web," but here's a thumbnail sketch. The Microsoft Personal Web Server (MS-PWS) turns your PC into a real, fully functional Web server. If your PC is online to the Internet, and the MS-PWS is running, the Webs you've stored on your machine are accessible to anyone with the server's current IP address, a PPP connection to the Internet, and a Web browser. There's nothing else you need at this basic level.

This means that you can dispense with installing your Web on your Internet Service Provider's server and run your Web site from your desktop. All you need to do is to set yourself up with a 24-hour modem connection. If you're really serious, you'll need to register your site to get a permanent IP address because your site's dynamic IP address, as set by your ISP, changes whenever you log off the ISP connection and log back on again, but that's really all there is to it.

▶ **See** Chapter 27, "Serving Your Web to the World with the Microsoft Personal Web Server," **p. 611**, for a detailed discussion of Web serving needs and techniques.

In fact, FrontPage 98 ships with two Web servers, the Microsoft Personal Web Server and the FrontPage Personal Web Server. Microsoft Personal Web Server is the recommended one and is the more powerful. FrontPage Personal Web Server (cleverly named to be as confusing as possible when compared with Microsoft Personal Web Server), has fewer features and less serving power. In fact, it is included with FrontPage 98 solely because it had been included since the very first version of FrontPage and Microsoft wanted to guarantee backward compatibility. If you don't need the older server, only install Microsoft PWS.

The FrontPage Personal Web Server is sufficient for testing your Webs and even for establishing a low traffic site, but the Microsoft PWS is more powerful because of its ability to serve more connections simultaneously and its ability to allow more active content in your Web pages than the FrontPage PWS. If you want a public Web site with lots of daily traffic and advanced interactivity features, you'll need a more powerful server altogether, such as Netscape's FastTrack or Enterprise Server, or Microsoft's Internet Information Server.

From Here...

You're off to a good start. You've installed FrontPage successfully, set up your administrator's username and password, and had a taste of both FrontPage Explorer and Editor. Now you can check out the following.

- Chapter 3, "Essential Tools for Webmasters," introduces you to some of the advanced interactivity features of FrontPage Web creation.
- Chapter 4, "Introducing FrontPage Editor," explores the features and capabilities of the easy-to-use FrontPage Editor program.

- Chapter 5, "Developing the Basic Page: Text, Lists, and Hyperlinks," gets you started on your Web page design.
- The remainder of Part II examines the advanced features of FrontPage Editor.

## CHAPTER 3

Essential Tools for Webmasters

Even in the brief time since the introduction of the first version of Microsoft FrontPage in early 1996, the needs of Webmasters and page designers for a greater variety of tools have grown. This need is particularly acute in the area of active content, such as Dynamic HTML, and in layout, with the growing use of Cascading Style Sheets.

FrontPage 98 addresses most, if not all, of these needs. As before, it includes the sophisticated site management tools of FrontPage Explorer, an excellent Web page editor, the Microsoft Personal Web Server, and WebBot technology (now called FrontPage Components) that relieve you of any need to write CGI scripts. Among the new features are: more powerful Web management tools in FrontPage Explorer; many additions to the FrontPage Editor such as Dynamic HTML, style sheets, and WYSIWYG frames and table editing; and an upgraded Image Composer for processing and creating Web graphics. In this chapter we take a brief overview of the major features of FrontPage 98. ■

Using FrontPage Components (also called WebBots)

Make your site interactive without writing CGI scripts.

Do-It-Yourself graphics

Assemble, edit, and create your own images with Image Composer.

Use ActiveX controls, scripts, and applets

Put active content on your pages with ActiveX components, Visual Basic and Java scripts, and Java applets.

Easy frameset creation

FrontPage 98's frames editor lets you create, populate, and arrange frames in a WYSIWYG environment.

Drawing tables

Now you can use a pencil to draw tables directly on a page, as well as create and delete individual cells, rearrange them, and resize them.

Understanding FrontPage Components

In earlier versions of FrontPage, these *Components* were called WebBots, but whatever their name, they were unique to FrontPage. They're very useful because they relieve you of having to write CGI scripts to make your site interactive. Without CGI scripts, or Components to fill in for them, people can visit your site, but they can't interact with it through forms, searches, discussions, or registrations. Much of the appeal of the World Wide Web is in this interactivity, and if your site doesn't have it, you're missing a lot. Until recently, though, getting your pages to be interactive was a headache because not everyone can (or wants to) write CGI scripts. Moreover, incorrectly written custom scripts can behave so badly that ISP administrators often won't allow them to be installed on their server. All that changed with the introduction of FrontPage 97 in 1996, and FrontPage 98 carries on the tradition.

So what's a FrontPage Component? It's really no more than a chunk of programming that you embed in your page to carry out the operation you want, and FrontPage comes with several of them. Some are designed for interactive applications; others are more modest and merely insert useful bits of information into your page. Let's have a quick look at one, so they won't be so mysterious.

Click anywhere on a document in the FrontPage Editor workspace and choose Insert, FrontPage Component. The Insert FrontPage Component dialog box opens with a list of the available Components. There are more of them than are listed because some do their work invisibly and you never see them. Select Comment and choose OK. A dialog box opens with a text box for you to type an annotation for whatever you need. Choose OK and the dialog box closes. The text of your comment appears, in purple, on the page.

Well, OK, that's nice, but you could have gone to the HTML mode in FrontPage Editor (more about this later) and typed the comment in yourself, so why bother with the previous procedure?

A couple of reasons: Comments in HTML source code can be easy to miss, unless you're looking for them, and inserting comments into raw HTML is always at the risk of a typo in the <!-- and --> tags. The Comment Component allows you to put important annotations about the page right into the FrontPage Editor workspace, where you and anyone else working on the page will see them. However, they aren't visible to anyone accessing the page in a browser. To demonstrate this, click the Preview tab at the bottom of the FrontPage Editor workspace and you'll see that the Comment text does not appear on the previewed page.

This is a minor example, but some Components are very powerful. They and FrontPage Editor together can relieve you of almost every programming chore; in fact, you could set up and run a Web site with FrontPage 98 and never write a line of HTML code.

Incidentally, if you put the cursor on top of the purple text, it turns into a little robot. That's the *Bot cursor*, and it tells you if there's a FrontPage Component or other at this particular spot in your page—sometimes you can't tell just by looking. Actually, some FrontPage Components don't appear in the Insert FrontPage Component menu (even though they're Components) and the Bot cursor shows up if the mouse pointer hovers over them. These tend to be the more frequently used elements, like the Timestamp Component, and are available from other menus.

With FrontPage Components, you can do the following:

- Comment your pages so you can see the comments, although visitors to your site won't.
- Make custom confirmation pages to reply to people who send you information.
- Put a Hit Counter on your page.
- Include the content of another page in the current page.
- Add nonstandard HTML code to your pages without using a text editor.
- Add a page banner.
- Make an image or a page appear in your site for a specified length of time (advertisers take note).
- Allow a visitor to search your site for key words or phrases (if your site is a reference or research site, this is important).
- Substitute your own page variables for standard ones.
- Set up a dynamic Table of Contents that changes automatically as your site changes (choose Insert, Table of Contents)
- Add a navigation bar (choose Insert, Navigation Bar).
- Add a timestamp to your page (choose Insert, Timestamp).

For more information on this, see Chapter 11, "Using FrontPage Components, Forms, and Interactive Page Templates."

Creating and Customizing Graphics

Images are integral to Web pages. For what you might call *utility images* such as lines, buttons, and icons, you can search around on the Web and likely find something that suits your needs. However, most people want to personalize their site and off-the-shelf graphics don't really contribute to this. So FrontPage 98 obligingly offers Image Composer version 1.5 to let you alter existing images and create new ones. This is an upgraded version from FrontPage 97 1.0.

Image Composer: A Very Brief Overview

Image Composer is a powerful graphics package, but you can learn the essentials quickly. The Typical installation gives you the application plus a tutorial and online help. A full installation adds to these basics a set of fonts plus over 200M (yes, megabytes) of photo samples and 18M of Web Art samples. These samples can be used as components to build custom graphics, rather like clip art.

Getting Acquainted with Image Composer

You may have been reluctant to install the full 200+ megabytes of art samples, depending on how much disk space you have. So for this quick look at the application, we'll assume you installed the tutorial and use the images that come with it. They're TIFF files, but once you've completed your work, you can save the results as a GIF or JPEG to use in your Web. (Actually, FrontPage Editor automatically converts to GIF for you unless you instruct it differently.)

T I P The supplied graphics in Image Composer are Tagged Image File Format (TIFF) files. This format is lossless; that is, it compresses the image without degrading image quality. It also stores images in True Color. Starting with an image of such high quality contributes to the quality of the GIF or JPEG that you eventually put on your Web page.

To get started, do the following:

1. Start Image Composer by selecting Show Image Editor from either FrontPage Explorer or FrontPage Editor. The Arrange box also automatically starts.

2. Close the Arrange box for now.

3. Select Insert, From File. Assuming a default installation, go to C:\Program Files\Microsoft Image_Composer\Tutorial. You'll see four TIFF files listed; we'll be using the flowers files.

T I P If you don't see these files, make sure you have selected either All Files or .TIF in the Files of Type text box.

4. Double-click DAISY.TIF. The image of the daisy appears in the workspace (see Figure 3.1).

FIG. 3.1
Image Composer's workspace with an image loaded and ready for editing.

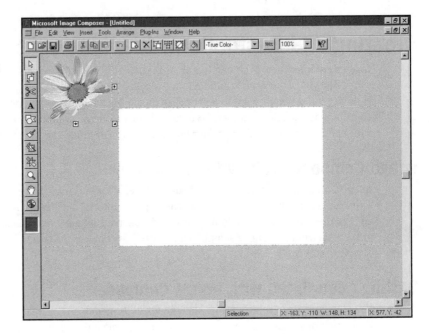

5. Move the daisy from the top left corner of your screen onto the white *paper* rectangle. Do this by positioning the cursor over the image until you see a four-arrow pointer and drag to the right.

6. Enlarge the daisy while maintaining its original proportions by holding down the Shift key, grabbing the arrow at the bottom right of the image, and dragging down and to the right. (If you don't hold the Shift key down, resizing may distort the image since its proportions aren't preserved.) Release the mouse button and the image resizes.

7. Choose Insert, From File and choose HIBISCUS.TIF to load another component into your image. Drag the hibiscus over the daisy and click outside the image area. You'll now have two components combined into one image.

8. Click and drag the rotation handle at the top right of the box to reorient the daisy part of the image. Put the side of the flower without petals at the top left of the box (see Figure 3.2).

FIG. 3.2

You can reorient components that are part of a complete image by dragging their rotation handles.

9. Now add a third component. Choose Insert, From File and choose TULIP.TIF. Move it on top of both of the other images at the edge of the daisy without petals. Right-click the tulip and choose Send to Back. This places it behind both of the other flowers. Click away from the flowers and you'll see your three-part image (see Figure 3.3).

10. Now sharpen the entire image. Select all three flowers by holding down the Control key and clicking each of them in succession (you can also select them all by using Ctrl+A). Choose Tools, Effects to open the Effects dialog box. Click the Effects tab and use the drop-down list box (labeled Category) to find and select Photographic.

FIG. 3.3
You can layer image components in any order.

11. Once you've selected Photographic, you'll see a list of available photographic effects appearing in the dialog box's Effects sheet. Scroll until you find Sharpen and click the parrot image. Now click <u>A</u>pply and close the Effects dialog box. You'll now have a sharper image.

12. At this point, give the whole image a different look. Select all the flowers and choose Tools, <u>E</u>ffects again. In the drop-down list box, find the Paint entry and select it. In the dialog box's Effects sheet, scroll until you find Fresco. Click the parrot, <u>A</u>pply, and close the dialog box. Your bouquet is now a frescoed image (see Figure 3.4).

When you're done, save the image as a GIF or JPEG file and import it into FrontPage Editor on the page of your choice.

Using ActiveX, Scripts, and Applets

FrontPage Editor 98 makes it easy to add ActiveX components, Visual Basic Scripts, and Java Scripts to your pages. Applets are, of course, more complex because you (or somebody) has to write the Java code for the applet and compile it so it can be used. However, the basic procedure is the same in each case.

Adding an ActiveX Control

ActiveX Controls combine the convenience of Java applets with the permanence and functionality of Netscape Navigator plug-ins. Like Java applets, ActiveX Controls can be automatically downloaded to your system if they are not currently installed or if the installed version isn't the most recent. Like plug-ins, ActiveX Controls remain available to your Web browser continuously once they are installed.

These controls build on Microsoft's highly successful Object Linking and Embedding (OLE) standard to provide a common framework for extending the capability of Web browsers. ActiveX Controls, however, are more than just a simple Web browser plug-in or add-in. Because of the nature of ActiveX Controls, they can be used to extend the functionality of Microsoft browsers and any programming language or application that supports the OLE standard.

To insert an ActiveX Control, do the following:

1. Start FrontPage Editor and load a document into the workspace.

2. Choose Insert, Advanced, ActiveX Control. When the dialog box appears, click the button at the right of the Pick a Control box to get the drop-down list of controls on your system. Notice that FrontPage 98 comes with a selection of controls already installed for you (see Figure 3.5).

3. Choose the control you want, and choose the Properties button to use the properties dialog boxes to customize the control to suit your purposes.

ActiveX Controls can be complicated to use; they all require parameters of one kind or another. For a detailed examination of setting parameter values, refer to Chapter 17, "Using ActiveX Controls."

FIG. 3.5
You can choose from among controls installed on your system.

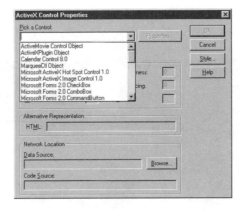

Adding Scripts

Microsoft has introduced its own scripting language, Visual Basic Script (VB Script), which is based on the Visual Basic and Visual Basic for Applications languages. Just as those two languages made it much easier to create applications for Windows and within the Microsoft Office suite, respectively, VB Script was designed as a language for easily adding interactivity and dynamic content to Web pages.

The JavaScript language—first introduced by Netscape in its Web browser, Netscape Navigator 2—gives Web authors another way to add interactivity and intelligence to their Web pages. JavaScript code is included as part of the HTML document and requires no additional compilation or development tools other than a compatible Web browser. Although FrontPage Editor on its own is an extremely capable page editor, its capabilities are enormously extended by adding scripts.

FrontPage Editor lets you insert either VBScript or JavaScript into your page by choosing the Insert, Advanced, Script command. When you do this, you get the Script dialog box (see Figure 3.6).

Within the Language section of this dialog box, you have several options, as follows:

- **VBScript**   Mark this option button if you want to write your script in VBScript. When your script is complete and you close the dialog box, FrontPage inserts the VBScript icon on the page to indicate that VBScript was placed at that point.

N O T E   The question of which scripting language to use has no ready-made answer. JavaScript resembles the Java language, while VBScript is derived from Visual Basic. Your familiarity with either of these languages may influence your choice. In the short term, however, JavaScript may afford broader compatibility, since both Netscape and Internet Explorer browsers understand it. Netscape browsers ignore VBScript. This question is explored at more length in Chapter 18, "Scripting with VBScript." ■

FIG. 3.6
Use the Script dialog
box to add inline
programming to your
pages.

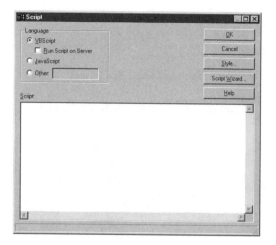

- **Run Script on Server**   This option directs the script to execute on a Microsoft Internet Information Server. This is oriented toward the use of ASP (Active Server Pages).

- **JavaScript**   Mark this button if you want to write your script in JavaScript. As with VBScript, when your script is complete and you close the dialog box, FrontPage inserts the JavaScript icon to indicate that a JavaScript was placed at that point.

- **Other**   This option is for scripting languages that may be developed in the future.

After selecting the language you want, click in the Script dialog box, type your code, and choose OK when finished.

You may prefer to use the Script Wizard to write your scripts. This is a point-and-click method of creating code; for more information refer to Chapter 18, "Scripting with VBScript."

Adding Applets

Applets are specialized Java programs, especially designed for executing within Internet Web pages. To run a Java applet, you need a Java-enabled Web browser such as Netscape Navigator 3.x or 4.x, or Microsoft's Internet Explorer versions 3.x or 4.x. These and other Web browsers are all capable of handling standard HTML, recognizing applet tags within an HTML Web page, and downloading and executing the specified Java program (or programs) in the context of a Java virtual machine.

Assuming you've created and compiled an applet, and it's installed at an appropriate location in your Web, use the Insert, Advanced, Java Applet command to open the Java Applet Properties dialog box (see Figure 3.7).

The Applet Source is the name of the source file; this almost always has a CLASS extension. The Base URL is the URL of the folder containing this file. You must add any parameter names and values required by the applet. For more detailed information on using applets, refer to Chapter 20, "Inserting Java Applets and Browser Plug-Ins."

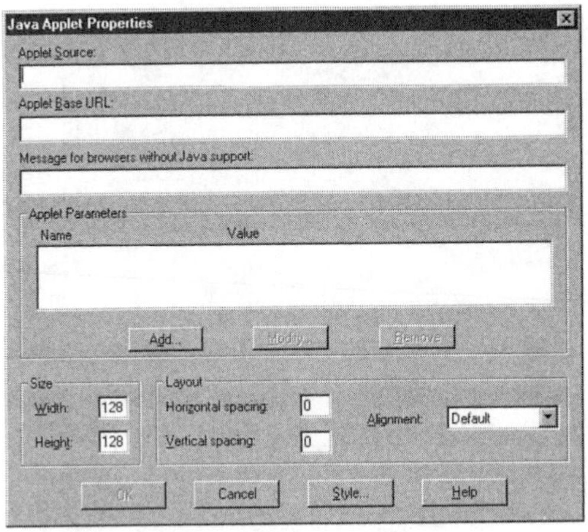

FIG. 3.7

To add an applet to a page and configure it quickly, use the Java Applet Properties dialog box.

Adding Netscape Plug-Ins

Starting with version 1 of Navigator, Netscape provided ways to enhance its browser with helper applications that support data formats beyond the built-in graphics and HTML. With Netscape Navigator Version 2, Navigator began supporting plug-ins, another way to extend the range of data types that can be presented on or with a Web page.

FrontPage Editor's plug-in insertion command generates the <EMBED> tag, which is recognized by both Navigator and Internet Explorer. Essentially, the <EMBED> tag is a type of link; objects specified by it automatically download and display when the document displays. To insert a plug-in, choose Insert, Advanced, Plug-In to open the Plug-In Properties dialog box (see Figure 3.8).

FIG. 3.8

Use the Plug-In Properties dialog box to embed objects in a Web page so that browsers that support plug-ins can use them.

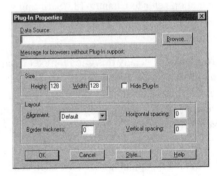

Into the Data Source box, type the name of the file you want embedded. The MIME type of the embedded file tells a user's browser which plug-in to use; if it's Netscape Navigator, and it doesn't have the right plug-in, it offers to download one for the user.

Using the New FrontPage 98 Frame Layout Tools

FrontPage 98 takes a new approach to creating and linking framesets and framed pages. Unlike the Frames Wizard approach of FrontPage 97, this technique allows you to see exactly what you're doing, while you're doing it.

In the next procedure, you'll create a frameset with two frames and populate it. Before beginning, ensure that the open Web has at least two pages in it—you'll need these to best illustrate WYSIWYG frameset behavior. You might also want to make sure the pages have some identifiable material in them, so you'll be able to identify them on sight.

To create a frameset with two frames and populate it:

1. Start FrontPage Editor and choose <u>F</u>ile, <u>N</u>ew to open the New dialog box. Click the Frames tab to display the available frame templates. For this example, select the Header template, which gives you an upper frame whose links change the page that displays in the lower frame. Choose OK. Now you have the screen shown in Figure 3.9.

FIG. 3.9

FrontPage 98 gives you a choice of several different frame layouts, such as this Header and Main Frame arrangement.

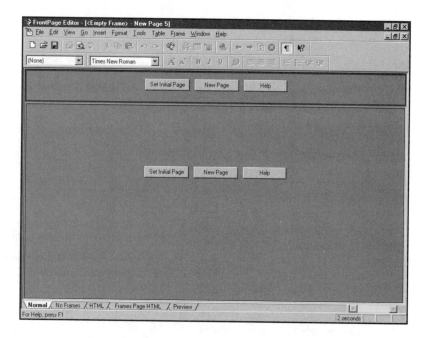

Part

I

Ch

3

2. Click the New Page button in the upper frame and a new blank page appears there. You'll use this page for the hyperlinks that control the display in the lower frame. Note that you can also insert an existing page into any frame.

3. Click the Set Initial Page button in the lower frame. This opens the Create Hyperlink dialog box. From the list box, select an existing page of the current FrontPage Web and click OK. The selected page opens in the lower window. (If you look in the FrontPage Editor title bar at this point, you'll see that two page titles are given; the first is that of the active page, the second is the title of the frameset file itself.)

4. Click in the upper frame. Type some text to serve as a hyperlink. Select it and choose Insert, Hyperlink to open the Create Hyperlink dialog box. In the dialog list box, select the page you chose in step 3 (in other words, link to the Initial Page, the page that currently appears in the lower frame).

5. Repeat step 4, but instead of linking to the page that currently appears in the lower frame, link to a different page in the FrontPage Web. Your screen should now resemble that shown in Figure 3.10.

FIG. 3.10

The frameset is being set up with two links in the upper frame.

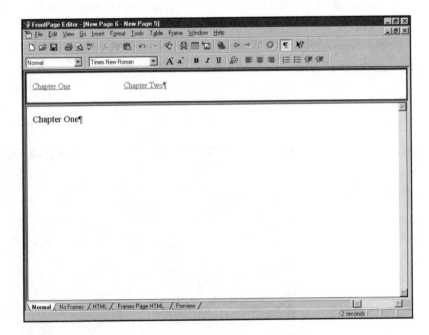

6. Use File, Save All to save the frameset file and the new or changed pages. You'll be asked to supply a name for the frameset file and a name for the new page you created in step 2.

7. Preview Mode does not support frame linking, so use the Preview In Browser command to test the frameset. Clicking the links in the upper frame should switch the page appearing in the lower frame.

To edit the frameset later, simply open the frameset file in FrontPage Editor. It will appear with its assigned initial pages displayed.

N O T E If you used the New Page button to create a new page within a frame, that frame does not show the new file the next time you open the frameset—for example, for editing. You must use the Set Initial Page button to make that new page into the initial page. ▪

If you want to save the frameset without saving the pages that display in it, click the Frames Page HTML tab at the bottom of the editor workspace while you're working on the frameset. When the HTML page appears, choose File, Save As and provide Page Title and file name.

If you want to establish your Web as a *framed* Web as soon as people access it, rename the frameset page with the file name default.htm.

Drawing a Table on a Page

Many Web page authors make heavy use of tables to control layout and Microsoft has gone to some lengths to improve table creation in FrontPage 98. The main improvement is a WYSIWYG drawing tool that makes table setup considerably more intuitive. To draw a simple table, do this:

1. Choose Table, Draw Table and the Table toolbar appears. When you move the mouse pointer into the workspace, it turns into the table drawing tool.

2. Drag the table drawing tool through the Editor workspace until you have a rectangle that's about the size of the table you want and release the mouse button. (It's the same technique as drawing rectangles in a simple paint program).

3. Drag within the cells to create new cells, columns, or rows. Figure 3.11 shows a partially completed table, with a row boundary being drawn in (shown by the dotted line).

Part

I

Ch

3

FIG. 3.11
Adding cells, rows, and columns is as easy as drawing with a pencil.

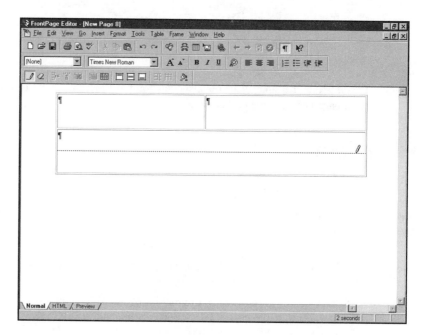

4. To resize a cell, place the drawing tool on top of any cell border until the pointer becomes a double-headed arrow. Drag this to adjust the size of the cell or the table.

5. To remove a border, click the Eraser button on the Table toolbar. The mouse pointer turns into an eraser. Hold the left mouse button down while dragging the eraser over the cell border you want to erase. When the border is selected, it is highlighted. Release the

mouse button and the cell border vanishes. (Note that in some configurations of cells, certain borders cannot be erased.)

You can adjust the table's properties further with the Table Properties dialog box. For example, if you're using the table as a layout aid, you likely won't want the borders to be visible. Right-click anywhere on the table and choose Table Properties from the shortcut menu to make the dialog box appear (see Figure 3.12). Modify any properties and choose OK.

FIG. 3.12

Use the Table Properties dialog box to fine-tune the appearance of the table.

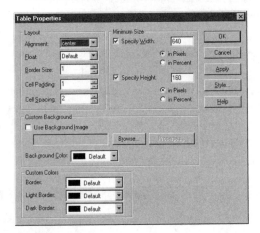

To add text to the table, place the insertion point in a cell and type. Cells can contain anything that a page can, including other tables.

From Here...

You're off to a good start. You've installed FrontPage successfully and had a look at WebBots and Image Composer. Now you have many other places you can go, among them:

- Part II, "Creating Your Web Pages with FrontPage Editor," covers the nuts and bolts of page design and creation, including chapters on text and hyperlinks, graphics, and multimedia, tables, frames, and templates.

- Part III, "Creating and Adapting Graphics with Image Composer," shows you the methods you use to make and modify your own graphics.

- Part IV, "Integrating Active Content into Your Web," explores the software technologies of ActiveX, VBScript and JavaScript, Java applets, and the Virtual Reality Modeling Language.

- Part V, "Building and Managing a Web," shows you how to integrate the pages you create into a sophisticated, well-organized Web site that will be the envy of your neighbors in cyberspace.

Creating Your Web Pages with FrontPage Editor

## CHAPTER 4

Introducing FrontPage Editor

FrontPage Editor 98 is a very powerful Web page editor. So powerful, in fact, that you'll seldom need to work directly with HTML text files. FrontPage Editor's interface and behavior resemble those of a word processor, and you'll find many advantages both in this resemblance and in FrontPage Editor's close integration with FrontPage Explorer. Furthermore, and very importantly, FrontPage Editor includes FrontPage Components, dynamic objects that you can insert into a page to produce elements like timestamps, confirmation fields, and searches. This all-in-one approach, combining FrontPage Explorer's overall view of a Web site, FrontPage Editor's WYSIWYG interface, several multimedia tools, and FrontPage Components to replace programming, helps you build an attention-getting and functional site with a minimum of time and difficulty. ■

FrontPage Editor 98 enhancements and new features

The new version of FrontPage brings you multimedia, better font resources, direct HTML editing, and much more.

Page creation

Create, save, and retrieve pages while using FrontPage Editor and Explorer together.

Applying a theme to an individual page

You can specify that certain pages have a different theme from that of the Web as a whole.

Workspace customizing

Change the FrontPage Editor screen display.

Preview in FrontPage editor

Use Preview mode and the Preview in Browser command to see what your pages will look like without connecting to the Internet.

HTML and coding by hand

What HMTL is, and how to use FrontPage Editor's HTML View to insert code by hand into your page.

HTML markup

Use the HTML Markup command to add unsupported HTML to a page.

What's New in FrontPage Editor 98?

The FrontPage 98 package contains significant enhancements and improvements over FrontPage 97. FrontPage Editor 98 has shared in this upgrade, and if you're used to FrontPage Editor 97, here are the major differences you'll notice.

- Supplied Themes that you can use to give a page an overall, coordinated *look*.
- A Preview mode that lets you evaluate the appearance of a page without using a browser.
- A new HTML editing mode that improves the way FrontPage Editor handles direct modification of the HTML code of a page.
- Support for Dynamic HTML, such as outlining, animated buttons, animated page transitions such as PowerPoint's, text animation, marquees, and multimedia.
- New image editing tools that let you crop, rotate, change contrast and brightness, and perhaps most useful of all, add text on top of a GIF image.
- Cascading Style Sheet support, now built into the editor.
- WYSIWYG frames creation and editing.
- A Table Drawing Tool that allows you to draw tables directly on the page in a WYSIWYG environment.
- Improved forms handling.

Using FrontPage Editor with FrontPage Explorer

Although FrontPage Editor is capable of running in stand-alone mode, this isn't usually recommended. Many of its features depend on it being used concurrently with Explorer and the Personal Web Server, and running FrontPage Editor by itself removes its more advanced functionality. Furthermore, using the two applications side by side lets you keep an eye on links among pages and within pages, lets you access image and page files with little fuss, and gives you an overall view of your Web as it grows from a single page to a full-scale Web site.

Server Considerations with FrontPage 98

After you start Explorer, you open a Web by selecting the Web's name from the list box in the Getting Started dialog box and choosing OK. If the Getting Started dialog box isn't visible, choose File, Open FrontPage Web to make it appear. If the Web name isn't in the list box, use the More Webs button to open the Open FrontPage Web dialog box and click the List Webs button to locate it.

When you've selected the Web and chosen OK, Explorer may ask you for a username and password. This happens if you didn't install the Microsoft Personal Web Server when you installed FrontPage. If you didn't install the Microsoft PWS, what did get installed (automatically) was the FrontPage Personal Web Server, a different piece of software. The FrontPage PWS always asks for a username and password before Explorer opens a Web. However, if you installed the Microsoft PWS, the Web simply opens and you won't be asked for identification.

Another obvious difference between the two servers is that the default home page created by the Microsoft PWS is named DEFAULT.HTM, and that created by the FrontPage PWS is named INDEX.HTM. Furthermore, with the FrontPage Personal Web Server, the Webs you create are automatically stored in the C:\FrontPage Webs\Content folder. With the Microsoft PWS, they are stored in C:\Webshare\Wwroot.

N O T E   Notice that the examples and screen shots in the Editor sections of this book assume the use of the Microsoft Personal Web Server, unless explicitly stated otherwise. ▨

After you've opened the selected Web, the display in Figure 4.1 shows what you might see in the earliest stages of the Web's construction. In the figure, Folder View was selected.

FIG. 4.1
Explorer's Folder View of a Web site is modeled closely on Windows 95's file display.

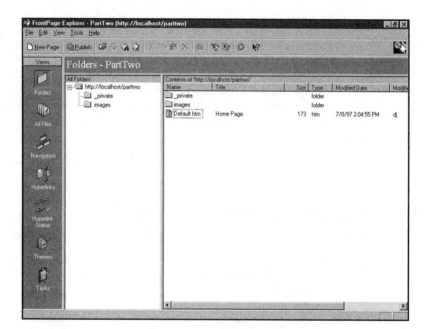

Part
II

Ch
4

N O T E   In Figure 4.1, note that the page title of the home page is Home Page, while the page file name is DEFAULT.HTM. Don't confuse the page title and the page file name—the file name is a regular file in the directory structure and must be treated as one. The page title is simply a label for the page. In fact, you can have identical page titles in the same Web, although you should avoid this. It's confusing for your audience because they will see the same page title for different pages, and also for you because you'll have to remember that identical page titles refer to different pages. ▨

CAUTION

The DEFAULT.HTM file, which automatically creates when you create a Web with FrontPage Explorer, acts as the default entry point for that Web. If you delete or rename DEFAULT.HTM, browsers display only a file index

continues

continued

of the pages of the Web, and your visitors won't see the home page unless they can figure out which file it is. However, some servers such as O'Reilly WebSite do use the INDEX.HTM name for the home page. If you're running your Web on such a server, you'll have to rename your home page to INDEX.HTM after all.

Creating a New Page with FrontPage Explorer

Page creation can be done either through FrontPage Explorer or FrontPage Editor. The Explorer method is quick but not very flexible, so you may prefer to use the Editor for most page creation.

If you do want to use the Explorer method, you can be in any of Explorer's Views. For the example, assume the use of Folder View (choose View, Folders if you aren't seeing it). Click the New Page button on the Explorer toolbar. A new page listing immediately appears in Explorer's right pane. It defaults to the file name NEWPAGE.HTM and a Page Title of "New Page." At this point, you should give the page a nondefault file name—in fact, Explorer encourages you to do so by placing the text insertion point at the end of NEWPAGE.HTM in the file listing. You can't change the Page title, however; to do this you must open the page in FrontPage Editor. You'll do this shortly.

A page created in this way takes on whatever theme has been applied to the currently open Web.

Creating a New Page with FrontPage Editor

To create a new page by using FrontPage Editor, use the following steps:

1. From the Explorer menu bar, choose Tools, Show FrontPage Editor; or click the FrontPage Editor button on the Explorer toolbar. The FrontPage Editor starts (see Figure 4.2).

N O T E If your FrontPage Editor screen doesn't look like the one in Figure 4.2, see "Changing the FrontPage Editor Screen Display" later in this chapter. ▪

2. After Editor starts, choose File, New. The New dialog box appears (see Figure 4.3).

N O T E If you click the New button on the FrontPage Editor toolbar, FrontPage Editor automatically opens a blank Normal Page and applies whatever theme has been applied to the currently open FrontPage Web. ▪

3. Select the Page Template or wizard.
4. Choose OK.

If you select a Normal Page, you immediately return to FrontPage Editor with a blank Normal Page opened for you. If you make another choice, you can create a specialized page from the template layout that appears; or, in the case of the Form Page Wizard, work through the process of creating a form. In all cases, the page inherits the theme chosen for the currently open Web. You can, however, change the theme used in an individual page.

FIG. 4.2

FrontPage Editor waits for you to create a new page.

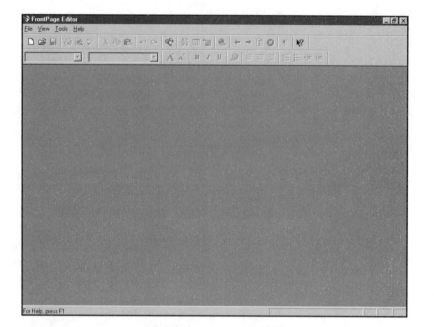

FIG. 4.3

You can create pages by using any one of several templates, or you can use the Form Page Wizard to automate the form creation process.

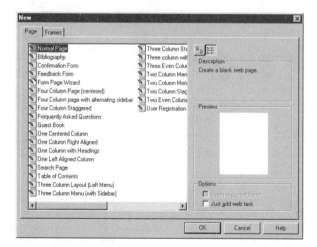

Changing the Theme of a Selected Page   You might have an overall theme for a Web, but prefer a different theme (or no theme at all) for particular pages. To change a page's theme:

1. With the target page open in FrontPage Editor, choose Format, Theme. The Choose Theme dialog box opens (see Figure 4.4).

FIG. 4.4

You use the Choose Theme dialog box to vary the themes within a Web.

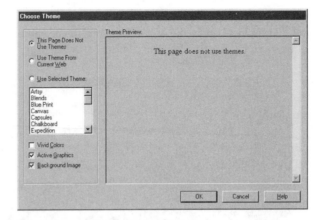

2. Mark the top option button if you don't want any theme. Mark the second one down if you want the current Web's theme to be used.

3. If you want to pick a different theme, mark the third option button, and choose a theme from the list box.

4. Mark the Vivid Colors option button to specify a brighter set of theme colors. Mark the Active Graphics option button to get active buttons, bullets, and similar graphical elements. Mark the Background Image option button if you want a background texture rather than a solid color.

   ▶ **See** Chapter 6, "Enhancing Pages with Themes, Graphics, and Multimedia," **p. 123**, for more detail on the options in Step 4.

5. When you're satisfied with the results that display in the Theme Preview window, choose OK, and the theme is applied to the page.

Creating a Page from a Template   If you select a Page Template, you simply use it as a pattern for laying out the page you want. As soon as you've made even a few additions to it, though, you should save it to avoid losing your work. To do this, choose File, Save or choose the Save button on the toolbar. The Save As dialog box appears (see Figure 4.5).

N O T E   Of the New Page Wizards supplied with FrontPage 97, only the Form Page Wizard has been carried over into FrontPage 98. The Form Page Wizard is examined in detail in Chapter 11, "Using FrontPage Components, Forms, and Interactive Page Templates." ▪

To finish setting up the new page, use the following steps:

1. Type a page title into the Title text box provided. It can be as long as you like, but don't make it too long; because of the size of browser title bars in low resolution displays, 60 characters is the practical maximum.

2. FrontPage Editor constructs a file name for the page, using nonblank characters from the Title box, and shows this name in the URL text box. Choose OK to accept this file name.

Or, you can type a different file name in the Page URL text box and choose OK. If you don't give the file name an HTM extension, FrontPage Editor supplies one.

FIG. 4.5

Use the Save As dialog box to save your new page with a descriptive page title and a suitable file name.

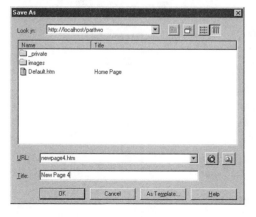

CAUTION

The file extension for a Web page file should almost always be HTM or HTML; if you give it another extension, browsers may not properly display that page. There are a couple of exceptions—Active Server Pages have the extension ASP, and linked Cascading Style Sheets have the extension .CSS.

The page is saved to the current, or active, Web. You can see the page title you just gave it by looking in the title bar. FrontPage Editor's behavior is different here from a word processor; the page title, not the page file name, appears in the title bar. If you click the FrontPage Explorer button on the toolbar, the Explorer views show you the new page you added (see Figure 4.6).

You could, of course, have accepted the default page title, which FrontPage Editor displays for you, but it's not very informative, and the page title is what your audience sees in the title bar when they're browsing your Web. People like to know what to expect in a page, so use your page titles to give them an idea of what they're looking at.

Editing an Existing Page

Start FrontPage Explorer and open the Web that contains the page you want to edit. To load and edit the page, use the following steps:

1. From the Explorer menu bar, choose Tools, Show FrontPage Editor or click the FrontPage Editor button on the Explorer toolbar.
2. After the Editor starts, choose File, Open or click the Open button on the Editor toolbar.
3. From the Open dialog box, select the title of the page you want to edit (see Figure 4.7).
4. Choose OK. The selected page appears in the Editor's workspace.

FIG. 4.6

Explorer shows your new page's icon and title in the right pane of the Folder View.

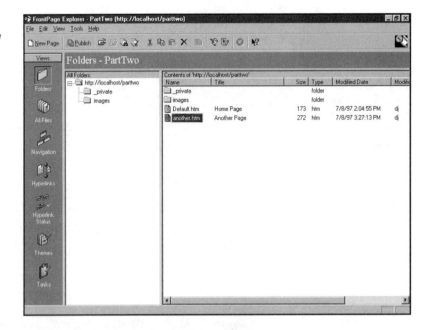

FIG. 4.7

The Open dialog box displays the page titles and file names of the pages that belong to the currently open Web.

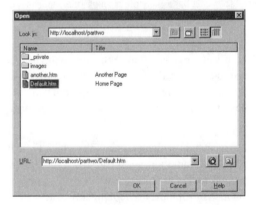

 If Editor isn't already running, you can double-click the icon of the page you want to edit in the right pane of either the Folder View or the Hyperlink View of FrontPage Explorer, or in FrontPage Explorer's All Files View. This starts Editor and automatically loads the page you double-clicked. Alternatively, right-click the page you want to edit and choose Open from the shortcut menu that appears.

 You can also open a page in FrontPage Editor by dragging its icon from any Explorer pane to FrontPage Editor's title bar. Don't drag the icon into Editor's workspace if there's a page already there because this creates a hyperlink between the page already in Editor and the page whose icon you're dragging.

Retitling or Renaming a Page

As your Web becomes large and elaborate, you'll likely run into situations where you need to change a page's title or URL (that is, its file name). This is pretty straightforward.

To change the page title, use the following steps:

1. Load the page into FrontPage Editor using whatever method you prefer.
2. Edit the page, if desired.
3. Choose File, Page Properties. The Page Properties dialog box appears (see Figure 4.8).

FIG. 4.8
You can change or edit a page title in the Page Properties dialog box.

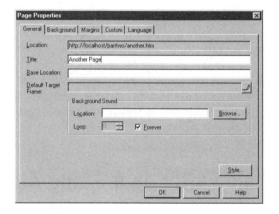

4. Choose the General sheet tab if it isn't already chosen and type the title you want into the Title text box.
5. Choose OK.

The new page title appears in FrontPage Editor's title bar.

N O T E Changing the page title doesn't affect the file name or the URL in any way. The file name and URL stay as they are until you change them to something else. ■

You can also give the page a different file name. To do so, use the following steps:

1. Choose File, Save As. The Save As dialog box appears.
2. Type the file name you want in the URL text box. If you don't type in the HTM extension, FrontPage Editor supplies it for you.
3. Choose OK.

To see the effect of this, make FrontPage Explorer the active window, with Folder View selected. Your page is present under its new title and with its new file name in the right pane. However, the original page, the one you began with, is still present. If you want to delete it, use the following steps:

Part
II

Ch
4

1. In FrontPage Explorer (in any pane that shows page icons), click the name or icon of the file to select it.
2. Choose Edit, Delete. The Confirm Delete dialog box appears.
3. Choose Yes. The file is deleted and the Explorer screen is updated.

> **CAUTION**
>
> When deleting a page, don't accidentally select the Delete FrontPage Web command in Explorer's File menu. Once you delete a Web, it's gone for good!

N O T E If you create a template-based page (not a Normal Page) and save it with the template's default file name and page title, and then create a second page from the same template, Explorer queries you when you attempt to save the second page. This is because the default file name of both pages is the same. The query lets you either overwrite the first page with the second or cancel the action entirely. Of course, you can have identical file names as long as they're in different Webs or folders. This does not happen if you are creating new Normal Pages because FrontPage Editor numbers them sequentially as they are created. ■

Running FrontPage Editor as a Stand-Alone HTML Editor

As stated, this is not a recommended procedure because the sophisticated functionality of FrontPage Editor is lost. However, if you feel the method suits your needs (for example, if you want to edit pages that are not going to be installed in a FrontPage Web), here's how to do it:

1. Start FrontPage Explorer, but don't open a Web. If the Getting Started dialog box is visible, you'll have to click its Cancel button to clear it.
2. Choose Tools, Show FrontPage Editor. When the editor opens, you can switch to FrontPage Explorer and close it.
3. Use FrontPage Editor to open the HTML file you want to edit, or you can create new pages with the New command.
4. When you have created and/or edited the page, save it. As long as you stick to plain vanilla HTML 3.2, you'll get good results. However, server-dependent features such as FrontPage Components (in FrontPage 98, called FrontPage Components) will not behave. You'll need to experiment.

 To bypass FrontPage Explorer entirely, use Windows Explorer to go to the C:\Program Files\Microsoft FrontPage folder. Here, you'll find a shortcut icon to FrontPage Editor. Use the shortcut from this folder or copy it to the desktop for quicker access.

N O T E Microsoft Internet Explorer 4's Active Setup program provides the option of downloading and installing a free Web authoring tool called FrontPage Express. This is essentially a "lite" version of FrontPage Editor, and lacks the latter's advanced features such as WYSIWYG tables and WYSIWYG frames. It also does not include the site management tools provided by FrontPage Explorer, or the image processing capabilities you get with Image Composer. If you already have FrontPage on your system, you don't need FrontPage Express. ▪

Changing the FrontPage Editor Screen Display

FrontPage Editor doesn't allow extensive customization of its display. You're restricted to turning on or off the following elements:

- Toolbars: Standard, format, image, forms, advanced, table
- Status Bar
- Format Marks: Hard line returns, bookmarks, and form outlines

You can hide or show all these from the View menu (see Figure 4.9).

FIG. 4.9
Use the View menu to choose the screen elements to be displayed.

To hide or show individual screen elements, use the following steps:

1. Choose View from the FrontPage Editor menu bar.
2. Click the name of the toolbar you want to hide or show.
3. Turn the status bar on or off by clicking Status Bar on the menu.
4. Turn line break symbols, paragraph marks, and HTML Markup icons on or off by clicking Format Marks on the menu.

Directly Editing HTML

One of the tabs at the bottom of the FrontPage Editor workspace is the HTML tab. If you click this, you leave the Normal mode (where you do most of your page editing) and enter HTML mode, where you can edit the HTML of the page directly (see Figure 4.10).

FIG. 4.10

With FrontPage Editor 98, you can work directly with the active page's HTML code.

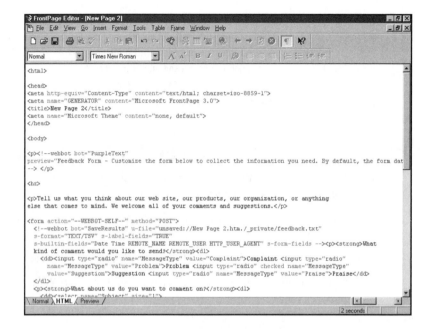

CAUTION

You may find some unpredictable behavior if you try to add unsupported code by using this technique. There's usually no problem with supported code (assuming no syntax errors) but for unsupported HTML, it's much safer to use the HTML Markup command. FrontPage 97 was criticized for its rough handling of directly entered HTML, and Microsoft has been at some pains to correct the problem, so FrontPage 98's behavior is distinctly improved in this area. However, the direct editing procedure and the HTML Markup command do not flag errors in the code, although FrontPage Editor does attempt to rectify glaring mistakes.

Previewing Your Work

FrontPage Editor 98 makes page editing more convenient by giving you a quickly available Preview mode, as well as the Preview in Browser command that first appeared in FrontPage 97.

You use the Preview tab at the bottom of the FrontPage Editor workspace to switch to Preview mode. This mode shows you the page as it displays in a Microsoft Internet Explorer browser. At the time of writing (August 1997), the browser version installed with FrontPage 98 was Internet Explorer 3.0, although presumably FrontPage 98 will quickly be updated with the IE 4.0 browser. This is because the latter supports Dynamic HTML and the former does not.

Using the Preview in Browser command is straightforward; you don't even have to be connected to the Internet. You don't have to install your system's browsers into FrontPage, either, because when FrontPage 98 sets itself up, it finds the browsers you have on your machine and ties them into FrontPage Editor. You'll see this when you use the command for the first time. To do so, open the page you want to look at, and choose File, Preview in Browser to open the Preview in Browser dialog box (see Figure 4.11).

FIG. 4.11

It's easy to assess your work in any browser you have on your system.

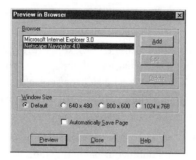

N O T E If you have two browsers of the same type on your machine, FrontPage puts the latest version into the Preview in Browser list. That is, if you have both Navigator 3 and Navigator 4 installed, only the Navigator 4 is available by default. To use Navigator 3 as a preview browser, you must add it manually, using the Add command. ▨

You can set the window size to simulate what your visitors will see in different screen resolutions. (The Default selection uses the current resolution of your display.) Select the desired resolution, then select the desired browser and choose Preview. The browser starts and loads the page for you to view. When you've seen as much as you like, close the browser to return to FrontPage Editor.

Updating your system when you add or remove browsers is done with the Add, Edit, and Delete buttons. These take you to dialog boxes where you can make the following adjustments:

- ▨ **Add**   Click Add to open the Add Browser dialog box to add another browser to the list of available ones.
- ▨ **Edit**   Select a browser and click Edit to open the Edit Browser dialog box to change information about a browser you have added. You cannot edit information about a browser that FrontPage automatically detects and adds to the Preview in Browser dialog box during installation.
- ▨ **Delete**   Select a browser and click Delete to remove it. However, you cannot remove a Web browser that FrontPage has already detected and added during installation.

Because the browser reads the page from the disk rather than from the Editor workspace, it's important to save the page before opening it for preview in a browser. To force this to happen without your intervention, mark the check box labeled Automatically Save Page.

Part
II

Ch
4

Understanding HTML

The Hypertext Markup Language (HTML) is a subset of the Standard Generalized Markup Language, a standard for typesetting. HTML is not complex; when you look at an HTML file in an editor, it is plain text. However, this text includes special embedded command codes that the browser understands. These commands give you control of how your page looks with respect to layout and content.

The command codes are always embedded in angled brackets (the symbols for less than and more than: < >). Some HTML commands are paired; others are not. These commands or codes are called *tags*. Basic HTML is understood by all browsers, although the language is evolving so rapidly that earlier browser versions may not display the results of more recently developed tags.

You don't have to know any HTML to get started with FrontPage, because FrontPage Editor generates the HTML code for you as you build your page. If you do need to do some fine-tuning of your code, you can modify the actual HTML by using FrontPage Editor's HTML view. We'll look at this later; first, though, we'll briefly explore the basics of HTML itself.

Understanding the HTML File Structure

The basic structure of all HTML files, no matter how complex they are, is the same. Every file has three parts: the HTML container that encloses all the other parts of the page; the Head section; and the Body section. Each section is defined by a tag pair, as follows: the HTML container by the opening tag <HTML> and the closing tag </HTML>; the Head section by the opening and closing tags <HEAD> and </HEAD>; and the Body section by the opening and closing tags <BODY> and </BODY>. Not all HTML tags have to be closed, but most are; the closing tag is always identified by the forward slash in front of the tag text. The case of the tag makes no difference; <HEAD> and <head> are functionally identical.

Thus the structure of the simplest possible HTML file is this (it would produce a blank page):

```
<html>
<head>
</head>
<body>
</body>
</html>
```

Understanding the Head/Body Structure

As previously described, every HTML page begins with the HTML tag <html>, and ends with the closing tag </html>. These two tags tell the browser where the page begins and ends.

Between the HTML tags, every page has two sections: the head and the body. Both sections must be defined for the browser to display the page properly. The head is everything between the <head> and </head> tags; the body is anything between the <body> and </body> tags.

A slightly more complex page than the preceding listing might read:

```
<html>
<head>
<title>MY HOME PAGE</title>
</head>
<body>
</body>
</html>
```

In this, you'll notice a line that says, `<title>MY HOME PAGE</title>`. The browser will display the words between those title tags in the title bar of the browser's display. This is an important consideration; while the average visitor won't pay much attention to the title bar while visiting, text within the title tag is what browsers usually save with a bookmark or "Favorites." If you do title your HTML document, "My Home Page," that's how it will look in a bookmark file or in a World Wide Web catalog such as Lycos. Therefore, choose your title text carefully; it's probably how you'll be recalled for future visits.

Other codes can also appear in the head section of an HTML document. For example, you could use a link tag here, to define a relationship between the document and yourself as the owner or manager of the document. Your link could look like this:

```
<LINK rev=made href="mailto:yourid@youraddress">
```

Another tag you may want to put in the Head section is the `<meta>` tag. The `<meta>` tag is a generic tag; you can use it to embed information about your document that does not fit in the other HTML tags. It's usually used to give the page keywords for indexing in catalogs. An example would be

```
<meta keywords= coffee, food, retail>
```

Everything else in the HTML document is part of the body; this is enclosed in the `<body>` and `</body>` tags.

Useful Tags for the Body Section

Most HTML tags are used in the body section of the page. Some must be paired as the preceding tags, such as:

`<I>` and `</I>` to begin and end italicized text

`<B>` and `</B>` to begin and end bold text

`<BIG>` and `</BIG>` for large type

`<A HREF=xxxx>` and `</A>` for a hypertext link to another file or a bookmark within this file

`<Address>` and `</Address>` to begin and end a formatted section for contact information

`<ul>` and `</ul>` for unnumbered lists

`<dl>` and `</dl>` for definition lists

`<dt>` and `</dt>` for defined terms in definition lists

`<dd>` and `</dd>` for the definitions in definition lists

`<em>` and `</em>` for emphasized text

Part II

Ch 4

<strong> and </strong> for extra emphasis

<H#> and </H#> for headlines, usually from H1 (the largest) to H6 (the smallest)

Others do not have to be paired, such as:

<IMG SRC=xxxxx> for placing an image

<li> for list items

<P> for a paragraph break, a line break, and a blank line

 for a line break, but no blank line

<HR> for a rule between sections

These are just a few of the tags in HTML, but they are enough to give you an idea of how the code works.

Hand-Coding HTML in FrontPage Editor

You're bound to run into situations where you need to modify a page's HTML code directly. One simple real-world example: You're using FrontPage Editor as a stand-alone editor to create a page for a nonFrontPage Web, and you want to remove the FrontPage-proprietary META tags from the HEAD section.

To do this, open the page you want to modify. Then click the HTML tab at the bottom of the workspace to switch to HTML view. You can see a simple example of this in Figure 4.12.

FIG. 4.12
Use the HTML tab to switch to HTML view, to make direct adjustments to the HTML of a page.

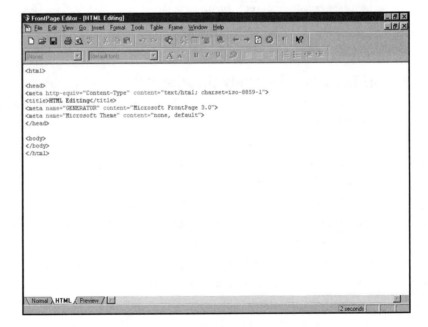

The HTML view provides what is essentially a text editor. In the suggested example, where you want to remove the META tags, you would first select the tag text along with its angle brackets. Pressing the Delete key then removes the META tag.

The editing tools are fairly basic, but all the essentials are available: Cut, Copy, Paste, Select All, Find, and Replace. The File menu commands are also fully functional, but for a complete editing environment you have to switch back to Normal view.

 TIP With Copy and Paste, you can take HTML code from one file and paste it into another. This is a very useful way of recycling code from other sources.

By default, the displayed HTML is color-coded. To turn this feature on and off, right-click in the editor workspace to open the shortcut menu, and toggle the Show Color Coding command on or off. With color coding switched on, you will notice that as soon as you put in a beginning angle bracket, everything after that changes color until you add the closing bracket. This helps ensure you haven't left off important brackets.

CAUTION
FrontPage Editor does some basic syntax checking of any HTML inserted through the HTML view. If it spots what it thinks is a mistake, it will try to correct it, often by inserting <P> tags into and around the offending code. Unfortunately, if you insert valid HTML code that is not recognized by FrontPage Editor, the editor will still "correct" this code even though it's perfectly legal. If you find this happening to your inserted code, you'll have to use the HTML Markup command, as described in the next section.

Part
II

Ch
4

Using the HTML Markup Command

This is the only safe way to include HTML code that FrontPage doesn't directly support. Code inserted with the HTML Markup command is left strictly alone by FrontPage Editor, even if the code is incorrect. To use the command, do this:

1. Switch to Normal view. Choose Insert, FrontPage Component to open the Insert FrontPage Component dialog box.
2. Select Insert HTML from the dialog's list box, and choose OK. This opens the HTML Markup dialog box (see Figure 4.13).

FIG. 4.13

Use the HTML Markup dialog box to add unsupported HTML to a page.

3. Type the desired HTML into the text box. When you are finished, choose OK to close the dialog box.

After you close the dialog box, you don't actually see the output of the inserted code; instead, you get a yellow question mark icon at the place where the code was inserted. This icon appears even if the code is recognized by FrontPage, and actually signals the presence of the HTML Markup FrontPage Component. To edit the inserted HTML code, double-click the question mark icon to open the HTML Markup dialog box again.

TIP

If you don't see the yellow icon, your Format Marks are turned off. Choose View, Format Marks to turn them on.

Although FrontPage supports most current HTML code, the extensions are forever becoming more diverse and powerful. By using the HTML Markup command, you can include all the newest features in your FrontPage Web pages.

From Here...

You've now covered the options that FrontPage Explorer and FrontPage Editor give you for creating and managing pages. Now it's time to move on to the creative stuff. That can get complicated too, but it's worth it.

■ Chapter 5, "Developing the Basic Page: Text, Lists, and Hyperlinks," describes the basics of good page design and starts you out making a basic page with text entry and layout, lists, and hyperlinks.

■ Chapter 6, "Enhancing Pages with Themes, Graphics, and Multimedia," takes you further into page design with image handling, color usage, image maps, sound, and inline video.

■ Chapter 7, "Using Dynamic HTML, Active Elements, Shared Borders, and Navigation Bars," shows you how to use these new, active components to give more life to your pages.

Developing the Basic Page: Text, Lists, and Hyperlinks

FrontPage's value lies in its all-in-one approach to Web site construction, page creation, and site maintenance. Carry this sense of integration with you as you use FrontPage Editor to compose and link pages; that is, you should keep in mind that the particular page you're working on doesn't stand in isolation. It should fit seamlessly into the larger pattern of your site. This chapter deals with what makes a good page and with the essentials of using FrontPage Editor to compose and link pages. ■

Page design

Design your pages to please your visitors, keep them around, and make them want to come back, with attractive graphics, well-planned content, and fast downloads.

Text entry and layout

Add headings, text, and font variety to your page. Use text formatting, such as bold and italic, for emphasis; set off sections with horizontal lines; indent or center paragraphs.

Lists

Use lists, including bulleted lists, numbered lists, nested lists, and glossary lists. Now you can customize bullets, using your own images or theme images.

Decorative elements

Use text and background colors. Define custom colors, set a consistent color scheme across your pages, and change the color of selected text.

Hyperlinks

Understand and install hyperlinks within your Web, to sites on the World Wide Web, or to files on the host machine. Use the e-mail link, and learn to edit existing hyperlinks.

Thinking Through Your Page Design

Compared to writing HTML code with a text editor, making a page with FrontPage Editor is easy. You can drop in a few headers, some paragraphs of text, three or four images (and maybe an imagemap), a list, a form, a table, an animation or two, some sound, and as many hyperlinks as you please, all in a very short time. Now you've got a home page. Then you do another page, and another, and soon you've got a wonderful Web site ready for the world to visit. Don't you?

Well, maybe, but bad design is the nemesis of many, many Web pages, and you risk producing an unattractive page if you don't know and follow a few common sense guidelines. Most importantly, you have to think about your visitors and how they're likely to experience your site.

Planning for Your Visitors

If you've spent any time browsing the Web, you've already encountered plenty of sites you won't revisit because the first page you went to had one or more of the following problems:

- Took too long to load.
- Had no clear purpose.
- Was poorly laid out or badly written.
- Had obscure navigational tools.
- Didn't link to other sites as it said it would.
- Had no useful information.

Obviously, you don't want people to have that experience with your work, but how do you make sure they don't? The short answer is to put yourself in your visitor's shoes and think like the audience you want to have. Any author, in print, multimedia, or Web design has to do this or risk failure.

For illustration, consider your own experience. When you open a new book or magazine or see an unknown Web page appearing in your browser, what's in the back of your mind? You may be barely aware of it, but it's always there, and it's, "What's in this for me?" You want something from this page: information, entertainment, aesthetic pleasure, or intellectual stimulation, depending your tastes and the needs of the moment. If you sense in the first minute or two that you're not going to get it, you very quickly go elsewhere—and so will your viewers if they get that feeling from the first Web page they see on your site.

Keeping Your Visitors Around for More

This danger of losing the audience on the first page is something all professional authors worry about. The tool they use to prevent it is called *the hook*, and they try very hard to find the best hook for whatever it is they're producing. The idea of the hook is simple: it goes at the very beginning of a work, and it's carefully designed to seize the reader's attention. More than that, it's designed to make the reader want to go on paying attention, to read the rest of this page, and the next, and the next. As an author of Web pages, you're going to want to keep your audience's attention; otherwise, why are you bothering to make the pages at all? So, put yourself in the mind of the person who's seeing your site for the first time, and ask, "What's here for me?" If the honest answer is, "Not much," you need to rethink your approach. You need a better hook, one that makes your viewer want to look around the rest of your site; but, how do you make one?

Avoiding the Extremes

The first temptation is to pull out all the stops on the technology. That's a considerable temptation because it's gotten a lot simpler to produce decorative or animated marvels on a Web page, and it's fun. The trouble is that it's likely more fun for the page designer to do than it is for the audience to experience. It's true that a visually spectacular page keeps a viewer's interest for a while (assuming the viewer waits for it to download), but if there's nothing to it but spectacle, it's a failure as a page (see Figure 5.1).

FIG. 5.1
Avoid the errors here: a large image that downloads slowly, clumsy layout, no obvious navigation tools, and a distracting and pointless GIF animation (the frog). There's a misspelling, too!

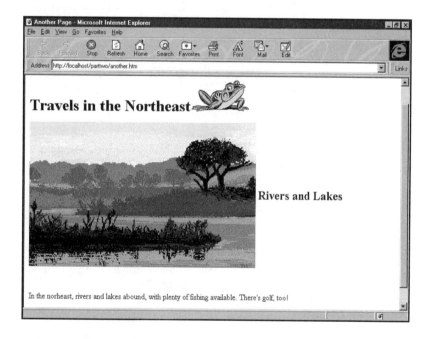

At the other extreme, a page crammed with solid text, scrolling on and on without whitespace or other elements to relieve the eye, is almost as bad. You may feel that the important information you give is enough of a hook. But even if the information the reader wants is there, will she stick around to find it? Her browser controls are in easy reach, and she may decide to go elsewhere for what she's after (see Figure 5.2).

Finding a Balance

When you're trying to identify the best hook for your site, ask yourself, What does my viewer want, and how do I show the viewer, in a hurry, that it's there? Reversing the earlier list of reasons for not staying on a Website, you get the following:

- The first page appears quickly.

- Its purpose is immediately and clearly identified.

- It's well laid out and well written.

- Its links accurately suggest what the viewer will find.

- Its links behave as advertised when the viewer does use them.

- It supplies the content the viewer expects or a quick path to that content.

FIG. 5.2
Filling screen after screen with solid print is hard on your reader's eyes.

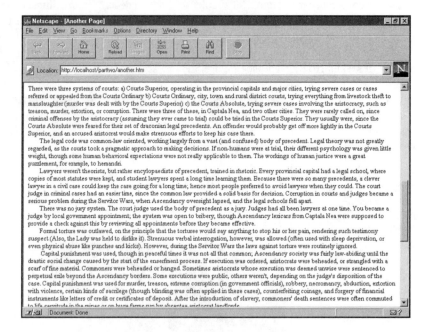

Using these suggestions will produce a successful hook for a Web site. Following these guidelines goes a long, long way toward making all your pages, and therefore your entire site, both pleasing and useful. In short, your key to success is really a balance of presentation and content. An example of such balance appears in Figure 5.3.

You can also produce a very efficient and useful page without using many images and graphical controls. This is a good approach if your intended audience uses a wide range of browsers, including text-only ones like LYNX. The example in Figure 5.4 is almost entirely text, but its content is balanced by a presentation that directs the user quickly and efficiently to the resources.

Letting Visitors in by the Side Door

You need to keep in mind another important fact about Web authoring. With other media, the author has some control over where the audience is going to start. People read novels from page one; movie goers try to reach the theater before the opening credits roll; magazine readers may flip through the magazine, but they usually start reading an article at its beginning.

With a Web site, though, your readers may enter at any page, depending on which link sent them there. This means that you should design every page with the same care that you lavished on your home page. Because people usually like to have a look at the home page (it helps them get oriented), it's a good idea to include a go-to-home-page control on all your pages. This is especially true if you have a large or complex site or one whose organization isn't obvious when a person enters it at some point other than the home page.

FIG. 5.3

This page integrates images, text, and navigation links to make an attractive and functional whole.

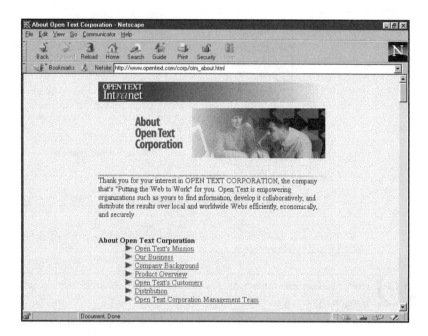

Tips for Quality Pages

Web authoring is a young art, but already there is some agreement about its basic principles. The following guidelines list the fundamentals of text layout and hyperlink design.

- Use lots of white space with a text-heavy page.
- Avoid very long pages that require endless scrolling.
- Give your page a title that helps the user figure out where she is and what she's looking at.
- Write clearly and pay close attention to spelling and grammar. Nothing undermines a page's authority as much as confusing language and bad spelling. Even typos suggest that the author couldn't be bothered to check the work, and what does that say about the other information that's offered?
- If you modify the colors of unvisited and visited links, test the results very carefully to make sure the two states can be distinguished in any display the viewers are likely to use. When in doubt, keep the link colors at their defaults.

Part
II

Ch
5

FIG. 5.4
This text-based page is laid out clearly and economically. It also includes a version you can download for printing, a thoughtful touch on the part of its designer.

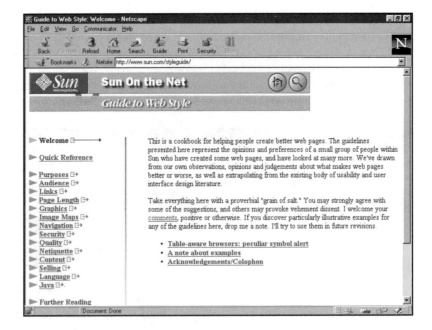

■ Keep your navigation controls uniform in appearance; for example, a go-to-home-page button should look the same everywhere on your site.

http://www.sun.com/styleguide, Sun Microsystem's Website, offers useful general advice on page layout and writing style.

http://info.med.yale.edu/caim, the Yale Center for Advanced Instructional Media, gives extensive information about page design with a leaning toward the production of scholarly documents.

Testing

The importance of testing can't be emphasized too much. Your pages may look flawless in your favorite browser, but how do they look in another kind of browser? Different browsers, even different versions of the same browser, modify the general appearance of a page, and all recent versions can be user-configured to make drastic changes to the display. Although you can't allow for every possible variation, comprehensive testing ensures that most people can use your site. Just as important, it tells you that your pages are behaving properly, before anybody else sees them. Here are some ways of getting things right the first time:

■ Test each page with the default settings of Netscape 3.0, Netscape 4.0 (also known as Communicator), Microsoft Internet Explorer 3.0, and Microsoft Internet Explorer 4.0. These are now the dominant browsers. In addition, test using the lowest common denominator of display, which is 640×480 in 16 colors, on a 14" monitor.

- Vary the browsers' configurations to see if this drastically changes the appearance of your pages.

- Put in alternate text for images and graphical navigation controls. Remember that many people run their browsers with images turned off to download pages faster.

- Speaking of speed, always test your page's downloading time with a phone line connection through your ISP. Simply opening the page in your browser as a local file, or retrieving it via an ISDN line, is much faster than most real-world situations. Assume that your viewers are using a 14.4 kps modem and plan your page accordingly.

- Get user feedback during testing. Like any author, you're too close to your material to catch every flaw.

- Print your pages and inspect them. Hard copy often reveals problems with the writing in a way that a screen image (for some mysterious reason) doesn't.

- Remember that long, complicated pages are harder to maintain than short, simple ones.

- After making even a minor change to your page, test it thoroughly.

- When everything is working perfectly, test it again.

Creating a Page Based on the Normal Template

Now that you've had a look at some basic design principles, the rest of this chapter explores how to place text and hyperlinks on a clean page. The page to start with is the home page of a single page Web, which you'll generate with Explorer. You've learned to create Webs and apply themes earlier, but the procedure is reviewed briefly here. To create a one-page Web, use the following steps:

1. Start FrontPage Explorer. Choose File, New, FrontPage Web, and when the New FrontPage Web dialog box appears, select One Page Web.

2. Type a title for the Web in the text box labeled Choose a Title, and choose OK.

3. Change the theme, if you wish, when the Explorer display of the Web appears. For clarity in the figures in this chapter, the theme of the example Web was set to This Web Does Not Use Themes.

FrontPage Explorer generates the Web, and the Home Page icon (a house) appears in Hyperlink View's left pane. Now, with the new Web open, start FrontPage Editor. The quickest way to do this, and at the same time load the page you want, is to double-click the page icon in Hyperlink View's right pane. Or, double-click its Name entry in Folder View's right pane, or its Name entry in the All Files View. Whichever you do, FrontPage Editor appears with the chosen page in the editing window (see Figure 5.5). Now you're ready to start!

N O T E FrontPage Editor makes it convenient to move among pages you've opened. Choose Window, and the lower section of the menu shows the currently open documents. Click the one that you want to display it. To flip rapidly to the previous page or the next page, you can use the Forward and Back buttons on the Standard toolbar.

Part
II

Ch
5

FIG. 5.5
FrontPage Editor retrieves the blank home page, ready for you to start composing. Notice the default title Home Page in the title bar.

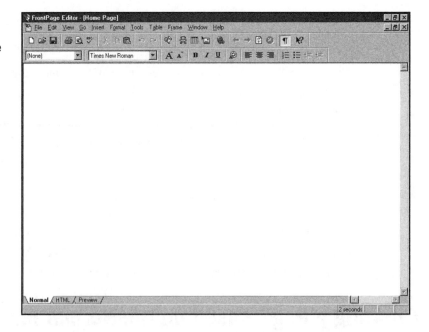

Web pages, as you know, can be very elaborate. However, all you need to keep in mind at this point is that the bulk of every page is made up of combinations of the following three basic elements:

- Text
- Hyperlinks
- Images

There's also active content, of course, like JavaScript, ActiveX, animations, and so on. These aren't basic in the sense that they're required for a pleasing, functional page, so they will be discussed in later chapters.

▶ **See** Chapter 7, "Using Dynamic HTML, Active Elements, Shared Borders, and Navigation Bars," **p. 157**.

▶ **See** Chapter 17, "Using ActiveX Controls," **p. 343**.

▶ **See** Chapter 18, "Scripting with VBScript," **p. 369**.

▶ **See** Chapter 19, "Scripting with JavaScript" **p. 417**.

▶ **See** Chapter 20, "Inserting Java Applets and Browser Plug-Ins," **p. 459**.

Giving Your Page a Title that Works

Before you start adding content to any page, you should give it a meaningful title. You can always modify the title later. You ought to put some thought into this because a person new to your page usually reads its title for hints about where he is and what he's looking at, and the default titles of most pages just won't help much. In fact, there are two more reasons for taking pains with your title. First, it's what your visitor's browser records in its Bookmark list (Netscape) or Favorites folder (Internet Explorer) if he marks the page; an informative title jogs his memory later about the nature of your site. Second, Internet search programs read the title for indexing and retrieval purposes, and presumably you want your site to show up in their lists.

To change the page title to a more useful one, use the following steps:

1. Choose File, Page Properties, or right-click in the workspace and choose Page Properties from the shortcut menu. The Page Properties dialog box appears (see Figure 5.6).

FIG. 5.6

You can change your page title in the Page Properties dialog box.

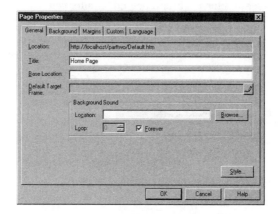

2. Type the new page title into the Title text box. You can use any characters you want. The title can also be any length, but remember that your visitors may be using a lower screen resolution than you are. A width of 60 characters is about the practical maximum.

3. Choose OK.

Your new page title appears in the FrontPage Editor title bar.

 Remember that your home page isn't the only one in your site that needs a functional title. Every page should have such a guidepost for its viewers. A title like "Page 31" or "Section 17" isn't much use in keeping a viewer oriented.

Previewing Your Edited Page

Now that you've made a change to the page, you may want to see what it's going to look like in a browser. Here you have two choices.

You can simply click the Preview tab to see how a Microsoft browser (at the time of writing, IE 3.0) displays the page. This won't help much for other browsers, though, so you'll certainly also want to use the Preview in Browser command. As you may remember from the discussion

Part

II

Ch

5

in Chapter 4, FrontPage automatically sets up preview browsers when you install it. To use them:

1. Choose File, Preview in Browser. The Preview in Browser dialog box appears (see Figure 5.7).

2. Click the name of the browser you want to use in the Browser list box.

3. Mark the option button for the resolution you want. The Default uses the current resolution of your display.

4. Choose Preview. The selected browser loads and displays the page currently active in FrontPage Editor.

5. Close the browser to return to FrontPage Editor after you've checked your work.

 TIP   A convenient feature of this preview command is that you can set the browser to save the page before loading it. Mark the Automatically Save Page check box in the Preview in Browser dialog box to enable this feature.

FIG. 5.7
You use the Preview in Browser dialog box for fast and easy previewing of a page you're working on.

 TIP   If you make a mistake, you can choose Edit, Undo to undo your last action.

TROUBLESHOOTING

I edited a page, previewed it, and everything was fine. To save time, I didn't close the previewing browser. I did another edit and switched back to the browser, but it didn't show the new edit even when I clicked the Refresh or Reload buttons. Why not? The previewing browser retrieves the page from the file it's stored in, not from the FrontPage Editor workspace. If you don't mark the Automatically Save Page check box in the Preview in Browser dialog box, you will have to save the page each time you want to preview it and then use the browser's Reload or Refresh buttons to display the new version of the page.

Using the Format Menu to Add Headings

You use headings to mark off major divisions and subdivisions of meaning within a page. FrontPage Editor offers the six levels of headings that are standard with HTML. To place one on a page, use the following steps:

1. Type the heading text at the place you want it. Do not press Enter when you're done.

2. Choose Format, Paragraph. The Paragraph Properties dialog box appears (see Figure 5.8).

FIG. 5.8

FrontPage Editor offers multiple levels of headings.

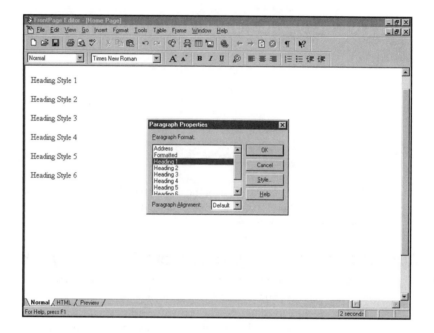

Part

II

Ch

5

3. Select Heading 1 and choose OK. The text changes to the largest heading style. Press the Enter key to put the insertion point on the next line.

4. Follow steps 1 through 3 and each time select a different heading type from the Paragraph Properties list box. Figure 5.9 shows the full range, using Preview mode.

Removing a Heading and Its Style

To delete a heading, use the following steps:

1. Make sure you are in Normal mode and select the heading you want to delete.

2. Press the Delete key or choose Edit, Clear to make the heading text disappear.

The line containing the insertion point still retains the heading style. To remove this, choose Format, Paragraph, and then select Normal from the list box and choose OK. The style of the line returns to Normal (default) style.

FIG. 5.9

FrontPage Editor
supplies very large
(1) to very small
headings (6).

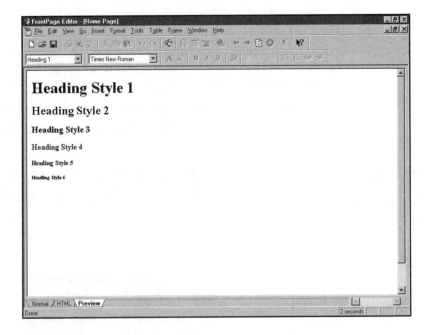

The heading style, unlike some of the other styles in FrontPage Editor, is not retained after you press the Enter key. When you press Enter at the end of a heading-style line, the style of the next line returns to Normal.

Applying Paragraph Styles with the Change Style Box

A faster and more convenient way to change heading levels is with the Change Style drop-down list box, which lets you choose from all the heading levels and text styles available. (If you've used styles in Microsoft Word, the technique is immediately familiar.) To see the styles, click the arrow button at the right of the Change Style drop-down list box (see Figure 5.10).

FIG. 5.10

You can apply styles
easily by selecting from
the list in the Change
Styles box.

To use this method to change a paragraph style, use the following steps:

1. Select the paragraph you want to modify by placing the insertion point anywhere inside it.

2. Click the arrow button at the right of the Change Style drop-down list box. The list of styles appears.

3. Click the style you want. All the text of the paragraph takes on the new appearance.

As you've already guessed, this method works for all styles, not just for headings. In some cases, you might want to compose most of the text of your page in the Normal style (the default) and then use the Change Style drop-down list box to modify certain sections.

 TIP Don't overuse the larger heading styles on a single screen. If you do, a visitor to your site may feel shouted at. Think of headings as signaling divisions and subdivisions of content, rather than as a method of emphasis.

Adding Paragraphs of Normal Text

In FrontPage Editor, you produce most text with the Normal style, which by default is set to the Times New Roman font. Because FrontPage Editor supports the <font face = > and </font> tags, however, you aren't limited to Times New Roman for Normal text—you can change fonts with the Format, Font command. The available fonts are whatever TrueType fonts you have installed on your system.

Before using different fonts, though, be aware that only recent browsers (MS Internet Explorer 3.0 and later and Netscape 3.0 and later) that support these <font face = > and </font> tags will display the font you choose. In older browsers, it shows up in whatever proportional font the browser's user has selected. Still, the font-capable browsers are widely used now, and in most circumstances you can comfortably use a range of fonts.

FrontPage Editor's Normal style produces text in the HTML paragraph style, as defined by the <P></P> tag pair. Unfortunately, there is an ongoing debate over exactly what *paragraph* means in Web authoring, and in fact, FrontPage Editor's Paragraph Format dialog box distinguishes four styles (or *formats*) of paragraphs: Normal, Formatted, Address, and Heading. You'll look at the behavior of the Normal style paragraph first, leaving its font at the default of Times New Roman.

To write your text, use the following steps:

1. Place the cursor where you want the text to begin.

2. Start typing if the Change Style box says (none) and the style defaults to Normal. If the box says something other than (none) or Normal, you must select the Normal style. Click the arrow button at the right of the box and select Normal from the drop-down list.

3. Type your text. When you reach the end of a paragraph, press Enter. This starts a new paragraph, still in the Normal style. Finish typing.

You can see an example of Normal text in Figure 5.11. Both FrontPage Editor and browsers automatically insert a blank line before the start of each paragraph. You can't change this behavior, but a method for closing up the white space between paragraphs is discussed later in the next section, "Using Line Breaks to Control Text Formatting."

FIG. 5.11
You use the Normal
style to generate
paragraphs of
ordinary text.

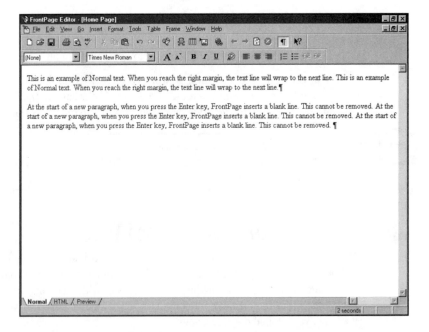

What if you want extra white space between paragraphs, in addition to the automatically inserted blank line? You can't put in blank lines merely by pressing the Enter key. White space shows up in the editing window just fine, but browsers ignore it.

With FrontPage Editor, the blank lines you get by pressing the Enter key *do* appear in recent browsers. FrontPage Editor achieves this by inserting an   (an escape sequence) whenever you press the Enter key. Browsers that recognize this escape sequence (including Netscape 2.0 and later, NCSA Mosaic 2.1 and later, and Microsoft Internet Explorer 2.0 and later) don't *crunch* the white space; they let it show up. You'll find this word processor-like feature to be a great improvement over earlier Web page editors that demand that you insert a line-break element to generate white space between paragraphs.

 Sometimes you need a nonbreaking space to force two words or a word and a number to stay together on one line (January 17, for example). Use Shift+Spacebar to insert such a space.

Using Line Breaks to Control Text Formatting

It's convenient that FrontPage Editor simplified using white space between paragraphs, but what about the opposite problem? You may need short lines of text all kept together (quoting poetry, for example). How do you keep FrontPage Editor from putting blank lines between these one-line paragraphs? If you try pressing Enter where you want the text to break, you'll always get a blank line. The solution is to insert line breaks. The line break orders a browser to jump to the very next line of its window.

The procedure is simple: to keep short lines of text together, press Shift+Enter when you reach the end of each line. This inserts an HTML line break tag into the text stream, which orders a browser not to leave a blank line before the start of the next line of text (see Figure 5.12). If you've turned on Format Marks (either with the View menu, or the Show/Hide Format Marks toolbar button), you'll see a line-break symbol in the FrontPage Editor work space. These symbols, of course, don't show up in a browser.

FIG. 5.12

You use line breaks to arrange text in short lines.

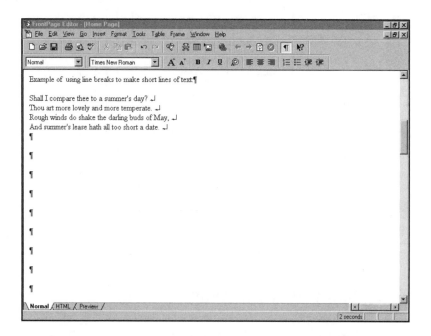

These line breaks don't define the end of a paragraph. Changing the paragraph style affects all the text between the end of the previous paragraph and the start of the next, and completely ignores the presence of the line breaks.

N O T E Choosing Insert, Break provides specialized line breaks as well as the basic one you get with Shift+Enter. These special breaks are discussed in the "Using Line Break Properties with Images" section in Chapter 6, "Enhancing Pages with Themes, Graphics, and Multimedia." ▪

Enlarging and Shrinking Normal Text

Sometimes you need to increase or decrease the size of text within a paragraph for emphasis or design purposes. You can't do this with a heading because headings are styles, so they affect all of a paragraph, not just part of it. The way around this problem is to use the Increase and Decrease Text Size buttons on the Formatting toolbar (see Figure 5.13). Select the text and click the Increase or Decrease Text Size button. Keep clicking until the text is close to the size you want. It may not be exactly what you want because the point size of the type isn't fully adjustable, as it is in a word processor. The sizes available, in terms of points, are 8, 10, 12, 14, 18, 24, and 36.

The size of *Normal* text defaults to 12 points in the Netscape Navigator and the Internet Explorer browsers. The seven point sizes correspond to the seven HTML-defined type sizes.

FIG. 5.13
Enlarging or shrinking text is simple with the Increase and Decrease Text size buttons.

Enlarged Twice

Shrunken Twice

Increase Text Size Button

Decrease Text Size Button

Bold Button

Italic Button

Underline Button

Change Color Button

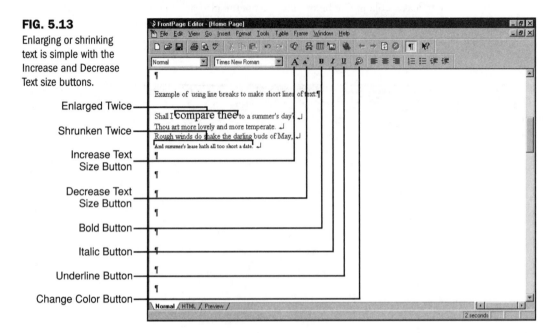

Adding Character Formatting

The physical appearance of words on a page gives your readers clues about what those words are for, and how important they are relative to everything else. (All your words are important, but some are more important than others, right?) Italics are for emphasis, but also for book titles and certain kinds of citations. Headings signal blocks of related information. Bold is another emphasis, but subtly different from italic. Typewriter font gives another effect. In Web publishing (as in conventional publishing), you won't go wrong if you stick to normal typographical conventions, especially the one that says "don't overdo it." If half your page displays in italic and half in bold, your reader can't tell the difference between what's important and what's really important.

With FrontPage Editor, you can apply all these character formats and change the text color simply by selecting and clicking. Figure 5.13 shows the buttons you use to apply these effects, using normal word processing practices. Select the text you want to modify and click the appropriate button to apply the effect. If you're starting new text, click the button, type the new text, and click the button again when you want to turn the effect off. The effects can be *layered*; that is, you can have text that is bold, italic, underlined, and in color.

Usage of bold, underline, and italic in page design is pretty conventional and easy to grasp. Color usage, however, is a more complex matter, and you'll consider it at more length later in this chapter, in the section "Changing Background and Text Colors."

Choosing Fonts with the Change Font Box

Using different fonts can add enormously to the impact of a page. Fonts do have what you might call (no pun intended) *character*; that is, they suggest a certain mood to the reader. Ornate fonts (TrueType Algerian would be an example) suggest a different atmosphere from the formal air that surrounds a traditional font like Bookman Old Style. Combinations of fonts lend both variety and pacing to the flow of the text on your page.

A common mistake of fledgling typographers, however, is to become overexcited at the vast range of fonts available and change them at the least opportunity. This usually leads to a visual mess. Instead of doing this, start by figuring out the *mood* of the page or of your site as a whole. Is it to be traditionally businesslike? High-technology? Whimsical? Highly personal? Artistic? Counterculture? Of course, the nature of the audience you hope to attract will help define the mood you want to create.

When you've got that worked out, look for fonts that reflect this mood. Experiment with them on the page to see if they work together or cause visual chaos. You'll likely end up with a small selection of fonts: a couple for titles and/or main headings, one for body text, and one or two others for specialized purposes, which will depend on the nature of your site. Properly selected, this range of fonts contributes to giving your page (and site) a feeling of unity and focus. This, in turn, adds conviction to what you want to say. When in doubt, go for fewer fonts, not more.

The simplest way to change fonts is with the Change Font list box (see Figure 5.14).

FIG. 5.14

Use the Change Fonts box to select different fonts.

Part

II

Ch

5

To switch to a new font for new text, click the arrow button at the right end of the Change Font box and select the font you want from the drop-down list. Whatever you type from that point on is in the new font until you either change it or place the insertion point within text of a different font.

To change the font of existing text, select the text to be modified and choose the new font from the Change Font box. The selected text changes accordingly.

Using the Font Dialog Box

These methods are useful shortcuts. However, you can also control your fonts and add additional effects with the Font dialog box. Choose Format, Font to open it. Figure 5.15 shows what it looks like.

This dialog box has two sheet tabs: Special Styles and Font, but for now you'll consider just the Font sheet. With it, you can do the following:

FIG. 5.15
With the Font dialog box, you can not only change fonts and their sizes, but add effects such as strikethrough.

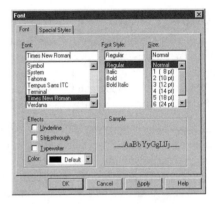

- Select the font name from the Font list box.

- Use the Font Style list box to apply regular, bold, italic, and bold italic character styles.

- Choose the font size from the Size list box.

- Use the Effects section to apply effects for Underline, Strikethrough, and Typewriter (which is actually monospaced Courier font).

- Use the Color drop-down list to apply color to a font or to generate a custom color for the font.

- See what the font will look like in the Sample box.

To make the font look as you want it, select from among the various options and choose OK. Selected text takes on these characteristics, or you can start typing new text with them. Generating custom colors is discussed later in this chapter, in the section "Changing Background and Text Colors."

The Future of Fonts on the Web

What happens if you designate a font with the FONT FACE parameter and design your page layout to depend on its look or proportioning, and the person viewing the page doesn't have that font installed on his machine? He'll see either the default of Times New Roman or whatever fonts he's set for his browser preferences. This may ruin your careful work.

The only immediate solution for this problem is sticking with the most common fonts; but help is on the way. In early 1997, Microsoft and Adobe Systems announced the OpenType extension to the True Type font format. When fully implemented, this technology will allow Open Type fonts to be embedded into a Web page, so that the font is downloaded, along with the page, to the user's browser. The browser must also support the technology; Microsoft Internet Explorer 4 (although not 3) does so. Because technology is in its usual state of flux, there is some uncertainty about the degree of Netscape's future support for OpenType. However, Netscape is working with both True Type and Dynamic Fonts, so compatibility across browser platforms will not likely be an issue.

Assuming a OpenType-supporting browser is on the target machine, the Web page designer— or Help author—is able to specify in precise detail what the end user sees on the screen, regardless of the fonts on the target system or the preference settings of the browser. The OpenType fonts is also optimized for screen display as well as for printing. Just as important, with regard to page download speed, is the fact that the OpenType technology allows the embedding into a Web page of only the characters actually used in that page. OpenType also uses MicroType Express, a lossless, on-the-fly font compression technology from Agfa, targeted at World Wide Web text-generation systems. When combined with selective embedding, this compression significantly reduces page size and therefore download time.

Getting Rid of Character Formatting

If you've been experimenting with character formatting on a large section of text and have messed it up and want to start all over again, you can easily do so. Select the offending text and choose Format, Remove Formatting. Character size, font, color, and attributes (such as bold) all revert to the default of Times New Roman, size 3 (12 point), regular typeface, color black.

Using FrontPage Editor's Other Paragraph Styles

So far in this chapter, you've looked at FrontPage Editor's Heading and Normal styles, which produce the page elements that formal HTML calls the heading and the paragraph. On top of that, FrontPage Editor's Paragraph Properties dialog box gives you two other styles: *formatted* and *address*.

N O T E Because Web publishing is such a new phenomenon, some of its terminology hasn't yet settled down to a standard. FrontPage Editor uses its own vocabulary for certain elements of HTML to make the interface software function more like a word processor. This shows especially in FrontPage Editor's use of *styles* of text, and you may find it easier to think in terms of styles rather than HTML references such as *preformatted text* or *blockquote*. For consistency with the software, we'll stick with FrontPage Editor's word processor model and refer most of the time to styles. ◼

Using Tabs and Embedded Spaces with Normal Text

The formal HTML definition of Normal text does not allow such text to have tabs or strings of spaces placed within the <p> and </p> tags that define it. In FrontPage Editor 98 (not 97) this limitation no longer applies. You can now use tabs and embedded strings of spaces when you are typing Normal text. To see how this works, add tabs or spaces within a paragraph and go to HTML mode. You'll see that FrontPage Editor is inserting the escape sequence   within the text, and each escape sequence forces a space. Pressing the Tab key inserts a string of three of these escape sequences. Netscape 3.0 and higher, and Internet Explorer 3.0 and higher, display these extra spaces and tabs correctly.

This actually does away with much of the need for the Formatted style, which, until FrontPage Editor 98, was the only simple way to get tabs and spaces into text. However, the Formatted style is still available, so you'll examine it in the next two sections.

Using the Formatted Style with New Text

Why would you need the Formatted style? It allows the embedding of tabs or strings of spaces within in it as well as character attributes, such as bold or italic, and most other HTML elements, such as links.

However, when it comes to breaking off a line, the Formatted style behaves just as the Normal style does. That is, if you use the Enter key to break a line while you're typing text, you'll get a blank line before the start of the next Formatted paragraph. To break a line without having this happen, use a line break (press Shift+Enter).

A typical use of the Formatted style is with text that needs several levels of indentation, or that needs various short lines indented (see Figure 5.16). One of its drawbacks is that it uses 8-space tabs, which may be too much if you have several levels of indentation.

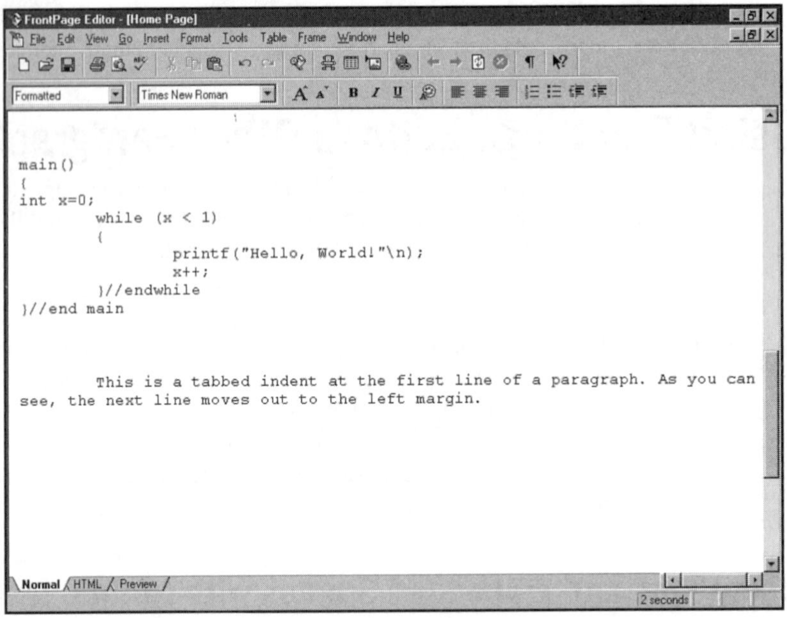

FIG. 5.16
The Formatted style preserves your program code indenting and lets you indent the first lines of paragraphs. Format marks have been turned off for clarity.

To write new text using the Formatted style, use the following steps:

1. Place the cursor where you want the new text to begin.

2. Choose Format, Paragraph and choose Formatted from the drop-down list in the Paragraph Properties dialog box (or simply use the Change Styles box to select the Formatted style). The Change Styles box shows you're in Formatted style.

3. Type the text you want, using tabs or strings of spaces as you need them. Remember to use Shift+Enter to keep lines together.

As you can see from Figure 5.16, the default Formatted style does have another drawback, although it's an aesthetic rather than a functional one. Until recently, most browsers displayed

Formatted text in a monospaced font like Courier, which is rather ugly, and that's the default font FrontPage Editor uses. With FrontPage Editor's support of font face tags, however, you're no longer limited to Courier. Choose the Formatted style and select the font you want to use. You'll find that the Formatted style's convenience of tabs and strings of spaces is still available, even though you're not using Courier. Browsers that don't support the font face tags, of course, still show the text in Courier.

TROUBLESHOOTING

I wanted to change from Normal to Formatted style when I was part of the way through a paragraph. When I used the Paragraph Properties dialog box to do this, the whole paragraph changed to Formatted style. The same thing happened when I tried using the Change Styles box. What's going on? Changing a paragraph style isn't the same as changing character style (for example, selecting Bold or a font). Character style changes affect only selected text or whatever characters you type after the change. However, when you select a paragraph style (the selection method makes no difference), the style is always applied to the entire paragraph. You can't break the paragraph into chunks, each chunk having a different style.

Importing Existing Text by Using the Formatted Style

Another use for the Formatted style is to make sure that imported ASCII text retains its indenting and any padding it does with spaces. (Of course, if the text starts out in another format, you'll have to convert it to an ASCII text file first. If you do this, be sure to save it as text with line breaks.)

To insert an existing text file into your page, position the cursor where you want the text to start and use the following steps:

1. Choose Insert, File. The Select a File dialog box appears.
2. Use the dialog box to find and select the file you want to insert and then choose Open. The Convert Text dialog box appears (see Figure 5.17), giving you four options.
3. Mark the option button that corresponds to the Formatted result you want. (Depending on the format of the source file, you may want to experiment with the various choices.) Choose OK.

FrontPage Editor inserts the file into the page and preserves space padding, line breaks, and tabs. Format marks have been turned off for clarity.

Part

II

Ch

5

FIG. 5.17

You can insert a file as either Formatted or Normal text, with options for paragraphing.

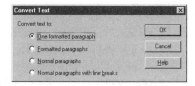

Using the Address Style

This is a simple style used to put the author's address on the page. Browsers usually display it in italics. To insert it, choose Format, Paragraph and choose Address from the list box. Alternatively, type your address, make sure the cursor is within the text, and select Address from the Change Styles box.

 T I P It's considered good Web manners to include your name and e-mail address, along with the last revision date of the page, at the end of each page.

Laying Out Text Effectively

Just getting words onto the page isn't enough. Good text layout affects a page's attractiveness and readability. FrontPage Editor has several tools to help you enhance the appearance of your pages: horizontal lines, centering, block indentation, and special character formatting.

N O T E If you've made a complicated edit that didn't work out, and you want to discard the changes before you go on, you can use FrontPage Editor's Refresh command. Choose View, Refresh (or click the Refresh button on the toolbar) and FrontPage Editor reloads the file as it was before the edit. You'll be asked if you want to save the changes you did make; assuming you don't, answer No. ■

Using Horizontal Lines

Paragraphs are units of meaning, and a new paragraph signals the reader that a new unit has begun. However, the horizontal line is effective if you want to announce a more significant shift of emphasis or subject. It's often used with headings, especially to set off the *headline* of a page or to begin a major section within the page. It is also a design element because it adds visual interest or relief from long blocks of text.

You place a line on a page by choosing Insert, Horizontal Line. The resulting default line, which all graphics-capable browsers display, is a shadowed line that stretches the width of the browser window. Incidentally, it forces a blank line above and below it, so you can't get text to snuggle up close to it.

N O T E If you want to position text right next to a line, you have to use a graphic line, which you insert as an image. ■

You can vary the line's appearance somewhat by adjusting its properties. These variations were originally Netscape extensions, which FrontPage Editor and the Microsoft browsers also support. To modify a line's appearance, click the line and choose Edit, Horizontal Line Properties; alternatively, right-click the line and choose Horizontal Line Properties from the shortcut menu. You can change the line's width, align it, adjust its weight by changing its height in pixels, change it to a solid, unshaded line, or give it a color (see Figure 5.18). You can see various line styles in Figure 5.19.

FIG. 5.18

You use the Horizontal Line Properties dialog box to modify the appearance of a line.

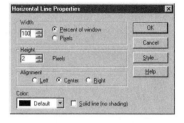

FIG. 5.19

Shaded or black lines of varying weight and width can add visual impact to sections of your page.

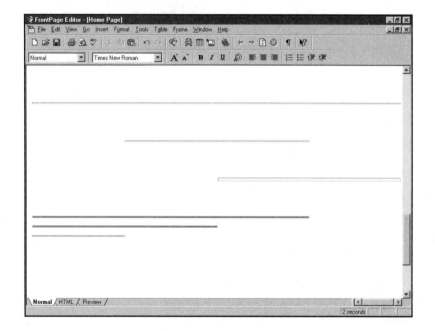

 TIP A well-designed page isn't littered with lines. Use them only when they serve a purpose (organizational or decorative). Also, it's better to determine the line width in percentage, not in pixels. That way its width will appear to a visitor as you designed it, independent of the screen resolution she's using.

Aligning Text Horizontally

You'll often want headings or other text to be somewhere other than at the left margin. To do this, use the following steps:

1. Click anywhere in the text you want to align.
2. Choose Format, Paragraph. The Paragraph Properties dialog box appears.

3. Click the arrow button at the right of the Paragraph Alignment drop-down list box. The alignment options list appears (see Figure 5.20).

4. Select the alignment you want and choose OK.

FIG. 5.20

Use the list of alignment options to left align, right align, or center text.

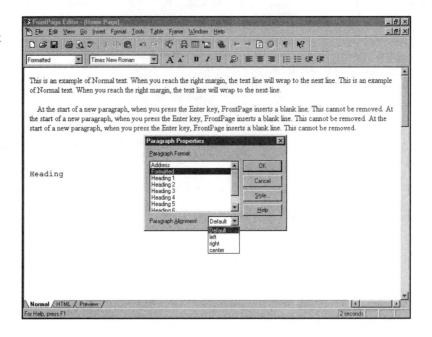

N O T E The Left alignment and the Default alignment both put text against the left margin. There is no functional difference between them, unless the user has set his browser so that (for example) the default alignment is right-aligned. ■

 A quick way to align text is to use the Align Left, Center, and Align Right buttons on the formatting toolbar.

Indenting Blocks of Text

In print documents, a chunk of text is sometimes set off from its surroundings by indenting its left margin. You often see this in long quotations. To get this result, you place the cursor in the desired paragraph and click the Increase Indent button on the formatting toolbar. The indentation increases each time you click the button. To decrease it, click the Decrease Indent button on the toolbar.

Applying Special Styles with the Font Dialog Box

When you worked with the Font dialog box earlier, you may have noticed a second sheet called Special Styles. These character styles represent the HTML approach to character formatting, which distinguishes between logical and physical styles.

The distinction initially can be confusing, but what it boils down to is this. If a browser sees the HTML tags for italic or bold characters (physical styles), it puts italic or bold on the screen, no matter how the browser preferences are set. But if it sees the emphasis or strong HTML tags (logical styles), it checks its preference settings to see how its user wants emphasized or strong text to appear. The default for the browser usually displays this text as italic and bold, respectively. However, if the user changed the *emphasized* preference setting to 14-point Caslon, the browser dutifully displays Caslon instead of italic. In short, logical styles are flexible at the browser end and physical ones aren't.

In the Font dialog box, the Font Style box on the Font sheet specifies only logical styles and so do the toolbar buttons for these character styles. If you want physical styles for bold or italic, you have to use the Special Styles sheet to force this condition. This sheet also provides logical styles such as Citation and Sample. Choose Format, Font, and click the Special Styles tab to see the sheet (see Figure 5.21).

FIG. 5.21

You use the Special Styles sheet to apply HTML physical styles for certain types of character formatting.

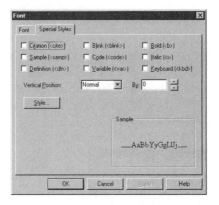

Part

II

Ch

5

As usual, you can apply these styles by selecting text and choosing the style you want. Tables 5.1 and 5.2 give more detail about how Web browsers display them. For most of your page creation work, you'll likely use the Font sheet to specify the look of your text.

Table 5.1 Physical Character Styles in FrontPage Editor

Style	Effect
Bold	Forces browser to display bold.
Italic	Forces browser to display italic.
Underlined	Forces underlining.
Typewriter font	Forces monospaced font, default Courier.

Table 5.2 Logical Character Styles in FrontPage Editor

Style	Effect
Strong	Bold unless changed by browser options.
Emphasis	Italic unless changed by browser options.
Strikethrough	Strike through characters.
Citation	Italic for citing references.
Sample	Output sample (resembles typewriter font).
Definition	Italic for definitions.
Blink	Blinks text.
Code	HTML code (resembles typewriter font).
Variable	Usually italic for defining a variable.
Keyboard	Indicates user-supplied text (resembles typewriter font).

 To quickly format one or more characters, select them, right-click the selection to open the shortcut menu, and click Font Properties to make the Font dialog box appear.

If you need superscripts or subscripts, you can also find these in the Special Styles sheet. To apply the formatting to selected or new text, click the arrow button at the right of the Vertical Position box and select from Superscript or Subscript. The By box lets you specify how much the affected text is offset from the text baseline (see Figure 5.22). Note that the number in this box is negative if you're using a subscript.

FIG. 5.22
You can make text into superscript or subscript.

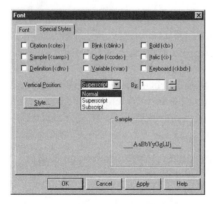

Using Symbols

From time to time, you need characters that don't appear on the keyboard, such as, the copyright or trademark symbols. To insert such a character, place the cursor where you want the symbol to appear and choose Insert, Symbol. The Symbol dialog box appears (see Figure 5.23). Click the character you want (a larger representation of it appears beside the Insert button), choose Insert and then choose Close. Clicking the Insert button twice inserts the character twice, and so on.

FIG. 5.23

When you need specialized symbols, you find them in the Symbol dialog box.

Setting Page Margins

At the time of writing, margins show up only in Internet Explorer 3.0 and later and Navigator 4.0. You set them by choosing File, Page Properties and going to the Margins sheet in the Page Properties dialog box. Mark the check box for the margin you want (left or top) and type a value into the size box. The units are in pixels.

Using Lists to Present Your Content

Part
II

Ch
5

As discussed earlier, the content and presentation of your pages should be in balance. That is, all the elements in a well-designed page support and reinforce each other so that the whole is greater than the sum of its parts. (This goes for a well-designed Web site, too.)

Lists are excellent for helping you achieve this synergy in your pages because they are good at integrating presentation and content. They're very adaptable, too, because you can combine different kinds of lists to organize different kinds of information. It's because of this flexibility that lists are everywhere in everyday life, from the humble loaf-of-bread-and-quart-of-milk version to the fantastically complicated checklists that govern the missions of interplanetary probes. In fact, lists are probably the oldest written documents of civilization. Scribes, 45 centuries ago, were already recording how many bushels of barley the local farmers owed to the king in taxes.

We don't use clay tablets today, but our electronic pages do contain lists by the dozens. They not only organize things for our visitors, they also help us organize our thinking as we put them together. What makes lists even more useful is that you can put hyperlinks, styles, and character formatting into them. You're not limited to a fixed font and type size, for instance, and you can nest lists of one kind inside lists of another.

The trouble with coding lists in HTML is that the work is so exact; one tag out of place in a nested list, and terrible things happen to your page. Fortunately, FrontPage Editor relieves you of this picky stuff so you can concentrate on what the list says, rather than how it's put together. You also have a full range of listing tools at your disposal, from bulleted to definition.

Making a Bulleted List

You use a bulleted list for items that need no particular order, although there's sometimes an implied grading of importance within it. (Formally, these are called unordered lists.) Bulleted lists can summarize important points in an argument or emphasize key items of information. They're the most common list type on the World Wide Web, partly because they're visually attractive, and partly because they're good for so many different things.

If you use a theme, the bullets are images attached to that theme. To make the simplest kind of bulleted list, without using theme bullet images, use the following steps:

1. Remove a theme if you are using one from the current page. Choose Format, Theme and mark the option button labeled This Page Does Not Use Themes. Choose OK. You can skip this step if you're not using a Theme. When the Choose Theme dialog box closes, put the insertion point where you want the list to start.

2. Choose Format, Bullets and Numbering. The List Properties dialog box appears (see Figure 5.24) with three tabbed sheets, two of which offer varied bullet styles.

FIG. 5.24

With the List Properties dialog box you can choose between Numbered Lists and Bulleted lists.

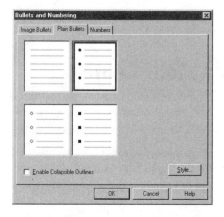

3. Click the Plain Bullets tab and choose the page icon with the bullet style you want (or choose the nonbulleted page icon to turn off bullets).

N O T E The Enable Collapsible Outlines check box in the Bullets and Numbering dialog box is to make collapsible lists for Dynamic HTML-enabled browsers (specifically Internet Explorer 4.0). This type of list is treated in Chapter 7. ▮

4. Choose OK. The dialog box vanishes and a bullet appears on the page.

5. Start typing your list and press Enter at the end of each item.

6. Press Enter twice to stop inserting bulleted items when you've finished.

7. Position the insertion point immediately to the right of the preceding item, press Enter, and type the new item if you need to insert an item into the list (see Figure 5.25).

FIG. 5.25
A bulleted list that is about to have a new item inserted after the third entry.

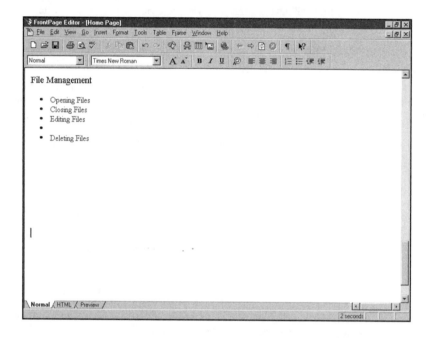

 A fast way to start a list (of any kind) is to use the Change Style drop-down list box. It contains all the types of lists that FrontPage Editor supports. Alternatively, click the Bulleted List button or the Numbered List button to start a list of that type.

Deleting a List or a List Item

To delete the whole list, select it and press the Delete key, or choose Edit, Clear. After deletion, one bullet remains; to get rid of it, press the Backspace key.

To delete an item in a list, select it and press the Delete key or choose Edit, Clear. Press the Delete key again to remove the remaining bullet.

Making a Bulleted Sublist Under a Top-Level Bulleted List

You use a sublist (called a nested list) to arrange less important points or headings under more important ones. If you've used the outlining tools in applications like WordPerfect, Word, or PowerPoint, this principle is familiar to you. It's a powerful method of organizing information. To start a nested list under a top-level list, use the following steps:

1. Place the cursor at the end of the line beneath which the nested list will appear. This can be within an existing list or at the end of the last item of an existing list.

2. Press the Enter key to make a new bullet but don't type anything.

3. Click the Increase Indent button twice. The first bullet of the nested list appears; this bullet will have a different style from those in the superior list.

3. Type the items of the nested list.

4. End the nested list by pressing Enter to get a bullet without any text. Press the Delete key and the insertion point returns to the top-level list.

5. Go on with the top-level list and place the insertion point at the end of the appropriate item, press the Enter key, and continue typing items. If you are finished with the top-level list, press the Delete key to get a bullet with no item and press the Delete key again.

Lists with more than two levels are a bit trickier. If you are typing items in a third-level list, for example, how do you continue the second-level list after you've ended the third-level one? You can't use the step 4 procedure because this returns you to the top-level list. To get a new second-level bullet to follow the last item of the third-level list:

1. Press Enter to get a third-level bullet without any text.

2. Press the Backspace Key twice (or click the Decrease Indent button twice). A second-level list bullet appears beneath the third-level list item.

3. Continue adding items to the second list.

4. Use any of the steps in this procedure or the previous procedure to complete the list.

You can see a nested list with three levels in Figure 5.26. Incidentally, you can create more levels for a list than you're ever likely to need.

FIG. 5.26

You use nested lists to arrange less important points or headings under more important ones. Here, an item is about to be added at the end of the third-level list.

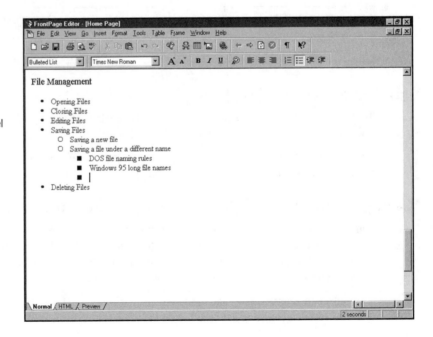

T I P It's easy to *promote* a list item to the superior list above it. Place the insertion point inside the item and click the Decrease Indent button twice. Similarly, to *demote* an item to the list below it, place the insertion point inside the item and click the Increase Indent button twice.

Changing Bullet Styles in Nested Lists

Nested lists by default change their bullet appearance. This may not be what you want, though. For example, you might want all the bullets in the lists of Figure 5.26 to be round, solid ones. To make such changes, do the following:

N O T E The next procedure only works with pages that do not use themes. On a page with a theme, the bullet images are fixed and can't be modified. ▪

1. Place the insertion point inside the nested list whose bullets you want to change.
2. Choose F**o**rmat, Bullets and **N**umbering. The List Properties dialog box appears.
3. Click the Plain Bullets tab and click the type of bullet you want.
4. Choose OK. The nested list immediately acquires the new bullets.

This also works for the topmost list, not only for the nested lists below it.

Using Image-Based Bullets

The trouble with the bullets used thus far is that they're boring. Themes, of course, supply much more interesting bullets, but you may not like any of those, either. The answer is to select your own bullet images.

To make this happen:

1. Choose F**o**rmat, Bullets and **N**umbering to open the Bullets and Numbering dialog box and click the Image Bullets tab (see Figure 5.27).

FIG. 5.27

Specify your own bullet image by using the Image Bullets dialog box.

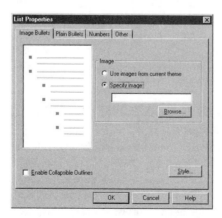

2. Mark the Specify Image option button. If you know the file name of the image you want, type it into the text box under the option button. Alternatively, choose Browse to open the Select Image dialog box (see Figure 5.28).

FIG. 5.28

Use the Select Image dialog box to locate the bullet image you want.

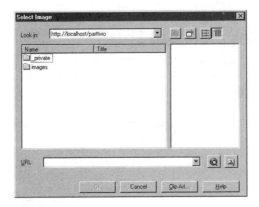

3. Assuming the bullet image is stored on your machine somewhere, click the rightmost icon on the right end of the URL text box (the folder and magnifying glass icon). This opens a standard Windows 95 file open dialog box, titled Select File. You'll be seeing a lot more of this dialog box in the next chapter.

4. Use this dialog box to locate and select the bullet image, then choose Open. When you return to the Bullets and Numbering dialog box, choose OK. The selected image is the first bullet of the list.

The bullet is applied only to the current level of the current list. If you want a bullet image (even the same one) to apply to a sublist, this image needs to be selected by using the previous procedure.

When you save the page, you are asked if you also want to save the image as an embedded file. If you want to copy the image file to the current FrontPage Web so the page can access it from there, answer OK. You'll be examining image handling in much more detail in the next chapter.

N O T E Changing a page's theme automatically changes all the bullets on that page. However, selecting a bullet image, as you just did, does not affect existing bulleted lists. ■

Adding Paragraph Styles and Character Formatting

You can vary a list's paragraph style and character format. In Figure 5.29, some text is in bold and line breaks separate the items of the topmost list. Additionally, the third-level nested list contains a hyperlink. Again, avoid assuming that the Normal mode displays an accurate representation of the real appearance of the page; in the Figure 5.29 example, two blank lines are between the top list items, but in Preview mode, there's only one. Note also that you need two Line Breaks to force a single blank line in a browser view of the page.

FIG. 5.29
You can use character formatting, line breaks, and hyperlinks inside lists. Format marks have been turned on to show the paragraph and line break symbols.

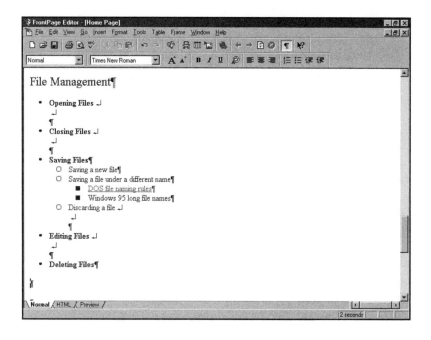

Making a Numbered List

These are somewhat less common on the Web than bulleted lists. They're used for tables of contents, establishing a rank order from highest to lowest, a set of instructions, or any data where relative importance needs to be shown. Because of the numbering, they're formally called ordered lists.

You make a numbered list just as you make a bulleted list. Choose Format, Bullets and Numbering and click the Numbers sheet tab. Here you have several different numbering styles that you can arrange into a hierarchy (see Figure 5.30). Themes have no effect on the appearance of numbered lists.

FIG. 5.30
The Numbers sheet gives you five numbering styles and the *unnumbered* option.

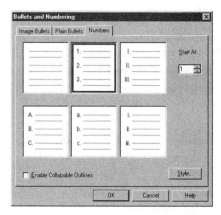

Part
II

Ch
5

Usually, your list starts with 1, or a, and so on. However, if it must start at a higher number, adjust the number in the Start At box accordingly. If you put 2 in the box, for example, and choose the a,b,c type list, the list starts at b.

When you've selected the numbering type, choose OK and the first item of the numbered list appears. FrontPage Editor inserts a new number every time you press Enter. To end the list, press Enter twice. You can use paragraph styles, character formatting, and hyperlinks within numbered lists.

You start a numbered nested list the same way you start a bulleted nested list. Place the cursor at the end of the item before the nested list and press Enter to get a new number. Click the Increase Indent button twice and the nested list starts. Complete it and press Enter once to get a blank entry and click the Decrease Indent button twice. The insertion point returns to the superior list. FrontPage Editor adjusts all numbering to match the additions or deletions.

When you try this, you'll notice that FrontPage Editor doesn't automatically supply a hierarchy of numbering formats. If your superior list uses Arabic numerals, so will your nested list, unless you specify otherwise.

You change the style of the nested list numbering by using the following steps:

1. Place the insertion point inside the nested list and choose Format, Bullets and Numbering.
2. Click the Numbers sheet tab.
3. Click the page icon that shows the style you want.
4. Choose OK. The nested list takes up the new style.

You can see an example of an ordered, nested list in Figure 5.31.

To delete the list or parts of it, or to promote or demote list items, use the methods applied earlier to bulleted lists. (See "Deleting a List or a List Item" and "Making a Bulleted Sublist Under a Top-Level Bulleted List.")

Changing the Style of an Existing List

You may put a bulleted list together and then decide it would be more useful as a numbered one. To make this change, do the following:

1. Place the insertion point somewhere inside the list and choose Format, Bullets and Numbering. The List Properties dialog box appears.
2. Click the Numbers sheet tab. On the numbers sheet, click the page icon that shows the desired numbering style.
3. Choose OK. The list immediately takes on the new style. You use this procedure going the other way, too, to change a numbered list to a bulleted list.

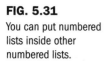

FIG. 5.31

You can put numbered lists inside other numbered lists.

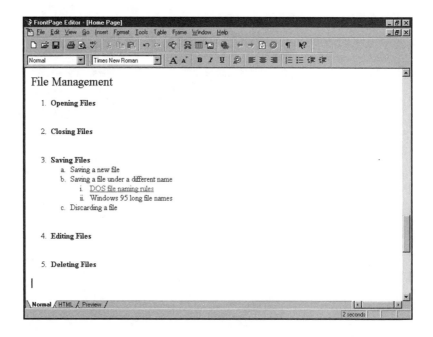

Combining List Types Within a List

You can mix types of lists to fine-tune your presentation of content. For example, you can include a nested list of numbered instructions inside a bulleted list (see Figure 5.32) by following these steps:

1. Place the insertion point at the end of the line before the new nested list. Press Enter but don't type anything.
2. Click the Increase Indent button twice.
3. Choose Format, Bullets and Numbering to open the List Properties dialog box.
4. Select the type of list you want (numbered, in this example) from the available sheets. Select the format you want and choose OK. The new list format appears.
5. Type the list. When finished, press the Enter key to make a blank item but don't type anything.
6. Click the Decrease Indent button twice. The list symbol for the superior list appears.

Using the List Buttons or Change Style Box to Modify Existing Lists

You can use either the Numbered List or the Bulleted List button to manipulate existing lists. To change a list or nested list from one type to another, place the insertion point anywhere in the list and click the appropriate button. Only that list changes; lists subordinate or superior to it aren't affected. If you want to change the formatting of the bullets or numbers, choose

Part
II

Ch
5

Format, Bullets and Numbering to display the List Properties dialog box and make your changes from there.

FIG. 5.32

You can use mixed lists to put different types of information together.

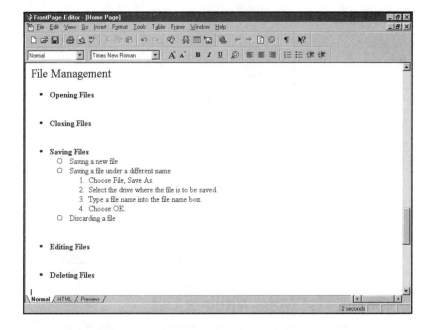

Alternatively, place the insertion point inside the list and choose the new list type from the drop-down list in the Change Styles box.

Modifying the Properties of One Item in a List

You won't want to do this often, but here's what you do if you want to mix numbers and letters inside a numbered list:

1. Right-click the item whose list property you want to change. The shortcut menu appears.

2. Click List Item Properties. The List Properties dialog box appears.

3. Click the page icon of the new format you want and choose OK. The item gets its new property, but the other items in the list are unaffected. Notice that you can't mix bullets and numbers.

 TIP To get to the List Properties dialog box in a hurry, right-click inside the list and click List Properties to make the dialog box appear.

Removing a List Format

If you decide your list should be ordinary text, you can get rid of the list style by selecting the entire list and clicking the Decrease Indent button. If you have nested lists, they won't be affected until you click the Decrease Indent button individually.

Making Directory or Menu Lists

The appearance of both directory and menu list types depends on the tags the browser supports. If you make either list in FrontPage Editor, they will look exactly like bulleted lists. Netscape 2.0 and later, Internet Explorer 3.0, and Mosaic also show them as bulleted lists. Internet Explorer 2.0, however, displays them as indented lists without bullets.

A browser that does support directory lists shows the entries evenly spaced across the screen. Neither the Netscape nor the Microsoft browser supports the directory tag, so if you want the effect, use a table. The menu list, in browsers that support this option, shows a list without bullets, and nested lists are simply indented.

You're unlikely ever to need the menu list or the directory list. In fact, the new HTML 4 standard discourages these types of lists, and they will soon be history.

▶ **See** Chapter 8, "Creating Tables," **p. 179**

Definition Lists

Also called glossary lists, definition lists are a useful reference format. You can see a typical example of a definition list in Figure 5.33.

FIG. 5.33

Definition lists provide structured lists made up of terms and their definitions.

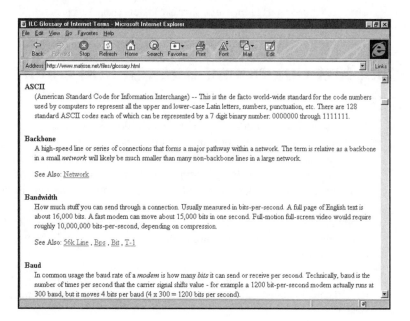

A definition list is a collection of entries, and each entry is made up of a term and its definition. Naturally, this structure isn't only for formal definitions; you can use it for anything that needs a short heading term and one or more indented paragraphs of information beneath this. For the sake of appearance, the term should be short enough to fit on one line of a browser display, but the definition text can be as long as you like. To start a new definition list, use the following steps:

1. Select Defined Term from the Change Style box.
2. Type the term to be defined and press Enter. The insertion point automatically indents.
3. Type the definition and press Enter.
4. Note that the Change Style box says Defined Term again. Repeat steps 2 and 3 until you're finished. Press Enter three times to end the list.

Definition lists are that simple. You can embed other lists inside definition lists, and vice versa. Definition lists can contain hyperlinks and whatever character formatting you want.

N O T E   Converting lists to and from definition lists causes more problems than it solves. When you convert a list to a definition list, what you get is a list made completely of definitions, so you have to add the terms by hand. If you go from a definition list to a bulleted or numbered list, both terms and definitions convert to first-level bullets or numbers. ■

CAUTION

Don't use heading styles inside lists. This style forces line breaks and can leave your list looking very fragmented. If you want to emphasize parts of a list, use character formatting.

Using Text Colors and Background Colors on Your Page

Both content and presentation are important in Web pages, just as they are in any form of communication. However, content is what most people are after, and you should remember this when you're adding colors to a page. If most of the content of the page is in the text (and often it is), don't allow that text to be obscured by even the most stunning visual effects. White text in normal size on a black background, for example, is excruciatingly hard to read; if you want this combination, be prepared to allocate space to a large font or heading style. Some color combinations, like orange and green, or purple and yellow, seem to vibrate, and instantly detract from whatever your words are trying to say. So be careful when selecting background colors and text colors.

Don't bother using color depths over 8-bit (256 colors) either. Most people's systems are set up for 256 colors at most, and the extra bandwidth needed to transmit more than this is simply wasted.

Always remember to test with different browsers and resolutions.

N O T E Pages with themes have their background color and background image fixed. You can't modify these by using the procedures that follow. As for text color, you can't modify that globally to the page, although you can change the color of selected text.

Changing the Background and Text Colors on Non Theme Pages

Both these changes can be made at once from the same dialog box, so you will consider them together. To change text or background color, use the following steps:

1. Choose File, Page Properties. When the Page Properties dialog box appears, click the Background tab to bring that sheet to the front.
2. Mark the Specify Background and Colors option button.
3. Click the button at the right of the Background drop-down list box. A drop-down list of available colors appears (see Figure 5.34).

FIG. 5.34

Use the Background sheet of the Page Properties dialog box to modify the background color or text color of your pages.

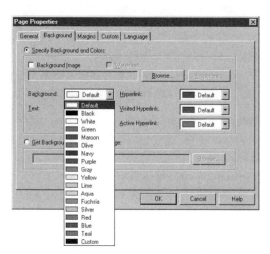

4. Click the color you want. Click OK and the dialog box vanishes, and your page background immediately assumes that color.
5. Click the button at the right of the Text drop-down list box to set the text color. The same color list appears. Select the color you want and click OK.

All new text and existing text not already colored with character formatting or the Text Color button takes on the color you selected in Step 5.

Defining Custom Colors

If the range of colors available from the drop-down list isn't enough, you can mix your own hue by using the Custom color selection at the bottom of the list. Follow Steps 1 to 3, but instead of

Part
II

Ch
5

clicking a color, click the Custom rectangle at the bottom of the list. The Color dialog box appears (see Figure 5.35).

FIG. 5.35
The Color dialog box lets you either pick from predefined colors or define your own.

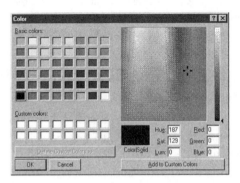

You create a new color in one of the following three ways:

1. Drag the mouse pointer over the large colored rectangle on the right of the dialog box. This changes the color in the Color/Solid box. When you see the color you want, stop dragging. You can change the color's luminance by dragging the black triangle that's next to the vertical bar beside the color box.

2. Adjust the numbers in the boxes for Red, Green, and Blue.

3. Adjust the numbers in the boxes for Hue, Saturation, and Luminance.

After you've adjusted the color, close the dialog boxes by choosing OK in each box until they all disappear. The page background now has the color you chose.

This doesn't save your custom color, however. If you want to save it to a custom palette, click the Add to Custom Colors button in the Color dialog box before you leave this box.

CAUTION

Custom colors may look great in your 256-color or higher display, but they won't appear to the same effect (or at all) on a 16-color system. Using them is more likely a waste of time than an enhancement, unless you are sure that most of your audience will be able to see them.

Changing the Color of Part of Your Text

You can make non global changes of text color even if the page has a theme. Select the text to be changed and do the following:

1. Choose Format, Font to open the Font dialog box.

2. Click the arrow button on the Font sheet at the right of the Color box. A drop-down list of colors appears. (It's the same list as the one you saw in the previous procedures.)

3. Click the color you want. The dialog box closes and the selected text takes on the new color.

Naturally, you can create new text in the new color by following the steps just listed and typing the text. You can also make custom colors by clicking the Custom choice to open the Color dialog box and using the procedures described earlier.

Finally, the Text Color button on the toolbar opens the Color dialog box, and you can specify colors from there.

The best way to understand the effects of these changes is to experiment and see the results through the eyes of your visitors. What will the person using a 16-color, 640×480 display make of your ingeniously coordinated color scheme? Or, if she's got a 256-color display, does she really want to read three screens of yellow text on a black background? Or worse, red on purple?

CAUTION

The Background sheet of the Page Properties dialog box is also where you change the default link colors to custom colors (for non theme pages only). You should think very hard about this before you do it. How would you react to a map that used blue for the land and green for the water, just because the cartographer decided it looked better that way? Furthermore, viewers might not recognize a custom-colored link as being a link.

N O T E Many applications, including browsers, have a built-in set of colors, called a color table, that they use for screen display. If a downloaded page contains a color that isn't in the browser's table, the browser either substitutes a similar color or dithers multiple colors from its table to get as close as it can. If you make up a custom color, it may not appear in a browser as it does in FrontPage Editor. As always, test your work. ▨

Making Colors Consistent Across Pages

Even if (and perhaps *especially* if) you don't use themes, you may want to get a consistent *look* across your site or part of it, and it's a little inconvenient to define the background color and text color for each page as you create it. To get around this, first set up a model page with the color combination you want. Then, for each new or existing page that is to have that combination, open the Page Properties dialog box and go to the Background sheet. Mark the option button called Get Background and Colors from Page and type the file name of the model page into the text box (or use the Browse button to locate the page). Choose OK and the color combination is applied to the current page.

Using the Text-Editing Tools

Just as word processors do, FrontPage Editor provides commands for spell-checking, finding and replacing words or strings of words, and a thesaurus. None of these tools is a substitute for careful proofreading and competent writing, but they help.

Spell-Checking Your Work

When you've finished writing the text of your page, you can check it for spelling errors. Choose Tools, Spelling (or click the Check Spelling button on the toolbar) and the Spelling dialog box appears. The first possible error is already showing in the Not in Dictionary box (see Figure 5.36).

FIG. 5.36

Using the spell checker to find suspected errors.

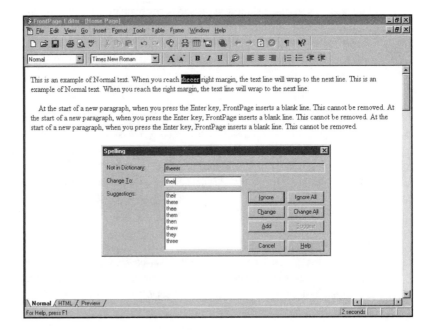

You can accept the suggested change that appears in the Change To box, or select a different change from the Suggestions list box, or type your own correction into the Change To box. Whichever you do, choose the Change button when you're ready to make the change. You can also do one of the following:

- Choose Ignore to bypass the word, or Ignore All to bypass this and all later occurrences of it (you do this if the word is correct but you don't want to add it to the spell-checker's custom dictionary).

- Choose Change All to change this and all other occurrences of the word.

- Choose Add to add the new word to the custom dictionary. If you do this, it won't get flagged as an error in this or any other document.

- Choose Suggest to get other spelling suggestions from the dictionary. This choice isn't available unless you select a word from the Suggestions list box.

Choosing the Change, Change All, Ignore, or Ignore All buttons immediately takes you to the next possible error, until the page has been checked completely.

Using Find and Replace

These related commands work just as they do in a word processor. To find occurrences of a string of text, choose Edit, Find. The Find dialog box appears (see Figure 5.37).

FIG. 5.37

You can search for occurrences of a word with the Find dialog box.

The search direction can be specified by marking the option buttons, and you can make the search case-sensitive by marking the Match case check box. Depending on what you're looking for, you may want to mark the Match Whole Word Only check box, as well; if you don't, the command finds all occurrences of the text pattern even if it's embedded inside a word.

To search and replace a word or text string, choose Edit, Replace to open the Replace dialog box (see Figure 5.38).

FIG. 5.38

The Replace command is handy for selective or global replacement of a text string.

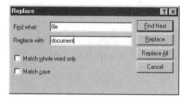

Type the search string into the Find What box, and the replacement text into the Replace With box. Here you should consider carefully whether you need to mark the Match whole Word Only check box. If it's unchecked, and you replace "led" with "brought" (for example), you'll discover that "filed" becomes "fibrought" after the replacement. This may be amusing, but is counterproductive! If it happens, choose Edit, Undo immediately to cancel the changes.

You can automatically replace all occurrences of the search string by choosing Replace All. To replace selectively, choose Find Next, and if you want to replace, choose the Replace button. If you don't want the replacement, choose Find Next again to go on to the next occurrence of the search string until you've finished the document.

Using the Thesaurus

Mark Twain said that "The difference between the right word and the almost-right word is the difference between lightning and the lightning bug." If you're staring at the almost-right word and can't think of the right one, try using FrontPage Editor's thesaurus to find it.

Position the insertion point immediately before the word that's giving you trouble and do the following:

1. Choose Tools, Thesaurus to open the Thesaurus dialog box (see Figure 5.39).

FIG. 5.39

Use the Thesaurus when you're having trouble finding the exact word for what you want to say.

2. Choose Replace if you like the suggested word in the Replace with Synonym box. The dialog box closes, and the original word is automatically replaced with the new one.

3. Select a better one, if the suggested word isn't right, from the right list box and choose Replace.

4. Select a similar meaning from the Meanings list box if that list box doesn't show you what you want. More words appear in the right-hand list box. Select one of these and choose Replace.

5. Select any word from either list box and choose Look Up if you are still not satisfied. More words will appear in the list boxes. (To go back to the previous list, choose Previous.)

6. Keep doing this until you find the word you're after and choose Replace.

You can also use the Thesaurus to find antonyms, the opposite of synonyms. The word "antonym" sometimes appears at the bottom of the list in the Meanings list box; select this to get a list of opposites.

There are two problems with using the Thesaurus. A minor one is that it's easy to become so fascinated with words that you just keep wandering among them—it's harmless, though, and good for your vocabulary. The other, more serious problem, has to do with style. You don't want to become infected with the disorder known as *thesaurusitis*. You know you've contracted the disease when you start replacing words like "image" with "simulacrum" and "help" with "succor." The effect is often pretentious and may also obscure your meaning. When it comes to style, simple is usually best.

Previewing and Printing Your Pages

Printing your pages is a good idea because language errors seem to stand out better on paper than they do on a screen. Hard copy also gives you another perspective on your page design. You can preview a page before sending it to your printer by choosing File, Print Preview. You print by choosing File, Print or by clicking the Print button on the toolbar.

Understanding Hyperlinks

Without hyperlinks there would be no World Wide Web, just a multitude of isolated pages like unknown islands in an uncharted sea. It's not for nothing that people speak of *navigating* the Web; it really is like a vast and ever-expanding collection of islands, and the hyperlinks are like the trade and communications routes that bind them together across the electronic deeps.

Less poetically, *hyperlink* generally refers to the highlighted words (or specially defined images) that you click in a Web page to access a different resource on the Web or the Internet. Tucked away behind this highlight or image is a string of HTML code that gives your browser the URL for the new location and directs the browser to jump to that location. FrontPage Editor generates this code automatically when you tell it to set up a hyperlink.

Using Hyperlinks Effectively

Most of your hyperlinks will made up of words rather than images. When you're choosing which words to use for the link, think about them from your readers' point of view. It helps if the link itself suggests what happens if you follow it. An ambiguous link, which a reader must follow to discover whether he really wants to go there, is a potential waste of time. An ambiguous link says "Click here for HTML 3.2;" a clear one says "HTML 3.2 Command Reference." You can make the purpose of a link even clearer by wording the surrounding text to give it context.

▶ **See** Chapter 6, "Enhancing Pages with Themes, Graphics, and Multimedia," for detailed information on using images as links.

Also, hyperlinks by their very nature stand out from their background. They drag the reader's eye toward them, and if they're not well chosen or there are too many of them, their presence can overpower the meaning of the surrounding text. You should also avoid links that are so short that they're meaningless (*back*) or are very long, like a full sentence. Additionally, you should think hard before you change the default link colors. People expect the defaults, so they can easily tell what links they've visited. If you fool around with the link colors, they'll have to adjust to a different standard, and they may resent it.

If your page is longer than a couple of screens, you should consider repeating the navigation links at suitable points. This is so that the reader doesn't have to scroll all the way back to the top of the document to get at any links there. You will often find textual navigation controls repeated at the bottom of a home page, along with corresponding graphical controls.

 T I P Avoid using the *forward* label for navigation links because it depends on how a person reached your site.

Setting Up a Hyperlink

The simplest use of a hyperlink is to take your visitor to the top of another page in your Web site. To set this up, make sure you have at least two pages in your current FrontPage Web, one to be the hyperlink page and the other to be the destination page and do the following:

1. Open the hyperlink page in FrontPage Editor. In the hyperlink page, select some text to be the hyperlink.

2. Choose Edit, Hyperlink or click the Create/Edit Link Button on the toolbar. The Create Hyperlink dialog box appears, as in Figure 5.40.

Part
II

Ch
5

The list box displays all the pages in the Web. Some pages may appear twice, once with a standard page icon, and once with a red quill pen and page icon. This last icon simply means the page is currently open in FrontPage Editor.

3. Select the desired destination page by clicking its name and choosing OK.

FIG. 5.40
You use the Create Hyperlink dialog box to select the destination for a hyperlink.

The dialog box closes, and you've now set up the hyperlink. The text you used as the hyperlink is now highlighted and underlined with the default link color. To test it, click the link and choose Go, Follow Hyperlink. (Or you can use CTRL+click the link to get the same result.) The destination page should appear in the FrontPage Editor workspace.

Another way of checking the link is to switch to Preview mode and click the link. The destination page appears. Finally, you can also test the link by using the File, Preview in Browser command; remember to make the hyperlink page the active one, and make sure it's saved before you do this.

 If you put the cursor over a hyperlink but don't click it, the URL of the destination appears in the FrontPage Editor status bar. This is handy for identifying the link destination without actually having to go there.

Deleting Hyperlinks

If you decide the link isn't worthwhile or if its destination has vanished, you may want to delete a hyperlink. To do this, click anywhere in the link text and choose Edit, Unlink. The link is deleted. Saving the file updates the Explorer display.

Extending the Reach of Your Hyperlinks

As stated earlier, hyperlinks are the key element of the Web and its most powerful tool. From any location in your currently open Web, you can link to one of the following:

- The top of any page in the open Web (as we did earlier)
- A specified location in any page in the open Web (*bookmarking*)
- A page in another Web on the same host machine
- A resource anywhere in the Web or the Internet (pages at other Web sites, FTP sites, Gopher sites, and so on)

Hyperlinks and bookmarks give you tremendous flexibility in structuring your Web. For instance, you could keep a table of contents on a single page and set up links to other pages that hold the information itself. In general, hyperlinks make it unnecessary to produce monster pages. This has at least two advantages: shorter pages are easier to maintain, and it's easier to keep navigational aids handy for the reader. Also, most readers start to lose their way if they have to keep scrolling through screen after screen of information.

Linking to Bookmarks

As with all links, you need the hyperlink itself and its destination in order to create a link to a bookmark. In this case, our destination can be either a specific place on the current page or a specific place on a different page. Because it models itself on a word processor, FrontPage Editor refers to this destination as a *bookmark*, which is a common tool in major Windows word processors. This makes sense because you're working with pages, anyway.

You can link to a bookmark from any page in your Web, and you can establish bookmarks in any page that you have permission to modify. The formal term for a bookmark is *named anchor*.

N O T E The term *bookmark* is also used in Netscape to mean an entry in a quick-access list of Web or Internet sites. FrontPage Editor uses bookmark differently, to mean a page location rather than a site address. ■

Part

II

Ch

5

To set up the bookmark, which is the destination of the link, use the following steps:

1. Open the destination page in FrontPage Editor and make it the active page. Select an appropriate word or phrase anywhere in the destination page to be the bookmark. An image cannot be used as a bookmark.

2. Choose Edit, Bookmark. The Bookmark dialog box appears (see Figure 5.41).

FIG. 5.41
Use the Bookmark dialog box to define the destination of a hyperlink.

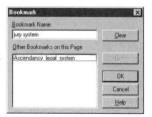

3. Choose the selected text that shows up in the Bookmark Name text box or type something else.

4. Choose OK. A dashed underline appears under the bookmarked text (this underlining does not appear in a browser).

 T I P To clear a bookmark, click anywhere in the marked text and choose Edit, Bookmark, Clear. The Bookmark vanishes.

With the bookmark defined, set up the hyperlink itself, as follows:

1. Make the origin page active and select the text you want to make into the hyperlink.

2. Choose Edit, Hyperlink or click the Create or Edit Link button on the toolbar. The Create Hyperlink dialog box appears.

3. Select the page that has the bookmark in the dialog box. This page has two icons because it's open in FrontPage Editor. You can select either entry.

4. Use the arrow button in the Bookmark box to display the Bookmark list for that page (see Figure 5.42).

5. Select the bookmark you assigned to the destination point. When you do, its name appears in the Bookmark text box.

6. Choose OK.

FIG. 5.42

You can choose among a page's bookmarks by using the Bookmark list in the Open Pages list box.

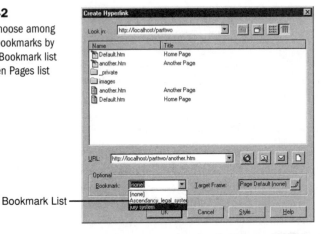

Bookmark List —

The hyperlink text is now highlighted and underlined with the default link color. Now switch to the origin page and test the link by using one of the methods described earlier. The destination page should appear with the bookmark at the top of the browser window.

 T I P When you put the cursor on top of a link, FrontPage Editor's status bar displays the name of the bookmark that is the link destination (if the destination is a bookmark, of course). In the status bar, the bookmark name is preceded by a pound sign (#), which is the HTML code to indicate a named anchor.

TROUBLESHOOTING

I want to use an image as a bookmark, and I can't find a way to do it. Is there one? No, there isn't. An HTML page doesn't actually contain the image data, but rather a *pointer* to the file where the image is stored. HTML doesn't let you define such a pointer as a named anchor, which is what a bookmark actually is. To get around this, use some text near the image (the caption, if there is one) as the bookmark.

Linking to a New Page

FrontPage Editor allows you to create a new page and make a hyperlink to it at the same time. It's a timesaver. To use the feature, carry out the following steps:

1. Open the origin page in FrontPage Editor and select some text or an image for the hyperlink. Choose Edit, Hyperlink.

2. Look at the row of icons to the right of the URL text box (shown in Figure 5.41). The fourth one is a white sheet of paper, which the ToolTip labels as *Create a Page and Link to the New Page*. Click this icon.

3. Select a page type in the New dialog box. Choose OK and the new page opens in the FrontPage Editor workspace.

4. Edit and save it with whatever file name and Page Title you need. Now, when you switch back to the origin page and inspect the link, you'll see that the link points to your new page.

Linking to the World Wide Web

It's now that you'll get a real sense of the power of hyperlinks. Local hyperlinks are useful things, but connecting your pages to the Web puts vast resources at your disposal. Remember, though, that it's your visitors who count. They'll use the resources you've selected, so you've got a lot of responsibility to them.

Like the links you've just explored, links to the Web are set up through the Create Hyperlink dialog box. If you know the URL of the Web site and/or the specific page within it, you can simply type that into the URL text box and choose OK. If, you want to actually access the Web site to make the link, however, you can do that as well. This a much surer way of making a valid link, especially if the site URL is long and complicated.

Here's how to do this:

1. Log onto your ISP, set up your connection to the Internet, and open the origination page (the one that will host the link) in FrontPage Editor. Select some text or an image to be the link.

2. Choose Edit, Hyperlink, to open the Create Hyperlink dialog box. The first button to the right of the URL text box has a globe and magnifying glass on it (see Figure 5.42). The

ToolTip identifies it as "Use Your Web Browser to Select a Page." Click the button. Your system's default browser opens with an instructional message to "Browse to the page of file you want to use, then return to Microsoft FrontPage to continue."

3. Access the page you want. *Without* closing the browser, switch back to FrontPage Editor.

4. Choose OK when you see the URL of the remote Web site in the URL text box, and save the page.

5. Close the browser. Leave your Internet connection active and use either Follow Hyperlink, Preview mode or the Preview In Browser command to test the link.

Your links to the World Wide Web work in the same way as the links within your own Web. Clicking a link that references a page somewhere else in the Web will take the visitor there. Likewise, clicking a link to an image file that resides on another server will display that image in a window all by itself.

Linking with Drag and Drop

A quick way to set up a link to a current page is to go to the right-hand pane of either Hyperlink View or Folder View in FrontPage Explorer. Find the page or image in Explorer that you want linked to the current page and drag it into FrontPage Editor's workspace. As you drag onto FrontPage Editor, the shortcut cursor appears. Put this cursor where you want the link to be, and when you release the mouse button, the page title of the linked page appears in the workspace as the hyperlink. You can also edit the link text.

Furthermore, if Explorer shows a link to another Web site, the icon for that can be dragged onto the current page. The link text is the remote site's URL, but it can be edited. This method is very simple and powerful.

 Another fast way to make a link is to choose Insert, Hyperlin<u>k</u> from the FrontPage Editor menu bar (without selecting any text for the link before you do this). In the Create Hyperlink dialog box, choose the page you want to link to and choose OK. FrontPage Editor automatically inserts a new text hyperlink onto the current page; this text is the Page Title of the page being linked to.

Creating a Mailto Link

A very common element of a Web page is an e-mail link, which the page visitor can use to send e-mail to the site's management. To add a mailto link to your page, do this:

1. Open the origin page in FrontPage Editor. Select some text or an image to be the link.

2. Look at the four buttons to the right of the URL text box. The third one has an envelope on it. Click this button. The Create E-mail Hyperlink dialog box opens (see Figure 5.43).

3. Type the appropriate e-mail address into the text box.

4. Choose OK and you return to the Create Hyperlink dialog box. You'll now see the e-mail address in the URL text box. Choose OK again and the link is established.

FIG. 5.43

Add a mailto link to your page by using the Create E-mail Hyperlink dialog box.

Now, when a visitor to the page clicks the mailto link to open the default mail program, the address you chose is already inserted as the recipient's address. The visitor types the message and sends it to the mailbox you specified.

Editing Links

To Edit a link , click anywhere in the link text and choose Edit, Hyperlink. The Edit Hyperlink dialog box appears. Except for the dialog box title, it's exactly the same as the Create Link dialog box. Make any changes you want and choose OK.

Keeping Your Visitors out of Dead Ends

The Web is a place people like to move around in. Well, chosen navigational links laid out in a useful way give your Web pages a professional gleam. But trying to keep visitors at your site by making it hard for them to leave is counterproductive.

A major error to avoid is leaving your visitor at a dead end—a page he can't leave without using his browser's Back button. As an example, suppose a visitor turns up at your site, but the link he used to get there brings him to a page that isn't your home page. Suppose also that you didn't bother to establish a link from this page back to your home page or to any other location in your site. So, when he's finished viewing this page, he's stuck. He can only go back to the site he came from, and it's not your site. He won't get a chance to see what else you have to offer him. For this reason alone, you should have a link at least to your home page in every page on your site.

Part

II

Ch

5

From Here...

You've covered an enormous amount of material in this chapter, and you have already acquired many of the tools you need to create good Web pages. But there's much more. Look to the following chapters for further ways to enhance your site:

Chapter 6, "Enhancing Pages with Themes, Graphics, and Multimedia," is where you learn to use images and imagemaps, get the most from graphics file formats, lay out text and images effectively, and use sound and inline video.

Chapter 7, "Using Dynamic HTML, Active Elements, Shared Borders, and Navigation Bars," gives you advanced tools for enlivening your Web pages.

Chapter 8, "Creating Tables," shows you how to use FrontPage 98's new WYSIWYG tables to organize and present information.

Enhancing Pages with Themes, Graphics, and Multimedia

Many books and some magazines present the reader with long blocks of unbroken text. This works fine on the printed page, but dense text doesn't look good on computer monitors. Even the best screen resolutions don't come near the clarity of print on paper, and studies have shown that people read a screen more slowly than they do a printed page. As a result, most people dislike slogging through screens crammed with words, so if that's all your Web site offers them, they'll get tired of it and go elsewhere. You need visual interest (and perhaps sound) to prevent them from leaving, and in this chapter you'll carry out a thorough exploration of how to use FrontPage Editor to add graphical and multimedia content to your Web pages. ■

Using images well

Design your pages to get the most out of graphics.

Image basics and image processing

Place images on pages, use non-local images and clip art, and use FrontPage 98's new image-manipulation tools.

Images and text

Position text and images coherently and use backgrounds as well as floating images and alternative text.

Images as hyperlinks

Use images to link inside and out-side your site, create navigational tools, and use thumbnails.

Image file formats

Convert GIF and JPEG image file formats, use interlacing, and make transparent GIFs.

Multimedia

Use sound, inline video, and video clips to give your pages life.

Themes

Even if you've applied a theme to a whole Web, you can still individual-ize pages with other themes, or no theme at all.

Getting the Most Out of Images

Images add visual interest, provide information, amplify the meaning of text, break text into manageable chunks, and (very important) give your site character. They're a resource no Web page author should willingly do without.

However, getting the best results from them takes some thought. If you have an artist's eye, you're already ahead of the game. If you're not trained in design, though, all is not lost. Before you start throwing pictures at a page, ask yourself the following questions:

- What purpose should the image or images serve?
- What content best suits this purpose?
- How big are the images (that is, how long to download)?
- How many should there be?
- How well do they relate to any text and to each other?
- Where do they look best on the page?

Working out these answers helps you avoid building pages that are a hodgepodge of unrelated elements. Once you've decided what images to use, keep the following in mind as you choose or create them:

- Don't use a background image that makes your text and graphics hard to see.
- Don't use huge graphics that take forever to download. If you want to make such an image available, put in a thumbnail with a link to the larger image. The largest single image you should consider is 25K, unless there's a very, very good reason to go bigger. Keep the total size of all graphics on a page to 30K or less.
- Speaking of size, be careful about using really wide graphics. If your visitors are running their browsers at less than full screen, or their hardware supports only VGA (640×480) resolution, the image may be lopped off at the side. Keep the image width to less than five or six inches, and test your results.
- When designing imagemaps, be sure the clickable areas are easily identified.
- Don't overuse *special effects* such as blinking text, fades, dissolves, and crawls. After the novelty wears off, many people are irritated by a page that flashes, squirms, and slithers. In particular, if you want somebody to concentrate on the meaning of a section of text, don't distract them with something bouncing around right next to it.

Understanding Image Basics

Graphics inserted into a Web page are called *inline images*. The two most common graphic file formats for Web publications are GIF (Graphics Interchange Format), and JPEG (Joint Photographic Experts Group). All graphics-capable browsers support these two formats and display them without fuss. However, several other formats exist, examples being TIFF, PCX, BMP, and PNG. More recent versions of the Netscape and Mosaic browsers handle these as well by calling up helper applications, which are programs designed to display images stored in these formats.

N O T E   PNG (Portable Network Graphics format) is a new graphics format that is becoming more common on the World Wide Web. It supports True Color, which makes it better for photographic images than GIF; also, unlike JPEG, its compression is lossless. ■

Which format, GIF or JPEG, should you use in your pages? Each has its own strengths. The advantage of GIF is that it's the bread-and-butter format for the Web, at least for the time being. Browsers decompress it quickly, so it's reasonably brisk about showing up on your visitor's screen. It's the format of choice for line art; that is, art without continuous shading of tones—photographs, for instance. It provides up to 256 colors and can simulate more by dithering. You can also go in the other direction because a useful characteristic of GIFs is that you can use image editors to reduce the number of different colors in them. This reduces the file size. Then again, you can simply reduce the size of the image with a graphics editor. This is a possibility with JPEGs, too.

GIF image files do tend to be larger than equivalent JPEG ones, so what you gain in fast GIF decompression you lose (somewhat) in having to store bigger files on your site. On the other hand, JPEG files, although they're smaller, decompress slower than GIF files. Their advantage over GIFs is that they support up to 16.7 million colors, so that continuous-tone images reproduce better on the screen. However, there's as yet no point in using actual High Color or True Color images on a Web page. It's true that this display technology is more widely used than it was a year ago, but most people are still looking at 256 colors, so the extra quality is probably wasted.

With JPEG images you can also adjust the compression level (in FrontPage Editor this is referred to as quality) to reduce the size of a graphic. If you do this, inspect the results because the higher the compression, the more the image is degraded. You have to find the right balance of size and quality.

N O T E   For best results, you should scale the compression of a JPEG graphic by using a native graphics program (such as Lview or Image Composer) rather than FrontPage Editor's Quality command. ■

FrontPage 98 ships with its own Clip Art Gallery of some 1,000 images, and if Microsoft Office is installed on your machine, you will also have access to the Office Clip Art. Some images, especially of icons and buttons, are also available on the Internet for free use. However, to individualize your own Web site, you'll likely want unique graphics. Original artwork can be produced either with graphics packages, such as the Image Composer software included with FrontPage 98, or by more traditional means like paint or photography. (If you're not an artist or a photographer, you may want to enlist the skills of someone who is.) Photographs and artwork must be scanned to make the required graphics files, which you can then insert into your pages.

▶ **See** Part III, "Creating and Adapting Graphics with Image Composer," **p. 275**

Part
II

Ch
6

Putting an Image onto a Page

FrontPage at its default settings stores your Web in an appropriately named folder inside the **C:\Webshare\Wwwroot** folder (assuming you installed the Microsoft Personal Web Server). Within your Web's folder are several more folders, and one of these is the images folder. This is the most convenient place to keep the graphics for your Web because having all your images in one place makes it easier to stay organized.

N O T E   When you reference a graphic that is stored outside the current Web, and then save the page that displays the graphic, FrontPage Editor asks if you want to copy that graphic to the current Web. If you say yes, the graphic ends up in the Web's root directory, not in the images folder. To copy the graphic to the images folder, you must supply the relative path name for that folder.

Once you've added a graphic to the images folder, use the following steps to insert it into your page:

1. Place the cursor where you want the image to appear.
2. Choose Insert, Image. The Image dialog box appears. In the list box, double-click the images folder icon to make the list of image files appear (see Figure 6.1).
3. Select the image file you want by clicking its name in the list. Notice that you get a preview of the image in the small window at the right of the dialog box.
4. Choose OK. FrontPage Editor inserts the image into the page (see Figure 6.2).

FIG. 6.1
Using the Image dialog box to select an image from the images folder.

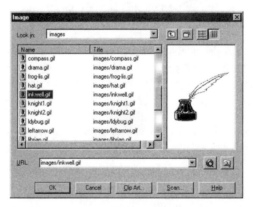

T I P   If you want to edit an image that's already on a page, double-click the image. This opens Image Composer and loads the image file.

Deleting an Image

Oops! You didn't want that image there. To get rid of it, first click it to select it (you know it's selected when the sizing handles appear on its borders). Choose Edit, Clear or press the Delete key and the image vanishes. Alternatively, you can right-click the image and choose Cut.

FIG. 6.2
The image you've selected appears at the cursor position.

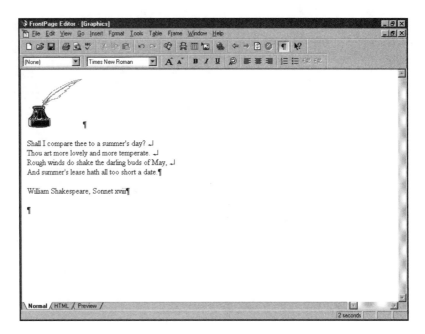

Using Images Not in the Current Web

Sometimes, the image file you want isn't in the images folder of the Web you're working on. FrontPage Editor gives you a quick way to import images from somewhere else on your host machine. Place the cursor where you want the image and use the following steps:

1. Choose Insert, Image so that the Image dialog box appears. Look at the URL text box and you'll see two buttons at its right end. The second button, with the folder and magnifying glass on it, is the one you want (its ToolTip is Make a Hyperlink to a File on Your Computer). Click the button.

    The Select File dialog box appears. This is the standard dialog box in Windows 95 to open a file.

2. Find and select the name of the image file you want and choose Open. All dialog boxes close, and the image appears on your page at the cursor position.

3. Continue editing the page until you're finished. Choose File, Save. Because you inserted an image which is not (yet) in the current Web, the Save Embedded Files dialog box appears (see Figure 6.3).

4. To save the new image to the root folder of the current Web, select the file, and choose OK.

5. To save the file to the current Web's images folder, select the file and choose the Change Folder Button. This opens the Current Web dialog box (see Figure 6.4).

Part

II

Ch

6

FIG. 6.3

Use the Save Embedded
Files dialog box to add
a graphic to your Web.

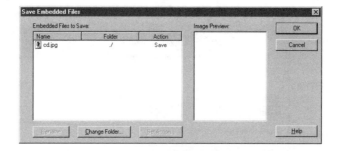

FIG. 6.4

Specify the save
location of an image file
by using the Current
Web dialog box.

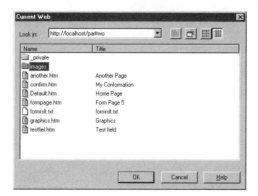

6. Double-click the images folder to select it in the Current Web dialog box (the folder name should appear in the Look In text box). Choose OK. When you return to the Save Embedded Files dialog box, images/ appears in its list box in the Folder column.

7. Choose OK to save the file to the images folder. You can, of course, use this procedure to save the file to any folder in the current Web.

If you now check Explorer's Folder View and click the images folder (or the root folder, depending on the path name you saved with), you'll see that the graphic has been added to your Web. Note that this is a copy of the original—you only copy the graphic and don't move it.

Sometimes you don't want the image to be saved to the current Web and want to leave it where it is. In this case, begin by following Steps 1 through 4 of the previous procedure and then do the following:

1. Click the file in the Save Embedded Files dialog box to select it and choose the Set Action button to open the Set Action dialog box.

2. Mark the option button labeled Don't Save.

3. Choose OK. When you return to the Save Embedded Files dialog box, choose OK again. The image file is now the destination of a hyperlink and is not stored in the current Web.

If you have added several graphics to a page before saving it, the Saved Embedded Files list box will list all the unsaved files. You can select and work with these files on an individual basis. Notice that you can rename them, as well—just select the target file and click the Rename button.

Inserting Images from a Remote Site

You can also access images at other sites, both in Webs on your local host and on the World Wide Web. To do this, open the Image dialog box and type the URL of the remote image into the URL text box. When you choose OK, FrontPage Editor establishes a link to the image and preserves the link when you save the page. If you look at Explorer's Hyperlink View with the Hyperlinks to Images option turned on, you'll see an icon for that remote image. (You may need to choose FrontPage Explorer's View, Refresh command to update the display.)

However, many URLs are long and complicated, and when typing them you're prone to errors. To use a more cumbersome but much more reliable linking method, first connect to the Internet. Click the first button to the right of the URL text box, the button with the globe and magnifying glass. This starts an Internet Explorer-type browser, which opens with a message: "Browse to the page or file you want to use, then return to FrontPage Editor to continue."

Use the browser to find the image you want. *Without* closing the browser, switch back to FrontPage Editor and the Image dialog box. The URL of the image now appears in the URL text box. Choose OK to create the link. You can now close the browser. You might want to test the link with Preview in Browser before disconnecting from the Internet.

 The danger in referencing another site is that it may become inaccessible, may vanish entirely, or its Webmaster may delete the image. If it's at all possible, make your images safe by downloading them to your host machine.

CAUTION

Remember that copyright law applies to the Internet and the Web; many images are for free use, but not all. Don't use the latter without permission from the owner.

Adding a Clip Art Image

Shipping with FrontPage 98 is an upgraded clip art interface and clip art gallery, which, at the time of this writing, Microsoft indicated would include about 1,000 clips. If you have Microsoft Office installed on your host machine, you have access to the Office clip art gallery. These galleries now include videos, photographic images, and sound, as well as traditional clip art.

To use clip art, do the following:

1. Choose Insert, Clip Art (you can retrieve the clip art via the Image dialog box). The Microsoft Clip Gallery 3.0 dialog box opens (see Figure 6.5).

2. Click one of the four tabs (Clip Art, Pictures, Sounds, and Videos), and select the category from the list box. The dialog box shows you previews of the items in that category in the preview box. Videos and sounds will play.

3. Scroll through the previews until you find the one you want. Click to select it and choose Insert. The clip art item inserts into your page.

FIG. 6.5

Choose from a selection of clip art to enliven a page.

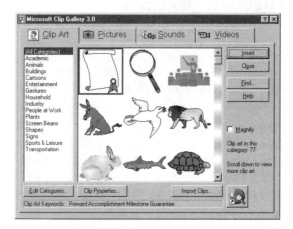

You're not limited to the supplied clip art. You can customize the collection by importing items into the clip art categories. Click the Import Clips button and use the dialog boxes to select an item and add it to a category of your choice.

When you save a page into which you have inserted a piece of clip art, you automatically see the Save Embedded Files dialog box. The default name of the clip is useful only to a computer; use the Rename button to give it a better name. Don't use the Set Action button to set up a link to the clip, either. If you do, the clip gets stored in FrontPage's TEMP folder, which is a very poor place to store files.

Inserting a Scanned Image

This capability is dependent on your hardware, but assuming you have a TWAIN-compatible device attached to your host machine, open the Image dialog box and choose Scan. In the Camera/Scanner dialog box, click the Source button to select the device. When it's selected, choose Acquire and the scanned image inserts into the active page.

Using FrontPage 98's Image Processing Tools

You've likely noticed by now that when you select an image, the Image Toolbar immediately appears. This toolbar has several very useful image manipulation tools on it, and you'll look at these in the next few pages.

To get started, place an image on a page and select it. You see the Image Toolbar with its tool buttons (see Figure 6.6).

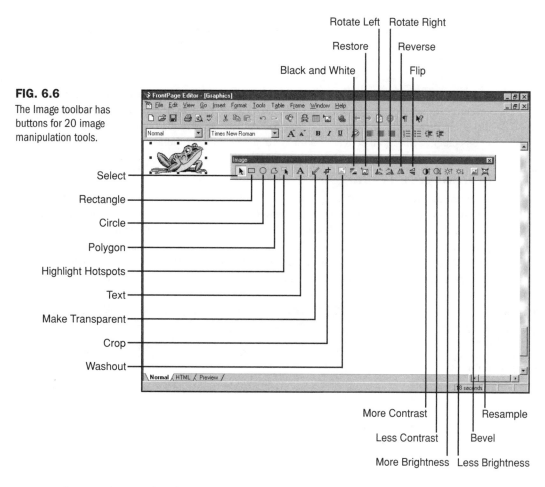

FIG. 6.6

The Image toolbar has buttons for 20 image manipulation tools.

Some of these tools fall into classes, so you'll examine them in groups when suitable. The first five buttons are actually for making imagemaps, so you'll see their discussion after images-based hyperlinks and navigational controls are covered later in this chapter.

Adding Text to a GIF

This is an easy way of custom labeling buttons, but you can also use it for any situation where placing text over an image is necessary (it doesn't work with JPEGs, however).

To add the text, first insert the GIF onto the page. Select it and choose the Create Text Label or Hotspot button. A text box appears on the image. You can resize this box with the sizing handles or drag it to any position on the GIF.

With the text box in place, you can type your label text into it, formatting the text with any of the text tools such as font, sizing, color, and so on. Note, however, that you can't mix fonts or font characteristics in one text box—if you change the font or the font color while the insertion point is in the box, for example, the effect is applied to all text in the box.

N O T E   Text over GIFs is programmed by a WebBot included in the page. Because of this, text over
GIFs will work only if the server hosting the Web has the FrontPage 98 server extensions
installed. ▨

You can also apply more than one text box to the same image. This is especially useful for
creating text labels that are also hyperlinks; in other words, you can set up an imagemap by
using text boxes, and their contained text, as hotspots. Hyperlinked hotpots are discussed later
in this chapter when you do a full treatment of image map creation.

Making Transparent Images

You want to give your pages a unified and harmonious appearance, and you achieve this
through your choice of images, text, and layout. You can add to this sense of unity by using
transparent GIF images (only GIFs support this option; it doesn't work with JPEGs). A transparent image lets the page background appear through parts of the graphic, as though the
picture were painted on acetate instead of paper. This embeds the image into its surroundings
and gives a sense of integration. You can see the difference in effect in Figure 6.7.

FIG. 6.7

The upper, transparent
GIF is better harmonized
with its surroundings
than the one below it,
which is opaque.

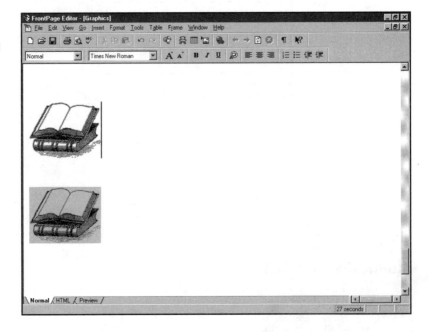

If you feel that a graphic looks better if a particular color is transparent, you can get this effect
with the Make Transparent tool from the Image toolbar. To make a particular color invisible,
use the following steps:

1. Select the graphic and click the Make Transparent button.

2. Put the cursor (it looks like the eraser end of a pencil) on the color you want to do delete, and click. All instances of that color in the graphic become transparent.

 TIP When you first look at the image properties for some graphics, the Transparent check box is grayed out because the graphic contains no transparent colors. To establish a transparent color, use the Make Transparent tool, from the Image toolbar.

Conversely, you may want to make a transparent graphic into an opaque one. To achieve this effect, select the image and go to the General sheet of the Image Properties dialog box. Clear the Transparent check box in the Type section. Choose OK and the graphic becomes opaque. You can't check the box again, though, to bring back the transparency. To do that, you have to use the Make Transparent tool, just described.

Using the Restore Button

This is quick to explain, but it's so important that it deserves a section to itself. If you apply one or more of the tools to an image and you don't like the results, click the Restore button. This isn't an undo—it actually re-inserts the original of the image.

Cropping an Image

Select the image and click the Crop button. A gray rectangle with outlined sizing handles appears on the image. Drag and size the rectangle to select the area of the image that you want to keep and double-click within the rectangle. The image is now cropped.

Note that if it had transparent areas, you'll have to restore them with the Make Transparent tool. Also, when you save the page, you see the Save Embedded Files dialog box. In this dialog box, give the cropped image a new name to distinguish it from the original. At the time of writing, FrontPage Editor did not warn you if you were inadvertently about to replace the uncropped image with the cropped one.

Using Resample

This is an extremely useful tool. It allows you to resize an image larger or smaller. In addition, making a smaller image also reduces the size of the graphic file.

Select the image and resize it by using the sizing handles. Click the Resample button. When you save the page, you'll see the Save Embedded files dialog box. Give the modified file a new name or a different save folder, unless you want it to replace the original. When you choose OK, the resized file is saved to your Web.

Using the Other Image Tools

These tools have the following effects on a selected image:

- Washout washes the image out by 50 percent. If you click the button again, it has no effect.

Part
II

Ch
6

■ Black and White changes the image to monochrome.

■ The rotate, reverse, and flip buttons change the image orientation.

■ The increase and decrease contrast and brightness buttons incrementally adjust these values with each click.

■ Bevel creates a beveled outline around the image. Because the beveling is white and gray, it shows up better on a background color or image than on a gray or a white page.

Coordinating Images and Text

If you've experimented with simple pages where you put blocks of text with an image, you've noticed that the text lines up with the image's bottom edge. Sometimes, this is what you want, but it's typographically limiting—you need more than that to lay out a good-looking page. What about centering images, putting them at the right margin, and getting multiple lines of text to flow down an image's side? FrontPage Editor lets you do all these things.

Positioning Text Around an Image

As we just observed, if you add Normal text beside an image or insert an image into an existing line of Normal text, the text lines up with the image's bottom edge. If you don't want this effect, you can change it. To do so, use the following steps:

1. Click the image to select it.

2. Choose Edit, Image Properties from the FrontPage Editor menu. The Image Properties dialog box appears.

3. Choose the Appearance tab. In the Layout area, click the arrow button at the right of the Alignment box (see Figure 6.8).

FIG. 6.8

You change text position relative to an image by choosing from the Alignment options.

4. Click bottom, middle, or top depending on which alignment you want.

5. Choose OK. The text moves to the appropriate position beside the image (see Figure 6.9).

FIG. 6.9

FrontPage Editor lets you align text with the bottom, middle, or top of an image.

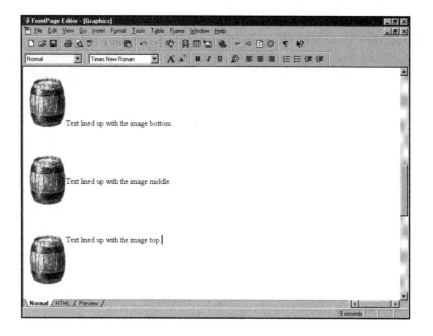

T I P You can get to the Image Properties dialog box quickly by right-clicking the image whose properties you want to change and choosing Image Properties from the shortcut menu.

Aligning and Floating Images

Centering or right-aligning an image is simple. You select the image and choose Format, Paragraph. When you reach the Paragraph Properties dialog box, open the Paragraph Alignment drop-down list box and pick the alignment you want. After you choose OK, the image is repositioned. An even faster method is to click the Align Left, Center, or Align Right buttons on the toolbar.

Often you'll want to wrap text around an image. FrontPage Editor lets you *float* an image so that this happens. To make an image float against the left or right margin so that existing or future text wraps around it, use the following steps:

1. Select the image.

2. Choose Edit, Image Properties to open the Image Properties dialog box. Choose the Appearance sheet tab.

3. Click the arrow button beside the Alignment drop-down list box to open the list of alignment options (refer to Figure 6.8).

Part

II

Ch

6

4. Select the Left or Right option.

5. Choose OK. The image moves to the appropriate margin, and any text present flows around it (see Figure 6.10).

FIG. 6.10

Text wraps around a *floating* image for better layout.

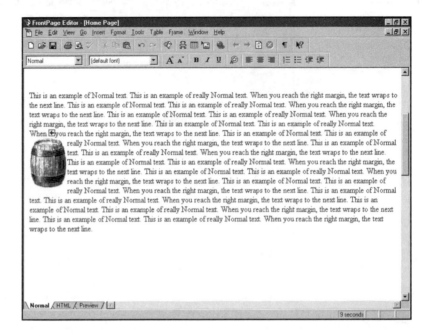

The Image Properties dialog box has an Edit button. Click this button to start Image Composer and automatically load the selected image.

Deleting a Floating Image

If you carefully inspect the text near the image, you'll see a small arrow icon the height of the text line. (Depending on how you assembled the text and image, the arrow may not be adjacent to the image but embedded in the text nearby.) Be careful not to delete this arrow icon; if you do, the image is also deleted. The marker doesn't show up in a browser.

TROUBLESHOOTING

I used the Right alignment option from the Paragraph Format dialog box to position an image at the right margin. But my text isn't wrapping around it. What's wrong? You may understandably think that the Left and Right alignment options in the Paragraph Properties dialog box are the same as the Left and Right alignment options in the Image Properties dialog box. They aren't, although they use exactly the same wording. The difference is that the paragraph alignments don't allow text wrapping; they merely position the image. Incidentally, don't apply mixed Image Properties alignments and

Paragraph Format alignments to the same image. A graphic with a Right paragraph alignment and a Right Image Properties alignment may behave unpredictably. There's no practical reason to mix the alignment types, anyway.

Using Other Alignments

You have four other Netscape-originated alignments for lining up text and images. All are accessible from the Alignment drop-down list box in the Image Properties dialog box. Table 6.1 describes what they do.

Table 6.1   Netscape *align* Extensions

Option	Effect
Texttop	Aligns tallest text with image top
Absmiddle	Aligns image with middle of current line
Absbottom	Aligns image with bottom of current line
Baseline	Aligns image with baseline of current line

These extensions actually make little discernible difference in a browser display.

Using Line Breaks with Images

So far, you've found out how to align a single line of text at the top, middle, or bottom of an image. You also know how to make text flow around an image that floats against the right or left margin. But how do you put just a few lines next to an image, for instance, if you want a two-line caption beside a graphic that's several lines high?

This effect is an important typographical tool, and fortunately it's supported by FrontPage Editor. You adjust the text layout by inserting special types of line breaks.

Let's say you start out with a page that looks like the one in Figure 6.11. The image captioning looks very awkward; you want both lines of text beside the image, not broken up as they are.

To get the desired layout, first change the image properties of the graphic to a left or right floating alignment and do the following:

1. Place the cursor where you want the special line break to occur. In the example in the figures, it was put right after the "Join our Reading Week" line.

2. Choose Insert, Line Break. The Break Properties dialog box appears (see Figure 6.12).

3. Choose Clear Left Margin or Clear Right Margin, depending on where your image is. If you're using a left-floating image and a right-floating image opposite each other, choose Clear Both Margins. (In the example, the text wraps around a left-floating image. As just stated, the break goes after "Join our Reading Week.")

4. Choose OK.

Part

II

Ch

FIG. 6.11

An image sits against the left margin with a caption positioned using the Default Image Property alignment (at the bottom).

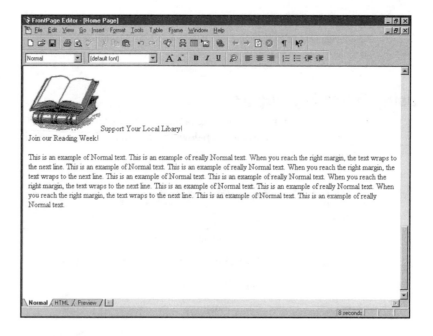

FIG. 6.12

Specialized line breaks give you more control of the relationship between images and text.

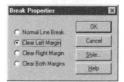

The text following the special line break moves down until it's past the bottom of the image, and then slides over to the appropriate margin (see Figure 6.13). If you have images of unequal size opposite each other, the Clear Both Margins option moves the text down to clear the bottom edges of both images.

Spacing Between Text and Image

You know that whitespace is an important component of any page, and you may dislike the way text gets crowded close to your images. Fortunately, you can adjust the text-to-image spacing with the Horizontal Spacing and Vertical Spacing boxes in the Appearance sheet of the Image Properties dialog box. The values you fill in here determine the spacing; a value of 10 in each gives the result shown in Figure 6.14.

Adjusting Image Size

Also on the Appearance sheet, you can mark the Specify Size check box to set the width and height of the graphic in pixels or percent. Fiddling with this can give weird results, especially if the image is a floating image. The adjustments don't affect the size of the image file, however, so don't try to use this feature to reduce image download times. It's likely most useful for making minor adjustments to balance the relationship of image and text.

FIG. 6.13

A specialized line break forces the text after it to drop below a floating image.

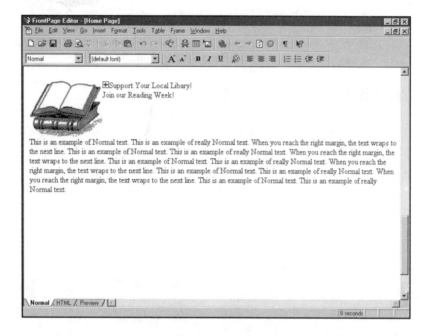

FIG. 6.14

Adding whitespace around an image keeps it from seeming crowded by surrounding text. Here the image is also a floating one, so the text wraps around it.

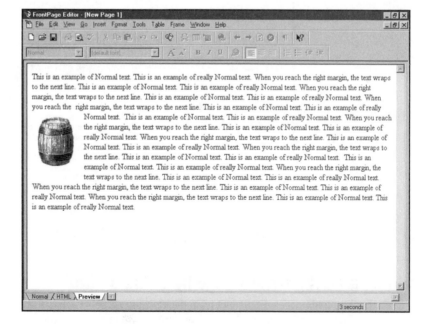

Part

II

Ch

6

Adding Borders to an Image

You might want a visible boundary around a graphic, although such boundaries aren't used much. When they are, they're often understood to indicate a clickable image. If you want one, there's not much variety; you're stuck with a simple solid line rectangle. You can only vary its line thickness. To add a border, go to the Appearance sheet of the Image Properties dialog box and type a nonzero value into the Border Thickness box.

Providing Alternative Text

This is important because you must tell people who are running their browsers with images turned off or who are using a text-only browser that there's an image on the page. Even if they have images turned off, they might like to see your graphic, so they have to know it's there.

You add alternative text by using the General sheet of the Image Properties dialog box. In the Alternative Representations section, use the Text box to type the word or phrase that stands in for the graphic. You can elect to accept the supplied default, which conveniently provides the image size in bytes. Choose OK. Remember to test the results! Don't try to give an elaborate description of the picture because a few, well-chosen words are plenty. Figure 6.15 shows what alternative text looks like.

FIG. 6.15

Tell your readers about the presence and nature of a graphic by including alternative text.

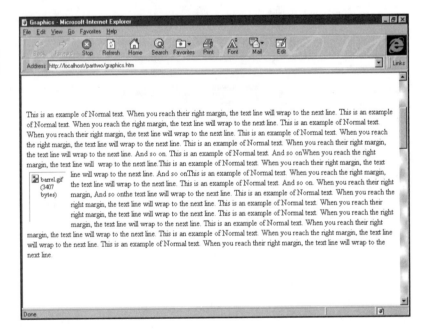

Adding a Background Image by Using a File

Background images, as distinct from background colors, are actual graphics that sit behind your text and your foreground images. You use them to add texture, color, site identification, or other visual effects to your pages. Aesthetics and legibility are important, but remember that it is only a background and should not distract from your content or diffuse the impact of your foreground images.

FrontPage Editor lets you use any graphics file as a background (it doesn't have to be a GIF). A few banks of appropriate images are available on the Web, and you can download them for your own use. Clip art also ships with FrontPage 98, and if you have MS Office installed on your system, you can use its clip art as well.

 Two such image resources are:

Randy's Icon and Image Bazaar at

http://www.iconbazaar.com/backgr/

and the Netscape resource at

http://home.netscape.com/assist/net_sites/bg/backgrounds.html

CAUTION

If you use a Web or Internet resource (other than simply linking to it), find out whether the site wants an acknowledgment that it supplied the resource. Copyright laws apply on the Internet, just as they do elsewhere. Besides, acknowledging someone else's contribution to your work is good manners. Incidentally, I'd be very wary of using obviously copyrighted images, such as cartoon figures. If you put a Disney character on your page, for example, you're asking for trouble.

Once you've obtained the image, you can make it into your background. FrontPage Editor does this by treating the image like a tile and laying enough identical tiles to cover everything in sight. To put in the image, use the following steps:

1. Choose File, Page Properties to open the Page Properties dialog box. Click the Background sheet tab and mark the Background Image check box.

2. Click the Browse button. The Select Background Image dialog box appears. Because the dialog box is identical to the Image dialog box (except for its title), you already know how to use it.

3. Select the name of the background file and return to the Background sheet by choosing OK or Open, depending on context.

   The image tiles across the page to produce your background (see Figure 6.16).

Part
II

Ch
6

 A real time saver is using the Get Background and Colors from Page check box in the Background sheet of the Page Properties dialog box. This copies all the color choices and the background image from another page into the current one. It's very handy for keeping your pages' appearance consistent.

FIG. 6.16
This dark background is striking with the white heading, but the white text may be almost impossible to read on some browsers and monitors.

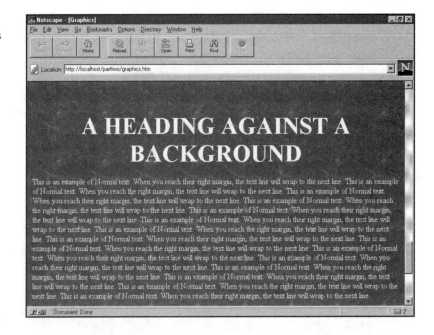

Remember that using a background image from another site puts your page's appearance at someone else's mercy. If the site's URL changes or its Webmaster deletes the image file, you'll lose your background. You're better off downloading the image and storing it locally.

 When you use a background image, also set the page's background color so that it's close to the predominant hue of the image. Why? So that a browser running with images turned off (which includes background images) displays your page similar to its intended appearance.

Using Watermarked Background Images

Your background images scroll in a browser, along with the foreground objects and text. Marking the Watermark check box on the Background sheet keeps the background image still, while the foreground material moves across it.

 If your page has a background image, you can edit it quickly by choosing View, Image Toolbar without selecting a foreground image. When the toolbar appears, you can use it to edit the background image. Not all of the tools are available, but the essential ones are.

Using Images with Hyperlinks

With FrontPage Editor, image-based hyperlinks are just as easy to make as text-based ones. Such images are frequently used as navigational controls within a site, as well as serving as links to remote locations.

Creating Image-Based Hyperlinks

If you know how to make a text hyperlink, you already know how to construct one from an image. Do the following:

1. Insert the image into the page using any of the methods you learned earlier.

2. Click the image to select it and choose Edit, Hyperlink to open the Create Hyperlink dialog box.

3. Set up the link with any of the procedures you learned in Chapter 5, "Developing the Basic Page: Text, Lists, and Hyperlinks."

That's all there is to it! To edit the link, select the image and choose Edit, Hyperlink.

▶ **See** Chapter 5, "Developing the Basic Page: Text, Lists, and Hyperlinks," **p. 71**

Making Navigational Controls

The Web is a place in which people like to move around. Well-chosen navigational tools laid out in a useful way give your Web pages a professional gleam. (And, as stated before, trying to keep visitors at your site by making it hard for them to leave is counterproductive). Buttons are the most common navigational symbols, and dozens of places on the Web offer these simple images for free-use downloading. Put them into your page in an organized way, link them to their destinations, and they'll tie your site together so that it'll be a pleasure to visit.

Be consistent with button usage, though; a button that has function X on one page shouldn't have function Y on another. Always provide alternative text for them, in case your visitor has images turned off or is using a text browser. Also consider putting a visible text label with each button. It makes life easier for your visitors, and they'll like you for it.

Using Imagemaps to Make Graphical Hyperlinks

Creating an imagemap by hand-coding it in HTML can be a real headache. FrontPage's capability to help you make imagemaps and link them easily is one of its most powerful features. The imagemaps it creates, by the way, are client-side. That is, the information about the map structure is embedded in the Web page that's downloaded to the browser client; the information does not reside on the server.

What is an *imagemap*? Functionally, it's a graphic that has hotspots in it; when a viewer clicks a hotspot, they are automatically sent to another location on the Web or in the current site. To put it another way, imagemaps are graphics with embedded hyperlinks. A good example is Yahoo!'s Yahooligans page, at **http://www.yahooligans.com/** (see Figure 6.17).

Because you're creating a Web site with its own character and needs, you probably will create or assemble the major imagemap graphics yourself. Before you start, though, think about what the graphic should look like, and especially remember that hotspots don't stand out as such in a browser window. This means you have to let people know where the hotspots are and what will happen if they click them.

FIG. 6.17

An image with clearly defined clickable regions (shown here as the round buttons in the heading image) is a good way to approach imagemap design.

Clickable regions ——

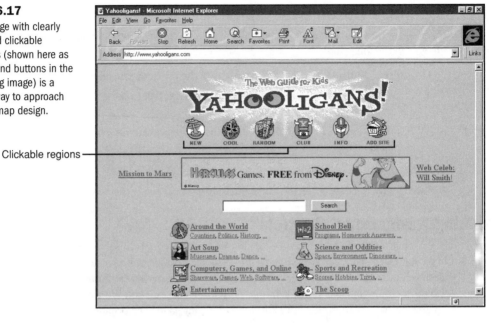

The first thing to do is design the graphic so that it has obvious *clickable* areas. Often the best way to do this is to make those hotspot regions look like buttons, as in the example in Figure 6.17. Another thing to consider is whether the destination of the link is made clear by the hotspot. If it isn't, you should consider adding text to describe what will happen if someone follows the link. Alternatively, modify the image itself to make its destination clearer. Try hard to see the imagemap as if you were coming across it for the first time, and try even harder to imagine how it can be misunderstood. (A corollary to Murphy's Law says that if something can be misunderstood, it will be.)

Another thing: Don't jam too many hotspot links into one image. Small hotspots, a few pixels across, are hard for users to point to, and an image with a dozen clickable regions starts to be confusing.

Finally, set up text links that duplicate the imagemap's hotspot destinations. This is for people who are running their browsers with images turned off.

CAUTION

If your Internet Service Provider (ISP) doesn't have the FrontPage server extensions installed on the server, your imagemaps probably will not work properly when you copy your Web from your PC to the server. If that happens, go to FrontPage Explorer's Web Settings dialog box in the Tools menu. The Advanced tab gives some alternate imagemap styles; try Netscape. If this also gives problems or you're concerned about browsers that don't support Netscape-like behavior, contact your ISP administrator to discuss using the CERN or NCSA styles.

Creating an Imagemap   To make an imagemap, you need an image. It can be in any file format, although you should remember that GIF or JPEG are the formats recognized by all browsers, without the need for plug-ins or helpers. Begin by inserting the image into the page. Select the image and use the following steps:

1. Decide whether you want the hotspot to be a rectangle, a circle, or a polygon. From the Image toolbar, select the appropriate drawing tool button (refer to Figure 6.6 for button identification).

N O T E   If you can't see the Image toolbar, toggle it on by choosing View, Image Toolbar. When it appears in the toolbar area, drag it to the place you want it.

2. Put the cursor on the image. The cursor changes to a crayon.
3. Hold down the left mouse button and drag to get the outline you want and then release the mouse button (the black rectangles on the outline are sizing handles). The Create Link dialog box appears.
4. Establish the link by using the techniques you learned in Chapter 5.

That's all you need to do. If you want to edit the link, select the image, click the hotspot, and choose Edit, Link.

T I P   A quick way to edit an imagemap link is to right-click the hotspot and select Image Hotspot Properties from the shortcut menu.

The nature of imagemaps is to have more than one hotspot in the graphic. To get them to fit neatly, resize each hotspot by dragging its sizing handles or move it around by putting the mouse pointer on its border and dragging it.

Deleting a Hotspot   Click the image so that the hotspot borders appear. Click the hotspot you want to delete and either press the Delete key or choose Edit, Clear.

Linking to Images

You now know how to link to pages, bookmarks, and remote locations. Linking to an image is pretty straightforward. Select the text, image, or hotspot you want for the link, and choose Edit, Hyperlink.

Now use the Create or Edit Hyperlink dialog boxes to find the name of the image to which you want to link. Complete the link and choose OK. When the link is clicked in a browser, the browser window clears and the image downloads and displays in that window. That is, the image isn't fitted into or overlaid on the page from which it was called.

Using Thumbnails

By now you may be somewhat paranoid about keeping your visitors waiting around for graphics to download, but attractive images are much of the appeal of a good Web site. How do you resolve this conflict between art and efficiency?

In two words: Use thumbnails. This is much easier in FrontPage 98 than it was in FrontPage 97 because of the Auto Thumbnail command. To use it:

1. Insert the full-sized graphic into the page and select it.

2. Choose Tools, Auto Thumbnail.

   FrontPage automatically reduces the size of the image and links it to the original in the original's current location.

3. Save the page. You'll see the Save Embedded Files dialog box with a default name for the thumbnail image. Use the techniques you learned earlier to save the thumbnail to your satisfaction. When you test the page, clicking the thumbnail should display the full size graphic in its own browser window.

 Choose Tools, Options to go to the Auto Thumbnail sheet, where you can customize the size and appearance of the thumbnail image. For example, if you don't want a border around the thumbnail, you can specify this.

The results of using thumbnails can be significant: a GIF that is 340×500 pixels in 256 colors reduces from a file size of 168K to 31K. It downloads (all other things being equal) in less than a fifth of the time the original took.

Thumbnails are also good audience psychology—your visitors can judge from the smaller image whether they want to look at the big one, and they won't feel that you've inflicted a finger-drumming wait on them if they choose to download the original. If you've got many images, you can put a whole gallery of thumbnails onto a page and let your visitors wander among them.

The thumbnail should be kept in the images/folder. Where you keep the full size pictures is up to you, but remember that if they're out on the World Wide Web, they may disappear without warning.

Making the Most of Image File Formats

Web images are almost all JPEG or GIF files, with the balance at the moment tending heavily toward the GIF format. You can manipulate these formats, to a limited degree, with the tools FrontPage Editor gives you (see Figure 6.18). You do this to control image quality and influence download speed.

Converting Image File Formats

When you insert an image, FrontPage Editor checks to see if it's GIF or JPEG. If it is neither GIF nor JPEG, and it is 256 colors or less, FrontPage Editor automatically converts it to GIF; if more than 256 colors, to JPEG.

If you want to store a file in the other format, you mark the appropriate check box for GIF or JPEG. Then, when you save the page, the image converts. If you go from GIF to JPEG, you also get a chance to adjust the quality of the stored JPEG image by typing a number from 1 to 99 into the Quality box (75 is the default). With the best quality (99), you get the lowest file compression and slowest downloading; with the lowest quality (1), you get the highest file compression and the fastest downloading. There's no free lunch, is there?

FIG. 6.18
Modify image file behavior by using the options in the General sheet of the Image Properties dialog box.

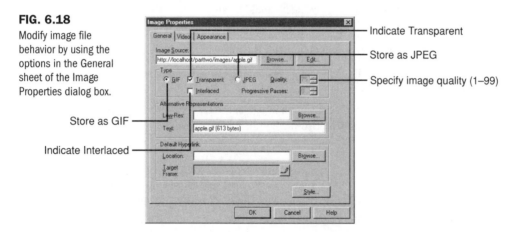

Indicate Transparent
Store as JPEG
Specify image quality (1–99)

Store as GIF
Indicate Interlaced

> **CAUTION**
> Once you've set the Quality setting and saved the image, you can't change that setting again, even if you delete the image and reinsert it from the saved page. So if you're experimenting, keep a backup!

 People sometimes link to images on other servers so they won't have to store many large images on their own Web host. If your Internet service provider limits the disk space you can use for your Web, this may be the only thing you can do to get the image resources you want.

Using Interlaced or Progressive Images for Speed

A browser that supports interlaced GIF images or progressive JPEG images (GIF only) builds up such an image in four passes, with the picture becoming clearer with each pass. On the first pass, the text and links of the page are also displayed, so that the viewer can start reading (or clicking a link) without waiting for the image to complete. Again, it's all in the interest of speed.

You can create an interlaced GIF from a non-interlaced one by marking the Interlaced check box in the Image Properties dialog box. When the page is saved, the image stores as an interlaced GIF. If you want to produce your own interlaced GIFs, Image Composer saves its GIF files in this format.

The analogous JPEG file treatment is to make it a progressive JPEG. This also downloads the image in a series of passes, and you can specify the number of passes in the Progressive Passes text box.

Part
II

Ch
6

Using Low Res for Speed

Another tool in your speed-up kit is the Low Res (low resolution) option. To employ this, first use a graphics program to make a lower-resolution version of the original, and then save that graphic to your images folder. This version should be smaller than the original; a common trick to achieve this is to change it to black and white.

When you want to use the Low Res option, use the following steps:

1. Select the original, full-resolution image and go to the General sheet of the Image Properties dialog box.

2. Insert the name of the low-resolution image in the Low-Res box in the Alternative Representations section (the Browse button is handy here).

3. Choose OK.

Now when someone goes to the page, their browser loads the low-resolution image and the page text first; only after that does the browser go back and display the high-resolution version of the image. This speeds things up. Notice that you don't have to do any linking here, as you do with the thumbnail technique. The HTML generated by FrontPage Editor takes care of everything for you.

Multimedia

Multimedia is moving swiftly onto the Web. Such effects certainly increase page appeal, but they're time-consuming to download, and active content like JavaScript presents security questions. Keep these factors in mind when you're deciding which (if any) special effects to add to a page.

Understanding and Using Sound

Sound does have its drawbacks. If you're going to use it, keep it under control and remember that not everyone has the same audio tastes that you do. Actually, many people still think sound is a gimmick, and a fairly useless one at that. This will change when the Web becomes a fully powered information delivery system with short downloads and solid, informative audio content, but that time isn't here yet.

A bit of well-chosen and unobtrusive sound can indeed enhance your page, at least for people who have recent browsers that handle audio. (Not everybody has a sound card installed, either, although that's changing fast.) Probably the best design advice is: don't make the sound clip too loud and don't loop it and loop it and loop it—unless it is a very soft, unobtrusive background noise.

From the technical point of view, the worst problem with sound is that even a few seconds' worth of audio takes a significant time to download; a minute or two of it, depending on the file format and quality, produces downloads in the multi-megabyte range. As a rule of thumb, keep audio clips short enough to make file sizes of 20K or less. Some audio file types do allow compression, which helps, although there's always the no-free-lunch factor—the higher the compression, the smaller the file, but the worse the quality. These compression formats are as follows:

- **AIFF-C** (6:1 compression)   The acronym stands for Apple Audio Interchange File Format, and the C indicates the extended version that supports compression (plain AIFF doesn't). The format produces stereo sound at high fidelity and is usually found on Macintosh platforms. The DOS/Windows file extension is AIF, which doesn't actually distinguish these files from the uncompressed version of the format, AIFF.

- **MPEG** (up to 20:1 compression)   This format, which is the international standard for both video and audio compression, was designed by the Moving Pictures Expert Group, hence MPEG. It provides stereo sound at high quality, and the files can be quite a lot smaller than equivalent ones in uncompressed formats. The DOS/Windows file extensions are usually MPG or MP2.

The uncompressed formats are:

- **AIFF**   It's essentially the same as AIFF-C (just mentioned) except without the compression. For DOS/Windows, the extension is also AIF.

- **AU**   This is from Sun Microsystems and is very common on the Web. It's as good as telephone quality, which makes it a reasonable choice for sound bites that are mostly speech. The DOS/Windows extension is AU.

- **SND**   This is a plain vanilla sound format, supporting both stereo and mono. The DOS/Windows extension is SND.

- **WAV**   This is a Microsoft format and another common one. It's useful for both stereo and mono, and the quality is good. The DOS/Windows file extension is WAV.

- **MIDI**   This Musical Instruments Digital Interface isn't actually a file format; instead, it's a file of instructions that are sent to an electronic sound synthesizer to tell it what to play and how to play it. The computer receiving the file must have a MIDI player for the sound to be heard. MIDI files do, however, allow complex sounds to be stored in relatively small files. The DOS/Windows file extension is MID.

Adding Background Audio to Your Page   Background audio is a sound file that plays automatically when someone downloads a page, assuming the person's browser supports the feature. Adding background sound is fairly simple even in HTML, but FrontPage Editor makes the task even easier. Do the following:

1. Choose File, Page Properties Insert. The Page Properties dialog box appears.

2. Choose the General tab and click the Browse button to open the Background Sound dialog box. Except for the dialog box title, this is the standard file location and opening dialog box used by FrontPage Editor.

3. Locate and open the file; its URL appears in the Location dialog box of the Background Sound section of the Page Properties dialog box.

4. Type the number of repetitions into the Loop box to make the sound repeat; to keep it going, mark the Forever check box (and remember that forever is a long time).

Part

II

Ch

6

5. Choose OK. The background audio is now inserted into the page. An inconvenience of the way FrontPage Editor handles this is that there's no indication in the editor workspace that a background sound is embedded in the page.

> **N O T E** The <LOOPDELAY> attribute, which sets a delay between repeats of the sound file, is not directly implemented in FrontPage Editor. What you must do, if you want the delay, is to use HTML mode to manually add the attribute. For example:
>
> `<BGSOUND SRC = "SOUND.WAV" LOOP = 10 LOOPDELAY=30>`
>
> Internet Explorer does not support the LOOPDELAY tag, so there won't be a pause between repeats. ▇

Now test the page in Internet Explorer 2.0 or 3.0, which support the HTML BGSOUND tag (that's what FrontPage Editor uses to insert this type of audio). Netscape 3.0 and later require Java applets to play background sound.

Removing Background Audio   To get rid of audio in the background, open the General sheet of the Page Properties dialog box and delete the file name from the Location box in the Background Sound section. Choose OK and the audio is gone.

Linking to a Sound File   Set this up as you would any other link, with the target of the link being the desired sound file. When visitors click the link, assuming their browser has the plug-in or helper application that plays the file format, they'll hear the playback of the file (see Figure 6.19). Internet Explorer 3 and higher, as previously noted, supports the BGSOUND tag, so they don't need plug-ins or helpers.

FIG. 6.19
Netscape's WAV player
plays back a sound file
when the link is clicked.

Understanding and Using Video

The basic principle of adding video clips to a page is the same as adding audio clips. Video comes in files of various formats, but they all have one thing in common: they're big. Even with heavy compression, and in a small playback window, a minute of video requires megabytes of data. When linking to such a file, you should be sure to indicate how big it is, so people can decide for themselves whether they want to wait for it to download.

The major video formats on the Web now are MPEG Levels 1 and 2, and Apple's Quicktime. Hot on their heels is Microsoft's AVI (also known as Video for Windows), which is making steady inroads into the domain. All these offer video compression, the highest ratio being that of the two MPEG formats, which offer good results at ratios even of 20:1.

Whatever scheme is used, though, all video must play back at 30 images (or frames) per second for full motion effects. The larger the images, the more processing power is required of the playback machine, the more storage space the file requires, and the longer the download time. Because of this, full screen video is uncommon on the Web. If you're selecting videos, or making your own, remember that smaller is faster in every respect. It's a matter of the inverse-square law—an image at 320×240 pixels (which is still pretty big) is one-fourth the size of an image at 640×480.

Using Inline Video   We owe this development to Microsoft, and at the time of writing (mid 1997), only Internet Explorer 3.0 and higher support this method of displaying AVI video clips. It's an alternative to the much more common method of having visitors play back a clip by using the plug-in application installed in their browsers. All the factors of file size and playback image size apply, however; inline video doesn't gain you anything in these respects. Of course, the viewer must be using a browser that supports the method. How quickly Netscape embraces the option remains to be seen; so for the moment, the effect is available only to users of Internet Explorer.

The engaging part of inline images is that, once downloaded, they can remain on a page until they are needed. They perform only when called upon, which makes them less distracting than infinite-loop GIF animations. There are a few sources of AVI files on the Web for you to download and experiment with; one is The Monster List at **http://www.islandnet.com/~carleton/ monster/monster.html**.

To install an AVI clip into a page, do the following:

1. Choose Insert, Active Elements, Video. The Video dialog box appears with the familiar file location and selection dialog box.

2. Use the dialog box to find the video file you want and choose Open to return to the page. FrontPage Editor inserts the first frame of the video to show where the clip will appear.

3. Save the page and use Preview mode or the Preview in Browser command to test the clip in Internet Explorer. (If it's a new file, you'll get the Save Embedded File dialog box.)

    As soon as the browser opens, the playback begins and runs until it ends.

4. Click anywhere in the picture to restart; to stop or restart part way through, click in the picture.

You can control the behavior of the clip by using the Image properties dialog box. To do this, select the still image by clicking it and choose Edit, Image Properties. When the Image Properties dialog box opens, choose the Video tab (see Figure 6.20).

These controls allow you to browse for another video file and allow more viewer control of the clip, as follows:

- Show Controls in Browser puts a set of simple playback controls on screen with the clip.

- Loop and Forever determine how many times the playback of the clip repeats.

- Loop Delay determines the time interval between repeated playbacks.

- On File Open tells the browser to start playing as soon as the clip file loads.

- On Mouse Over, if checked when On File Open is unchecked, halts playback except when the mouse pointer is on top of the image.

Part

II

Ch

6

FIG. 6.20

You can adjust characteristics of the video playback, such as looping and display of controls.

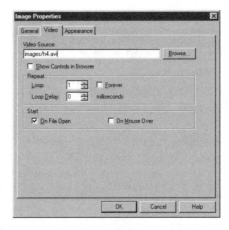

- On Mouse Over and On File Open, if both checked, causes the playback to run to completion as soon as the file loads, and then waits until the mouse pointer is on top of it before it runs again.

When the viewer sees the video clip in their browser, and the Show Controls in Browser check box is marked, the clip has simple stop-go controls available with it (see Figure 6.21).

FIG. 6.21

Microsoft Internet Explorer playing an inline AVI file. The browser controls are turned on.

Inline Video with Browsers that Don't Support It This works for people who are using Internet Explorer, but if you preview the video-equipped page in Netscape, you see an ugly, blank rectangle where the clip resides.

In this case, you need to put a plain graphic in to provide for browsers that don't handle inline images. To do this, return to the Image Properties dialog box and select the General sheet (see Figure 6.22).

FIG. 6.22

Use the Image Properties dialog box to insert a substitute for a video clip.

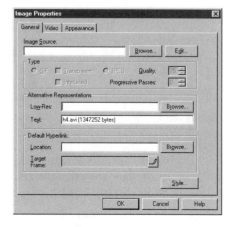

Use the <u>B</u>rowse button to locate a GIF or JPEG file to use as the substitute and choose OK. From now on, non-Internet Explorer browsers will display the graphic instead of the empty box, while IE browsers automatically play the clip.

 The most efficient way to set up a clip is to insert the graphic placeholder first, then use the Video sheet of the Image Properties dialog box to place the associated video clip on the page. You don't actually need the <u>I</u>nsert, Active <u>E</u>lements, <u>V</u>ideo command at all.

Linking to a Video Clip   That's one problem solved, but what about people using nonInternet Explorer browsers who want to see the clip? The answer is to give them a link so that their browser's plug-ins can play it for them. This assumes they know about the clip; your substitute graphic should tell them that it's available.

You might think it efficient to make the substitute image itself into the link. This seems like a good idea at first, but it has a major pitfall: IE-equipped users who click the clip to stop or start it will not only do that, they'll also activate the link! This gives them a second playback of the clip in an AVI player window. Good as the clip may be, this is probably too much of a good thing.

So, make the link from some nearby text or a clearly labeled graphic. Any file you use for inline video should be reasonably fast to load, but it's polite to indicate the file size with the link, anyway.

Finally, you can include noninline clips in your pages by setting up a link to them so they can be played back in a browser. As just mentioned, nonAVI clips must be displayed that way because only AVI can be used for inline video.

Part
II

Ch
6

Designing for Animated GIFs   Recently, animated GIFs have proliferated on the Web. Although they can add vivacity to a page—some are attractively whimsical—they can also distract from the content. There's been some heated debate over their use, and a few basic principles are emerging, as follows:

- Don't overuse them. One per screen is enough, if not more than enough.
- Text is almost always where the information is located. Keep a balance between moving images and static words, and remember that motion always draws attention.
- Because of this point, don't place animations too close to highly important text.
- Consider running the animation sequence once or twice, and then stopping it.
- Don't flash; change the animation slowly.
- When a design decision is in doubt, go for simplicity.

Making an Animated GIF   An animated GIF works on the essential principle of any animation: a series of slightly differing images that, when viewed in quick succession, give the impression of movement. Image Composer 1.5, an optional install with FrontPage 98, includes the Microsoft GIF animator in its Tools menu.

Making these little creatures is more complex than their appearance suggests, and producing good ones is a lot of work. Still, they're fun, and a clever one properly used can catch a new visitor's attention in a way that little else can.

Working with Themes

Themes give your site a unified appearance, which can be difficult to do if you're putting a large site together from the ground up. However, it is the mark of a professional approach to site construction. They provide a consistent navigational structure, along with predefined settings such as text, heading, background, and link colors, as well as predefined bullets, icons, banners, buttons, and lines.

FrontPage's approach to Themes is fairly strict. Fonts and font colors of an applied theme can be changed on a select-the-text basis (for example, not globally) but the graphical elements, such as bullets and background images or colors, cannot. Thus, you are limited in the amount of tweaking you can do. You can't create new Themes through FrontPage Editor or Explorer, either; although at the time of writing, Microsoft had implied that the FrontPage Software Developers' Kit (SDK) might provide some ability to produce custom themes. Also, Microsoft and third-party developers will likely produce theme packages that you can buy and/or download and use, for greater variety in the appearance of your Webs.

This subject actually overlaps into FrontPage Explorer, because if you want to apply a single theme to all the pages in a FrontPage Web, you specify the theme in the FrontPage Explorer interface. This is simply a convenience so that you don't have to apply the same Theme individually to every page in the Web. Once you know how to apply and modify themes to a single page, you'll know how to do so for a whole FrontPage Web—the dialog boxes and procedures are almost identical in both situations. The main difference is that in the Explorer version of the dialog box, you click an Apply button to begin the process of applying the theme to the entire current FrontPage Web.

Applying a Theme to a Page

Back in Chapter 4, "Introducing FrontPage Editor," you went through the procedure of applying a theme to a page, but for convenience, you're seeing it again here:

1. Open the target page in FrontPage Editor and choose Format, Theme. The Choose Theme dialog box opens (see Figure 6.23)

FIG. 6.23

You use the Choose Theme dialog box to vary the themes within a Web.

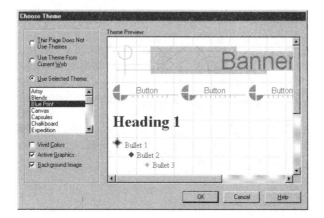

2. Mark the top option button if you don't want any theme at all. Mark the second one if you want the current Web's theme to be used.

3. Mark the third option button if you want to pick a different theme, and choose a theme from the list box.

4. Mark the Vivid Colors option button to specify a brighter set of theme colors. Mark the Active Graphics option button to get active buttons, bullets, and similar graphical elements (many of these only show up in Dynamic HTML-enabled browsers). Mark the Background Image option button if you want a background texture rather than a solid color.

5. Choose OK when you're satisfied with the results as displayed in the Theme Preview window, and the theme is applied to the page.

If you use FrontPage Editor to change the theme of an individual page, this page's theme is not affected by theme changes carried out in FrontPage Explorer. Thus, if you changed the theme of an entire Web in FrontPage Explorer and want to reset an individual page to use the overall theme, mark the Use Theme From Current Web option button in the Choose Theme dialog box. Choose OK.

If you do this, be aware that if you apply a theme to a page customized with your own backgrounds and colors, and then remove the theme, your customization will not be restored.

Part

II

Ch

6

Adjusting the Theme's Appearance

As was noted earlier, you can't tweak a theme very much. However, it does provide some scope for variation. These variations were noted briefly in the procedure just mentioned, but here's more detail:

- If the background image is too *busy*, you can remove it by clearing the Theme dialog box's Background Image check box. If the Vivid Colors check box is marked (this makes the background into a solid color, which is fixed), you can't modify it even in the Page Properties dialog box because the Background options aren't available in that dialog box if you use a theme. However, if the Vivid Colors check box is cleared, and the Background Image check box is cleared, you get a plain white or default gray background, depending on the theme.

- As indicated earlier, the Active Graphics aren't active unless the viewing browser supports JavaScript. Fortunately, this includes IE 3.0 and higher, and Navigator 3 and higher. Even if the browser doesn't animate them, they do look different from the graphics you get if the check box is cleared—they're more colorful and complex. Clearing the Active Graphics check box gives a more conservative look and feel to the images, if that's what you prefer. Also, your page might have other active elements on it, and you don't want the extra moving parts provided by the theme's busy little images.

- Marking the Vivid Colors check box changes the page color scheme of some themes to a somewhat less conservative one.

Getting Rid of a Theme

In the Choose Theme dialog box, mark the option button labeled This Page Does Not Use Themes and choose OK. This restores your full control over every page element. If you had theme bullets, they are replaced by generic ones, and navigation buttons are replaced by textual links.

From Here...

In the last two chapters, you covered the essentials of text, hyperlinks, and graphics. Now, you can move on to new territory, which includes tools for page and site organization, and customizing *boilerplate* pages for your own purposes. You'll do all this in:

Chapter 7, "Using Dynamic HTML, Active Elements, Shared Borders, and Navigation Bars," where you learn to use tools like collapsible outlines, text animation, and page transitions.

Chapter 8, "Creating Tables," which shows you how to design, set up, and modify tables to enhance the organization of your pages.

Chapter 9, "Enhancing Web Sites with FrontPage Frames," which guides you through the complexities of setting up a *framed* site, and shows you how to use frames with graphics, hyperlinks, and frame templates.

## CHAPTER 7

Using Dynamic HTML, Active Elements, Shared Borders, and Navigation Bars

Introducing DHTML

Understand what DHTML is, what it does, and where it came from.

Collapsible outlines

This DHTML tool lets you invisibly cram large amounts of information into small spaces.

Page transitions

Now you can fade, dissolve, and wipe between pages, just like a PowerPoint slideshow.

Animations

Animations allow you to "fly" text and images onto the page.

Active elements

These DHTML-based tools give you hover buttons, banner ad managers, marquees, and hit counters.

Shared borders and navigation bars

These heavy-duty tools help organize the relationships among pages in a Web site, provide consistency in the site's navigational tools, and automate the creation of hyperlinks among the site's pages.

The enhancements you can apply to your pages using graphical elements and themes were discussed in the last chapter. This chapter explores even more sophisticated things you can do.

Dynamic HTML (DHTML) is an important new software technology—or collection of technologies—that give Web content providers the ability to create pages that can change their structure, content, or appearance in response to user input, without requesting any data from the server. To be a little more precise, DHTML lets content providers get at and change any element on an HTML page without resorting to the capabilities of the server. This removal of server round-trip time for page modification results in faster response time for the user, plus less load on the server.

Another set of significant enhancements—unlike DHTML, these are unique to FrontPage—are several Active Element features, plus the new Navigation Bars and Shared Borders tools. Active Elements give you neat tools like hover buttons and a banner ad manager. Navigation Bars automate the creation and maintenance of links within your site, whereas Shared Borders help you improve the look of your pages with customizable border elements, which can be applied on a site-wide or a page-by-page basis. ■

What Is Dynamic HTML?

Dynamic HTML (DHTML) is a new software development that allows on-the-fly modification of a Web page, provided that the browser displaying that page is a DHTML-enabled browser. In such a browser, a DHTML page can change its appearance and its behavior in response to actions undertaken by the person using the browser—such as mouse or keyboard activity. This enhanced ability to respond to users' input is the reason for characterizing this development of HTML as *dynamic*.

The specification for this extension of HTML has been laid down in a preliminary way by the Word Wide Web Consortium (W3C), the organization responsible for trying to standardize the HTML language. This specification is referred to formally as the *Document Object Model* (DOM). This originated with Netscape in the first version of JavaScript used in Navigator 2.0; Microsoft and SoftQuad have since extended the DOM in anticipation of W3C's specification of a DOM standard. This specification had not, as of mid-1997, been formally adopted by the W3C.

Netscape has tended to take its own approach to DHTML, which unfortunately will lead to browser compatibility problems down the road (although the Netscape Navigator 4 browser works properly with the W3C specification for Cascading Style Sheets). The behavior of Microsoft's new Internet Explorer 4 browser, naturally enough, follows the DOM specification, but Navigator 4 tends to use more proprietary methods of doing things. These methods, such as JavaScript Style Sheets and TrueDoc layering and font technology, are not supported by IE 4. However, as the DOM standard develops at W3C, Netscape will no doubt move toward compatibility with that standard.

N O T E The reference page for Netscape's version of DHTML is: **http://developer.netscape.com/ library/documentation/communicator/dynhtml/index.htm**

The reference page for Microsoft's version of DHTML is: **http://www.microsoft.com/workshop/ author/dynhtml** ■

FrontPage 98 also uses Microsoft's DHTML approach; in other words, it follows rather closely the proposed DOM requirements that are now before the W3C. That being the case, you will notice that the DHTML effects produced by FrontPage 98 work best (or only) in IE 4.

The W3C Document Object Model

The W3C has this to say about the model, and about DHTML:

"The Document Object Model is a platform- and language-neutral interface that will allow programs and scripts to dynamically access and update the content, structure and style of documents. The document can be further processed and the results of that processing can be incorporated back into the presented page…[The term] 'Dynamic HTML' is a term used by some vendors to describe the combination of HTML, style sheets and scripts that allows documents to be animated. W3C has received several submissions from members companies on the way in which the object model of HTML documents should be exposed to scripts. These submissions do not propose any new HTML tags or style sheet technology. The W3C DOM WG is working hard to make sure interoperable and scripting-language neutral solutions are agreed upon."

You can get up-to-date information on the DOM spec at:

http://www.w3.org/pub/WWW/MarkUp/DOM/

The best way to understand DHTML is to actually use it, so that's what you'll do next. You can start to explore them, but keep in mind that only DHTML-enabled browsers show many of these effects, and that overuse of dynamic elements on a page can be irritating and distracting. DHTML and its effects are a means to an end, not an end in themselves. There should be a constructive purpose for every piece of DHTML included in your Web.

N O T E *Cascading Style Sheets* are often considered part of, or at least closely integrated with, DHTML. Style sheets are so important that they deserve a whole chapter to themselves (see Chapter 12, "Using Style Sheets with Pages and Web Sites").DHTML also includes *Data Binding* that allows pages to be dynamically updated from changing data sources. This Microsoft-proprietary feature is discussed in Part IX: Advanced Database Connectivity.

Using Collapsible Outlines

Anyone familiar with the outlining tools of any high-end word processor or document-processing application recognizes *collapsible outlines*. The DHTML version allows you to create an interactive outline so that clicking a topic heading displays the information under that heading, and clicking it again makes the information vanish. Headings can be nested so that a large amount of information can reside on one screen—it's invisible when it's not needed, and visible, at the user's command, when it is.

> **CAUTION**
> Collapsible Outlines do not function in Netscape Navigator 4.0. The full text of all the lists is visible, but sublists cannot be made to vanish and reappear.

In FrontPage 98, the collapsible outline is built around lists, either bulleted or numbered. You may remember (from our examination of lists in Chapter 5, "Developing the Basic Page: Text, Lists, and Hyperlinks") that in the List Properties dialog box there was a check box labeled Enable Collapsible Outlines. This is the option you use.

Begin by setting up a list with at least one sublevel list (a nested list). Figure 7.1 shows a list with two levels of nesting; when fully collapsed, it shows only the top-level headings. Just for your interest, the example uses image bullets from the Industrial Theme.

FIG. 7.1

This set of nested lists collapses and expands in a DHTML-enabled browser such as Microsoft Internet Explorer 4.

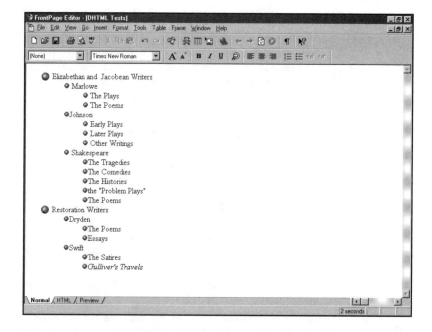

Place the insertion point in any list item in the topmost list and choose Format, Bullets and Numbering. When the List Properties dialog box appears, mark the Enable Collapsible Outlines check box. This means that the list(s) subordinate to any element in this list vanishes or appears as the element is clicked. Note that each list that is to have collapsible sublists must be marked as collapsible in the List Properties dialog box—in other words, enabling collapsible outlines for one list level does not automatically enable them for the list levels below or above it. Furthermore, remember that each sublist below a list item is treated as a separate list. In the example in Figure 7.1, the sublist containing "Marlowe," "Johnson," and "Shakespeare" is independent of the sublist containing "Dryden" and "Swift." If you wanted each of these sublists to be collapsible, you would have to enable collapsible outlines for each one.

Assume that you've created the bulleted list shown in Figure 7.1, and you've enabled collapsible outlines for the headings of the top level and for each sublist under each of the top level's headings. When you open the page in IE 4, the entire list is visible (this is to allow for nonDHTML browsers). Click any top-level heading, and all the second-level headings below it vanish. Click it again, and they reappear. Click one of these, and their subordinate levels vanish, and so on.

NOTE There is a good chance that authors of Help systems will, over the next year or two, be moving away from the WinHelp authoring environment toward the new HTML Help authoring environment. The collapsible outline is a natural for Help authors, because it allows them to cram a lot of information into a small Help window—the window can display just the topic subheadings, but when the Help user clicks on such a subheading, the text for it appears. For more information on HTML Help systems, see **http://www.microsoft.com/workshop/author/htmlhelp/** ■

Using Page Transitions

As you move away from bare bones Web page presentations, the creative itch grows stronger in Web authors. Why, for example, should pages just appear? Why shouldn't an author be able to do neat things with *transitions*, the way they can with slide transitions in PowerPoint?

> **CAUTION**
>
> Page Transitions do not function in Netscape Navigator 4.0. The page changes fine, but with no transition effect.

Well, now it can be done. Begin by opening the page where you want to apply the transition and choose Format, Page Transition to open the Page Transitions dialog box (see Figure 7.2).

FIG. 7.2
You have over 20 possible transitions (plus "none," to turn transitions off) to apply to a page entry or exit to a site entry or exit.

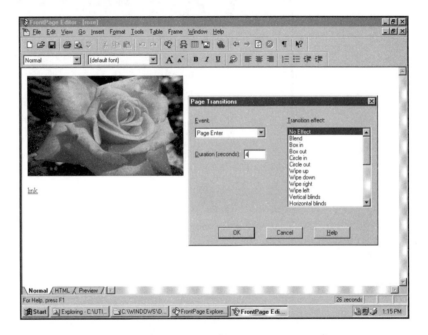

In the Event drop-down list box, specify whether you want the effect to take place on Page Entry or Exit, or Site Entry or Exit. In the Transition Effect list box, select the particular transition you want, and in the Duration text box, type the number of seconds over which the effect is to take place. You can apply two different effects to the same page, one for entry and one for exit—the Entry effect takes place as the page appears, and the Exit effect takes place as the page vanishes from the user's browser. The Site Entry and Site Exit options create the effect when the user enters or exits the Web site via the page to which the effects have been applied.

Part
II

Ch
7

N O T E   If you set up a new page transition, and then use Preview in Browser to view it in Internet Explorer 4, the transition will display properly. However, if you then edit the transition and try to view it again in IE 4, the change you made to the transition may not appear. If this happens, use IE 4 to open a page unrelated to the transition. Then manually clear the browser cache and try viewing the transition again.

Using Animations

Strictly speaking, this isn't an animation because the page element itself is not animated, but its entry onto the page is lively. You can invoke the effect by selecting the text or image you want to animate and choosing Format, Animation to open the Animation submenu (see Figure 7.3).

FIG. 7.3

The Animation menu gives you many ways to move text or an image onto your page.

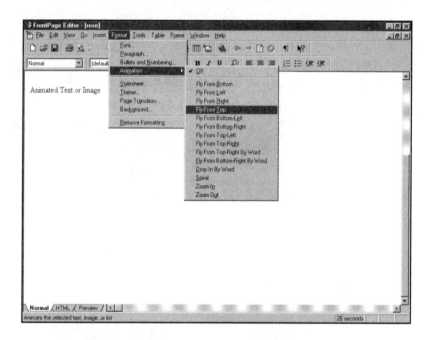

> **CAUTION**
>
> Animations do not function in Netscape Navigator 4.0. The animated element simply appears on the page with no animation effects.

The first eight animations are just linear animation. The *By Word* animations shows the text one word at a time, falling in from various directions. *Spiral* is a curved path, like the corresponding effect in PowerPoint. The *Zoom* animations are based on changing the size of the element as well as the animation path.

Select the effect you want and the menus will close. You can use Preview or the Preview in Browser command to test the behavior of the effect. To remove the animation, select the animated element, and choose Format, Animations and select Off from the menu.

Using Active Elements

Several of the Active Elements you'll examine in the following sections are actually Java applets that FrontPage Editor automatically generates for you, in response to your input. The *Hit Counter* is a FrontPage Component, and the *Marquee* is a tag that was introduced with FrontPage 97.

Using Hover Buttons

Hover buttons are animated buttons whose colors and outlines change when the mouse pointer hovers over them. They are intended specifically as navigation buttons. Because they are Java applets, they work fine in Internet Explorer 3 and Netscape 3.0 and 4.0.

To use one, place the insertion point where you want the button to be and choose Insert, Active Elements, Hover Button to open the Hover button dialog box (see Figure 7.4).

FIG. 7.4
With the Hover button dialog box, you can choose from seven different effects and change colors and button text.

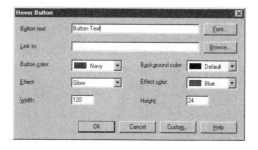

The dialog box allows you to:

- Use the Button Text text box to change the wording on the button. The Font button lets you change the font size, face, and color.
- Use the Link To text box to set up a hyperlink to the button's destination page.
- Use the Button Color and Effect Color drop-down list boxes to choose the colors for these two attributes.
- Use the Effect drop-down list to select among color fill, color average, glow, reverse glow, light glow, bevel out, and bevel in.
- Specify the Background Color of the button. This is to allow you to match its background color to the page background color, and it is mainly applicable if you are using custom images (see Figure 7.5).
- Specify Width and Height of the button.

Part
II

Ch
7

In this same dialog box, you can choose Custom to set up the Hover button with sound or a custom image (see Figure 7.5).

FIG. 7.5

You can customize the Hover Button with sound and your own images.

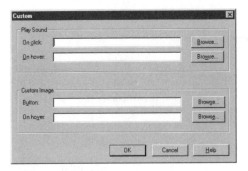

In the Play Sound section of this dialog box, you can specify a sound file to play when the button is clicked or when the mouse pointer hovers over it. Similarly, you use the Custom Image section of the dialog box to specify your own button images. The Button text box allows you to specify your own image for the button. The On Hover text box lets you select a hover image for the button; if you supply this, that image appears when the mouse pointer hovers on the button. In both instances, the effects applied to the button in the Hover Button dialog box are overridden.

If you use two custom images of different sizes (one for the button and one for the hover effect) you may need to adjust the background color to match the page background color so that the smaller graphic doesn't have colored edges.

N O T E   Hover buttons with custom images vanish from the Normal view but are still present (though invisible) in the page. They appear properly in Preview mode. ▪

Using the Banner Ad Manager

This FrontPage Component uses a list of images and displays each one for a preset number of seconds. It then switches to the next image, and the next, until it is finished with the list, and then it starts over again from the beginning. As its name suggests, the *Banner Ad Manager* is designed for advertising, but your imagination can no doubt come up with other uses. Because it's a Java applet, the ad manager works properly in Netscape 3 and 4, as well as in IE 3 and 4.

Before placing the banner on the page, prepare the images it will use and store them in a suitable folder. Make a note of the height of the tallest ad in pixels, and the width of the widest ad in pixels. These values might not be from the same ad, however. For best results, all the images should be close to the same size. Choose Insert, Active Elements, Banner Ad Manager to open the Banner Ad dialog box (see Figure 7.6).

FIG. 7.6

The Banner Ad Manager gives you extensive control over the appearance and behavior of advertisements.

To set up the rotating ads, do this:

1. Type the width of the widest image and the height of the tallest image into the appropriate text boxes of the dialog box. Images that are narrower or shorter than these values will display on a neutral background in a window sized with these values. If an image is bigger than the maximums, it is cut off.

2. Use the Effect drop-down list box to select the kind of effect you want for the transition between the images. You have a choice of dissolve, horizontal or vertical blinds, box in or out, or none.

3. Use the Show Each Image For text box to specify how long, in seconds, the ad should display.

4. Use the Link To text box to set up the URL to which the ad will point. If a user clicks on the ad, they are taken to that URL.

5. Click the Add button to specify the images that are to rotate through the banner. This opens the standard FrontPage 98 file location and selection dialog box. Use it to select images from the clip art gallery, your local system, or the World Wide Web. After you've selected the images, the URLs or path names appear in the Images To Display dialog box.

6. Select the ad you want to move and click the Move Up or Move Down buttons to rearrange the order in which the ads cycle. To remove an ad from the display, click the Remove button.

7. Choose OK when you're finished. A JavaScript placeholder now appears in the page that shows the positioning of the banner.

When you preview the banner in a browser, you'll see the images appear and vanish according to the specified effects and duration.

Part

II

Ch

7

CAUTION

The Banner Ad applet will not work unless its images are stored in the current Web. If you reference an image for the applet and this image is not in the current Web, then when you save the page you will get the Save Embedded Files dialog box. Make sure you save the image file to a folder in the current Web; in other words, don't use the Set Action button to force the image reference to remain external to the Web.

Using the Hit Counter

Hit counters in various formats are in just about every Web site these days, or at least in those that want a public display of how many times visitors have dropped by. To deploy FrontPage 98's counter, choose Insert, Active Elements, Hit Counter to open the Hit Counter Properties dialog box (see Figure 7.7).

FIG. 7.7

The Hit counter is an easily placed module for tracking visits to a page.

You can choose from five different display formats or choose a custom GIF of your own design. Such a custom GIF must include a full set of the digits 0–9. Make sure the digits are evenly spaced; some adjustment of the GIF may be necessary for best results.

You can also use the Reset Counter check box and text box to reset the counter to whatever number you please, as well as use the Fixed Number of Digits check box and text box to specify how high the counter will count before it starts over.

The Hit Counter functions properly in Netscape 3 and 4 as well as in IE 3 and 4.

Using Marquees

Marquees are those boxes that have text moving through them. Opinions vary on their best use; some people keep the text moving, others prefer to slide it into view and then leave it static. Your own design sense is your best guide.

CAUTION

The <MARQUEE> tag is specific to Internet Explorer browsers and does not work in Netscape browsers; the text of the marquee appears, but does not scroll. Netscape implements marquees through Java applets. For more information on this, see Chapter 20, "Inserting Java Applets and Browser Plug-Ins."

To insert a marquee, choose Insert, Marquee to open the Marquee Properties dialog box (see Figure 7.8).

FIG. 7.8

Customize the scrolling text with the Marquee Properties options.

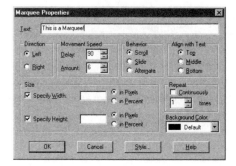

Type the text you want to scroll in the Text box and adjust the marquee properties as follows:

- The Left and Right option buttons determine the direction of scroll.
- Amount sets the speed of the scroll. Delay is an adjustment that essentially makes the scroll move smoothly or in slight increments.
- Slide moves the text onto the screen and stops it.
- Alternate scrolls the text onto the screen and then bounces it back and forth.
- If there's text beside the marquee, the Align with Text option buttons place it at the middle, the top, or the bottom of the marquee height.
- The Width and height of the marquee can be set as a percentage of the page or as pixels.
- The repetitions of the marquee movement are set with the Repeat section.
- The Background Color determines the color of the marquee box where the text appears. Default keeps the box the same color as the page, so the text appears to float across the page surface.

You can align the marquee on the page by using the alignment buttons on the toolbar. You can also use the Format, Font command to change the marquee font—click the marquee text to select the marquee field and change the font with the usual procedures. Note that you don't make the change with the Marquee Properties dialog box.

To make nonfont changes to the marquee, right-click the marquee and select Marquee Properties from the shortcut menu.

Part

II

Ch

7

Including a PowerPoint Animation

This procedure assumes you have already created a PowerPoint Animation file from a slide presentation. To include it in the page, choose Insert, Active Elements, PowerPoint Animation. This opens the PowerPoint Animation dialog box (see Figure 7.9).

FIG. 7.9
You can insert a PowerPoint Animation file as either an ActiveX component or as a Netscape plug-in.

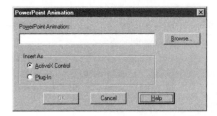

Locate and select the animation file. Mark one of the two option buttons in the dialog box to indicate whether the file is to be inserted into the page as an ActiveX control or as a Netscape plug-in.

 T I P You may want to include a page with each type of insertion, to allow as many users as possible to see the presentation.

Using Shared Borders and Navigation Bars

Shared Borders provide a quick and convenient way to give your Web a consistent appearance. *Navigation Bars*, which reside within these borders, greatly simplify creating and maintaining the links within a Web. You can apply Shared Borders and Navigation bars to an entire site at once, from FrontPage Explorer, and then (if you need to) individualize the borders of single pages within the Web.

A handy thing about Shared Borders is that you can modify a border in FrontPage Editor, and that modification will apply to all pages in the current Web. Pages whose borders you have modified on an individual basis, however, do not change.

Shared Borders and Navigation bars, incidentally, work in Navigator 3 and 4 as well as in IE 3 and 4.

Creating Shared Borders for the Current Web

To create a shared border for the current Web, open the desired FrontPage Web in FrontPage Explorer and choose Tools, Shared Borders. The Shared Borders dialog box appears (see Figure 7.10). Mark the check boxes for all or some of the borders you want to apply and choose OK.

FIG. 7.10

You can selectively add top, bottom, left, or right borders to an entire Web at once.

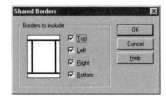

 The borders are stored as HTML files in the hidden folder named _borders. To see the hidden folders, go to FrontPage Explorer and choose Tools, Web Settings. Go to the Advanced sheet and put a check mark in the Show Documents in Hidden Directories check box.

Now, when you open an existing page or create a new page, these borders are automatically applied. The top and the left borders contain Navigation Bars, and the right and the bottom borders contain Comment FrontPage Components.

The appearance of the Navigation Bars depends on the theme chosen for the Web. If there is no theme, the navigation bars appear entirely as text. The links established through the navigation bars are determined by the Web's structure as set up in Navigation View. However, if you haven't set up a Web structure in Navigation View, the navigation bars will be too generic to be of much use. What it boils down to is this: the most useful combination of tools is to use Navigation View to set up the Web's linkage structure and then apply Shared Borders to that structure.

A detailed explanation of how to use Navigation View appears later in this book. You might find it useful to glance over the topic before proceeding with this chapter. To get you started, though, we'll briefly cover the basics of Navigation View in the next section.

▶ **See** Chapter 24, "Working with an Existing Web," **p. 557**

 Clearing the check boxes in the Shared Borders dialog box does not actually remove the HTML border files from the _borders folder. If you really mess up the edit of a border and want to begin over, you should uncheck the appropriate check box or boxes in the Shared Borders dialog box and go to the _borders folder and delete the appropriate border file. Reapply that particular border with FrontPage Explorer's Tools, Shared Borders command.

Working with Navigation Bars and Shared Borders

To create a navigational structure for a Web, go to FrontPage Explorer and click the Navigation icon in the left taskbar. This opens Navigation View, which has two panes. Drag page icons from the lower pane to the upper, placing the page in the correct relation to the home page and/or other pages. The Page Title of an existing page supplies the title of the icons in the upper pane. These icon titles are used as the page banners in the top Shared Borders of the pages.

Let's assume for the moment that the Navigation View of the current Web looks like the one in Figure 7.11 and that the Web does not use themes.

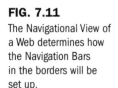

FIG. 7.11

The Navigational View of a Web determines how the Navigation Bars in the borders will be set up.

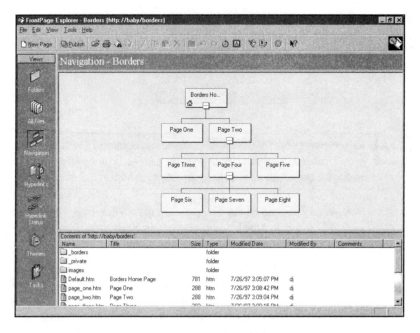

Now use FrontPage Explorer to apply all four borders to the pages in the Web. It doesn't matter whether you apply borders before or after creating the navigational structure.

Having done so, open one of the pages in FrontPage Editor—the example uses the home page, DEFAULT.HTM, as shown in Figure 7.12.

Working with the Top Shared Border   The top border has two default elements, one of which is the page banner—in the example, "Borders Home Page." The banner text is supplied from the page icon title in Navigation View.

This banner is actually inserted onto the page by a FrontPage Component, as you'll see from the little robotic cursor that appears after you click the banner and hover the mouse pointer over the banner text. If you accidentally delete this banner and its Component, you also delete the banners for all the other pages in the Web, so be careful. If you do need to change the text on the banner, you must go to Navigation View and edit the title of the page icon in the upper pane (right-click the icon and choose Rename from the shortcut menu).

N O T E   Although the Navigation View icon title is initially obtained from the Page Title, editing the icon title will *not* change the Page title. Also, using the Page Properties dialog box to change a Page Title does not change an existing icon title in Navigation View. ▨

If you want to change the look or orientation of the banner, highlight it, then right-click it and choose the Paragraph Properties dialog box or the Font Properties dialog box to make the changes.

FIG. 7.12

The top and left borders automatically supply navigation links and a banner, both as defined in Navigation View.

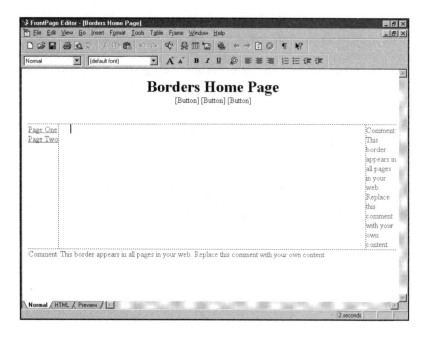

You notice, too, that the bracketed word [Button] appears three times under the banner. This second default element, a Navigation Bar, is inserted by a Navigation Bar Component and is actually a set of hyperlinks. We'll take a closer look at this FrontPage Component shortly.

When you use FrontPage Editor to view a page at the top of the Navigation View hierarchy (the Home Page, in this example), you'll see that the top border's navigation bar has [Button] placeholders for navigation buttons. You can simply leave these placeholders alone; they do show up in a browser, although they do in Preview mode. Don't try to delete them. If you do, you will delete the top border's navigation bar not only in this page, but in every page of the current Web!

Working with the Left Shared Border   If you look at the left border of the example in Figure 7.12, you see that it has two preset text links: Page One and Page Two. FrontPage Editor obtained the link text from the page icon titles in Navigation View, and this link text can be changed by editing the icon titles in that View.

You can also change the hyperlinks themselves by going to Navigation View and dragging the page icons to different orientations and connections. It's a good idea to close all pages in FrontPage Editor before you do this so that their links are properly updated when you reopen them.

Part
II

Ch
7

CAUTION

When you want an accurate assessment of Shared Border and Navigation Bar behavior, use the Preview in Browser command, not Preview mode. The latter can be misleading—for instance, it shows [Button] placeholders, which don't actually show up in a browser.

Working with Borders with Complex Linkages   Now consider a page with more complicated linkages, such as Page Four from the navigational structure example in Figure 7.12. When you open such a page in FrontPage Editor, it resembles the example shown in Figure 7.13.

FIG. 7.13

A page from the middle of a Web has more complex navigation bars than the Home Page.

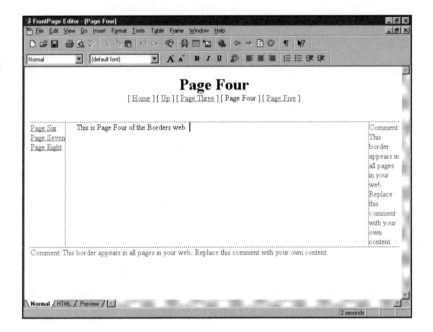

You see that the top border possesses multiple, automatically generated links:

- A Home link that takes the viewer to (where else?) the Home page
- An Up link that takes the viewer to Page Two, the page immediately above Page Four in the Navigation View hierarchy
- Links to Pages Three and Five, which are at the same level as Page Four in the Navigation View hierarchy

To let the user go downward in the Navigation View hierarchy, the left border provides automatically generated links to Pages Six, Seven, and Eight, which are below Page Four in the hierarchy (as you can see from Figure 7.12).

Editing Navigation Bars   You can add your own links—and any other page element—to the navigation bars. Click in the bar to place the insertion point there and use the normal FrontPage editing tools. Do not accidentally delete the Navigation Bar FrontPage Component!

You can adjust the links included in the navigation bar with the *Navigation Bar FrontPage Component*. To use it, click in the navigation bar to select it. Put the mouse cursor on the bar so that the Bot cursor appears, right-click, and choose FrontPage Component Properties from the shortcut menu. The Navigation Bar Properties dialog box appears (see Figure 7.14).

FIG. 7.14

You can change the linkages of a navigation bar with the Navigation Bar Properties dialog box.

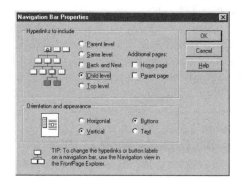

From this dialog box, you can specify which position in the hierarchy the link will lead to:

- Parent Level inserts links to all the pages in the hierarchy level immediately above the current page.

- Same Level inserts links to all the pages at the same level as the current page. This is the default for the top border navigation bar.

- Back and Next inserts links that allow the user to move across the pages in a level and back again. These links don't let you move outside that level.

- Child Level inserts links to all pages in the level below the current page. This is the default for the left border navigation bar.

- Top Level inserts a link to any page other than the Home Page, at the hierarchical level of the Home Page.

- You can also add a link to the Home Page or to the Parent Page. The latter is not quite the same as using Parent Level because it links only to the parent page, not to all pages at the parent level (assuming there might be more than one page at that level). It supplies a link named UP.

You can use the Orientation and Appearance section to specify whether the navigation links are buttons or text, and whether they run vertically or horizontally. If the Web uses no themes, though, you only get text—even if you mark the Buttons option button.

Part

II

Ch

7

CAUTION

When you use FrontPage Editor to view a page at the bottom level of the Navigation View hierarchy, you'll see that the left border's navigation bar has [Button] placeholders for navigation buttons. You should leave this border and its navigation bar as they are—the placeholders do not show up in a browser, although they do appear in Preview mode. Don't try to delete them—if you do, you delete the left border and its navigation bar not only in this page, but in every page of the current Web!

Working with the Right and Bottom Borders   These are simpler entities than the other two borders, since they don't have navigation controls in them. They default to Comment Components with purple Comment text. To add your own page elements, click inside either border, which selects the purple comment text. Insert any elements you like (the first element you insert replaces the comment text). Remember that the changes you make will appear in the borders of all pages on the Web site. The exception to this is if you individualize a page's borders. We'll examine this procedure later in this chapter.

Using Borders and Navigation Bars with Themes

So far, for simplicity, adding a theme to the borders and navigation bars has been avoided. You can do this now.

Assuming you want the theme to appear in all the pages in the Web, open the Web in FrontPage Explorer and use the method you learned in Chapter 6 to apply the theme. The one chosen for the examples that follow is the Global Marketing Theme, with the background image turned off for clarity. In Figure 7.15 you can see the results as they appear in Internet Explorer 4.0.

▶ **See** Chapter 6, "Enhancing Pages with Themes, Graphics, and Multimedia," **p. 123**

As you can see, the navigation buttons are supplied by the theme. You cannot customize Navigation Bar buttons with your own button images.

Sometimes you may want to change the banner so that it's plain text and doesn't use the theme image. To do this, right-click the banner and choose FrontPage Component Properties from the shortcut menu. This opens the Page Banner Properties dialog box where you can select either Image or Text option buttons. The Text option button will replace the banner image with plain black text.

You get an equivalent effect if you open the Navigation Bar Properties dialog box and mark the Text option button. This replaces the buttons with textual links, as they appeared when the pages had no theme. In the same dialog box, marking the Horizontal or Vertical option buttons changes the orientation of the button strip on the page, but only the orientation of the buttons in the top border. The buttons in the left border are not affected by this option.

Individualizing a Page's Borders

From time to time, you may want a page treatment different from that applied by the Web's Shared Borders. You get this result by individually customizing the borders of each page.

FIG. 7.15

A browser display of a page using both Shared Borders and Navigation Bars.

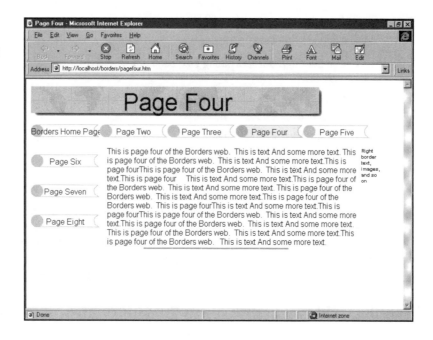

To do so, open the desired page in FrontPage Editor and choose Tools, Shared Borders. The Page Borders dialog box appears (see Figure 7.16).

FIG. 7.16

Customization of a page's borders begins with the Page Borders dialog box.

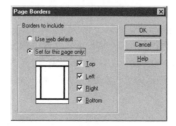

Assuming the Web already has borders applied, the Use Web Default option button will be marked. Change this by marking the Set for This Page Only option button and then mark or clear the check boxes that correspond to the borders you want to remove or keep. Choose OK, and the unwanted borders disappear from that page only.

> **CAUTION**
>
> The Set For This Page option is somewhat misleading. With this option you can only remove or add a particular page's borders; you can't edit that page's borders on a border-by-border basis. So, even if you mark the Set For This Page Only option button, any changes you make to the content of any border of a page will be repeated in the corresponding border of all the other pages of the Web.

Part

II

Ch

7

If the Web has a theme, the borders that remain will reflect that theme. To make the borders on a page use a different theme:

1. Use the Page Borders dialog box, seen in Figure 7.16, to remove all the borders from the page.

2. Choose Format, Theme and in the Choose Theme dialog box, select This Page Does Not Use Themes. Choose OK.

3. Use the Page Borders dialog box, when the nontheme page appears, to specify the borders you want on the page.

4. Choose OK. After you select the borders you want, the borders will appear with the selected theme applied to them. Only the borders on the current page are affected.

Of course, if you want a page with borders that don't depend on any theme for their appearance, remove the borders and the theme by choosing This Page Does Not Use Themes in the Choose Theme dialog box and reapply the borders you want. The drawback is that you're forced to use the supplied text links for navigation—as mentioned above, you can't edit the content of a border, even when you've specified that the borders are to affect this page only.

Creating New Pages in a Shared Borders Environment

Inevitably, you need to create more pages to go into a Web that has Shared Borders. Open FrontPage Editor and choose File, New and select the kind of page you want. When the new page appears, it has [Button] placeholders in the top and left borders, although the content of the right and bottom borders is the correct content.

To set up the top and left borders properly, save the page with a suitable Page Title and file name. Close it and go to FrontPage Explorer. In Navigation View, drag the new page to its correct position in the hierarchy in the upper pane. When you return to FrontPage Editor and open the page, the banner and links appear as they should.

▶ **See** Chapter 24, "Working with an Existing Web," **p. 557**, for information on creating a page while in FrontPage Explorer.

> **CAUTION**
>
> In case you haven't looked at the Help Page for Shared Borders yet, it strongly suggests that you not use Shared Borders with frames pages.

Inserting a Navigation Bar Without Shared Borders

You can place a navigation bar on a page without using Shared Borders. To do this, choose Insert, Navigation Bar. This opens the Navigation Bar Properties dialog box you saw in Figure 7.14. Specify the navigation bar properties you want, and choose OK to make the bar appear on the page. The bar's appearance is determined by the theme of the page, or it will be a textual navigation bar if no theme is present. Adding a navigation bar to one page does not add a navigation bar to any other page.

From Here...

The next three chapters provide you with yet more powerful tools for building a sophisticated Web. If you like this idea, go on with:

■ Chapter 8, "Creating Tables," shows you how to design, set up, and modify tables to enhance the organization of your pages. New for FrontPage 98 is the Table Drawing Tool that allows you to draw tables directly on the Web page.

■ Chapter 9, "Enhancing Web Sites with FrontPage Frames," is where you find out about designing a *framed* site, about using frames with links and images, and how to create ready-made framed environments with frame templates. The best part is that frames in FrontPage Editor are now WYSIWYG!

■ Chapter 10, "Creating Pages with FrontPage Editor Templates," shows you how you can use these organizational and presentation tools to generate real-world documents based on a wide selection of preset layouts.

Creating Tables

Tables are a powerful method of presenting page content in an accessible and understandable way. They're especially useful in the World Wide Web environment because of the limitations of our hardware. Most of us peer at relatively small screens, and a screen's resolution is much less than that of a printed page. Any tool that helps us compress information into small, organized areas is a very useful one, and tables fill this specification perfectly. Most Web authors make moderate to heavy use of tables as layout grids for their pages so most of the page templates provided with FrontPage 98's Editor, as well as the themes, are built around tables.

Versions of FrontPage prior to FrontPage 98, unfortunately, made the use of tables as a design aid much more of a chore than it needed to be. The introduction of FrontPage 98's near-WYSIWYG table drawing feature will significantly ease a Web author's burden so that they can now concentrate on the look of the table as it's created, rather than tediously switching between workspace and dialog box to see if the table looks right. ■

Table setup

Use the Table Drawing Tool to create the basic table framework to organize your information.

Table editing

Modify row and column structure and cell layout.

Cell editing

Format your cell content effectively with alignment and varying cell widths.

Decorative elements

Use cell and table background colors and images.

Using Tables for Better Content Organization

Like lists, tables are common in our lives, especially in business and science. Web pages can contain text and images, just as printed tables do, and you can use them to arrange text in parallel columns or to set an explanatory block of text beside the image that resides in the adjacent cell. You can insert lists into cells and even insert tables into other tables. All this gives you tremendous flexibility in arranging data and images (see Figure 8.1).

FIG. 8.1

In this FrontPage Editor page view in Preview mode, an image is in the left cell of the table's top row and a bulleted list in the right. Table borders are shown for clarity; they're optional.

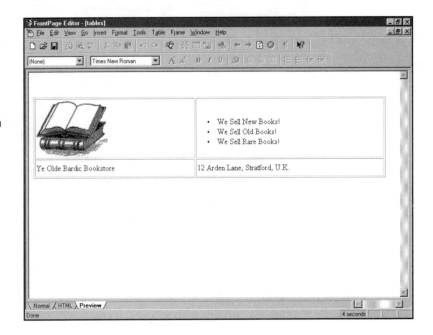

Tables can also contain hyperlinks to other resources, which gives them a whole new dimension. For example, you can make a table containing thumbnails of images and link these to the larger versions.

▶ **See** "Using Thumbnails," **p. 123** in Chapter 6, "Enhancing Pages with Themes, Graphics, and Multimedia."

In another example, each entry in a periodic table of the elements can be linked to a resource that gives detailed information about that element. You can also insert forms or FrontPage Components into a cell, which makes a table an interactive tool.

You can see this in Figure 8.2, where the bulleted hyperlinks are actually contained inside the cells of a two-column table. (In this example, the cell and table boundaries don't show.)

 TIP To understand better how tables work in FrontPage Editor, you can save a World Wide Web page to a file, import that file into a FrontPage Web, and then manipulate the table properties to see what happens.

FIG. 8.2

Here, the two-column bulleted list at the bottom of the screen is contained in the cells of a two-column table. The cell contents are hyperlinks.

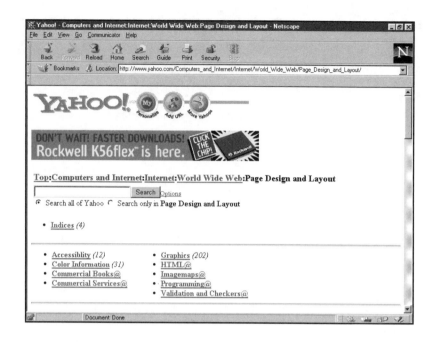

Tables are supported by the major browsers (Netscape 2.0 and later, and Internet Explorer 2.0 and later), so feel free to include them in your pages. Different browsers treat visible cell borders differently, though, so you should check to see what the borders look like in each browser before you settle on a design. Equally important, remember that many people cruise the Web at 640×480 resolution so if you create tables that take advantage of the width of a 1024×768 display, your visitors using a lower resolution may not see what you envisioned.

Setting Up a Table

FrontPage Editor gives you many options for table appearance, but don't begin a complicated table by plunging right into FrontPage Editor. Begin by planning it, if only by roughing it out on paper, to organize the data and its presentation. You'll save yourself a lot of time and revision.

Once you've worked out the table's content and structure, use the following steps:

1. Choose Table, Draw Table and the Table toolbar appears. When you move the mouse pointer into the workspace, the pointer turns into the table drawing tool.

2. Drag the table drawing tool through the Editor workspace until you have a rectangle that's about the size of the table you want. When you release the mouse button, the table border appears with a default thickness of 1 pixel.

3. Drag the drawing tool within the cells to create new cells, columns, or rows. You can tell where the new border is going to be because a dotted line snaps into position as you drag the drawing tool (see Figure 8.3). Don't start dragging while the drawing tool is on a cell boundary, or you will actually create a new table inside the current one.

FIG. 8.3

You get a *pilot line* while dragging the drawing tool which shows where the cell boundary is going to be.

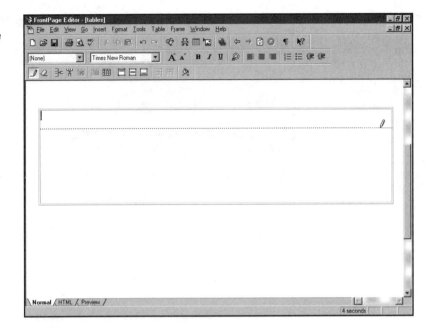

4. Place the drawing tool on top of any cell border until the pointer becomes a double-headed arrow. Drag this to adjust the size of the cell or the table.

5. Select the Eraser tool from the Table toolbar if you've made a mistake. Hold the left mouse button down while dragging the eraser over the cell border you want to erase. When the border is selected, it is highlighted. Release the mouse button and the cell border vanishes. (Note: in some configurations of cells, certain borders cannot be erased.)

If you prefer not to use the drawing tool, you can create a table by using the Table, Insert Table command. You also use this command to insert a table into an existing table because you can't use the drawing tool to insert tables inside tables.

When you use this command, the Insert Table dialog box appears (see Figure 8.4). Here, you can establish the essential characteristics of the table:

1. Specify the number of rows and columns in the Rows and Columns text boxes.

2. Specify whether you want the table against the left margin, centered, or against the right margin in the Alignment drop-down list box.

3. Specify how many pixels thick the cell and table borders are to be in the Border Size text box. A value of zero specifies no borders.

4. Specify how many pixels of space you want between the cell contents and the inside edge of the cell boundary in the Cell Padding text box.

5. Specify how many pixels of space you want between cells in the Cell Spacing text box.

FIG. 8.4

The Insert Table dialog box is an alternative way of creating a table.

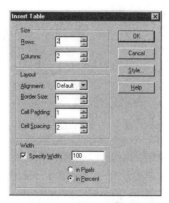

6. Specify how wide you want the table to be, either in pixels or as a percentage of the browser window in the Specify Width text box.

7. Choose OK when you are done and the table appears. If you chose a Border Size of zero, the cells are outlined, in dotted lines in the FrontPage Editor workspace, in Normal mode. These dotted cell boundaries don't appear in a browser or in Preview mode.

To put content into a cell, click in the cell and, if it's text you want, just start typing. The text wraps when it reaches the cell margin, pushing the bottom of the whole row down so that you can keep going. To insert images, other tables, lists, or any other page element, click in the cell and use the appropriate menus to insert the component. The cells resize to suit the content.

N O T E The appearance of the table in FrontPage Editor's Normal mode is not exactly WYSIWYG. To see an accurate picture of the table, use Preview mode. ■

Using the Table Menu

Now that you have a table, you can get a better look at the Table menu. (Except for Draw Table and Insert Table, the entries for the Table menu were grayed out when you last saw them.) Click anywhere in the table and choose Table to make the menu appear (see Figure 8.5).

Many of the operations you perform on table elements require you to select those elements. You can use the menu to select cells, rows, and columns, or the entire table. You can also drag across table elements to select them.

T I P You can also select a row or a column by placing the cursor on the table border to the left of that row or above that column. When the cursor changes to a small black arrow, click once to select the row or column.

FIG. 8.5

Use the Table menu to manipulate and select parts of a table.

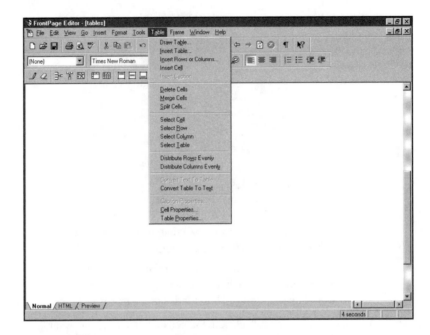

Modifying the Properties of an Existing Table

As you work on a table, you may discover that you need to change some of its characteristics. To do this, click anywhere in the table and choose Table, Table Properties. The Table Properties dialog box appears, as shown in Figure 8.6.

FIG. 8.6

Change the settings for an existing table with the Table Properties dialog box.

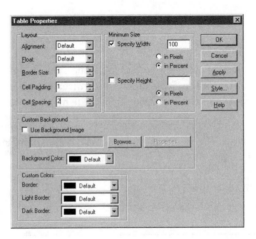

The Table Properties dialog box duplicates part of the Insert Table dialog box. You can modify the table layout and the width of the table by using the same procedures (minimum width is a value that is discussed later in this chapter). The Float option under the Alignment text box, when selected, allows text to wrap around the table, just as floating images allow the same effect.

You can also apply colors to the table; you will see this procedure a little later, in the section "Adding Colors and Backgrounds to Tables and Cells."

 TIP To get to the Table Properties dialog box quickly, right-click anywhere in the table and select Table Properties from the shortcut menu.

Deleting a Table or Parts of a Table

When you're experimenting, you need to know how to delete an experiment gone wrong. To get rid of a table entirely, click anywhere in it and choose Table, Select Table and press the Delete key. Another way is to double-click in the left margin to select the entire table and press the Delete key or choose Edit, Clear.

You remove columns or rows by the same method: select and then delete. However, if you delete a cell (as distinct from deleting its content), all the cells to its right slide over to fill the empty space, and a gap is left at the right side of the table (see Figure 8.7).

FIG. 8.7

Deleting a cell leaves a blank area in the table because the cells to its right move into the space left by the deleted cell.

Space caused by deleted cell in center of middle row

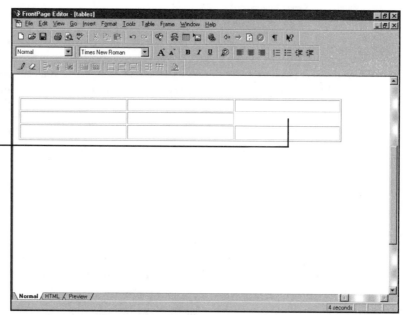

 TIP Another way to delete a cell, row, or column is to select it and click the Delete Cell button on the Table toolbar.

Adding Rows or Columns

Even with the best planning, you sometimes discover a class of information you didn't allow for, and you need a new row or column for it. To add either one, select the existing row or column that is to be adjacent to the new one. Choose Table, Insert Rows or Columns. The Insert Rows or Columns dialog box appears, as shown in Figure 8.8. Fill in the data for the number of rows or columns to insert and where they should go relative to the selection you made and choose OK.

FIG. 8.8
Use the Insert Rows or Columns dialog box to add data space to your tables.

 You can use the Table toolbar as a shortcut to column and row insertion. Select a row and click the Insert Row button. A blank row appears above the selected row. Use the Insert Column button similarly to insert a column left of the selected column. If you select two rows or two columns, two new rows or columns are added, and so on.

Inserting a Cell

If you deleted a cell and decide you want its real estate back, you can insert a new cell by using the Table, Insert Cell. Where the new cell appears is governed by the following:

- If the cursor is in an empty cell, the new cell is added immediately to the left of the current cell.

- If the cursor is at the left end of any data in a cell, the new cell is added on the left of the current cell.

- If the cursor is at the right end of any data in a cell, the new cell is added on the right of the current cell.

Adding and Formatting a Caption

To add a caption, click inside the table and choose Table, Insert Caption and the insertion point moves to the line immediately above the table's first row. The caption you type will center itself automatically.

You have some flexibility with its placement and appearance. To make adjustments, click anywhere in the caption and choose Table, Caption Properties to open the Caption Properties dialog box (see Figure 8.9). Mark the appropriate option button to place the caption above or below the table. For lateral placement, click the Left Align, Center, or Right Align buttons on the toolbar.

FIG. 8.9
Captions can go above
or below a table.

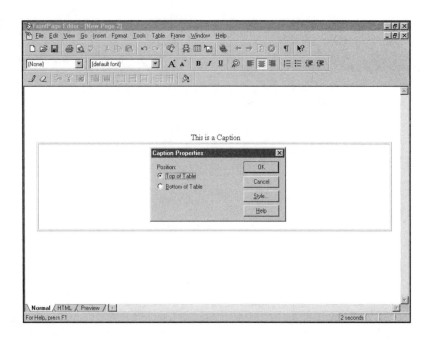

To change the caption font, select the text and choose Format, Font to make the changes with the Font dialog box. You can also use the character formatting buttons on the toolbar for bold, italic, underline, or color.

To delete a caption, select it and press the Delete key twice.

Inserting a Table into an Existing Table

You can get an interesting and powerful effect by putting a table inside a cell of another table. To do this, click the cell where you want the subtable to appear and choose Table, Insert Table. Set up the subtable properties as you like and choose OK. You can see an example of a table in another table's cell in Figure 8.10.

Splitting and Merging Cells

A perfectly regular grid of cells may not exactly match the way your data needs to be laid out. To change the cell patterns so that they serve your purposes better, you can split or merge them. To split a cell, click in it and choose Table, Split Cells. The Split Cells dialog box appears, as shown in Figure 8.11.

Now you have a choice of dividing the cell into columns or rows. Set up whichever you want and choose OK. Splitting the cells leaves the data intact in the left cell (row split) or the upper cell (column split). In Figure 8.12, you can see a table with both row-split and column-split cells.

To put cells together, select them and choose Table, Merge Cells. The data is intact in the resulting cell, although you may have to do some reformatting.

Part
II

Ch
8

FIG. 8.10

Placing a table within the cell of another table gives a subdivided effect.

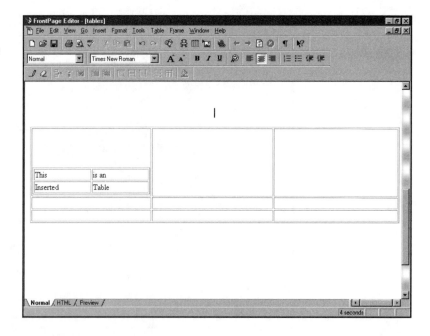

FIG. 8.11

You can change a table's cell subdivisions by splitting cells.

T I P Use the Split Cells or Merge Cells buttons on the Table toolbar as shortcuts for joining and dividing cells.

Modifying the Table's Appearance

A plain-vanilla table is good at organizing content, but you also need to think about presentation. Using column and row headers, captions, color, and suitable alignment of cell content can make your tables pleasing to the eye.

Adding Headers

Most tables have column headers to denote the kind of data in each column; many tables also have row headers. An example would be a sales report with product names as row headers, and sales for each quarter as column headers. You often want to emphasize such headers, and one way is to select the text and use character formatting. Another method is to change the cell properties. To do this, select the cell or cells you want as header cells and choose Table, Cell

Properties to display the Cell Properties dialog box (see Figure 8.13). Mark the Header Cell check box and choose OK.

FIG. 8.12

The top-right cell has been split into two rows and the bottom-left cell into three columns.

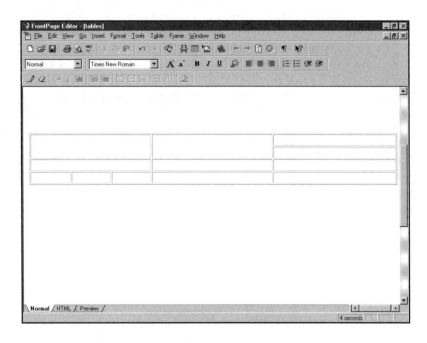

TIP   To reach the Cell Properties dialog box quickly, select the cell and press Alt+Enter.

FIG. 8.13

The Cell Properties dialog box lets you make a cell into a header cell.

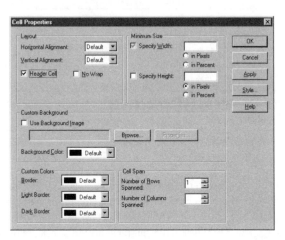

The text in the selected cell is rendered in bold. If you want to remove the header formatting, reopen the Cell Properties dialog box and deselect the Header Cell check box.

Aligning the Content of a Cell

Depending on your cell content, you may want it positioned in different places. An image, for example, usually looks better if it's centered within the cell borders. You can also get these effects by using the Cell Properties dialog box. In the Layout section, you can specify horizontal and vertical text alignment with the drop-down list boxes. Figure 8.14 shows an image with the Horizontal Alignment set to Center and Vertical Alignment set to Middle.

FIG. 8.14
Centering images and text in cells may improve their appearance.

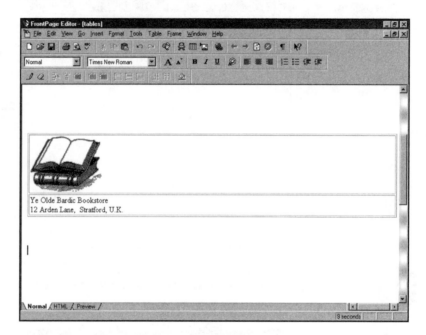

N O T E The alignments show up best in Preview mode, not Normal mode. ■

  The Align Top, Center Vertically, and Align Bottom buttons on the Table toolbar are shortcuts to locating cell content vertically within the cell.

Using No Wrap

The No Wrap check box, if marked, prevents word wrap from being applied to the contents of a cell. However, even with the box checked, and while you are in FrontPage Editor, a long line of text continues to wrap within the cell. That is, the "no wrap" effect does not actually appear until you view the page in a browser. This can have profound effects on a table's layout, so be sure to check your work in a browser if you do use the No Wrap option.

Specifying Minimum Cell Width

The Cell Properties dialog box gives yet another way to proportion cells, or in this case, full columns. As usual, you should keep the minimum width units set to percent, not pixels, to allow for different resolutions your viewers may be using.

 TIP   Sometimes the pixel measurement is a better choice than percentage, for example if you are basing the cell width on the absolute width of an image.

A three-column table has the default minimum cell widths set at 33%, that is, the cells take up at least 33% of the total table width each (to be precise, 33%, 33%, and 34%, from left to right). Changing these percentages lets you adjust the width of a whole column, independent of other columns, as shown in Figure 8.15. Getting the cell width percentages coordinated with the table width percentage can be tricky, and will take some experimentation and some browser previewing.

FIG. 8.15
You create columns of differing widths by using Minimum Width cell settings.

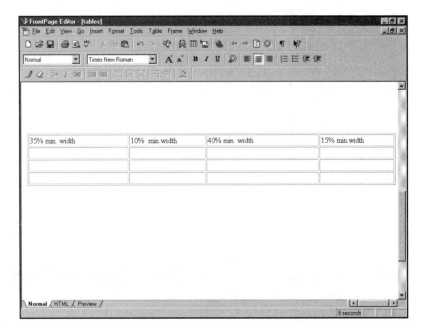

Evening Out Row and Column Proportions

If you've done a lot of dragging and fitting of row and column boundaries, they may not be as evenly proportioned as you'd like them to be. To make an even distribution of rows and columns, select the ones you want to be affected and click either the Distribute Rows Evenly button or the Distribute Columns Evenly button on the toolbar. There are also menu commands for these operations on the Table menu.

Making Cells Span Rows and Columns

Another way of modifying your table's grid is to make a cell bigger or smaller. This is called spanning, and you change a cell's span by selecting a cell and using the Cell Properties dialog box. In the Cell Span section, enter the number of rows or columns you want the cell to stretch across and choose OK. The ultimate effect of this can be very similar to merging or splitting cells. The difference is that when you span a cell, the cells it spans across are pushed down or sideways, as if you had inserted cells. You can delete these extra cells, of course. In the example in Figure 8.16, the large center cell was produced by setting its span at 2 rows and 2 columns. The cells that were pushed out to the right and downward by this were then deleted.

FIG. 8.16

Using cell spanning lets you customize your table's appearance.

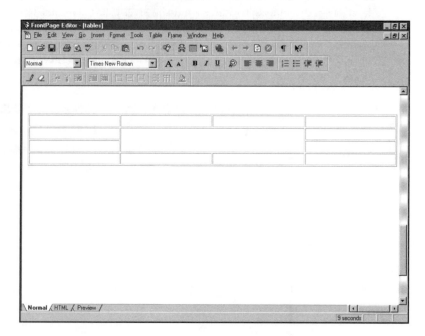

Adding Colors and Backgrounds to Tables and Cells

Both the Table Properties dialog box and the Cell Properties dialog box have sections for you to specify background colors, images, and border colors (unless the page has a theme). Because these sections are identical in both cases, they are considered together.

Figure 8.17 shows the Table Properties dialog box with the Color list for the Background Color displayed. This list is identical to those used elsewhere in FrontPage Editor, including the ability to mix a custom color, and also appears when you want to set the border color parameters in the Custom Colors sections of these two dialog boxes.

The major difference is that using the Table Properties dialog box sets the colors for the entire selected table, while using the Cell Properties dialog box sets the colors for the selected cell only.

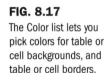

FIG. 8.17
The Color list lets you pick colors for table or cell backgrounds, and table or cell borders.

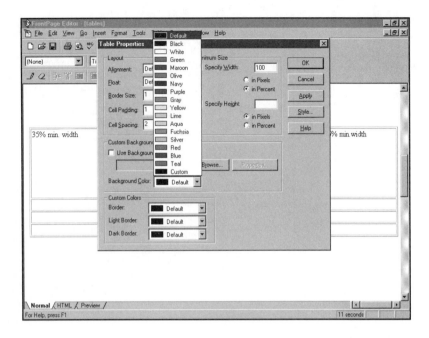

Entire tables or selected cells can have a background image, which you choose by marking the Use Background Image check box and inputting the file name of the desired image in the text box. The procedure is identical to the one you learned in Chapter 6, "Enhancing Pages with Themes, Graphics, and Multimedia."

Finally, a word about design: don't make the backgrounds of your tables too busy or their colors garish and distracting. The table is a means to an end, not an end in itself—the information it organizes is the most important thing.

N O T E   Background colors or images for tables will cover up any background color or image for the page that normally would appear behind the table. ■

Inserting Page Elements into a Table

To add text to a table, click in the cell and start typing. All of FrontPage Editor's text formatting tools are at your disposal.

As for images, links, and multimedia components, you add these to a table cell by clicking in the cell and continuing as if the new element were standing by itself on the page. The fact that it's in a table makes no difference at all. Again, don't make your table too busy.

As discussed at the beginning of this chapter, tables are a powerful organizational tool. In Figure 8.18, you can see a page that puts a series of elaborately equipped tables to good use.

FIG. 8.18

The tables on this page put a lot of information into well organized spaces.

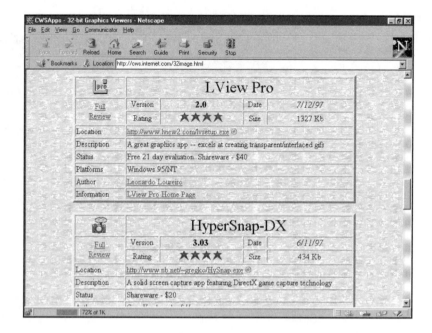

Included in each table are graphics, a graphical hyperlink in the top-left corner, text hyperlinks, and variously sized cells and columns. The author has also used different fonts to suggest different types of information, but hasn't gone overboard with them. Not used are table cell colors or backgrounds, which in this case is good—there's a lot of information here, and adding such decorative elements (because the page already has a background image) would have been too much.

From Here...

In this chapter, you explored the way FrontPage 98 helps you arrange and present your information by using tables. With these, and with everything else you've covered so far, you can build a well organized, efficient, and visually attractive Web site. But you aren't finished yet.

- Chapter 9, "Enhancing Web Sites with FrontPage Frames," is where you find out about designing a framed site, about using frames with links and images, and how to create ready-made framed environments with frame templates.

- Chapter 10, "Creating Pages with FrontPage Editor Templates," shows you how you can use these organizational and presentation tools to generate real-world documents based on a wide selection of preset layouts.

- Chapter 11, "Using FrontPage Components, Forms, and Interactive Page Templates," shows you how to use that other great organizational tool, the fill-in form.

Enhancing Web Sites with FrontPage Frames

Frames were originally developed by Netscape, and their use in Web sites is expanding steadily. Simply put, *framing* is a method of placing two or more windows on the screen and giving the viewer individual control of none, some, or all of them. Frames can even contain other frames, and the page within a frame can reference other pages independently of the rest of the display. This gives a Web designer great flexibility in choosing how to organize and present information, whether it's text, graphics, or active content.

To see what this means, look at the example in Figure 9.1. The narrow, black fixed frame at the top of the screen contains navigation controls and the leftmost frame contains a scrollable menu. The pages referenced by the menu items appear in the largest frame. ■

Strategies for frame design

Although frames are potentially very useful to your pages, poorly constructed frame design can turn users away faster than a 500K graphic on your main page.

Using FrontPage 98's WYSIWYG frames

This easy-to-use feature detours you around any need to use HTML for your frames.

Linking among frames

Interframe linking demands a well organized site because a badly designed one is confusing to set up and very difficult to maintain.

Using Frames with images and imagemaps

These graphical links are just as easy to make as text links, and can provide useful visual aids to navigation.

Using the FrontPage frame templates

Templates are a fast and efficient way to create framed sites.

FIG. 9.1

Frames allow different pages to appear and behave independently in the browser screen.

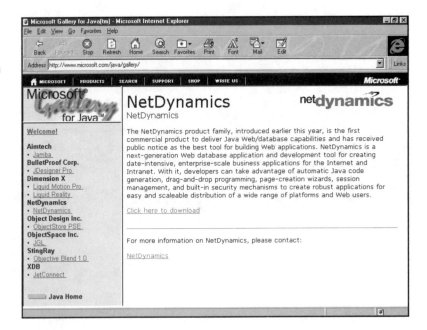

Why Use Frames?

You should use frames if you want your user's browser window to display both static and dynamic elements. A *static element* remains visible no matter what your user does; the *dynamic element* changes according to their input. In Figure 9.1, the menu frame is static and the scrollable window is dynamic.

One great advantage of the frame environment is the way it can keep your visitor oriented. The static part keeps a map of the site (or part of it) in front of him, and the dynamic elements show different parts of the site, on command. So the user doesn't have to scroll up or down, for example, to find the hyperlink that returns him to the home page or to another major section of the site. The links are always there, right in front of him. You can also present an image within one frame and give your visitor several screens' worth of information about it in an adjacent frame. While they scroll within the information frame, the image remains visible at all times. The only way to do this without frames would be to repeat the image for each screen of data, which is obviously a waste of space, time, and energy.

Back in 1995/1996, when many people used nonframe browsers, it was important to provide nonframed pages to meet their needs. The use of frame-supporting browsers is now so widespread, however, that this is much less of a consideration. Still, many people do not like frames—especially if their viewing area is limited to a 14" display. This may also change, but until it does, you should be aware of these differences of opinion when you're creating a framed environment. At the very least, don't cram a lot of frames into the same screen.

Designing for the Framed Environment

As with tables, handmade frame creation with HTML coding is a picky business. The introduction of a WYSIWYG frameset creation environment in FrontPage 98 makes setting up and managing frames immeasurably easier. This environment works with *framesets*, which is what FrontPage Editor calls several frames that appear together in a browser display. You don't actually insert framesets into a page; a frameset acts like a scaffolding to relate pages to each other.

Part
II
Ch
9

Even before you start creating a frameset, though, you need to think about how (or even if) you're going to use the frame environment. Keep the following in mind:

- Use frames only if you need them, not just because they're decorative (and they're only decorative for people who have browsers with frame support).

- Don't crowd a page with frames. This obviously reduces their sizes. In particular, a viewer shouldn't have to scroll to see an entire image; the practical maximum is three frames.

- Use static frames sparingly. Use them for navigational tools, table of contents information, or for site identification such as a logo. Static frames are like the instrument panel of a car, which drivers indeed need to refer to—but drivers spend most of their time looking through windshields.

- Commit most of the screen area to dynamic frames where information can be retrieved and displayed.

- Don't develop your frame layout for monitors with screens bigger than 15". Most people—and many businesses—don't use the larger screens yet, especially in the consumer market. Even a 15" monitor has about 20% more viewing area than a 14". In fact, you'd be wise to assume your visitor has a 14" monitor running at 800×600 resolution in 256 colors at best, and plan accordingly.

Using the WYSIWYG Frame Environment

In this next sequence, you'll create a frameset with two frames and populate it. To best illustrate WYSIWYG frameset behavior with this frameset, you'll need two or more pages, so create any you require, give them titles and file names, and save them.

Begin by choosing File, New to open the New dialog box and click the Frames tab to display the available frame templates (see Figure 9.2). You'll get a concrete example of how the procedure works by working through setting up a specific frameset.

Now do these steps:

1. Select the Header frameset which produces an upper frame whose links change the page displayed in the lower frame. After selecting, choose OK. The WYSIWYG frame environment appears (see Figure 9.3).

2. You can insert an existing page into any frame, but for purposes of illustration, you'll create a new one for the upper frame. In the upper frame, click the New Page button and

a new, blank page appears there. You'll use this page for the hyperlinks that control the display in the lower frame.

FIG. 9.2

FrontPage 98 gives you a selection of pre-defined framesets.

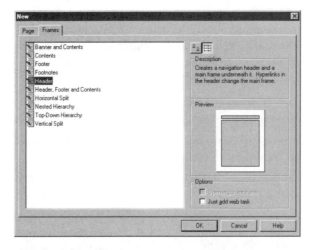

FIG. 9.3

The WYSIWYG frame environment lets you lay out your frames visually so you can see how the design and proportions look.

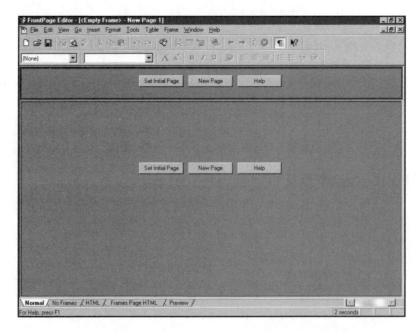

3. In the lower frame, click the Set Initial Page button. This opens the Create Hyperlink dialog box. From the dialog box list box, select an existing page and click OK. This existing page opens in the lower window. (If you look in the FrontPage Editor title bar at this point, you see that there are two page titles given: the first is that of the active page, the second is the title of the frameset file itself.)

4. Click in the upper frame. Insert a hyperlink to the page that is currently appearing in the lower window. While you are still in the upper frame, insert a second hyperlink to a different page.

5. Use File, Save All to save the frameset file and the new or changed pages. You'll be asked to supply names for any new files. You can tell the frameset page file (it's not strictly a page, but more of a scaffolding) because its default file name is FRAMESET.HTM.

Test the frameset by using the Preview In Browser command. It should resemble the one in Figure 9.4. Clicking the links in the upper frame should change the pages in the lower frame.

Part

II

Ch

9

FIG. 9.4

The results of creating a two-frame frameset with a navigation pane in the upper frame.

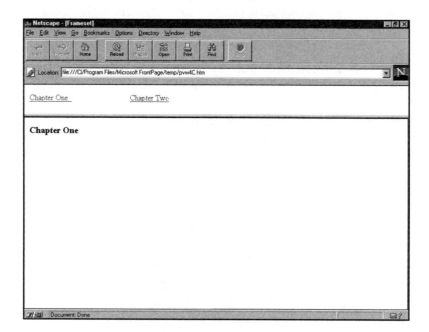

Editing a Frameset

You can adjust the appearance of the frameset during the previous procedure or in a later editing session. To edit the frameset later, open the frameset file in FrontPage Editor and it appears with its initial pages displayed.

N O T E   If you used the New Page button to create a new page within a frame, that frame does not contain the new page when you next open the frameset—what you see is the Set Initial Page, New Page, and Help buttons. Just use the Set Initial Page button to make that new page into the initial page, save the frameset, and from then on the correct initial page appears in the frame.

Next is a listing of the other frame-handling tools available directly from the WYSIWYG frame environment.

- To work on a page appearing in a frame, click that page. You know which page is active by the thick dark line around its frame.

- To adjust the proportions of the frames, drag their boundaries.

- To view the HTML of the frameset file itself, click the Frames Page HTML tab at the bottom of the editor workspace while you're working on the frameset.

- To view the HTML of a page within a frame, click it and then click the HTML tab.

- To edit the message that appears in a browser that does not support frames, click the No Frames tab. Edit the default warning message normally. This message gets saved with the frameset file, so you don't have to take any further action.

- To add frames to an existing frameset, you can split a frame into further rows or columns choose Frames.

- To establish your Web as a framed Web as soon as people access it, rename the frameset page with the file name DEFAULT.HTM.

Modifying a Frame of a Frameset

Just listed are the basic editing tools; however, there are two sets of properties of framesets that you might need to modify from time to time: those for the individual frames within a frameset, and those for the frameset itself.

Look at the individual frame properties by clicking in the frame whose properties you want to change. Choose Frame, Frame Properties to open the Frame Properties dialog box (see Figure 9.5).

FIG. 9.5

With the Frame Properties dialog box, you set specifications for features like scrolling and for the page that will be the frame's initial page.

In this dialog box, you can:

- Specify the frame Name. This is NOT the name of the page that is contained in the frame, but the label of the frame itself, and is used to identify the individual frame of the frameset. You use this name in various FrontPage dialog boxes (such as the Create Hyperlink dialog box) to specify the *target frame* in which a page should appear. Changing these target frames can be a confusing process, and is treated at length later in this chapter.

- Specify the frame size as *fixed* (that means the user can't resize it by dragging the frame border) by clearing the Resizable in Browser check box. To allow users to resize the frame, mark the check box.

- Specify scrollbar behavior by choosing If Needed, Never, or Always from the Show Scrollbars drop-down list.

- Specify frame width or height (if the selected frame belongs to a column or row of frames), as relative to that of other frames, as a percentage of the size of the window, or as a set number of pixels. Click the drop-down list boxes in the Frame Size section to choose among Relative, Percent, or Pixels.

- Adjust the Margin Width and Margin Height, which control the separation of the frames in a browser.

- Specify the URL of the initial page that is to be contained in the frame by typing the page URL into the Initial Page text box (or use the Browse button to locate and identify the page).

Modifying Frameset Properties

To do this, either choose Frame, Frames Page Properties, or click the Frames Page button in the Frame Properties dialog box. Either way, you get the Page Properties dialog box with one extra sheet because this is a frameset page (see Figure 9.6).

FIG. 9.6
The Frame sheet lets you change just two values: spacing and borders.

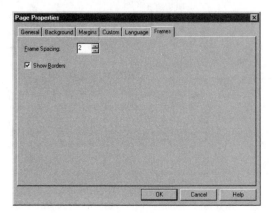

Here you can specify whether the frames have borders (clear the Show Borders check box to remove them) and set the frame spacing in pixels. Frame spacing determines the amount of padding to display between frames when they are viewed in a browser.

Creating Custom Frameset Layouts

The basics of this are quite simple, but can get confusing when you start customizing the target frames for the pages that show up in the frameset. Because of this, a concrete example will be used to illustrate (among other things) the use of *static frames*, those that don't get written over by other frames, so that you can use them to hold navigation aids.

There will be one frameset, which you'll eventually call FRAMESET.HTM, and five pages, one of which will be a navigation page containing links and will reside in the static frame; the others will be content pages. In the example, the page file names and their titles are:

- NAVIG.HTM   Contents
- CHAP01.HTM   Chapter One
- CHAP02.HTM   Chapter Two
- NOTES.HTM   Notes
- BIBLIO.HTM   Bibliography

Begin by choosing File, New and switching to the Frames sheet. Select the Contents template and choose OK. You now have a page that looks like the one in Figure 9.7.

FIG. 9.7

The best way to create a custom frameset is to start with a template similar to the one you want.

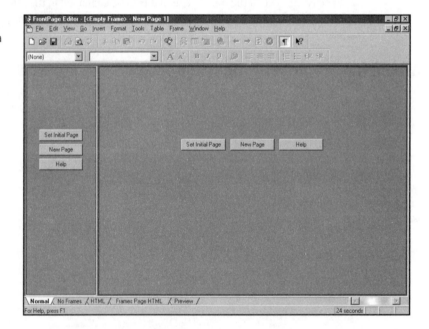

This frameset is going to be modified so that the links in the content frame (on the left) will change the page in an upper right frame, and the links in the upper right frame will change the page in a lower right frame.

Before going on, right-click in the left frame and choose Frame Properties from the shortcut menu. You see from the Frame Properties dialog box that this frame's name is CONTENTS. Do the same in the right frame and observe that its frame name is MAIN.

Now, to make the two, right frames, click in the existing single right frame to select it and choose Frame, Split Frame. The Split Frame dialog box appears (see Figure 9.8).

FIG. 9.8
You can change the
frameset layout with the
Split Frame dialog box.

N O T E You can also delete a frame. Click in it to select it and choose F<u>r</u>ame, <u>D</u>elete Frame.

You want a horizontal split, so mark the Split into <u>R</u>ows option button and choose OK. You now
have two right frames that are stacked one above the other. Check the frame names of your
new right-hand frames (right-click and choose Page Properties, as you just did) and you see
that the upper is still named MAIN, but the lower is MAIN1. You can, of course, change these
names, but for convenience, leave them at their default values.

Now, in the left frame, click Set Initial Page. The Create Hyperlink dialog box appears. Select
NAVIG.HTM and choose OK.

Similarly, in the top-right frame, click Set Initial Page and make the initial page CHAP01.HTM.
Use the same method in the lower-right frame to make the initial page NOTES.HTM.

In the left window, create a link to CHAP01.HTM. While the Create Hyperlink dialog box is
open, look at the text box labeled <u>T</u>arget Frame. The value in this box is Page Default(main).
The main is the important piece of information—it tells you that the page is going to appear in
the MAIN frame, which is the top-right frame. This target frame is also labeled a default because MAIN is the Default Target Frame property for this page.

N O T E It's necessary to distinguish between a *Target Frame*, which is an attribute of a link and is
specified in the hyperlink dialog box, and the *Default Target Frame*, which is a Page
Property and specifies the frame where the links in that page display their destinations. In effect,
setting the Default Target Frame of a page also sets the Target Frame of any hyperlink created on that
page.

If you wanted CHAP01.HTM to appear in the lower-right frame, you'd change this Target
Frame value to MAIN1. You'll examine how to do this in a minute, but for the moment, leave
the value as it is. Complete the Chapter One link and create a hyperlink to CHAP02.HTM, still
using the left frame.

Now click in the top-right frame. Create some text there to be a hyperlink to BIBLIO.HTM,
select the text and choose <u>E</u>dit, Hyperlin<u>k</u>. Select BIBLIO.HTM in the list box. Notice the
Target frame text box. It reads Page Default(none). This none means the link's destination
page will appear in the same frame as the page that owns the link—in other words,
BIBLIO.HTM replaces CHAP01.HTM in the upper-right frame.

Assume that you don't want this to happen—you want to be able to see both CHAP01.HTM
and BIBLIO.HTM at the same time. In other words, you want the upper-right frame to be a
static frame with respect to the lower-right frame so that the pages opened by links on the

upper-right frame don't overwrite what's already there. To achieve this, click the pencil icon button at the right of the Target Frame text box. The Target Frame dialog box appears (see Figure 9.9).

N O T E Of course, the upper-right frame is not a static frame with respect to the Contents (left) frame because the Contents frame's links do change the pages that appear in the upper-right frame. The Contents frame, though, is a true static frame—nothing alters it. To make a fully static frame, just be sure that it is not the target frame of any hyperlink in the current Web. ▓

FIG. 9.9

The Target Frame dialog box makes selecting a target frame as easy as clicking in it.

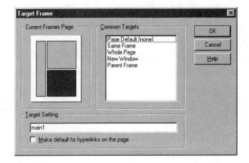

To specify where the destination page of the link should appear, click the desired frame in the small preview display, as Figure 9.9 shows for this example.

 T I P Marking the check box labeled Make Default for Hyperlinks on the Page specifies that any destination pages linked from the active page appear in the selected frame.

In the upper-right frame, place a link to the NOTES.HTM page, and change the target frame of NOTES.HTM to MAIN1 as well. To complete the example, open CHAP02.HTM and add to it the same links you added to CHAP01.HTM.

Choose Save All and you'll be asked for a file name and Page Title for the frameset file. In the example, it was christened (not very originally) FRAMES.HTM and Frameset.

The completed frame layout resembles that in Figure 9.10. The Contents frame links will change the page in the upper-right frame, and the links in the upper-right frame will change the page in the lower-right frame.

Creating a Custom Frameset Template

If the frame layout is one you use often, you may want to save the frameset file as a template. For the procedures for creating templates, see the section "Creating Custom Templates" in Chapter 10, "Creating Pages with FrontPage Editor Templates." The procedure is the same for both page templates and frameset templates. Note that only the frameset file is saved as the template, even if you have inserted Initial Pages into it.

FIG. 9.10
A three-frame display with navigation links in two of the frames.

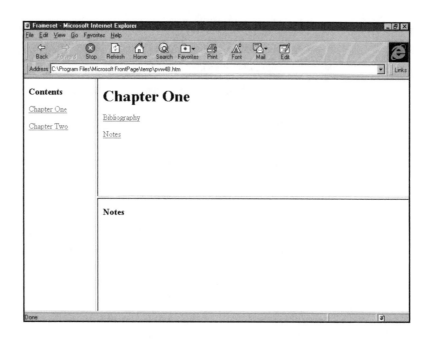

Part
II

Ch
9

Special Target Frames

There are also four special target types you can use. Typing one of these into the Target Frame box of the Create or Edit Hyperlink dialog boxes will have the following effects:

■ **New Window** The page the link points to loads into a new browser window. HTML for this target is _blank.

■ **Same Frame** The page the link points to overwrites the page where the calling link resides, but the frame layout in the browser window is not disturbed. HTML for this target is _self. This is the default.

■ **Parent Frame** The page the link points to overwrites the page where the calling link resides. The browser window is reset. HTML for this target is _parent.

■ **Whole Window** The page the link points to loads into the whole window of the browser, replacing the frameset. HTML for this target is _top.

> **CAUTION**
> If your link loads the destination page into the same frame as the origin page, it's extremely important to avoid a dead end at the destination. If users can't find a way out of a frame, its contents will sit there until they move to another site entirely. It tells them that you designed your site carelessly. Make sure you add a link to such a page, to keep it from becoming a dead end.

Incorporating New and Existing Pages into a Frameset

This is where the Default Target Frame specification, which you'll find in the Page Properties dialog box for any page, becomes especially important.

There are two likely situations. One is the case where you have a frameset, and you want to create new pages for it. The best way to do this is to open the frameset file where the page is going to appear and then:

1. Select any frame—it doesn't matter which one—and choose File, New. In the New dialog box, make sure you mark the Open in Current Frame check box. Select the page template you want and choose OK. The new page opens in the selected frame.

2. Right-click the page to get the shortcut menu and choose Page properties. The Page Properties dialog box appears.

3. Click the button at the right of the Default Target Frame text box and the Target Frame dialog box appears (see Figure 9.9). Just as you did in the procedure, "Creating Custom Frameset Layouts," select the frame you want for the page's default target frame and choose OK. When you return to the Page Properties dialog box, the frame name appears in the Default Target frame text box.

4. Choose OK again. Links created on this page now have the specified frame as their default target.

If you're wondering why you went to the trouble of opening the frameset and creating the page in that, the answer is that if you don't do it that way, you don't get the handy Target Frame dialog box that shows the small graphic of the frame layout. You get the dialog box without the graphic and have to type the frame name into the Target Setting text box, which is prone to errors.

The other situation in which you need to set the Default Target frame of a page is when you have some pages that never were part of the framed environment, and you want to include them in it, with their own Default Target Frames.

To achieve this, open the frameset, select any frame, and choose File, Open. The Open dialog box has the Open in Current Frame check box, just as the New dialog box did. Check the box on and choose OK and the page opens in the frame. Now follow steps 2 through 4.

CAUTION

If you get the Default Target Frame name wrong in the Page Properties dialog box, FrontPage won't warn you. You'll learn about your mistake when testing. When you click such a faulty link in the source page, you get the destination page showing up full page in a new browser window. There's no harm done, however, except to your pride. Go back and edit the page properties to fix the problem.

More About Static Frames

Now that you've had a look at Default Target frames, you can elaborate a little further on static frames. These are important entities because you often have frames on a page (navigation areas are a good example) that must not be changed.

To create a static frame (one whose content is not changed by the content of any other frame), specify a Default Target Frame for the page that displays in the static frame. Once you've done this, the content of the static frame is fixed (see the next Caution). Only the display in the target frame changes as links are clicked.

> **N O T E** This can be worded as a general principle: If a Default Target Frame is specified for a page, every link on that page displays its destination in the target frame only. ■

> **CAUTION**
>
> You can overwrite a static frame's content in two ways. If another page's Default Target Frame specifies the static frame, that will do it—so will specifying the static frame as the target frame of a hyperlink. Of course, you may encounter situations where you actually do want to overwrite the content of the static frame.

Using Target Frames and Hyperlinks in the Current Web

So far, you've concentrated on using the Default Target Frame of a page to determine where its linked pages show up, but you can also specify the display frame of a page by creating or editing the link that calls it. To do this, open the page in the frameset and select some text or an image for the link and choose Edit, Hyperlink. (Or set up to edit an existing link; the procedure is identical for both new and existing links.)

Assuming you're working with the current Web, select the destination page. Click the button at the right of the Target Frame text box to open the Target Frame dialog box (see Figure 9.9). Select the target frame for the link, choose OK, and OK again to return to the FrontPage Editor workspace. The hyperlink now displays the destination page in the specified frame, overriding the Default Target Frame of the page where the hyperlink resides.

> **N O T E** You may be wondering why you have two ways of deciding what frame a destination page displays in. After all, if you can specify the target frame for each link, why do you need the Default Target Frame option in the Page Properties dialog box? Convenience is the answer. This Page Properties option enables you to specify the target frames for all links on that page so you don't have to set them individually. Because it's merely a default, you override it when you specify the target frame for a particular link. ■

Using Target Frames and Text Links with World Wide Web URLs

This task is the same as setting up a target frame for the current Web, just as you did, except that you use the techniques from Chapter 5, "Developing the Basic Page: Text, Lists, and

Hyperlinks," to set up the link to the remote site. The Web site's page shows up in the frame you specify. Remember, however, that it has less room for display and it may look cramped.

Using Target Frames and Bookmarks

Bookmarks and frames don't really have much to do with each other, although you can specify both when creating or editing a link. The destination page simply scrolls to the bookmark when it displays in the named frame.

Coping with Browsers that Don't Support Frames

This situation rapidly is becoming less common, but you may still need to consider it—if for no other reason than that a lot of people haven't gotten used to frames, and don't like them. The best thing to do (apart from not using frames) is to supply an alternative area of your Web that works properly without frames. When your visitor links to the framed part of your Web, he should be notified that there is a nonframe alternative so that he has the choice of using it.

Should I Set Up My Home Page as a Frameset?

You should not set up your home page as a frameset unless you're determined to force people with frame-capable browsers to view frames from the moment they reach your home page. If this is what you really want, you can set up a framed home page by creating an empty Web and then creating a frameset for it. Give this frameset the file name DEFAULT.HTM, and that's your framed home page.

Using Target Frames with Images and Imagemaps

Setting up image-based links to use target frames is very similar to the procedure for establishing text links. Choose Edit, Hyperlink and use the hyperlink dialog box to choose the frame name for the Target Frame box.

▶ **See** Chapter 5, "Developing the Basic Page: Text, Lists, and Hyperlinks," **p. 71**.

▶ **See** Chapter 6, "Enhancing Pages with Themes, Graphics, and Multimedia," **p. 123**.

Likewise, drawing a *hotspot* (the portion of an image that acts as the link) on an image brings up the Create Hyperlink dialog box, and you use the dialog box to enter the target frame name in the Target Frame box.

Using Image Properties with Frames

If you open the Image Properties dialog box for an image, you find a Default Hyperlink section at the bottom. Use its Location box (with the Browse button, if appropriate) to set a default destination for the image's hyperlink. Use the Target Frame box to specify the frame where the destination page will appear (see Figure 9.11).

N O T E   Are you wondering why you'd use Image Properties to set a default destination and target frame for an image's hyperlink, when you can get the same result by specifying both when you establish a link? The answer: You'd do this when the image has hotspots, to set a default if the user clicks an area not covered by the hotspot. ■

FIG. 9.11
The Default Hyperlink area is where you specify the Location and Target Frame of an image's link.

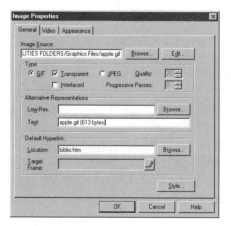

Putting Forms into Frames

You can instruct a form to send its results to a frame. You do this with the Form Properties dialog box, where you type the name of the target frame into the Target Frame box and click OK.

Floating Frames

Although FrontPage Editor doesn't support it, there is an alternate way to create compound documents: You can place frames in your HTML document by using the IFRAME element. Called *floating frames*, this design technique allows you to insert HTML documents into your document in the same way you insert images by using the IMG element. This means you can use the ALIGN= attribute just as you do with IMG to align the frame with the surrounding text. The following example aligns a frame at the left margin and wraps subsequent text around the right side of the frame:

```
<IFRAME SRC="xx.htm" ALIGN=LEFT>
</IFRAME> Here's some text to the right of a frame.
<BR CLEAR=LEFT>Here's some text beneath the frame.
```

The IFRAME syntax may not be compatible with all browsers, specifically with the Netscape browser. In that case, you can use a FRAME element within the IFRAME tags to provide an alternative presentation. For example:

```
<IFRAME SRC="xx.htm" ALIGN=LEFT>FRAME SRC="xx.htm"
<IFRAME>
```

In the previous example, the text of xx.htm will display in a floating frame in either an IFRAME or nonIFRAME-compatible browser. Remember that you set the attributes of IFRAME and FRAME independently. For example, if you want to specify position or size, you include those attributes in both the IFRAME tag and the FRAME tag.

Deleting a Frameset

You can delete a frameset with FrontPage Explorer. The frameset file, with an HTM extension, appears in the Explorer display just as a page would; you simply select it and choose Edit, Delete. However, if you delete a frameset, you must also remove all frame target entries in Page Properties and in links that referenced the deleted frameset. If you don't, browsers become confused about where they're supposed to be looking and give unpredictable results.

Using FrontPage's Frame Templates

FrontPage Editor supplies 10 templates to help you create different framesets.

- A bannered, two-column document in which the links in the banner change the left (contents) frame.
- A Table of Contents with a left frame that changes the frame on the right.
- A Footer document; links on the footer change the main frame.
- A document with footnotes; links in the main frame change the footnotes.
- A Header document where links in the header change the main frame.
- A Header, Footer, and Contents document where header and footer links change the man frame.
- A horizontal split with independent top and bottom frames.
- A nested, three-level hierarchy.
- A top-down, three-level hierarchy.
- A vertical split with independent left and right frames.

Creating your own custom framesets is so easy that you may prefer that approach if you use frames to any extent. Take a look at the templates, because they can be very useful.

Using the Banner and Contents Template

Use File, New to create a frameset from this template. Assuming you create and save a page for each frame, you end up with four new files: the frameset file itself and three ordinary pages—one to populate the banner frame, one for the contents frame, and one that will appear in the main (right lower) frame and change according to the links in the contents frame.

In a real site, naturally, there would be many different pages appearing in the main frame. To put the frameset into service, use FrontPage Editor to add page elements to the banner page and the contents page, and create as many main pages as you need. Figure 9.12 shows an example of how the results look in a browser.

Using the Contents Template

This is actually a simpler version of the template discussed earlier. The banner frame has been removed, but the links in the left frame still change the pages that appear in the right frame.

FIG. 9.12

Your visitors can use the left Table of Contents frame to see other pages without losing the Table of Contents itself.

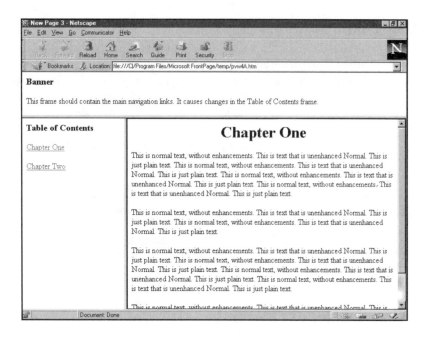

Part

II

Ch

9

Using the Footer Template

The display produced by this template looks like the one in Figure 9.13. The links in the footer frame change the content of, the large main frame.

FIG. 9.13

Use the Footer template to put navigational controls at the bottom of the browser display.

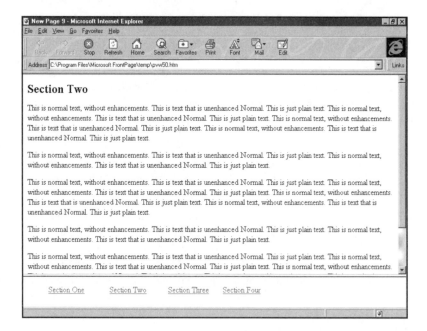

Using the Footnotes Template

This is the same as the Footer template, but the links go in the opposite direction. Clicking the footnoted text in the upper frame makes the footnote appear in the scrolling lower frame. The virtue of this for your visitor is that it's much more convenient than flipping back and forth through a single page—or linking to another full screen page—every time he wants to read a footnote. The viewer just clicks a footnote entry in the main document and the note appears at the bottom of the screen. To implement this application, put all the footnotes on one page, bookmark each one, and link to the bookmarks from the appropriate places in the main document.

N O T E As you know, the traditional footnote indicator is a superscript number. You can get these by going to FrontPage Editor's Font dialog box, choosing the Special Styles sheet, and using the Vertical Position box. However, a footnote superscript in a printed document is really just a link to the bottom of the page. Because the reader can already see a Web link, do you really need superscripts in a Web page to indicate a footnote? Probably not. Moreover, using superscripts in FrontPage Editor makes line spacing slightly uneven. ▪

Using the Header Template

This was discussed earlier in this chapter.

Using the Header, Footer, and Table of Contents Template

This is the most elaborate in appearance of the templates, but is merely built on the simpler ones. It gives you static frames at the top and bottom of the page, and is a good starting point for a complex, framed environment that requires extensive navigational tools. For example, one static frame could be a site identification area and the other could be the navigation control panel. Your imagination can certainly fill in other possibilities.

Two more frames lie between these two static areas: The left might be a Table of Contents, and the right would usually be the main data display area. Again, you can use your imagination to work out other uses for the arrangement.

This is a more complex frameset than you've looked at so far. The links in the upper static frame make their destination pages appear in the left frame (the TOC frame) and the links in the TOC frame and in the bottom frame make their destination pages appear in the right frame (the main frame). Links in the main frame—unless you set them otherwise—make their targets replace the current page in that frame.

You can change all this, as you know. For example, you can reset the page properties of the page in the top static frame to make its target document appear in the bottom frame (but then the bottom frame wouldn't be static) and so on. With a frameset as potentially complicated as this one, you'd need to do some careful page and data organization. You would also need even more careful testing if you decided to modify the targets of the various frames.

Using the Top-Down Hierarchy Template

Use the top-down hierarchy template for all or part of a site whose page and data organization is, as the name suggests, hierarchical in nature.

The frameset establishes the hierarchy as follows:

- The default target of the top frame is the middle frame.
- The default target of the middle frame is the bottom frame.
- The bottom frame's default target is itself.

So you'd use this scheme to go from broad categories to more precisely distinguished ones, to fine detail. Depending on how much information you had for each entry, you would use either full pages or bookmark entries within pages. An example of a hierarchical information structure is shown in Figure 9.14.

Part

II

Ch

9

FIG. 9.14
A hierarchical frame structure gives a cascade effect—in this case, from general information to more specific to quite detailed.

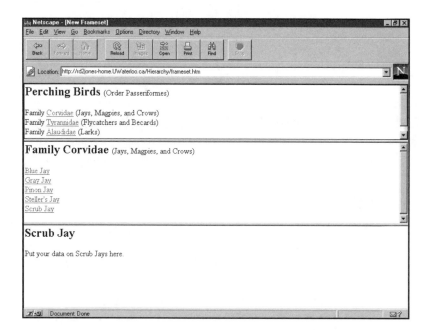

Using the Nested Hierarchy Template

The nested hierarchy template is similar in approach to the previous frameset, but the hierarchy works from left to top-right and then down.

In practice, the links in the left frame display their destination pages in the top-right frame; those in the top-right frame display their destination pages in the bottom-right frame. In Figure 9.15, you can see a nested version of the pages that appeared earlier in the top-down hierarchy. The visual characteristics of your page content (such as large or small images, number of images, quantity of text) influence which frame layout you choose.

FIG. 9.15
A nested hierarchy gives a different effect from a vertically organized heirarchy.

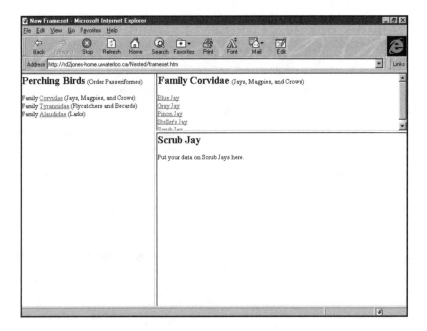

Using the Horizontal and Vertical Split Templates

These are identical except in their orientation. The two frames are independent of each other—the links in each frame simply overwrite the current contents of that frame.

From Here...

In this chapter, you learned the somewhat complicated craft of making and managing frames. Frames are still finding their way into the World Wide Web, of course, so everyone will be watching to see whether they fulfill their early promise of a more adaptable and flexible interface. Explore the following while you're waiting to find out:

- Chapter 10, "Creating Pages with FrontPage Editor Templates," which steps you through FrontPage 98's supplied templates. These templates speed up the creation of pages with preset formats for many different types of layouts.

- Chapter 11, "Using FrontPage Components, Forms, and Interactive Page Templates," which explains what FrontPage Components are and how to use them. You also learn about forms, and about the specialized templates that help you make your pages interactive.

Creating Pages with FrontPage Editor Templates

Content templates

FrontPage provides useful templates for bibliographies and FAQs.

Layout templates

This is where FrontPage templates really shine, giving you a wide selection of preset layouts—such as two-, three-, and four-column layouts, or layouts with sidebars and menu sections—that provide the basis of most of your layouts.

Custom templates

When you have a special page layout that you want to use over and over, create your own template. FrontPage Editor makes it a straightforward operation.

You've already found out from your travels on the World Wide Web that certain page types and formats are repeated from site to site. Some are content-oriented, such as guest books, bibliographies, glossaries, and the like, but many are layout-oriented. Whichever they are, these common content types and layout formats are the basis of FrontPage Editor's templates. Templates, being standardized arrangements of page content and/or layout elements, may be very useful tools to save you time and energy; you don't have to keep reinventing the wheel.

Each template provides a mockup for the layout and overall appearance of the completed page. You can either insert your own data into the appropriate areas; or, by using the methods you've already learned, customize the page as much or as little as you like. Although FrontPage's templates aren't suited to every Web project, they can help you get started and even get you past the dreaded Web author's block. Furthermore, you can create and save your own templates to speed up the process of developing a site that has many similar pages. ■

Using the Content-Oriented Templates

FrontPage Editor offers three basic, commonly used templates that are oriented to particular forms of information: bibliographies, frequently asked questions, and guest books.

N O T E The New dialog box lists more templates than are covered in this chapter. These other templates are oriented to the production and use of forms, and are discussed in Chapter 11, "Using Frontpage Components, Wizards, and Interactive Page Templates." ▪

Using the Bibliography Template

In the world of research, bibliographies are taken very seriously. They not only give credit to the sources you used, but also allow other people to refer easily to these sources. On the World Wide Web, bibliographies are fairly static documents and usually imitate their paper-based counterparts. A bibliography has a strict format (which one depends on the discipline), so FrontPage provides a template that conforms to a widely accepted style.

 FrontPage's bibliographic format represents only one of many permissible styles. You may need to refer to a reference manual such as the MLA (Modern Languages Association) Handbook for more complex formats.

You start any template-based page in the same way. Because of this, we'll go through it just once and not mention it again. Choose File, New and select the template you want from the list box; in this case, Bibliography. Choose OK and the template immediately opens in FrontPage Editor's workspace (see Figure 10.1). To help you further, the template includes instructions for use in the form of a Comment, which is the purple text. Comments don't show up in browsers, so you don't have to remove this one unless you want to.

If you've ever struggled with bibliographic formatting, you'll appreciate the help the template gives you. You have A, B, and C before LastName to indicate that all entries must appear in alphabetic format from A to Z down the page. From this point, replace the LastName, initial, title, city, state, and publisher with those that correspond to your particular references. Remember to retain the punctuation and italicization the template has set up for you.

With the formatting you also get bookmarks: ALastName, BLastName, and CLastName have the dotted underlines that signal these link targets. Once you link to them from the original document page, your reader can inspect your reference materials with hardly any effort.

When the page is complete, save it. Remember (and remember with all the templates) to use the Page Properties dialog box to give the page a meaningful title and make sure you change its file name to something other than the default.

You can see a real-world example of a bibliography in Figure 10.2.

FIG. 10.1
This bibliography template can be customized according to your particular needs.

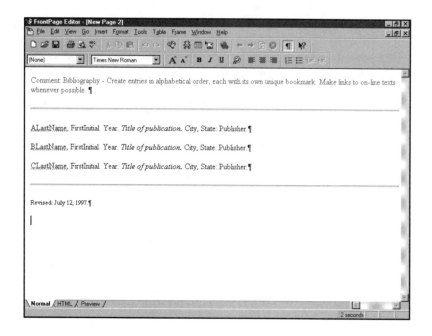

N O T E Although not all of the real-world examples in this chapter have been prepared with FrontPage, they show you design approaches that can easily be reproduced with FrontPage's editing tools.

FIG. 10.2
This formal bibliography refers you to the documents cited in the Web site (**http://www.newciv.org/ISSS_Primer/biblio.html**).

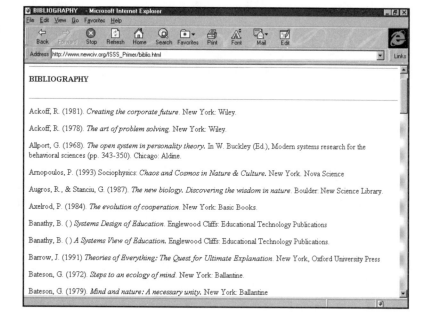

Part
II

Ch
10

The author compiling this bibliography did not use hyperlinks to other documents because these were exclusively print references. However, hyperlinking in bibliographies will become more common as more and more resources are put online. Notice that the citation style closely follows that of the FrontPage Editor template.

Creating a Frequently Asked Questions (FAQ) Page

With so many people browsing through the tangles of the World Wide Web, the number of questions posed to Webmasters increases by the minute. FAQ lists target the most frequently repeated questions and provide a single, thorough answer. So many answers are needed that FAQ lists now accompany almost every newsgroup and mailing list on the Net and the Web. To help you set up one of your own, FrontPage offers you a template. Open it to get the screen shown in Figure 10.3.

FIG. 10.3
With the FAQ template, you get a Table of Contents menu ready for customization.

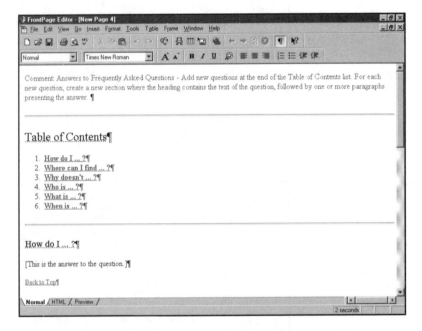

The FAQ template provides users with an introductory area from which they can access all major sections of the FAQ page. The Table of Contents hyperlinks work like the This Month, Last Month, and Previous Month divisions in the Press Release Directory, giving readers suitable points of entry to information areas of the site.

If you plan on only a few questions and responses, the FrontPage Editor template is adequate. However, if your FAQ page is extensive, you should consider setting up separate pages for each class of question and linking to bookmarks in them. As usual, this is to enhance response speed.

You can see an example of a large FAQ site in Figure 10.4. It offers a header area from which you can access mirror sites in several languages, and from which you can download the FAQ answers in several file formats. The Contents entries are links to bookmarks farther down the page. These bookmarked areas, in turn, each have Tables of Contents, and each entry in these subtables is a link to a page where you find the answers to the question. These pages have further hyperlinks to places where you can get even more information on the subject.

FIG. 10.4
This site classifies questions into specialized areas for more efficient access to information (**http://www.boutell.com/faq/#intro**).

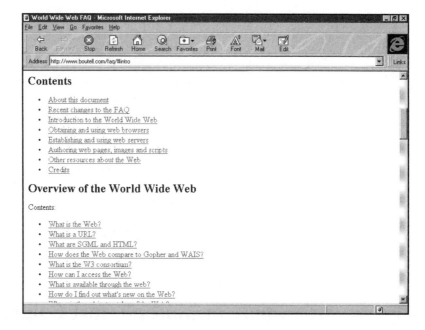

 TIP When wording the responses to your FAQs, remember that you may be addressing a newcomer to the Internet, or at least a newcomer to your site. Avoid highly technical answers that could confuse people, or worse, encourage more questions.

Using FrontPage Editor's Layout Templates

Over a dozen layout templates fall into groups. These are:

- Layouts with single or multiple text columns
- Layouts with single or multiple text columns with menus or sidebars
- Layouts with multiple staggered columns

The secret of all these layouts is that they are specified by tables. As you saw in Chapter 8, "Creating Tables," tables are a very efficient way of controlling the arrangement of a page. One principle to remember, when you're using table layouts, is that just because a table column, row, or cell exists, it doesn't need to have something in it. With cell borders turned off, as they are in all these layouts, such a cell just looks like blank space.

In the next few sections, you'll look at some representative samples of each group. As you select different templates, you can get an idea of what the page will look like by examining the Preview pane in the New dialog box.

Simple Layouts with Single or Multiple Text Columns

The layouts in this category are:

- **One Centered Column**   This is a three-column table with one row; you can adjust the width of the center column to whatever you like, and type your text in that.

- **One Column with Headings**   This is a more complex table. If you inspect it in FrontPage Editor, you'll see that the hanging indent of the heading text is created by making the heading text's cell occupy the whole width of the table, whereas the text under the heading is pushed to the right by an empty cell on the table's left margin. Notice how an empty, full width cell is inserted to establish the spacing between the main title and the first section title.

- **Two Even Columns**   Here, you have a reorganization of the One Centered Column layout. In the two-column arrangement, the main text area of the table has three columns, but the center column is squashed thin to provide the white space between the two text columns. Empty cells again are used to create spacing between the page title and the text area.

- **Three Even Columns**   This layout actually has five columns in the main text area; three are for text, and two are spacers. Empty rows again are used to control vertical spacing between page elements.

Layouts with Single or Multiple Text Columns with Menus or Sidebars

This group consists of:

- **One-Column Right Aligned**   This template has no title area; it simply presents three columns of varying widths. The left is the sidebar area, the middle is for text, and the right is white space.

- **One-Column Left Aligned**   This merely reverses the layout just described and adjusts the column widths by dragging the cell boundaries.

- **Two-Column Left Menu**   At the top is a title area. In the main informational area, the leftmost column is essentially a navigation section, suitable (for example) for a site map. The middle column is extremely narrow and serves as a spacer. The right column is for text, and anything else you want to put there, as the template graphic suggests.

- **Two-Column Right Menu**   This is essentially a mirror image of the previous layout, but has four main columns. The leftmost column serves to provide a margin of white space, the next is the main information column, the third is a spacer, and the fourth and rightmost column is the navigation section.

- **Three-Column Left Menu**   An elaboration of the Two-Column Left Menu, this layout has five columns. The leftmost column is the navigation section, followed by a spacer column and two main information columns again separated by a spacer column.

- **Three-Column Menu with Sidebar**   Another five-column table, this one reserves the leftmost column for the navigation section, puts the text into the wide center column, and reserves the rightmost column for a sidebar (populated by graphics, in the template). There are narrow spacer columns between the three main ones.

- **Three Columns with Right Sections**   This is five columns, too, but takes a different organizational approach. There is a title area, and under that is (leftmost) the main text area. A spacer column follows, then a column populated by (suggested) graphical hyperlinks. There's another spacer and a column for a text sidebar.

- **Four Columns Centered**   This actually does set up just four columns but reserves the center two for the main text area and gives the outside columns over to other purposes. In the basic template, the leftmost column could be a menu area with hyperlinks to other sections of the page, while the rightmost functions as a text or image sidebar.

Layouts with Multiple Staggered Columns

These provide visual variety by avoiding a strictly linear arrangement. The layouts in this group are:

- **Two-Column Staggered**   The table has four columns (the outside two providing white-space margins) and multiple rows. Alternating blank cells with filed ones in each column give the staggered effect.

- **Three-Column Staggered**   The table again has four columns, but does away with the margin columns. The leftmost two columns alternate page elements with white space by breaking the columns into rows. A spacer column separates these columns from the main text area, which has one row and thus isn't staggered.

- **Four Columns with Alternating Sidebar**   This might equally belong in the section on sidebar layouts, but it's here because it staggers the sidebar content. Here you have five columns, two of which are spacers. The two leftmost columns are broken into rows to provide a staggered-entry navigational section. The main central column is for text, and a suggested graphical sidebar occupies the rightmost column.

- **Four-Column Staggered**   This is about as elaborate as you should get, with six columns, two of which are spacers. The leftmost column has one row and is the navigational area. The rightmost column is a sidebar column. The two large center columns are broken into rows, allowing page elements to be inserted in a staggered arrangement.

What a Real-World Example Looks Like

Figure 10.4 shows how the Two Column Left Menu template might be applied as the basis of a layout in a real Web site. This page is from the Yale C/AIM Style Manual, an excellent guide to the principles of Web page design, which you can find at:

Part

II

Ch

10

http://info.med.yale.edu/caim/manual/

The page is shown in the FrontPage Editor workspace, so that the table boundaries are visible as dotted lines. This page's arrangement differs from the FrontPage Editor template only in the addition of two narrow spacer columns on the left of the table, and one spacer at its right. The leftmost spacer is margin white space, and the one next to it provides a hanging indent for the section title ("Page Design"). Next comes the main navigation area in the third column, a spacer, the main text area, and the right margin spacer. You can see from this how using tables is a very efficient way of organizing information on a page.

FIG. 10.5
The Yale C/AIM Style Manual uses tables to control the arrangement of page elements.

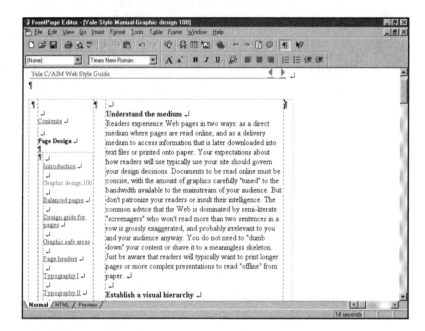

Creating Custom Templates

This is basically a page-editing task, although it may be a long and complicated one, depending on how elaborate your template is. Begin by loading the template that will serve as the basis for your own, or by creating an entirely customized page. Once the template page is completed to your satisfaction, take the following steps:

1. Use the Page Properties dialog box to give the template page an appropriate title.

2. Choose File, Save As. The Save As dialog box appears.

3. Choose the As Template button. The Save as Template dialog box appears (see Figure 10.6).

4. Edit the template's Page Title in the Title box if you wish and then type a file name into the Name box. You don't need to add an extension; FrontPage will add a TEM extension by default.

FIG. 10.6

You can save a page layout and design as a custom template.

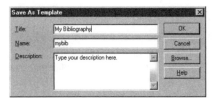

5. Type a description of the template into the <u>D</u>escription box. This appears in the New Page dialog box when you choose the template to create a page.

CAUTION

The Description is required, so if it isn't there, the OK button is grayed out. But, if you insist on not entering a description, go to Windows Explorer, open C:\Program Files\Microsoft FrontPage\Pages, open the appropriate template folder, and edit the .inf file.

6. Choose OK.

N O T E Because a template is merely an HTML file, any page can be a template. That means you can open any page from the Web, save it, and use it as such. ▪

Assuming a default installation, the custom template will be saved in the C:\Program Files\Microsoft FrontPage\Pages folder, within a subfolder bearing the name you assigned to the template. This name has a TEM extension. From now on, whenever you choose FrontPage Editor's <u>F</u>ile, <u>N</u>ew command, the custom template's name appears in the list box. If you want to remove the template, both from the system and from the New Page list box, use Windows Explorer to go to the Pages folder and delete the folder bearing that name.

Using the templates described in this chapter, you can also create hybrid templates. Open the templates you want to use and cut and paste the appropriate parts of them into the new template. Save the new template as a custom one, using the previous procedure. It's no more complex than cutting and pasting with a word processor.

Of course, you can add themes and Shared Borders to pages created with the FrontPage Editor templates, and you can also add these to custom templates. Use the procedures described in Chapter 7, "Using Dynamic HTML, Active Elements, Shared Borders, and Navigation Bars."

About the Pages Folder and Its Templates

All FrontPage Editor's templates are stored in their own folders in the C:\Program Files\Microsoft FrontPage\Pages folder. When you save an HTML page as a template, its unique folder is created with the name you assigned to the template. Unlike most folder names, this one has an extension, TEM (for template, obviously). It's this extension that makes the template accessible through the New command, and if it isn't there, the template won't appear in the New Page list box. Within the folder is the template file itself, which is simply an HTML file. The template folder name must match this

continues

Part

II

Ch

10

continued

file's name. Also in the folder is an INF file. This is a text file storing the name and description of the template, as well as the path names of any separate files (such as image files) required by the template file. There's no officially stated limit on the number of templates you can have. It's probably as large as your hard drive has room for.

From Here...

The page types you've explored in this chapter are useful, and you'll get a lot of mileage out of them. You can incorporate many of their features into *scratch* pages you begin with the Normal template. More sophisticated features are available that you can add to the pages of your site. To find out how, see the following chapters:

- Chapter 11, "Using FrontPage Components, Wizards, and Interactive Page Templates," discusses FrontPage Components and how they help make your Web interactive. You also learn about forms and using specialized templates to make your pages interactive.

- Chapter 12, "Using Style Sheets with Pages and Web Sites," shows you how to use this technique for developing and maintaining a consistent and easily modified look for an entire site or for a set of pages.

Using FrontPage Components, Forms, and Interactive Page Templates

FrontPage Components

These code modules (*component*) relieve you of the task of writing CGI scripts.

Designing FrontPage forms

Effective forms are organized, brief, and attractive.

Customizing forms

Customizing lets you use fields, text, and images of your choice.

Using templates

FrontPage templates provide a quick way to set up interactive pages.

This chapter discusses one of the most important facets of the World Wide Web: its interactivity. Without this, the Web would be similar to channel browsing on television—you'd get to look, but you'd never get to talk to anybody. On the Web, however, you can talk to your heart's content, and if you've got something useful or entertaining to say, you may find that a lot of people are listening to you. ■

Understanding FrontPage Components

These components (which were simply called WebBots in FrontPage 97) are a key part of FrontPage because they automate certain procedures that other Web authoring tools require you to hand code in HTML or in a scripting language such as Perl. FrontPage puts several different kinds of components at your disposal.

What exactly is a FrontPage Component? A component represents a chunk of programming that gets embedded into the HTML code of a page when you insert the component. Depending on the type of component, the program it represents executes when one of the following happens:

- The author saves the page.
- A visitor to the site accesses the page.
- The visitor clicks an interactive portion of the page, such as the Submit button for a form.

You use some components only with forms whereas others are what you might call "utility" component because they carry out useful, routine tasks that streamline page and site creation. A few are almost invisible because they execute automatically when you tell FrontPage Editor to do something but they don't show up in FrontPage Editor or a browser. An example of the last type is the imagemap component. If you inspect the HTML code for an imagemap, you'll see the word "bot" tucked away in it. That's as close as you ever get to this particular component.

You use the Insert menu to put most of the visible components into a page. You'll look at some of the simple utility Component first, just to get acquainted with component behavior.

Using the Comment Component

The *Comment Component* lets you insert text that appears only in FrontPage Editor. It works much like a comment or annotation in a word processor in that it's invisible to end users. In our context, that means that when someone views the page in their Web browser, they don't see the comment text.

The Comment Component is extremely useful, especially if different people are editing the same Web page and they need to leave explanations for each other. In fact, FrontPage Editor sometimes does exactly this, for your benefit. Several of its Wizards and templates have Comment Components embedded in them to prompt you about how to use features of the page.

To insert a Comment, use the following steps:

1. Position the cursor where you want the comment to appear.
2. Choose Insert, FrontPage Component. The Insert FrontPage Component dialog box appears (see Figure 11.1).
3. Select Comment from the list and choose OK. The Comment dialog box appears with a text box where you enter your comment (see Figure 11.2).

FIG. 11.1

Choose Comment from the list of FrontPage Components to open the Comment dialog box.

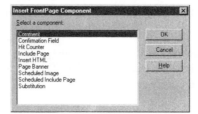

4. Enter the text you want for the comment and choose OK. The Comment dialog box closes, and the comment appears in the FrontPage Editor workspace in purple text (assuming that you are using the defaults).

FIG. 11.2

Use the Comment dialog box's text box to enter the text of the comment.

Now position the cursor on top of the comment text. The cursor becomes an arrow attached to a small, robot-like figure. This is the component cursor, and it appears whenever the ordinary cursor is in a region of the workspace where there's a component. Even if you can't see the component itself, the cursor appears to tell you it's there.

If you want to change the text of the comment, click it. This automatically selects the entire text block. Now choose Edit, FrontPage Component Properties, and the Comment dialog box appears. Make your changes and choose OK (or you can just double-click the component to edit it).

 You can also right-click while the component cursor is visible, and choose Comment Properties from the shortcut menu.

N O T E This chapter doesn't cover all the possible selections available from the Insert FrontPage Component dialog box. This is because some of these components (such as Insert HTML) are more suitably covered in other chapters. ■

Using the Include Page Component

The Include Page Component inserts the contents of a file into an existing page. You use this if you have several pages in a Web that need identical formatting for one or more elements, such as a standard heading at the top of each page. By using the Include Component, you can include this heading on as many pages as you like. Furthermore, if you need to change it (inserting a new logo, for example), you can make the change in only one file instead of editing every page where the element appears. Each page using the Include Component is updated automatically when the included file changes.

To use the Include Page, choose Insert, FrontPage Component. This opens the FrontPage Component dialog box. Select Include Page and choose OK. The Include Page Component Properties dialog box appears (see Figure 11.3).

FIG. 11.3
Specify the included file with the Include Page Component Properties dialog box.

Enter the URL of the file to be included, either by typing it or by selecting Browse to search the current Web. Notice that you can only enter page URLs, not image URLs.

Using the Scheduled Image Component

The Scheduled Image Component inserts a graphic file from the Web and displays it for a specified period of time. If the time period has not arrived or has elapsed, one of the following happens:

- A message such as Expired Scheduled Image appears in FrontPage Editor. When the page is viewed from a browser, nothing appears.
- A specified alternate image appears in both FrontPage Editor and Web browser.

The Scheduled Image is particularly useful for advertising or displays that only run for a period of time. With a Scheduled Image, you can, for example, insert a client's advertisement for a day or week and, after the time expires, replace it with a specified alternative.

To put a scheduled image into your page, select that component from the Insert FrontPage Component dialog box. The Scheduled Image Component Properties dialog box appears (see Figure 11.4).

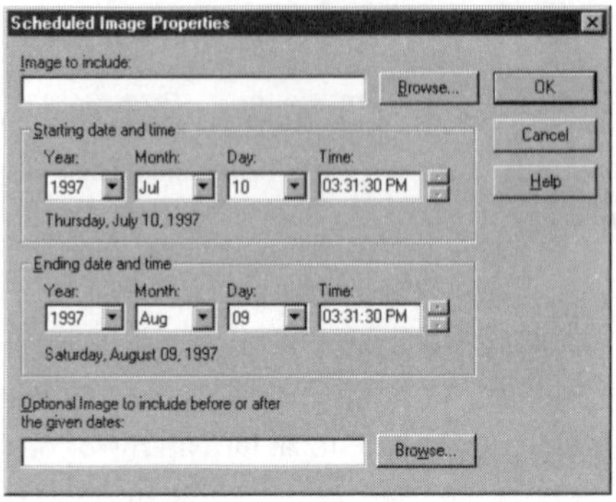

FIG. 11.4
Use the Scheduled Image Properties dialog box to specify how long an image will be included on your page.

Then use the following steps:

1. Use the <u>B</u>rowse button to select an image from the Web, or type in the URL of the image.

2. Specify the starting and ending date and time for the image to appear. The defaults are today's date for the starting date and one month later for the ending date.

3. Specify optionally an image to be displayed before or after the dates given in step 2. If this field is left empty and the system date is outside the specified range, nothing shows up when a user views the page in their browser.

4. Choose OK. If the current system date is within the date range specified in step 3, the image appears on the page in the FrontPage Editor workspace. If the date falls outside the range, a text message appears in the workspace to state that it is expired.

A scheduled image has the following behaviors:

■ Although the image looks like a normal one, you can't select it and edit the image properties, such as borders, image type, or alignment. Attempting to open the Image Properties dialog box leads you to the Component Properties box instead. In other words, the object on the page is really a Component, not an image.

■ If the computer's system date falls outside the range given by the start and end dates you specified, and if there is no optional image specified, the message Expired Scheduled Image appears in FrontPage Editor in place of the image. Of course, the image and this message do not appear in a browser.

■ You can link or unlink the scheduled image or the optional image by using <u>E</u>dit, Hyperlin<u>k</u> (or U<u>n</u>link) and the usual linking methods.

Using the Scheduled Include Page Component

You insert a Scheduled Include Page just as you do a Scheduled Image (the dialog boxes are identical in function, so the box isn't shown again as a figure). The difference here is that an HTML page file is inserted into the document.

Because you're inserting a page, you have some options for making it appear as you want it. Although you can't edit the inserted material directly (trying this just displays the Scheduled Include Properties dialog box), you can edit the component's source page. Because of this, the Scheduled Include Page Component is more versatile and configurable than the Scheduled Image. You can create notices, newsletters, limited time offers, holiday pages, and in-depth advertisements and include them as pages. You can also specify an optional page to display outside the date range specified.

N O T E Sometimes it's better to use the Scheduled Include Page method for inserting an image than the Scheduled Image method. Even though it takes slightly more work to do (you have to create a HTML page and insert the image into it), inserting an image with the Scheduled Include Page Component allows you to create hotspots on the image as well as modify its properties. ■

Part

II

Ch

11

Using the Search Form Component

When you insert a Search Form Component, a simple form appears allowing a reader to search all pages in the current Web or in a discussion group for a string of words.

To insert a Search Component, choose Insert, Active Elements and from the pop-up menu, choose Search Form. This opens the Search Form Properties dialog box (see Figure 11.5).

FIG. 11.5

Use the Search Form Properties dialog box to establish the parameters of a search.

N O T E The Search Component searches only the current Web. It isn't intended as a search engine for locations beyond that Web. ▨

The dialog box has two sheets. On the Search From Properties sheet, you can modify the form's properties in the following ways:

- Put your own text, such as "Search My Web For:," in the Label for Input text box.
- Set the maximum Width in Characters for the search string.
- Customize the Clear and Start button labels.

When you have these to your liking, click the Search Results tab to move to the Search Results sheet. Here you specify the Word List to Search to set the search range. ALL (the default) searches all the pages of the current Web. If you've set up a discussion group, you can enter its directory name here, and the Search Component searches all entries in that discussion group directory. If you want to exclude some pages from a search, you must store these in a hidden directory.

▶ **See** the section "Using Hidden Directories with FrontPage Components," in this chapter, **p. 232**

You can also use the check boxes to display the closeness of the match, the last update of a matched page, and the matched page's size in kilobytes (see Figure 11.6).

When a visitor to your site submits words to search for, the Search Component returns a list of pages on which the words appear. If your Web is complex or large, your visitors will appreciate an easily accessible search form.

FIG. 11.6
You determine the search range and other basic information in the Search Results sheet.

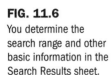

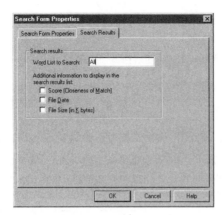

FIG. 11.6
You determine the search range and other basic information in the Search Results sheet.

Using the Substitution Component

The Substitution Component inserts the value of a page configuration variable, such as the original author, the person who modified the page, the page URL, or the page description (which can be free-form text). Also listed are any page configuration variables you added in FrontPage Explorer.

To use the component, choose Insert, FrontPage Component, and select it from the Insert FrontPage Component dialog box. This opens the Substitution Component Properties dialog box. Click the button at the right of the Substitute With list box, select the name of the variable you want, and choose OK. Its value as defined for the current FrontPage Web appears on the page.

Using the Table of Contents Component

This component creates a table of contents (TOC) for your Web site. To use it, choose Insert, Table of Contents. The Table of Contents Properties dialog box appears (see Figure 11.7).

FIG. 11.7
Using the Table of Contents Component helps you set up this essential part of a Web.

With this component, you can do the following:

- Select the page that is the starting point of the TOC. On execution, the component follows all links from this page. If you want a list of all pages on your Web, assign the home page as the starting point.

Part

II

Ch

11

- Choose the heading size for the table of contents. The TOC heading is taken from the Page Title of the starting page.
- Mark the Show Each Page Only Once check box to keep the same page from appearing over and over in the TOC. With the check box deselected, you'll get a TOC entry for the page for each link to it.
- Mark the Show Pages with No Incoming Links check box to include all pages on the site, even orphan pages with no links to them.
- Mark the Recompute Table of Contents When Any Other Page Is Edited check box to update the TOC every time you edit a page in the Web. Large Web sites can take a long time to update, so mark this box only if you can wait. To manually update a table of contents, open the page containing the Table of Contents Component and resave it.

TROUBLESHOOTING

I inserted a Table of Contents Component, but it's not showing the actual TOC in the FrontPage Editor in either Normal mode or Preview mode. It just shows three dummy entries, which I can't even edit. What have I done wrong? You haven't done anything wrong. You don't see the real TOC unless you access the page through a Web server, and neither the Normal mode nor the Preview mode uses a server. To see what the actual TOC will look like, you must use the Preview in Browser command, because this goes through the Personal Web Server to retrieve and display the page. Admittedly, this makes page layout a little more difficult because you can't see directly what the page is going to look like. Remember, however, that this TOC page is inevitably fluid because it changes as your site gains and loses pages.

Using a Timestamp Component

The Timestamp automatically inserts the last date the page was saved or updated. It can, optionally, also include the time of either of these events.

It's a simple component, which you insert by choosing Insert, Timestamp. Use its Properties dialog box to select whether it gives the date of the last edit or the date the page was updated. An update is either the last edit or when the page's URL was regenerated because of a change in the structure of the Web.

Using Hidden Directories with FrontPage Components

Hidden directories are important to Web security and component behavior. Hidden-directory names are indicated by a leading underscore character.

When you create a new Web, FrontPage Explorer puts the special directory _PRIVATE into it. Browsers can't directly read files in this or any other hidden directory. For example, if a site visitor tries to access the location **http://www.mysite/_private/header.htm**, they are prompted for a user name and password.

By default, FrontPage Explorer and Editor do not show files stored in hidden directories. Search Component do not search hidden directories, and the Table of Contents Component does not add links to pages in hidden directories. However, you can configure FrontPage Explorer to show the content of hidden directories. In the FrontPage Explorer menu bar, choose Tools, Web Settings. When the Web Settings dialog box appears, select the Advanced tab and mark the Show Documents in Hidden Directories check box on the Advanced tab.

The _PRIVATE directory is often used with the two Include Component. For instance, you may want a standard header file for each page in the Web but don't want people to be able to access that header file directly. Put it into the _PRIVATE directory and call it from there with the appropriate component.

 TIP If you want to create a link to a file in a hidden directory, mark the Show Documents in Hidden Directories check box so that you can use Browse buttons to locate the file.

Forms: Why Bother?

Nobody knows who invented the first form (he or she must have been a bureaucrat, though) but they've been proliferating like weeds ever since. There's a good reason for this: they're useful. In a society like ours, which depends so heavily on the processing of information, they're essential for organizing both the way the information is gathered and how it's presented. If a census-taker merely asks a person to "tell me all about your household," she'll probably get some of the data she's after, but she'll miss at least some, and receive unwanted information. In this disorganized state, the information is almost useless. But give the same census-taker a form to guide the data collection, and life suddenly becomes much easier.

Designing Effective Forms

Because you intend for your forms to gather information, you have to persuade people to fill them out. Almost on principle, people dislike forms, and if the form is badly organized, too long, and filled with irrelevant questions, nobody will touch it. The following are a few things you can do to create user-friendly forms:

■ If you can, create an enticement to complete the form. Remember how people ask, "What's in this for me?" when they first enter your site? This inclination is multiplied when they run into a form.

■ Keep the length of the form short. List the form's objectives and ask only for data that applies to them. Don't get sidetracked by nice-to-know items—stick to the need to know. If a form takes more than a minute or two to fill out, most people won't bother.

■ Briefly tell the reader why you want the data and how it is to be used. If she understands the form in this context, she'll be more likely to fill it out correctly. But don't overburden her with explanations; a couple of sentences should summarize your intentions adequately.

- Ask general questions first, starting with a couple of easy ones and then go for the detail. Ask demographic questions (age, income, sex, education, occupation, and so on) last of all. Don't ask them anything unless it is necessary. Too many personal questions make the reader apprehensive about submitting the form.

- Nobody reads forms carefully, so ask your questions as briefly and clearly as you can. If the question takes multiple sentences to ask, find a way to shorten it, and don't ask two questions at the same time. Remember that if something can be misunderstood, it will be.

- Avoid ambiguous questions, such as, "Do you find our service good?" That's brief, admittedly, but it's a badly designed query. Is the "service" your delivery speed, your customer response line, or what? What is "good"? Fast but expensive? Slow but cheap?

- Avoid leading questions, where the wording influences the answer. They're unethical, for one thing, and they can give you results you don't want or intend. If you ask "Is our aggressive Web advertising campaign offensive?" you're almost asking for a Yes answer because many people disagree with the idea of advertising on the Web, especially aggressive advertising.

- Before putting the form into service, test it on some real live people and use the feedback to modify it. Even professional form and survey designers don't get it right on the first try.

Understanding World Wide Web Forms

When a visitor to your site fills out a form and clicks the Submit button, this action sends the information to a program on the Web server. The server program must exist, because without it, nothing happens and the data doesn't get saved anywhere.

When the data comes in, the server program processes it. This processing can be as simple as saving the data to a file, or as complex as sorting the data and calculating results from it before the information is sent to the intended recipient. The program also sends the respondent a confirmation that the information was received.

The software standard that controls how your visitors interact with your site is called the *Common Gateway Interface* (CGI). The server programs that deal with such incoming information are called CGI scripts and are written to conform to the CGI specifications. When your visitor clicks that Submit button on your form, the data goes to the script and the script processes it according to the way the script was written.

Without FrontPage, you have to write a CGI script to handle your forms and install that script on the Web server. Writing these scripts is a headache for anyone without some programming experience; worse, badly written ones can cause severe misbehavior at the server end, and many ISPs won't let you put your own scripts in their servers. Fortunately, FrontPage enormously simplifies the whole messy business. You don't have to write any CGI scripts because certain FrontPage Component take their place. FrontPage calls these components *Form Handlers*.

CAUTION

To use forms generated by FrontPage, your Web pages must reside on a server that runs the proper FrontPage extensions. If the Web server doesn't have these extensions, it won't have the software that evaluates the submitted information, and your forms won't work. If this happens, contact your ISP administrator.

If you're already familiar with programming and compiling CGI scripts, though, you'll be happy to know that FrontPage fully supports them. However, you'll need them only when adding specialized features or when a page dependent on a CGI script is imported from another Web server.

CAUTION

Like writing GCI scripts, CGI security is far beyond the scope of this book. However, you should be aware that, because CGI opens the door to end user interaction (in fact, that's its purpose), there's always the possibility that an aggressive and unethical user could submit statements and codes that, in effect, control your Web server's behavior. For more on CGI security issues, see

http://hoohoo.ncsa.uiuc.edu/cgi/security.html

and

http://www.go2net.com/people/paulp/cgi-security/

Part
II

Ch
11

N O T E For an exhaustive treatment of CGI scripting, refer to Que's *Special Edition Using CGI.* ■

Understanding FrontPage Forms

With FrontPage forms, you can get just about any information you want from your visitors (assuming they're willing to give it). You can also instruct FrontPage to save the data in various HTML or text formats, allowing viewing and manipulation by various external software applications and macros.

Every FrontPage form has the same basic structure: at least one question, one or more fields for the reader to enter information, a Submit button to send the information to the server, and a Clear (or Reset) button to remove existing entries from the fields. Also associated with the form, at the server end, is some component-generated software to process the submitted data.

You can create a FrontPage form in any of three ways: with the Forms Wizard, by designing a custom form of your own, or with a template. You'll explore each of these in the next sections.

 Do a draft on paper before starting the form in FrontPage Editor. This forces you to organize and visualize the form and you'll create the software version with less backtracking and revision.

Creating a Form with the Form Page Wizard

The Form Page Wizard lets you easily and quickly create many of the forms you need. The wizard takes a lot of the drudgery out of the work, supplies you with suitable formatting and inserts the required Component Form Handlers for you.

To start the Wizard, choose File, New to open the New dialog box. From the New sheet, select Form Page Wizard and choose OK. The first dialog box of the Form Page Wizard appears.

No input from you is required for the first dialog box, so choose Next to move to the second one. In this second dialog box, you should supply a suitable Page URL and Page Title. Do so and choose Next to go on.

N O T E You might not want the form to stand on a page by itself. To insert it into an existing page, complete it on its own page, copy just the form to the Windows Clipboard, and paste it at the appropriate place. ■

Adding Questions to Your Form The third dialog box is where you get down to business and start asking questions of your respondents (see Figure 11.8).

FIG. 11.8

Use the Form Page Wizard dialog box to specify the questions for your form. This one shows contact and ordering information.

When you choose Add, the Wizard opens a list box where you can pick the type of input this question collects. The list is pretty comprehensive. You can see what it does by reading the Description section of the dialog box. If the Description section lists several items (that is, form fields), don't worry. You can customize the form later as much as you like.

The Edit Prompt for This Question text box shows the default wording of the question. Depending on which input type you select, the prompt differs. You can edit it if you need to. When you have the prompt right, choose Next.

Specifying Fields for the Input Type Now you decide which data items to collect from users (see Figure 11.9). These chunks of data are assigned to fields. From the user's viewpoint, fields are simply the text boxes on the form to type input. The wizard uses terms like value, field name, and variable. For our purposes, think of the name of the variable as being the same as the field name, and the value of the variable as being the data itself. Better yet, think of the variable as a bucket with the field name painted on it, and the value as whatever someone pours into the bucket.

FIG. 11.9
You can choose several data items and two subtypes in this section of the Form Page Wizard.

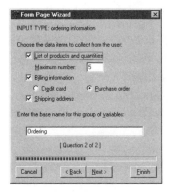

Although this dialog box is slightly different for each input type (ordering, account, and so on), it's always divided into three parts: a section that reminds you of the input type, a section that lets you choose data items, and a section that lets you specify the base name for this particular group of form variables.

No matter what the input type, the second section is always set up the same way. A check box adds a field and the option buttons and text boxes modify what the field looks like. For example, marking the Billing Information check box in Figure 11.9 tells the wizard to insert fields for billing information. The Credit Card and Purchase Order option buttons further define what type of fields appear. If you don't want a particular data item to be asked for, clear the check box.

Usually you needn't worry about changing the contents of the Enter the Base Name for This Group of Variables text box. This is what the wizard uses to help organize the field structures of the form. Changing it merely changes the standard prefix of the field names.

When everything is to your satisfaction, choose Next or Finish. If you choose Finish, FrontPage Editor immediately generates the form page. If you choose Next, you go back to the dialog box shown in Figure 11.7 so that you can add another input type to the form, edit an input, or get rid of it (be careful of the Clear List button; it removes everything).

Go through this cycle until you have all the input types you want, and return to the dialog box shown in Figure 11.8. If you have several input types, you can change the order of presentation by using the Move Up and Move Down buttons.

If you choose Finish at this point, FrontPage Editor immediately generates the form. However, there are some refinements you can add. To do this, choose Next instead of Finish.

Finishing the Form with Presentation Options   When you use the Next button to leave the dialog box shown in Figure 11.8, you find yourself looking at another dialog box in the Form Page Wizard (see Figure 11.10).

Part
II

Ch
11

You can format your questions as one of the following:

- Normal paragraphs
- Numbered lists
- Bulleted lists
- HTML Definition lists

You can also create a table of contents for the form. Do this if your form has many sections; otherwise, don't bother. Remember that if you have a form that long, you may have difficulty getting anybody to use it!

You can automatically create tables to keep the form fields aligned. If you don't want this to happen (because browsers' handling of forms differs somewhat), clear the Use Tables to Align Form Fields check box.

When you are finished with this dialog box, you can choose Finish to generate the form immediately. However, you'll likely want to choose Next because that's how you get to decide a very important part of the whole information-gathering process: how to save the data so that you can look at it.

N O T E   If you're wondering if you can edit a template-based form, you can. Form customization is discussed a little later in this chapter. ■

Specifying Form Output Options   The dialog box shown in Figure 11.11 allows you to choose how the data will be saved. You have the following three options:

- **Save Results to a Web Page**   This creates an HTML file in the Web. Whenever a user clicks the Submit button on the form, the name/value pair of each field is added to that file. The *name* is the name of the field (such as ORDER_QTY) and the *value* is whatever data the user typed into that field on the form.
- **Save Results to a Text File**   This does the same as choosing Save Results to a Web Page, except that the output is in plain ASCII text. Use this if you want to import the data into another application, such as a database or spreadsheet.

- **Use Custom CGI Script** This tells FrontPage that a CGI script, which you have to write, accepts the data and produces a results file.

FIG. 11.11

In this dialog box you determine the results file format.

The Enter the Base Name of the Results File text box is where you type the name of the file that stores the output (avoid using the default). *Base name* simply means that this is the name to which the appropriate extension is added: HTM, TXT, or CGI, depending on the kind of output you asked for.

At last you can choose Next, then Finish, and let FrontPage Editor create the form. You're not quite done, though. You'll need to edit the `This Is an Explanation...` section at the top of the form to suit your needs. You might also want to modify the form title and probably the copyright information at the bottom of the form. (Notice that there's a Timestamp Component included with the copyright data.) When you've finished, save the form page.

Getting at the Information that People Send You If you told the wizard to save the results as a Web page, take a look at FrontPage Explorer. You'll see that you now have a results page. Its default Page Title is pretty cumbersome, so you should change it with the Page Properties dialog box.

This results page stores the data sent when a user fills out the form and clicks the Submit button. To see the information that somebody sends you, open the results page in an application compatible with the data storage format, and look at it.

If you told the wizard to save the results as a text file, the file shows up in FrontPage Explorer. However, if you open it from Explorer, it is retrieved into whatever application handles TXT files on your system (the default is Windows Notepad). If you chose Use Custom CGI Script, that script processes the information and stores it as the script instructs. Whatever you did to save the data, you now have it and can use it as needed.

Part
II

Ch
11

Getting Started on Customized Forms

The forms that FrontPage Editor generates for you are generic; they're good, but they're not great. You can customize them extensively by editing the text, inserting images, adding or removing text boxes, and modifying the form's properties or you can begin from scratch and build a form from the ground up.

Before you begin, there's an important point about form pages. If you inspect any form, you see a dashed line surrounding it. This identifies the form boundary. If you insert a form field onto the page outside this boundary, you're actually starting a new form, so be careful.

> **N O T E** You can customize a form created by the Form Page Wizard. Everything about customization, as described in the following paragraphs, also applies to modifying forms you've created with the wizard. ■

Rough out your form design on paper first to get an idea of how it should look. Then open a new page, and you're ready to start. You insert and edit text and images with the standard editing and insertion tools. At this stage, creating the form is just like creating any kind of page. When you start adding the form fields, though, life is going to get a little more complicated.

Before adding the form fields, you need to look more closely at how the software actually handles the data returned from these fields. With the wizard, you only needed to decide the format for the saved information or whether it should be passed to a custom CGI script. But, for custom forms, you need to understand how the Save Results Component works.

Understanding the Save Results Component

The Save Results Component (formally, the *WebBot Save Results Component*) is the most common form handler used in FrontPage. This component takes the information submitted by a form and saves it to a file in a format you select. These are various flavors of HTML, text, and database formats.

To specify the behavior of the Save Results component for a particular form, right-click any field in the form and select Form Properties from the shortcut menu to open the Form Properties dialog box (see Figure 11.12).

If needed, you can change the destination file of the form results. More importantly, you can set up many other options. Before you consider them, take a look at a new feature of FrontPage 98—the ability to direct form results to an e-mail address.

Sending Form Results to E-mail   Many Web site managers prefer to get user feedback through e-mail rather than through results files, which can be cumbersome to handle and maintain. Setting this up is as simple as filling in the target e-mail address in the E-mail address text box of the Form Properties dialog box. This e-mail is handled on the server and is transparent to the user. The server-side processing takes the form results, encodes them for e-mail, and transmits them on to an e-mail server. You'll look at options for configuring e-mail submission of form results a little later in this chapter.

FIG. 11.12

The Form Properties dialog box is the starting place for extensive customization of the way form results are recorded and acknowledged.

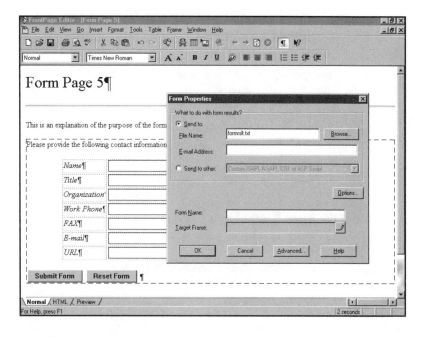

Using the Form Properties Options In the Form Properties dialog box, click the Options button. This opens a tabbed, four-sheet dialog box entitled Options for Saving Results of Form. This dialog box defaults on opening to the File Results sheet.

Using the File Results Sheet You use this sheet (see Figure 11.13) as follows:

FIG. 11.13

With the File Results sheet, you specify the destination file and format of the user-submitted information.

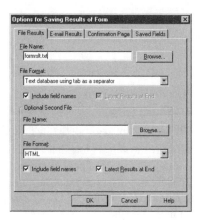

■ In the File Name text box, enter the name of the file where the form data will be stored. Supply an absolute path name if you want to save the file outside the Web but in the server (for example, C:\TEMP\RESULTS.HTM).

■ Use the File Format drop-down list box to select the format for the result file. Mark the Include Field Names in Output check box to also save the variable name and value of each field in the results file.

■ The Optional Second File section allows you to specify another file in which the user-submitted information will also be stored. This is useful if you need to store submitted data in one format to suit a database, and in another format for human readability.

■ Marking the Latest Results at End check box puts the latest submitted information at the bottom of the results file, but only if it is an HTML file. With a text file, results are always appended at the end, and this can't be changed.

■ Marking the Include Field Names in Output check box saves both the name and the value of each form field. If the box is unmarked, only the values are saved.

Using the E-mail Results Sheet   This sheet lets you specify the e-mail results address, which actually duplicates the E-mail text box in the Form Properties dialog box (see Figure 11.14).

FIG. 11.14

The E-mail sheet provides options for mail formatting and message headers.

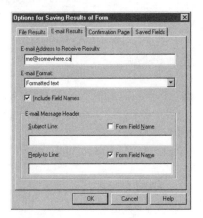

On this sheet, you can also:

■ Specify the e-mail format. Formatted text is the default, which is the preferred format for most e-mail programs.

■ Include field names along with the data by marking the Include Field Names check box.

■ In the Subject Line text box, specify the subject line that should appear in the e-mail message header. This is, of course, to help you figure out what form the information came from, and why you were collecting it. If you want the subject line to contain the results of a form field, mark the Form Field Name check box and type the name of the field into the Subject Line text box.

■ Use the Reply-to Line text box to specify the form field whose value should appear in the e-mail's reply-to line. If you don't want this result, clear the Form Field Name check box (it's marked on by default) and type the desired text into the text box.

Using the Confirmation Page Sheet   In the URL of Confirmation Page text box, you can enter an optional confirmation page. A standard HTML confirmation page is sent to the reader's browser automatically if this text box is left blank. You optionally use the URL of Validation Failure box to send a page telling the submitter that the information submitted is invalid.

Using the Saved Fields Sheet   You can use the Saved Fields sheet to specify which form fields to include in the results file. When this sheet is first opened, the Form Fields to Save list box displays the names of all the fields on the form (see Figure 11.15). You can delete or rearrange these fields. Whatever fields you make appear in the list box are written to the results file in the order of their appearance.

FIG. 11.15
Use the Saved Fields sheet to specify the fields to be saved and the order of their appearance in the results file.

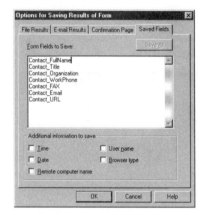

Using Hidden Fields   Also in the Form Properties dialog box is a provision for hidden fields. (To access it, click the Advanced button). These fields don't show up in a browser but are sent to the form handler as a field name plus the value in that field. This is called a *name-value pair*. You create name-value pairs by choosing Add and filling in a field name and a value for the field in the Name/Value Pair dialog box. You can modify or remove the entry once it's created.

Now that you've sorted all that out, you can continue to put more form fields onto your page.

N O T E   The Target Frame text box deals with a framed environment. For details, see Chapter 9, "Enhancing Web Sites with FrontPage Frames." ▪

Selecting Fields to Add to Your Form

To insert a field, choose Insert, Form Field and select the desired kind of field from the submenu that appears. The field inserts at the cursor position. You have eight field types, ranging from one-line text boxes to labels. You'll explore each of them next.

 You can select all the form field types, except Image and Label, from the Forms toolbar.

Adding a One-Line Text Box. The one-line text box gives you a field one-line high and up to 999 characters long. You use it for short answers, such as name, phone number, or e-mail address. When you select it, a text box appears on the screen inside a dotted form boundary. You can now type any text you want to label the box for its users.

T I P You can use the Increase Indent and Decrease Indent buttons to line up blocks of fields. Remember that you can use tables inside forms to arrange your form fields.

What about configuring the form field content? You do this by clicking the field to select it and choosing Edit, Form Field Properties and the Text Box Properties dialog box appears (see Figure 11.16).

FIG. 11.16

Use the Text Box Properties dialog box to set up the parameters for the form field.

You set up a text box by using the following steps:

1. Assign a name to the Text Box field by entering an appropriate name in the Name text box. This is the *name* part of the name/value pair associated with the field. (It has nothing to do with the prompt or question text that appears on the form itself.)

2. Type that text into the Initial Value text box if you want the box to start off with specific text. If you don't want an initial value, leave the text box blank.

3. Type a number into the Width in Characters text box to set the width of the box when it appears on the form.

4. Choose the Yes option button in the Password Field section if you want a password.

If you are targeting Internet Explorer 4 as the main browser, you can specify a Tab Order in this or in any other Form Field dialog box by entering a number in the Tab Order box.

Tab Order works like this: if you have five fields in a column in a form, and you gave the top field the tab order **2** and the third field the tab order **1**, the insertion point starts off in the third field. Pressing the Tab key moves the insertion point to the top field (because you designated it as tab order **2**). Remember that this only works with IE 4. To remove the field from the tab order, enter **-1**.

Now comes a very important step: data validation. This allows you to reject spurious data at the browser or client side of the information transaction. If you do this, the server isn't burdened with validation, thereby relieving it of much of its data-processing load. Choose the Validate button to open the Text Box Validation dialog box (see Figure 11.17).

FIG. 11.17

Validate your users' input before it's sent to the server.

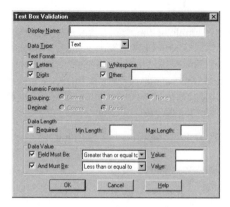

The Display <u>N</u>ame dialog box is used to specify a name the user sees in error dialog boxes if the internal field name isn't the one that the user sees on the form. Make this name the same as the one the form shows for the field, and the user will know which field to correct.

The other fields here are self-explanatory. You can specify the kind of data type (no constraints, text, numeric, integer), the kinds of text allowed, the numeric format, minimum, maximum, and required data length, and the data value ranges. To get this right, you have to have a thorough understanding of the information formats you want. Plan ahead and test, test, test.

Once you've specified the validation parameters, choose OK to return to the Text Box Properties dialog box, and choose OK again to place the completed field on the form. When a user types the wrong kind of data into a field (numbers instead of text, for example) and presses the Submit button, a message will ask for a specified correction.

> **CAUTION**
>
> If you specify a validation failure page in the Confirm sheet of the Settings dialog box in the Forms Properties dialog box, users don't see error messages if they try to submit an incorrect form. Instead, the validation failure page appears.

 When you click a text box, sizing handles appear. You can change the size of the box, within limits, by dragging them.

Adding a Scrolling Text Box This field lets the user type in multiple lines of text. The Scrolling Text Box Properties dialog box resembles that of the one-line text box, except that you can specify the number of lines allowed for a scrolling text box. Setting the properties for a scrolling text box is similar to setting them for a one-line text box, except that you can specify the number of lines, but no password. The validation procedure is identical.

 To open a field's Properties dialog box quickly, double-click the field in the FrontPage Editor workspace.

Part
II

Ch
11

Adding a Check Box   You use check boxes for a list of fields that can be selected or not selected (see Figure 11.18). For example, if you want to know which books on a supplied list a reader owns, the viewer can check several fields, one, or none. You can specify the field's initial state as marked or not marked. The default value is ON, which means that if the check box's initial state is not marked, when someone does mark it, the value returned to the form handler is ON. If the box remains unmarked, a null value is returned. You use these values to figure out which fields are true or false for a given respondent.

As a check box returns only ON or null, no validation is required.

FIG. 11.18

Use the Check Box Properties dialog box to set the returned data values.

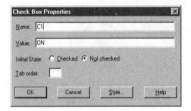

Adding Option Buttons   You use option buttons instead of check boxes when the reader must give one, and only one, answer from a list. One button in a group of buttons is always selected; clicking another one selects that one instead. You have to have more than one button for the tool to be useful; a single button will always be on, which doesn't tell you much.

You use the Option Button Properties dialog box to set up the group (see Figure 11.19). All the buttons that work together must have the same group name, which you enter in the Group Name text box. In the Value text box, type the value that the field returns when somebody clicks it. The Initial State can be Selected or Not Selected.

FIG. 11.19

Option buttons must be grouped into sets with the Option Button Properties dialog box.

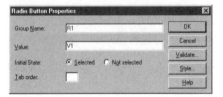

There is also a validation procedure for option buttons; if the Data Required check box is marked, the user must actively check one of the option buttons. The Display Name box serves the same purpose as with the one-line text box.

Using a Drop-Down Menu   A drop-down menu is another way to give choices to a user. The Drop-Down Menu Properties dialog box is a little more complicated than the others (see Figure 11.20).

FIG. 11.20
You can give the user a menu by using the Drop-Down Menu field.

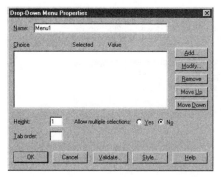

Set up a drop-down menu by using the following steps:

1. Type a name for the menu in the Name text box.

2. Choose Add and the Add Choice dialog box appears. In the Choice text box, type the menu entry as it appears to the user.

3. Leave the Specify Value check box blank if you want the form to return the value specified in the Choice text box. If you mark it, a new, untitled box automatically opens so you can type the value that is returned instead. The user's menu entry remains the same, however, as in the Choice text box.

4. Click Selected or Not Selected to specify whether the menu entry is highlighted in the user's browser. Selected returns the value in the Choice text box; Not Selected returns a null value.

5. Choose OK to return to the Drop-Down Menu Properties dialog box. Repeat steps 2 through 4 until the menu is complete.

6. Select Yes or No in the Drop-Down Menu Properties dialog box to enable or disable multiple selections by the user.

7. Specify the height of the menu box. The menu behavior varies depending on the browser, so experiment.

8. Modify or rearrange the entries, if necessary, with the Modify, Move Up, and Move Down buttons.

9. Use the Validation button to go to the Validation dialog box and set the required conditions, if any, for the data.

10. Choose OK to insert the menu field into the form.

Adding a Push Button   Finally, life gets a little simpler with the Push Button Properties dialog box (see Figure 11.21). Assign the button a name and type the label you want into the Value/Label box and mark the appropriate option button to choose whether it's a Normal, Submit, or Reset button (Submit you know about; Reset clears all the form's fields). A Normal button is a generic one that does nothing until you assign a script to it. Choose OK and the button appears on the form.

Part
II

Ch
11

N O T E You can also use Style Sheets with the button text. For more information on Style Sheets, **see** Chapter 12, "Using Style Sheets with Pages and Web Sites," **p. 255**

FIG. 11.21

The Push Button
Properties dialog box
gives you a bit of control
over the look of the
Reset and Submit
buttons.

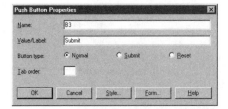

Adding an Image Field You might think that inserting an image field has the same purpose as inserting an image, but it doesn't. An image field does exactly the same things a Submit button does. When you insert an image field, you give it a name in its Field Properties dialog box, edit its image properties if needed, and choose OK. You can't edit its link, though, because an image field cannot have a link. It's really just a fancy Submit button.

Adding a Form Label This command assigns the label text to the VALUE attribute of the <LABEL> tag. To use it, insert the form field and type some text next to it to be the field label. Select both the form field and the label text and choose Insert, Form Field, Label to carry out the command. If you inspect the HTML for the page, you'll see that the <LABEL> </LABEL> container is applied to the text of the field label.

Changing the Form Properties Changing the form's properties is the final way of customizing a form. Right-click anywhere inside the form boundaries and then select Form Properties from the shortcut menu. This opens the Form Properties dialog box that you looked at in detail earlier.

Creating a Custom Confirmation for Your Visitors

When someone visiting your site submits a form, FrontPage automatically returns to them a confirmation of what he entered. This is a bare-bones confirmation, and you might like something a little more decorative. You achieve this with the Confirmation Field Component, which you use in a confirmation page you create.

To do this, use FrontPage Editor to go to the form the visitor will use and double-click any field you want to confirm. Write down the field name that appears in the Name text box and click Cancel. Do this until you have a list of all the field names you're going to confirm.

You can then create a new Normal page and edit it to have the look you want. At each place you want a confirmation to appear, use the following steps:

1. Choose Insert, FrontPage Component. From the list box, choose the Confirmation Field. The Confirmation Field Properties dialog box appears.

2. Type the name of a field from your written list in the Name of Form Field to Confirm text box and choose OK. The field name appears in your page.

3. Repeat steps 1 and 2 until you've entered all the confirmations and save the page.

4. Go to the form you want to confirm. Right-click it and select Form Properties. The Form Properties dialog box appears.

5. Choose the Options button. When the Options for Saving Results dialog box appears, click the Confirmation Page tab.

6. Insert the URL of the confirmation page you just created in the URL of Confirmation Page text box. Choose OK and then choose OK again to close the Form Properties dialog box.

7. Enter the URL of the validation failure page (which you must create) in the lower text box if you want invalid input to open a validation failure page rather than to display error messages.

8. Save the page and test it. When you submit the form, you should see your custom confirmation (or validation failure page for invalid input) in your browser.

Understanding the Discussion Form Handler

You've likely noticed that the Form Properties dialog box offers a grayed-out text box next to a option button labeled Send To Other. Mark this option button to make the text box active, and click the arrow button at the right of the text box. This option lets you send results to a script or to two specialized form handers, one of which is the Discussion handler.

This *Discussion handler* is specifically designed to handle inputs from a discussion Web, which you create by using the Discussion Web Wizard in FrontPage Explorer. This is certainly the best way to set up a discussion group. However, you might want to modify some of the properties of such pages, and you do this in FrontPage Editor.

To change the look of the page, use the normal editing tools; a discussion group page is like any other except in its form handler and some of its properties. To modify the properties, right-click within any form boundary and choose Form Properties. When the Form Properties dialog box appears, choose the Options button. This opens the Options for Discussion Form Handler dialog box, which has three tabbed sheets. The dialog box defaults to showing the Discussion sheet.

Understanding the Discussion Sheet   You use this sheet to specify how the discussion Web behaves in normal operation (see Figure 11.22) as follows:

■ Use the Title text box to edit the name of the discussion group. This name appears on all articles.

■ Use the Directory text box to specify the directory where FrontPage stores all the articles. This directory must be hidden.

■ Use the Table of Contents Layout section to customize the look of the TOC, which automatically regenerates every time someone submits an article. You can modify what appears in the TOC's subject descriptions by typing field names into the Form Fields text box. You can have more than one field; just separate them with spaces. Marking the Time and Date check boxes displays the date and time of submission for each article.

Marking the Remote Computer Name and User Name check boxes displays remote computer names and the usernames of the authors, respectively. Finally, you can decide if the articles appear from oldest to newest or the reverse.

FIG. 11.22
The Discussion sheet lets you customize the group title, TOC appearance, and confirmation page.

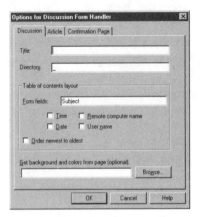

Understanding the Article and Confirmation Page Sheets The Article tab establishes additional information to show up in each article. You can specify the URLs of your standard header and footer, time and date of the article's submission, and remote computer name and author name. If you want a custom confirmation or validation failure page, insert the URL of these into the appropriate boxes on the Confirm sheet.

Understanding Registration Forms

A Registration Form gives you some control over who gets into a particular Web on your host. The basic procedure is this: a new user accesses a registration form stored in the root Web of your site and registers with a username and password for a particular child Web of the root Web. This isn't very tight security. However, it does make it unnecessary for registered users to keep entering their name into some types of form fields because the server finds out who they are when they log on. Also, there's some assurance to others that it's really you communicating with them, and not an impostor.

Creating a Registration Form Begin by using FrontPage Explorer to open the Web for which you want to register users; when you've finished, this will be a protected Web. After the Web is open, use the following steps:

1. Choose Tools, Permissions to move to the Web Permissions dialog box.

2. Choose the Settings tab and click the Use Unique Permissions for This Web option button. Click the Apply button and then click OK.

3. Choose Only Registered Users Have Browse Access in the Users tab. Click Apply and then click OK.

4. Open the server's root Web while remaining in FrontPage Explorer. (All registration forms must reside in the root Web to work properly, even though users are registering for a child Web.)

5. Switch to FrontPage Editor with the root Web still open. Choose File, New and select the User Registration template from the list box.

6. Use the instructions included with the template as a guide to modifying it. After that, change the title and heading of the page to suit the Web that it's for. If you want more information from the registrant, add form fields to collect it.

7. Once you are satisfied with the form, right-click any form field and select Form Properties to open the Form Properties dialog box. Notice that the form handler is automatically set to be the Registration Form Handler.

8. Click the Options button in the Form Properties dialog box. This opens the Options for Registration Form Handler dialog box, which has four tabbed sheets. The Registration sheet is the default.

9. In the FrontPage Web Name box of the Registration sheet, type the name of the protected Web for which the users are registering.

10. In the User Name Field text box, provide the name of the field where the user types his user name.

11. In the Password Field text box, provide the name of the form field into which the user will type a password.

12. In the Password Confirmation Field text box, provide the name of the form field where the user confirms his password.

13. Mark the Require Secure Password check box to force the user to specify a password with at least six characters, and which does not partially match his username.

14. Give the URL of the page the user sees if his registration fails in the URL of Registration Failure Page. If you leave this box blank, a default failure page is used.

15. Choose OK. The File Results, Confirmation Page, and Saved Fields sheets are identical to ones you saw earlier. Use them as desired to set other parameters for the form.

16. Choose OK again to close the Form Properties dialog box and save the page. The Web is now set up to accept only registered users.

Part

II

Ch

11

N O T E In step 7, we referred to the Registration For Handler's appearance in the Send to Other text box, in the Form Properties dialog box. This handler is specifically written to handle registration forms. Don't change this setting, or the forms won't work. ■

Using the Registration Form   To register for the protected Web, users have to access the root Web and complete the form page for the protected Web. This includes choosing a username and password so if you have more than one protected Web, you need a Registration Form for each one, and the registrants have to have access to these forms.

The security check is actually made at the browser level. When a user's browser contacts the URL of the page, a username and password box appears in the browser window. The user can't get into the Web unless he knows both of these items. Once he's in, however, all pages in that Web are accessible to him, even if he leaves the Web and returns. The security isn't enforced again until the browser is shut down and then restarted.

Using Templates to Create Interactive Pages

FrontPage supplies five templates that have WebBot Components or similar interactive elements installed in them. The way the templates use these components and form fields gives you useful examples to follow when you're setting up the interactive parts of your site. Now that you know a lot more about how your visitors can communicate with you through your site, it's time to have a look at these types of pages. The templates are:

> **CAUTION**
>
> When you use the templates, remember to use their Form Properties to rename the files where they store their results (if applicable). Leaving the result files at their default names may cause data to be overwritten or jumbled.

- The Guest Book template uses a scrolling text box to gather comments about a site. It sends the data with the username of the commentator to a file named GUESTLOG.HTM. This file is displayed in the lower part of the page by an Include Page Component, so the visitor can see what other people had to say about the site. This page also has a Comment Component at the top to give instructions for use, and a Timestamp at the bottom. All the templates have these two Bots so they won't be mentioned again.

- The Search Page template uses the Search Component to find instances of a text string in the current Web's public pages. The page includes two bookmarks for navigation and a section that describes how to use the query language.

- The Table of Contents template is nothing more than a page with a Table of Contents Component in it. Remember you don't see the real TOC unless you view the page in a browser.

- The Feedback Form template is really an elaborated example of the Guest Book. An interesting addition is the set of four option buttons that help classify the kind of feedback being given. Inspect these buttons' properties to see how default button values are used.

- The Confirmation Form template is a general-purpose tool for letting users know that you've recorded the information they sent you. The template uses several Confirmation Field Components. To use it, type its name into the URL of Confirmation Page text box of the page you want confirmed.

▶ **See** "Using the Comment Component," in this chapter, **p. 226**

▶ **See** "Using the Timestamp Component," in this chapter, **p. 232**

▶ **See** "Using the Search Form Component," in this chapter, **p. 230**

▶ **See** "Creating a Custom Confirmation for Your Visitors," in this chapter, **p. 248**

From Here...

In this chapter, you've learned a lot about the interactive side of the Web, the side that turns it into a vast forum for the interchange of ideas, information, and even some wisdom. It's a lot to digest, and you'll likely want to take some time for experimentation. When you're ready to go on, see the following chapters:

- Chapter 12, "Using Style Sheets with Pages and Web Sites," which shows you how to use this technique for developing and maintaining a consistent and easily modified look for an entire site or for a set of pages.

- Chapter 13, "Getting Started with Image Composer," which introduces you to the new version of this powerful graphics package.

Part

II

Ch

11

Using Style Sheets with Pages and Web Sites

Microsoft's Internet Explorer 3.0 was the first browser to support Cascading Style Sheets, and the capability has been extended in Internet Explorer 4. Netscape Navigator 3 won't handle style sheets, but Navigator 4 does, plus the latter browser supports Netscape's own version of style sheets called JavaScript Style Sheets (JSSS).

Style sheets are important, from the page designer's point of view, because they provide a shorthand for page formatting, much in the way that styles do for the major word processors. Unlike its predecessor, FrontPage 98 directly supports style sheets, so that you can add these entities to your pages and Web sites with a minimum of hand-coding in HTML. ■

What style sheets are

Find out about these useful Web tools and their syntax.

The syntax of style sheets

Understand inline, embedded, and linked style sheets and how their coding works.

Cascading style sheets

Understand the hierarchy of different style sheet levels.

Creating style sheets with FrontPage Editor

Use FrontPage 98's new editing tools to create style sheets.

Style sheet attributes

Use this reference list to compose your own style sheets.

What Are Style Sheets?

A style sheet is a page styling template you create yourself; it embeds special commands within HTML formatting tags to specify the appearance of a Web page, or pages. Style sheets provide:

- More complex formatting capabilities, especially greater control over text appearance and placement. These formatting effects can be achieved without complex and awkward HTML workarounds.

- More flexible and simpler control of the formatting across multiple pages. You don't need to turn tags on and off to change the look of individual page elements, and the reduced number of tags makes your HTML code much easier to read and follow.

- Fast changes to the formatting of a page or pages, by changing a few parameters in a linked style sheet. This lets you make major changes to the appearance of a whole site, without the drudgery of modifying every page the site contains.

- Greater potential for sophisticated page design, based on a style sheet standard which all browsers will (eventually) be able to recognize.

The implementation of style sheets in FrontPage 98 is based on that of the World Wide Web Consortium's working draft on the enhancement. You can access this at

http://www.w3.org/pub/WWW/TR/WD-css1.html

N O T E   You can use a style sheet on a page without much fear of blowing up nonsupporting browsers. When the styling parameters are properly embedded within tags, a nonsupporting browser simply ignores them and applies its default formatting. This design feature of the style sheet specification allows you to provide styling directives to style-compatible browsers without messing up the display of noncompatible browsers. ▪

The term *"cascading style sheets"* refers to the fact that you can use multiple styles to determine how your page looks. A style sheet-supporting browser follows a set hierarchy to determine which formatting elements get displayed and which don't.

With IE 3 and 4, and Netscape Navigator 4, you have three different approaches to employing style sheets: linked styles, embedded styles, and inline styles. All three styling methods work with these browsers, and behave as follows:

- **Linked style sheets**   Your regular Web pages link to such a sheet (this is actually just a text file with a CSS extension) which determines how they'll look. With this method, you can change the look of many pages by changing only the style sheet file.

- **Embedded style sheets**   You actually insert a style sheet specification into a particular page. Changing a parameter modifies the look of the complete page.

- **Inline styles**   These modify the behavior of a single tag, a group of tags, or a block of information on a single page.

You can mix these approaches on a single page, too—using one doesn't preclude the use of others. The rules of precedence for the different style sheets are described later in this chapter in "Understanding Cascading."

No doubt you're eager to explore the tools provided by FrontPage 98 for the creation of style sheets. You'll get to this, but the way FrontPage Editor handles style sheets will make much more sense if you examine the underlying syntax of style sheet HTML. The next few sections will cover this, and then you'll go on to using FrontPage Editor.

Understanding Style Sheet Syntax

With linked and embedded style sheets, you include at least one definition of the style in the HEAD section of the page. The style definition format is as follows:

```
<ANY HTML TAG>{property1 name: property1 value; property2 name: property 2
value}</ANY HTML TAG>.
```

Note that curly braces were used to set off the definition itself. Within these braces, there can be as many properties as you like. The style definitions are enclosed in the <STYLE> </STYLE> tags. Where these are placed within the HTML file depends on the kind of style sheet you're using.

Using Embedded Styles

Embedding a style sheet is straightforward. Insert a <STYLE> </STYLE> tag pair into the document between the <HEAD> tags. This styling block controls the appearance of the entire Web page in which it's embedded. IE 3 and 4 automatically register the MIME media type for style sheets, so you can include the TYPE="text/css" parameter within the style tags to direct nonsupporting browsers to disregard the style sheet.

In addition, to make sure nonsupporting browsers don't display the text of the style definitions, you comment out the style block with <!-- and -->.

Here's an example of what it looks like:

```
<HTML>
<HEAD><title>Some Styles</title>
<STYLE TYPE="text/css">
<!--
BODY {font: 10pt "Arial"; color: maroon}
H1 {font: 24pt "Book Antiqua"; color: blue}
P {font: 10pt "Arial"; color: red}

-->
</STYLE>
</HEAD>
<BODY>
<h1>A HEADING </h1>
<p>Some Text</p>
</BODY>
</HTML>
```

If you edit this directly into a page, and then use Preview or the Preview in Browser command, you'll see a 24-point blue heading in Book Antiqua font, and the words "Some Text" in Arial, 10 point, in red.

T I P   You would assign styles to the <BODY> tag to set the overall appearance of your page, as in the previous example. These effects take place globally. Then, to set individual styles for particular elements, you define these in the rest of the <STYLE> block, as is done with the <P> and <H>1 tags.

The values inside the curly braces next to the H1 define the style for all Heading 1 headings in the page; the values inside the curly braces next to the P do the same for all paragraph (normal) text in the page. You can change the global look of the page by changing the values within the curly braces.

Using Inline Styles

You use inline styles to set the properties of a single tag and its contents. To do this, you place the style attributes within the tag itself. To set the color and attributes of a Normal paragraph of text, you'd use this syntax:

```
< P STYLE ="color:green;font-style:italic">
This text is green and in italics.
</P>
```

As you can figure out for yourself, the result is green, italicized text. Note that curly braces aren't used here, but quotation marks, to define the attributes list.

Note also that if an inline style differs from the embedded style block of the page, or from a linked style, the inline style takes precedence. In the previous example, no matter how the <P> tag is defined in the page's <STYLE> block, the inline style will make the text of this paragraph into green italics.

Sometimes you want to change the look of a large block of a page, and inserting the same inline attributes for each tag within that block would be tedious and error-prone. For this, you use the <DIV> tag. For example:

```
<DIV STYLE = "font-size: 14pt; color: red">
. . . block of HTML code . . .
</DIV>
```

This makes a global color and font size change to all the text contained within the <DIV> tags. In other words, if you have several <P> sections and a <UL> section or two, you don't have to set inline styles for each tag. However, if you do add an inline style to one tag of that larger block, the style will override the <DIV>-defined style and apply the different appearance to the part enclosed in that tag (only).

Another handy inline style tag is the <SPAN> tag. This is used to affect text within a block element, such as the <P> element. You can use it as an inline attribute, as follows:

```
<P>This is black text. This is <SPAN STYLE="color:red">RED TEXT</SPAN> and now
this is black text. </P>
```

The result of this HTML will be the phrase RED TEXT appearing in red within a line of black text.

SPAN can also be used within the STYLE block. Within the block, write "SPAN {color:lime}" and then use the <SPAN> </SPAN> tag pair to wrap some text within some text. The wrapped text will be a pale green. Similarly, "SPAN.lime {color:lime}" would define a class.

These principles can also be applied to the <DIV> tag.

Grouping Tags

Sometimes you want several different tags styled the same way. You can define the styles individually for each tag in the embedded style section, but there's a shortcut. If you wanted formatted and normal text to have the same look, for example, you'd write:

```
H1,H2,H3 {font-style: italic; color: blue}
```

and this would affect all three heading styles. You *must* use the commas to separate the tags, or the grouping won't work.

Using Linked Style Sheets

To set this up, create a file with the desired style definitions, using exactly the same techniques you use for embedded styles. Save the file with a CSS extension, and link to it from the page that is to have that style. In practice, if you wanted all the pages in your Web to have the same style, you'd link each one to the style sheet. The syntax is as follows:

```
<HEAD>
<TITLE> Title of Page </TITLE>
<LINK REL=STYLESHEET HREF= "mystyles.css" TYPE="text/css">
</HEAD>
```

The forward link type REL=STYLESHEET indicates that LINK specifies a link to a style sheet, and that this style sheet is to be applied to the page where the forward link resides (for example, the page where the LINK statement appears).

Part
II

Ch
12

Specifying a Style Class or ID

Creating a class lets you make up variations on a base tag (like <P>) and use these variations either globally on a page (if the class definition is in an embedded style) or globally in the Web (if the style definition is in a linked style sheet).

Let's say you want three types of <P> text, one bold, one italic, and one bold and green. The code for this would be:

```
<STYLE>
<!--
P.bold {font-weight:bold}
P.italic {font-style:italic}
P.boldgreen {font-weight:bold; color:green}
-->
</STYLE>
```

You would place this either in the Style block at the head of the page (for embedded styles) or in the linked style sheet (for linked styles). Then, when you want to use the tag classes on the page, you would write:

```
<P CLASS=bold>Bold is easy using the class attribute.</P>
<P CLASS=italic>Italic is easy using the class attribute.</P>
<P CLASS=boldgreen>Bold and green are easy using the class attribute.</P>
<P> This text is unaffected by any styles.</P>
```

The bold, italic, and boldgreen are arbitrarily chosen labels for the class. You could have a class label of P.aardvark if you wanted to.

IDs are assigned on an individual basis to define the style of an element. An ID is specified by using the indicator # to precede a label for the identifier. ID syntax looks like this:

#xyz { color:red }

This would be referenced in HTML by the ID attribute:

```
<P ID=xyz >Red Text</P>
```

IDs are most useful in scripts because they can be used to reference page elements so that the script can change them.

Specifying Leading

Leading (pronounced "ledding") is the adjustment of the space between lines of text, measured from text baseline to text baseline. Typographers use leading to make subtle changes to the text density on a page. To set leading in your page, use the line-height style attribute. For example, to set the <P> tag to produce Normal text with 24 points between text baselines, you'd use the attribute as follows:

```
P {line-height:24pt}
```

If you were doing a lot of variable line spacing, using the CLASS attribute would be useful. You'd insert some modified <P> tags into a STYLE block, like this:

```
<STYLE>
<!--
P.12 {line-height:12pt}
p.18 {line-height:18pt}
p.24 {line-height:24pt}
-->
</STYLE>
```

Then you'd use them in your text, like this:

```
<P CLASS=18>This line is 18 points from its baseline to the baseline of the line
above it.</P>
```

Understanding Cascading

If you use several style sheets whose definitions conflict, the results are settled by cascading. This means that a page author's styles will take precedence over readers' style sheets (supported at this writing only by IE 4 and Navigator 4) which in turn take precedence over the browser defaults. The W3C working draft on Cascading Style Sheets specifies that within each member of this hierarchy, inline styles take precedence, followed by embedded styles, followed by linked styles.

Creating Style Sheets with FrontPage Editor

Stylesheet use in FrontPage Editor is not exactly WYSIWYG, but it is certainly easier than coding the HTML by hand. Essentially, you insert styling code into a STYLE block, using preset choices from a dialog box. Alternatively, you can add inline styles to a page element by using the CLASS sheet of the Style dialog box. Finally, you can create a linked style sheet and reference it from the other pages in your Web.

Creating an Embedded Style

As you'll remember from our discussion earlier in this chapter, embedded styles are those you define with the STYLE block inside the HEAD section of the page. An example of creating such a style block is given in the following procedures. The example sets up a page that uses the Courier New font as default, with maroon as the default text color (in other words, the <BODY> tag is to have these style attributes). Furthermore, the style block will set all H1 level headings to appear in black Arial, bold italic, with a solid-line border; and all paragraphs will have a left margin of 16 pixels.

Setting Fonts and Colors   FrontPage Editor's method of creating a style sheet requires you to type in the page element tag by hand; the software will then fill in the attributes you want for the page element, using a set of styling dialog boxes. To get started, do the following:

1. Open the page that is to have the style applied to it. Then choose Format, Stylesheet. The Format Stylesheet dialog box appears.

2. Place the insertion point right after the <!-- marker in the dialog box workspace, and press Enter a couple of times to get yourself some working room.

3. Begin by setting up the default appearance of the page. Type **BODY**, then **a space**. (The space isn't strictly necessary—it's just for readability). The dialog box will now appear as shown in Figure 12.1.

FIG. 12.1

In the Format Stylesheet dialog box, you type the page element names so that their attributes can be added by FrontPage Editor.

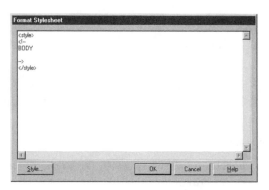

4. With the insertion point on the same line as BODY, choose the Style button at the lower-left of the Format Stylesheet dialog box. This opens the Style dialog box. In the Style dialog box, click the Font tab. In the scrolling list box under the Primary Font text box,

scroll until you find Courier New, and select it. However, don't click OK just yet (see Figure 12.2).

FIG. 12.2

Use the Font sheet to specify the font of a style.

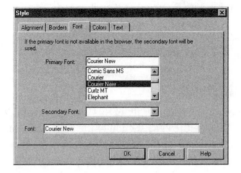

5. Click the Colors tab to open the Colors sheet (see Figure 12.3). In the Foreground Color drop-down list, find and select Maroon.

6. Now click OK. When you return to the Format Font dialog box, you'll see that the style code now reads **BODY {font-family: Courier New; color: rgb(128,0,0);}**. However, don't choose OK yet in the Format Stylesheet dialog box—you have to remain in this dialog box to complete the STYLE block.

FIG. 12.3

You set the foreground and background colors of the page with the Colors sheet.

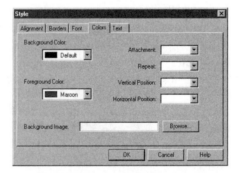

You've now established the font and the font color of the BODY element, thus establishing the default font and font color of the page as a whole. Here's a short reference section on what the other tools on the Font and Colors sheets can do.

In the Font sheet, you can:

■ Use the Primary Font drop-down list to specify the font of the page, provided that font is available to the viewer's browser.

■ Use the Secondary Font drop-down list to specify the font that will be used for the page if the Primary Font isn't available in the user's browser. Given the default fonts supplied with Windows 95, you'll always be safe if you select a font-family such as serif to be the secondary font.

In the Colors sheet, you can determine properties for the background and foreground of the page, as follows:

- Set the Background color, which will be applied behind the element. This will display on top of any background color specified in the Background sheet of the Page Properties dialog box.
- Set the Foreground Color, which applies to foreground elements—text, normally.
- Specify a background image, using the Browse button or typing the image URL into the Background Image text box.
- Set the Attachment of the background image. The list box gives you Scroll or Fixed which determine whether the background image moves along with scrolling text, or stays put (if the latter, it's also called a *watermark*).
- Set the background image's Repeat value; the drop-down list gives you repeat, repeat-x, repeat-y, and none. Repeat (the first value) tiles the image over the entire screen. Repeat-x tiles the image horizontally only, while repeat-y tiles it vertically only.
- Set Vertical and Horizontal position of the background image with respect to the top-left corner of the page.

 TIP The Styles dialog box supplies RGB values for the various colors. Any colors defined this way appear properly in IE 4 and Navigator 4, but they don't do so in Internet Explorer 3 (Navigator 3, as you'll remember, does not support style sheets). The workaround for this is to hand-substitute color names for the RGB values; in the previous example, you would write color:maroon.

 TIP You can create styles for text attributes, too. For example, to apply the color red to italicized text (italicized text has the <EM> tag in FrontPage Editor), put this line into the STYLE block : **EM {color:red}.** When you select some text and click the italic button, that selected text will turn red as well as being italicized.

Setting Up Text and Border Attributes   You remember from the introduction to this section that the H1 headings of this page are to be in bold, italic, and the Arial font. Now make sure the insertion point is at the end of the line reading **BODY {font-family: Courier New; color: rgb(128,0,0);}** and then press the Enter key to get a new blank line, and do this:

1. Type **H1** just as you typed the BODY tag earlier, then type **a space**.
2. Choose the Styles button. Use the Font sheet, as you did earlier, to specify Arial as the Primary Font. Don't choose OK yet.
3. Click the Text tab to display the Text sheet (see Figure 12.4). In the Weight drop-down list, choose Bold.
4. Choose Italic in the Style drop-down list.
5. Click the Borders tab to go to the Borders sheet (see Figure 12.5). In each of the Left, Right, Top, and Bottom drop-down lists, select Solid.

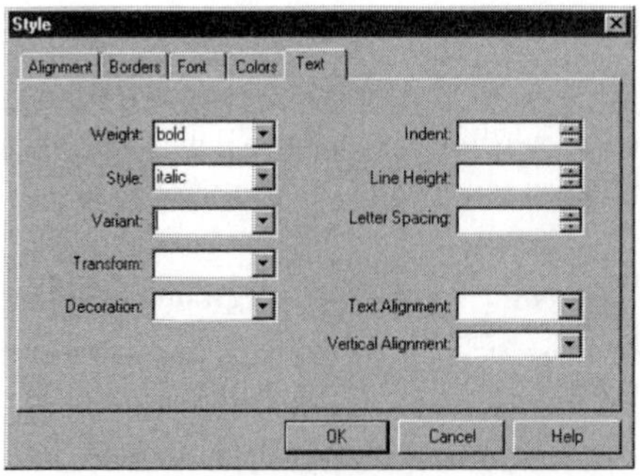

FIG. 12.4

In the Text sheet, you can modify the appearance and alignment of the text.

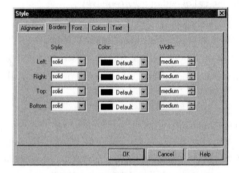

FIG. 12.5

The Borders sheet lets you create and decorate the borders of a page element.

6. Choose OK. The H1 entry in the STYLE block will now read **H1{font-family:Arial; font-weight:bold; font-style:italic; border:medium solid;}**.

There are more selections available than you used. Here are the other attributes you can set from these two sheets:

From the Text sheet:

- Weight can be normal, bold, bolder, lighter or a series of graduated weights from 100 to 900. Experiment to see which looks best.
- Style can be normal, italic, or oblique. There is no easily visible difference between the latter two.
- Variant can be normal or small caps.
- Decoration can be none, underline, overline, line-through, or blink.
- The Indent text box lets you set the indent (in pixels) of the first formatted line. Note that this affects the first line only—it is not the same as using Increase Indent on the formatting toolbar.
- The Line Height text box lets you set leading, as discussed earlier in this chapter.
- The Letter Spacing text box lets you adjust the spacing between letters, in pixels. This amounts to *kerning*.

- Text Alignment can be left, center, right, or justify.
- Vertical alignment can be baseline, sub, super, top, text-top, middle, bottom, text-bottom. These specify the placing of the text relative to the text baseline.

From the Borders sheet, you can:

- Specify the four borders of the element, with seven different line styles or none at all.
- Set the color for each of these borders.
- Set the thickness of each of these borders.

Setting Alignments   You're still in the Format Stylesheet dialog box, or should be. Place the insertion point on a blank line after the H1 line you just finished. Then do this:

1. Type P followed by a space and then choose the <u>S</u>tyle button.
2. Enter **16** into the Left Margin text box in the Alignment sheet (see Figure 12.6).

FIG. 12.6

You specify alignments of the page element using the Alignment sheet.

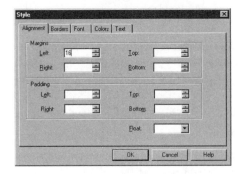

3. Choose OK. The style line in the Format Stylesheet dialog box's workspace will read **P {margin-left:16}**.
4. Choose OK again to close the Format Stylesheet dialog box.

Part

II

Ch

12

Test the effects of this stylesheet by typing some H1 headings and some Normal text. Headings will be colored maroon (because the BODY style specified this) and will be bold, italic, Arial. Paragraphs will have a margin of 16 pixels, and will also be in maroon.

Referring to the Alignment sheet again, notice that it lets you specify all margins for the element. Note also that these aren't page margins, but element margins—a <P> top margin of 60 pixels (for example) simply moves the top line of a Normal text paragraph to a position 60 pixels below the bottom of the immediately preceding page element. The four Padding text boxes control the spacing between the element and its surrounding border. The <u>F</u>loat options (none, left, right) dictate how text will wrap around the selected element. This is analogous to the Left and Right floating alignments for images, which was covered in Chapter 6, "Enhancing Pages with Themes, Graphics, and Multimedia."

Changing Existing Style Attributes

Suppose you made a mistake in the previous example and wanted the BODY foreground color to be something other than maroon? Corrections are quite simple. Do this:

1. If you have already closed the Format Stylesheet dialog box, open it again with Format, Stylesheet. The style block will appear in the dialog box workspace.

2. Find the curly brackets that contain the incorrect attribute, and put the insertion point anywhere within these curly brackets. Note that you don't need to select the incorrect attribute.

3. Choose the Style button to open the Style dialog box. Select the appropriate sheet for the correction, make the correction, and choose OK in the Style dialog box to return to the Format Stylesheet dialog box.

4. In the Format Stylesheet dialog box, you'll see that the new value of the attribute has replaced the old one. Choose OK again to close the Format Stylesheet dialog box, and the change will immediately take place.

Creating a Linked Style Sheet

A linked style sheet is essentially a page with nothing on it but a Style block. After you save such a page, use FrontPage Explorer to change its extension to CSS; this defines a style sheet. To apply the styles of this stylesheet to an HTML page, insert into the <HEAD> section of that HTML page the following line (where MYSTYLE.CSS stands for the name of the style sheet):

```
<LINK REL="STYLESHEET" HREF="MYSTYLE.CSS" TYPE="TEXT/CSS">
```

Save the HTML page, and from then on it will use the styles supplied to it by the CSS file, unless you override those styles by adding a style block or inline styles to the HTML page.

Using Style Classes with FrontPage Editor

The basic principles of embedded stylesheet usage are pretty simple. Using the previous procedures, you specify the styles you want for various page elements, and when you insert the elements into the page, the styles are automatically applied. So, using our example stylesheet from the previous sections, you'd get maroon Courier New text whenever you put Normal text on the page. That's the basic use of embedded styles—you get one style per element.

But suppose you need several different styles for paragraphs, or for any other element for that matter? That's where classes come in—you create them with FrontPage Editor, then apply them.

The class creation procedure is exactly the same as you used earlier to create styles for tags—it just involves a tiny bit more typing to add the class name to the tag name. For example, to create an H1 class called H1.bigred, you put the insertion point on a blank line within the <!-- and --> markers, and type "H1.bigred." Then you use the various sheets in the Style dialog box to set the attributes of this class.

Let's say you use this technique to create three paragraph classes in the STYLE block, as follows:

> P.green {color:green}
>
> P.red {color:red}
>
> P.blue {color:blue}

That's easy enough, but how do you actually apply the required style to a paragraph? To do this:

1. Type the paragraph, or part of it. Click anywhere in the text, and choose Format, Paragraph. In the resulting Paragraph Properties dialog box, click the Style button.

2. The Style dialog box appears. Notice that it has a new sheet, the Class sheet. This sheet has a list box that shows the style classes defined for the current page (see Figure 12.7).

FIG. 12.7

You use the Class sheet to apply embedded style values to individual page elements.

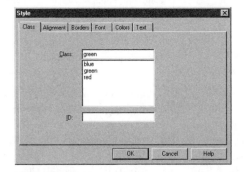

3. Select the desired class name from the list box. Using our example classes, you might pick **green**; the class name **green** then appears in the Class text box. Alternatively, you can type the desired class name into the Class text box.

4. Choose OK, then OK again to close the Paragraph Properties dialog box. The paragraph will now be green. This style will be continued across paragraphs until you change it. If you click the HTML tab, you'll see that the lead-in tag of the paragraph says <p class="green">.

N O T E If you defined an ID in the STYLE block, you can alternatively type its name into the ID text box. Use of the ID attribute for style sheets is discouraged by the W3C, however, as it leads away from the structural approach to style sheets. IDs are recommended for scripting and other uses on the page; for style sheets, you should stick to using Classes. ■

You can apply the Class specification to any page element whose Properties sheet has a Style button. Fortunately, FrontPage Editor is smart enough to know where to put the CLASS= instruction. Suppose, for example, that you want some of your bulleted lists to be green, others blue. Insert into the STYLE block the code:

```
UL.green {color:green}
UL.blue {color:blue}
```

To apply blue to a bulleted list, just click in it and choose Format, Bullets and Numbering. Then choose the Style button from the dialog box and use the Class sheet as just described. When you inspect the HTML code, you'll see <ul class="blue" type=disc> (the "disc" merely refers to the kind of bullet being used).

Similarly, using the Page Properties dialog box to specify a Class inserts the CLASS= instruction into the <BODY> tag.

N O T E If you want to apply a Class to an element, the Class must have been defined for that element. That is, if you have a class P.xyz, and try to use the Class dialog box to apply the xyz style to anything but Normal text, it will have no effect. However, you can actually define a class that is not associated with a tag. Simply write into the STYLE block (for example) .xyz {color:red}, with no tag designated ahead of the period. The xyz style can now be applied to any element, using the Class dialog box. ■

Using Inline Styles

Inline styles are those applied to an HTML tag directly, without using a STYLE block. You'd use these for isolated instances of a style, ones which apply only to a few sections of the page. To apply an inline style, right-click inside the element (such as a paragraph) that needs the style. Then choose the element's Properties entry from the shortcut menu. When the Properties dialog box appears, choose the Style button. This opens the Style dialog box, with the sheets for Class, Alignment, Borders, Font, Colors, and Text. Ignore the Class sheet, and use the others as you did in the earlier procedures, when you created a STYLE block.

In this case, however, you don't create a STYLE block—as soon as you choose OK, the style attributes are inserted directly into the tag of the page element. An example would be <P STYLE = "color:green;font-style:italic">. You can observe this insertion by inspecting the HTML for the element.

Style Sheet Properties Supported by Internet Explorer 3 and 4

The following section provides reference information as to the CSS properties that can be safely used with IE 3.0 and later. At the time of writing, Netscape had stated that its Netscape Communicator suite (which includes the Navigator 4 browser) "fully supports cascading style sheets" as defined by the W3C. This suggests that the bulk of the attributes in Table 12.1 are usable in Navigator 4.

Properties Supported by Internet Explorer 3.0

The style sheet properties supported by Internet Explorer 3 are shown in Table 12.1.

Table 12.1   Internet Explorer 3-Supported Properties

Attribute	Description	Values	Example
font-size	Sets text size	points (pt) inches (in) centimeters (cm) pixels (px)	{font-size: 12pt}
font-family	Sets typeface	typeface name	{font-family: courier}
font-weight	Sets type thickness	extra-light light demi-light medium demi-bold bold extra-bold	{font-weight: bold}
font-style	Italicizes text	normal italic	{fontstyle: italic}
line-height	Sets the distance between baselines	points (pt) inches (in) centimeters (cm) pixels (px) percentage (%)	{line-height: 24pt}
color	Sets color of text	color-name RGB triplet	{color: blue}
text- decoration	Underlines or highlights text	underline italic line-through none	{text-decoration: underline}
margin-left	Sets distance from left edge of page	points (pt) inches (in) centimeters (cm) pixels (px)	{margin-left: 1in}
margin-right	Sets distance from right edge of page	points (pt) inches (in) centimeters (cm) pixels (px)	{margin-right: 1in}
margin-top	Sets distance from top edge of page	points (pt) inches (in) centimeters (cm) pixels (px)	{margin-top:-20px}

Part

II

Ch

12

continues

Table 12.1   Continued

Attribute	Description	Values	Example
text-align	Sets justification	Left center right	{text-align: right}
text-indent	Sets distance from left margin	points (pt) inches (in) centimeters (cm) pixels (px)	{text-indent: 0.5in}
background	Sets background images or colors	URL, color-name RGB triplet	{background: #33CC00}

The named colors you can use are:

black	silver	gray	white
maroon	red	purple	fuschia
green	lime	olive	yellow
navy	blue	teal	aqua

T I P   To place a background image in a style sheet, specify the URL in parentheses with the BODY tag:

BODY {background: URL(books.gif)}

Internet Explorer 4-Supported Style Properties

Internet Explorer 4 supports the following style sheet attributes in addition to those in Table 12.1. For more detailed information, refer to the Microsoft Dynamic HTML Web site at **http://www.microsoft.com/workshop/author/dynhtml/**from which much of the following data is drawn.

- **background-attachment**   If a background image is specified, the value of background-attachment determines if it is fixed with regard to the canvas or if it scrolls along with the content.
  Syntax: { background-attachment: scroll| fixed}

- **background-color**   Sets the background color of an element.
  Syntax:{ background-color: <color> | transparent}

- **background-image**   Sets the background image of an element.
  Syntax:{ background-image: <url> | none}

- **background-position**   If a background image has been specified, the value of background-position specifies its initial position.
  Syntax:{ background-position: [<position> | <length>]{1,2} | [top | center | bottom] || [left | center | right]}

■ **background-repeat** If a background image is specified, the value of `background-repeat` determines how/if the image is repeated.
Syntax: {background-repeat: repeat| repeat-x | repeat-y | no-repeat}

■ **border** Specifies the border to display around the element. The `border` property sets the border for all four sides while the other border properties only set their respective side.
Syntax: { border: <border-width> || <border-style> || <color>}

■ **border-bottom** Specifies the bottom border.
Syntax: { border-bottom: <border-bottom-width> || <border-style> || <color>}

■ **border-bottom-width** Sets the width of an element's bottom border.
Syntax: { border-bottom-width: thin | medium| thick | <length>}

■ **border-color** Sets the color of the four borders.
Syntax: { border-color: <color> Syntax: {1,4}}

■ **border-left** Sets the left border.
Syntax: { border-left: <border-left-width> || <border-style> || <color>}

■ **border-left-width** Sets the width of an element's left border.
Syntax: { border-left-width: thin | medium| thick | <length>}

■ **border-right** Sets the right border.
Syntax: { border-right: <border-right-width> || <border-style> || <color>}

■ **border-right-width** Sets the width of an element's right border.
Syntax: { border-right-width: thin | medium| thick | <length>}

■ **border-style** Sets the style of the four borders.
Syntax: { border-style: none | solid}

■ **border-top** Describes the top border.
Syntax: { border-top: <border-top-width> || <border-style> || <color>}

■ **border-top-width** Sets the width of an element's top border.
Syntax: { border-top-width: thin | medium| thick | <length>}

■ **border-width** This is a shorthand property for setting `border-width-top`, `border-width-right`, `border-width-bottom`, and `border-width-left` at the same place in the style sheet.
Syntax: { border-width: [thin | medium | thick | <length>] {1,4}}

■ **font-variant** Sets the variant of the font to normal or small caps.
Syntax: { font-variant: normal| small-caps}

■ **height** This property can be applied to text, but it is most useful with inline images and similar insertions. The height is to be enforced by scaling the image if necessary. When scaling, the aspect ratio of the image should be preserved if the 'width' property is 'auto'.
Syntax: { height: <length> | auto}

■ **left** Sets the left position when in a 2-D canvas.
Syntax: { left: <length> | <percentage> | auto}

Part
II

Ch
12

■ **letter-spacing**   The length unit indicates an addition to the default space between characters. Units are in ems.
Syntax: { letter-spacing: normal| <length>}

■ **margin-top**   Specifies the top-margin for the text.
Syntax: { margin-top: [<length> | <percentage> | auto]}

■ **margin-bottom**   Specifies the bottom-margin for the text block.
Syntax: { margin-bottom: [<length> | <percentage> | auto]}

■ **position**   Specifies whether the element can be positioned.
Syntax: { position: absolute | relative | static}

■ **text-transform**   Transforms the text.
Syntax: { text-transform: capitalize | uppercase | lowercase | none}

■ **top**   Sets or Returns the top position for elements that are positioned absolutely or relatively.
Syntax: { top: <length> | <percentage> | auto}

■ **vertical-align**   Affects the vertical positioning of the element.
Syntax: { vertical-align: baseline| sub | super | top | text-top | middle | bottom | text-bottom | <percentage>}

■ **width**   This property can be applied to text elements, but it is most useful with inline images and similar insertions. The width is to be enforced by scaling the image if necessary. When scaling, the aspect ratio of the image should be preserved if the 'height' property is 'auto'.
Syntax: { width: <length> | <percentage> | auto}

■ **z-index**   Specifies the z-index for the element. Positive z-index is above the text, negative z-index is rendered below the text.
Syntax: { z-index: number}

N O T E   At the time of writing, Microsoft was still updating and adding to the CSS attributes supported by IE 4.0. For the latest set of attributes, check the IE 4 technology pages at **http://www.microsoft.com/sitebuilder/workshop/prog/ie4/**. ■

Unsupported CSS Attributes

The following CSS attributes are not supported in IE 4.0:

■ word-spacing

■ !important

■ first-letter pseudo

■ first-line pseudo

■ white-space

From Here...

This chapter completes most of our work on basic page design and layout. Now you have a choice of several directions:

- Part III, "Creating and Adapting Graphics with Image Composer," is the place to go if you want detailed information on using this powerful graphics package to develop your own graphics or customize existing ones to your needs.

- Part IV, "Integrating Active Content into Your Web," explores the exciting new software technologies of ActiveX, VBScript and JavaScript, Java applets, and the Virtual Reality Modeling Language.

- Part V, "Building and Managing a Web," shows you how to integrate the pages you create into a sophisticated, well-organized Web site that will be the envy of your neighbors in cyberspace.

Part
II

Ch
12

Creating and Adapting Graphics with Image Composer

## CHAPTER 13

Getting Started with Image Composer

In Chapter 6, "Enhancing Pages with Themes, Graphics, and Multimedia," you learned to insert graphic images on your Web site to create attractive and useful pages. You also learned to use images as site maps to help your visitors navigate your site in an intuitive way. FrontPage does include a nice selection of clip art, but in order to create really unique images, you need a graphics product powerful enough to create and edit sophisticated images, and one that integrates smoothly with FrontPage. Enter the Microsoft Image Composer—a powerful graphics design program that is bundled with the FrontPage bonus pack. ■

Installing Microsoft Image Composer

Image Composer is included in the FrontPage 98 Bonus Pack. Make sure that Image Composer has been installed, making it easy to open image files.

Launching Image Composer from FrontPage

You can start Microsoft Image Composer directly from the FrontPage Explorer.

Navigating the Image Composer environment

Control the Image Composer screen and sort through the tools and palettes.

Creating sprites

Create the basic building blocks of every graphic image in Image Composer.

Sending Image Composer files to FrontPage

Once you've edited an image, send it back to FrontPage to be included on a Web page.

Editing clip art in the Image Composer

You get to edit clip art by using Image Composer to make it unique.

What Can Image Composer Do?

Microsoft Image Composer is powerful enough to create flashy logos, subtle background textures, expressive artistic text, and a wide variety of other graphic images. Image Composer is not simply a tool for creating Web graphics. You can design images to include in printed documents, to insert in PowerPoint presentations, or to copy into any other application.

Image Composer is, however, uniquely suited to creating Web site graphics. One powerful feature, that we will explore in Chapter 16, "Tailoring Your Images for FrontPage Documents," is the ability to maintain relatively consistent colors regardless of what Web browser your visitors are using.

All the aesthetic considerations you explored in Chapter 6, "Enhancing Pages with Themes, Graphics, and Multimedia"—where you learned to insert graphic images—apply at a different level when you create your own images with Image Composer. The difference is creating your own images gives you far more power to control the look and feel of your Web site. Looking for a subtle button to place on your site that will whoosh visitors to a sophisticated art gallery? The tools are here in Image Composer. Looking for a flashy, wild logo that expresses your noncorporate image? You can do this all yourself. How much artistic talent do you need? You be the judge—but Image Composer will do its best to help you transform a scanned image, an original graphics file, or a vision in your head into an image ready to place on your Web site.

Microsoft Image Composer is bundled with the bonus pack version of FrontPage 98. It is installed from the same CD that you used to install FrontPage.

Using Microsoft Image Composer with FrontPage

Typically, you may well work on your Web site with the FrontPage Explorer and FrontPage Editor running, and Image Composer open as well. The real fun comes when you switch seamlessly back and forth between the FrontPage Editor and Image Composer, editing image content, adding graphical text, changing image color, and tweaking your graphic images so that your site has the look you want.

Once you have installed Image Composer, you can open it directly from the FrontPage Explorer. You can also open Image Composer from the FrontPage Editor by selecting Tools, Show Image Editor or by double-clicking the image. Once you open Image Composer, it is often handy to keep it open while you edit your Web page. That way, you can use your Taskbar to toggle back and forth.

In this chapter, you'll explore two ways to send your edited image to a FrontPage Web, using the File option to do that, or just copying the image through the Clipboard. You'll see these options later in this chapter.

Installing Image Composer

If you installed Microsoft Image Composer as part of installing Microsoft FrontPage 98, it's already there, and you can skip right on ahead to the next section of this chapter. If you elected not to install Image Composer during your original FrontPage 98 setup, or if you're not sure whether or not you installed Image Composer, you can do that easily from your FrontPage 98 installation CD.

To install Image Composer, place the CD in your CD drive and select Start, Run from the Taskbar. In the Open area type **E:\Setup.exe** and OK the Run dialog box. See Figure 13.1.

You'll be given the option of installing Image Composer.

> **TIP** Unless you have unlimited hard disk space, you are better off pulling clip art image files off the FrontPage 98 CD as needed.

Starting Image Composer

You can start Image Composer from your Taskbar, just as you would any other application. But if you are working in FrontPage, the easiest way to start editing a graphic is to launch Image Composer directly from the FrontPage Explorer.

There are two ways to start Image Composer from the FrontPage Explorer. If you are creating a *new* graphic image for your Web site, you can start the Image Composer by clicking the button in the FrontPage Explorer toolbar. See Figure 13.2.

If you wish to edit a graphic image that you have already imported into your Web site (as you learned to do in Chapter 6, "Enhancing Pages with Themes, Graphics, and Multimedia"), you can double-click that image in the FrontPage Explorer Folder view or Hyperlink view.

> **TIP** You should take care to close Microsoft Image Composer when you are done editing an image, because launching an image a second time starts a separate instance of the program (unfortunately). Microsoft recommends against having more than three copies of Image Composer running on your computer to prevent using too much system memory at any given time.

Associating Your Image Files with Image Composer

By default, Image Composer establishes itself as FrontPage's default image editor when you install it. However, if for any reason it is not the default, and you wish it to be, you can change the file associations accordingly. This means establishing Image Composer as the default editor for your GIF and JPG image files, the two primary image file types in Web sites.

Change the default image editor by selecting Tools, Options from the FrontPage Explorer menu. This will yield the Options dialog box shown in Figure 13.1. Click the Configure Editors tab and select the file format that you wish to associate with Image Editor (for example, GIF files or JPEG files). Use the Modify button to change the associated image editor to Image Composer.

Part
III

Ch
13

FIG. 13.1

Through the Configure Editors sheet, you can specify that Image Composer handle your GIF and JPEG files.

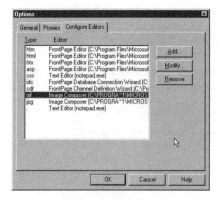

Getting Started with Image Composer

What do you need to start creating or editing an image by using Image Composer? The short answer is nothing. You can create a graphic image from scratch in Image Composer.

However, if you have an image you wish to edit, you can import an image file. Image Composer will import with any of the following file types:

- A scanned photo in TIF file format.
- A GIF image file.
- A Targa file.
- A JPEG image file.
- A bitmap file (*.bmp or *.dib).
- An Adobe Photoshop file.
- A file created in Altamira Composer.

You can open files from any of these formats in Image Composer. If you created an image in a graphics program that is not on this list, chances are overwhelming that your graphics program will allow you to export your image to one of those formats.

Exploring Image Composer Tools and Palettes

Image Composer is a richly featured program. Like all graphics programs, however, its interface can be quite intimidating, especially if you've rarely or never used a serious graphics package before. If you're familiar with graphics programs, however, Image Composer will present no difficulties whatsoever.

Besides the image editing area, there are five parts of the Image Composer screen, each part movable or removable, including the top toolbar, the left toolbox, the Color Swatch, the Status bar, and the color Palette. See Figure 13.2 to identify these components.

FIG. 13.2
All the toolbars on the
Image Composer
screen can be moved
to any location you
wish.

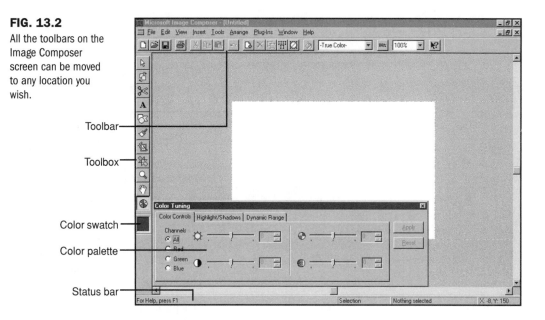

Toolbar

Toolbox

Color swatch

Color palette

Status bar

A Look at the Toolbar

Much of the Image Composer Toolbar will look familiar to users of FrontPage and other
Microsoft Office applications. There are the same file management tools—New, Open, Save.
The Print button looks familiar as does the undo button.

What's new are tools that let you select and work with *Sprites*. We'll come back to what Sprites
are momentarily, but for now we'll go with a quick definition: *Sprites* are graphic image objects
that you import or create in Image Composer. See Table 13.1 for a list of Image Composer tools.

Table 13.1   The Image Composer Toolbar

Tool	Tool Name	Description
	New	Creates a new Image Composer file.
	Open	Allows you to open or manage existing image files.
	Save	Saves the current file. If the file has been named, the file is resaved with the same name.
	Print	Opens the Print dialog box.

Part

III

Ch

13

continues

Table 13.1   Continued

Tool	Tool Name	Description
	Cut	Removes selected objects and places them in the Clipboard to be pasted.
	Copy	Copies selected objects into the Clipboard, to be pasted.
	Paste	Places the contents of the Clipboard on the page.
	Undo	Undoes the last command you performed.
	Insert Image File	Opens the Insert from File dialog box, allowing you to place saved graphic image files from a list of formats.
	Delete	Deletes the selected object(s) from the page.
	Duplicate	Creates a duplicate of the selected object(s), offset down and to the right of the original.
	Select All	Selects all objects on the page.
	Clear Selection	Deselects whatever objects are selected.
-True Color-	Color Format	Pick from a list of color formats
	Color Fill	Fills the selected region with the specified color
100%	Actual Size	Resets an imported image back to its original size.
100%	Zoom Percent	Zoom in to make objects appear larger, or press Ctrl+click to zoom out and see more objects.
	Help	Click, then point to any part of the screen for help on that feature.

The Toolbox to the Left of the Screen

The Image Composer Toolbox is where you find all the real goodies. Most of them won't get explored in depth until Chapter 14, "Working with Sprites," and Chapter 15, "Using Effects for Maximum Impact," but we'll take a peek at them now. See Table 13.2 for a list of Toolbox tools.

Table 13.2   The Image Composer Toolbox

Toolbox Tool	Tool Name	Description
	Arrange	Sizes, Rotates, Moves Sprites front to back, or Aligns Sprites.
	Cutout	Lets you cutout shapes from a sprite to produce a separate sprite consisting of that shape.
	Text	Lets you create and edit text.
	Shapes	Draws rectangles, ovals, and polygons.
	Paint	Paints images with a large variety of brush stroke types.
	Effects	Opens the Effects dialog box for applying accents, blurs, and other special effects.
	Texture	Lets you copy properties Transfer) Transfer of one sprite to another.
	Zoom	Like the Zoom List in the Toolbar, zooms in on part of the page.
	Pan	Let's you adjust the section of the page being viewed.
	Color Tuning	Allows you to tune highlights Tuning) and shadowing.
	Color Swatch	Lets you select the default fill color.

TIP One of the things that makes the Image Composer seem a little chaotic at first is that the Palettes change depending on what tool you have selected from the toolbox. If you find the Palette changes distracting, you can turn them off by selecting Tools, Options and using the Tool Palettes tab in the Options dialog box, and deselect the Show New Tool Palette on Change check box.

Part
III

Ch
13

Creating Sprites

Sprites are sort of the atoms of the Image Composer Universe—the smallest object that you create. Or is there a smallest object in the universe? The analogy has its limits but think of sprites as the basic building blocks of a file in Image Composer. Later in this chapter, you'll investigate the relationship between these little (or big) sprites, and Image Composer files. But for now, you'll create a cute little sprite and play with it for a while. To do that, you'll pick up a tool or two from the Image Composer toolbox.

Creating and Editing Sprites with Tools in the Toolbox

To the left of the screen is the toolbox. The 10 tools allow you to accomplish all kinds of image editing. It will take the next three chapters to try experiments with all these tools, but you can look at some of the tools right away.

As you select different tools in the Toolbox, you will notice different *palettes* appear in the lower portion of your Image Composer window. Palettes change depending on what Toolbox tool you are working with.

To Create a Square   The Shape tool in the Toolbox allows you to create ovals, rectangles, and other polygons. You'll explore shapes in detail in the next chapter, but you can experiment with one quickly now.

1. Click the Shapes tool in the toolbox. The tooltip will help you find the tool.

 When you select the Shapes tool in the Toolbox, the Shapes Palette opens in the lower part of the screen.

2. Select the square-looking rectangle tool in the Shapes-Geometry Palette.
3. Draw a rectangle in the drawing area (see Figure 13.3).
4. Click the Create button in the Shapes Palette.

To Resize a Selected Object

1. Click the lower-right handle—an arrow pointing down and to the right.
2. Click and drag down to the right to enlarge the selected sprite.

To Rotate a Selected Object

1. Click the first tool in the toolbox—the Arrange tool. The Arrange tool Palette shows the selected sprite's location, alignment, and rotation angle.
2. Click the rotation handle—the upper-right of the right corner and side arrows. Notice that the upper-right handle looks different. It is used to rotate an object (see Figure 13.4).
3. Drag up slightly on the rotation handle to angle the selected object.

FIG. 13.3
The rectangle tool lets you draw free-form rectangles and adjust for hard/soft appearance.

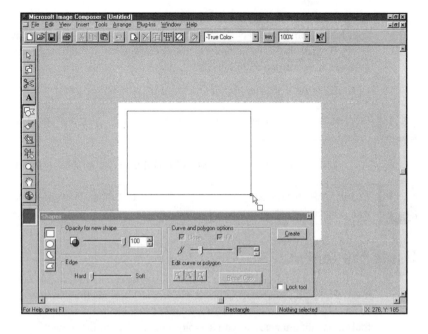

FIG. 13.4
The Arrange palette gives you extensive control over the position of your object.

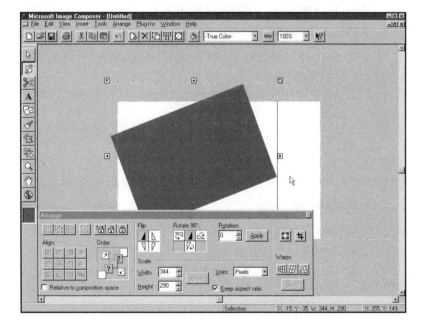

Part
III

Ch
13

Warps and Filters   No, warps and filters are not tools to stretch your backbone and screen your lungs from harmful contaminants in the air. But they do let you have a lot of fun with a selected sprite. Before you explore other components of the Image Composer environment, try getting a little warped and filtered.

1. Click the Warps and Filters tool in the Toolbox.

 TIP Here's another chance to note how the Palette changes as you select a different tool from the Toolbox.

2. Click the Escher warp and click the <u>A</u>pply button in the Warps and Filters dialog box.

 TIP You'll do some serious filtering and warping in Chapter 15, "Using Effects for Maximum Impact." If you want to experiment with something safe now, try adding an Edge outline to the sprite.

Using the Toolbar

The toolbar at the top of the Image Composer screen includes tools familiar to everyone who has worked with Microsoft Office applications—buttons to open new and saved files, a button to save files, and buttons to cut, copy, and paste objects. Nothing too scary here. The rest of the tools help edit images, and you'll explore most of them in the next two chapters as you need them. But you can try a couple of them now.

To Zoom In on an Image

1. Click the Zoom Percent list in the Toolbar and select a percentage to enlarge the view of your image.

2. You will often need to use the horizontal and vertical scroll bars to find your image once you have zoomed in or out.

3. Hold down the Ctrl key while you click with Zoom selected. Ctrl+Click zooms out, allowing you to see more, but smaller objects.

4. To return to a normal-sized image, select <u>V</u>iew, <u>A</u>ctual Size from the menu, click the 100% button on the toolbar, or select 100% from the Zoom Percent list on the toolbar.

To Duplicate an Image

1. Click Duplicate from the Edit menu.

2. You can undo the duplicate image by clicking the Undo button.

3. Try duplicating the image again. You can do this several times to experiment (see Figure 13.5).

FIG. 13.5

The Duplicate feature lets you create multiple copies, but be careful not to get confused by having too many.

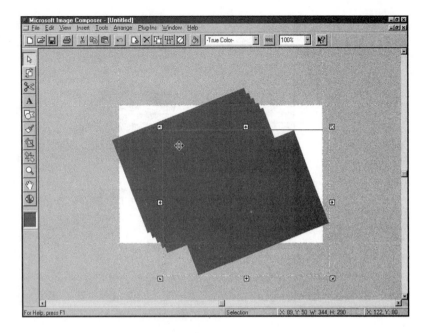

Using the Color Swatch to Select Colors

When you click the Color swatch, you can assign colors to any object. Identify that little square in the lower-left corner of your screen. That's it.

1. Click the Color Swatch.
2. Select a color in the Color Picker palette.
3. Lighten or darken the color hue by clicking the vertical bar next to the color palette in the Color Picker.
4. When you have selected a color, click OK in the Color Picker dialog box.
5. Draw another rectangle and render it. The fill color will reflect your selection from the Color Swatch.

Changing Colors for a Selected Sprite

You can reassign a new color to a selected sprite. The Patterns and Fills tool in the Toolbox allows you to do all kinds of fun things with fills, but it can also fill a selected sprite with the currently selected color fill.

1. Select the sprite to which you want to assign the selected color swatch.
2. Click the Colors and Fills tool in the Toolbox.
3. Select Current Color Fill from the Patterns and Fills list, and set the Opacity Spin Box to 100 (see Figure 13.6).

Part

III

Ch

13

FIG. 13.6
Selecting a Color Fill and Opacity.

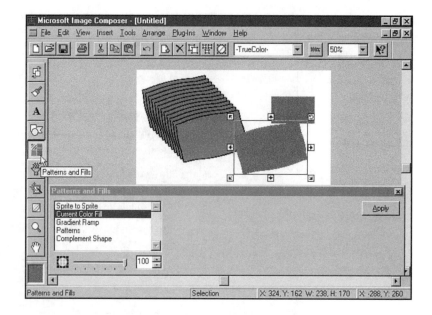

Interpreting the Status Bar

The strip of information on the bottom of the screen is the Status Bar. It indicates, first of all, whether or not you have a sprite selected. If not, the message is simply "Nothing Selected." Try clicking off your sprite. The Status Bar still indicates pixel coordinates as you move your cursor around the screen—how many pixels up (Y axis) or to the left (X Axis) where your cursor is located.

When you select a sprite, the Status Bar indicates the size and location of that object. You'll explore the significance of size and location more in Chapter 14, "Working with Sprites."

Making Palettes Go Away

As you've seen, Palettes change depending on which Toolbox tool is selected. What if you would just like a nice, clear screen to work with? You can simply close any Toolbox Palette by clicking the close button in the title bar, or the F2 function key will toggle between a displayed and a disappeared Palette.

Sprites, Composition Guides, and Files

It is not necessary to save a sprite, or a bunch of sprites, in order to place them in a FrontPage Web. You can simply copy them into a page in the FrontPage Editor and then save the Web page. As you save the page, the images you have copied onto the page will be saved as files in the Web site.

In many cases, you will create images with the Image Composer, copy them onto a page, and simply close Image Composer without saving the files.

Does this mean you can never edit those images in Image Composer? Not at all. You can open an image from the FrontPage Explorer *in Microsoft Image Composer* simply by double-clicking the file in the Hyperlink or Folder View.

Why then, would anyone want to bother saving a file in Image Composer? One good reason is that you may create a file with many sprites, not all of which you want to copy into a Web. You can save many sprites by saving the file that they are a part of.

When you do save a file, you can control the size of that file by editing the size of the *Composition Guide*. The Composition Guide does not necessarily take up the entire Image Composer Workspace. Like the sprite (or sprites) that sit on it, the Composition Guide area can be sized.

Selecting a size for the Composition Guide area, and arranging sprites within that, gives you control over how your image will appear on your Web site.

When a file in Image Composer is saved, only the sprites that are within the Composition Guide are saved. When you select the Send to FrontPage feature in Image Composer, only sprites within the Composition Guide get sent to the open FrontPage Web site.

The *entire* Composition Guide area gets sent to FrontPage when you select the Send to FrontPage feature. Sometimes that's not so helpful. It requires that your sprite (or sprites) be aligned just right on the Composition Guide, or the image won't look right on the Web site.

There are a couple ways to resolve this problem. You can resize your Composition Guide area and arrange your sprite (or sprites) within it properly. Or, the other option is to simply copy your sprite into the FrontPage Editor via the Clipboard. Both these options have advantages, as you'll see.

CAUTION

Don't forget that you're dealing with two files here and to save your image file in the more appropriate place. If you create a sprite in Image Composer, copy and paste it on a FrontPage Editor Web page, then close both the FrontPage Editor and the Image Composer without saving, you'll lose your sprite. If you know or suspect that you'll need to fiddle with the sprite itself, it might be simpler to save it in Image Composer. If you don't plan on making any sprite changes, saving the pasted sprite in the FrontPage Editor Web page will most likely be sufficient.

Part
III

Ch
13

Copying Sprites

Since copying a sprite to a Web page is the simplest way to put an image on your FrontPage Web Site, let's explore that first.

You can simply select a sprite and use the Copy tool in the Image Composer toolbar to copy that image to the FrontPage Editor. The procedure is:

1. Right-click a sprite or select several sprites at once by clicking the Arrange tool in the Image Composer toolbox and drawing a marquee around all the sprites you wish to select.

2. Click the button in the toolbar.

3. Use the Taskbar to open, or switch to an open page, in the FrontPage Editor.

4. Place your insertion point on a Web page and click the Paste button in the FrontPage Editor toolbar.

5. Save the FrontPage Editor file. You will be prompted to assign a file name to your imported image.

Defining Composition Guides

You can specify the size of your Composition Guide in the Composition Properties dialog box.

You can place sprites outside of the Composition Guide. However, if you save your file in a format other than a Microsoft Image Manager file, only sprites inside the Composition Guide are saved. If you print your file, you have the option of printing only the sprites inside the Composition Guide, or the entire view.

Deciding on whether or not to save your file as an Image Composer file or another format, handling the relationship between sprites and the Composition Guide can get a little tricky. Here are three examples:

- If you created several sprites, but were only using one in a Web site, you could save the entire file (including sprites outside the Composition Guide) as a Microsoft Image Composer file. You could then open that file any time you wished by using Image Composer, and copy and paste *any* of the sprites into FrontPage.

- If you created a file with only one sprite, and you wished to send that sprite/file directly to FrontPage, you should resize your Composition Guide so that it matches the size of the sprite. Save the file as either an Image Composer file or a GIF (or JPEG file). Then use the Send to FrontPage option in the file menu.

  ▶ **See** Chapter 6, "Enhancing Pages with Themes, Graphics, and Multimedia," **p. 123**.

- If you want to save a sprite with a separate background, you can define the Composition Guide, assign it a color and size, and then define the sprite(s) on that guide—and move them around on the guide. You'll see how to use this last, useful option shortly.

- If you feel that this is all too complicated, no problem. Just copy your sprites into FrontPage and don't even worry about saving files. When the day comes that this method doesn't give you enough freedom to work with files in the most efficient way, try out the other options.

To Define the Size of a Composition Guide Composition width is defined in pixels—those tiny dots that make up a monitor viewing area. You can define a Composition Guide to be any number of pixels wide or high. The default is 640 pixels by 480. This is the size of many VGA monitors.

1. Define Composition Guide size by right-clicking a blank part of the editing area and selecting Properties from the shortcut menu.
2. Enter width and height in the Composition Properties dialog box.

To Define the Background Color of a Composition Guide

1. Right-click a blank part of the editing area.
2. Select Properties from the shortcut menu.
3. Enter up to 255 in the Red, Green, and Blue areas of the Composition Properties dialog box.

TIP Entering 255 for all three colors produces a white background for the Composition. Entering 0 for all three colors creates a black background.

You can click the current color box (the preview of the current color) to display the palette.

Arranging Sprites in a Composition Guide

If you wish to put together a sprite (or more than one) on a Composition Guide and send that to FrontPage, you need to size your Composition Guide and then arrange your sprites on it.

You can arrange Sprites on a Composition Guide by selecting them and dragging them onto the Composition Guide.

In Figure 13.7, the three Sprites don't quite fit in the Composition Guide. Figure 13.8 shows what happens when you select File, Send to FrontPage.

In Figure 13.9, the Composition Guide has been made wider by about 80 pixels.

Now, when the file is sent to FrontPage, the entire Composition Guide will fit, and all three sprites will fit in the image.

Editing Inserted Clip Art

In Chapter 6, "Enhancing Pages with Themes, Graphics, and Multimedia," you learned to insert clip art images onto your page. That helped jazz things up a bit. But let's face it, visitors to your Web site are going to recognize that clip art. Sometimes that's fine—familiar icons help visitors feel at home at your site and help them navigate around.

Sometimes it's appropriate to be more creative. If your creative skills or confidence level aren't quite at the point of creating images from scratch, modifying someone else's image is a good way to add some variety and spice to your site.

Part
III

Ch
13

FIG. 13.7
Two and a half Sprites
in the Composition
Guide.

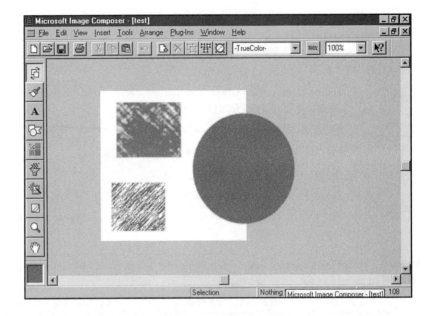

FIG. 13.8
Composition Guide
Truncating Sprites
sent to FrontPage.

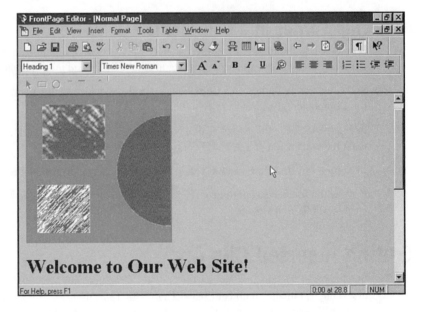

FIG. 13.9

Composition Guide Including Sprites sent to FrontPage.

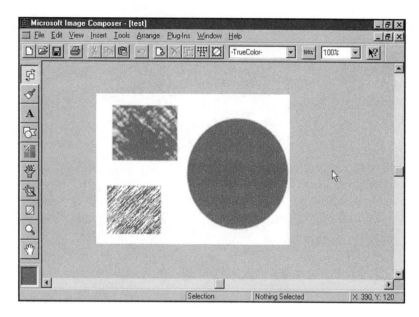

To Edit Clip Art in Image Composer

Earlier you learned to insert clip art images directly onto a Web page by using the FrontPage Editor. When you save your page, the inserted clip art file is saved to the Web site.

▶ **See** Chapter 6, "Enhancing Pages with Themes, Graphics, and Multimedia," **p. 123.**

One you have inserted a clip art image on your page and saved the page, you can edit that clip art directly from the FrontPage Explorer. Simply switch to the FrontPage Explorer (the Show FrontPage Explorer button in the FrontPage Editor toolbar), and then double-click the clip art image in the Folder or Hyperlink view.

As soon as you double-click the image file in the FrontPage Editor (Folder or Hyperlink view), Image Composer opens with the selected file ready for editing.

As soon as you launch Image Composer by double-clicking an image, you're there! Your graphic image is ready to edit (see Figure 13.10).

You can experiment with any of the editing features you've looked at in this chapter, and then send your image back to FrontPage. Instead of reinserting a new graphic image, you can just select View, Refresh from the FrontPage editor menu, and the image will be updated. Figure 13.11 shows the large "New" clip art image with a little touching up in Image Composer.

Part

III

Ch

13

FIG. 13.10

Image Composer
launched from the
FrontPage Editor.

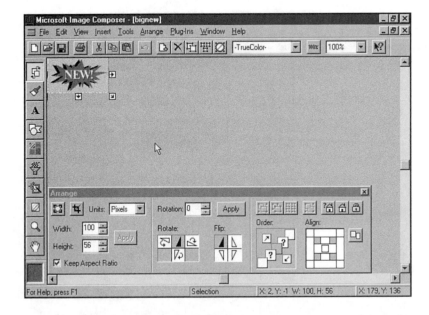

FIG. 13.11

Clip art edited in Image
Composer.

From Here...

In this chapter, you explored the Image Composer environment, and even had a little fun editing a bitmap image. You investigated different ways to take Image Composer graphic images into FrontPage. Hopefully all this has whetted your appetite for some serious (or unserious) image creation and editing. The fun part comes next.

Look to the following chapters for further ways to create and edit graphic images:

- Chapter 14, "Working with Sprites," will give you the ability to create new graphic images by using text, drawings, and imported images.
- Chapter 15, "Using Effects for Maximum Impact," will cover the wide range of image effects available by using Patterns and Fills, more Warps and Filters, Art Effects, and Color Tuning.
- Chapter 16, "Tailoring Your Image for FrontPage Documents," will examine different options for making your Image Composer files work well with your Web site.

Part
III

Ch
13

## CHAPTER 14

Working with Sprites

In Chapter 13, "Getting Started with Image Composer," you began to examine sprites. You saw that they are the basic building blocks of Image Composer graphical objects. Remember that an Image Composer file can be composed of one or many sprites.

Microsoft Image Composer allows you to create, edit, shape, warp, align, and combine sprites in ways that open up whole new vistas for your FrontPage Web site. Image Composer allows, you to present text styles and text patterns not available from the font list in FrontPage. Image Composer shapes, combined with arranging tools, allow you to create attractive and intuitive symbols, icons, and graphical guides for visitors to your site. In this chapter, you'll explore the process of creating custom icons, special bullets, and helpful graphical clues that can make your FrontPage-created Web site comfortable and fun for your visitors. ■

Working with graphical text

Stretch, rotate, and warp text to create imaginative text presentations.

Drawing with shapes

Create your own custom designs.

Painting sprites

Touch up sprites with brushstrokes.

Arranging sprites

Combine shapes and text to design custom buttons, tools, and link icons.

Creating imagemaps

Let visitors to your site navigate via an entertaining and intuitive imagemap.

Graphical Text

Microsoft Internet Explorer 3.0 supports a nice variety of fonts. In Chapter 5, "Developing the Basic Page: Text, Lists, and Hyperlinks," you learned to format text in fonts besides standard Times Roman. Those fonts will display when your site is visited if your visitors are using Internet Explorer 3.0. Unfortunately, not everyone is using I.E. 3.0 so you're still constrained in what you can do with text. All the font selections in the world won't let you tilt text, stretch text, or fill text with fun gradient fills and shading, but Image Composer will. And from there, it's a simple matter to send or copy that graphical text to FrontPage.

N O T E Internet Explorer 4.0, scheduled to be in final release when this book is published, also includes support for dynamic fonts. ■

Since this is so much fun, why not do most or all of your text in Image Composer, jazz it up to the max, and then zip it over to the FrontPage Editor? The drawbacks are that you are working with graphical image files, with all the implications for speed that were discussed in Chapter 6, "Enhancing Pages with Themes, Graphics, and Multimedia." Editing text is much simpler using the word processing power of the FrontPage Editor so the choice is yours. Be sure to use text from Image Composer sparingly—and to good effect.

Composing Text

You can compose text in the Text Palette by clicking the Text tool in the Image Composer Toolbox. This yields the Text palette, which lets you choose font, font size, font style, anti-aliasing, and opacity (see Figure 14.1). Click in the composition space to establish a text box and type your text. If you click outside the text box, the box becomes a movable, resizable sprite.

The changes you make in the Text Palette aren't applied until you click the text box itself. You can do this with each change, and then double-click the text box to bring the Text Palette back up. If, after you apply an effect, you don't like the way your text looks, simply click the Undo button in the toolbar.

If you want to get rid of your text sprite, click it and press the Delete key.

Opacity

Opacity is technically a measure of the ratio between solid and opaque (filled in) pixels. Opacity ranges from 100 percent—fully colored—to 0 percent. Zero percent opacity is fully transparent, so if you choose it, you won't be able to see the sprite. Anything below 10 percent, in fact, will be extremely faint.

You set opacity by dragging the opacity slider between 0 percent and 100 percent, or you can set opacity by entering a number in the Spin box.

 T I P An opacity setting of 100 makes your text completely opaque, or nontransparent. An opacity setting of less than 10 makes your text filmy, translucent, and light.

FIG. 14.1
The text dialog box allows you to control whether or not you want your fonts smoothed out via antialiasing.

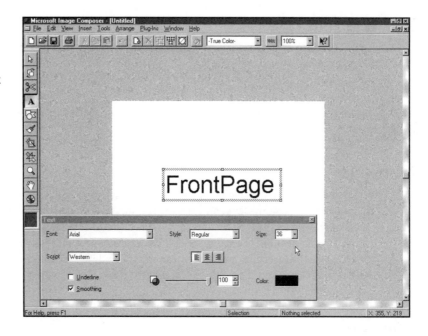

Font Colors

One advantage of creating graphical text in Image Composer is that you have an unlimited array of colors and fills to use. The whole spectrum of colors available from the Color Picker can be applied to text. When you compose text using the Text Palette, you can click the Color box in the lower-right corner of the Text Palette to yield the Color Picker and choose a color (Figure 14.2). You apply colors to a selected sprite by clicking the Color box and selecting colors and hues from the range offered. A shortcut is to right-click the Color box and select your color from the resulting color palette.

FIG. 14.2
The Color Picker offers a virtually unlimited range of colors, or you can customize your own.

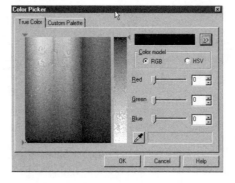

Part
III

Ch

14

Selecting Font Type

You can choose from a list of fonts by clicking the Font drop-down menu on the Text Palette. Click the font you wish to display and click in the text box in the composition space to see what it looks like.

 T I P You can also select font size in the Font dialog box. We'll explore another way to adjust font size later on in this chapter.

Editing Text

After you have shaped, shaded, stretched, rotated, and generally distorted text beyond recognition, you can still edit the text content easily. Simply click the text box in the composition space and click the Text tool in the toolbox, or, double-click the text box and the Text Palette will appear. If you only want to change the text itself, not its properties, single-click in the text box, click to place the insertion point where you want it, and type whatever you want. The new text will automatically adopt the properties of the text that's already in place. Click outside the text box to set the text in place.

Sizing Text

You can select text size from the Text Palette, but you have even more flexibility to size text by using the handles on a text sprite once you have created it.

You can compress text horizontally by dragging in on either side handle (see Figure 14.3).

FIG. 14.3

The box handles let you resize text to whatever size you want.

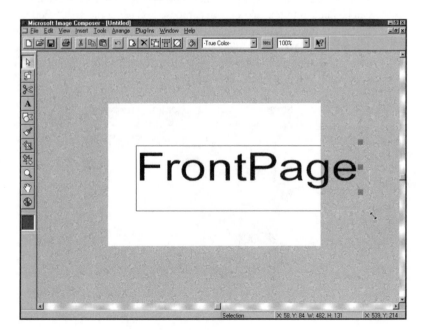

You can also compress a text sprite vertically by dragging in on the top or bottom handles, and you can stretch text by dragging *out* on any of the handles.

Of course, if you stretch too far, compress too much, or just plain wreck your text, there's always the Undo button in the toolbar to get you back to square one.

Rotating Text

You can rotate a text sprite the same way we learned to rotate sprites in Chapter 13, "Getting Started with Image Composer," by clicking the rotation handle in the upper-right corner of the sprite and pulling down (to rotate clockwise) or up (to rotate counterclockwise). Rotated text can be a helpful component in buttons and imagemaps, and even for spicing up a Web page.

Using Graphical Text in a FrontPage Web

The sprites you create by using the Text tool in Image Composer have the same graphical image properties as any other image. You can copy them into the FrontPage Editor or send them into a Web site.

▶ **See** Chapter 13, "Getting Started with Image Composer," for copying sprites to the FrontPage Editor or sending Composition Guides to a FrontPage Web site." **p. 277**

Once you copy or send your image into FrontPage, you can apply all the image-editing features available in FrontPage Editor, including sizing, floating, and wrapping text around your new image. The entire spectrum of effects in Editor's image toolbar is available to you to enhance the text sprite.

Working with Shapes

Image Composer allows you to create rectangles and squares, ovals and circles, straight and curved lines, freehand drawings, and objects with any number of sides. Table 14.1 lists the tools in the Shapes Palette, which is shown in Figure 14.4.

Table 14.1   The Shapes Palette

Tool	Tool Name	What It Does
(Pic of Rectangle)	Rectangle	Draws squares or rectangles. To draw a square, hold down the Ctrl key while you draw the rectangle.
(Pic of circle)	Oval	Draws circles or ovals. To draw a circle, hold down the Ctrl key while you click and drag a rectangular shape that will frame the circle or oval.
(Pic of Curve)	Splines	Draws curved lines, freehand drawings, shapes, and filled-in shapes.
(Pic of Polygon)	Polygon	Creates shapes with any number of sides. Click to set a point, double-click to complete the polygon.

Part
III

Ch
14

FIG. 14.4
The Shapes Palette lets
you create and edit
standard and freeform
shapes.

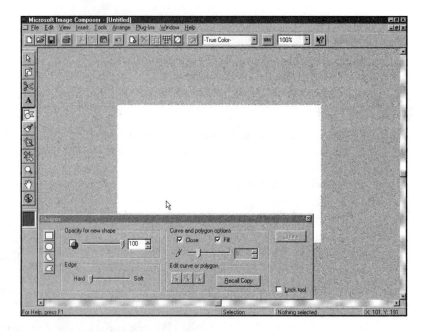

Locking Shape Tools   If you are going to be drawing more than one oval, rectangle, polygon, or curve, you can select the Lock Tool check box in the Shapes Palette. With the Lock Tool box selected, your selected shape remains the default until you pick another shape, and you can draw circles, squares, or lines repeatedly. With the Lock Tool box deselected, each time you render a shape, you need to pick a Shape tool before you can begin to draw.

Working with Rectangles

In Chapter 13, "Getting Started with Image Composer," you learned the basics of creating rectangles. You can make a rectangle square by holding down the Ctrl key as you click and drag the rectangle outline.

Circles and Ovals

To draw a circle or an oval, first select the Shapes tool in the Image Composer Toolbox and click the Oval tool in the Shapes Palette.

Once you have selected the Oval tool, click the Render button.

Curves

In Image Composer, curves are more than just lines that bend. Curves can include sprites with wavy or rounded edges. Image Composer's curves are a flexible and utilitarian tool for creating all kinds of shapes. You can set the width of a curve, edit nodal points within it, and elect to fill the closed curve or leave it open. Figure 14.5 shows one example of the kind of curve you can create.

FIG. 14.5

By using a combination of nodal points on the curve, you can shape it to whatever shape you want.

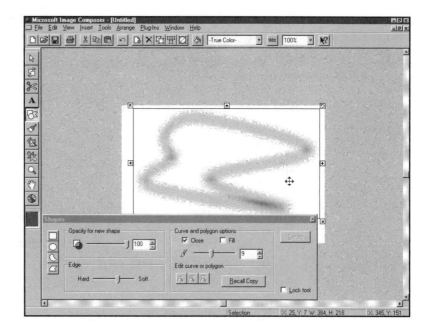

Setting the Width of a Line   If you elect not to fill your curve, you can adjust the width of the outline by dragging the Line Width Slider. The Line Width Slider is in the Spline and Polygon Defaults area of the Shapes-Geometry Palette (it's associated with the small brush icon), and becomes active only when you deselect the Fill check box.

Unlike other shapes, curves and polygons can be closed or not closed. If you deselect the Close check box in the Shapes Palette, you can draw freehand lines and curves that do not form a closed shape.

Drawing a Straight Line   Before you experiment with some of the trickier shapes, explore the most basic type—a nice straight line. Straight lines can be copied into a FrontPage Editor document to create unique, customized horizontal lines.

1. Select the Curve Tool in the Shapes-Geometry Palette.
2. Click the starting point for the line.
3. Click the ending point of the line.
4. Click the Create button in the Shapes-Geometry Palette.

You can then move your line by selecting the Arrange tool in the Toolbox and dragging the middle of the sprite to a new location. You can rotate your line by dragging clockwise or counterclockwise on the rotate handle in the sprite. See Figure 14.6.

Making Waves   Sprites allow you to create smooth curves and wavy lines. Each point on the wave can then be individually edited.

Part

III

Ch

14

FIG. 14.6
Rotating a Straight Line
Spline is identical to
rotating any Image
Composer sprite.

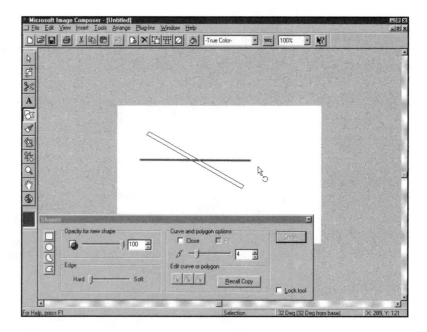

To draw a wavy line, do the following:

1. Select the Curve button in the Shapes Palette.

 TIP   If you are creating many examples of the same shape, or you need many attempts to create a shape, click the Sticky check box to retain a default shape.

When you are drawing a spline, your cursor takes on a special wavy icon appearance.

2. Click the starting point for your curved line.
3. Click the next nodal point in the spline.
4. Continue to click at nodal points until you have marked all the nodal points for your wavy line. See Figure 14.7.
5. Before you Create the line, you can click the Edit Points button in the Spline and Polygon Defaults area of the Shapes-Geometry Palette, and edit any of the nodal points. See Figure 14.7.
6. Before you Create the line, you can adjust the Spline Line Width and the Hardness or Softness of the edges.
7. Click the Create button when everything is set.

Odd Shapes and Zigzag Lines

You can use the Polygon tool to create closed shapes of any configuration. You can also use the Polygon tool to create zigzag lines.

FIG. 14.7
You can edit Nodal
Points on a Curve
before clicking Create.

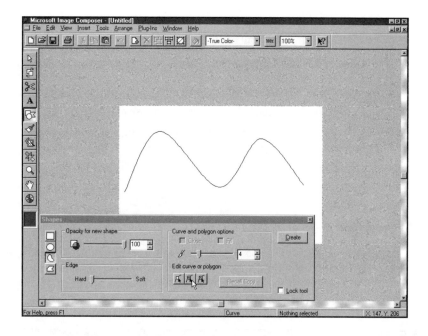

Drawing zigzag lines with the Polygon tool is very similar to drawing wavy lines with the Curve tool. Deselect the Closed check box and click to place nodal points, select line width, edit points as necessary, and then render the line. See Figure 14.8 for an example of a result.

FIG. 14.8
A Zig-Zag polygon with
slightly soften edges.

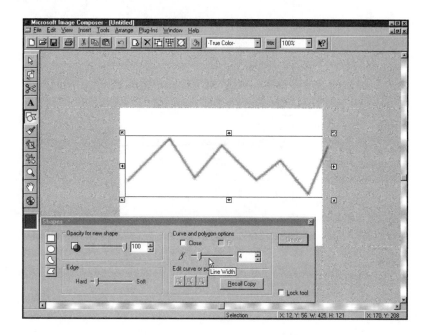

Part
III

Ch
14

To draw a closed shape, select the Closed check box in the Shapes Palette. Using the Polygon tool, click each nodal point of the shape. Click Create to set the polygon in place.

Closed and Filled Polygons and Curves   By *not* selecting the Close check box in the Shapes Palette, you can use the Polygon or Curve tool to draw zigzag or wavy lines. You can create closed shapes (where the end nodal point is automatically continued to the starting nodal point) that are not filled in by selecting the Close check box, but *not* the Fill check box.

You can also create closed and filled polygons. When you do, the closed areas of the shape are filled with the selected color swatch. The process of drawing a closed filled polygon is similar to creating a closed polygon without a fill—just click the Fill check box before you render the shape.

Arranging Sprites

Once you begin to compose graphic images from more than one sprite, you will find it necessary to arrange sprites. Sprites can be aligned so that a group of images is on the same horizontal or vertical plane, or even all centered together. You can also position sprites in front of or behind each other. This technique is often used to place text on top of a shape. See Figure 14.9.

FIG. 14.9

This figure shows a text box on top of a polygon sprite.

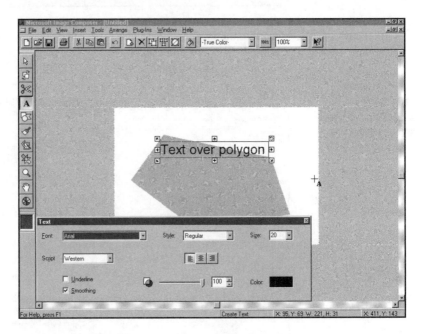

The Arrange Palette, shown in Figure 14.10, also lets you manipulate sprite properties in other useful ways, as follows:

FIG. 14.10
The Arrange Palette lets
you determine which
sprite appears in which
position.

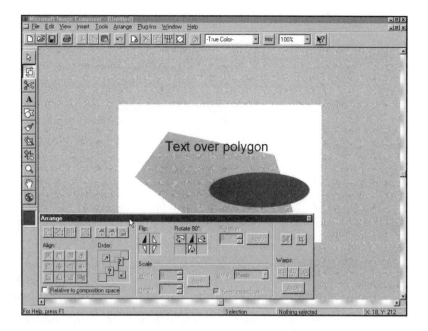

Fit sprites to a Bounding Box

Crop sprites

Group sprites

Size sprites by percent

Rotate sprites precisely

Assign a default location to a sprite.

Taken together, these features allow you to create imagemaps and navigational buttons to
which you can attach hotspot hyperlinks. The resulting imagemaps allow visitors to your page
to jump to hyperlinked bookmarks or Web pages by pointing and clicking at one element in a
larger picture.

▶ **See** Chapter 6, "Enhancing Pages with Themes, Graphics and Multimedia," for instructions on
assigning hyperlinks to images, **p. 123**

Moving Sprites Forward and Backward

By arranging sprites front and back, you can place text against a shape to create an effective
navigational button.

You will find buttons to move selected sprites in front of and behind each other in the Order
area of the Arrange Palette. When you point at the buttons, tooltips will identify those buttons.
Those buttons are listed in Table 14.2.

Part
III

Ch
14

Table 14.2 Moving Sprites Forward and Backward

Ordering Tool	What It Does
Send Forward	Moves the selected sprite one level above the other sprites that share the same space.
Send Backward	Moves the selected sprite one level behind other sprites that share the same space.
To Back	Sends the selected sprite all the way to the back of (behind) all other sprites that share the same space.
To Front	Brings the selected sprite all the way to the front of all other sprites that share the same space.

Ordering Three Sprites   Let's say you have three sprites that you wish to combine into a button that will be used as a hyperlink in your FrontPage Web. Those three sprites might be an oval, a polygon, and text. See Figure 14.10 for an example of such a sprite collection.

You can move one sprite on top of another by selecting it and dragging from the middle of the sprite. When you do so, the sprite you're dragging is placed on top of the target sprite. In graphics terminology, that means it is at the *Front*.

There are times when you will drag one sprite on top of another, but you want the target sprite to be on top of the pile. If this is the case, select the sprite you want to move one layer back, and click the Send Backward tool in the Order area of the Align Palette.

CAUTION
Clicking the Send to Back button will send the selected object *all the way* to the back of the stack of sprites.

When in doubt, experiment. You can arrange objects in any order to create an effective image.

Aligning Sprites

Aligning sprites is handy when you are creating a row of buttons or tools to let visitors navigate your site. You can center a text sprite horizontally and vertically within a shape. You can align several buttons along a horizontal line to make a nice neat row of buttons.

The first step in aligning a group of sprites is to select the Arrange tool from the Toolbox and draw a marquee around all the sprites you wish to align. You do so by clicking in the composition space outside the sprites and dragging the mouse until it encompasses all of them. See Figure 14.11.

FIG. 14.11
This demonstrates the selection of all three sprites with a Marquee.

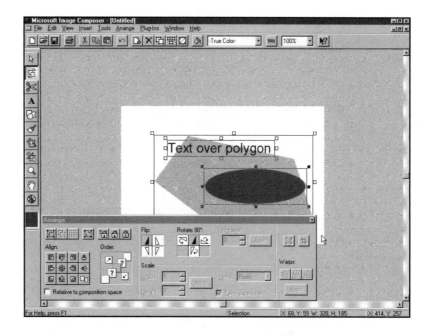

CAUTION

Before aligning sprites, make sure you have selected *all* the sprites to be aligned.

You can align sprites in the following ways:

> By upper-left corners
>
> By upper-right corners
>
> By lower-left corners
>
> By lower-right corners
>
> By tops
>
> By bottoms
>
> By left sides
>
> By right sides
>
> By centers
>
> By centers vertically
>
> By centers horizontally
>
> By touching edges

Part
III

Ch
14

To Align Sprites: The process of aligning sprites is basically the same no matter what kind of alignment you want. The two steps are:

1. Select all the sprites to be aligned.

2. Click one of the Alignment options in the Align area of the Arrange Palette.

Centering Sprites   Centering is particularly useful for creating buttons. You can select a background and text—or more objects—and align their centers to create a button.

After you select all the sprites which are to be center-aligned, Image Composer will prompt you to select one of the images to act as the center for centering. All other sprites will be aligned so that they share the same center as the sprite you select (see Figure 14.12.)

FIG. 14.12
Selecting a center for the sprites in order to create a button.

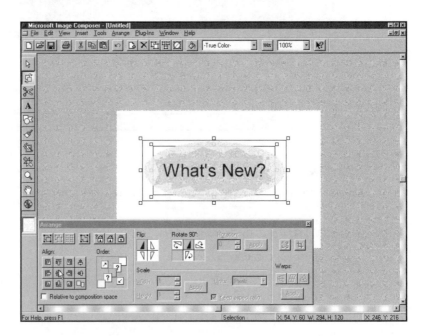

Aligning Sprites Horizontally and Vertically   You align sprites horizontally and vertically in much the same way you center sprites. Select all the sprites to be aligned and click the Tops, Bottoms, Right Side, or Left Side, tools in the Align area of the Arrange Palette.

Centering Sprites Horizontally and Vertically   Not only can you align centers, tops, or bottoms (or lefts and rights) of selected sprites, you can align the centers of selected sprites *horizontally* or *vertically*.

Grouping Sprites

Once you have arranged two or more sprites, you can group them. Grouping Sprites allows you to move and size them together. For example, if you created a button out of three sprites, you could group those three sprites and move and duplicate the button as you would a single sprite. Most formatting features, however, cannot be applied to grouped sprites.

After you group sprites, you can ungroup them and edit any of the single sprites individually. To group two or more sprites, do the following:

1. Select the Arrange Palette.
2. Draw a marquee around the sprites you wish to group, or hold the Shift key down and click more than one sprite.
3. Click the Group button just above the Order area in the Arrange Palette.

Once you have grouped sprites, you can move the new (grouped) sprite just as you would any other sprite. However, if you want to edit the features of one of the sprites, you need to ungroup first by clicking the grouped sprite and clicking the Ungroup button in the Align Palette.

 TIP One handy technique for creating a set of buttons is to group all the sprites used in a model button, duplicate the button, and ungroup and edit the text in each button (see Figure 14.13.)

FIG. 14.13
Buttons created by grouping and ungrouping duplicated sprites.

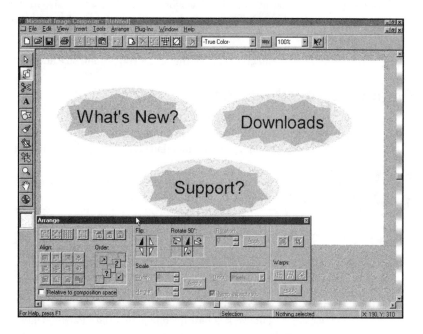

Flattening Sprites

Grouped sprites can still be ungrouped at any time—and their individual component sprites edited, deleted, or moved within the group. However, grouped sprites cannot be edited. If you want to edit a grouped sprite, you can flatten it. Flattening combines the sprites in the group, creating a new sprite. This new sprite can then be resized.

Part
III

Ch
14

Any number of sprites or grouped sprites can be included in a flattened sprite. The flattened sprite can be edited, *but it cannot be unflattened,* so before making the plunge, be sure you want to flatten a group of sprites permanently.

Fitting Sprites to a Bounding Box

The Fit to Bounding Box tool in the Arrange Palette crops any unnecessary pixels out of the area around your sprite. This is a handy tool to use before copying your sprite onto your Web page.

Cropping Sprites

You can crop any sprite by selecting the Crop tool in the Arrange Palette and dragging in on the special crop handle that appears. You need to click the Crop tool each time you want to crop because it does not stay selected.

Sizing Sprites by Percent

If you want your sprite to fill half a visitor's Web page, set the size to 50 percent. For three-quarters of a page, set to 75 percent. You can set sprite size in percent by selecting Percent from the Units list in the Arrange Palette.

To assign the percentage size, click the Sprite you wish to size and select a percent value.

Rotating Sprites Precisely

In Chapter 13, "Getting Started with Image Composer," you learned to rotate sprites by dragging clockwise or counterclockwise on the rotation handle. If you want to assign an exact angle to a rotation, you can do that in the Rotation area of the Arrange Palette.

 T I P   If you want to align an angled line or shape with angled text, select both sprites and assign them the same rotation angle.

You can also flip a selected sprite or sprites by using the Rotate and Flip buttons in the Align Palette.

Giving a Sprite a Home

If you want to fix a set location in Composition Guide for a sprite, click the Home button—the one that looks like a house at the right edge of the Align Palette. Once you set a home location for your sprite, then whenever you have moved it, you can click the Return to Home Position button to zip the sprite back to its home. If you don't want the sprite moved, you can click the Lock Position button.

Clicking the Lock Position button a second times toggles this feature off.

Creating Imagemaps

You can combine sprites in a group and bring them into FrontPage to function as an imagemap. Imagemaps are becoming a standard feature on Web sites these days and with the tools you've acquired in this chapter, you can create your own. Once the imagemap has been created in Image Composer, copy it into a page in the FrontPage Editor and assign hyperlinks to different parts of the image.

▶ **See** Chapter 6, "Enhancing Pages with Themes, Graphics and Multimedia," for assigning hyperlinks to imagemaps. **p. 123**.

Designing your imagemap in Image Composer gives you a tremendous amount of freedom to control the content and style. Using just the tools we've covered in this chapter, you can create functional and friendly imagemaps with buttons, icons, or, if you're really artistic, drawings that will send the visitor to just where he or she wants to go.

From Here...

In this chapter, we explored a wide variety of ways you can create, edit, and combine sprites. Look to the following chapters for further ways to creatively work with graphic images:

- Chapter 15, "Using Effects for Maximum Impact," will cover the wide range of image effects available using Patterns and Fills, more Warps and Filters, Art Effects and Color Tuning.

- Chapter 16, "Tailoring Your Image for FrontPage Documents," will examine different options for making your Image Composer files work well with your Web site.

Part
III

Ch
14

Using Effects for Maximum Impact

Microsoft Image Composer is loaded with an arsenal of fun effects that you can use to enhance your graphic images. Tasteful but creative, and provocative but friendly image editing can make your site unique and expressive.

In Chapter 14, "Working with Sprites," you explored using graphical text and combining text with image sprites to make customized buttons. By applying the effects that come with Image Composer, you can also transform your text into a whole series of fun, scary, impressive, and eye-catching looks.

With the addition of special fills, your images can glow, shine, and take on 3-D effects and rainbow-like shadings. Other artistic options include altering imported photos to give the impression that they were created by using water-color paints, charcoal, pencil, and other artistic tools. ■

Use special fills

Fill selected sprites with everything from palette colors to checker-boards. Lift fills from one sprite and place them in another.

Outlining and enhancing colors

Add a variety of outlines to any sprite, including 3-D shading.

Edit imported photos

Enhance colors, bring pictures into focus, change tints, turn gray hair black, and change burnt toast to perfectly done.

Get artistic

Use Art Effects such as paint and charcoal to give imported photos, text, and shapes unique textures and looks.

Working with Special Patterns and Fills

You can use just about anything for a fill pattern in Image Composer. You can change the color of any sprite. You can apply gradient fills to give your sprite that ethereal look of fading off into the somewhere. You can place patterns inside your sprite. You can use Complement Fills to create a cookie-cutter effect. And, you can steal a fill from one sprite, perhaps from an imported photo, and use it for a fill in another sprite.

Changing Colors

After you create a sprite, you can change the fill with the Fill button on the Image Composer main toolbar. To do this, select the sprite you wish to recolor and click the Color Picker in the Color Swatch to select a fill color and hue. Click the Fill button and the change is immediately made. If the recoloring masks the sprite too much, click the Undo button.

Applying Gradient Effects

Gradient effects allow you to make the color in your sprites fade from one color to another. The term *gradient* is a metaphor for gradual change—like the ramp that takes you from one level of a parking garage to another. Applied to shades or colors, a gradient creates a rainbow-like series of colors that transition from the start to the finish color.

You can assign a total of four colors to a Gradient fill so that they will blend into each other. To apply a Gradient fill, do the following:

1. Select the sprite or sprites to receive the fill.
2. Click the Effects tool in the Toolbox and select Gradient from the Category drop-down list. Click the Details tab of the Effects Palette.
3. Experiment with 19 preconfigured shading patterns that come with Image Composer. Scroll through the list of Gradient fills in the Ramp Name list and select one.
4. Click Apply to apply the Gradient Ramp fill to your selected sprite(s). See Figure 15.1.

Customizing Gradient Ramps You can create your own custom Gradient effects by selecting two, three, or four colors in the Pick Color swatches of the Gradient area of the Effects Palette.

Often Gradients will use the same color on top or on one side, and a second color on the bottom or the other side but you can mix and match up to four colors. The best way to determine what you need is to experiment. Some Gradient fills work best as backgrounds; others work fine as fills for text.

Using Pattern Fills

Image Composer comes with a set of Pattern fills that can be used in any selected sprite. As with other fills, select the sprite(s) to be filled and then access the Patterns and Fills Palette from the Toolbox.

When you select the Patterns category from the Effects Palette, you can choose from a list of patterns. If you apply a Stripes pattern, you can set the width and spacing of the stripes by using the tools behind the Details tab. See Figure 15.2.

FIG. 15.1
Applying a preconfigured gradient effect to a filled polygon.

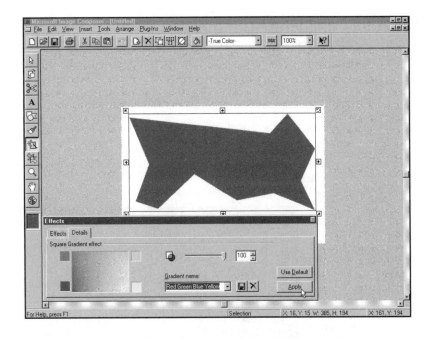

FIG. 15.2
Setting stripe width and spacing.

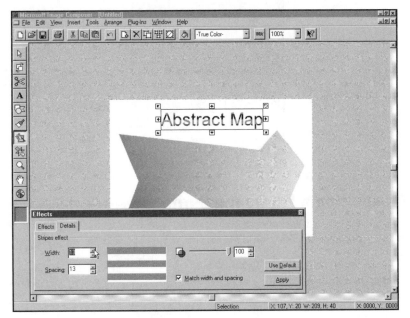

Creating Complement Shapes

Complement Shapes look like you used your original sprite as a cookie cutter to cut a piece out of a background. The background accepts the fill that has been applied to the sprite, and in effect, is a negative image of that sprite.

There are two steps to creating a Complement Shape, as follows:

1. Select the sprite to apply the Complement fill to, duplicate it, and drag it off the original sprite.

2. Using the Photographic Category of the Effects Palette, choose the Negative icon and click Apply. See Figure 15.3.

FIG. 15.3
A Complement fill showing a negative image.

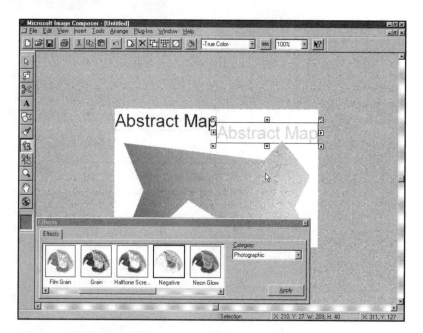

Transferring a Fill from a Sprite

Any sprite can provide a fill for another sprite—even a photo. This opens up some very interesting possibilities for filling drawings, but especially for textured text. See Figure 15.4.

To fill one sprite from another one:

1. Be sure that the target sprite is on top of the source sprite.

2. Select both sprites.

3. Click the Texture Transfer tool in the Image Composer toolbox and choose Transfer Full from the icons. Click Apply.

FIG. 15.4
Transferring a fill from sprite to sprite.

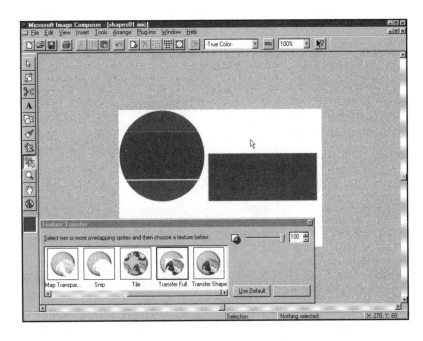

 TIP If you want your source sprite to fill your entire target sprite, the source sprite must fill the entire area behind the target sprite.

After you transfer the source sprite fill to the target, you can pull the target sprite off the source and use the two sprites in any combination you wish—or you can simply delete the source sprite once you've borrowed its fill.

You can experiment with different transfer options from the Sprite Texture Type list, but you will probably find that the Transfer Full option works best to transfer a fill to a selected sprite.

Outlining, Filtering, and Enhancing Sprites

In Chapter 13, "Getting Started with Image Composer," you experimented with some of the fun features on the Warps and Filters Palette; but, that was only the beginning. The Warps and Filters Palette contains a number of hidden utilitarian goodies, including the ability to apply outlines, filter images, and enhance photos and other sprites.

Outlining Sprites

Outlines can help frame an image. Combining outlines with subtle fills can produce attractive text. Outlines can also be used for shaded 3-D effects.

The Outline list in the Effects Palette has five different types of outlines (see Table 15.1).

Table 15.1   Outline Effects

Effect	What It Does
Drop Shadow	Can be adjusted through the Details tab to provide different angles of 3-D–style shading (see Figure 15.5)
Edge	Outlines images with a line by using the selected color swatch and line thickness (Details tab) (see Figure 15.5)
Edge Only	Creates an outline for the selected sprite, and then clears the fill
Recess	Creates a shadow above and to the left of the selected sprite
Relief	Creates a shadow below and to the right of the selected sprite

FIG. 15.5

The graphic here shows an Edge outline on the left and a Drop Shadow to the top-right corner on the right.

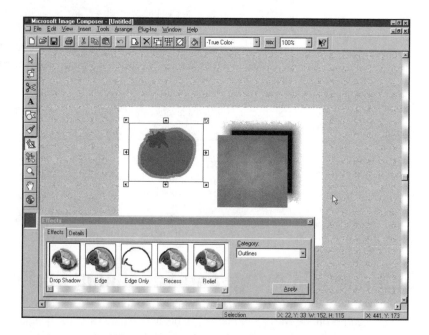

Placing a Shadow   To place a shadow on a selected sprite, select the Effects Palette and choose Outlines from the Category List. Click Drop Shadow and then click Details. Choose the desired direction of the shadow from the Drop Shadow Effect area and click the desired Distance, Angle, Color, Hardness/Softness, and Opacity. When finished, click Apply.

You can change the color of the shadow by clicking the Color Swatch and selecting a color from the palette and reduce the opacity of the shadow with the Opacity slider.

▶ **See** Chapter 14, "Working with Sprites," for a discussion of Opacity, **p. 297**

When you have defined the offsets and the color for the shadow, click the Apply button.

CAUTION

Each time you apply an outline, the new effect is added to the existing effects so reapplying an outline will double the thickness of the outline.

Placing an Edge   Placing an edge is similar to adding a shadow to a selected sprite. The difference is that there is no offset—the outline is uniform all around the sprite.

Outlines are effective in making faint images sharply defined. Often outlines are placed around light colored or filled text for effect.

T I P   Remember that FrontPage Editor allows you to place borders around graphic images; so, if you want to place a border around an image, you can do so there. Any border you attach to a sprite in Image Composer cannot be removed in the FrontPage Editor.

Placing an Edge-Only Outline   Edge-only outlines work exactly like regular outlines, except that they remove all fills from the target sprite.

Recessing a Sprite   Recessing a sprite is a form of applying a shadow outline. The Recess outline is calculated to create an effect of an embedded or notched image. See Figure 15.6.

FIG. 15.6

The tomato has been recessed.

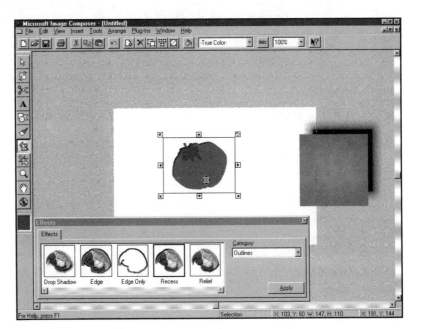

Unfortunately, there are no offsets, line thickness, colors, or opacity settings for the Recess outline—they are all preset.

Placing a Sprite in Relief   Placing a sprite in relief creates an illusion that the object is set off from the page. Relief is another form of applying a shadow outline. The Relief outline also comes with preset offsets, line thickness, colors, and opacity. Relief outlines give an edge and 3-D feel to any image. Relief outlines can often be used to good effect with imported photos. See Figure 15.7.

FIG. 15.7
Placing a sprite in relief.

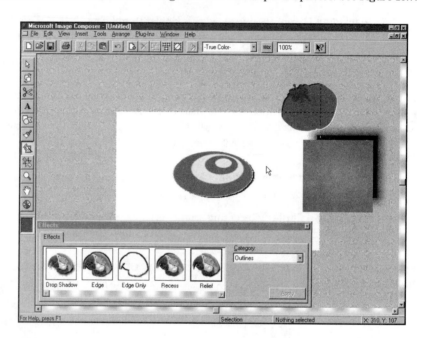

Photographic Effects

Photographic effects can be used to touch up photos for various artistic effects. Photographic effects include the following:

Blur

Diffuse Glow

Film Grain

Grain

Halftone Screen

Negative

Neon Glow

Sharpen

Sharpen Lite

Soften

Transparent

Usually, you will want to experiment with photographic effects to find one that will enhance your imported photo image.

To experiment with photographic effects, select an imported photo image and apply the photographic effect. These effects can also be applied to text, for example, to create that annoying blurry text that says "Focus Here" on T-shirts. See Figure 15.8.

FIG. 15.8
Had your glasses
checked lately?

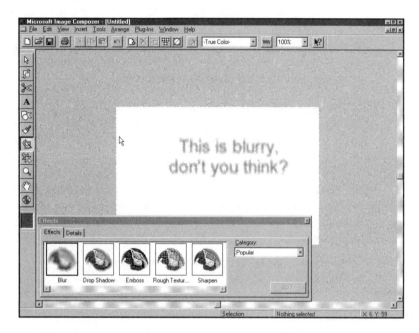

The higher the settings in the Horizontal and Vertical Blur Details boxes (Details tab), the blurrier your sprite will become.

> **CAUTION**
> Using too much blurry text can be bad for your eyes and can annoy your visitors. Use it judiciously for a public Web site.

Color Tuning

The Color Tuning Palette allows you to adjust the colors and brightness of an imported photo as follows:

1. The Brightness Slider in the Color Tuning Palette lets you recolor a photo. Here's where you can perform miracles of hair coloring, change a pink house to green, or change burnt toast to golden brown.

2. The Contrast Slider in the Color Tuning Palette works like the contrast dial on your TV or computer monitor. You can sharpen up or lighten the contrast in a selected sprite.

3. The Hue Slider adjusts the hues in the selected sprite. Hue is the most unique component of a color.

4. Saturation changes the amount of gray in a color.

Enhancing Sprites

Not only can you turn a focused object blurry, you can actually sharpen up a blurry sprite with Image Composer. Use the Sharpen option from the Photographic category in the Effects Palette to bring out-of-focus photos into better focus.

N O T E   The Sharpen option doesn't really refocus an out-of-focus sprite, it increases the contrast between pixels. As the contrast increases, the different parts of the image appear "sharper" as the pixels stand out more against their neighbors. You still have an out-of-focus image, but it doesn't appear quite so blurry. ■

The Sharpen Lite effect is similar to Sharpen, but Sharpen Lite applies a subtler contrast between pixels. You can apply either Sharpen or Sharpen Lite more than once, further increasing pixel contrast. Applied repeatedly, Sharpen causes graininess; with Sharpen Lite, graininess is less pronounced.

The more you apply the Sharpen or Sharpen Lite effects, the more detail is emphasized. Keep your finger ready to click the Undo button when you go too far!

Distortions

Cataloguing every single effect provided by Image Composer is beyond the scope of this book. There is an almost unlimited combination of effects you can create by using various effects on top of each other. One group of effects we cannot skip is under the Distort category of the Effects Palette.

Once you've tried Distortions, you'll be hooked on them. Just remember that your Web site visitors may not find them as much fun as you do if you overuse them. One per Web site is about the limit on these wild effects.

Waving a Flag   The Wave effect can be selected from the Distort icons in the Effects Palette. You can experiment with different settings in the Frequency % and Amplitude % (Details tab). You can wave only vertically (the Y Only option button), horizontally (the X Only option button), or both. Your wave can also be symmetrical or asymmetrical.

The wave effect applies a sine wave warp. When you select a higher Frequency %, you increase the number of waves within the target sprite. When you select a higher number in the Amplitude % Spin box, you increase the height of the individual waves. In short, you need to experiment. One setting to try is to set the Amplitude to 10 percent or less and select a Y Only Wave Axis. This setting can be used to wave a rectangle (see Figure 15.9).

FIG. 15.9

The original image for both sprites is on the left. In the middle is a Wave Distortion; on the right, a Fisheye Distortion.

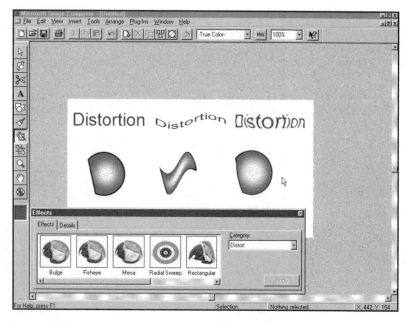

Interactive Warps

Interactive Warps are available from the Warps group in the Arrange Palette.

Interactive Warps are called *interactive* because once you select one of these effects, you tug and stretch, pull and push on parts of the selected sprite to warp and transform it.

Each Interactive Warp works differently, and each one has an infinite number of permutations, depending on how you stretch and pull on the selected sprite after applying a Warp. All Interactive Warps are applied in two steps, as follows:

1. Select the target sprite and choose one of the Warps from the Warps list in the Arrange Palette.

2. Click and drag on the corners or center of the marquee that appears around the sprite. Some Interactive Warps are applied by dragging on corners of the sprite, others by dragging on the middle. See Figure 15.10.

By liberal use of the Undo key and lots of experimentation, you can apply just the right Interactive Warp effect to enhance the message emanating from your Web site. You can also apply more than one interactive Warp effect to a sprite.

FIG. 15.10
Warping a sprite by using the Arrange Palette.

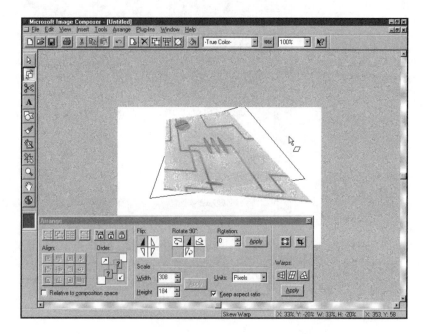

Art Effects

Art effects can be applied to any sprite, but they are frequently used to transform imported photos into what appear to be drawings, paintings, sketches, charcoal images, and so on. A grainy black-and-white photo can become a sharply etched line drawing.

There is truly an unlimited array of Art effects available in the Effects Palette. Some are available in the Arts and Crafts category, some in the Paint category, and others in other Effects categories. You can experiment with applying them to imported photos to create various artistic effects. A color photo of a parrot's head can become an impressionist watercolor painting. See Figure 15.11.

Art effects can be applied to text sprites as well as graphics sprites, but many of the effects from the Paint and Sketch categories are a little too subtle to have much impact on text display. They are often best used to transform an imported photo into a simulated painting, sketch, or drawing (see Figure 15.12).

FIG. 15.11

Graphic on left transformed into a watercolor painting on right.

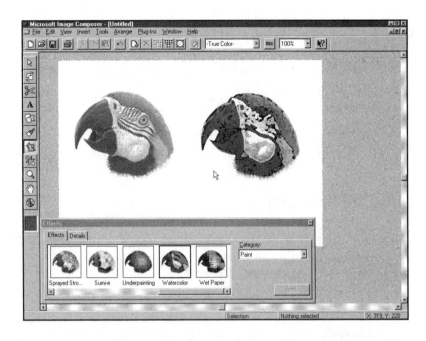

FIG. 15.12

Photo transformed into a technical pen drawing.

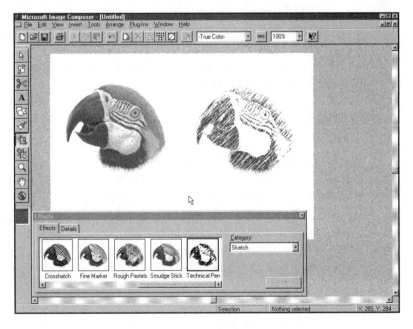

Using the Paint Palette

The Paint Palette provides you with a wide range of tools with which to create Paint effects. These Paint tools all differ in their effect, but the process of applying Paint effects generally takes three steps, as follows:

1. Select the Paint effect from the buttons on the left side of the Paint Palette.

2. Select a brush or effect size from the grid in the middle of the Paint Palette.

3. Select a sprite and apply the Paint effect by painting over all or part of the sprite with the selected Paint tool.

Using the Paintbrush

The Paintbrush, along with the brush size you pick in the Size grid, can be used to paint over sections of the selected sprite by using the color selected in the Color Picker swatch.

Using the Airbrush and Pencil

The Airbrush tool is similar in effect to the Paintbrush tool, but this tool applies color in a more airy, spray-painted mode.

The Pencil tool applies the selected Color Picker color in a thin line as you draw over a selected sprite. It can be used to apply a very fine "paint-over" to a sprite.

The Smear tool is not the most attractive of paint effects. Smear pretty much muddies up the coloring of the selected sprite as you color over it. You'll find a way to use it someday—like when you are creating a Web site for the Muddy Creek Chamber of Commerce, and the photo they give you comes out too clear.

Erasing and Tinting Effects

When opacity is set to 100 percent, the Erase tool wipes out everything it paints over.

The Tint tool tints images with the selected color swatch as you click and drag over the selected sprite. For example, select a light pink or rose color from the Color Picker and paint over an image to give it a rosy glow.

The Colorize tool changes color to the selected swatch color as you paint over parts of the selected sprite. By reducing the Opacity setting, you can touch up a photo and by cranking up the Opacity, you paint over the old colors.

The Dodge-Burn tool is an intriguing paint effect that lightens or darkens as you paint over a sprite. Try it. For those of you who develop and print your own photos, these effects are similar to dodging or burning a photo as you print it. *Dodging* can be used to reduce the exposure of a selected area of the photograph. *Burning* increases the exposure of the selected elements of the photo. Dodging lightens the selected area of the image and burning darkens the areas where it is applied.

Use the Contrast tool to make an image sharper or to give it less contrast. Depending on how you set the Step Contrast Slider, this effect sharpens or blurs the contrast on a selected sprite as you paint over it.

Transferring and Using the Rubber Stamp

The Rubber Stamp effect lets you pick up the color of a sprite and stamp it on another sprite, producing a very blurry effect.

The Transfer effect is similar to Rubber Stamp—it copies part of a sprite onto other parts of the sprite.

From Here...

In this chapter, we have reached into the far corners of Image Composer's ability to lend unique and creative effects to images. We used techniques that can be applied to imported photo files or sprites created in Image Composer, including text sprites.

Look to the following chapter for further ways to create and edit graphic images:

- Chapter 16, "Tailoring Your Images for FrontPage Documents," examines different options for making your Image Composer files work well with your Web site.

Tailoring Your Images for FrontPage Documents

In the previous three chapters, you explored a wide variety of tools and effects available in Microsoft Image Composer. In many cases, all that will be required to place your graphic image creations in a FrontPage 98 Web site is to copy selected sprites from Image Composer to the FrontPage Editor.

There are some additional ways to take advantage of Image Composer creations. While FrontPage 98 comes with a useful selection of clip art to use as background images, a truly unique Web site might require a customized background and other customized graphics. In this chapter, you'll explore Image Composer's potential to solve these needs.

You can achieve some additional control over the quality and speed of JPEG images by tweaking the compression in Image Composer before sending the file to FrontPage, so we'll take a look at that as well. Similarly, you can add transparent attributes to GIF files directly in Image Composer, even before you send the image to the FrontPage Editor. You'll then take a look at the advantages of Image Composer's Sample Sprite Catalog. ■

Creating custom background fills

Create a custom background on-the-fly, directly from the FrontPage Editor.

Adjusting JPEG compression

A larger degree of image compression causes a JPEG image to resolve more quickly, but decreases image quality.

Saving GIF images with transparent backgrounds

You can add transparent background attributes right in Image Composer.

Using Image Composer's sample sprite catalog

Image Composer includes a color format designed to make your colors look consistent regardless of what browser visitors are using to view your FrontPage Web site.

Creating Custom Background Fills

Your Web page backgrounds are a crucial part of setting the tone for your site. They exude an atmosphere like the paint on your living room walls or the music in the air when someone visits your home.

You can create customized background fills for your FrontPage Web by using the FrontPage Editor and Image Composer. In Chapter 6, "Enhancing Pages with Themes, Graphics, and Multimedia," you learned to select custom background colors and fills, and you saw that FrontPage has a large set of images that can be used as attractive backgrounds.

You can also use Image Composer to create fully customized backgrounds and fills for your Web pages. All of the fills and effects that are explored in Chapter 13, "Getting Started with Image Composer," Chapter 14, "Working with Sprites," and Chapter 15, "Using Effects for Maximum Impact," can be combined to create background fills. It is important to avoid the temptation to make your page background so flashy or distracting that it overshadows your Web site content—you may have noticed a site or two with this problem in your travels.

The following is a list of five things to avoid in backgrounds:

- Dark colors combined with dark text fonts. Eyes and brains just don't cope well with a lack of contrast between foreground and background objects.

- Distracting images that overshadow the site contents. When push comes to shove, what are you really trying to "sell": the content of your pages or the graphics? Sites that seem more intent on showing off every cool graphic that could possibly be crammed on one page can actually turn visitors away.

- Image files so large that visitors wait too long for the page background to resolve. You may have a T1 line that downloads anything in seconds, but your readers may well be operating with a 14.4 modem. If you don't have consideration for your visitors' time, are you sure they'll stay interested to check out the rest of your site?

- Backgrounds that clash with your images. Again, eyes and brains don't like discomfort when reading. If your visitors see that you don't have taste in your color combinations, they may figure that you won't have taste in your content, either.

- Unattractive background images (get a second opinion when in doubt). You're trying to appeal to a large audience and tastes vary. You can have broadly appealing background images without losing artistic and graphic value. In addition to second opinions, check out other Web sites to see what works well.

What Backgrounds Are Made of

The background of your Web site page is the width of a screen, and its length depends on how long your page is—it could be very, very long. When you create a background image, you do not create one large image that will be big enough to paper over the entire page. You create a small image, and from the standpoint of downloading speed, the smaller the better. This small image is then tiled—that is, little images are placed side by side and top to bottom so that they cover the entire page.

Background image files are generally in JPEG format. This is because JPEG images support far more colors than GIF files, and resolve more quickly because they are compressed. The advantages of GIF files—interlacing and transparency—are not really useful for background image files since you rarely want them to be transparent, and interlacing your background would be distracting in the extreme.

▶ **See** Chapter 6, "Enhancing Pages with Themes, Graphics, and Multimedia," for a full discussion of the relative benefits of GIF and JPEG image formats.

Since backgrounds are composed of small JPEG image files, we can create them in Image Composer and send them right into an open FrontPage Web.

Launching Image Composer to Create a Custom Background

Let's say you are working in the FrontPage Editor, and the time comes to select a custom background to mesh aesthetically with your Web page. You look at the nice selection of background clip art, but there's nothing there that will really add a dynamite background. No problem, you can create a custom background image by using Image Composer.

You may have noticed, back in Chapter 6, that custom background graphic image files are *tiled*—that is, rather than one super-large image file filling the entire page background, a small image file is repeated over and over, like tiles on a floor. This method produces a much smaller, more manageable, and faster image file than trying to save a huge image large enough to fill the entire background of your page.

Since the sample clip art background images that come with FrontPage 98 are a very nice size, a good technique is to pick one, rename it, and edit it in Image Composer to create a unique, customized background. Let's do that.

1. With a Web open in the FrontPage Explorer, and a Web page open in the FrontPage Editor, right-click the page.
2. Select Page Properties from the Shortcut menu.
3. Click the Background tab in the Page Properties dialog box.
4. Select the Background Image check box.
5. Click the Browse button.
6. Click the Clip Art tab in the Select Background Image dialog box.
7. Select Web Backgrounds from the Category list.
8. Select *any* background image—we're going to change the image. See Figure 16.1.
9. Click OK in the Select Background Image and Page Properties dialog box.
10. Save your page in the FrontPage Editor and click OK on the prompt to save your new image(s).
11. Switch to the FrontPage Explorer, and in Folder view, rename the background image with a custom name, like BK1.GIF. You will be prompted to update your links so that this renamed file becomes the background image for linked pages. Do that.
12. Double-click the renamed image to open that file in Image Composer.

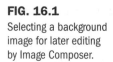

FIG. 16.1

Selecting a background image for later editing by Image Composer.

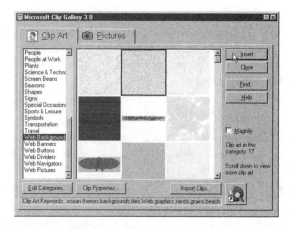

Designing a Background Image in Image Composer

When you launch Image Composer by double-clicking a renamed background image in the FrontPage Explorer, the file is opened in Image Composer. The image file opens with a single sprite and a composition space. Both the sprite size and the composition space can be adjusted, but this is a nice, small size for a background image tile, so there's no reason to do so.

You can edit the fill of the rectangular (square, to be precise) sprite. Look back over the effects and fills covered in Chapters 13, 14, and 15 ("Getting Started with Image Composer," "Working with Sprites," and "Using Effects for Maximum Impact," respectively) and experiment until you have a fill that you think will look good tiled in the background of your Web site. A good technique is to combine one fill—Gradients often work well—with one effect (see Figure 16.2).

When you are satisfied with the image, select File, Save for the Web. This will open the Save for the Web wizard, the second step of which is shown in Figure 16.3. You'll be asked for the format of the file (either GIF or JPEG will do).

Once the wizard is finished, go to FrontPage Explorer and use File, Import to bring your saved image into the Web. If you changed the file name in the process of saving it through Image Composer, return to FrontPage Editor and select this new file as your background image. Refresh FrontPage Editor by pressing F5, and your new background will appear.

There's no substitute for trial and error here. See how the image looks behind your FrontPage Web page. You may want to test your background using your Web browser. That way, you will know how long it takes to load the background image.

If you don't like the image, you can reopen the file in Image Composer, double-click the background image file in the FrontPage Explorer, and send it back into Image Composer.

FIG. 16.2
Creating a background image tile with a gradient fill.

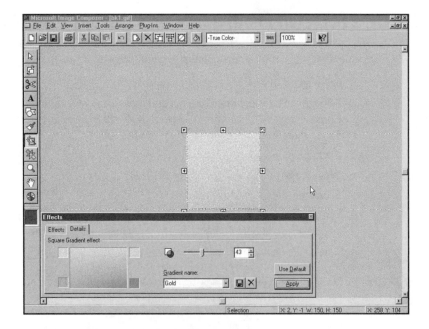

FIG. 16.3
The Save for the Web Wizard takes you through the steps of saving an image for use on the Web site.

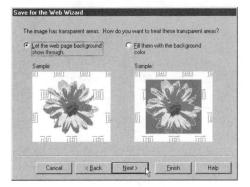

Adjusting JPEG Compression

The spectrum of JPEG compression basically runs from fast with low quality to slow with good quality. The more compression you select, the faster the image will compose when a visitor comes to your site. However, a larger amount of compression generally means less quality to the picture.

Here, again, there is often no avoiding trial and error. You can try saving an imported photo with very little compression. Then you can send the image to FrontPage, test the site with your browser, and see if the wait is too long.

Saving a Selected Photo Sprite as a Compressed JPEG File

You can open a photo saved to TIF format and save it as a JPEG file in Image Composer. When you do that, you can select the amount of compression.

1. Open an existing or new Image Composer file.

2. Select Insert, From File to insert a photo file from your disk or a CD-ROM. Image Composer comes with a nice selection of photos you can use, or you can open a scanned file or photo from a disk or CD-ROM of photos.

3. Click the photo Sprite and select File, Save Selection As.

4. From the Save File as Type list, select JPG.

5. Select the Compression check box.

6. You should generally start with a low compression ratio—try 10 percent at first. Set the compression ratio by dragging on the Amount slider. See Figure 16.4.

7. Enter a file name and click Save.

FIG. 16.4
Select a specific compression ratio when saving a photo in JPEG format.

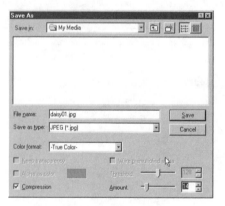

Testing Image Resolution Speed

Once you have saved a selection, you can close your current Image Composer file and open the just-saved one. This file will have the composition space matched to the sprite size.

You can let FrontPage 98 estimate the download time for your page. This is calculated and displayed on the right side of the FrontPage Editor status bar as you work on your page.

If you want a more exact test of download time, you can test the resolution speed by saving the Web page and previewing the page in your Web browser. If the image takes too long to resolve, you can resave the file with a higher compression ratio.

Saving GIF Images with Transparent Backgrounds

In Chapter 6, "Enhancing Pages with Themes, Graphics, and Multimedia," you learned how to apply transparency to GIF files by using the Make Transparent tool in the Image toolbar. You can also assign transparency in Image Composer and with more control over the level of transparency.

To assign transparency to an Image Composer file, you must save it in GIF format. JPEG files cannot be transparent. Assign transparency by saving (or resaving) a file as a GIF file. Enter a file name, if necessary, and click the Transparent color check box.

You can change the color that will become transparent by clicking the Transparent color Color Swatch and selecting a color from the palette. See Figure 16.5.

FIG. 16.5

Selecting a transparency color and threshold amount.

You can also regulate the degree of transparency using the Threshold Slider. Threshold determines just how transparent your image will be. Higher Threshold levels mean your image is less transparent.

Using Image Composer's Sample Sprite Catalog

Once you know how to create your own sprites, you can appreciate and take advantage of the sample sprite photos and other sample image files that come with Image Composer.

You can view thumbnail images of the sprites on the Image Composer CD-ROM by selecting Help, Sample Sprites Catalog. The Index tab in the Sample Sprites Catalog dialog box shows an alphabetical list of sample sprites. Looking for a picture of an almond? Scroll down the list and find one.

To view a sample sprite, click the Display button in the Sample Sprites Catalog dialog box (see Figure 16.6).

FIG. 16.6

Use the sprite catalog's Display command to view a sample sprite.

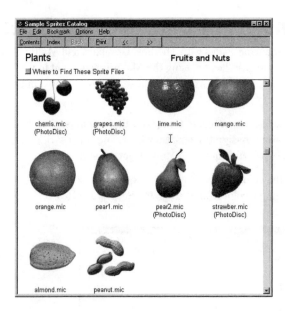

You can also look for sample sprites by category. You do this from the Contents tab of the Sample Sprites dialog box. Select either photos or Web images by double-clicking one of those two icons.

The Web images include:

- Web—Backgrounds
- Web—Bullets
- Web—Buttons
- Web—Counters
- Web—Horizontal Rules
- Web—Navigational Controls

The photos are even more extensive. On the CD-ROM, you'll find:

- Amimals
- Backgrounds—Abstract
- Backgrounds—Food
- Backgrounds—Marble and Paper
- Backgrounds—Objects
- Backgrounds—Other
- Backgrounds—Outdoor Scenes
- Backgrounds—Patterns and Textures

- Backgrounds—Plants and Wood
- Backgrounds—Rock and Sand
- Backgrounds—Sky and Water
- Buttons and Icons
- Clothes
- Dividers and Decorations
- Entertainment
- Flags
- Food and Dining
- Gestures
- Healthcare and Medicine
- Household—Kitchen
- Household—Miscellaneous
- Household—Personal
- Household—Recreation
- Household—Utility
- Industry
- Metaphor—A to L
- Metaphor—M to Z
- Music
- Nature
- Office
- Plants—Flowers
- Plants—Fruits and Nuts
- Plants—Leaves and Petals
- Plants—Miscellaneous
- Plants—Vegetables
- Shapes
- Symbols

From these categories, you'll find hundreds of images to spruce up your site. You may even find some that are as good as ones you make yourself!

Once you find an image you like, double-click the file in the file list to insert that image into your open Image Composer file. Of course, you can edit these images and resave them to create custom tools, buttons, and backgrounds.

T I P   Once you find the name of a sample sprite in the catalog, you can zip to it in the Index tab and double-click to open the file.

From Here...

Now that you've had a comprehensive look at the capabilities of Image Composer, you may want to explore the sophisticated tools that let you add active content to your pages. You can find out about this kind of content in the chapters that follow, such as:

- Chapter 17, "Using ActiveX Controls," which teaches you the ins and outs of employing this Microsoft technology to enliven your Web pages.

- Chapter 18, "Scripting with VBScript," where you find out about the components of the VBScript language, and how you use Visual Basic scripts to interact with Microsoft Internet Explorer.

- Chapter 19, "Scripting with JavaScript," which explores JavaScript language elements and syntax, and shows how you can use this scripting language to interact with Web page elements and users.

Integrating Active Content into Your Web

## CHAPTER 17

Using ActiveX Controls

Microsoft introduced ActiveX Technologies in 1996 at the time it released Internet Explorer 3. By building on its highly successful Object Linking and Embedding (OLE) technology, Microsoft has attempted to set a standard for adding active content to Web pages. This standard allows the capabilities of the Web browser to evolve continually, and also allows data and information from existing applications to be easily accessed.

ActiveX Controls combine the convenience of Java applets with the permanence and functionality of Netscape Navigator plug-ins. Like Java applets, ActiveX Controls can be automatically downloaded to your system if they are not currently installed or if the installed version is not the most recent. Like plug-ins, ActiveX Controls remain available to your Web browser continuously once they are installed.

This chapter introduces you to ActiveX Controls, shows you examples of the available controls, and demonstrates how you can install them into your pages with FrontPage Editor. ∎

Learn about Microsoft's ActiveX Controls

This chapter discusses Microsoft's ActiveX Controls and how you use them with FrontPage Editor to increase the capabilities of Internet Explorer 3 and other compatible applications.

Find out how ActiveX Controls are made secure

Learn why it is a good idea to use only *signed* Controls and how they decrease the risk of tampering.

Find out what ActiveX Controls mean for FrontPage users and programmers

Find out what ActiveX Controls mean to the users and developers of World Wide Web software, information, and products.

See what ActiveX Controls can do in a Web page

Find out what some of the ActiveX Controls can do.

What Are ActiveX Controls?

ActiveX Controls are more than simple Web browser plug-ins or add-ins. Because of the nature of ActiveX Controls, not only can they be used to extend the functionality of Microsoft's Web browser, but they also can be used by any programming language or application that supports the OLE standard. For example, an ActiveX Control could be written to enable Internet Explorer 3 or 4 to automatically search Usenet newsgroups for specific information and, at the same time, perform a similar function through integration into Microsoft Office products such as Excel or Access. Netscape Navigator plug-ins, on the other hand, can be used only in Web browsers and often work only with those that are Netscape-based; although, to be fair, ActiveX controls sometimes don't work properly outside a Microsoft browser environment.

As with Netscape Navigator's plug-ins, ActiveX Controls are dynamic code modules that exist as part of Microsoft's *Application Programming Interface* (API) for extending and integrating third-party software into any OLE-compliant environment. The creation of (and support for) ActiveX Controls by Microsoft is significant, primarily because it allows other developers to integrate their products seamlessly into the Web via Internet Explorer or any other OLE application, without having to launch any external helper applications.

For Internet Explorer users, ActiveX Controls support allows you to customize Internet Explorer's interaction with third-party products and industry media standards. Microsoft's ActiveX Control API also attempts to address the concerns of programmers, providing a high degree of flexibility and cross-platform support.

What ActiveX Controls Mean for End Users

For most users, integrating ActiveX Controls is transparent because they open up and become active whenever an ActiveX-enabled browser is opened. Furthermore, you will often not even see ActiveX Controls at work because most ActiveX Controls are not activated unless you open up a Web page that initiates them. For example, after you install the Shockwave for Macromedia Director ActiveX Control, you will notice no difference in the way Internet Explorer functions until you come across a Web page that features Shockwave.

Once an ActiveX Control is installed on your machine and initiated by a Web page, it manifests itself in one of the following three potential forms:

- Embedded
- Full-screen
- Hidden

Embedded Controls   An embedded ActiveX Control appears as a visible, rectangular window integrated into a Web page. This window may not appear any different from a window created by a graphic, such as an embedded GIF or JPEG picture. The main difference between the previous windows supported by Internet Explorer 3 and 4 and those created by ActiveX Controls is that ActiveX Control windows support a much wider range of interactivity and movement, and thereby remain live instead of static.

In addition to mouse clicks, embedded ActiveX Controls also can read and take note of mouse location, mouse movement, keyboard input, and input from virtually any other input device. In this way, an ActiveX Control can support the full range of user events required to produce sophisticated applications.

Full-Screen Controls A full-screen ActiveX Control takes over the entire current Internet Explorer window to display its own content. This is necessary when a Web page is designed to display data that is not supported by HTML. An example of this type of ActiveX Control is the VRML ActiveX Control available from Microsoft. If you view a VRML world using Internet Explorer 3 with the VRML ActiveX Control, it loads into your Web browser like any other Web page, but it retains the look and functionality of a VRML world, with 3-D objects that you can navigate through and around.

Hidden Controls A hidden ActiveX Control doesn't have any visible elements, but works strictly behind the scenes to add some features to Internet Explorer 3 that are not otherwise available. An example of a hidden control would be the Preloader Control, discussed later in this chapter. This ActiveX Control is used to preload a graphic, sound, or other element that is subsequently viewed by the Internet Explorer user. Because the element is downloaded while the user is browsing through the current Web page, the response time of the element appears to be much shorter.

Regardless of which ActiveX Controls you are using and whether they are embedded, full-screen, or hidden, the rest of Internet Explorer's user interface should remain relatively constant and available. So even if you have a VRML world displayed in Internet Explorer's main window, you'll still be able to access the browser's menus and navigational controls.

What ActiveX Controls Mean for Programmers

For programmers, ActiveX Controls offer the possibility of creating Internet Explorer add-on products by using existing ActiveX Controls to assemble Internet-based applications. Creating a custom ActiveX Control requires much more intensive background, experience, and testing than actually using one. If you are a developer or are interested in creating an ActiveX Control, the following discussion will be useful.

The current version of the ActiveX Control Application Programming Interface (API) supports four broad areas of functionality.

ActiveX Controls can do the following:

- Draw into, receive events from, and interact with objects that are a part of the Internet Explorer 3 object hierarchy.
- Obtain MIME data from the network via URLs.
- Generate data for consumption by Internet Explorer 3, by other ActiveX Controls, or by Java applets.
- Override and implement protocol handlers.

ActiveX Controls are ideally suited to take advantage of platform-independent protocols, architectures, languages, and media types such as Java, VRML, and MPEG. ActiveX Controls should

be functionally equivalent across platforms as well as complementary to platform-specific protocols and architectures.

When the Internet Explorer 3 or 4 client launches, it knows of any ActiveX Controls available
through the Windows 95 Registry, but does not load any of them into RAM. Because of this, an
ActiveX Control resides in memory only when needed, but many ActiveX Controls may be in
use at one time, so you still need to be aware of memory allocation. By having many ActiveX
Controls readily available, without taking up any RAM until just before the time they are
needed, the user is able to view seamlessly a tremendous amount of varied data. An ActiveX
Control is deleted from RAM as soon as the user moves to another HTML page that does not
require it.

Integration of ActiveX Controls with the Internet Explorer client is quite elegant and flexible,
allowing the programmer to make the most of asynchronous processes and multithreaded
data. ActiveX Controls may be associated with one or more MIME types, and Internet Explorer
3 may, in turn, create multiple instances of the same ActiveX Control.

At its most fundamental level, an ActiveX Control can access an URL and retrieve MIME data
just as a standard Internet Explorer client does. This data is streamed to the ActiveX Control
as it arrives from the network, making it possible to implement viewers and other interfaces
that can progressively display information. For instance, an ActiveX Control may draw a
simple frame and introductory graphic or text for the user to look at while the bulk of the
data is streaming off the network into Internet Explorer's existing cache. All the same bandwidth considerations adhered to by good HTML authors need to be accounted for in ActiveX
Controls.

Of course, ActiveX Controls can also be file-based, requiring a complete amount of data to be
downloaded first before the ActiveX Control can proceed. This type of architecture is not en-
couraged due to its potential user delays, but it may prove necessary for some data-intensive
ActiveX Controls. If an ActiveX Control needs more data than can be supplied through a single
data stream, multiple simultaneous data streams may be requested by the ActiveX Control, so
long as the user's system supports this.

If data is needed by another ActiveX Control or by Internet Explorer 3 while an ActiveX Control
is active, the ActiveX Control can generate data itself for these purposes. Thus, ActiveX Controls not only process data, they also generate it. For example, an ActiveX Control can be a data
translator or filter.

ActiveX Controls are generally embedded within HTML code and accessed through the OBJECT
tag.

N O T E   Whereas creating an ActiveX Control is much easier to do than, say, writing a spreadsheet
application, it still requires the talents of a professional programmer. Third-party developers
offer visual programming tools or BASIC environments that provide ActiveX Control templates, making
the actual coding of ActiveX Controls much less tedious. However, most sophisticated ActiveX Controls
are, and will be, developed in sophisticated C++ environments, requiring thousands of lines of
code. ■

ActiveX Control Security

ActiveX Controls are pieces of software; therefore, all of the dangers of running unknown software apply to them as anything you may download from the Internet. ActiveX Controls are unlike Java applets, which run in an environment designed to ensure the safety of the client and can usually cause trouble only by exploiting bugs or flaws in the Java runtime security systems. ActiveX Controls, on the other hand, can do anything on the client computer. Although this increases their potential to perform functions within your Web browser and other compatible applications, it also poses an added security risk. How do you know that a downloaded ActiveX Control won't erase your hard drive?

To address this concern, Microsoft's Internet Explorer Web browsers (version 3.02 and later) support *Authenticode code-signing technology.* This enables vendors of ActiveX Controls and other software components to digitally *sign* these components. When they are downloaded and the digital signature is recognized, a code signature certificate, like that shown in Figure 17.1, is displayed on the screen. This certificate ensures that the software component is coming from the named source and that it hasn't been tampered with. At this point, you can choose to install the software component.

FIG. 17.1

Authenticode technology in Microsoft's Internet Explorer browsers helps ensure that downloaded software components are genuine and come from a trusted source.

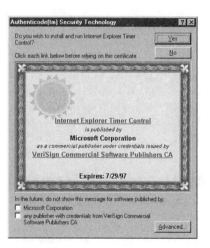

Internet Explorer 3 and 4 both provide graduated levels of security in dealing with downloadable components like ActiveX. By default, Internet Explorer 3 installs in *High* security mode. In this mode, downloaded software components that are unsigned, or whose signatures can't be verified, are not installed. In this case, an Alert box displays that reads something like: "This page contains active content that is not verifiably safe to display. To protect your computer, this content will not be displayed. Choose Help to find out how you can change your safety settings so you can view potentially unsafe content." Note that in high security mode, the user doesn't even have the option of installing software components whose authenticity can't be verified.

Internet Explorer 4 has more elaborate security arrangements, which are also more customizable than those in IE 3 (see Figure 17.2). IE 4 automatically installs at the Medium security level, which warns you before you download and run potentially dangerous content. Knowledgeable users can select Custom and click the Settings button, which opens a dialog box where you can specify precisely how much security is to be applied to signed controls, unsigned controls, and so on. You can also set up "zones" of sites, each of which has a different security level.

FIG. 17.2
In Internet Explorer 4, Medium security level puts the burden on the user—you will be warned of potential security risks, but you are given the option to continue.

CAUTION
You should almost never select the Low security level, because this leaves your system completely unprotected from malevolent or poorly written software. Only select this level if you are certain that all the sites you are visiting are safe.

HTML Implementation of ActiveX Controls

Implementing ActiveX Controls in HTML Web pages requires the use of the HTML <OBJECT> and <PARAM> tags to include and configure each desired control. Although not too difficult, the syntax for using these controls and determining the correct configuration parameters for each—particularly now, with the technology in its infancy—can be an intimidating task. This is all the more so since IE 4 implements plug-ins, applets, and ActiveX with the <OBJECT> tag.

FrontPage Editor 98 makes the process a lot easier through its point-and-click method of control installation. If you've used Microsoft's freeware ActiveX Control Pad, the method is familiar, because FrontPage Editor uses a version of that software. Before we begin, however, a brief discussion of how ActiveX works in a page will be helpful.

As just stated, including ActiveX Controls in HTML documents requires use of the <OBJECT> tag to embed the control within the page. Controls are configured through the attributes of the <OBJECT> tag, and configuration parameters set using the <PARAM> tag within the <OBJECT>...</OBJECT> container.

Using FrontPage Editor, any locally installed ActiveX Control can be placed within a Web page. Individual Label Controls can be displayed as they would appear, as will images and other elements. FrontPage Editor also allows you to configure the many options of each embedded ActiveX Control—set the <OBJECT> and <PARAM> configuration values—using a simple dialog box customized for each control. When control configuration is complete, the HTML code needed to implement the control in your Web page is written into the HTML document.

The *<OBJECT>* Tag

Part
IV

Ch
17

ActiveX Controls are embedded in HTML documents through use of the HTML <OBJECT> tag and are configured through use of the <PARAM> tag. Listing 17.1 is an example of using the ActiveX Marquee Control, embedded within an HTML Web page. The attributes of the <OBJECT> tag itself determine the ActiveX Control (or other Web object) used, as well as its size and alignment on the Web page. The <OBJECT>...</OBJECT> container tags also enclose the <PARAM> tags that are used to set the Control-specific parameters.

On their own, neither Netscape Navigator nor Communicator supports ActiveX Controls and will ignore any controls embedded in a Web page through the use of the <OBJECT> tag. However, with one of the Ncompass Labs plug-ins installed, Netscape browsers do support ActiveX Controls and will interpret embedded objects correctly.

N O T E   NCompass only works with Navigator 3.0 running ActiveX if <EMBED> is used within <OBJECT>. ▨

ON THE WEB

http://www.ncompasslabs.com/   This site gives all the information you need and shows some examples of using Microsoft's ActiveX Technologies in Netscape Navigator through the Ncompass Labs plug-ins.

The next sections discuss each of the important attributes of the <OBJECT> tag and some of the possibilities for using the <PARAM> tags.

Listing 17.1   Marquee.htm—Example Using the ActiveX Marquee Control Object

```
<HTML>
<HEAD>
<TITLE>Marquee Example</TITLE>
</HEAD>
```

continues

Listing 17.1 Continued

```
<BODY BGCOLOR=#FFFFFF>
<CENTER>
<HR>
<OBJECT
    ID="Marquee1"
    CLASSID="CLSID:1A4DA620-6217-11CF-BE62-0080C72EDD2D"
    CODEBASE="http://activex.microsoft.com/controls/iexplorer/marquee.ocx
[ic:ccc]#Version=4,70,0,1161"
    TYPE="application/x-oleobject"
    WIDTH=100%
    HEIGHT=100
>
<PARAM NAME="szURL" VALUE="queet.gif">
<PARAM NAME="ScrollPixelsX" VALUE="2">
<PARAM NAME="ScrollPixelsY" VALUE="2">
<PARAM NAME="ScrollStyleX" VALUE="Bounce">
<PARAM NAME="ScrollStyleY" VALUE="Bounce">
</OBJECT>
<HR>
</CENTER>
</BODY>
</HTML>
```

ID   The ID attribute of the <OBJECT> tag is used to give the ActiveX Control a name that can be used within the Web browser (or other application) environment. This is the easiest way for the parameters of the ActiveX Control to be accessed and manipulated by other elements running within the Web browser (usually VBScript or JavaScript applications). For example, in Listing 17.1, a VBScript to change the background color of the Marquee Control to red, if clicked, would look like the following:

```
Sub Marquee1_OnClick()
   Marquee1.BackColor = 16711680
End Sub
```

CLASSID   The CLASSID attribute is perhaps the most intimidating looking piece of the <OBJECT> tag of an ActiveX Control. However, it is simply the identification code for the ActiveX Control being used. It is what Internet Explorer uses to load the correct ActiveX Control code module from your computer, and its value is set for each control by the control's author. The code for the ActiveX Marquee Control, displayed in Listing 17.1, is "CLSID:1A4DA620-6217-11CF-BE62-0080C72EDD2D".

CODEBASE   Unlike Netscape Navigator plug-ins, ActiveX Controls can be automatically down-loaded and installed when Internet Explorer 3 (or another compatible application) encounters a document that makes use of them. The key to this feature is the CODEBASE attribute. The CODEBASE attribute defines the URL from which the ActiveX Control can be downloaded, and defines the version of the control used. Then, when Internet Explorer attempts to render the Web page on a client machine, the CODEBASE attribute checks if each ActiveX Control embedded in the HTML document exists on that machine, and checks if it is the latest version. If a more recent version exists at the URL defined by the CODEBASE attribute, it is automatically downloaded and installed, subject to the security settings in place in the local copy of Internet Explorer being used.

 T I P Whenever possible, only use ActiveX Controls that have been digitally signed by their vendors in your Web pages. This helps to ensure that these controls can be downloaded and installed on your users' machines without a problem.

TYPE The TYPE attribute defines the MIME type of the ActiveX Control. In general, this will be application/x-oleobject. For other object types embedded in an HTML document using the <OBJECT> tag, the value of this attribute will be different.

WIDTH and HEIGHT The WIDTH and HEIGHT attributes of the <OBJECT> tag define the size of the ActiveX Control within the Web page. For hidden Controls, such as the Timer or Preloader Controls, these attributes can be kept at their default values of 0. For controls such as the Marquee or Label Controls, these attributes need to be sized correctly for their desired appearance.

The <PARAM> Tags

The <PARAM> tags are used to configure the appropriate parameters of each ActiveX Control. In general, the syntax of the <PARAM> tag is as follows:

```
<PARAM NAME="ParameterName" VALUE="ParameterValue">
```

For instance, in the Marquee Control example shown in Listing 17.1, the URL of the document being placed in the marquee is given by:

```
<PARAM NAME="szURL" VALUE="queet.gif">
```

To make use of an ActiveX Control effectively, you need to know the names and possible values of all of its parameters that can be set with the <PARAM> tag. One of the benefits of using FrontPage Editor for creating Web pages that use ActiveX Controls is that the software knows what parameters are used by each control.

Using Microsoft ActiveX Controls in FrontPage

Microsoft provides a set of ActiveX Controls with Internet Explorer 3 and 4 and hosts an ActiveX Gallery Web site to show them off, along with ActiveX Controls from other vendors. This Web site is located at **http://www.microsoft.com/activex/controls/**.

Many of the Microsoft-produced controls are also included with FrontPage 98. (If they appear only as placeholders when you try them out, you'll need to download them from this site.) The following sections demonstrate how you use FrontPage Editor to place them on your pages and describe the workings of several of these controls.

N O T E At the time of writing, Microsoft was intending to remove this component gallery and replace it with links to third-party sites that develop ActiveX controls. Presumably, Microsoft will still make its own controls available somewhere on its site. ▪

Part
IV

Ch
17

Adding an ActiveX Control

Start off by choosing Insert, Advanced, ActiveX Control. Alternatively, click the Insert ActiveX Control button on the Advanced toolbar. The ActiveX Control Properties dialog box appears (see Figure 17.3). Then do the following:

1. Click the arrow button at the right of the Pick a Control box. The list of available controls appears.

2. Select the control you want. In the Name box, type a name for the component. This isn't necessary, but it makes it easier to figure out what each control is doing if you look at the HTML code later.

3. Type the HTML code for this alternative into the HTML box if you want an alternate representation for the control (for browsers not supporting ActiveX). For instance, `<img src="inkwell.jpg" width="116" height="103">` in this box produces a JPEG image in Netscape in place of the control.

4. Choose OK. The dialog box closes and the component appears on the page.

FIG. 17.3

You can select from the ActiveX Controls on your system with the ActiveX Properties dialog box.

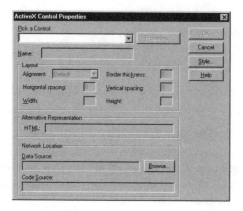

You can set the alignment, width, spacing, and border thickness of the control in the Layout section of this dialog box. The Data Source and Code Source boxes in the Network Location section are used for the following:

- Specifying a data file for controls that require or optionally take information from such a file. The file formats vary from control to control.

- Specifying the Code Source defines the URL from which the ActiveX Control can be downloaded and defines the version of the control used. This is actually an alternate method of specifying the CODEBASE parameter for the control (see the Object Tag section for more on CODEBASE).

Setting ActiveX Control Properties

ActiveX Controls usually need to be customized; this customization is largely a matter of editing the parameters to suit your needs.

To start an edit session for a new control, choose the Properties button in the ActiveX Properties dialog box after you've selected and named the control. To edit an existing Control, double-click it to open the dialog box and choose the Properties button. Either way, you get the two windows where you do your editing (see Figure 17.4).

FIG. 17.4
The Edit ActiveX Control and Properties dialog boxes allow you to set the Control parameters and appearance.

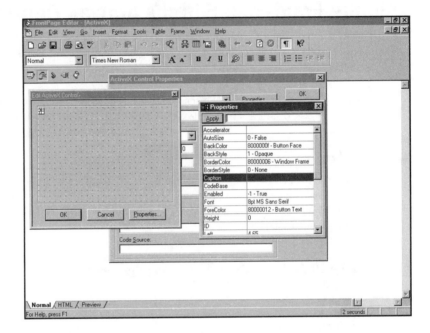

Part
IV

Ch
17

N O T E   There are a few controls for which you get a single window where you manually type in parameters and their values, instead of the two windows just referred to. ■

The first is the Edit ActiveX Control window, which gives a WYSIWYG (what-you-see-is-what-you-get) representation of the current configuration of the ActiveX Control. This is most evident for controls such as the Label Control—for hidden controls, this window merely shows the current size for which the control is configured, which may be zero by zero.

The other window is the Properties dialog box for the specific ActiveX Control chosen. This dialog box gives you the ability to set all the necessary parameters of the <OBJECT> and <PARAM> tags needed to configure the ActiveX Control. You don't need to know the class ID code, and you don't need to remember the specific parameter names that must be configured—FrontPage Editor does it all for you. To change a parameter in the Properties box, click the parameter in the list box, type in a new value in the text box (or select one from a drop-down or pop-up menu, if one appears), and click the Apply button.

N O T E   It is difficult to determine the appropriate size for some controls, such as the Animated Button Control. This difficulty exists because the controls need to be sized to fit an animation file that FrontPage Editor isn't able to show you. Some trial and error may be necessary. ■

When you've finished entering the parameters, close the Edit ActiveX Control and Properties windows. At this point, the HTML code needed to implement the control, using the parameters you selected, is automatically generated and placed in the HTML document.

Exploring FrontPage Editor's ActiveX Controls

The selection of ActiveX Controls that ships with FrontPage 98 (or can be downloaded from the Microsoft site) includes both general utility-type controls and a set of form components. In the following sections we'll look at a representative sample.

N O T E   FrontPage Editor's ActiveX Control Properties list box refers to many of these controls as objects. Objects and Controls, in our present context, mean the same thing. ■

Label Control

The ActiveX MCSiLabel Control, shown in Figure 17.5, allows text to display within a Web page by using any installed font, with any style and color, and at an arbitrary angle. In the example shown in Figure 17.5 (whose code is shown in Listing 17.2) the angle of the text changes whenever the region is clicked.

Listing 17.2   HTML Example Showing the Label Control

```
<HTML>
<HEAD>
<TITLE>Label Example</TITLE>
<SCRIPT LANGUAGE="VBS">
Sub Label1_Click
   Label1.Angle = (Label1.Angle + 15) mod 360
End Sub
</SCRIPT>
</HEAD>
<BODY BGCOLOR=#FFFFFF>

<H1>Label Example</H1>
<HR>

<object width="181" height="127" id="Label1"
classid="clsid:40F07A91-8E6F-11D0-8A0A-00A0C90C9B67">
  <param name="ForeColor" value="16777215">
  <param name="BackColor" value="4227072">
  <param name="Alignment" value="4">
  <param name="Appearance" value="1">
  <param name="BackStyle" value="1">
  <param name="Text" value="FrontPage 98">
  <param name="Angle" value="0">
```

```
     <param name="BorderStyle" value="2">
     <param name="FontName" value="Arial">
     <param name="FontSize" value="14">
     <param name="FontBold" value="0">
     <param name="FontItalic" value="0">
     <param name="FontUnderline" value="0">
     <param name="FontStrikethrough" value="0">
     <param name="FontCharset" value="0">
</object>

<HR>
This example of the ActiveX Label Control demonstrates the ability of the
Control to display text at an arbitrary position and orientation. A VBScript
changes the orientation of the text whenever the Control is clicked.
</BODY>
</HTML>
```

FIG. 17.5

The Label Control gives the Web author the ability to place text arbitrarily on the Web page, without having to resort to graphics.

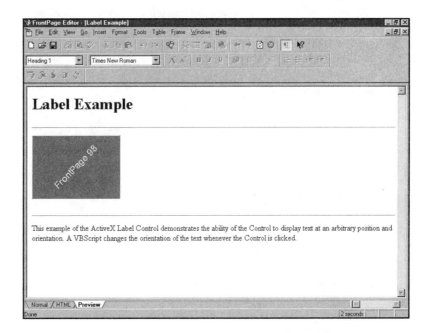

Microsoft's parameter descriptions for the MCSiLabel Control are as follows:

- **Alignment**[= integer] Returns or sets the alignment of text. The settings for integer are: 0: Top left; 1: Top centered; 2: Top right; 3: Left centered; 4: Centered; 5: Right centered; 6: Left bottom; 7: Center Bottom; 8: Right bottom.

- **Angle**[= integer] Used to set the angle of rotation of the text, where integer represents the angle of text rotation in the range of 0 to 359 degrees in increments of 1 degree.

- **Appearance**[= flag] Used to set the visual appearance of the label. Flag can be 0 = flat, 1 = 3-D.

- **Backcolor**[= color] Returns or sets the background color of the label.

- **Forecolor**[= color]   Returns or sets the foreground color of the label.
- **BackStyle**[= integer]   Returns or sets the background style, where integer: 0 = transparent, 1 = opaque.
- **BorderStyle**[= style]   Returns or sets the style of the border. The settings for style are: 0: Raised outer edge; 1: Sunken outer edge; 2: Raised inner edge. 3: Sunken inner edge; 4: Raised inner and raised outer edge; 5: Raised inner and sunken outer edge; 6: Sunken inner and raised outer edge; 7: Sunken inner and sunken outer edge.
- **Font**   Specifies the characteristics of the font used to display the cells in the control.
- **Text** [= string]   Returns or sets the text contained in a MCSiLabel control.

Menu Control

The ActiveX Menu Control enables you to create drop-down menus within a Web page. Items selected from these menus can be set up to trigger events as well as JavaScript or VBScript functions. Listing 17.3 shows example code that is used to construct two simple drop-down menus. In this example, no events are triggered by selection of the items (see Figure 17.6). Notice that the code uses the BtnMenu control, not the Ikonic Menu Control—you may see both of these listed if you are using the Pick a Control text box in the ActiveX Control Properties dialog box.

Listing 17.3   HTML Example Showing the Menu Control

```
<HTML>
<HEAD>
<TITLE>Menu Example</TITLE>
<SCRIPT Language="VBS">
<!— Hide script from incompatible browsers!
Function Timer_Timer()
   If IsObject(mnuEdit) Then
     Timer.Enabled="0"
     mnuFile.Caption="File"
     mnuFile.AddItem "New", 1
     mnuFile.AddItem "Open", 2
     mnuFile.AddItem "Save", 3
     mnuFile.AddItem "Save As...", 4
mnuEdit.Caption="Edit"
     mnuEdit.AddItem "Cut", 1
     mnuEdit.AddItem "Copy", 2
     mnuEdit.AddItem "Paste", 3
     mnuEdit.AddItem "Delete", 4
   End If
End Function
<!— —>
</SCRIPT>
</HEAD>
<BODY BGCOLOR="#FFFFFF">
<CENTER>
<H1>Menu Example</H1>
<HR>
```

```
<OBJECT
   ID="mnuFile"
   CLASSID="CLSID:52DFAE60-CEBF-11CF-A3A9-00A0C9034920"
   CODEBASE="http://activex.microsoft.com/controls/iexplorer/btnmenu.
➡ocx#Version=4,70,0,1161"
   TYPE="application/x-oleobject"
   WIDTH=60
   HEIGHT=30
>
</OBJECT>
<OBJECT
   ID="mnuEdit"
   CLASSID="CLSID:52DFAE60-CEBF-11CF-A3A9-00A0C9034920"
   CODEBASE="http://activex.microsoft.com/controls/iexplorer/btnmenu.
➡ocx#Version=4,70,0,1161"
   TYPE="application/x-oleobject"
   WIDTH=60
   HEIGHT=30
>
</OBJECT>
<OBJECT
   ID="timer"
   CLASSID="clsid:59CCB4A0-727D-11CF-AC36-00AA00A47DD2"
   CODEBASE="http://activex.microsoft.com/controls/iexplorer/ietimer.
➡ocx#version=4,70,0,1161"
   TYPE="application/x-oleobject"
   ALIGN=middle
>
<PARAM NAME="Interval" VALUE="100">
<PARAM NAME="Enabled" VALUE="True">
</OBJECT>
</CENTER>
<HR>
This example of the ActiveX Menu Control demonstrates the ability of the
Control to create and support menus within the Web browser.
</BODY>
</HTML>
```

Part IV Ch 17

Delayed ActiveX Control Configuration Using the ActiveX Timer Control

Look through Listing 17.3 to see a curious use of the ActiveX Timer Control. At first glance, it is not obvious what the Timer Control is doing nor why it is doing it.

The Timer Control is continuously running through its count sequence, from its Interval parameter of 100 milliseconds to zero. Each time it hits zero, it triggers the Timer_Timer() VBScript function. This function checks to see if the mnuEdit object is defined, and if it is, the function sets the menu and item names for the two drop-down menus and disables the Timer Control. If the mnuEdit object doesn't exist, the function does nothing and the Timer Control continues to operate.

Why is this necessary? It's because the CODEBASE attribute of the <OBJECT> tag is used to allow the ActiveX Control to be automatically downloaded and installed if it doesn't exist on the client computer or if a more recent version of it exists at the source. This means that there might be a considerable delay before the ActiveX Menu Control object becomes defined and active. If the

continues

continued

VBScript required to configure the menu objects runs before completion of this download and installation, an error occurs because the menu objects are not yet defined.

So the Timer Control and the corresponding `Timer_Timer()` VBScript function are used to check periodically to see if the menu object has been defined. Once it is defined, the function runs to configure it, and the Timer Control is disabled.

FIG. 17.6

Drop-down menus can be created, changed on-the-fly, and used to trigger scripted events, all within a Web page.

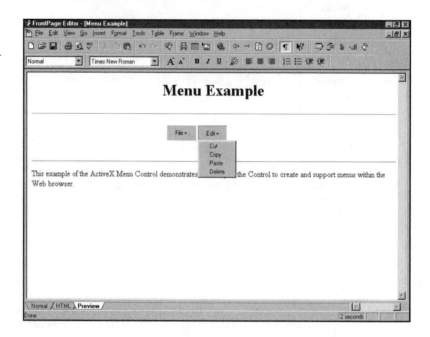

Microsoft's parameter descriptions for the Menu Control are as follows:

- **ItemCount** The number of menu items in the current menu (read only).
- **Caption** The caption to be displayed.
- **Menuitem** The menu item to be displayed.
- **AboutBox** Displays the About dialog box.
- **PopUp([in] int x, [in] int y)** Pops up the menu. If no value is passed for X or Y position (or both), the current mouse position is used to display the pop-up menu. The x and y values are relative to the window, not to the screen.
- **Clear** Clears off all menu items.
- **RemoveItem ([in] int index)** Removes the specified item. If the menu item does not exist, nothing is done.
- **AddItem ([in] String, [in/optional] int index)** Adds the passed menu item at the specified index. If no index is passed, the item is appended to the menu.

- **Select(int item)** Indicates the menu item selected.
- **Click** No menu items were present, and the button was clicked.

Popup Menu Control

The ActiveX Popup Menu Control is similar to the Menu Control described previously, except that it displays pop-up menus rather than drop-down menus. The example in Listing 17.4 shows how VBScript is used to dynamically change the menu by using the RemoveItem() and AddItem() methods of the Popup Menu Control. Figure 17.7 displays the initial configuration of the Popup Menu Control, which is triggered by clicking the Show Menu button.

Listing 17.4 popmenu.htm—HTML Example Showing the Popup Menu Control

```
<HTML>
<HEAD>
<TITLE>Popup Menu Example</TITLE>
</HEAD>
<SCRIPT Language="VBS">
Sub Iepop1_Click(ByVal x)
    Alert "Item #" & x & " SELECTED!!!"
    Call Iepop1.RemoveItem(x)
    Call Iepop1.AddItem("Item #" & x & " SELECTED!!!",x)
End Sub

Sub ShowMenu_onClick
    Call Iepop1.PopUp
End Sub
</SCRIPT>
<BODY BGCOLOR=#FFFFFF>
<CENTER>
<H1>Popup Menu Example</H1>
<HR>
<OBJECT
    ID="iepop1"
    CODEBASE="http://activex.microsoft.com/controls/iexplorer/iemenu.
➥ocx#Version=4,70,0,1161"
    TYPE="application/x-oleobject"
    CLASSID="clsid:7823A620-9DD9-11CF-A662-00AA00C066D2"
    WIDTH=1
    HEIGHT=1
>
<PARAM NAME="Menuitem[0]" value="One">
<PARAM NAME="Menuitem[1]" value="Two">
<PARAM NAME="Menuitem[2]" value="Three">
<PARAM NAME="Menuitem[3]" value="Four">
<PARAM NAME="Menuitem[4]" value="Five">
</OBJECT>
<INPUT TYPE="button" NAME="ShowMenu" VALUE="Show Menu" ALIGN=RIGHT>
</CENTER>
<HR>
This example of the ActiveX Popup Menu Control demonstrates the ability of
```

continues

Listing 17.4   Continued

```
the Control to create and support pop-up menus within the Web browser.
</BODY>
</HTML>
```

FIG. 17.7

By attaching the Popup Menu Control to the onClick() method of the Show Item HTML Forms button, the menu appears whenever the button is clicked.

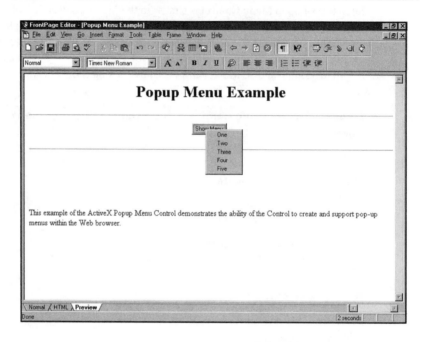

Once an item is selected from the Popup Menu Control, the Click() method of the control is triggered via the VBScript Iepop1_Click() subroutine. This subroutine removes the selected item and replaces it with one that reflects that this menu item slot has been previously selected and displays an Alert box to display what item was picked. The next time the Popup Menu Control is selected the updated menu item is displayed (see Figure 17.8).

Microsoft's parameter descriptions for the Popup Menu Control are as follows:

- **ItemCount**   The number of menu items in the current menu (read only).
- **Menuitem[]**   The menu item to be displayed.
- **AboutBox**   Displays the About dialog box.
- **PopUp ([in] int x, [in] int y)**   Pops up the menu. If no value is passed for X or Y position (or both), the current mouse position is used to display the pop-up menu. The x and y values are relative to the window, not to the screen.
- **Clear**   Clears off all menu items.
- **RemoveItem ([in] int index)**   Removes the specified item. If the menu item does not exist, nothing is done.

■ **Additem ([in] String, [in/optional] int index)** Adds the passed menu item at the specified index. If no index is passed, the item is appended to the menu.

■ **Click(int item)** Item clicked is one of the parameters passed.

FIG. 17.8

The Popup Menu Control allows menus and menu items to be changed dynamically.

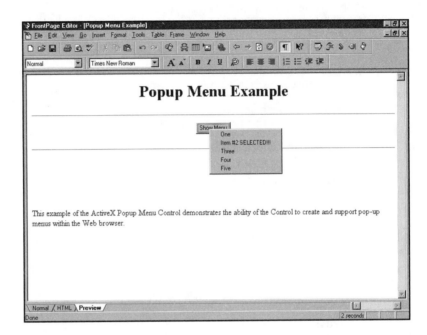

Popup Window Control

The ActiveX Popup Window Control enables you to preview Web pages displayed in their own pop-up window. The HTML displayed is subject to the same limitations as those used with the Marquee Control. For example, hypertext links, though displayed correctly, are not active, and embedded objects do not appear. Listing 17.5 shows an example of using the Popup Window Control to provide a preview of a page, specifically the INDEX.HTM page of a Web (see Figure 17.9). Notice that the VBScript StrGetUrlBase() function is used to parse the base (everything other than the document name itself) from the URL of the current document.

> **CAUTION**
>
> To try out the code in the listing, you have to access the pop-up-enabled page from outside the FrontPage environment. Start a browser and use its File, Open command to open the page hosting the pop-up window. Also make sure that the file you want to pop up in the window is named INDEX.HTM.

Part

IV

Ch

17

Listing 17.5   HTML Example Showing the Popup Window Control

```
<HTML>
<HEAD>
<TITLE>Popup Window Example</TITLE>
<SCRIPT Language="VBSCRIPT">
Sub Label0_MouseMove(ByVal s, ByVal b, ByVal x, ByVal y)
    PopObj.Popup strGetUrlBase & "index.htm", True
End Sub
Function StrGetUrlBase()
    Dim strBase, strSlash, idx

    strBase = Location.HRef
    If (Left(strBase,5)) = "file:" then
      strSlash = "\"
    ElseIf (Left(strBase,5)) = "http:" then
      strSlash = "/"
    Else
      strBase = ""
      strSlash = "/"
    End If

    idx = Len(strBase)
    While idx > 0 And Mid(strBase, idx, 1) <> strSlash
      idx = idx - 1
    Wend

    strBase = Left(strBase,idx)

    StrGetUrlBase = strBase
End Function
</SCRIPT>
</HEAD>
<BODY BGCOLOR=#FFFFFF>
<CENTER>
<H1>Popup Window Example</H1>
<HR>
<A ID="Link1" href="index.html">
<OBJECT
    ID="label0"
    CLASSID="clsid:99B42120-6EC7-11CF-A6C7-00AA00A47DD2"
    CODEBASE="http://activex.microsoft.com/controls/iexplorer/ielabel.
➥ocx#version=4,70,0,1161"
    TYPE="application/x-oleobject"
    WIDTH=400
    HEIGHT=20
    VSPACE=0
    ALIGN=center
>
<PARAM NAME="Angle" VALUE="0">
<PARAM NAME="Alignment" VALUE="4" >
<PARAM NAME="BackStyle" VALUE="1" >
<PARAM NAME="BackColor" VALUE="#F0F000" >
<PARAM NAME="Caption" VALUE="Move the cursor here to preview my home page.">
<PARAM NAME="FontName" VALUE="Times New Roman">
```

```
<PARAM NAME="FontSize" VALUE="16">
<PARAM NAME="ForeColor" VALUE="#000000" >
</OBJECT>
</A>
<OBJECT
    ID="PopObj"
    CLASSID="clsid:A23D7C20-CABA-11CF-A5D4-00AA00A47DD2"
    CODEBASE="http://activex.microsoft.com/controls/iexplorer/iepopwnd.
➥ocx#Version=4,70,0,1161"
    TYPE="application/x-oleobject"
    WIDTH=400
    HEIGHT=20
>
</OBJECT>
</CENTER>
<HR>
This example of the ActiveX Popup Window Control demonstrates the ability of
the Control to display Web pages in a pop-up window. In this example, the pop-up
window is attached to a MouseMove event on the displayed ActiveX Label
Control, and appears when the cursor touches the Label object.
</BODY>
</HTML>
```

FIG. 17.9
The Popup Window Control allows you to present previews of HTML Web pages within their own window.

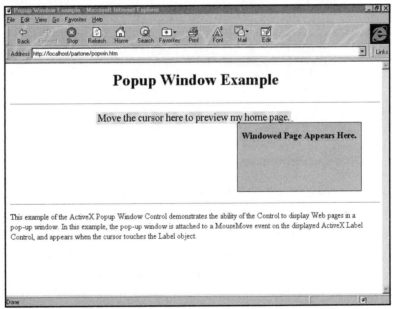

Microsoft's parameter descriptions for the Popup Window Control are as follows:

- **AboutBox** Displays the About dialog box.
- **Popup** Brings up the pop-up window. This method accepts the following parameters.
  - **URL** The URL location of the page to be displayed.
  - **URL Scale** optional Boolean value:

- **True**   Scale the display to fit in the pop-up window.
- **False**   Don't scale; clip display to fit in the pop-up window.
- **Dismiss**   Removes the pop-up window, if one is currently being displayed.

Preloader Control

The ActiveX Preloader Control can be used to speed up the apparent throughput of a Web session by allowing Internet Explorer 3 to preload graphics, video, audio, or other HTML elements while a user is reviewing a given page.

Normally, the Web author would use the Preloader Control to quietly preload images or other HTML elements while the user is reading the current Web page. Then, when the user wants to go to the next page in the Web site, or when the user wants to view an image file, hear a sound, or watch a video clip, the Internet Explorer will already have downloaded it to the cache, and the user can view it without any further delay. Listing 17.6 shows an excerpt of how the Preloader Control is set up to download an image file into the cache.

Listing 17.6   HTML Code to Implement the Preloader Control

```
<OBJECT
    ID="PreLoader"
    CLASSID="CLSID:16E349E0-702C-11CF-A3A9-00A0C9034920"
    CODEBASE="http://activex.microsoft.com/controls/iexplorer/iepreld.
➥ocx#Version=4,70,0,1161"
    TYPE="application/x-oleobject"
    WIDTH=1
    HEIGHT=1
>
<PARAM NAME="URL" VALUE="bigimage.gif">
<PARAM NAME="Enable" VALUE="1">
</OBJECT>
```

Microsoft's parameter descriptions for the Preloader Control are as follows:

- **URL**   URL to be downloaded.
- **Enable**   Enables (Enable=1) or disables (Enable=0) the Control.
- **CacheFile**   File name of the local cached file (read only).
- **Bytes**   The amount of data read so far in bytes (read only).
- **Percentage**   The amount of data read so far in percentage (read only).
- **AboutBox**   Displays the About dialog box.
- **Complete**   Fired when the download has been completed.
- **Error**   Fired when the download could not be completed.

Stock Ticker Control

The ActiveX Stock Ticker Control is used to display scrolling stock ticker information across a Web page. Listing 17.7 shows a typical way the control would be coded to be included in a Web page.

Listing 17.7 HTML Code to Implement the Stock Ticket Control

```
<OBJECT
   ID=iexr2
   TYPE="application/x-oleobject"
   CLASSID="clsid:0CA4A620-8E3D-11CF-A3A9-00A0C9034920"
   CODEBASE="http://activex.microsoft.com/controls/iexplorer/iestock.
➡ocx#Version=4,70,0,1161"
   WIDTH=300
   HEIGHT=50
>
<PARAM NAME="DataObjectName" VALUE="stocks.dat">
<PARAM NAME="DataObjectActive" VALUE="1">
<PARAM NAME="scrollwidth" VALUE="5">
<PARAM NAME="forecolor" VALUE="#ff0000">
<PARAM NAME="backcolor" VALUE="#0000ff">
<PARAM NAME="ReloadInterval" VALUE="5000">
</OBJECT>
```

The data file (STOCKS.DAT, in the listing) used by the ActiveX Stock Ticker Control can be dynamically changed to allow the information displayed to be continuously updated. In text format, the data file will be of the form:

```
name1TABvalue1TABvalue2...CR/LF
name2TABvalue1TABvalue2...CR/LF
...
```

You can also specify an OLE object that generates data in the XRT format.

Microsoft's parameter descriptions for the Stock Ticker Control are as follows:

- **DataObjectName** Name of the data source. This can be a URL or an OLE object.
- **DataObjectActive** Indicates whether the data source is active. 1: active, 0: inactive. The Ticker Control displays data only when `DataObjectActive` is 1.
- **ScrollWidth** The amount in which the display is scrolled for each redraw.
- **ScrollSpeed** The intervals at which the display is scrolled.
- **ReloadInterval** The interval at which the URL is reloaded periodically.
- **ForeColor** Foreground color.
- **BackColor** Background color.

■ **OffsetValues**   The value (in pixels) by which the value will be offset from the name in the vertical direction.

■ **AboutBox**   Displays the About dialog box.

Using the Microsoft Forms 2.0 Objects

FrontPage Editor gives you several ActiveX Controls that are oriented toward forms. These add flexibility and interactivity not readily available in the static forms components you get from the Forms Toolbar. To make these objects work together and provide the results you want, some programming will be required.

The form objects available are as follows:

■ **Check Box**   Inserts a check box next to an independent option that you select or clear. Multiple choices with several options chosen are supported.

■ **Combo Box**   Inserts a combination text box and list box. Users can either type in an entry or select one from a list. This box includes a scroll bar.

■ **Command Button**   Inserts a command button that carries out an operation.

■ **Frame**   Inserts a box in which you can group related choices. To be able to move the frame and the controls it contains together, insert the frame before you insert the controls.

■ **Image**   Inserts a graphic with options for appearance.

■ **Label**   Inserts a label.

■ **List Box**   Inserts a box that displays available choices. If the list is bigger than the box, the user is provided with a scroll bar.

■ **Option Button**   Inserts an option button next to each item in a group of choices that are mutually exclusive.

■ **Scrollbar**   Inserts a scroll bar next to a list box that contains more items than are visible.

■ **Spin Button**   Inserts a Spin Control that lets a user increment or decrement a value.

■ **Tab Strip**   Provides tabbed or buttoned file folders.

■ **Text Box**   Inserts an edit field or Edit Control that displays text typed by the user.

■ **Toggle Button**   Inserts a toggle button that switches between two states.

From Here...

You've had a look at one type of active content you can add to pages on your site. However, there are more resources than just ActiveX. For an exploration of these, see:

■ Chapter 18, "Scripting with VBScript," where you find out about the components of the VBScript language and how you use Visual Basic scripts to interact with Microsoft Internet Explorer.

■ Chapter 19, "Scripting with JavaScript," which explores JavaScript language elements and syntax, and shows how you can use this scripting language to interact with Web page elements and users.

■ Chapter 20, "Inserting Java Applets and Browser Plug-Ins," where you can learn about MIME media types, Netscape plug-ins, and get an overview of the Java programming language.

Part

IV

Ch

17

## CHAPTER 18

Scripting with VBScript

In addition to Netscape's JavaScript language, there now exists for Web programmers Microsoft's own scripting language, Visual Basic Script (VBScript), which is based on the Visual Basic and Visual Basic for Applications languages. Just as these two languages made it much easier to create applications for Windows and within the Microsoft Office suite, respectively, VBScript was designed as a language for easily adding interactivity and dynamic content to Web pages. VBScript gives Web authors the ability to use Internet Explorer 3.x and 4.x, and other compatible Web browsers and applications, to execute scripts that perform a wide variety of functions. These functions include verifying and acting on user input, customizing Java applets, interacting with and customizing ActiveX Controls and other OLE-compatible applications, and many other things. ■

Find out about Visual Basic (VB) Script

In this chapter, you'll find out about using Visual Basic Script, Microsoft's own scripting language, with FrontPage 98.

VBScript is related to Visual Basic for Applications

Find out how VBScript is related to Microsoft's Visual Basic for Applications and Visual Basic programming environments.

VBScript language components

Learn about the different components, statements, and functions of the VBScript programming language.

Use VBScript to interact with Web browsers

Learn how to use VBScript to interact with Internet Explorer through the Internet Explorer object model.

VBScript in HTML documents

See examples of VBScripts used in HTML documents to add increased interactivity, functionality, and an interface to other Web objects.

Use FrontPage Editor's Script Wizard

Add VBScript to your pages the easy way.

Using FrontPage Editor to Add Scripts to a Page

Whereas FrontPage Editor on its own is an extremely capable page editor, its capabilities are enormously extended by adding scripts. Before getting started with investigating VBScript itself, you'll likely want to know how you persuade FrontPage Editor to insert scripts in an HTML document. It's quite simple; use the following procedure:

1. Choose Insert, Advanced, Script, or click the Insert Script button on the Advanced toolbar. The Script dialog box appears (see Figure 18.1).

FIG. 18.1
Use the Script dialog box to choose and compose the type of script you want.

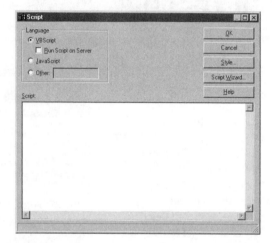

2. Mark the option button for the kind of script you want and mark the check box if you want the script to run on a Microsoft Internet Information Server.

3. Type the code into the workspace of the dialog box and choose OK. The script inserts into the page.

The workspace in this dialog box is just that of a text editor, and absolutely no syntax checking is done. You don't need to include the <SCRIPT> tags; they're inserted when you choose OK to close the dialog box and add the script.

N O T E You'll know there's a script in your page because a small script icon (coffee cup for Java; movie clapboard for VBScript) appears in the FrontPage Editor workspace to indicate its presence. ▨

The Script Wizard, also available through this dialog box, makes it unnecessary (much of the time) for you to type code in by hand. The use of the Script Wizard is discussed later in this chapter.

Background: Microsoft's ActiveX Scripting

Since Microsoft began its big push into the Internet and World Wide Web arena in December 1995, it has been hotly pursuing Netscape, the industry leader in browsers. Not content to play catch-up with Netscape, Microsoft has introduced its own new technologies and innovations, particularly in Internet Explorer versions 3.x and 4.x. Among its biggest innovations has been a collection of technologies called ActiveX; one of these technologies is ActiveX Scripting, which includes support for JavaScript and Microsoft's own Visual Basic Script (VBScript). ActiveX technology is now in the public domain, by the way, and has a standards committee.

▶ **See** Chapter 17, "Using ActiveX Controls," **p. 343**

However, ActiveX Scripting is more than just support for VBScript and JavaScript. Microsoft has developed a standard to allow its Web browser and other compatible applications to support arbitrary scripting engines. Vendors can develop scripting engines of their own that can be used with Internet Explorer, as long as they conform to the ActiveX Scripting standard.

ON THE WEB

Microsoft discusses ActiveX Scripting in greater detail within the Internet Explorer Web site at **http://www.microsoft.com/ie/ie3/activescript.htm**
and under its Internet developer Web site at **http://www.microsoft.com/intdev/sdk/docs/olescrpt/**.

The first two examples of ActiveX scripting languages are VBScript and JScript, Microsoft's implementation of the JavaScript language.

▶ **See** Chapter 19, "Scripting with JavaScript," for more information on JavaScript. **p. 417**

Part
IV

Ch
18

What Is VBScript?

Like JavaScript, VBScript allows you to embed commands into an HTML document. When a user of a compatible Web browser (currently only Internet Explorer browsers, or Netscape Navigator 3 or 4 with the appropriate ScriptActive plug-ins from Ncompass Labs) downloads your page, your VBScript commands are loaded by the Web browser along with the rest of the document, and are run in response to any of a series of events. Again, like JavaScript, VBScript is an *interpreted* language; Internet Explorer interprets the VBScript commands when they are loaded and run. They do not first need to be *compiled* into executable form by the Web author who uses them.

N O T E The NCompass plug-in cannot natively read ActiveX unless the object tag contains the appropriate *embed* information. ■

VBScript is a fast and flexible subset of Microsoft's Visual Basic and Visual Basic for Applications languages, and it is designed to be easy to program in and quick in adding active content to HTML documents. The language elements are mainly those that are familiar to anyone who has programmed in just about any language, such as If...Then...Else blocks, Do, While, and For...Next loops, and a typical assortment of operators and built-in functions. This chapter takes you to the heart of the VBScript language and shows you examples of how to use it to add interaction and increased functionality on your Web pages.

N O T E If you are acquainted with JavaScript, parts of this chapter will be very familiar. That's because JavaScript and VBScript are similar languages with similar syntax, which can perform many of the same functions. If you're torn between them, check the "What Scripting Language Should You Use?" section at the end of this chapter. ▨

Why Use a Scripting Language?

Although HTML provides a good deal of flexibility for Web page authors, it is static by itself; once written, HTML documents can't interact with the user other than by presenting hyperlinks. Creative use of CGI scripts (which run on Web servers) has made it possible to create more interesting and effective interactive sites, but some applications really demand programs or scripts that are executed by the client.

VBScript allows Web authors to write small scripts that execute on the users' browsers instead of on the server. For example, an application that collects data from a form and then posts it to the server can validate the data for completeness and correctness before sending it to the server. This can greatly improve the performance of the browsing session, because users don't have to send data to the server until it's been verified as correct.

Another important use of Web browser scripting languages like VBScript comes as a result of the increased functionality being introduced for Web browsers in the form of Java applets, plug-ins, ActiveX Controls, and VRML objects and worlds. Each of these things can be used to add extra functions and interactivity to a Web page. Scripting languages act as the glue that binds everything together. A Web page might use an HTML form to get some user input and then set a parameter for an ActiveX Control based on that input. Usually it's a script that will actually carry this out.

What Can VBScript Do?

VBScript provides a fairly complete set of built-in functions and commands that allows you to perform math calculations, manipulate strings, play sounds, open new windows and new URLs, and access and verify user input to your Web forms.

Code to perform these actions can be embedded in a page and executed when the page is loaded. You can also write functions that contain code that's triggered by events you specify. For example, you can write a VBScript method that is called when the user clicks the Submit button of a form, or one that is activated when the user clicks a hyperlink on the active page.

VBScript can also set the attributes, or *properties*, of ActiveX Controls, Java applets, and other objects present in the browser. This way, you can change the behavior of plug-ins or other objects without having to rewrite them. For example, your VBScript code could automatically set the text of an ActiveX Label Control based on what time the page is viewed.

VBScript, Visual Basic, and Visual Basic for Applications

VBScript is a subset of the Visual Basic and Visual Basic for Applications languages. If you are familiar with either of these two languages, programming in VBScript will be easy. Just as

Visual Basic was meant to make the creation of Windows programs easier and more accessible, and Visual Basic for Applications was meant to do the same for Microsoft Office applications, VBScript is meant to give an easy-to-learn yet powerful means for adding interactivity and increased functionality to Web pages.

How Does VBScript Look in an HTML Document?

VBScript commands are embedded in your HTML documents, just as with JavaScript and other scripting languages. Embedded VB scripts are enclosed in the HTML container tag `<SCRIPT>...</SCRIPT>`. The LANGUAGE attribute of the `<SCRIPT>` tag specifies the scripting language to use when evaluating the script. For VBScript, the scripting language is defined as LANGUAGE="VBS".

VBScript resembles JavaScript and many other computer languages you may be familiar with. It bears the closest resemblance, as you might imagine, to Visual Basic and Visual Basic for Applications because it is a subset of these two languages. The following are two of the simple rules for structuring VB scripts:

- VBScript is case insensitive, so function, Function, and FUNCTION are all the same.
- A single statement can cover multiple lines if a continuation character, a single underscore, is placed at the end of each line to be continued. Also, you can put multiple short statements on a single line by separating each from the next with a colon.

VBScript Programming Hints

You should keep a few points in mind when programming with VBScript. These hints ease your learning process and make your HTML documents that include VB scripts more compatible with a wider range of Web browsers.

Hiding Your Scripts   Because VBScript is directly supported only by Internet Explorer 3 and 4, you'll probably be designing pages to be viewed by Web browsers that don't know what to do with it. To keep those browsers from misinterpreting your VB script, wrap your scripts as follows:

```
<SCRIPT LANGUAGE="VBS">
<!-- This line opens an HTML comment
VBScript commands...
This line closes an HTML comment -->
</SCRIPT>
```

The opening `<!--` comment causes Web browsers that do not support VBScript to disregard all text they encounter, until they find a matching `-->`, so they don't display your script. Make sure that your `<SCRIPT>...</SCRIPT>` container elements are outside the comments, though; otherwise, even compatible Web browsers will ignore the script.

Comments   Including comments in your programs to explain what they do is usually good practice for most scripting languages—and VBScript is no exception. The VBScript interpreter ignores any text marked as a comment, so don't be shy about including them. Comments in VBScript are set off by using the REM statement (short for remark) or by using a single

Part
IV

Ch
18

quotation mark (') character. Any text following the REM or single quotation mark, until the end of the line, is ignored. To include a comment on the same line as another VBScript statement, you can use either REM or a single quotation mark. However, if you use REM, you must separate the statement from the REM with a colon. Some of the ways of including HTML and VBScript comments in a script are shown in the following script fragment:

```
<SCRIPT LANGUAGE="VBS">
<!-- This line opens an HTML comment
REM This is a VBScript comment on a line by itself.
' This is another VBScript comment
customer.name = "Jim O'Donnell"        'Inline comment
customer.address = "1757 P Street NW"  :REM Inline REM comment (note the :)
customer.zip = "20036-1303"
<!-- This line closes an HTML comment -->
</SCRIPT>
```

Elements of the VBScript Language

As a subset of Visual Basic and Visual Basic for Applications, VBScript doesn't have as much functionality. It is intended to provide a quick and simple language for enhancing Web pages and servers. This section discusses some of the building blocks of VBScript and how they are combined into VBScript programs.

You can get up-to-the-minute information on the language at the Microsoft VBScript Web site at **http://www.microsoft.com/vbscript/**.

VBScript Identifiers

An *identifier* is just a unique name that VBScript uses to identify a variable, method, or object in your program. As with other programming languages, VBScript imposes some rules on what names you can use. All VBScript names must start with an alphabetic character and can contain both uppercase and lowercase letters and the digits 0 through 9. They can be as long as 255 characters, although for readability you probably don't want to go much over 32 or so.

Unlike JavaScript, which supports two different ways for you to represent values in your scripts, literals and variables, VBScript has only variables. The difference in VBScript, then, is one of usage. You can include literals—constant values—in your VBScript programs by setting a variable equal to a value and not changing it. Literals and variables will be referred to as distinct entities, although they are interchangeable.

Literals and variables in VBScript are all of type *variant*, which means that they can contain any type of data that VBScript supports. It is usually a good idea to use a given variable for one type and explicitly convert its value to another type as necessary. The following are some of the types of data that VBScript supports:

- **Integers** These types can be one, two, or four bytes in length, depending on how big they are.
- **Floating Point** VBScript supports single- and double-precision floating point numbers.

- **Strings**   Strings can represent words, phrases, or data, and they're set off by double quotation marks.
- **Booleans**   Booleans have a value of either `true` or `false`.
- **Objects**   A VBScript variable can refer to any object within its environment.

Objects, Properties, Methods, and Events

Before you proceed further, you should take some time to review some terminology that may or may not be familiar to you. VBScript follows much the same object model followed by JavaScript, and uses many of the same terms. In VBScript, just as in JavaScript—and in any object-oriented language for that matter—an *object* is a collection of data and functions that have been grouped together. An object's data is known as its *properties*, and its functions are known as its *methods*. An *event* is a condition to which an object can respond, such as a mouse click or other user input. The VBScript programs that you write make use of properties and methods of objects, both those that you create and those objects provided by the Web browser, its plug-ins, ActiveX Controls, Java applets, and the like.

T I P   Here's a simple guideline: an object's *properties* are the information it knows, its *methods* are how it can act on that information, and *events* are what it responds to.

N O T E   A very important but rather confusing thing to remember is that an object's methods are *also* properties of that object. An object's properties are the information it knows. The object certainly knows about its own methods, so those methods are properties of the object right alongside its other data. ■

Using Built-In Objects and Functions   Individual VBScript elements are objects. For example, *literals* and *variables* are objects of type *variant*, which can be used to hold data of many different types. These objects also have *associated methods*—ways of acting on the different data types. VBScript also allows you to access a set of useful objects that represent the Web browser, the currently displayed page, and other elements of the browsing session.

You access objects by specifying their names. For example, the active document object is named `document`. To use `document` properties or methods, you add a period and the name of the method or property you want. For example, `document.title` is the `title` property of the `document` object.

Using Properties   Every object has properties—even literals. To access a property, just use the object name followed by a period and the property name. To get the length of a string object named `address`, you can write the following:

```
address.length
```

You get back an integer that equals the number of characters in the string. If the object you're using has properties that can be modified, you can change them in the same way. To set the color property of a house object, just write the following:

```
house.color = "blue"
```

You can also create new properties for an object just by naming them. For example, say you define a class called customer for one of your pages. You can add new properties to the customer object as follows:

```
customer.name = "Jim O'Donnell"
customer.address = "1757 P Street NW"
customer.zip = "20036-1303"
```

Because an object's methods are just properties, you can easily add new properties to an object by writing your own function and creating a new object property by using your own function name. If you want to add a Bill method to your customer object, you can write a function named BillCustomer and set the object's property as follows:

```
customer.Bill = BillCustomer;
```

To call the new method, you just write the following:

```
customer.Bill()
```

VBScript Variables

VBScript *variables* are all of the type *variant*, which means that they can be used for any of the supported data types. The types of data that VBScript variables can hold are summarized in Table 18.1.

Table 18.1   Data Types that VBScript Variables Can Contain

Type	Description
Empty	Uninitialized and is treated as 0 or the empty string, depending on the context
Null	Intentionally contains no valid data
Boolean	true or false
Byte	Integer in the range –128 to 127
Integer	Integer in the range –32,768 to 32,767
Long	Integer in the range –2,147,483,648 to 2,147,483,647
Single	Single-precision floating point number in the range –3.402823E38 to –1.401298E-45 for negative values and 1.401298E-45 to 3.402823E38 for positive values
Double	Double-precision floating point number in the range –1.79769313486232E308 to –4.94065645841247E-324 for negative values; 4.94065645841247E-324 to 1.79769313486232E308 for positive values
Date	Number that represents a date between January 1, 100 to December 31, 9999
String	Variable-length string up to approximately 2 billion characters in length
Object	Any object
Error	Error number

Expressions

An *expression* is anything that can be evaluated to get a single value. Expressions can contain string or numeric variables, operators, and other expressions, and they can range from simple to quite complex. For example, the following is an expression that uses the assignment operator (more on operators in the next section) to assign the result 3.14159 to the variable pi:

```
pi = 3.14159
```

By contrast, the following is a more complex expression whose final value depends on the values of the two Boolean variables Quit and Complete:

```
(Quit = TRUE) And (Complete = FALSE)
```

Operators

Operators do just what their name suggests: they operate on variables or literals. The items that an operator acts on are called its *operands.* Operators come in the two following types:

- **Unary**   These operators require only one operand, and the operator can come before or after the operand. The Not operator, which performs the logical negation of an expression, is a good example.

- **Binary**   These operators need two operands. The four math operators (+ for addition, - for subtraction, x for multiplication, and / for division) are all binary operators, as is the = assignment operator you saw earlier.

Assignment Operators   *Assignment operators* take the result of an expression and assign it to a variable. One feature that VBScript has that most other programming languages do not is that you can change a variable's type on the fly. Consider the example shown in Listing 18.1.

Part
IV
Ch
18

Listing 18.1   Pi-fly.htm—VBScript Variables Can Change Type On-the-Fly

```
<HTML>
<HEAD>
<SCRIPT LANGUAGE="VBS">
<!-- Hide this script from incompatible Web browsers!
Sub TypeDemo
    Dim pi
    document.write("<HR>")
    pi = 3.14159
    document.write("pi is " & CStr(pi) & "<BR>")
    pi = FALSE
    document.write("pi is " & CStr(pi) & "<BR>")
    document.write("<HR>")
End Sub
<!-- -->
</SCRIPT>
<TITLE>Changing Pi on the Fly!</TITLE>
</HEAD>
<BODY BGCOLOR=#FFFFFF>
If your Web browser doesn't support VBScript, this is all you will see!
```

continues

Listing 18.1   Continued

```
<SCRIPT LANGUAGE="VBS">
<!-- Hide this script from incompatible Web browsers!
TypeDemo
<!-- -->
</SCRIPT>
</BODY>
</HTML>
```

This short function first prints the (correct) value of *pi*. In most other languages, though, try-ing to set a floating point variable to a Boolean value either generates a compiler error or a runtime error. Because VBScript variables can be any type, it happily accepts the change and prints pi's new value: `false` (see Figure 18.2).

FIG. 18.2
Because VBScript variables are all of type *variant*, not only their value can be changed, but also their data type.

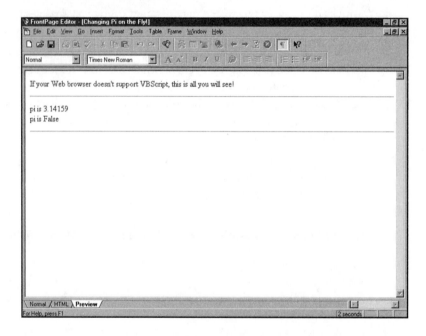

The assignment operator, =, simply assigns the value of an expression's right side to its left side. In the preceding example, the variable pi gets the floating point value 3.14159 or the Boolean value `false` after the expression is evaluated.

Math Operators   The previous sections gave you a sneak preview of the math operators that VBScript furnishes. As you might expect, the standard four math functions (addition, subtrac-tion, multiplication, and division) work just as they do on an ordinary calculator and use the symbols +, -, x, and /.

VBScript supplies three other math operators as follows:

■ \—The backslash operator divides its first operand by its second, after first rounding floating point operands to the nearest integer, and returns the integer part of the result. For example, 19 \ 6.7 returns 2 (6.7 rounds to 7, 19 divided by 7 is a little over 2.71, the integer part of which is 2).

■ Mod—This operator is similar to \ in that it divides the first operand by its second, after again rounding floating point operands to the nearest integer, and returns the integer remainder.

■ ^—This exponent operator returns the first operand raised to the power of the second. The first operand can be negative only if the second, the exponent, is an integer.

Comparison Operators Comparing the value of two expressions to see whether one is larger, smaller, or equal to another is often necessary. VBScript supplies several *comparison operators* that take two operands and return true if the comparison is true and false if it's not. Table 18.2 shows the VBScript comparison operators.

Table 18.2 VBScript Comparison Operators

Operator	Read It As	Returns *true* When
=	Equals	The two operands are equal.
<>	Does not equal	The two operands are unequal.
<	Less than	The left operand is less than the right operand.
<=	Less than or equal to	The left operand is less than or equal to the right operand.
>	Greater than	The left operand is greater than the right operand.
>=	Greater than or equal to	The left operand is greater than or equal to the right operand.

Part
IV

Ch
18

 The comparison operators also can be used on strings; the results depend on standard lexicographic ordering.

Thinking of the comparison operators as questions may be helpful. When you write:

(x >= 10)

you're really saying, "Is the value of variable x greater than or equal to 10?" The return value answers the question, true or false.

Logical Operators Comparison operators compare quantity or content for numeric and string expressions, but sometimes you need to test a logical value—like whether a comparison operator returns true or false. VBScript's *logical operators* allow you to compare expressions that return logical values. The following are VBScript's logical operators:

■ **And** The And operator returns true if both its input expressions are true. If the first operand evaluates to false, And returns false immediately, without evaluating the second operand. Here's an example:

```
x = TRUE And TRUE      ' x is TRUE
x = TRUE And FALSE     ' x is FALSE
x = FALSE And TRUE     ' x is FALSE
x = FALSE And FALSE    ' x is FALSE
```

■ **Or** This operator returns true if either of its operands is true. If the first operand is true, ¦¦ returns true without evaluating the second operand. Here's an example:

```
x = TRUE Or TRUE       ' x is TRUE
x = TRUE Or FALSE      ' x is TRUE
x = FALSE Or TRUE      ' x is TRUE
x = FALSE Or FALSE     ' x is FALSE
```

■ **Not** This operator takes only one expression and it returns the opposite of that expression, so Not true returns false, and Not false returns true.

■ **Xor** This operator, which stands for "exclusive or," returns true if either, but not both, of its input expressions are true, as in the following:

```
x = TRUE Xor TRUE      ' x is FALSE
x = TRUE Xor FALSE     ' x is TRUE
x = FALSE Xor TRUE     ' x is TRUE
x = FALSE Xor FALSE    ' x is FALSE
```

■ **Eqv** This operator, which stands for "equivalent," returns true if its two input expressions are the same—either both true or both false. The statement x Eqv y is equivalent to Not (x Xor y).

■ **Imp** This operator, which stands for "implication," returns true according to the following:

```
x = TRUE Imp TRUE      ' x is TRUE
x = FALSE Imp TRUE     ' x is TRUE
x = TRUE Imp FALSE     ' x is FALSE
x = FALSE Imp FALSE    ' x is TRUE
```

N O T E The logical implication operator Imp is the only logical operator for which the order of the operands is important. ■

Note that the And and Or operators don't evaluate the second operand if the first operand provides enough information for the operator to return a value. This process, called *short-circuit evaluation*, can be significant when the second operand is a function call.

N O T E All six of the logical operators can also operate on nonBoolean expressions. In this case, the logical operations described previously are performed bitwise, on each bit of the two operands. For instance, for the two integers 19 (00010011 in binary) and 6 (00000110):

```
19 And 6 =   2 (00000010 in binary)
19 Or 6  =  23 (00010111 in binary)
Not 19   = -20 (11101100 in binary) ■
```

String Concatenation The final VBScript operator is the *string concatenation operator* &. While the addition operator + can also be used to concatenate strings, using & is better because it is less ambiguous.

Controlling Your VBScripts

Sometimes the scripts that you write are very simple and execute the same way each time they are loaded—for example, a script to display a graphic animation. However, in order to write a script that can perform different functions, depending on different user inputs or other conditions, you will eventually need to add a little more sophistication to your script. VBScript provides statements and loops for controlling the execution of your programs based on a variety of inputs.

Testing Conditions VBScript provides one control structure for making decisions—the `If...Then...Else` structure. To make a decision, you supply one or more expressions that evaluate to `true` or `false`; which code is executed depends on what your expressions evaluate to.

The simplest form of `If...Then...Else` uses only the `If...Then` part. If the specified condition is `true`, the code following the condition is executed; if not, that code is skipped. For example, in the following code fragment, the message appears only if the variable x is less than pi:

```
if (x < pi) then document.write("x is less than pi")
```

You can use any expression as the condition. Because expressions can be nested and combined with the logical operators, your tests can be pretty sophisticated. Also, using the multiple statement character, you can execute multiple commands, as in the following:

```
if ((test = TRUE) And (x > max)) then max = x : test = FALSE
```

The `else` clause allows you to specify a set of statements to execute when the condition is `false`. In the same single line form shown in the preceding line, your new line appears as follows:

```
if (x > pi) then test = TRUE else test = FALSE
```

A more versatile use of the `If...Then...Else` allows multiple lines and multiple actions for each case. It looks something like the following:

```
if (x > pi) then
    test = TRUE
    count = count + 1
else
    test = FALSE
    count = 0
end if
```

Note that with this syntax, additional test clauses using the `elseif` statement are permitted. For instance, one more clause could be added to the previous example:

```
if (x > pi) then
    test = TRUE
```

```
        count = count + 1
elseif (x < -pi) then
        test = TRUE
        count = count - 1
else
        test = FALSE
        count = 0
end if
```

Repeating Actions   If you want to repeat an action more than once, VBScript provides a variety of constructs for doing so. The first, called a `For...Next` loop, executes a set of statements some number of times. You specify three expressions: an *initial* expression, which sets the values of any variables you need to use; a *final value*, which tells the loop how to see when it's done; and an *increment* expression, which modifies any variables that need it. Here's a simple example:

```
for count = 0 to 100 step 2
    document.write("Count is " & CStr(count) & "<BR>")
next
```

In this example, the expressions are all simple numerical values. The initial value is 0, the final value is 100, and the increment is 2. This loop executes 51 times and prints out a number each time.

The third form of loop is the `While...Wend` loop. It executes statements as long as its condition is true. For example, you can rewrite the first `For...Next` loop as follows:

```
count = 0
while (count <= 100)
    document.write("Count is " & CStr(count) & "<BR>")
    count = count + 2
wend
```

The last type of loop is the `Do...Loop`, which has several forms, that tests the condition either at the beginning or the end. The test can either be a `Do While` or `Do Until`, and can occur at the beginning or end of the loop. If a `Do While` test is done at the beginning, the loop executes as long as the test condition is true, similar to the `While...Wend` loop. Here's an example:

```
count = 0
do while (count <= 100)
    document.write("Count is " & CStr(count) & "<BR>")
    count = count + 2
loop
```

An example of having the test at the end, as a `Do...Until`, can also yield equivalent results. In that case, the loop looks like the following:

```
count = 0
do
    document.write("Count is " & CStr(count) & "<BR>")
    count = count + 2
loop until (count = 102)
```

One other difference between these two forms is that when the test is at the end of the loop, as in the second case, the commands in the loop are executed at least once. If the test is at the beginning, that is not the case.

Which form you prefer depends on what you're doing. `For...Next` loops are useful when you want to perform an action a set number of times. `While...Wend` and `Do...Loop` loops, while they can be used for the same purpose, are best when you want to keep doing something as long as a particular condition remains `true`.

N O T E The `For...Next` and `Do...Loop` loops also have a way to exit the loop from inside–the `End For` and `End Do` statements, respectively. Normally, these tests would be used as part of a conditional statement, such as:

```
for i = 0 to 100
    x = UserFunc()
    document.write("x[" & CStr(i) & "] = " & CStr(x) & "<BR>")
    if (x > max) end for
next
```

Other VBScript Statements

This section provides a quick reference to some of the other VBScript statements. The following formatting is used:

- All VBScript keywords are in a `monospace` font.
- Words in `monospace italics` represent user-defined names or statements.
- Any portions enclosed in square brackets ([and]) are optional.
- Portions enclosed in braces ({ and }) and separated by a vertical bar (¦) represent an option, of which one must be selected.
- The word `statements...` indicates a block of one or more statements.

The *Call* statement   The `Call` statement calls a VBScript `Sub` or `Function` procedure (see the next example).

Syntax:

```
Call MyProc([arglist])
```

or

```
MyProc [arglist]
```

Note that `arglist` is a comma-delimited list of zero or more arguments to be passed to the procedure. When the second form is used, omitting the `Call` statement, the parentheses around the argument list, if any, must also be omitted.

The *Dim* Statement   The `Dim` statement is used to declare variables and also to allocate the storage necessary for them. If you specify subscripts, you can also create arrays.

Syntax:

```
Dim varname[([subscripts])][,varname[([subscripts])],...]
```

The *Function* and *Sub* Statements The Function and Sub statements declare VBScript procedures. The difference is that a Function procedure returns a value, and a Sub procedure does not. All parameters are passed to functions *by value*—the function gets the value of the parameter but cannot change the original value in the caller.

Syntax:

```
[Static] Function funcname([arglist])
    statements...
    funcname = returnvalue
End
```

and

```
[Static] Sub subname([arglist])
    statements...
End
```

Variables can be declared with the Dim statement within a Function or Sub procedure. In this case, those variables are local to that procedure and can be referenced only within it. If the Static keyword is used when the procedure is declared, all local variables will retain their value from one procedure call to the next.

The *On Error* Statement The On Error statement is used to enable error handling.

Syntax:

```
On Error Resume Next
```

On Error Resume Next enables execution to continue immediately after the statement that provokes the runtime error. Or, if the error occurs in a procedure call after the last executed On Error statement, execution commences immediately after that procedure call. This way, execution can continue despite a runtime error, allowing you to build an error-handling routine inline within the procedure. The most recent On Error Resume Next statement is the one that is active, so you should execute one in each procedure in which you want to have inline error handling.

VBScript Functions

VBScript has an assortment of intrinsic functions that you can use in your scripts. Table 18.3 shows the functions that exist for performing different types of operations. (Some functions can be used for several types of operations, so they are listed multiple times in the table.)

Table 18.3　VBScript Functions

Type of Operation	Function Names
array operations	IsArray, LBound, UBound
conversions	Abs, Asc, AscB, AscW, Chr, ChrB, ChrW, Cbool, CByte, CDate, CDbl, CInt, CLng, CSng, Cstr, DateSerial, DateValue, Hex, Oct, Fix, Int, Sgn, TimeSerial, TimeValue

Type of Operation	Function Names
dates and times	`Date, Time, DateSerial, DateValue, Day, Month, Weekday, Year, Hour, Minute, Second, Now, TimeSerial, TimeValue`
input/output	`InputBox, MsgBox`
math	`Atn, Cos, Sin, Tan, Exp, Log, Sqr, Randomize, Rnd`
objects	`IsObject`
strings	`Asc, AscB, AscW, Chr, ChrB, ChrW, Instr, InStrB, Len, LenB, LCase, UCase, Left, LeftB, Mid, MidB, Right, RightB, Space, StrComp, String, LTrim, RTrim, Trim`
variants	`IsArray, IsDate, IsEmpty, IsNull, IsNumeric, IsObject, VarType`

VBScript and Web Browsers

The most important things you will be doing with your VBScripts are interacting with the content and information on your Web site and, through it, with your user. You have seen earlier in this chapter a little of one particular thing VBScript can do to your Web page—use `document.write()` to place information on the page itself.

VBScript interacts with your Web browser through the browser's object model. Different aspects of the Web browser exist as different objects, with properties and methods that can be accessed by VBScript. For instance, `document.write()` uses the `write` method of the `document` object. Understanding this Web browser object model is crucial to using VBScript effectively. Understanding how the Web browser processes and executes your scripts is also necessary. Such understanding is even more important with the advent of Dynamic HTML-enabled browsers such as Microsoft Internet Explorer 4 and Netscape Navigator 4, which use a much expanded Document Object Model to make every element on a Web page accessible to on-the-fly changes.

When Scripts Execute

When you put VBScript code in a page, the Web browser evaluates the code as soon as it's encountered. Functions, however, don't get executed when they're evaluated; they just get stored for later use. You still have to call functions explicitly to make them work. Some functions are attached to objects, such as buttons or text fields on forms, and they are called when some event happens on the button or field. You might also have functions that you want to execute during page evaluation. You can do so by putting a call to the function at the appropriate place in the page.

Where to Put Your Scripts

You can put scripts anywhere within your HTML page, as long as they're surrounded with the `<SCRIPT>...</SCRIPT>` tags. One good system is to put functions that will be executed more than once into the <HEAD> element of the page; this element provides a convenient storage place. Because the <HEAD> element is at the beginning of the file, functions and VBScript code that you put there will be evaluated before the rest of the document is loaded. You can then execute the function at the appropriate point in your Web page by calling it, as in the following:

```
<SCRIPT language="VBS">
<!-- Hide this script from incompatible Web browsers!
myFunction()
<!-- -->
</SCRIPT>
```

Another way to execute scripts is to attach them to HTML elements that support scripts. When scripts are matched with events attached to these elements, the script is executed when the event occurs. This can be done with HTML elements, such as forms, buttons, or links. Consider Listing 18.2, which shows a very simple example of attaching a VBScript function to the onClick attribute of a HTML forms button (see Figure 18.3).

Listing 18.2   Button1.htm— Calling a VBScript Function with the Click of a Button

```
<HTML>
<HEAD>
<SCRIPT LANGUAGE="VBS">
<!-- Hide this script from incompatible Web browsers!
sub Pressed
    alert "Stop that!"
end sub
<!-- -->
</SCRIPT>
<TITLE>VBScripts Attached to HTML Elements</TITLE>
</HEAD>
<BODY BGCOLOR=#FFFFFF>
<FORM NAME="Form1">
<INPUT TYPE="BUTTON" NAME="Button1" VALUE="Don't Press Me!"
        onClick="Pressed">
</FORM>
</BODY>
</HTML>
```

VBScript also provides you with several alternate ways to attach functions to objects and their events. The first is through the VBScript function name. To have a VBScript function execute when a given *event* occurs to an *object*, name the function *object_event*. For instance, Listing 18.3 shows an alternate way of coding Listing 18.2 by using this method. Another method for simple actions is to attach the VBScript directly to the attribute of the HTML form element, as shown in Listing 18.4. All three of these listings produce the output shown in Figure 18.3.

FIG. 18.3
VBScript functions can be attached to form fields through several different methods.

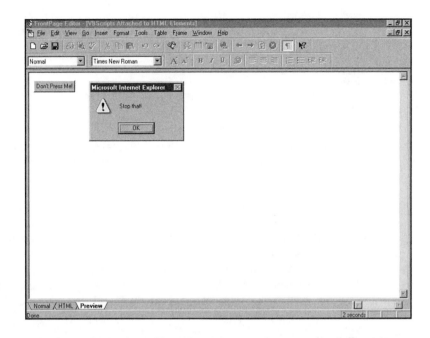

Listing 18.3   Button2.htm—VBScript Functions Can Be Named to Be Called Automatically

```
<HTML>
<HEAD>
<SCRIPT LANGUAGE="VBS">
<!-- Hide this script from incompatible Web browsers!
sub Button1_onClick
    alert "Stop that!"
end sub
<!-- -->
</SCRIPT>
<TITLE>VBScripts Attached to HTML Elements</TITLE>
</HEAD>
<BODY BGCOLOR=#FFFFFF>
<FORM NAME="Form1">
<INPUT TYPE="BUTTON" NAME="Button1" VALUE="Don't Press Me!">
</FORM>
</BODY>
</HTML>
```

Listing 18.4   Button3.htm—Simple VBScripts Can Be Attached Right to a Form Element

```
<HTML>
<HEAD>
<TITLE>VBScripts Attached to HTML Elements</TITLE>
</HEAD>
<BODY BGCOLOR=#FFFFFF>
<FORM NAME="Form1">
    <INPUT TYPE="BUTTON" NAME="Button1" VALUE="Don't Press Me!"
        onClick="alert('I said Don\'t Press Me!')">
</FORM>
</BODY>
</HTML>
```

Sometimes, though, you have code that shouldn't be evaluated or executed until after all the page's HTML has been parsed and displayed. An example is a function to print out all the URLs referenced in a page. If this function is evaluated before all the HTML on the page has been loaded, it misses some URLs. Therefore, the call to the function should come at the page's end. The function itself can be defined anywhere in the HTML document; it is the function call that should be at the end of the page.

 T I P   Or you can use the onLoad event handler in the BODY tag.

N O T E   Until the release of Microsoft Internet Explorer 4, VBScript code to modify the actual HTML contents of a document (as opposed to merely changing the text in a form text input field, for instance) had to be executed during page evaluation. With IE 4, due to the expanded Document Object model, page content can be modified at any time. ▇

Web Browser Objects and Events

In addition to recognizing VBScript when it's embedded inside a <SCRIPT>...</SCRIPT> tag, Internet Explorer 3 and other compatible browsers will also expose some objects, along with their methods and properties, that you can then use in your programs. The Web browsers can also trigger methods you define in response to events that are triggered when the user takes certain actions in the browser (for example, when a button is clicked). The examples shown in Listings 18.2, 18.3, and 18.4 all demonstrate this—a VBScript function is executed when a Web browser *object* (the form input field named Button1) responds to the onClick *event* (triggered by the user clicking the button).

Web Browser Object Hierarchy and Scoping

Figure 18.4 shows the page on the Microsoft Web site that gives the hierarchy of objects that the Web browser provides and that are accessible to VBScript. Window is the top-most object in the hierarchy, and the other objects are organized underneath it, as shown. The dashed lines show where more than one object of the given type can exist. Using this hierarchy, the full reference for the value of a text field named `Text1` in an HTML form named `Form1` would be `Window.Document.Form1.Text1.Value`.

FIG. 18.4
Objects defined by the Web browser are organized in a hierarchy and can be accessed and manipulated by VBScript.

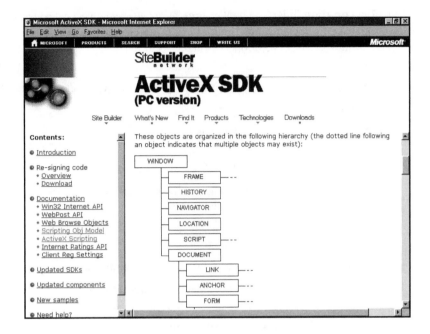

Part

IV

Ch

18

ON THE WEB

http://www.microsoft.com/intdev/sdk/docs/scriptom/   for complete specifications for Microsoft's implementation of the Web browser object model.

Because of the object scoping rules in VBScript, however, it is not necessary to specify this full reference. Scoping refers to the range over which a variable, function, or object is defined. For instance, a variable defined within a VBScript function is scoped only within that function—it cannot be referenced outside of the function. VBScripts are scoped to the current window but not to the objects below the window in the hierarchy. So, for the last example, the text field value could also be referenced as `Document.Form1.Text1.Value`.

Web Browser Object Model

Many events that happen in a browsing session aren't related to items on the page (such as buttons or HTML text). Instead, they're related to what's happening in the browser itself, like what page the user is viewing.

N O T E   Information about the VBScript language can be found through Microsoft's VBScript Web site at **http://www.microsoft.com/vbscript/**, and information about the Web browser object models can be found through the Netscape Navigator and Microsoft Internet Explorer Web sites. ▪

In this section, you get an overview of the most important browser objects, properties, methods, and events that are available—the ones you are most likely to use—and see some examples of their use.

The *Location* Object   The Web browser exposes an object called Location, which holds the current URL, including the hostname, path, CGI script arguments, and even the protocol. Table 18.4 shows some of the properties of the Location object.

Table 18.4   The *Location* Object Contains Information on the Currently Displayed URL

Property	What It Contains
href	The entire URL, including all the subparts; for example, **http://www.msn.com/products/msprod.htm**
protocol	The protocol field of the URL, including the first colon; for example, **http:**
host	The hostname and port number; for example, **www.msn.com:80**
hostname	The hostname; for example, **www.msn.com**
port	The port, if specified; otherwise, it's blank
pathname	The path to the actual document; for example, **products/msprod.htm**
hash	Any CGI arguments after the first **#** in the URL
search	Any CGI arguments after the first **?** in the URL

N O T E   Remember that VBScript is not case sensitive; so, for example, references to the following are all equivalent:

```
Location.HREF
location.href
location.Href
LoCaTiOn.HrEf
```

Listing 18.5 shows an example of how you access and use the Location object. First, the current values of the Location properties are displayed on the Web page (see Figure 18.5). As you can see, not all of them are defined. Additionally, when the button is clicked, the Location.Href property is set to the URL of my home page. This causes the Web browser to load that page.

Listing 18.5 Location.htm—The Location Object Allows You to Access and Set Information About the Current URL

```
<HTML>
<HEAD>
<SCRIPT LANGUAGE="VBS">
<!-- Hide this script from incompatible Web browsers!
sub Button1_onClick
    Location.Href = "http://www.rpi.edu/~odonnj/"
end sub
<!-- -->
</SCRIPT>
<TITLE>The Location Object</TITLE>
</HEAD>
<BODY BGCOLOR=#FFFFFF>
<SCRIPT LANGUAGE="VBS">
<!-- Hide this script from incompatible Web browsers!
document.write "Current Location information: <BR> <HR>"
document.write "Location.Href = " & Location.Href & "<BR>"
document.write "Location.Protocol = " & Location.Protocol & "<BR>"
document.write "Location.Host = " & Location.Host & "<BR>"
document.write "Location.Hostname = " & Location.Hostname & "<BR>"
document.write "Location.Port = " & Location.Port & "<BR>"
document.write "Location.Pathname = " & Location.Pathname & "<BR>"
document.write "Location.Hash = " & Location.Hash & "<BR>"
document.write "Location.Search = " & Location.Search & "<BR> <HR>"
<!-- -->
</SCRIPT>
<FORM NAME="Form1">
    <INPUT TYPE="BUTTON" NAME="Button1" VALUE="Goto JOD's Home Page!">
</FORM>
</BODY>
</HTML>
```

The *Document* Object   The Document object, as you might expect, exposes useful properties and methods of the active document. Location refers only to the URL of the active document, but Document refers to the document itself. Table 18.5 shows Document's properties and methods.

Table 18.5   The *Document* Object Contains Information on the Currently Loaded and Displayed HTML Page

Property	What It Contains
title	Title of the current page, or Untitled if no title exists
location	The document's address (read-only)
lastModified	The page's last-modified date
forms	Array of all the FORMs in the current page

continues

Part

IV

Ch

18

Table 18.5 Continued

Property	What It Contains
links	Array of all the HREF anchors in the current page
anchors	Array of all the anchors in the current page
linkColor	Link color
alinkColor	Active Link color
vlinkColor	Visited link color
bgColor	Background color
fgColor	Foreground color
all	A collection of all the document elements

Method	What It Does
write	Writes HTML to the current page

FIG. 18.5

Manipulating the Location object gives you another means of moving from one Web page to another.

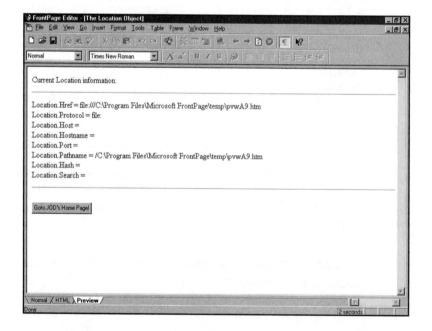

Listing 18.6 shows a VBScript that accesses and displays some of the properties of the Document object. Notice that the Links property is an array, one for each URL link on the current Web page. Figure 18.6 shows the results of loading this Web page.

Listing 18.6 Document.htm—The *Document Object* Allows You to Access and Set Information About the Current Document

```
<HTML>
<HEAD>
<TITLE>The Document Object</TITLE>
</HEAD>
<BODY BGCOLOR=#FFFFFF>
<A HREF="http://www.rpi.edu/~odonnj/">JOD's Home Page</A>
<A HREF="http://www.rpi.edu/~odonnj/Location.htm">The Location Object</A>
<HR>
<SCRIPT LANGUAGE="VBS">
<!-- Hide this script from incompatible Web browsers!
Dim n
document.write "Current Document information: <BR> <HR>"
document.write "Document.Title = " & Document.Title & "<BR>"
document.write "Document.Location = " & Document.Location & "<BR>"
document.write "Document.lastModified = " & Document.lastModified & "<BR>"
for n = 0 to Document.Links.Length-1
    document.write "Document.Links(" & Cstr(n) & ").Href = " & _
        Document.Links(n).Href & "<BR>"
next
document.write "Document.linkColor = " & Document.linkColor & "<BR>"
document.write "Document.alinkColor = " & Document.alinkColor & "<BR>"
document.write "Document.vlinkColor = " & Document.vlinkColor & "<BR>"
document.write "Document.bgColor = " & Document.bgColor & "<BR>"
document.write "Document.fgColor = " & Document.fgColor & "<BR> <HR>"
<!-- -->
</SCRIPT>
</BODY>
</HTML>
```

Part IV

Ch 18

FIG. 18.6
Document object properties contain information about the current document displayed in the Web browser.

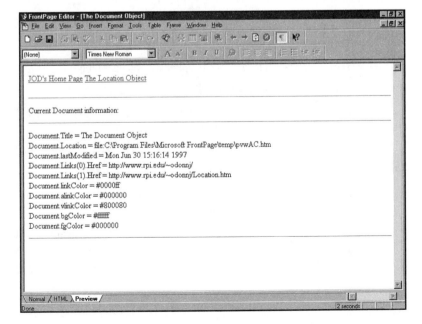

Some of the real power of the Document object, however, is realized by making use of the objects underneath it in the hierarchy, particularly the different HTML forms elements available. This is because these elements are the primary ways of interacting with the user of a Web page.

The *Form* Object

The HTML form object is the primary way for Web pages to solicit different types of input from the user. VBScript often works along with HTML forms in order to perform its functions. The object model for HTML forms includes a wide variety of properties, methods, and events that can be used to program VBScripts.

***Form* Methods and Events**   Table 18.6 shows some of the methods and events attached to HTML form objects. The methods and events can be used in VBScripts—the methods can be used to perform certain functions, and the events can be used to trigger VBScript functions. For instance, if there is a text area named Text1 as part of a form named Form1, the method Document.Form1.Text1.Focus() can be called in a VBScript to force the focus to move to that text area. On the other hand, if there is a button named Button1 in the same form, the event onClick can be used as an attribute to the <INPUT> tag to call a VBScript function when the button is clicked (an example of the different ways of doing this was shown in Listings 18.2, 18.3, and 18.4).

Table 18.6   Methods and Events that Allow You to Control the Contents and Behavior of HTML Elements

Method	What It Does
focus()	Calls to move the input focus to the specified object.
blur()	Calls to move the input focus away from the specified object.
select()	Calls to select the specified object.
click()	Calls to click the specified object, which must be a button.

Event	When It Occurs
onFocus	When the user moves the input focus to the field, either via the Tab key or a mouse click.
onBlur	When the user moves the input focus out of this field.
onSelect	When the user selects text in the field.
onChange	Only when the field loses focus and the user has modified its text; use this function to validate data in a field.
onSubmit	When the user submits the form (if the form has a Submit button).
onClick	When the button is clicked.

Note that `focus()`, `blur()`, `select()`, and `click()` are methods of objects; to call them, you use the name of the object you want to affect. For example, to turn off the button named Search, you type `Document.Form.Search.Disable()`.

In addition to the methods and events, `form` objects have properties that can be used by VBScripts. Table 18.7 lists the properties exposed for HTML `form` elements.

Table 18.7   HTML *Forms* Properties that You Can Use in Your VBScript Code

Property	What It Contains
name	The value of the form's NAME attribute
method	The value of the form's METHOD attribute
action	The value of the form's ACTION attribute
elements	The elements array of the form
encoding	The value of the form's ENCODING attribute
target	Window targeted after submit for form response
Method	**What It Does**
submit()	Any form element can force the form to be submitted by calling the form's submit() method.
Event	**When It Occurs**
onSubmit()	When the form is submitted; this method can't stop the submission, though.

Properties for Objects in a Form   A good place to use VBScript is in forms because you can write scripts that process, check, and perform calculations with the data the user enters. VBScript provides a useful set of properties and methods for text INPUT elements and buttons.

You use INPUT elements in a form to let the user enter text data; VBScript provides properties to get the objects that hold the element's contents, as well as methods for doing something when the user moves into or out of a field. Table 18.8 shows the properties and methods that are defined for text INPUT elements.

Table 18.8   Properties and Methods that Allow You to Control the Contents and Behavior of HTML *INPUT* Elements

Property	What It Contains
name	The value of the element's NAME attribute.
value	The field's contents.
defaultValue	The initial contents of the field; returns `""` if blank.

continues

Table 18.8   Continued

Method	What It Does
onFocus	Called when the user moves the input focus to the field, either via the Tab key or a mouse click.
onBlur	Called when the user moves the input focus out of this field.
onSelect	Called when the user selects text in the field.
onChange	Called only when the field loses focus and the user has modified its text; use this action to validate data in a field.

Individual buttons and check boxes have properties, too; VBScript provides properties to get objects containing a button's data, as well as methods for doing something when the user selects or deselects a particular button. Table 18.9 shows some of the properties and methods that are defined for button elements.

Table 18.9   Properties and Methods that Allow You to Control the Contents and Behavior of HTML Button and Check Box Elements

Property	What It Contains
name	The value of the button's NAME attribute
value	The VALUE attribute
checked	The state of a check box
defaultChecked	The initial state of a check box
Method	**What It Does**
click()	Clicks a button and triggers whatever actions are attached to it.
Event	**When It Occurs**
onClick	Called when the button is pressed.

As an example of what you can do with VBScript and the objects, properties, and methods outlined, you might want to put the user's cursor into the first text field in a form automatically, instead of making the user manually click the field. If your first text field is named UserName, you can put the following in your document's script to get the behavior you want
Document.Form.UserName.Focus().

An example of using VBScript with HTML forms is shown in the section, "VBScript Intranet Application."

Example VBScript Applications

As with most programming languages, you can learn best by doing, and the easiest way is to take a look at some examples. The listings shown so far have demonstrated some of the things you can do with VBScript. Next are two more examples, giving some more practical examples of VBScript in action.

VBScript Intranet Application

Unless and until VBScript becomes more widespread on the Internet, its best applications might be intranet applications, in companies or organizations that have adopted Microsoft Internet Explorer as their standard. In order to show some of the capabilities of VBScript and the kind of applications it can be used for, you will look at the design of an HTML form and VBScript for submitting a timesheet.

In my organization, we are required to fill out a timesheet every other week, detailing how many hours we worked each day on each of our projects. There are several guidelines that we have to follow when working and when filling out our timesheets: we have to account for eight hours a day of work or leave, and hours worked in excess of eight hours a day are considered overtime.

The goal of designing a Web page for the submission of a timesheet is to decrease the amount of paper flying around our office. Previously we filled out a timesheet that was initialed by our group leader and then used by the secretary to fill out a timecard. By putting the timesheet on the computer, we save a little time and paper.

Designing the HTML Form   The first step in the process is designing the HTML form for the timesheet. This is pretty simple. One form is used for the employee information and for the timesheet itself. The part of the form for the employee information is very straightforward, and the HTML to generate it looks like this:

```
<FORM NAME="TS" ACTION="mailto:odonnj@rpi.edu" METHOD=POST>
<TABLE BORDER>
<TR><TD ALIGN=RIGHT BGCOLOR=CYAN><B>EMPLOYEE NAME</B></TD>
    <TD BGCOLOR=YELLOW>
        <INPUT NAME="EmpName" TYPE="Text" VALUE="" SIZE=40 ></TD></TR>
<TR><TD ALIGN=RIGHT BGCOLOR=CYAN><B>ID NUMBER</B></TD>
    <TD BGCOLOR=YELLOW>
        <INPUT NAME="IDNum" TYPE="Text" VALUE="" SIZE=40 ></TD></TR>
</TABLE>
<TABLE BORDER>
```

This is used by the employees to enter their name and ID number. An HTML table is used to lay out the form, and a little color is added for appearance. We are careful to assign names to the form and to the two input fields, because they will be used by VBScript to reference those elements.

The timesheet part of the form is also pretty straightforward, although there is a lot more HTML code involved. Each line of the timesheet form requires 18 text fields, one each for the 14 days of the pay period, two for weekly totals, one for the pay period total, and one for the job order number of the project (or the numeric code for annual or sick leave). The top of this part of the form, showing the column headings and the first row of the timesheet, looks like:

```
<TR BGCOLOR=CYAN>
    <TH>Job Order Number</TH>
    <TH>SU</TH>
    <TH>MO</TH><TH>TU</TH><TH>WE</TH><TH>TH</TH><TH>FR</TH>
    <TH>SA</TH><TH>Week #1</TH>
    <TH>SU</TH>
    <TH>MO</TH><TH>TU</TH><TH>WE</TH><TH>TH</TH><TH>FR</TH>
    <TH>SA</TH><TH>Week #2</TH><TH>Pay Period</TH></TR>
<TR ALIGN=CENTER>
    <TD BGCOLOR=YELLOW><INPUT TYPE="Text" VALUE="" SIZE=16></TD>
    <TD><INPUT TYPE="Text" VALUE="" SIZE=1 onChange="Calc"></TD>
    <TD><INPUT TYPE="Text" VALUE="" SIZE=1 onChange="Calc"></TD>
    <TD><INPUT TYPE="Text" VALUE="" SIZE=1 onChange="Calc"></TD>
    <TD><INPUT TYPE="Text" VALUE="" SIZE=1 onChange="Calc"></TD>
    <TD><INPUT TYPE="Text" VALUE="" SIZE=1 onChange="Calc"></TD>
    <TD><INPUT TYPE="Text" VALUE="" SIZE=1 onChange="Calc"></TD>
    <TD BGCOLOR=RED>
        <INPUT TYPE="Text" VALUE="0" SIZE=2 onChange="Calc"></TD>
    <TD><INPUT TYPE="Text" VALUE="" SIZE=1 onChange="Calc"></TD>
    <TD><INPUT TYPE="Text" VALUE="" SIZE=1 onChange="Calc"></TD>
    <TD><INPUT TYPE="Text" VALUE="" SIZE=1 onChange="Calc"></TD>
    <TD><INPUT TYPE="Text" VALUE="" SIZE=1 onChange="Calc"></TD>
    <TD><INPUT TYPE="Text" VALUE="" SIZE=1 onChange="Calc"></TD>
    <TD><INPUT TYPE="Text" VALUE="" SIZE=1 onChange="Calc"></TD>
    <TD BGCOLOR=RED>
        <INPUT TYPE="Text" VALUE="0" SIZE=2 onChange="Calc"></TD>
    <TD BGCOLOR=RED>
        <INPUT TYPE="Text" VALUE="0" SIZE=2 onChange="Calc"></TD></TR>
    [etc...]
```

N O T E Don't worry, the complete listing for this VBScript application is shown a little later. ▨

You might notice a few things about the fields in this form that are different from the fields in the first form. First, the different fields are not named. If you name each field separately, the VBScript functions to process them would be very repetitive—after all, you will be doing the same operations on each row in the form. So rather than naming the fields, make use of the Elements property of the Form object. Elements is an array of the fields in the Form object in the order they are originally defined. So, for the first row of the previous form, the fields shown can be references with Document.Timesheet.Elements(0) through Document.Timesheet.Elements(17).

The second thing different about this form is that most of the fields set the onChange attribute of the <INPUT> tag to call the VBScript function Calc. Discussion of this tag is in the next section.

So, with a total of five rows for the timesheet, and additional rows for annual leave, sick leave, and overtime, you have the HTML document for a timesheet. The resulting Web page looks like Figure 18.7. (The Submit Timesheet button and text field beside it are explained next.)

FIG. 18.7
Using a combination of HTML forms and tables, setting up this timesheet is simple.

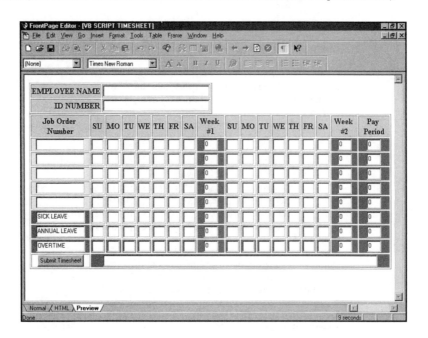

Adding VBScripts   At this point you could be done, and the employees filling out our Web page timesheet would be no worse off than when they were filling out the paper version. They could enter their name, ID number, job order number, hours worked, and total hours for the week and the pay period.

But you can use VBScript to perform some of these calculations automatically. As shown earlier, each form field in the `Timesheet` form (other than the ones for the job order number) has the VBScript function `Calc` attached to its `onChange` event. That means every time that form field changes value, `Calc` is called. Here is the VBScript for `Calc`:

```
Sub Calc
   Dim i,j,jmax,sum
   jmax = 7
   For k = 0 to 1
      For i = 0 to 6
         sum = 0
         For j = 0 to jmax-1
            If (IsNumeric(Document.TS.Elements(k*8+j*18+i+3).Value)) Then
               sum = sum + CDbl(Document.TS.Elements(k*8+j*18+i+3).Value)
            End If
         Next
         If (sum > 8 Or (sum > 0 And (i = 0 Or i = 6))) Then
            If (i = 0 Or i = 6) Then
```

Part
IV

Ch

18

```
                Document.TS.Elements(k*8+jmax*18+i+3).Value = sum
            Else
                Document.TS.Elements(k*8+jmax*18+i+3).Value = sum - 8
            End If
        Else
            Document.TS.Elements(k*8+jmax*18+i+3).Value = ""
        End If
    Next
Next
For j = 0 to jmax
    Document.TS.Elements(j*18+10).Value = 0
    Document.TS.Elements(j*18+18).Value = 0
    For i = 0 to 6
        If (IsNumeric(Document.TS.Elements(j*18+i+3).Value)) Then
            Document.TS.Elements(j*18+10).Value = _
                CDbl(Document.TS.Elements(j*18+10).Value) + _
                CDbl(Document.TS.Elements(j*18+i+3).Value)
        End If
        If (IsNumeric(Document.TS.Elements(j*18+i+11).Value)) Then
            Document.TS.Elements(j*18+18).Value = _
                CDbl(Document.TS.Elements(j*18+18).Value) + _
                CDbl(Document.TS.Elements(j*18+i+11).Value)
        End If
    Next
    Document.TS.Elements(j*18+19).Value = _
        CDbl(Document.TS.Elements(j*18+10).Value) + _
        CDbl(Document.TS.Elements(j*18+18).Value)
Next
Document.TS.Elements((jmax-2)*18+2).Value = "SICK LEAVE"
Document.TS.Elements((jmax-1)*18+2).Value = "ANNUAL LEAVE"
Document.TS.Elements(jmax*18+2).Value = "OVERTIME"
End Sub
```

Now, this looks trickier than it really is, so we'll go through it step by step. The first two lines:

```
Dim i,j,jmax,sum
jmax = 7
```

set up some local variables and set $jmax$ to the number of timesheet rows.

Next, there are two sets of nested For...Next loops to perform the calculations that you are interested in. The first set is used to add up each column of the timesheet to see if there were any overtime hours worked—overtime defined as any hours over eight worked on a weekday or any hours worked at all on a weekend. After this number is calculated, each cell in the overtime row is set appropriately.

The next set of For...Next loops allow us to process each row in the timesheet, including the extra row used for overtime, and total up the hours for that row. The two lines:

```
X.Elements(j*18+10).Value = 0
X.Elements(j*18+18).Value = 0
```

initialize the form elements for the weekly totals to zero. The inner For...Next adds up and sets each row's totals. The section of code that does this looks like the following:

```
If (IsNumeric(Document.TS.Elements(j*18+i+3).Value)) Then
   Document.TS.Elements(j*18+10).Value = _
      CDbl(Document.TS.Elements(j*18+10).Value) + _
      CDbl(Document.TS.Elements(j*18+i+3).Value)
End If
If (IsNumeric(Document.TS.Elements(j*18+i+11).Value)) Then
   Document.TS.Elements(j*18+18).Value = _
      CDbl(Document.TS.Elements(j*18+18).Value) + _
      CDbl(Document.TS.Elements(j*18+i+11).Value)
End If
```

This code does the following:

1. Determines if there is a number entered into the field.
2. Adds the number of hours worked to the total for that row.

This is done for each week, and then the last two lines in this `For...Next` loop add the two weekly totals to get the total for the pay period. The last thing performed by the function is to make sure the job order number fields of the annual leave, sick leave, and overtime rows are set equal to their correct values.

With this VBScript attached to the form fields of the timesheet, completing the sheet becomes a bit easier. Weekly and pay period totals are calculated automatically each time you enter a number and move the cursor. Overtime hours are added automatically when more than eight hours a day are worked. Obviously, the script could be made smarter—verifying that the correct number of hours per pay period are worked, for instance—but this is a good start.

Adding Memory with Cookies There's one more thing that this Web page could use, something that you do have with paper timesheets. With paper timesheets, each employee received a timesheet with his or her name, ID number, and the job order numbers of the most common projects they worked on already printed on it. One way you could do this would be to create a separate Web page for each employee. There is a better way, however, that requires only one Web page and stores the personal information on each employee's local computer. This can be done with *cookies*.

In this example, seven cookies are needed, one each for the employee name and ID number, and one each for the five job order numbers. Creating or changing a cookie is very simple and is included in the VBScript function that is called when the Submit Timesheet button is clicked:

```
Sub SubmitTS_onClick
   Document.Cookie = "EmpName=" & Document.TS.EmpName.Value & _
      ";expires=31-Dec-99 12:00:00 GMT"
   Document.Cookie = "IDNum=" & Document.TS.IDNum.Value & _
      ";expires=31-Dec-99 12:00:00 GMT"
   Document.Cookie = "JON1=" & Document.TS.Elements(2).Value & _
      ";expires=31-Dec-99 12:00:00 GMT"
   Document.Cookie = "JON2=" & Document.TS.Elements(20).Value & _
      ";expires=31-Dec-99 12:00:00 GMT"
   Document.Cookie = "JON3=" & Document.TS.Elements(38).Value & _
      ";expires=31-Dec-99 12:00:00 GMT"
```

Part
IV

Ch

18

```
    Document.Cookie = "JON4=" & Document.TS.Elements(56).Value & _
        ";expires=31-Dec-99 12:00:00 GMT"
    Document.Cookie = "JON5=" & Document.TS.Elements(74).Value & _
        ";expires=31-Dec-99 12:00:00 GMT"
    Document.TS.CookieTS.Value = Document.Cookie
    Document.TS.Submit
    MsgBox "Timesheet Submitted!"
End Sub
```

This function saves each of the seven cookies, displays the cookie in the long text field at the bottom of the timesheet (this isn't necessary of course, but is helpful for this example), submits the form, and pops up a message box to tell the user that the form has been submitted (see Figure 18.8).

FIG. 18.8

A VBScript message box is used to tell the user that the timesheet has been submitted.

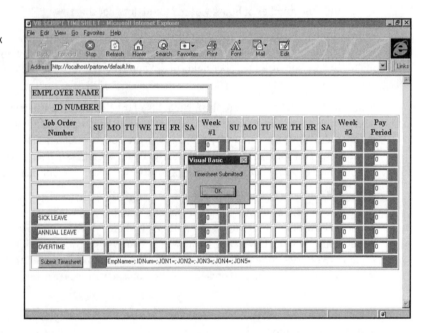

Once the cookie has been saved, whenever that Web page is loaded the cookie is available. It is still necessary to get the information out of the cookie and into the appropriate text fields. Use a VBScript (located at the bottom of the HTML document so that it executes after the rest of the page has been loaded) to search the cookie and put the appropriate information in each of the text fields:

```
<SCRIPT LANGUAGE="VBS">
<!-- Hide this script from incompatible Web browsers!
Document.TS.EmpName.Value = GetCookie("EmpName")
Document.TS.IDNum.Value = GetCookie("IDNum")
Document.TS.Elements(2).Value = GetCookie("JON1")
Document.TS.Elements(20).Value = GetCookie("JON2")
Document.TS.Elements(38).Value = GetCookie("JON3")
```

```
Document.TS.Elements(56).Value = GetCookie("JON4")
Document.TS.Elements(74).Value = GetCookie("JON5")
Document.TS.CookieTS.Value = Document.Cookie
<!-- -->
</SCRIPT>
```

The VBScript function GetCookie is used to search the cookie for each piece of it. A document cookie is essentially a long string with each piece included as CookieName=Value and separated from the next field by a semicolon. GetCookie uses VBScript string manipulation functions to search through the document cookie for a given piece and either returns its value, if defined, or an empty string.

```
Function GetCookie(CookieName)
    Dim Loc
    Dim NamLen
    Dim ValLen
    Dim LocNext
    Dim Temp

    NamLen = Len(CookieName)
    Loc = Instr(Document.Cookie, CookieName)

    If Loc = 0 Then
        GetCookie = ""
    Else
        Temp = Right(Document.Cookie, Len(Document.Cookie) - Loc + 1)
        If Mid(Temp, NamLen + 1, 1) <> "=" Then
            GetCookie = ""
        Else
            LocNext = Instr(Temp, ";")
            If LocNext = 0 Then LocNext = Len(Temp) + 1
            If LocNext = (NamLen + 2) Then
                GetCookie = ""
            Else
                ValLen = LocNext - NamLen - 2
                GetCookie = Mid(Temp, NamLen + 2, ValLen)
            End If
        End If
    End if
End Function
```

With this in place, the next time the Web page is loaded, the employee name, ID number, and job order numbers used on the last submitted timesheet are filled in automatically. In our example, the document cookie is also displayed in the lower text field (see Figure 18.9).

The VBScript Timesheet Web Page   The complete listing for the VBScript Web page is shown in Listing 18.7. As mentioned previously, the VBScript could be made a lot smarter, and the form could be customized pretty easily to add more timesheet rows or to include a dedicated annual and/or sick leave row.

Part
IV

Ch
18

FIG. 18.9

Using cookies allows a single Web page to serve multiple users, and customizes it with their particular information.

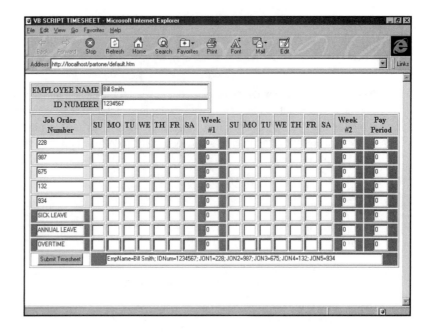

Listing 18.7 Timesheet.htm—VBScript Can Be Used to Automate Many User Input Functions

```
<HTML>
<HEAD>
<SCRIPT LANGUAGE="VBS">
<!-- Hide this script from incompatible Web browsers!
Sub Calc
    Dim i,j,jmax,sum
    jmax = 7
    For k = 0 to 1
        For i = 0 to 6
            sum = 0
            For j = 0 to jmax-1
                If (IsNumeric(Document.TS.Elements(k*8+j*18+i+3).Value)) Then
                    sum = sum + CDbl(Document.TS.Elements(k*8+j*18+i+3).Value)
                End If
            Next
            If (sum > 8 Or (sum > 0 And (i = 0 Or i = 6))) Then
                If (i = 0 Or i = 6) Then
                    Document.TS.Elements(k*8+jmax*18+i+3).Value = sum
                Else
                    Document.TS.Elements(k*8+jmax*18+i+3).Value = sum - 8
                End If
            Else
                Document.TS.Elements(k*8+jmax*18+i+3).Value = ""
            End If
        Next
    Next
```

```vbscript
    For j = 0 to jmax
        Document.TS.Elements(j*18+10).Value = 0
        Document.TS.Elements(j*18+18).Value = 0
        For i = 0 to 6
            If (IsNumeric(Document.TS.Elements(j*18+i+3).Value)) Then
                Document.TS.Elements(j*18+10).Value = _
                    CDbl(Document.TS.Elements(j*18+10).Value) + _
                    CDbl(Document.TS.Elements(j*18+i+3).Value)
            End If
            If (IsNumeric(Document.TS.Elements(j*18+i+11).Value)) Then
                Document.TS.Elements(j*18+18).Value = _
                    CDbl(Document.TS.Elements(j*18+18).Value) + _
                    CDbl(Document.TS.Elements(j*18+i+11).Value)
            End If
        Next
        Document.TS.Elements(j*18+19).Value = _
            CDbl(Document.TS.Elements(j*18+10).Value) + _
            CDbl(Document.TS.Elements(j*18+18).Value)
    Next
    Document.TS.Elements((jmax-2)*18+2).Value = "SICK LEAVE"
    Document.TS.Elements((jmax-1)*18+2).Value = "ANNUAL LEAVE"
    Document.TS.Elements(jmax*18+2).Value = "OVERTIME"
End Sub

Function GetCookie(CookieName)
    Dim Loc
    Dim NamLen
    Dim ValLen
    Dim LocNext
    Dim Temp

    NamLen = Len(CookieName)
    Loc = Instr(Document.Cookie, CookieName)

    If Loc = 0 Then
        GetCookie = ""
    Else
        Temp = Right(Document.Cookie, Len(Document.Cookie) - Loc + 1)
        If Mid(Temp, NamLen + 1, 1) <> "=" Then
            GetCookie = ""
        Else
            LocNext = Instr(Temp, ";")
            If LocNext = 0 Then LocNext = Len(Temp) + 1
            If LocNext = (NamLen + 2) Then
                GetCookie = ""
            Else
                ValLen = LocNext - NamLen - 2
                GetCookie = Mid(Temp, NamLen + 2, ValLen)
            End If
        End If
    End if
End Function

Sub SubmitTS_onClick
    Document.Cookie = "EmpName=" & Document.TS.EmpName.Value & _
```

Part

IV

Ch

18

continues

Listing 18.7 Continued

```
                        ";expires=31-Dec-99 12:00:00 GMT"
        Document.Cookie = "IDNum=" & Document.TS.IDNum.Value & _
            ";expires=31-Dec-99 12:00:00 GMT"
        Document.Cookie = "JON1=" & Document.TS.Elements(2).Value & _
            ";expires=31-Dec-99 12:00:00 GMT"
        Document.Cookie = "JON2=" & Document.TS.Elements(20).Value & _
            ";expires=31-Dec-99 12:00:00 GMT"
        Document.Cookie = "JON3=" & Document.TS.Elements(38).Value & _
            ";expires=31-Dec-99 12:00:00 GMT"
        Document.Cookie = "JON4=" & Document.TS.Elements(56).Value & _
            ";expires=31-Dec-99 12:00:00 GMT"
        Document.Cookie = "JON5=" & Document.TS.Elements(74).Value & _
            ";expires=31-Dec-99 12:00:00 GMT"
        Document.TS.CookieTS.Value = Document.Cookie
        Document.TS.Submit
        MsgBox "Timesheet Submitted!"
    End Sub
    <!-- -->
    </SCRIPT>
    <TITLE>VB SCRIPT TIMESHEET</TITLE>
    </HEAD>
    <BODY BGCOLOR=#FFFFFF>
    <FORM NAME="TS" ACTION="mailto:odonnj@rpi.edu" METHOD=POST>
    <TABLE BORDER>
    <TR><TD ALIGN=RIGHT BGCOLOR=CYAN><B>EMPLOYEE NAME</B></TD>
        <TD BGCOLOR=YELLOW>
            <INPUT NAME="EmpName" TYPE="Text" VALUE="" SIZE=40 ></TD></TR>
    <TR><TD ALIGN=RIGHT BGCOLOR=CYAN><B>ID NUMBER</B></TD>
        <TD BGCOLOR=YELLOW>
            <INPUT NAME="IDNum" TYPE="Text" VALUE="" SIZE=40 ></TD></TR>
    </TABLE>
    <TABLE BORDER>
    <TR BGCOLOR=CYAN>
        <TH>Job Order Number</TH>
        <TH>SU</TH>
        <TH>MO</TH><TH>TU</TH><TH>WE</TH><TH>TH</TH><TH>FR</TH>
        <TH>SA</TH><TH>Week #1</TH>
        <TH>SU</TH>
        <TH>MO</TH><TH>TU</TH><TH>WE</TH><TH>TH</TH><TH>FR</TH>
        <TH>SA</TH><TH>Week #2</TH><TH>Pay Period</TH></TR>
    <TR ALIGN=CENTER>
        <TD BGCOLOR=YELLOW><INPUT TYPE="Text" VALUE="" SIZE=16></TD>
        <TD><INPUT TYPE="Text" VALUE="" SIZE=1 onChange="Calc"></TD>
        <TD><INPUT TYPE="Text" VALUE="" SIZE=1 onChange="Calc"></TD>
        <TD><INPUT TYPE="Text" VALUE="" SIZE=1 onChange="Calc"></TD>
        <TD><INPUT TYPE="Text" VALUE="" SIZE=1 onChange="Calc"></TD>
        <TD><INPUT TYPE="Text" VALUE="" SIZE=1 onChange="Calc"></TD>
        <TD><INPUT TYPE="Text" VALUE="" SIZE=1 onChange="Calc"></TD>
        <TD><INPUT TYPE="Text" VALUE="" SIZE=1 onChange="Calc"></TD>
        <TD BGCOLOR=RED>
            <INPUT TYPE="Text" VALUE="0" SIZE=2 onChange="Calc"></TD>
        <TD><INPUT TYPE="Text" VALUE="" SIZE=1 onChange="Calc"></TD>
        <TD><INPUT TYPE="Text" VALUE="" SIZE=1 onChange="Calc"></TD>
```

```
        <TD><INPUT TYPE="Text" VALUE="" SIZE=1 onChange="Calc"></TD>
        <TD><INPUT TYPE="Text" VALUE="" SIZE=1 onChange="Calc"></TD>
        <TD><INPUT TYPE="Text" VALUE="" SIZE=1 onChange="Calc"></TD>
        <TD><INPUT TYPE="Text" VALUE="" SIZE=1 onChange="Calc"></TD>
        <TD><INPUT TYPE="Text" VALUE="" SIZE=1 onChange="Calc"></TD>
        <TD BGCOLOR=RED>
            <INPUT TYPE="Text" VALUE="0" SIZE=2 onChange="Calc"></TD>
        <TD BGCOLOR=RED>
            <INPUT TYPE="Text" VALUE="0" SIZE=2 onChange="Calc"></TD></TR>
<TR ALIGN=CENTER>
    <TD BGCOLOR=YELLOW><INPUT TYPE="Text" VALUE="" SIZE=16></TD>
    <TD><INPUT TYPE="Text" VALUE="" SIZE=1 onChange="Calc"></TD>
    <TD><INPUT TYPE="Text" VALUE="" SIZE=1 onChange="Calc"></TD>
    <TD><INPUT TYPE="Text" VALUE="" SIZE=1 onChange="Calc"></TD>
    <TD><INPUT TYPE="Text" VALUE="" SIZE=1 onChange="Calc"></TD>
    <TD><INPUT TYPE="Text" VALUE="" SIZE=1 onChange="Calc"></TD>
    <TD><INPUT TYPE="Text" VALUE="" SIZE=1 onChange="Calc"></TD>
    <TD BGCOLOR=RED>
        <INPUT TYPE="Text" VALUE="0" SIZE=2 onChange="Calc"></TD>
    <TD><INPUT TYPE="Text" VALUE="" SIZE=1 onChange="Calc"></TD>
    <TD><INPUT TYPE="Text" VALUE="" SIZE=1 onChange="Calc"></TD>
    <TD><INPUT TYPE="Text" VALUE="" SIZE=1 onChange="Calc"></TD>
    <TD><INPUT TYPE="Text" VALUE="" SIZE=1 onChange="Calc"></TD>
    <TD><INPUT TYPE="Text" VALUE="" SIZE=1 onChange="Calc"></TD>
    <TD><INPUT TYPE="Text" VALUE="" SIZE=1 onChange="Calc"></TD>
    <TD><INPUT TYPE="Text" VALUE="" SIZE=1 onChange="Calc"></TD>
    <TD BGCOLOR=RED>
        <INPUT TYPE="Text" VALUE="0" SIZE=2 onChange="Calc"></TD>
    <TD BGCOLOR=RED>
        <INPUT TYPE="Text" VALUE="0" SIZE=2 onChange="Calc"></TD></TR>
<TR ALIGN=CENTER>
    <TD BGCOLOR=YELLOW><INPUT TYPE="Text" VALUE="" SIZE=16></TD>
    <TD><INPUT TYPE="Text" VALUE="" SIZE=1 onChange="Calc"></TD>
    <TD><INPUT TYPE="Text" VALUE="" SIZE=1 onChange="Calc"></TD>
    <TD><INPUT TYPE="Text" VALUE="" SIZE=1 onChange="Calc"></TD>
    <TD><INPUT TYPE="Text" VALUE="" SIZE=1 onChange="Calc"></TD>
    <TD><INPUT TYPE="Text" VALUE="" SIZE=1 onChange="Calc"></TD>
    <TD><INPUT TYPE="Text" VALUE="" SIZE=1 onChange="Calc"></TD>
    <TD BGCOLOR=RED>
        <INPUT TYPE="Text" VALUE="0" SIZE=2 onChange="Calc"></TD>
    <TD><INPUT TYPE="Text" VALUE="" SIZE=1 onChange="Calc"></TD>
    <TD><INPUT TYPE="Text" VALUE="" SIZE=1 onChange="Calc"></TD>
    <TD><INPUT TYPE="Text" VALUE="" SIZE=1 onChange="Calc"></TD>
    <TD><INPUT TYPE="Text" VALUE="" SIZE=1 onChange="Calc"></TD>
    <TD><INPUT TYPE="Text" VALUE="" SIZE=1 onChange="Calc"></TD>
    <TD><INPUT TYPE="Text" VALUE="" SIZE=1 onChange="Calc"></TD>
    <TD><INPUT TYPE="Text" VALUE="" SIZE=1 onChange="Calc"></TD>
    <TD BGCOLOR=RED>
        <INPUT TYPE="Text" VALUE="0" SIZE=2 onChange="Calc"></TD>
    <TD BGCOLOR=RED>
        <INPUT TYPE="Text" VALUE="0" SIZE=2 onChange="Calc"></TD></TR>
```

Part
IV
Ch
18

continues

Listing 18.7   Continued

```
<TR ALIGN=CENTER>
    <TD BGCOLOR=YELLOW><INPUT TYPE="Text" VALUE="" SIZE=16></TD>
    <TD><INPUT TYPE="Text" VALUE="" SIZE=1 onChange="Calc"></TD>
    <TD><INPUT TYPE="Text" VALUE="" SIZE=1 onChange="Calc"></TD>
    <TD><INPUT TYPE="Text" VALUE="" SIZE=1 onChange="Calc"></TD>
    <TD><INPUT TYPE="Text" VALUE="" SIZE=1 onChange="Calc"></TD>
    <TD><INPUT TYPE="Text" VALUE="" SIZE=1 onChange="Calc"></TD>
    <TD><INPUT TYPE="Text" VALUE="" SIZE=1 onChange="Calc"></TD>
    <TD><INPUT TYPE="Text" VALUE="" SIZE=1 onChange="Calc"></TD>
    <TD BGCOLOR=RED>
        <INPUT TYPE="Text" VALUE="0" SIZE=2 onChange="Calc"></TD>
    <TD><INPUT TYPE="Text" VALUE="" SIZE=1 onChange="Calc"></TD>
    <TD><INPUT TYPE="Text" VALUE="" SIZE=1 onChange="Calc"></TD>
    <TD><INPUT TYPE="Text" VALUE="" SIZE=1 onChange="Calc"></TD>
    <TD><INPUT TYPE="Text" VALUE="" SIZE=1 onChange="Calc"></TD>
    <TD><INPUT TYPE="Text" VALUE="" SIZE=1 onChange="Calc"></TD>
    <TD><INPUT TYPE="Text" VALUE="" SIZE=1 onChange="Calc"></TD>
    <TD><INPUT TYPE="Text" VALUE="" SIZE=1 onChange="Calc"></TD>
    <TD BGCOLOR=RED>
        <INPUT TYPE="Text" VALUE="0" SIZE=2 onChange="Calc"></TD>
    <TD BGCOLOR=RED>
        <INPUT TYPE="Text" VALUE="0" SIZE=2 onChange="Calc"></TD></TR>
<TR ALIGN=CENTER>
    <TD BGCOLOR=YELLOW><INPUT TYPE="Text" VALUE="" SIZE=16></TD>
    <TD><INPUT TYPE="Text" VALUE="" SIZE=1 onChange="Calc"></TD>
    <TD><INPUT TYPE="Text" VALUE="" SIZE=1 onChange="Calc"></TD>
    <TD><INPUT TYPE="Text" VALUE="" SIZE=1 onChange="Calc"></TD>
    <TD><INPUT TYPE="Text" VALUE="" SIZE=1 onChange="Calc"></TD>
    <TD><INPUT TYPE="Text" VALUE="" SIZE=1 onChange="Calc"></TD>
    <TD><INPUT TYPE="Text" VALUE="" SIZE=1 onChange="Calc"></TD>
    <TD><INPUT TYPE="Text" VALUE="" SIZE=1 onChange="Calc"></TD>
    <TD BGCOLOR=RED>
        <INPUT TYPE="Text" VALUE="0" SIZE=2 onChange="Calc"></TD>
    <TD><INPUT TYPE="Text" VALUE="" SIZE=1 onChange="Calc"></TD>
    <TD><INPUT TYPE="Text" VALUE="" SIZE=1 onChange="Calc"></TD>
    <TD><INPUT TYPE="Text" VALUE="" SIZE=1 onChange="Calc"></TD>
    <TD><INPUT TYPE="Text" VALUE="" SIZE=1 onChange="Calc"></TD>
    <TD><INPUT TYPE="Text" VALUE="" SIZE=1 onChange="Calc"></TD>
    <TD><INPUT TYPE="Text" VALUE="" SIZE=1 onChange="Calc"></TD>
    <TD><INPUT TYPE="Text" VALUE="" SIZE=1 onChange="Calc"></TD>
    <TD BGCOLOR=RED>
        <INPUT TYPE="Text" VALUE="0" SIZE=2 onChange="Calc"></TD>
    <TD BGCOLOR=RED>
        <INPUT TYPE="Text" VALUE="0" SIZE=2 onChange="Calc"></TD></TR>
<TR ALIGN=CENTER>
    <TD BGCOLOR=RED>
        <INPUT TYPE="Text" VALUE="SICK LEAVE" SIZE=16 onChange="Calc"></TD>
    <TD><INPUT TYPE="Text" VALUE="" SIZE=1 onChange="Calc"></TD>
    <TD><INPUT TYPE="Text" VALUE="" SIZE=1 onChange="Calc"></TD>
    <TD><INPUT TYPE="Text" VALUE="" SIZE=1 onChange="Calc"></TD>
    <TD><INPUT TYPE="Text" VALUE="" SIZE=1 onChange="Calc"></TD>
    <TD><INPUT TYPE="Text" VALUE="" SIZE=1 onChange="Calc"></TD>
    <TD><INPUT TYPE="Text" VALUE="" SIZE=1 onChange="Calc"></TD>
```

```
        <TD><INPUT TYPE="Text" VALUE="" SIZE=1 onChange="Calc"></TD>
        <TD BGCOLOR=RED>
            <INPUT TYPE="Text" VALUE="0" SIZE=2 onChange="Calc"></TD>
        <TD><INPUT TYPE="Text" VALUE="" SIZE=1 onChange="Calc"></TD>
        <TD><INPUT TYPE="Text" VALUE="" SIZE=1 onChange="Calc"></TD>
        <TD><INPUT TYPE="Text" VALUE="" SIZE=1 onChange="Calc"></TD>
        <TD><INPUT TYPE="Text" VALUE="" SIZE=1 onChange="Calc"></TD>
        <TD><INPUT TYPE="Text" VALUE="" SIZE=1 onChange="Calc"></TD>
        <TD><INPUT TYPE="Text" VALUE="" SIZE=1 onChange="Calc"></TD>
        <TD BGCOLOR=RED>
            <INPUT TYPE="Text" VALUE="0" SIZE=2 onChange="Calc"></TD>
        <TD BGCOLOR=RED>
            <INPUT TYPE="Text" VALUE="0" SIZE=2 onChange="Calc"></TD></TR>
<TR ALIGN=CENTER>
    <TD BGCOLOR=RED>
        <INPUT TYPE="Text" VALUE="ANNUAL LEAVE" SIZE=16
            onChange="Calc"></TD>
        <TD><INPUT TYPE="Text" VALUE="" SIZE=1 onChange="Calc"></TD>
        <TD><INPUT TYPE="Text" VALUE="" SIZE=1 onChange="Calc"></TD>
        <TD><INPUT TYPE="Text" VALUE="" SIZE=1 onChange="Calc"></TD>
        <TD><INPUT TYPE="Text" VALUE="" SIZE=1 onChange="Calc"></TD>
        <TD><INPUT TYPE="Text" VALUE="" SIZE=1 onChange="Calc"></TD>
        <TD><INPUT TYPE="Text" VALUE="" SIZE=1 onChange="Calc"></TD>
        <TD BGCOLOR=RED>
            <INPUT TYPE="Text" VALUE="0" SIZE=2 onChange="Calc"></TD>
        <TD><INPUT TYPE="Text" VALUE="" SIZE=1 onChange="Calc"></TD>
        <TD><INPUT TYPE="Text" VALUE="" SIZE=1 onChange="Calc"></TD>
        <TD><INPUT TYPE="Text" VALUE="" SIZE=1 onChange="Calc"></TD>
        <TD><INPUT TYPE="Text" VALUE="" SIZE=1 onChange="Calc"></TD>
        <TD><INPUT TYPE="Text" VALUE="" SIZE=1 onChange="Calc"></TD>
        <TD><INPUT TYPE="Text" VALUE="" SIZE=1 onChange="Calc"></TD>
        <TD><INPUT TYPE="Text" VALUE="" SIZE=1 onChange="Calc"></TD>
        <TD BGCOLOR=RED>
            <INPUT TYPE="Text" VALUE="0" SIZE=2 onChange="Calc"></TD>
        <TD BGCOLOR=RED>
            <INPUT TYPE="Text" VALUE="0" SIZE=2 onChange="Calc"></TD></TR>
<TR ALIGN=CENTER BGCOLOR=RED>
    <TD><INPUT TYPE="Text" VALUE="OVERTIME" SIZE=16 onChange="Calc"></TD>
    <TD><INPUT TYPE="Text" VALUE="" SIZE=1 onChange="Calc"></TD>
    <TD><INPUT TYPE="Text" VALUE="" SIZE=1 onChange="Calc"></TD>
    <TD><INPUT TYPE="Text" VALUE="" SIZE=1 onChange="Calc"></TD>
    <TD><INPUT TYPE="Text" VALUE="" SIZE=1 onChange="Calc"></TD>
    <TD><INPUT TYPE="Text" VALUE="" SIZE=1 onChange="Calc"></TD>
    <TD><INPUT TYPE="Text" VALUE="" SIZE=1 onChange="Calc"></TD>
    <TD><INPUT TYPE="Text" VALUE="0" SIZE=2 onChange="Calc"></TD>
    <TD><INPUT TYPE="Text" VALUE="" SIZE=1 onChange="Calc"></TD>
    <TD><INPUT TYPE="Text" VALUE="" SIZE=1 onChange="Calc"></TD>
    <TD><INPUT TYPE="Text" VALUE="" SIZE=1 onChange="Calc"></TD>
    <TD><INPUT TYPE="Text" VALUE="" SIZE=1 onChange="Calc"></TD>
    <TD><INPUT TYPE="Text" VALUE="" SIZE=1 onChange="Calc"></TD>
    <TD><INPUT TYPE="Text" VALUE="" SIZE=1 onChange="Calc"></TD>
    <TD><INPUT TYPE="Text" VALUE="" SIZE=1 onChange="Calc"></TD>
    <TD><INPUT TYPE="Text" VALUE="0" SIZE=2 onChange="Calc"></TD>
```

continues

Listing 18.7 Continued

```
    <TD><INPUT TYPE="Text" VALUE="0" SIZE=2 onChange="Calc"></TD></TR>
<!--<TR><TD BGCOLOR=CYAN COLSPAN=18> </TD></TR>-->
<TR ALIGN=CENTER>
    <TD><INPUT NAME="SubmitTS" TYPE="Button"
            VALUE="Submit Timesheet"></TD>
    <TD COLSPAN=17 BGCOLOR=RED>
        <INPUT NAME="CookieTS" TYPE="Text" SIZE="110"></TD></TR>
</TABLE>
</FORM>
<SCRIPT LANGUAGE="VBS">
<!-- Hide this script from incompatible Web browsers!
Document.TS.EmpName.Value = GetCookie("EmpName")
Document.TS.IDNum.Value = GetCookie("IDNum")
Document.TS.Elements(2).Value = GetCookie("JON1")
Document.TS.Elements(20).Value = GetCookie("JON2")
Document.TS.Elements(38).Value = GetCookie("JON3")
Document.TS.Elements(56).Value = GetCookie("JON4")
Document.TS.Elements(74).Value = GetCookie("JON5")
Document.TS.CookieTS.Value = Document.Cookie
<!-- -->
</SCRIPT>
</BODY>
</HTML>
```

CAUTION

Because cookies need to go through a Web server to be processed, the cookie storage mechanism that is part of this Web page does not always work when the Web page is viewed locally. Unless you are running a local server, you may need to upload the HTML document to your ISP's system and view it with the ISP's Web server to see the cookies work.

Of course, once the forms are submitted, what to do with them at the receiving end is another question—one for a different chapter.

▶ **See** Chapter 11, "Using FrontPage Components, Forms, and Interactive Page Templates," **p. 225**

Interacting with Objects

This is an example of using VBScript to manipulate another Web browser object—in this case the ActiveX Label Control. The Label Control allows the Web author to place text on the Web page and select the text, font, size, and an arbitrary angle of rotation. One of the exciting things about the Label Control is that it can be manipulated in real-time, producing a variety of automated or user-controlled effects.

In the following example, text is placed on the Web page by using the Label Control, and form input is used to allow the user to change the text used and the angle at which it is displayed. Figure 18.10 shows the default configuration of the label, and Figure 18.11 shows it after the text and the rotation angle has been changed.

FIG. 18.10
The ActiveX Label Control allows arbitrary text to be displayed by the Web author in the size, font, position, and orientation desired.

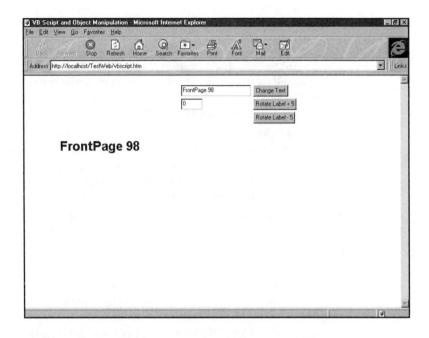

FIG. 18.11
VBScript's ability to manipulate Web browser objects allows the label parameters to be changed dynamically.

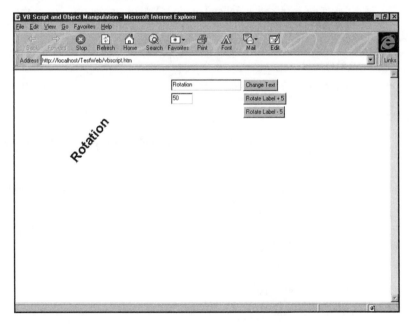

Listing 18.8 shows the code used to produce this example. The following are some things to notice about the example:

- The `<OBJECT>`...`</OBJECT>` container tag is where the ActiveX Label Control is included and its default parameters assigned. The `classid` attribute must be included exactly as shown. The `id` attribute is the object name used by VBScript to reference the Label Control object. The other attributes define the size and placement of the control.

- The `<PARAM>` tags within the `<OBJECT>`...`</OBJECT>` container allow the Web author to define attributes of the ActiveX Label Control. The `NAME`, `VALUE` pairs are unique to each ActiveX Control and should be documented by the ActiveX Control author. For the Label Control, they define various aspects of the appearance of the label. The `NAME` is also used to manipulate the value with VBScript.

- An HTML form is used to accept input and print output for information about the Label Control. The first text area is used to set the label text, whereas the second text area is used to output the current label text angle. The buttons call the appropriate VBScript routine to change the label text or angle.

- One final note about the placement of the VB scripts in this HTML document: the functions are defined in the `<HEAD>` section—this is not necessary, but it is common practice, so that they will be defined before used. The last `<SCRIPT>`...`</SCRIPT>` section, though, which initializes the value of the form text area showing the current angle, is placed at the end of the HTML document to ensure that the object is defined and value set before it is called.

CAUTION

The example in Listing 18.8 requires that you have the ActiveX Label Control on your system.

Listing 18.8   Object.htm—VBScript Can Interact with Objects

```
<HTML>
<HEAD>
<OBJECT classid="clsid:99B42120-6EC7-11CF-A6C7-00AA00A47DD2"
        id=lblActiveLbl
        width=250
        height=250
        align=left
        hspace=20
        vspace=0
>
<PARAM NAME="Angle" VALUE="0">
<PARAM NAME="Alignment" VALUE="4">
<PARAM NAME="BackStyle" VALUE="0">
<PARAM NAME="Caption" VALUE="Rotation">
<PARAM NAME="FontName" VALUE="Arial">
<PARAM NAME="FontSize" VALUE="20">
<PARAM NAME="FontBold" VALUE="1">
<PARAM NAME="ForeColor" VALUE="0">
```

```
</OBJECT>
<SCRIPT LANGUAGE="VBS">
<!-- Hide this script from incompatible Web browsers
Sub cmdChangeIt_onClick
    Dim TheForm
    Set TheForm = Document.LabelControls
    lblActiveLbl.Caption = TheForm.txtNewText.Value
End Sub
Sub cmdRotateP_onClick
    Dim TheForm
    Set TheForm = Document.LabelControls
    lblActiveLbl.Angle = lblActiveLbl.Angle + 5
    Document.LabelControls.sngAngle.Value = lblActiveLbl.Angle
End Sub
Sub cmdRotateM_onClick
    Dim TheForm
    Set TheForm = Document.LabelControls
    lblActiveLbl.Angle = lblActiveLbl.Angle - 5
    Document.LabelControls.sngAngle.Value = lblActiveLbl.Angle
End Sub
<!-- -->
</SCRIPT>
<TITLE>VBScript and Object Manipulation</TITLE>
</HEAD>
<BODY BGCOLOR=#FFFFFF>
<FORM NAME="LabelControls">
<TABLE>
<TR><TD><INPUT TYPE="TEXT" NAME="txtNewText" SIZE=25></TD>
    <TD><INPUT TYPE="BUTTON" NAME="cmdChangeIt" VALUE="Change Text">
    </TD></TR>
<TR><TD><INPUT TYPE="TEXT" NAME="sngAngle" SIZE=5></TD>
    <TD><INPUT TYPE="BUTTON" NAME="cmdRotateP" VALUE="Rotate Label + 5">
    </TD></TR>
<TR><TD></TD>
    <TD><INPUT TYPE="BUTTON" NAME="cmdRotateM" VALUE="Rotate Label - 5">
    </TD></TR>
</TABLE>
</FORM>
<SCRIPT LANGUAGE="VBS">
<!-- Hide this script from incompatible Web browsers
Document.LabelControls.sngAngle.Value = lblActiveLbl.Angle
Document.LabelControls.txtNewText.Value = lblActiveLbl.Caption
<!-- -->
</SCRIPT>
</BODY>
</HTML>
```

Part

IV

Ch

18

What Scripting Language Should You Use?

With a choice of scripting languages now available, the question of which to use quickly arises. JavaScript and VBScript have similar capabilities. Also, because they are both relatively new, you don't have much history to rely on for making a choice. The following are a few points to consider:

■ **What language are you more comfortable with?**   JavaScript is based on the Java and C++ languages; VBScript, on Visual Basic and Visual Basic for Applications. If you are proficient in one of these parent languages, using the scripting language that is based on it might be a good idea.

■ **What are you trying to do?**   Both languages are object-oriented and can interact with a compatible Web browser and other objects that it may have loaded, such as Java applets or ActiveX Controls. But if you will be primarily working with Internet Explorer 3 using a feature of Microsoft's ActiveX technologies, using VBScript is probably a good idea because it is designed with that use in mind.

■ **Who is your target audience?**   For general purpose uses—like processing form inputs or providing simple interactivity—the biggest question to answer is who will be the audience for your Web pages. Although Microsoft Internet Explorer has a growing share of the Web browser market, Netscape Navigator has the lion's share. Unless your Web pages are targeted at a specific audience that definitely use Internet Explorer, you will probably want to use JavaScript. At least for the present, using JavaScript will ensure maximum compatibility.

Using FrontPage Editor's Script Wizard

Now that you've explored VBScript as you might write it into the Script dialog box, you should investigate an easier way to do Visual Basic scripting. This is where the Script Wizard comes in. You still have to know your way around VBScript, though—the Wizard assumes this. The next, very simple example gives you the basis of how to use it.

N O T E   The Script Wizard can be used only for JavaScript or VBScript.   ■

Let's say that for design reasons, you've decided you don't want to use a plain old hyperlink to move visitors to a different page—for example, a page where they can play back a movie. Instead, you want to use a form field button to take them there. Here's how you'd do it.

1. Open the page where you want the button and install the button by choosing Insert, Form Field, Push Button. When the button appears on the page, double-click it to go to the Push Button Properties dialog box. By default, the button name is B1 and you can choose to leave it.

2. Type **Movie** for the button label in the Value/Label box. Mark the Normal option button to make this a generic button. (A generic button does nothing until you attach a script to it, which is what we're going to do.) Click OK and the relabeled button appears in the FrontPage Editor workspace.

   We're going to assume that there's another page in the current Web site called amovie.htm, which is where the movie is played back.

3. Choose Insert, Advanced, Script. When the Script dialog box opens, click the Script Wizard button and the Script Wizard dialog box appears.

   The upper-left pane of the dialog box is the Select an Event pane. The Event pane provides a hierarchical view of all the objects and events that you can script. In the hierarchy, objects are listed in alphabetical order by ID name. The icons represent different types of these events and objects.

When you click an event, the Script Wizard displays that event handler in the Insert Action pane—the pane at the upper right of the dialog box. (An event handler is code that is executed when a particular event occurs.)

In this example, the event that you want is part of the Unnamed FORM Element entry. (It's unnamed because you didn't bother to name the form.)

4. Click the plus sign at the left of Unnamed FORM Element to get to that event. Now you see an icon for B1. (B1 is the ID of the button.) At the left of this icon is also a plus sign. Click the plus sign, and an onClick event appears below B1. Click the onClick event to select it. Now the action that you choose next is attached to the onClick event.

5. Look at the Insert Action pane at the upper right of the dialog box. This pane provides a hierarchical view of the actions and properties you can use in the event handler, as well as the global variables and procedures defined for the page.

6. Double-click the Go To Page icon in the Insert Action pane because you want to move the visitor to a different page when the button is clicked. Now you see the Go To Page dialog box.

7. Type **amovie.htm** (assuming that this is the name of our destination page) into the Enter a Text String box and choose OK. Now, in the lowest pane of the Script Wizard dialog box, you'll see an event called Go To Page amovie.htm.

8. Mark the Code View option button at the bottom of the dialog box to see what this looks like in VBScript. The lowest pane now displays Window.location.href = 'amovie.htm'. You can also edit scripts directly in this window.

9. Choose OK, and preview the page in a browser. When the button is clicked, the destination page appears in the browser window.

This is a very simple example, but if you already know VBScript, you can use the Script Wizard effectively with just a moderate amount of practice.

From Here...

This rather long chapter gave you an introduction to one of the two major Web scripting languages. Now it's time to look at the other one: JavaScript. Take a look at the following chapters for more information on some of the issues touched on in this chapter:

- Chapter 19, "Scripting with JavaScript," tells you about the different JavaScript language elements, how you use JavaScript to interact with page elements and users, and how you can integrate it with FrontPage.

- Chapter 20, "Inserting Java Applets and Browser Plug-Ins," covers MIME media types and Netscape plug-ins, and gives you an overview of the Java programming language.

- Chapter 21, "VRML and Java," provides an introduction to the Virtual Reality Modeling Language and its connections to Java.

## CHAPTER 19

Scripting with JavaScript

The JavaScript language, which was first introduced by Netscape in its Web browser, Netscape Navigator 2, gives Web authors another way to add interactivity and intelligence to their Web pages. JavaScript code is included as part of the HTML document and requires no additional compilation or development tools other than a compatible Web browser. In this chapter, you learn about JavaScript, get an idea of what it can do, and learn to insert scripts into pages generated with FrontPage Editor. Whereas FrontPage Editor on its own is an extremely capable page editor, its capabilities are enormously extended by adding scripts. ▪

What is JavaScript and what can it do?

Learn about Netscape's JavaScript Web browser programming language and how you can use it with FrontPage.

How do you program your Web pages with JavaScript?

Learn how JavaScript can be used to interact with Web page elements and users.

What does JavaScript consist of?

Find out about the different JavaScript language elements and how to use them to add functionality to your Web pages.

What do JavaScript programs look like?

Examine sample JavaScript Web browser applications to see which kinds of things JavaScript is capable of doing.

N O T E   The "standard" form of JavaScript is likely going to be the one promulgated by ECMA, the European standardizing agency. Both Microsoft and Netscape have indicated that they will subscribe to this standard. You can get more information on this at **www.ecma.ch** (see draft 262). ■

Using FrontPage Editor to Add JavaScripts to a Page

This is the same procedure described early in Chapter 18, "Scripting with VBScript." In case you jumped ahead to Java scripting, it's repeated here. Use the following procedure:

1. Choose Insert, Advanced, Script, or click the Insert Script button on the Advanced toolbar. The Script dialog box appears (see Figure 19.1).

FIG. 19.1

Use the Script dialog box to choose the type of script you want and to compose it.

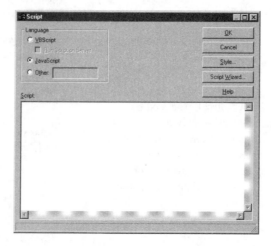

2. Mark the JavaScript option button.
3. Type the code into the workspace of the dialog box and choose OK. The script will be inserted into the page.

The workspace in this dialog box is just that of a text editor, and absolutely no syntax checking is done. You don't need to include the <SCRIPT> tags; they're inserted when you choose OK to close the dialog box and add the script.

The Script Wizard—also available through this dialog box—makes it unnecessary (much of the time) for you to enter code by hand. It functions with JavaScript in the same way that it does with VBScript.

▶ **See** Chapter 18, "Scripting with VBScript" **p. 369**

N O T E   You'll know there's a script in your page because a small script icon appears in the FrontPage Editor workspace where the script is located. ■

Introduction to JavaScript

JavaScript allows you to embed commands in an HTML page. When a compatible Web browser—such as Netscape Navigator 2 or higher, or Internet Explorer 3 or higher—downloads the page, your JavaScript commands are loaded by the Web browser as a part of the HTML document. These commands can be triggered when the user clicks on page items, manipulates gadgets and fields in an HTML form, or moves through the page history list.

Some computer languages are *compiled*; you run your program through a compiler, which performs a one-time translation of the human-readable program into a binary that the computer can execute. JavaScript is an *interpreted* language; the computer must evaluate the program every time it's run. You embed your JavaScript commands within an HTML page, and any browser that supports JavaScript can interpret the commands and act on them.

JavaScript is powerful and simple. If you've ever programmed in dBASE or Visual Basic, you'll find JavaScript easy to pick up.

N O T E Java offers a number of C++-like capabilities that were purposefully omitted from JavaScript. For example, you can access only the limited set of objects defined by the browser and its Java applets, and you can't extend those objects yourself. ▪

Why Use a Scripting Language?

FrontPage Editor provides great flexibility to page authors, but from time to time you may want to write small scripts that execute on the users' browsers instead of on the server. For example, an application that collects data from a form and then posts it to the server can validate the data for completeness and correctness before sending it to the server. This can greatly improve the performance of the browsing session because users don't have to send data to the server until it's been verified as correct.

Another important use of Web browser scripting languages like JavaScript comes as a result of the increased functionality being introduced for Web browsers in the form of Java applets, plug-ins, ActiveX Controls, and VRML objects and worlds. Each of these things can be used to add extra functions and interactivity to a Web page. Scripting languages act as the glue that binds everything together. A Web page might use an HTML form to get some user input and then set a parameter for an ActiveX Control based on that input. Usually this is actually carried out by a script.

Part
IV

Ch
19

What Can JavaScript Do?

JavaScript provides a fairly complete set of built-in functions and commands, allowing you to perform math calculations, manipulate strings, play sounds, open up new windows and new URLs, and access and verify user input to your Web forms.

Code to perform these actions can be embedded in a page and executed when the page is loaded. You can also write functions containing code that is triggered by events you specify.

For example, you can write a JavaScript method that is called when the user clicks the Submit button of a form, or one that is activated when the user clicks a hyperlink on the active page.

JavaScript can also set the attributes, or *properties*, of ActiveX Controls, Java applets, and other objects present in the browser, so you can change the behavior of plug-ins or other objects without having to rewrite them. For example, your JavaScript code could automatically set the text of an ActiveX Label Control based on what time the page is viewed.

> **CAUTION**
>
> JavaScript and VBScript are very similar, with similar syntax and capabilities. However, they are different languages, and you should be careful not to mix them up when you are programming. It is possible, though, to mix different scripts on a page if each Script tag is marked with the proper language reference.

What Does JavaScript Look Like?

As described earlier, you use FrontPage Editor's Script dialog box to embed JavaScript commands in your pages. Doing this requires only one new HTML element: <SCRIPT> and </SCRIPT>. The <SCRIPT> element takes the attribute LANGUAGE, which specifies the scripting language to use when evaluating the script.

> **CAUTION**
>
> Don't type the <SCRIPT> and </SCRIPT> tags into the Script dialog box workspace. These tags and the LANGUAGE attribute are added automatically.

JavaScript itself resembles many other computer languages. If you're familiar with C, C++, Pascal, HyperTalk, Visual Basic, or dBASE, you'll recognize the similarities. If not, don't worry—the following are some simple rules that help you understand how the language is structured:

- JavaScript is case sensitive.
- JavaScript is pretty flexible about statements. A single statement can cover multiple lines, and you can put multiple short statements on a single line—just make sure to add a semicolon at the end of each statement.
- Braces (the { and } characters) group statements into blocks; a block may be the body of a function or a section of code that gets executed in a loop or as part of a conditional test.

N O T E If you're a Java, C, or C++ programmer, you might be puzzled when looking at JavaScript programs—sometimes each line ends with a semicolon, sometimes not. In JavaScript, unlike those other languages, the semicolon is not required at the end of each line. However, you should use good programming habits and put a semicolon at the end of each line. ■

JavaScript Programming Conventions

Even though JavaScript is a simple language, it's quite expressive. In this section, you learn a small number of simple rules and conventions that will ease your learning process and speed your use of JavaScript.

Hiding Your Scripts   You'll probably be designing pages that may be seen by browsers that don't support JavaScript. To keep those browsers from interpreting your JavaScript commands as HTML—and displaying them—wrap your scripts as follows:

```
<SCRIPT LANGUAGE="JavaScript">
<!-- This line opens the comment
YOUR CODE GOES HERE
This line closes the comment -->
</SCRIPT>
```

The opening `<!--` comment causes Web browsers that do not support JavaScript to disregard all text they encounter until they find a matching `-->`, so they don't display your script. You do have to be careful with the `<SCRIPT>` tag, though; if you put your `<SCRIPT>` and `</SCRIPT>` block inside the comments, the Web browser ignores them also.

Comments   Including comments in your programs to explain what they do is good practice and JavaScript is no exception. The JavaScript interpreter ignores any text marked as comments, so don't be shy about including them. You can use two types of comments: single-line and multiple-line.

Single-line comments start with two slashes (`//`), and they're limited to one line. Multiple-line comments must start with `/*` on the first line and end with `*/` on the last line. Here are a few examples:

```
   // this is a legal comment
/ illegal -- comments start with two slashes
/* Multiple-line comments can
   be spread across more than one line, as long as they end. */
/* illegal -- this comment doesn't have an end!
/// this comment's OK, because extra slashes are ignored //
```

> **CAUTION**
>
> Be careful when using multiple-line comments—remember that these comments don't nest. For instance, if you commented out a section of code in the following way, you would get an error message:
>
> ```
> /* Comment out the following code
>  * document.writeln(DumpURL()) /* write out URL list */
>  * document.writeln("End of list.")
>  */
> ```
>
> The preferred way to create single-line comments to avoid this would be as follows:
>
> ```
> /* Comment out the following code
>  * document.writeln(DumpURL()) // write out URL list
>  * document.writeln("End of list.")
>  */
> ```

Using *<NOSCRIPT>* You can improve the compatibility of your JavaScript Web pages through the use of the <NOSCRIPT>...</NOSCRIPT> HTML tags. Any HTML code that is placed between these container tags does not appear on a JavaScript-compatible Web browser but will be displayed on one that is not able to understand JavaScript. This allows you to include alternative content for users who are using Web browsers that don't understand JavaScript. At the very least, you can let them know that they are missing something, as in this example:

```
<NOSCRIPT>
<H1>If you are seeing this text, then your Web browser
   doesn't speak JavaScript!<H1>
</NOSCRIPT>
```

The JavaScript Language

JavaScript was designed to resemble Java, which in turn looks a lot like C and C++. The difference is that Java was built as a general purpose object language, whereas JavaScript is intended to provide a quicker and simpler language for enhancing Web pages and servers. In this section, you learn the building blocks of JavaScript and how to combine them into legal JavaScript programs.

N O T E JavaScript was developed by the Netscape Corporation, which maintains a great set of examples and documentation for it. Its JavaScript Authoring Guide is available online at
http://home.netscape.com/eng/mozilla/3.0/handbook/javascript/index.html ■

Using Identifiers

An *identifier* is a unique name that JavaScript uses to identify a variable, method, or object in your program. As with other programming languages, JavaScript imposes some rules on what names you can use. All JavaScript names must start with a letter or the underscore character, and they can contain both upper- and lowercase letters and the digits 0 through 9.

JavaScript supports two different ways for you to represent values in your scripts: literals and variables. As their names imply, *literals* are fixed values that don't change while the script is executing, and *variables* hold data that can change at any time.

Literals and variables have several different types; the type is determined by the kind of data that the literal or variable contains. The following are some of the types supported in JavaScript:

- ■ **Integers** Integer literals are made up of a sequence of digits only; integer variables can contain any whole number value. Octal (base 8) and hexadecimal (base 16) integers can be specified by prefixing them with a leading "0" or "0x," respectively.

- ■ **Floating-Point Numbers** The number 10 is an integer, but 10.5 is a floating-point number. Floating-point literals can be positive or negative and they can contain either positive or negative exponents (which are indicated by an *e* in the number). For example, 3.14159265 is a floating-point literal, as is 6.023e23 (6.023×10^{23} or Avogadro's number).

- **Strings**   Strings can represent words, phrases, or data, and they're set off by either double or single quotation marks. If you start a string with one type of quotation mark, you must close it with the same type. Special characters, such as \n and \t, can also be utilized in strings.

- **Booleans**   Boolean literals can have values of either TRUE or FALSE. Other statements in the JavaScript language can return Boolean values.

Using Objects, Methods, and Properties

JavaScript is modeled after Java, an object-oriented language. An *object* is a collection of data and functions that have been grouped together. A *function* is a piece of code that plays a sound, calculates an equation, sends a piece of e-mail, and so on. The object's functions are called *methods,* and its data are called its *properties.* The JavaScript programs you write will have properties and methods and will interact with objects provided by the Web browser, its plug-ins, Java applets, ActiveX Controls, and other things.

N O T E   Alhough the terms *function* and *method* are often used interchangeably, they are not the same. A method is a function that is part of an object. For instance, writeln is one of the methods of the object document. ▨

T I P   Here's a simple guideline: an object's *properties* are the information it knows; its *methods* are how it can act on that information.

Using Built-In Objects and Functions   Individual JavaScript elements are *objects.* For example, string literals are string objects and they have methods that you can use to change their case, and so on. JavaScript can also use the objects that represent the Web browser in which it is executing, the currently displayed page, and other elements of the browsing session.

Part
IV

Ch
19

You access objects by specifying their names. For example, the active document object is named document. To use the properties or methods for document, you add a period and the name of the method or property you want. For example, document.title is the title property of the document object, and explorer.length calls the length member of the string object named explorer. Remember, literals are objects, too.

Using Properties   Every object has properties, even literals. To access a property, just use the object name followed by a period and the property name. To get the length of a string object named address, you can write the following:

```
address.length
```

You get back an integer that equals the number of characters in the string. If the object you're using has properties that can be modified, you can change them in the same way. To set the color property of a house object, just use the following line:

```
house.color = "blue"
```

You can also create new properties for an object just by naming them. For example, say you define a class called `customer` for one of your pages. You can add new properties to the `customer` object as follows:

```
customer.name = "Joe Smith";
customer.address = "123 Elm Street";
customer.zip = "90210";
```

Knowing that an object's methods are just properties is important. You can easily add new properties to an object by writing your own function and creating a new object property using your own function name. If you want to add a `Bill` method to your `customer` object, you can do so by writing a function named `BillCustomer` and setting the object's property as follows:

```
customer.Bill = BillCustomer;
```

To call the new method, you use the following:

```
customer.Bill()
```

Array and Object Properties　JavaScript objects store their properties in an internal table that you can access in two ways. You've already seen the first way—just use the properties' names. The second way, *arrays*, allows you to access all of an object's properties in sequence. The following function prints out all the properties of the specified object:

```
function DumpProperties(obj, obj_name) {
    result = ""     // set the result string to blank
    for (i in obj)
       result += obj_name + "." + i + " = " + obj[i] + "\n"
    return result
}
```

So, not only can you access all of the properties of the `document` object, for instance, by property name using the dot operator (for example, `document.href`), you can also use the object's property array (for example, `document[1]`, although this may not be the same property as `document.href`). JavaScript provides another method of array access that combines the two, known as *associative arrays*. An associative array associates a left- and right-side element, and the value of the right side can be used by specifying the value of the left side as the index. Objects are set up by JavaScript as associative arrays with the property names as the left side, and their values as the right. The `href` property of the `document` object could, therefore, be accessed by using `document["href"]`.

N O T E　JavaScript begins array numbering with 0, not 1. So the first element of an array is (for example) document[0]. ▪

Programming with JavaScript

JavaScript has a lot to offer page authors. It's not as flexible as C or C++, but it's quick and simple. Most importantly, it's easily embedded in your Web pages so that you can maximize their impact with a little JavaScript seasoning. This section covers the gritty details of JavaScript programming, including a detailed explanation of the language's features.

Expressions

An *expression* is anything that can be evaluated to get a single value. Expressions can contain string or numeric literals, variables, operators, and other expressions, and they can range from simple to quite complex. For example, the following are expressions that use the assignment operator (more on operators in the next section) to assign numerical or string values to variables:

```
x = 7;
str = "Hello, World!";
```

By contrast, the following is a more complex expression whose final value depends on the values of the `quitFlag` and `formComplete` variables:

```
(quitFlag == TRUE) & (formComplete == FALSE)
```

Operators

Operators do just what their name suggests: they operate on variables or literals. The items that an operator acts on are called its *operands*. Operators come in the two following types:

- **Unary operators**   These operators require only one operand, and the operator can come before or after the operand. The `--` operator, which subtracts one from the operand, is a good example. Both `--count` and `count--` subtract one from the variable count.

- **Binary operators**   These operators need two operands. The four math operators (+ for addition, - for subtraction, * for multiplication, and / for division) are all binary operators, as is the = assignment operator you saw earlier.

Assignment Operators   *Assignment operators* take the result of an expression and assign it to a variable. JavaScript doesn't allow you to assign the result of an expression to a literal. One feature of JavaScript that is not found in most other programming languages is that you can change a variable's type on the fly. Consider the HTML document shown in Listing 19.1.

Part

IV

Ch

19

Listing 19.1   Var-fly.htm—JavaScript Allows You to Change the Data Type of Variables

```
<HTML>
<HEAD>
<SCRIPT LANGUAGE="JavaScript">
<!-- Hide this script from incompatible Web browsers!
function typedemo() {
   var x;
   document.writeln("<HR>");
   x = Math.PI;
   document.writeln("x is " + x + "<BR>");
   x = false;
   document.writeln("x is " + x + "<BR>");
   document.writeln("<HR>");
}
```

continues

Listing 19.1 Continued

```
<!-- -->
</SCRIPT>
<TITLE>Changing Data Types on the Fly!</TITLE>
</HEAD>
<BODY BGCOLOR=#FFFFFF>
If your Web browser doesn't support JavaScript, this is all you will see!
<SCRIPT LANGUAGE="JavaScript">
<!-- Hide this script from incompatible Web browsers!
typedemo();
<!-- -->
</SCRIPT>
</BODY>
</HTML>
```

This short program first prints the (correct) value of pi in the variable x. In most other languages, though, trying to set a floating-point variable to a Boolean value would generate either a compiler error or a runtime error. JavaScript happily accepts the change and prints the new value for x: false (see Figure 19.2).

FIG. 19.2

Because JavaScript variables are loosely typed, not only their value can be changed, but also their data type.

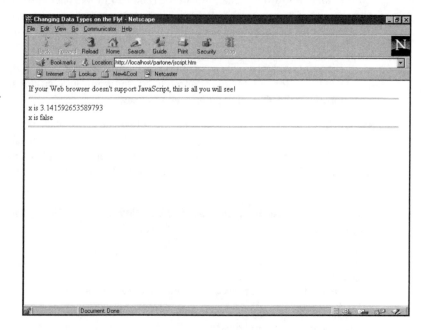

The most common assignment operator, =, simply assigns the value of an expression's right side to its left side. In the previous example, the variable x got the integer value 7 after the expression was evaluated. For convenience, JavaScript also defines some other operators that combine common math operations with assignment; they're shown in Table 19.1.

Table 19.1 Assignment Operators that Provide Shortcuts to Doing Assignments and Math Operations at the Same Time

Operator	What It Does	Two Equivalent Expressions
+=	Adds two values	x+=y and x=x+y
	Adds two strings	string += "HTML" and string = string + "HTML"
-=	Subtracts two values	x-=y and x=x-y
*=	Multiples two values	a*=b and a=a*b
/=	Divides two values	e/=b and e=e/b

Math Operators   The preceding sections gave you a sneak preview of the math operators that JavaScript furnishes. You can either combine math operations with assignments, as shown in Table 19.1, or use them individually. As you would expect, the standard four math functions (addition, subtraction, multiplication, and division) work just as they do on an ordinary calculator. The negation operator, -, is a unary operator that negates the sign of its operand. Another useful binary math operator is the modulus operator, %. This operator returns the remainder after the integer division of two integer numbers. For instance, in the expression:

```
x = 13%5;
```

the variable x would be given the value of 3.

JavaScript also adds two useful unary operators: -- and ++, called, respectively, the *decrement* and *increment* operators. These two operators modify the value of their operand, and they return the new value. They also share a unique property: they can be used either before or after their operand. If you put the operator after the operand, JavaScript returns the operand's value and then modifies it. If you take the opposite route and put the operator before the operand, JavaScript modifies it and returns the modified value. The following short example might help clarify this seemingly odd behavior:

```
x = 7;    // set x to 7
a = --x;  // set x to x-1, and return the new x; a = 6
b = a++;  // set b to a, so b = 6, then add 1 to a; a = 7
x++;      // add one to x; ignore the returned value
```

Comparison Operators   Comparing the value of two expressions to see whether one is larger, smaller, or equal to another is often necessary. JavaScript supplies several comparison operators that take two operands and return TRUE if the comparison is true, and FALSE if it's not. (Remember, you can use literals, variables, or expressions with operators that require expressions.) Table 19.2 shows the JavaScript comparison operators.

Part
IV

Ch
19

Table 19.2   Comparison Operators that Allow Two JavaScript Operands to Be Compared in a Variety of Ways

Operator	Read It As	Returns *TRUE* When
==	Equals	The two operands are equal
!=	Does not equal	The two operands are unequal
<	Less than	The left operand is less than the right operand
<=	Less than or	The left operand is less than equal to or equal to the right operand
>	Greater than	The left operand is greater than the right operand
>=	Greater than or	The left operand is greater equal to than or equal to the right operand

Thinking of the comparison operators as questions may be helpful. When you write the following:

```
(x >= 10)
```

you're really saying, "Is the value of variable x greater than or equal to 10?" The return value answers the question, TRUE or FALSE.

Logical Operators   Comparison operators compare quantity or content for numeric and string expressions, but sometimes you need to test a logical value, like whether a comparison operator returns TRUE or FALSE. JavaScript's logical operators allow you to compare expressions that return logical values. The following are JavaScript's logical operators:

- ◼ **&&, read as "and"**   The && operator returns TRUE if both its input expressions are TRUE. If the first operand evaluates to FALSE, && returns FALSE immediately, without evaluating the second operand. Here's an example:

```
x = TRUE && TRUE;      // x is TRUE
x = FALSE && FALSE;    // x is FALSE
x = FALSE && TRUE;     // x is FALSE
```

- ◼ **¦¦, read as "or"**   This operator returns TRUE if either of its operands is TRUE. If the first operand is TRUE, ¦¦ returns TRUE without evaluating the second operand. Here's an example:

```
x = TRUE ¦¦ TRUE;      // x is TRUE
x = FALSE ¦¦ TRUE;     // x is TRUE
x = FALSE ¦¦ FALSE;    // x is FALSE
```

- ◼ **!, read as "not"**   This operator takes only one expression, and it returns the opposite of that expression, so !TRUE returns FALSE, and !FALSE returns TRUE.

Note that the "and" and "or" operators don't evaluate the second operand if the first operand provides enough information for the operator to return a value. This process, called *short-circuit evaluation*, can be significant when the second operand is a function call. For example,

```
keepGoing = (userCancelled == FALSE) && (theForm.Submit())
```

If userCancelled is TRUE, the second operand, which submits the active form, isn't called.

String Operators   A few of the operators that were just listed can be used for string manipulation as well. All of the comparison operators can be used on strings too; the results depend on standard lexicographic ordering, but comparisons aren't case sensitive. Additionally, the + operator can also be used to concatenate strings. The expression:

```
str = "Hello, " + "World!";
```

assigns the resulting string Hello, World! to the variable str.

Controlling Your JavaScripts

Some scripts you write will be simple; they'll execute the same way every time, once per page. For example, if you add a JavaScript to play a sound when users visit your home page, it doesn't need to evaluate any conditions or do anything more than once. More sophisticated scripts might require that you take different actions under different circumstances. You might also want to repeat the execution of a block of code—perhaps by a set number of times, or as long as some condition is TRUE. JavaScript provides constructs for controlling the execution flow of your script based on conditions, as well as for repeating a sequence of operations.

Testing Conditions   JavaScript provides a single type of control statement for making decisions: the if...else statement. To make a decision, you supply an expression that evaluates to TRUE or FALSE; which code is executed depends on what your expression evaluates to.

The simplest form of if...else uses only the if part. If the specified condition is TRUE, the code following the condition is executed; if not, it's skipped. For example, in the following code fragment, the message appears only if the condition (that the lastModified.year property of the document object says it was modified before 1995) is TRUE:

```
if (document.lastModified.year < 1995)
    document.write("Danger! This is a mighty old document.")
```

You can use any expression as the condition. Because expressions can be nested and combined with the logical operators, your tests can be pretty sophisticated. For example:

```
if ((document.lastModified.year >= 1995) && (document.lastModified.month >= 10))
    document.write("This document is reasonably current.")
```

The else clause allows you to specify a set of statements to execute when the condition is FALSE, for instance:

```
if ((document.lastModified.year >= 1995) && (document.lastModified.month >= 10))
    document.write("This document is reasonably current.")
else
    document.write("This document is quite old.")
```

Repeating Actions   JavaScript provides two different loop constructs that you can use to repeat a set of operations. The first, called a for loop, executes a set of statements some number of times. You specify three expressions: an *initial* expression that sets the values of any

Part
IV

Ch
19

variables you need to use, a *condition* that tells the loop how to see when it's done, and an *increment* expression that modifies any variables that need it. Here's a simple example:

```
for (count=0; count < 100; count++)
   document.write("Count is ", count);
```

This loop executes 100 times and prints out a number each time. The initial expression sets the counter, count, to zero. The condition tests to see whether count is less than 100, and the increment expression increments count.

You can use several statements for any of these expressions, as follows:

```
for (count=0, numFound = 0; (count < 100) && (numFound < 3); count++)
   if (someObject.found()) numFound++;
```

This loop loops either 100 times or as many times as it takes to "find" three items—the loop condition terminates when count >= 100 or when numFound >= 3.

The second form of loop is the while loop. It executes statements as long as its condition is TRUE. For example, you can rewrite the first for loop in the preceding example as follows:

```
count = 0
while (count < 100) {
   if (someObject.found()) numFound++;
   document.write("Count is ", count)
}
```

Which form you use depends on what you're doing; for loops are useful when you want to perform an action a set number of times, and while loops are best when you want to keep doing something as long as a particular condition remains TRUE. Notice that by using curly braces, you can include more than one command to be executed by the while loop (this is also true of for loops and if...else constructs).

JavaScript Reserved Words

JavaScript reserves some keywords for its own use. You cannot define your own methods or properties with the same name as any of these keywords; if you do, the JavaScript interpreter complains.

 Some of these keywords are reserved for future use. JavaScript might allow you to use them, but your scripts may break in the future if you do.

JavaScript's reserved keywords are shown in Table 19.3.

Table 19.3 JavaScript Reserved Keywords Should Not Be Used in Your JavaScripts			
abstract	double	instanceof	super
boolean	else	int	switch

break	extends	interface	synchronized
byte	FALSE	long	this
case	final	native	throw
catch	finally	new	throws
char	float	null	transient
class	for	package	TRUE
const	function	private	try
continue	goto	protected	var
default	if	public	void
do	implements	return	while
	import	short	with
	in	static	

CAUTION

Because JavaScript is still being developed and refined by Netscape, the list of reserved keywords might change or grow over time. Whenever a new version of JavaScript is released, it might be a good idea to look over its new capabilities with an eye towards conflicts with your JavaScript programs.

Other JavaScript Statements

Part
IV
Ch
19

This section provides a quick reference to some of the other JavaScript commands. The commands are listed in alphabetical order—many have examples. Here's what the formatting of these entries mean:

- All JavaScript keywords are in monospaced font.
- Words in *monospace italics* represent user-defined names or statements.
- Any portions enclosed in square brackets ([and]) are optional.
- {*statements*} indicates a block of statements, which can consist of a single statement or multiple statements enclosed by curly braces.

The *break* Statement   The break statement terminates the current while or for loop and transfers program control to the statement following the terminated loop.

Syntax

break

Example

The following function scans the list of URLs in the current document and stops when it has seen all URLs or when it finds a URL that matches the input parameter searchName:

```
function findURL(searchName) {
    var i = 0;
    for (i=0; i < document.links.length; i++) {
        if (document.links[i] == searchName) {
            document.writeln(document.links[i] + "<br>");
            break;
        }
    }
}
```

The *continue* Statement   The `continue` statement stops executing the statements in a `while` or `for` loop, and skips to the next iteration of the loop. It doesn't stop the loop altogether, as the `break` statement does; instead, in a `while` loop, it jumps back to the condition, and in a `for` loop, it jumps to the update expression.

Syntax

```
continue
```

Example

The following function prints the odd numbers between 1 and x; it has a `continue` statement that goes to the next iteration when i is even:

```
function printOddNumbers(x) {
    var i = 0;
    while (i < x) {
        i++;
        if ((i % 2) == 0) // the % operator divides & returns the remainder
            continue;
        else
            document.write(i, "\n");
    }
}
```

The *for* Loop   A `for` loop consists of three optional expressions, enclosed in parentheses and separated by semicolons, followed by a block of statements executed in the loop. These parts do the following:

- The starting expression, `initial_expr`, is evaluated before the loop starts. It is most often used to initialize loop counter variables, and you're free to use the `var` keyword here to declare new variables.

- A `condition` is evaluated on each pass through the loop. If the condition evaluates to TRUE, the statements in the loop body are executed. You can leave the condition out, and it always evaluates to TRUE. If you do so, make sure to use `break` in your loop when it's time to exit.

- An update expression, `update_expr`, is usually used to update or increment the counter variable or other variables used in the condition. This expression is optional; you can update variables as needed within the body of the loop if you prefer.

- A block of statements is executed as long as the condition is TRUE. This block can have one or multiple statements in it.

Syntax

```
for ([initial_expr;] [condition;] [update_expr]) {
    statements
}
```

Example

This simple for statement prints out the numbers from 0 to 9. It starts by declaring a loop counter variable, i, and initializing it to zero. As long as i is less than 9, the update expression increments i, and the statements in the loop body execute.

```
for (var i = 0; i <= 9; i++) {
    document.write(i);
}
```

The *for...in* loop   The for...in loop is a special form of the for loop that iterates the variable variable-name over all the properties of the object named object-name. For each distinct property, it executes the statements in the loop body.

Syntax

```
for (var in obj) {
    statements
}
```

Example

The following function takes as its arguments an object and the object's name. It then uses the for...in loop to iterate through all the object's properties and writes them into the current Web page.

```
function dump_props(obj,obj_name) {
    for (i in obj)
        document.writeln(obj_name + "." + i + " = " + obj[i] + "<br>");
}
```

The *function* Statement   The function statement declares a JavaScript function; the function may optionally accept one or more parameters. To return a value, the function must have a return statement that specifies the value to return. All parameters are passed to functions *by value*—the function gets the value of the parameter but cannot change the original value in the caller.

Syntax

```
function name([param] [, param] [..., param]) {
    statements
}
```

Example

```
function PageNameMatches(theString) {
    return (document.title == theString)
}
```

The *if...else* Statement   The if...else statement is a conditional statement that executes the statements in block1 if condition is TRUE. In the optional else clause, it executes the

Part
IV

Ch
19

statements in `block2` if `condition` is `FALSE`. The blocks of statements can contain any JavaScript statements, including further nested `if` statements.

Syntax

```
if (condition) {
    statements
}
[else {
    statements}]
```

Example

```
if (Message.IsEncrypted()) {
    Message.Decrypt(SecretKey);
}
else {
    Message.Display();
}
```

The *new* Statement   The `new` statement is the way that new objects are created in JavaScript. For instance, if you defined the following function to create a `house` object:

```
function house (rms,stl,yr,garp) { // define a house object
    this.room = rms;        // number of rooms (integer)
    this.style = stl;       // style (string)
    this.yearBuilt = yr;    // year built (integer)
    this.hasGarage = garp;  // has garage? (boolean)
}
```

you could then create an instance of a `house` object by using the `new` statement, as in the following:

```
var myhouse = new house(3,"Tenement",1962,false);
```

A few notes about this example: first, note that the function used to create the object doesn't actually return a value. The reason it is able to work is that it makes use of the `this` object, which always refers to the current object. Second, although the function defines how to create the `house` object, none is actually created until the function is called by using the `new` statement.

The *return* Statement   The `return` statement specifies the value to be returned by a function.

Syntax

```
return expression;
```

Example

The following simple function returns the square of its argument, x, where x is any number.

```
function square( x ) {
    return x * x;
}
```

The *this* Statement   You use `this` to access methods or properties of an object within the object's methods. The `this` statement always refers to the current object.

Syntax

```
this.property
```

Example

If `setSize` is a method of the `document` object, then `this` refers to the specific object whose `setSize` method is called:

```
function setSize(x,y) {
   this.horizSize = x;
   this.vertSize = y;
}
```

This method sets the size for an object when called as follows:

```
document.setSize(640,480);
```

The *var* Statement   The `var` statement declares a variable *varname*, optionally initializing it to have *value*. The variable name *varname* can be any JavaScript identifier, and *value* can be any legal expression (including literals).

Syntax

```
var varname [= value] [, var varname [= value] ] [..., var varname [= value] ]
```

Example

```
var num_hits = 0, var cust_no = 0;
```

The *while* Statement   The `while` statement contains a condition and a block of statements. The `while` statement evaluates the condition; if *condition* is TRUE, it executes the statements in the loop body. It next reevaluates *condition* and continues to execute the statement block as long as *condition* is TRUE. When *condition* evaluates to FALSE, execution continues with the next statement following the block.

Part

IV

Ch

19

Syntax

```
while (condition) {
   statements
}
```

Example

The following simple `while` loop iterates until it finds a form in the current `document` object whose name is `"OrderForm"`, or until it runs out of forms in the document:

```
x = 0;
while ((x < document.forms[].length) && (document.forms[x].name
[ic:ccc]!= "OrderForm")) {
   x++
}
```

The *with* Statement   The `with` statement establishes *object* as the default object for the statements in `block`. Any property references without an object are then assumed to be for *object*.

Syntax

```
with object {
    statements
}
```

Example

```
with document {
    write "Inside a with block, you don't need to specify the object.";
    bgColor = gray;
}
```

JavaScript and Web Browsers

The most important thing you will be doing with your JavaScripts is interacting with the content and information on your Web pages, and through it, with your user. JavaScript interacts with your Web browser through the browser's object model. Different aspects of the Web browser exist as different objects, with properties and methods that can be accessed by JavaScript. For instance, document.write() uses the write method of the document object. Understanding this Web browser object model is crucial to using JavaScript effectively. Understanding how the Web browser processes and executes your scripts is also necessary.

When Scripts Execute

When you put JavaScript code in a page, the Web browser evaluates the code as soon as it's encountered. Functions, however, don't get executed when they're evaluated; they just get stored for later use. You still have to call functions explicitly to make them work. Some functions are attached to objects, like buttons or text fields on forms, and they are called when some event happens on the button or field. You might also have functions that you want to execute during page evaluation. You can do so by putting a call to the function at the appropriate place in the page.

Where to Put Your Scripts

You can put scripts anywhere within your HTML page, as long as they're surrounded with the <SCRIPT>...</SCRIPT> tags. One good system is to put functions that will be executed more than once into the <HEAD> element of their pages; this element provides a convenient storage place. Because the <HEAD> element is at the beginning of the file, functions and VBScript code that you put there will be evaluated before the rest of the document is loaded. You can then execute the function at the appropriate point in your Web page by calling it, as in the following:

```
<SCRIPT language="JavaScript">
<!-- Hide this script from incompatible Web browsers!
myFunction();
<!-- -->
</SCRIPT>
```

Another way to execute scripts is to attach them to HTML elements that support scripts. When scripts are matched with events attached to these elements, the script is executed when the event occurs. This can be done with HTML elements, such as forms, buttons, or links. Consider Listing 19.2, which shows a very simple example of attaching a JavaScript function to the onClick attribute of an HTML forms button (see Figure 19.3).

Listing 19.2   Button1.htm—Calling a JavaScript Function with the Click of a Button

```
<HTML>
<HEAD>
<SCRIPT LANGUAGE="JavaScript">
<!-- Hide this script from incompatible Web browsers!
function pressed() {
    alert("I said Don't Press Me!");
}
<!-- -->
</SCRIPT>
<TITLE>JavaScripts Attached to HTML Elements</TITLE>
</HEAD>
<BODY BGCOLOR=#FFFFFF>
<FORM NAME="Form1">
    <INPUT TYPE="button" NAME="Button1" VALUE="Don't Press Me!"
        onClick="pressed()">
</FORM>
</BODY>
</HTML>
```

FIG. 19.3

JavaScript functions can be attached to form fields through several different methods.

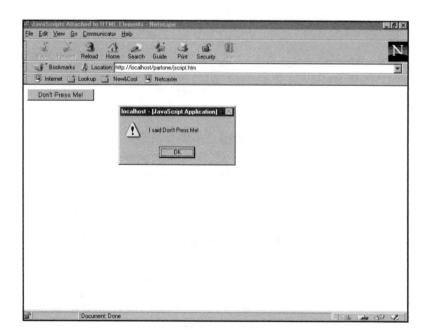

JavaScript also provides you with an alternate way to attach functions to objects and their events. For simple actions, you can attach the JavaScript directly to the attribute of the HTML form element, as shown in Listing 19.3. Each of these listings produce the output shown in Figure 19.3.

Listing 19.3   Button2.htm—Simple VBScripts Can Be Attached Right to a Form Element

```
<HTML>
<HEAD>
<TITLE>JavaScripts Attached to HTML Elements</TITLE>
</HEAD>
<BODY BGCOLOR=#FFFFFF>
<FORM NAME="Form1">
    <INPUT TYPE="button" NAME="Button1" VALUE="Don't Press Me!"
        onClick="alert('I said Don\'t Press Me!')">
</FORM>
</BODY>
</HTML>
```

Sometimes, though, you have code that shouldn't be evaluated or executed until after all the page's HTML has been parsed and displayed. An example would be a function to print out all the URLs referenced in the page. If this function is evaluated before all the HTML on the page has been loaded, it misses some URLs, so the call to the function should come at the page's end. The function itself can be defined anywhere in the HTML document; it is the function call that should be at the end of the page.

N O T E   Until recently, JavaScript code to modify the actual HTML contents of a document (as opposed to merely changing the text in a form text input field, for instance) had to be executed during page evaluation. The Dynamic HTML enhancements and the new Document Object Model have changed this, for browsers that support these technologies. Using them, just about anything in a page can be dynamically changed. ■

Web Browser Objects and Events

In addition to recognizing JavaScript when it's embedded inside a `<SCRIPT>` tag, compatible Web browsers also provide some objects (and their methods and properties) that you can use in your JavaScript programs. They can also trigger methods you define when the user takes certain actions in the browser.

Web Browser Object Hierarchy and Scoping

Figure 19.4 shows the hierarchy of objects that the Web browser provides and that are accessible to JavaScript. As shown, `window` is the topmost object in the hierarchy, and the other objects are organized underneath it as shown. Using this hierarchy, the full reference for the value of a text field named `text1` in an HTML form named `form1` would be `window.document.form1.text1.value`.

FIG. 19.4
Objects defined by the Web browser are organized in a hierarchy (as shown in the diagram in this Web page) and can be accessed and manipulated by JavaScript.

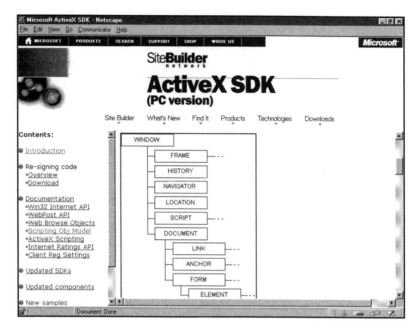

However, because of the object scoping rules in JavaScript, it is not necessary to specify this full reference. Scoping refers to the range over which a variable, function, or object is defined. For instance, a variable defined within a JavaScript function is only scoped within that function—it cannot be referenced outside of the function. JavaScripts are scoped to the current window, but not to the objects below the window in the hierarchy. So, for the previous example, the text field value could also be referenced as `document.form1.text1.value`.

Part
IV

Ch
19

Browser Object Model

Many events that happen in a Web browsing session aren't related to items on the page, like buttons or HTML text. Instead, they're related to what's happening in the browser itself, like what page the user is viewing.

The *location* Object Internet Explorer 3 exposes an object called `location`, which holds the current URL, including the hostname, path, CGI script arguments, and even the protocol. Table 19.4 shows the properties and methods of the `location` object.

Table 19.4 The *location* Object Contains Information on the Currently Displayed URL

Property	Type	What It Does
href	String	Contains the entire URL, including all the subparts; for example, **http://www.msn.com/products/msprod.htm**

continues

Table 19.4   Continued

Property	Type	What It Does
protocol	String	Contains the protocol field of the URL, including the first colon; for example, **http:**
host	String	Contains the hostname and port number; for example, **www.msn.com:80**
hostname	String	Contains only the hostname; for example, **www.msn.com**
port	String	Contains the port, if specified; otherwise, it's blank
path	String	Contains the path to the actual document; for example, **products/msprod.htm**
hash	String	Contains any CGI arguments after the first # in the URL
search	String	Contains any CGI arguments after the first ? in the URL
toString()	Method	Returns location.href; you can use this function to get the entire URL easily
assign(x)	Method	Sets location.href to the value you specify

Listing 19.4 shows an example of how you access and use the location object. The current values of the location properties are displayed on the Web page (see Figure 19.5). As you can see, not all of them are defined. Additionally, when the button is clicked, the location.href property is set to the URL of my home page. This causes the Web browser to load that page.

Listing 19.4   Loc-props.htm—The *Location* Object Allows You to Access and Set Information About the Current URL

```
<HTML>
<HEAD>
<SCRIPT LANGUAGE="JavaScript">
<!-- Hide this script from incompatible Web browsers!
function gohome() {
    location.href = "http://www.rpi.edu/~odonnj/";
}
<!-- -->
</SCRIPT>
<TITLE>The Location Object</TITLE>
</HEAD>
<BODY BGCOLOR=#FFFFFF>
<SCRIPT LANGUAGE="Javascript">
<!-- Hide this script from incompatible Web browsers!
document.writeln("Current location information: <BR> <HR>");
document.writeln("location.href = " + location.href + "<BR>");
document.writeln("location.protocol = " + location.protocol + "<BR>");
document.writeln("location.host = " + location.host + "<BR>");
document.writeln("location.hostname = " + location.hostname + "<BR>");
document.writeln("location.port = " + location.port + "<BR>");
document.writeln("location.pathname = " + location.pathname + "<BR>");
```

```
document.writeln("location.hash = " + location.hash + "<BR>");
document.writeln("location.search = " + location.search + "<BR> <HR>");
<!-- -->
</SCRIPT>
<FORM NAME="Form1">
   <INPUT TYPE="button" NAME="Button1" VALUE="Goto JOD's Home Page!"
      onClick="gohome()">
</FORM>
</BODY>
</HTML>
```

FIG. 19.5

Manipulating the location object gives you another means of moving from one Web page to another.

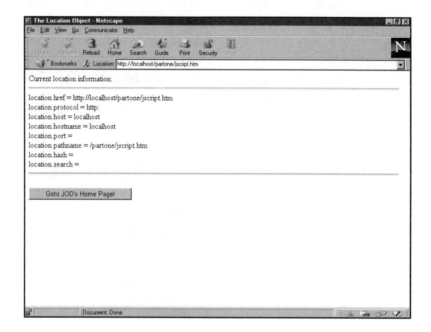

The **document** Object   Web browsers also expose an object called document. As you might expect, this object exposes useful properties and methods of the active document. The location object refers only to the URL of the active document, but document refers to the document itself. Table 19.5 shows document's properties and methods.

Table 19.5   The document Object Contains Information on the Currently Loaded and Displayed HTML Page

Property	Type	What It Does
title	String	Contains title of the current page, or Untitled if there's no title.
URL or Location	String	Contains the document's address (from its Location history stack entry); these two are synonyms.

continues

Table 19.5 Continued

Property	Type	What It Does
lastModified	String	Contains the page's last-modified date.
forms[]	Array	Contains all the FORMs in the current page.
forms[].length	Integer	Contains the number of FORMs in the current page.
links[]	Array	Contains all HREF anchors in the current page.
links[].length	Integer	Contains the number of HREF anchors in the current page.
write(x)	Method	Writes HTML to the current document, in the order in which the script occurs on the page.

The *history* Object   The Web browser also maintains a list of pages you've visited since running the program; this list is called the *history list*, and can be accessed through the history object. Your JavaScript programs can move through pages in the list by using the properties and functions shown in Table 19.6.

Table 19.6 The *history* Object Contains Information on the Browser's History List

Property	Type	What It Does
previous or back	String	Contains the URL of the previous history stack entry (that is, the one before the active page). These properties are synonyms.
next or forward	String	Contains the URL of the next history stack entry (that is, the one after the active page.) These properties are synonyms.
go(x)	Method	Goes forward x entries in the history stack if x > 0; else, goes backward x entries. x must be a number.
go(str)	Method	Goes to the newest history entry whose title or URL contains str as a substring; the string case doesn't matter. str must be a string.

The *window* Object   The Web browser creates a window object for every document. Think of the window object as an actual window, and the document object as the content that appears in the window. The following are a couple of the methods available for working in the window:

- ■ alert(*string*) puts up an Alert dialog box and displays the message specified in string. Users must dismiss the dialog box by clicking the OK button before Internet Explorer 3 lets them continue.

- ■ confirm(*string*) puts up a Confirmation dialog box with two buttons (OK and Cancel) and displays the message specified in string. Users can dismiss the dialog box by clicking Cancel or OK; the `confirm` function returns TRUE when users click OK and FALSE if they click Cancel.

The *form* Object   There are a series of object, properties, methods, and events associated with HTML forms when used in a Web page. Some of them you have already seen in the examples presented thus far in this chapter. All of the properties of the `form` object work the same way in JavaScript as in VBScript.

▶ **See** Chapter 18, "Scripting with VBScript" **p. 369**

Example JavaScript Applications

In this section, you'll see a couple of examples of JavaScript applications. A common scripting application generally involves interaction with HTML forms in order to perform client-side validation of the forms data before submission. JavaScript can perform this function very well. If you are interested in seeing an example of using JavaScript in this way, there is a JavaScript version on the CD-ROM that does much the same thing.

In order not to duplicate the forms discussion, the example shown in this chapter show how JavaScript can be used within a Web browser to interact with browser frames and windows. As usual, the interface between the user and the JavaScript code remains HTML forms elements —the examples also show you how to open, close, and manipulate Web browser windows and frames.

Manipulating Windows

This example shows how it is possible to create an HTML forms-based control panel that uses JavaScript to load and execute other JavaScripts in their own windows. This is done through the use of the `window` Web browser object and its properties and methods.

Listing 19.5 shows the *main program*, the top-level HTML document giving access to the control panel (see Figure 19.6). The JavaScript in this example is very simple, and is included in the `onClick` attribute of the forms `<input>` tag. Clicking the button executes the JavaScript `window` method open:

```
window.open('cp.htm','ControlPanel','width=300,height=250')
```

This creates a window named `ControlPanel` that is 300×250 pixels in size, and loads the HTML document CP.HTM.

Part
IV

Ch
19

Listing 19.5   Cpmain.htm—A JavaScript Attached Right to a Forms Button Will Create a New Window When Clicked

```
<HTML>
<HEAD>
<TITLE>JavaScript Window Example</TITLE>
</HEAD>
<BODY BGCOLOR=#FFFFFF>
```

continues

Listing 19.5 Continued

```
<CENTER><H3>Activate the control panel by clicking below</H3></CENTER>
<HR>
<FORM>
<CENTER>
<TABLE>
<TR><TD><INPUT TYPE="button" NAME="ControlButton" VALUE="Control Panel"
        onClick="window.open('cp.htm','ControlPanel',
                             'width=300,height=250')"></TD></TR>
</TABLE>
</CENTER>
</FORM>
</BODY>
</HTML>
```

FIG. 19.6

The Control Panel button calls a JavaScript and creates a new browser window.

When the button is clicked, CP.HTM is loaded into its own window, as shown in Figure 19.7 (notice that in this figure and the next, the windows have been manually rearranged so that they can all be seen). This HTML document uses an interface of an HTML form organized in a table to give access through this control panel to other JavaScript applications, namely a timer and a real-time clock. Listing 19.6 shows CP.HTM. The JavaScript functions openTimer(), openClock(), closeTimer(), and closeClock() are used to open and close windows for a JavaScript timer and clock, respectively. These functions are attached to forms buttons that make up the control panel. Notice that JavaScript variables timerw and clockw, because they are defined outside of any of the functions, can be used anywhere in the JavaScript document. They are used to remember whether or not the timer and clock windows are opened.

Listing 19.6   Cp.htm—This HTML Form Calls JavaScripts to Create and Destroy Windows for a Timer and or a Real-Time Clock

```
<HTML>
<HEAD>
<SCRIPT LANGUAGE="JavaScript">
<!-- Hide this script from incompatible Web browsers!
var timerw = null;
var clockw = null;
function openTimer() {
   if(!timerw)
      timerw = open("cptimer.htm","TimerWindow","width=300,height=100");
}
function openClock() {
   if(!clockw)
      clockw = open("cpclock.htm","ClockWindow","width=50,height=25");
}
function closeTimer() {
   if(timerw) {
      timerw.close();
      timerw = null;
   }
}
function closeClock() {
   if(clockw) {
      clockw.close();
      clockw = null;
   }
}
<!-- -->
</SCRIPT>
</HEAD>
<BODY BGCOLOR=#EEEEEE>
<FORM>
<CENTER>
<TABLE>
<TR><TD>To Open Timer...</TD>
    <TD ALIGN=CENTER>
       <INPUT TYPE="button" NAME="ControlButton" VALUE="Click Here!"
       onClick="openTimer()"></TD></TR>
<TR><TD>To Close Timer...</TD>
    <TD ALIGN=CENTER>
       <INPUT TYPE="button" NAME="ControlButton" VALUE="Click Here!"
       onClick="closeTimer()"></TD></TR>
<TR><TD>To Open Clock...</TD>
    <TD ALIGN=CENTER>
       <INPUT TYPE="button" NAME="ControlButton" VALUE="Click Here!"
       onClick="openClock()"></TD></TR>
<TR><TD>To Close Clock...</TD>
    <TD ALIGN=CENTER>
       <INPUT TYPE="button" NAME="ControlButton" VALUE="Click Here!"
       onClick="closeClock()"></TD></TR>
<TR><TD>To Open Both...</TD>
    <TD ALIGN=CENTER>
       <INPUT TYPE="button" NAME="ControlButton" VALUE="Click Here!"
```

Part

IV

Ch

19

continues

Listing 19.6   Continued

```
            onClick="openTimer();openClock();"></TD></TR>
<TR><TD>To Close Both...</TD>
    <TD ALIGN=CENTER>
        <INPUT TYPE="button" NAME="ControlButton" VALUE="Click Here!"
            onClick="closeTimer();closeClock();"></TD></TR>
<TR><TD></TD></TR>
<TR><TD>To Close Everything...</TD>
    <TD ALIGN=CENTER>
        <INPUT TYPE="button" NAME="ControlButton" VALUE="Click Here!"
            onClick="closeTimer();closeClock();self.close();"></TD></TR>
</TABLE>
</CENTER>
</FORM>
</BODY>
</HTML>
```

FIG. 19.7

JavaScript can create new Web browser windows with definable widths and heights.

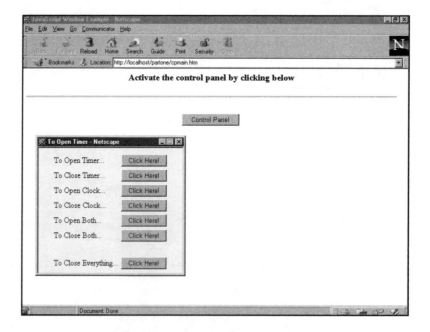

Listing 19.7 and Listing 19.8 show CPTIMER.HTM and CPCLOCK.HTM, the HTML documents to implement the JavaScript timer and real-time clock. Notice that each uses the properties of the JavaScript Date object to access time information. Figure 19.8 shows the Web page with the control panel, timer, and real-time clock windows all open.

Listing 19.7 Cptimer.htm—The JavaScript *Date* Object Can Be Used to Keep Track of Relative Time

```
<HTML>
<HEAD>
<SCRIPT LANGUAGE="JavaScript">
<!-- Hide this script from incompatible Web browsers!
var timerID = 0;
var tStart  = null;
function UpdateTimer() {
   if(timerID) {
      clearTimeout(timerID);
      clockID  = 0;
   }
   if(!tStart)
      tStart   = new Date();
   var tDate = new Date();
   var tDiff = tDate.getTime() - tStart.getTime();
   var str;
   tDate.setTime(tDiff);
   str = ""
   if (tDate.getMinutes() < 10)
      str += "0" + tDate.getMinutes() + ":";
   else
      str += tDate.getMinutes() + ":";
   if (tDate.getSeconds() < 10)
      str += "0" + tDate.getSeconds();
   else
      str += tDate.getSeconds();
   document.theTimer.theTime.value = str;
   timerID = setTimeout("UpdateTimer()", 1000);
}
function Start() {
   tStart = new Date();
   document.theTimer.theTime.value = "00:00";
   timerID = setTimeout("UpdateTimer()", 1000);
}
function Stop() {
   if(timerID) {
      clearTimeout(timerID);
      timerID  = 0;
   }
   tStart = null;
}
function Reset() {
   tStart = null;
   document.theTimer.theTime.value = "00:00";
}
<!-- -->
</SCRIPT>
</HEAD>
<BODY BGCOLOR=#AAAAAA onload="Reset();Start()" onunload="Stop()">
<FORM NAME="theTimer">
<CENTER>
<TABLE>
```

Part
IV

Ch
19

continues

Listing 19.7   Continued

```
<TR><TD COLSPAN=3 ALIGN=CENTER>
      <INPUT TYPE=TEXT NAME="theTime" SIZE=5></TD></TR>
<TR><TD></TD></TR>
<TR><TD><INPUT TYPE=BUTTON NAME="start" VALUE="Start"
           onclick="Start()"></TD>
   <TD><INPUT TYPE=BUTTON NAME="stop"  VALUE="Stop"
           onclick="Stop()"></TD>
   <TD><INPUT TYPE=BUTTON NAME="reset" VALUE="Reset"
           onclick="Reset()"></TD>
   </TR>
</TABLE>
</CENTER>
</FORM>
</BODY>
</HTML>
```

Listing 19.8   Cpclock.htm—The *Date* Object Can Also Be Used to Access the Real-Time Clock of the Client System

```
<HTML>
<HEAD>
<TITLE>Clock</TITLE>
<SCRIPT LANGUAGE="JavaScript">
<!-- Hide this script from incompatible Web browsers!
var clockID = 0;
function UpdateClock() {
   if(clockID) {
      clearTimeout(clockID);
      clockID  = 0;
   }
   var tDate = new Date();
   var str;
   str = "";
   if (tDate.getHours() < 10)
      str += "0" + tDate.getHours() + ":";
   else
      str += tDate.getHours() + ":";
   if (tDate.getMinutes() < 10)
      str += "0" + tDate.getMinutes() + ":";
   else
      str += tDate.getMinutes() + ":";
   if (tDate.getSeconds() < 10)
      str += "0" + tDate.getSeconds();
   else
      str += tDate.getSeconds();
   document.theClock.theTime.value = str;
   clockID = setTimeout("UpdateClock()", 1000);
}
function StartClock() {
   clockID = setTimeout("UpdateClock()", 500);
}
```

```
function KillClock() {
   if(clockID) {
      clearTimeout(clockID);
      clockID  = 0;
   }
}
<!-- -->
</SCRIPT>
</HEAD>
<BODY BGCOLOR=#CCCCCC onload="StartClock()" onunload="KillClock()">
<CENTER>
<FORM NAME="theClock">
   <INPUT TYPE=TEXT NAME="theTime" SIZE=8>
</FORM>
</CENTER>
</BODY>
</HTML>
```

FIG. 19.8

Multiple browser windows can be created by JavaScript, each running its own JavaScripts and performing its functions independently.

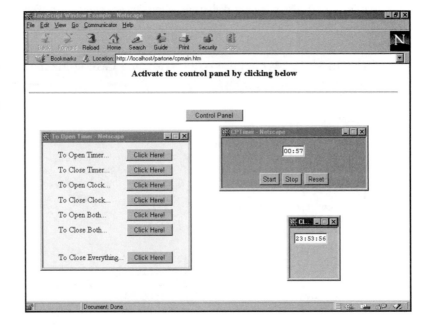

Part
IV
Ch
19

Web Browser Windows and Frames

In this example, you can see further examples of window manipulation by using JavaScript; in addition, you will see how different frames can be accessed and manipulated. Listing 19.9 shows WFMAIN.HTM. Like CPMAIN.HTM in Listing 19.5, this is the simple, top-level HTML document for this example. This one is even simpler, in that it doesn't contain any JavaScript at all but simply sets up the frameset and frames for the example and indicates the HTML documents, WFTOP.HTM and WFTEXT.HTM, to be loaded into each frame.

Listing 19.9   Wfmain.htm—This Main HTML Document Creates a Frameset and Loads Two Other Documents into the Resulting Frames

```
<HTML>
<TITLE>Windows and Frames</TITLE>
<FRAMESET ROWS="100,*">
   <FRAME SRC="wftop.htm"  NAME="frame1" SCROLLING="no" NORESIZE>
   <FRAME SRC="wftext.htm" NAME="frame2">
</FRAMESET>
<NOFRAMES>
</NOFRAMES>
</HTML>
```

The document that makes up the uppermost frame, shown in Listing 19.10, creates a button bar of functions that can be used to manipulate the frames and windows of this example. The initial contents of the lower frame give some quick instructions on what each button does (see Listing 19.11). The resulting Web page, when this is loaded into a Web browser, is shown in Figure 19.9.

Listing 19.10   Wftop.htm—The HTML and JavaScripts in this Web Page Allow the Manipulation of the Windows and Frames in This Example

```
<HTML>
<HEAD>
<TITLE>Windows and Frames</TITLE>
<SCRIPT LANGUAGE="JavaScript">
<!-- Hide this script from incompatible Web browsers!
function bottomColor(newColor) {
   window.parent.frames['frame2'].document.bgColor=newColor;
}
function topColor(newColor) {
   window.parent.frames['frame1'].document.bgColor=newColor;
}
function navi() {
   window.open('wfvisit.htm','Visit',
      'toolbar=no,location=no,directories=no,' +
      'status=no,menubar=no,scrollbars=no,resizable=no,' +
      'copyhistory=yes,width=600,height=200');
}
function Customize() {
var PopWindow=window.open('wfcolor.htm','Main',
      'toolbar=no,location=no,directories=no,status=no,' +
      'menubar=no,scrollbars=no,resizable=no,copyhistory=yes,' +
      'width=400,height=200');
   PopWindow.creator = self;
}
function ConfirmClose() {
   if (confirm("Are you sure you wish to exit Netscape?"))
      window.close()
}
<!-- -->
</SCRIPT>
```

```
</HEAD>
<BODY>
<CENTER>
<FONT COLOR=RED>
<H2>Windows and Frames</H2>
<FORM>
<INPUT TYPE="BUTTON" VALUE="Back"
    onClick="parent.frame2.history.back()">
<INPUT TYPE="BUTTON" VALUE="Visit Other Sites"
    onClick="navi()">
<INPUT TYPE="BUTTON" VALUE="Background Colors"
    onClick="Customize()">
<INPUT TYPE="BUTTON" VALUE="Forward"
    onClick="parent.frame2.history.forward()">
<INPUT TYPE="BUTTON" VALUE="Exit"
    onClick="ConfirmClose()">
</CENTER>
</FORM>
</BODY>
</HTML>
```

Listing 19.11 Wftext.htm—This Informational Web Page Also Provides the Jumping-Off Point to Another Site

```
<HTML>
<HEAD>
<TITLE>Windows and Frames Text</TITLE>
</HEAD>
<BODY BGCOLOR=#FFFFFF>
<CENTER>
<H2>Welcome to Windows and Frames Using JavaScript</H2>
</CENTER>
<B>There are 5 control buttons on the control panel:<BR>
<OL><LI>Forward: Takes you to the front of the frame. (This only works
        after you actually choose to go somewhere and come back.)
    <LI>Visit Other Site: This window will let you type a site address and
        you will be able to visit that specific site.
    <LI>Background Color: Lets you choose the top and the bottom frame's
        background color.
    <LI>Back: Takes you back on a frame.
    <LI>Exit: Exits from Netscape.
</OL>
</B>
<CENTER>
Let's check the "back/forward" buttons. Let's<BR>
<FONT SIZE="+2"><A HREF="http://www.microsoft.com">Go Somewhere!!!</A>
</BODY>
</HTML>
```

Part
IV

Ch
19

The intent of this example is to use the button bar and attached JavaScript functions of the top frame to manipulate the contents of the lower frame and the appearance of both. If you follow instructions and click the Go Somewhere!!! hypertext link in the lower frame, the URL included in the listing for that link (the Microsoft home page) is loaded into the lower frame (see Figure 19.10).

FIG. 19.9

JavaScript can use the browser window and frame objects to create and manipulate the browser and its frames.

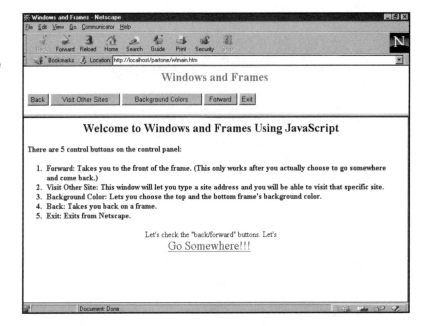

By using a JavaScript function navi(), the Visit Other Sites button creates a window and loads in the HTML document WFVISIT.HTM, shown in Listing 19.12. This document uses an HTML form to query the user for a URL (see Figure 19.11) and then makes use of the Web browser frame object to load the Web page referenced by that URL into the lower frame (see Figure 19.12).

Listing 19.12   Wfvisit.htm—The HTML and JavaScript in This File Allow Other Web Pages to Be Loaded into the Lower Frame

```
<HTML>
<HEAD>
<TITLE>Windows and Frames Navigator</TITLE>
<SCRIPT LANGUAGE="JavaScript">
<!-- Hide this script from incompatible Web browsers!
function visit(frame) {
```

```
    if (frame == "frame2")
        open(document.getsite.site.value,frame);
    return 0;
}
<!-- -->
</SCRIPT>
</HEAD>
<BODY BGCOLOR=#FFFFFF>
<CENTER>
<H2><B>Windows and Frames Navigator</B></H2>
<FORM NAME="getsite" METHOD="post">
<hR>
<INPUT TYPE="TEXT" NAME="site" SIZE=50>
<INPUT TYPE="BUTTON" NAME="gobut" VALUE="Go!"
    onclick="window.close();visit('frame2')">
<HR>
<INPUT TYPE="BUTTON" VALUE="Exit" onclick="window.close()">
</FORM>
</BODY>
</HTML>
```

FIG. 19.10

After you click the Go Somewhere!!! hypertext link you see the Microsoft Web site appear in the lower frame.

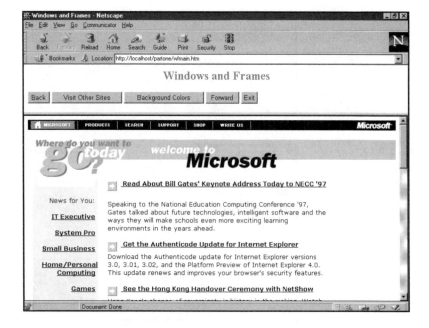

Part

IV

Ch

19

The Back and Forward buttons also call JavaScript functions that use the `frame` object to move the lower frame backward and forward through its history list.

Anther capability given by the upper frame toolbar is the ability to specify the background colors of either the upper or lower frame. Clicking the Background Colors button creates a window and loads the HTML document shown in Listing 19.13. This window uses HTML forms option buttons to allow you to select from five choices of background color for each frame. Note that the `creator` object and the `topColor()` and `bottomColor()` methods used in

Listing 19.13 to change the frame colors are set up in the `Customize()` function of the WFTOP.HTM HTML document (refer to Listing 19.10). Because this window is created by that function, it inherits those objects and methods, and can use them to change the frame background colors (see Figure 19.13).

FIG. 19.11

Any valid URL can be typed into this HTML form to be loaded into the lower frame of the main browser window (notice that you must include the protocol, for example, http://, to make it work).

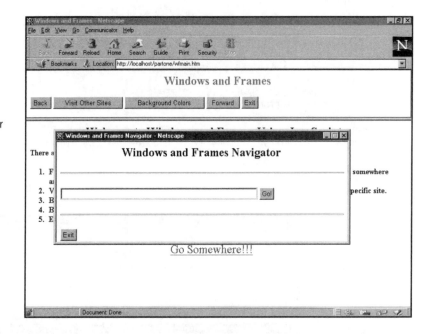

FIG. 19.12

Once a few documents have been viewed in the lower frame, the Back and Forward buttons in the upper frames can be used.

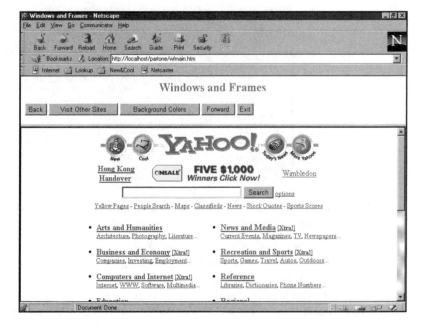

Listing 19.13 Wfcolor.htm—JavaScript Allows You to Manipulate the Appearance of Windows and Frames that Are Being Viewed

```
<HTML>
<HEAD>
<TITLE>Windows and Frames Custom Colors</TITLE>
</HEAD>
<CENTER>
1. <FONT COLOR="#000000">Black</FONT>
2. <FONT COLOR="#FF0235">Red</FONT>
3. <FONT COLOR="#6600BA">Purple</FONT>
4. <FONT COLOR="#3300CC">Blue</FONT>
5. <FONT COLOR="#FFFFFF">White</FONT>
<FORM NAME="background">
<FONT SIZE=4>
   Top Frame Colors<br>
   <INPUT TYPE="RADIO" NAME="bgcolor"
       onClick="creator.topColor('#000000')">1
   <INPUT TYPE="RADIO" NAME="bgcolor"
       onClick="creator.topColor('#FF0235')">2
   <INPUT TYPE="RADIO" NAME="bgcolor"
       onClick="creator.topColor('#6600BA')">3
   <INPUT TYPE="RADIO" NAME="bgcolor"
       onClick="creator.topColor('#3300CC')">4
   <INPUT TYPE="RADIO" NAME="bgcolor"
       onClick="creator.topColor('#ffffff')">5
   <BR>
   Bottom Frame<BR>
   <INPUT TYPE="RADIO" NAME="bgcolor"
       onClick="creator.bottomColor('#000000')">1
   <INPUT TYPE="RADIO" NAME="bgcolor"
       onClick="creator.bottomColor('#FF0235')">2
   <INPUT TYPE="RADIO" NAME="bgcolor"
       onClick="creator.bottomColor('#6600BA')">3
   <INPUT TYPE="RADIO" NAME="bgcolor"
       onClick="creator.bottomColor('#3300CC')">4
   <INPUT TYPE="RADIO" NAME="bgcolor"
       onClick="creator.bottomColor('#FFFFFF')">5
   <p>
   <INPUT TYPE="BUTTON" VALUE="Exit" onClick="window.close()">
</FONT>
</FORM>
</CENTER>
</BODY>
</HTML>
```

Part
IV

Ch
19

The final button of the upper frame toolbar calls a JavaScript function that gives the user the ability to exit from the Web browser after first getting confirmation (see Figure 19.14).

FIG. 19.13

The choices in this box allow you to dynamically change the background color of each frame.

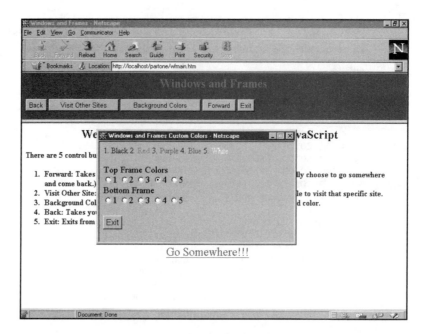

FIG. 19.14

The upper frame's Exit button includes a JavaScript confirmation dialog box.

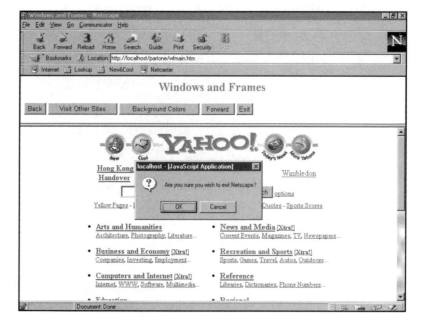

From Here...

In the last few chapters, you've looked at ActiveX, VBScript, and JavaScript. There are two more ways of getting active content into a page, though, and you'll have a look at those in the following chapters:

- Chapter 20, "Inserting Java Applets and Browser Plug-Ins," covers MIME media types and Netscape plug-ins, and gives you an overview of the Java programming language.
- Chapter 21, "VRML and Java," provides an introduction to the Virtual Reality Modeling Language and its connections to Java.

Or, if you've had enough active content for a while and would like to do something else, take a look at the chapters in the following parts of this book:

- Part III, "Creating and Adapting Graphics with Image Composer," explores the methods you use to make and modify your own graphics.
- Part V, "Building and Managing a Web," shows you how to integrate the pages you create into a sophisticated, well-organized Web site that will be the envy of your neighbors in cyberspace.

Part
IV

Ch
19

## CHAPTER 20

Inserting Java Applets and Browser Plug-Ins

Although HTML is the backbone of any Web page, some effects and functionality can't be added to a page with HTML itself. To obtain some of these sophisticated features and to provide for browsers that do and don't support them, you'll need two more tools—Netscape plug-ins and Java applets. In this chapter, you learn about these components and how you use FrontPage Editor to add them to your pages. ■

Understanding Netscape Plug-Ins

Get acquainted with why Netscape has plug-ins, and how the browser uses them.

About MIME media types

Knowing the media type of your content is essential when setting up a Web page.

Plug-Ins on your pages

Learn the tricks of using plug-ins with FrontPage Editor to embed features in your Web page.

Java overview

Take a look at the strengths of Java and what it means to the World Wide Web and to your Webs.

Basic Java language constructs

Assess the language itself to understand its power.

FrontPage Editor and Java applets

Learn how to use FrontPage Editor to install Java applets in your pages and configure them.

Understanding Netscape Plug-Ins

High-end browsers, such as the Netscape browsers and Microsoft Internet Explorer, handle many different media types, but no browser can handle everything. Both Netscape and Microsoft put *hooks* in their products to allow programmers to write code that extends the media types supported by the browser. Netscape browsers depend on *helpers* and *plug-ins*. (Internet Explorer browsers use ActiveX technology, rather than plug-ins, to achieve similar effects.)

Starting with version 1 of Navigator, Netscape provided ways to enhance its browser with helper applications, which support data formats beyond the built-in graphics and HTML. With Netscape Navigator version 2, Navigator began supporting plug-ins, another way to extend the range of data types that can be presented on or with a Web page. This continued with Navigator 3 and has been carried into the latest browser version, Navigator 4 (which Netscape refers to as Communicator).

To see why plug-ins are useful, go to the desktop of a Macintosh or Windows 95 computer and double-click a few documents. If you choose a document that your system associates with a particular application, that application launches; but, if you double-click a document whose type and creator are unknown, you'll get a dialog box like the one shown in Figure 20.1.

FIG. 20.1

A Windows 95 user is invited to *associate* a file extension with an application.

On the whole, Apple and Microsoft have developed workable schemes for mapping documents to applications. Even most UNIX vendors provide something similar with the X Windows system.

But today, the user's world goes far beyond their local hard drive. The user may have files on a file server on the local area network and may access files on a coworker's machine on the other side of the room or, through a company intranet or the Internet, the other side of the world.

When a Netscape 3 user attempts to open a document that the browser does not recognize, the user gets the dialog box shown in Figure 20.2. This dialog box allows the user to select an external viewer application with the Pick App button or to save the file.

FIG. 20.2

A Navigator 4 user attempts to open an unrecognized file type.

NOTE Netscape Communicator (a.k.a. Navigator 4) is much more adaptable and looks for an installed application that can handle the file. For example, if you have WinZip on your machine and try to open a ZIP file in Communicator, Communicator automatically calls WinZip instead of opening the Unknown File Type dialog box. (In the example for Figure 20.2, the host machine did not have WinZip installed, so the Unknown File Type dialog appeared.) ▪

External viewers, also known as *helper applications*, allow the Web user to see a variety of data types that are not built into browser. The downside of helper applications is that they are, indeed, applications. This means that they are fully separate programs launched outside the browser, whereas plug-ins work more or less seamlessly within the browser environment. Therefore, to view a file with a helper application, the user's machine must start a whole new program. This fact means the following:

- The user has to wait while the new program loads.
- The user may run out of memory and not be able to launch the new program.
- If the helper application launches, the document will appear in its own window, out of context from the Web document.
- There's no interaction between the Web document and the external file—for example, if the external file is a movie, there's no provision to allow the user to use buttons on the Web page to control the movie viewer.

Understanding MIME Media Types

To understand helper applications and plug-ins, you must first understand MIME media types, formerly known as MIME types. Multimedia Internet Message Extensions, or MIME, were developed to allow users to exchange files by e-mail. Although the Web does not use the full MIME standard, it is convenient to use media types to tell a Web browser how the file is formatted.

MIME is described in detail in Request for Comments (RFC) 1590. RFC 1590 updates the registration process originally described in RFC 1521. Although MIME was originally intended for use in e-mail systems, and RFC 1521 was written with that application in mind, today's user encounters MIME in a variety of multimedia settings.

NOTE RFCs are supervised by the Internet Engineering Task Force (IETF), which is the protocol engineering and development arm of the Internet. The IETF is a large open international community of network designers, operators, vendors, and researchers concerned with the evolution of the Internet architecture. For more information on the IETF and RFCs, go to **http://www.ietf.org/**. ▪

Part
IV

Ch
20

MIME is designed to have a limited number of top-level types, such as application, text, and video, which can be extended by subtypes. Table 20.1 shows some typical MIME-compliant media types.

Table 20.1   MIME Types Consist of a Type and a Subtype

Type	Subtype	Meaning
application	msword	Format of Microsoft Word documents
application	rtf	The Rich Text Format for word processors
application	octet-stream	A catchall type for a collection of bytes
application	zip	The compressed-file format of PKZIP and its kin
application	pdf	Adobe's Portable Document Format
audio	aiff	An audio interchange format developed by Apple Computer
audio	midi	A music format based on instruments
audio	wav	The RIFF WAVE sound format developed by Microsoft and IBM
image	cgm	Computer Graphics Metafile image format
image	gif	Graphics Interchange Format image format
image	jpeg	File interchange format of the Joint Photographic Experts Group
text	plain	ASCII text
text	html	The Hypertext Markup Language
video	mpeg	Video format of the Motion Picture Experts Group
video	quicktime	Format developed by Apple Computer

When a Web browser requests a document from a server, the server sends several header lines before it sends the document itself. One of the headers is Content-type. This header line contains the MIME type and subtype, separated by a slash. Thus, most Web pages are preceded by the following line:

```
Content-type: text/html
```

N O T E   MIME media types are assigned by the Internet Assigned Numbers Authority (IANA) in response to a formal request process. If you plan to develop your own plug-in, check out the list of IANA-approved MIME types at **ftp://ftp.isi.edu/in-notes/iana/assignments/media-types/media-types**.

If you need a private MIME media type for use on an intranet or in a limited distribution application, use the most appropriate type and select a subtype that begins with the characters x-. For example, application/x-myType is an acceptable name for a private type.

For information about how to register your own media type and how to program a plug-in, see *Netscape Plug-Ins Developer's Kit* (Que Corp., 1996). ▪

How Netscape Browsers Process Plug-Ins

When the Microsoft Windows versions of Navigator 3 or Communicator start, they look in the directory that holds the browser executable for a directory called Program. Inside that directory, they look for a directory named Plug-ins. They next examine the files in the plug-ins folder and read out the MIME type. You can see which plug-ins either browser found by choosing Help, About Plug-ins.

 TIP On a Windows machine, the names of the plug-in files must begin with the characters np or Netscape browsers will not recognize them as plug-ins.

Later, when the Netscape browser encounters a Content-type header with a type it does not recognize, it looks through the list of MIME types registered by the plug-ins. If it finds a match, it loads that plug-in Dynamic Link Library (DLL) into memory and passes the contents to the plug-in.

If none of the plug-ins on the list match, the browser looks at the list of helper applications. If none of those match, the browser starts the plug-in assisted installation process. (Figure 20.2 shows the installation dialog box as used by Navigator 3.)

Using FrontPage Editor to Invoke a Netscape Plug-In

FrontPage Editor's plug-in insertion command generates the <EMBED> tag, which is recognized by both Netscape browsers and Internet Explorer. Essentially, the <EMBED> tag is a type of link; objects specified by it automatically download and display when the document is displayed. To insert a plug-in, do the following:

1. Choose Insert, Advanced, Plug-in. The Plug-In Properties dialog box appears (see Figure 20.3).
2. Type the path name of the data file to be loaded in the Data Source box, or use the Browse button to locate the file. (The Data Source is the file the browser tries to read with its plug-in.)
3. Using the Message box, type a message that browsers that don't use plug-ins can display.
4. Specify the size and height of the plug-in region (in pixels) that you want in the browser window. If you don't want any visible evidence of the plug-in region in the browser, mark the Hide Plug-in check box.

Part
IV

Ch
20

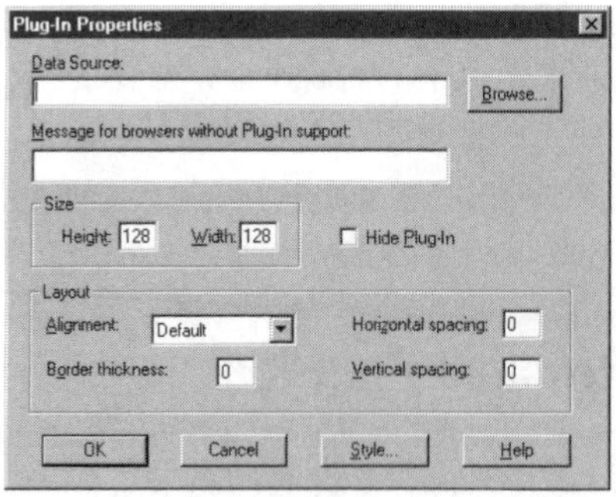

FIG. 20.3

The Plug-In Properties dialog box lets you specify the behavior of the plug-in.

5. Use the Layout section to specify where the plug-in will sit in relation to text, its border thickness, and its spacing away from text.

6. Choose OK. A generic plug-in placeholder appears in the FrontPage Editor workspace.

The workings of such an embedded object can be a little confusing. (For this example, you'll assume a default Netscape Navigator or Communicator installation without any third-party plug-ins.) If you plug in an object whose MIME type is supported directly by either browser (such as a WAV file) and view it in Navigator 3 or Communicator, a WAV audio player automatically loads with the page and is embedded in the page from which it was called. The user can now play the file with the controls (see Figure 20.4).

FIG. 20.4

You can embed a WAV player in a Netscape-displayed page by using the <EMBED> tag.

This result of using the <EMBED> tag is quite different from using a link to access the data source file: in the latter case, the WAV player appears only when the viewer clicks the link, and it is not integrated with the page on which the link resides.

An interesting side effect of making the WAV plug-in hidden is that the sound file automatically plays when the page loads in a Netscape browser. This is a workaround for getting background sound into these browsers without using an applet, although they don't enable you to loop the sound for continuous playback.

As was noted in Chapter 6, "Enhancing Pages with Themes, Graphics, and Multimedia," Navigator 3 and Communicator don't support inline video with AVI files, as IE 3 and 4 do. If you simply use the Insert, Video command to put the animation file into the page, the Netscape browsers won't display it. However, if you use a plug-in and make the data source the AVI file, Navigator 3 or Communicator display the animation without the user needing to click a link to go to it. Don't hide the plug-in, though, or you'll get an error message that the window could not be created.

With Netscape browsers, if you use a MIME type for which the user's browser has no plug-in, an icon appears in the browser window at the plug-in location, and when the user clicks the icon, the message shown in Figure 20.5 appears. In this case, the MIME type was MPEG, and the Navigator 3 installation being used didn't have an MPEG plug-in. (Using the same page, IE 3.0 provided an MPEG player as soon as the MPEG file was downloaded.) After clicking the Get the Plugin button, a user is linked directly to Netscape's plug-in resource site.

FIG. 20.5

Netscape asks if the user wants to download a plug-in for an unsupported MIME type.

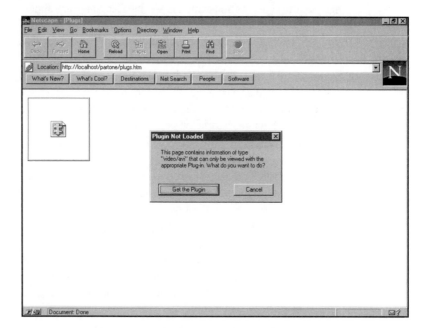

Part

IV

Ch

20

Browser responses to embedded data sources vary considerably with the MIME types used and the capabilities and configurations of the browsers, so you'll have to do some experimenting to get things just right.

Java: An Overview

"Java," to quote Sun on the subject, "is a simple, robust, object-oriented, platform-independent, multithreaded, dynamic, general-purpose, programming environment."

Although this rather immodest sentence was meant as a humorous reference to all the marketing buzzwords and hoopla surrounding Java, the authors quite seriously go on to back up each of their claims. You can read the entire white paper from which this quote was taken at Sun Microsystems' Web site at **http://java.sun.com/allabout.html.**

What Exactly Is Java?

Depending on whom you talk to, the term Java can mean any of several completely different things, such as the following:

- **JavaScript** JavaScript is an adaptation of Netscape's own scripting language. It consists of Java-like commands embedded directly into your HTML document. Rather than download a precompiled Java executable (more on this later), JavaScript is interpreted on-the-fly, right along with your Web page's HTML, inline images, and so on. Although many of the concepts and syntax in the Java language are applicable to JavaScript, the two are quite separate entities. Strictly speaking, JavaScript and Java are two separate things. Please refer to Chapter 19, "Scripting with JavaScript," for a complete discussion of JavaScript.

- **Stand-alone Java programs** The Java programming language was originally designed and implemented as a language for programming consumer electronics. Stand-alone Java programs do not need to be run from inside a Web page. In fact, things like URLs and the Internet don't necessarily enter into the picture at all!

  Because of Java's inherent runtime safety and platform independence, stand-alone Java language programs can easily enjoy as much success in areas such as embedded systems software and database access middleware as Java applets are already enjoying among Web developers. Two good examples of stand-alone Java programs are the HotJava Web browser and the Jigsaw HTTPD Web server.

- **Java applets** *Applets* are specialized Java programs designed for executing within Internet Web pages. To run a Java applet, you need a Java-enabled Web browser such as Netscape Navigator or Microsoft's Internet Explorer. These and other Web browsers are all capable of handling standard HTML, recognizing applet tags within an HTML Web page, and downloading and executing the specified Java program (or programs) in the context of a Java virtual machine.

  Java applets are a specialized subset of the overall Java development environment. Although you won't see writing code for Java applets in this chapter (refer to Que's

Special Edition Using Java 1.1, Third Edition), you will work through the procedure for including Java applets in your pages.

Why Java?

At the time of this writing (mid 1997), the Internet is still in its infancy as a medium for dynamic mass communications.

The basic technology that makes up the Internet has been around for many years, but it was the introduction of a simple graphical user interface—the Web browser—that suddenly made it so incredibly popular among millions of users worldwide.

Most Web pages now seen on the Internet, however, have a relatively primitive, static character. Take away all the gaudy flying logos and ticker tapes, and you're usually left with one of the following:

- Static HTML, passively displayed by your Web browser
- Simplistic HTML forms
- Graphical imagemaps

N O T E   The advent of Dynamic HTML, the use of the Document Object Model, and more widespread scripting will combine to add much more interactivity to Web pages, as these technologies are adopted by authors. ■

Although forms and imagemaps allow a measure of user interaction, all of the main processing is done remotely on the Web server. For any frequently used site (such as **www.netscape.com**), this incurs a considerable load on the server. Moreover, the final result of all of the server's hard work is more static HTML, which is downloaded only to be passively displayed by your Web browser.

This kind of interaction is not the style of computing preferred by a generation of users weaned on productivity tools such as VisiCalc, Aldus Pagemaker, Microsoft Word, PowerPoint, Lotus Notes, and, above all, PGA Golf. We are accustomed to the benefits of running our applications locally on our own personal computers.

Java promises an alternative model for Web content—a model much closer to the spirit of computer programs people are running on their own PCs. The crucial difference between a Java-based program and a traditional PC application is that Java programs are, by nature, network-aware and truly distributed. As creatures of the Internet, Java programs offer all the benefits of locally executed programs: responsiveness, the capability to take advantage of local computing resources, and so on. Yet at the same time, Java programs break the shackles of being tied to a single PC. Users can suddenly take advantage of computing resources from the entire, global Internet! You'll get a taste of this awesome potential as you continue to learn about writing Java applets.

In the context of the Web, Java applets offer the following advantages:

- Java applets are dynamic, whereas native HTML is relatively static (though this will change as use of Dynamic HTML becomes more common).

Part
IV

Ch
20

- Because they run on the client, not on the server, Java applets can make better use of computing resources.

- Java is designed to be *architecture-neutral*. This is the software equivalent of "one size fits all." For vendors, it means larger potential markets, fewer inventory headaches, and the elimination of costly software porting efforts. For consumers, it means lower costs, increased choices, and greater interoperability between components.

- Although other languages can be considered architecture-neutral, Java programs can typically execute much faster and more efficiently.

   Because a Java program consists of bytecodes, it tends to be smaller and lends itself better to transferring across the Internet. The bytecode scheme also lends itself to far greater levels of runtime optimization than scripting languages. The *Just In Time* Java compilers built into newer Web browsers can make Java programs run almost as fast as native executables.

Basic Language Constructs

Java syntax is very similar to C and C++. At first glance, this makes the language immediately accessible to the millions of practicing C/C++ programmers. However, although Java and C look very much alike, they are not identical and sometimes apparent similarities can be misleading.

The following four tables, 20.2 through 20.5, summarize Java's basic language constructs.

Table 20.2   Basic Language Constructs (Java Types)

Type	Example	Notes
boolean	boolean flag = false;	A Java boolean is just true or false. It cannot be cast to char or int
char	char c[] =	A Java char is a 16-bit {'A','\uu42','C'}; Unicode character. You'll usually use the Java class String instead
byte	byte b = 0x7f;	8-bit signed integer (–127 .. 127)
short	short s = 32767;	16-bit signed integer (–32,768 .. 32767)
int	int i = 2;	32-bit signed integer
long	long l = 2L;	64-bit signed integer. Note the suffix L is be required for a long (decimal) literal
float	float x = 2.0F;	32-bit IEEE754 number. Note the suffix F is required for a float literal
double	double d = 2.0;	64-bit IEEE754 number (15 significant digits)

TIP

Java is a *strongly typed* language. You must explicitly declare the *type* of every single variable that you use, and you can't arbitrarily mix or interconvert types as easily as you can in C++ or Basic.

Java was deliberately engineered this way. In the long run, the use of strong typing tends to eliminate many common bugs and yields safer, more robust software products. But for novice Java programmers, the compiler's strict typing rules can be a source of frustration.

It, therefore, is best to focus on *classes* instead of primitive data types. By thinking at this higher level (at the *class* level), you'll probably need fewer primitive types and they'll be less likely to interact with each other in troublesome ways. By forcing yourself to think in terms of Java classes, you'll save yourself some headaches, and you'll probably end up with simpler, more robust program designs, too!

Table 20.3   Basic Language Constructs (Java Operators)

Operator	Description
.	Member selection
[]	Array subscript
()	Parenthesis/Function call
++, —	Auto-increment/Auto-decrement
*, /, %	Arithmetic: multiply, divide, modulo
+, -,	Arithmetic: add, subtract
<<, >>, >>>	Bitwise: shift left, arithmetic shift right and logical shift right
<=, <, >, >=	Equality: less than or equal to, less than, greater than, greater than or equal to
==, !=	Equality: equal to, not equal to
&, |, ^, ~	Bitwise: AND, OR, Exclusive Or (XOR) and NOT
&&, ||, !	Logical: AND, OR and NOT
? :	Conditional expression
=	Simple assignment
*=,/=, %=, +=, -=, &=, |=, ^=, <<=, >>=,>>>=	Complex assignment

TIP

The operators in Table 20.3 are arranged in order of precedence. For example, the compiler treats the expression 2 + 2 * 2 ^ 2 as 2 + (2 * (2 ^ 2)) by executing 2 XOR 2 first, 2 * the result next, and so on.

In your own Java code, always make liberal use of parentheses to state explicitly the order in which you want the operations in your expression to be carried out. Using parentheses instead of relying on the default precedence hierarchy will help you avoid a common source of bugs.

Table 20.4 Basic Language Constructs (Control Flow)

Construct	Example
if...then...else	if (i >= salesGoal) { ... }
for	for (i = 0; i < maxItems; i++) {...}
while	while (i < salesGoal) { ... }
do...while	do { ... } while (i < salesGoal);
switch (...) case	switch (i) { case 1: ... break; }
break	while (i < salesGoal) { if (I==10) break;...}
continue	while (i < salesGoal) { if (I==10) continue; ... }
labelled break	while (i < salesGoal) { if (I==10) break my_label;...}

Table 20.5 Basic Language Constructs (Java Comments)

Comment style	Format	Notes
C comments	/*...*/	Can span multiple lines
C++ comments	//...	Comment stops at the end of the line; less prone to error
Javadoc comments	/**...*/	Appropriate for header comments; lets you autogenerate program documentation

ON THE WEB

http://java.sun.com/docs/   This site gives you all the details on Sun's official Java documentation, including reference manuals and language tutorials.

Leveraging Java Classes and Packages

Although operators and data types are obviously very important in Java, classes are where the real action is.

In his book, *Object-Oriented Modeling and Design*, James Rumbaugh defined a "class" as describing "...a group of objects with similar properties (attributes), common behavior (operations), common relationships to other objects, and common semantics." An object, on the other hand, is simply an *instance* of a class, dynamically created by the program during runtime. In other words, *classes* are definitions; *objects* are the real thing.

In Java, everything is a class. Unlike C and C++, Java has no structs and no free subprograms. (A free subprogram is a subroutine or function that exists independently of a class.) Most of the power of C++ stems from the simple notion of extending C's basic struct into the notion of a

C++ class, which encapsulates both state (program data) and methods (a program's algorithms) into a single logical entity. Java completes this transition by recognizing that, after you have the power of classes, structs become irrelevant!

Java was designed to be both a simpler and a safer language than C++. Many features of C++ such as multiple inheritance were deliberately left out of Java because Java's authors felt that they could make their new language less complex and make Java programs less prone to common C++ programming and design errors.

Table 20.6 gives a brief overview of Java classes in comparison to C++.

Table 20.6   Java Class versus C Class Constructs

Construct	C++	Java
Class	Yes	Yes
Single Inheritance	Yes	
Multiple Inheritance	Yes	No
Constructors	Yes	Yes
Destructors	Yes	No
Templates	Yes	No
Packages	No	Yes
Interfaces	No	Yes
Packages	No	Yes

Basically, traditional methods force you to think like the machine and break things down into modules, variables, parameters, and the like. Object-oriented methods allow you to think at a much higher level—in terms of objects, their behavior, and how they relate to each other.

The interesting thing is that Java (unlike, for example, C++) forces you to think in an object-oriented style. When you work with Java, you will probably find yourself spending most of your development time figuring out what objects your program needs, and browsing to see if your library already has existing (canned) classes that you can inherit from, thus reusing existing code with little or no additional effort on your part!

Part
IV

Ch
20

This is a marked contrast from traditional programming styles in languages such as FOR-TRAN, C, or Pascal, where the bulk of your effort goes into *decomposing* a problem into modules, and then creating algorithms the modules use to process data. In many subtle (and many not-so-subtle) ways, Java almost forces the programmer to abandon old procedural habits in favor of a more object-oriented perspective.

You'll return to this discussion later. For now, let's get on with the fun stuff—coding and running our very first Java applet!

Where to Get Java Tools

Many tools for creating Java applications now exist. Symantec's Café and Visual Café, Borland C++ 5.0, and Microsoft Visual J++ come immediately to mind as excellent, GUI-based development tools. If you want to start with the basics, the original Java tools are freely available from the creators of Java, Sun Microsystems. These tools are as follows:

■ **javac**   The Java compiler

■ **appletviewer**   A Java virtual machine for testing and debugging your applet

■ **javadoc**   Automatically generates an online manual documenting your program's classes

You can download a free copy of the Java Developer Kit at **http://www.javasoft.com/**.

 Java requires a 32-bit operating system and support for long, case-sensitive file names. In the PC arena, Java supports only Windows 95 or Windows NT.

Using FrontPage Editor and Java Applets

The overview of Java helps you decide whether or not you want to pursue learning the language. In the following, we assume you've learned it and have written, compiled, and tested a few Java applets. Now it's time to use FrontPage Editor to add them to your pages. To do this, use the following procedure:

1. Copy the applet file into the same folder as the page that will include the applet. (The applet file likely has the extension CLASS or CLA; but see the next Caution.) Also, copy into this folder any other files the applet needs to work properly.

2. Choose Insert, Advanced, Java Applet. The Java Applet Properties dialog box appears (see Figure 20.6).

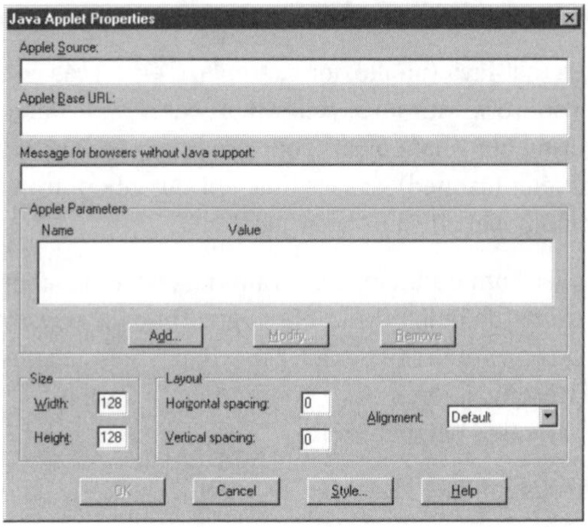

FIG. 20.6

The Applet Properties dialog box lets you install and fine-tune Java applets and their parameters.

3. Type the name of the source file into the Applet Source box and the Applet Base URL if the applet isn't stored in the Web site's root folder.

4. Type an appropriate message in the Message for Browsers without Java Support box.

5. Use the Applets Parameters section to add any required parameter values needed by the applet. Because Java does not provide a mechanism for displaying what the parameters and values are for a given applet, you'll have to consult the documentation that comes with the applet (if you didn't write it yourself) to learn the correct parameter names and the legal values for each parameter.

6. Type values for the applet's size and layout into the appropriate boxes and choose OK. A placeholder for the applet appears.

7. Use the Preview in Browser command to test the applet.

A calculator applet is shown in Figure 20.7. This is a simple applet in the sense that it doesn't use any parameters to modify its appearance or behavior. The HTML code to insert the applet into the page is:

```
<applet code="PocketCalc.class" width="395" height="179"></applet>
```

FIG. 20.7

A simple calculator applet running in a page.

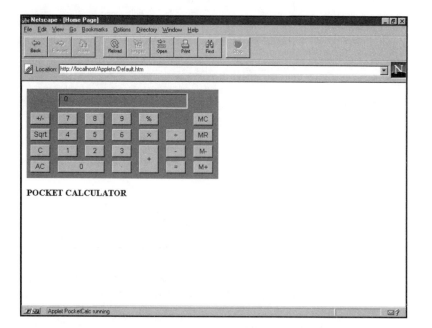

POCKET CALCULATOR

Note that the values for the width and height of the applet, in pixels, must be specified by using the Applet Properties dialog box. This is because the screen area needed by an applet isn't detected automatically by FrontPage Editor and you have to get this information from the applet documentation and add it by hand.

CAUTION

When typing the name into the Applet Properties dialog box, you have to preserve the case and spelling exactly as it is given in the applet documentation. Renaming the applet file in FrontPage Explorer and using that name in the page will cause errors. This is especially important to remember if you unzipped a downloaded applet with an unzip utility that doesn't preserve case or long file names. If this happens, you must restore the correct case and file name before using the applet. In the previous example, the correct applet name is POCKETCALC.CLASS. Calling the applet with POCKETCA.CLA will not work, even if that's the way the applet's name appears in the Web folder.

Two instances of a digital clock applet are shown running in Figure 20.8. This is a somewhat more interesting example because the applet displays parameters can be changed.

FIG. 20.8

Two instances of the same applet showing the differences obtainable by changing the applet parameters.

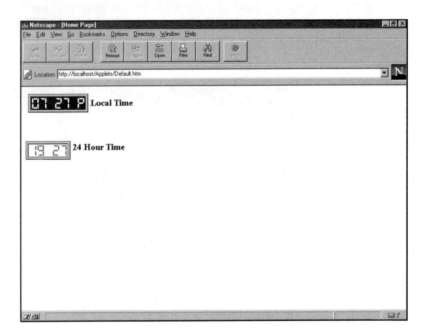

The upper applet uses white LEDs on a black background; the lower is 24-hour time with red LEDs on a white background. The HTML coding for the upper applet is as follows:

```
<applet code="curtime.class" align="absmiddle"
width="126" height="37">
<param name="LEDColor"value="255,255,255">
<param name="MilitaryTime" value="0">
Clock
</applet>
```

Clock in the code is the text that is displayed by browsers that don't support Java. The HTML for the lower applet is as follows:

```
<applet code="curtime.class" align="absmiddle" width="94"
height="37">
<param name="24HourTime" value="1">
<param name="BackColor" value="255,255,255">
<param name="LEDColor" value="255,0,0">
Clock
</applet>
```

Remember that the names of the parameters are defined by the applet code; you have no control over these names. There may be required out-of-bounds values for some parameters, so check the applet documentation. As is clear from the preceding examples, you don't have to write your own applets to begin experimenting with them. There is a growing number of applets, which you can use in your own pages, available for download from the Web. The following are a few of those applet sites:

Gamelan: **http://www.gamelan.com**

Java Applet Rating Service (JARS): **http://www.jars.com/25.htm**

Cup O'Joe: **http://www.cupojoe.com/applets/**

Café Del Sol (Sun Microsystems): **http://www.xm.com/cafe/**

From Here...

As you can see from the last few chapters, there are now some very powerful tools for integrating active content into Web pages. As the Web develops, such content becomes more and more widespread. Active page components do require a lot of bandwidth, though, so remember to use them only when they truly enhance your site. But now it's time to move on, so you can head for the following:

- Chapter 21, "VRML and Java," provides an introduction to the Virtual Reality Modeling Language and its connections to Java.
- Chapter 22, "Building a Web," is where you get down to the business of starting a new Web site by using the FrontPage 98 New Web Wizard to help you get up and running quickly and efficiently.
- Chapter 23, "FrontPage's Web Templates and Wizards," shows you around the creation of specialized Web sites for customer support, projects, and discussion groups.

Part
IV

Ch
20

## CHAPTER 21

VRML and Java

Virtual Reality. You've seen it depicted in television shows, movies, and read about it in the news. You've heard that it's cool, amazing, and the future of computing. Well, it isn't quite at the level Hollywood would like us to believe right now, but VR is definitely for real and there are a lot of impressive things being done with it including games, simulations, and even live 3-D interactive events.

Virtual Reality on the WWW is accomplished by using the Virtual Reality Modeling Language, or VRML, a standard format for the display of 3-D virtual worlds on various computing platforms. As VRML grows in popularity and capability, the Web is being moved beyond the flat 2-D page and into the 3-D, interactive, multiuser VR future.

In this chapter, you will learn about VRML's humble beginnings to where it is today, in addition to being given a glimpse of VRML's future. ■

What VRML Is All About

Learn where VRML came from and where it's going.

Using VRML with FrontPage

Link your FrontPage documents to VRML worlds.

VRML 2.0 data structures and syntax

Learn how VRML works and take a look at the actual syntax of the language.

Coordinate systems and transforms

Transforms are used to position, scale, and rotate objects in a three-dimensional world.

Shapes, sounds, and lights

Discover the basic building blocks of every VRML world.

Java interactivity

Learn to make your VRML world interactive with Java.

The future of VRML

VRMLScript, the External Authoring Interface, and more VRML developments will be covered.

What VRML Is All About

VRML (pronounced "vermal") is the standard file format for creating 3-D graphics on the World Wide Web. Just as HTML is used for text, JPEG and GIF are used for images, WAV is for sounds, and MPEG is used for moving pictures; VRML is used to store information about 3-D scenes. VRML files are stored on ordinary Web servers and are transferred using HTTP.

VRML files are just ordinary text files that have an extension of WRL. A Web server that serves up VRML files needs to be configured to use the MIME type of x-world/x-vrml or the newer model/vrml. If the Web server is not set up correctly to serve VRML files, the end user will only see a text file containing a bunch of scene coordinates. If you have any problems with this, make sure to see the section on server configuration elsewhere in this book.

When a user retrieves a VRML file (by clicking a link in an HTML document, for example), the file is transferred onto the user's machine and a VRML browser is invoked. If the file is embedded into the page using either the <EMBED> or <OBJECT> tags, it may be displayed inline by an ActiveX control or a plug-in. As long as the user has a VRML browser correctly installed and configured on his or her machine, it will launch and retrieve the WRL file from the Web server. Once the scene is loaded, the VRML browser allows the user to travel through it at will, with no further data being transferred from the server.

There are other VR technologies on the Web that are not VRML, but may be confused with it. Apple QuickTimeVR is its own separate technology for VR that is not in any way related to VRML. There is also VRML+ and other extensions to VRML 1.0 from several companies. These extensions are not part of the VRML specification and will not work with VRML 2.0 browsers.

Current releases of both Netscape Communicator and Internet Explorer come equipped with VRML browsers to save you the trouble of downloading one. If you are running an older version of Netscape or IE, or some other browser, you may or may not have a VRML browser. A section at the end of this chapter contains links to sites where you can download some of the more popular VRML browsers.

A Brief History of VRML

The basic idea for VRML originated with Mark Pesce back in 1993. He saw the potential for 3-D graphics on the Web, and realized that a standard file format would be needed. Basically, he wanted to create the VR equivalent of HTML. He got together with Tony Parisi, and together they created Labyrinth, the first crude 3-D Web browser. They demonstrated it at the very first conference on the World Wide Web, and received an enthusiastic response from everyone who saw it.

The next step was the creation of an electronic mailing list, which *Wired* magazine offered to host. After several months of discussion, it was decided to base the first version of the VRML file format on an existing language. Several proposals were put forward, and OpenInventor from Silicon Graphics Incorporated (SGI) was selected.

OpenInventor was extremely large and complex, so a subset of the language was used and extensions were added to make it suitable for use on the Web. Gavin Bell of SGI joined Pesce and Parisi in writing the specifications for VRML 1.0, and people all over the world set about creating VRML browsers.

This was a good first step, but VRML 1.0 was a far cry from *The Lawnmower Man*. VRML 1.0 had many weaknesses, some of which it inherited from OpenInventor, some of which were part of the limited scope of the VRML 1.0 project.

N O T E *The Lawnmower Man* is a movie that contains stunning virtual reality graphics and effects.

First off, by using OpenInventor as its foundation, VRML 1.0 inherited some of that language's weaknesses. The state-accumulation approach that is part and parcel of OpenInventor turned out to be difficult to implement on many platforms. It was also difficult to implement the full lighting model that the spec required. No two VRML browsers would produce exactly the same results for a given scene. Sometimes the results varied dramatically.

Worse than that, however, was the fact that there was no interactivity or movement of any kind beyond navigating the scene and clicking objects to use as hyperlinks to other places on the Web. There was no way to program intelligence or even basic movement into a VRML 1.0 world—so frankly, it was boring. VRML 2.0 changed that state of affairs dramatically.

N O T E VRML 1.0 had no programing capability whatsoever and this seems like an odd omission, but was actually intentional. There was little agreement on programming languages to use for the Web back then, as Java had not yet been invented.

The limitations and problems of VRML 1.0 were clear enough that work began immediately on the creation of VRML 2.0. Several companies created their own proprietary extensions to VRML 1.0 that allowed for some of the interaction and movement, but it was generally agreed that trying to fix VRML 1.0 would be a difficult chore and that a major redesign was required. Half a dozen proposals came in, including some from Microsoft, IBM, Apple, SGI, and Sun. After much discussion and debate, the "Moving Worlds" proposal was selected as the basis for VRML 2.0.

VRML 2.0 resembles VRML 1.0 in syntax, although the semantics are very different.

CAUTION

This chapter is only going to discuss VRML 2.0. VRML 1.0 is not recommended for usage and there is very little reason to even want to create VRML 1.0 content anymore. It is strongly recommended that you only create VRML 2.0 content.

Part

IV

Ch

21

Using VRML with FrontPage

You can link from your Web document to a VRML world as easily as you would link to any other type of document on the Web. Within FrontPage, choose Edit, Hyperlink, or click the Create or Edit Hyperlink button on the toolbar. The Create Link dialog box should appear. When it does, click the World Wide Web tab and enter the URL of the VRML file into the URL field. Make sure you include the WRL extension. Finish creating the link as you would normally.

That's all there is to it. When a user clicks the link you've created, her browser will automatically transfer the VRML world from the server and start up the appropriate plug-in or helper application to let the user view the world and navigate through it.

Creating the link is the easy part; building the world itself is much more complex. FrontPage contains no VRML authoring capability at all, but there are lots of graphical VRML authoring tools out there. I've included links to quite a few of them in the resources section at the end of this chapter. The rest of this chapter will focus on how to create VRML 2.0 worlds from scratch, using nothing more than a text editor such as Notepad. Even if you do not want to hand code all of your VRML, it is valuable to understand how it works. In fact, many people use the graphical world builder programs to do the lion's share of the work and then fine tune their worlds in a text editor.

Once you've built your world, you can simply put it on your Web site the way you would an HTML document, a GIF or JPEG image, or a WAV file.

An Introduction to VRML 2.0

To get some sort of idea how large and complex VRML is, imagine what would be involved in describing the size, location, shape, texture, lighting, and behavioral characteristics of every object in the room with you right now. Now try and put that in a text file so a computer can recreate it. Sounds complicated? It is. Due to that fact, it isn't possible to cover it in any detail in this one chapter. However, this chapter will give you at least a basic understanding of the language and the concepts involved modeling 3-D worlds. If you need to create more sophisticated VRML worlds (and you will!), you should refer to Que's *Special Edition Using VRML*. There are several good online references for VRML as well and the resources section at the end of this chapter will point towards some of the better ones. OK, now let's dig in to building 3-D worlds.

Basic 3-D Modeling Concepts

Before we go head first into VRML syntax, it would be appropriate to discuss 3-D coordinate systems. Because VRML describes scenes in three dimensions, you need to understand how 3-D coordinate systems work in order to use VRML effectively.

As you can see by looking at Figure 21.1, the 3-D coordinate system consists of the X, Y, and Z axes. The X axis goes from left to right, the Y axis goes from bottom to top and the Z axis extends from the the X-Y plane toward the viewer. The place where all three axes intersect is called the *origin*.

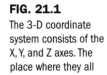

FIG. 21.1
The 3-D coordinate system consists of the X, Y, and Z axes. The place where they all meet is the origin.

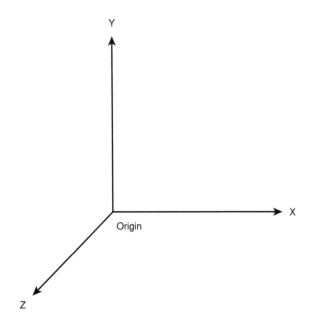

Every point in 3-D space can be specified using three numbers: the coordinates along the X, Y, and Z axes. The origin is located at (0 0 0). In VRML, distances are always represented in meters (a meter is about three feet). If a particular point in a VRML world is at (15.3 27.2 –4.2), then it's 15.3 meters along the X axis, 27.2 meters along the Y axis, and 4.2 meters backwards along the Z axis. This system of coordinates is referred to as the Cartesian coordinate system.

VRML Scene Structure

The most basic building blocks of any VRML scene are *nodes*. Nodes are blocks of text in the VRML file that represent something in the scene. Nodes can represent visible and invisible things. For example, a node can represent a sphere in the scene, a light source, or the behavior something exhibits when touched. The basic VRML data structure is an inverted tree that is composed of nodes.

There are two basic types of nodes: *leaf* and *grouping*. To understand this concept a little better, imagine a wooden chair. Each leg of the chair is its own piece of wood with its own color, shape, and texture, yet all the pieces of wood combined make one individual object, the chair. This is how grouping and leaf nodes work. A leaf node could be used to represent a leg of the chair, while a grouping node allows all the individual legs, as well as the other pieces of wood in the chair, to be treated as one object by combining them. Each grouping node can contain leaf nodes and additional grouping nodes. The result look like an inverted tree.

Leaf nodes generally correspond to the sorts of things you'd expect to find in a 3-D world: shapes, sounds, lights, and so forth. They have a direct effect on your experience of the virtual world by being either visible or audible. A table or chair might be represented by a Shape node,

Part
IV

Ch
21

the ticking of a clock would be created using a Sound node, and the scene would be made visible using one or more Lighting nodes.

Grouping nodes, on the other hand, are completely invisible. You can't see a grouping node when you view a VRML world, but it's there and it has an effect on the positioning and visibility of the leaf nodes below it in the tree. The most common type of grouping node is a Transform, which is used to position shapes, sounds, and lights in the virtual world.

Nodes that are attached to another node are referred to as the *children* of that node, and that node is the *parent* of each of the children. Occasionally, nodes that share a common parent are referred to as *siblings*. Note that in VRML 2.0, the order of children is generally irrelevant, because sibling nodes don't affect each other the way they did in VRML 1.0. However, the ordering of children is still important in certain types of grouping nodes, such as Switch or LOD, which are beyond the scope of this chapter.

There are also nodes that are not really "in" the tree structure, although they're stored there for the sake of convenience. Among these nodes is the Script node, which will be examined in detail in the second half of this chapter.

There are a number of different types of nodes in VRML 2.0 (54 at last count!), and it's possible to define new nodes using the prototype mechanism. Each of these nodes does something specific; fortunately, you don't have to learn very many of them in order to start building simple VRML worlds.

Each type of node has a set of fields that contain values. For example, a Lighting node would have a field that specifies the intensity of the light. If you change the value of that field, the light changes brightness. That's the essence of what behavior in VRML is all about—changing the values of fields in nodes.

VRML Syntax

VRML files are human-readable text, and they use the Unicode character set. Because these files are text, you can print them out and read them, modify them with a text editor, and so forth. IBM, Apple, and a company called Paragraph International have announced that they're working together to create a binary format for VRML 2.0, which will make VRML files much smaller and faster to download. However, this format will still be semantically equivalent to the text format, so world-builders won't have to worry about it.

Everything after a # on any line of a VRML file is treated as a comment and ignored. The only exception is when a # appears inside a quoted string. The # works just like // in a Java program.

The first line of every VRML 2.0 file looks like the following:

```
#VRML V2.0 utf8
```

Notice that this first line begins with a #, so it's a comment. The V2.0 means, "This file conforms to Version 2.0 of the VRML specification." The utf8 refers to the character set encoding.

The rest of the file consists mostly of nodes, as described previously. Each node contains a number of fields that store the node's data, and each field has a specific type. For example, Listing 21.1 shows a typical PointLight node.

Listing 21.1   A *PointLight* Node

```
PointLight
    {
    on TRUE
    intensity 0.75
    location 10 -12 7.5
    color 0.5 0.5 0
    }
```

This node contains four fields. The fact that they're on separate lines is irrelevant; VRML is completely free-format, and anywhere you can have a space, you can also have a tab or a new line. You could just as easily have said:

```
PointLight { on TRUE intensity 0.75 location 10 -12 7.5 color 0.5 0.5 0 }
```

but it would have been harder to read.

The word PointLight indicates what type of node this is. The words on, intensity, location, and color are field names, and each is followed by a value. Notice that the values are different for each field; the on field is a Boolean value (called an SFBool in VRML), and in this case, it has the value TRUE. The intensity field is a floating-point number (an SFFloat in VRML terminology). The location is a *vector*—a set of X, Y, and Z values (called an SFVec3f in VRML), and the color is an SFColor containing the red, green, and blue components of the light.

In other words, the point light source is turned on at 75 percent of its maximum intensity. It's located at 10 meters along the positive X axis (right), 12 meters along the negative Y axis (down), and 7.5 meters along the positive Z axis (toward us). It's a reddish-green color because the red and green values are each at 50 percent of their maximum value and the blue value is set to zero.

Note that any fields which aren't given values have default values assigned to them, as described in the VRML specification. For example, you could have left out the on TRUE because the on field has TRUE as its default value.

You can assign a name to a node using the DEF (for "define") syntax. For example:

```
DEF Fizzbin PointLight { intensity 0.5 }
```

would create a PointLight and assign it the name Fizzbin. You'll see later in this chapter how these names get used when we discuss Instancing.

Types of Fields

VRML supports a number of different types of fields, many of which correspond to data types in Java. Table 21.1 shows the correspondence between Java types and VRML types.

Part
IV

Ch
21

Table 21.1 The Correspondence Between Java Types and VRML Types

Java Type	VRML Type
boolean	SFBool
float	SFFloat
int	SFInt32
String	SFString

As mentioned previously, there are also special data types for 3-D vectors (SFVec3f), colors (SFColor), and rotations (SFRotation). There are also 2-D vectors (SFVec2f). A special data type is used for time (SFTime) and another for bitmapped images (SFImage).

In addition to these single-valued fields (which is what the SF prefix stands for), there are multiple-valued versions of most of the fields (which begin with MF). These multiple-valued fields are arrays of values; for example, an array of vectors would be an MFVec3f. If more than one value is specified for a particular field, the values are surrounded by square brackets, like the following:

```
point [ 0 0 0, 1.3 2.57 -14, 12 17 4.2 ]
```

One other field type that turns out to be very useful is SFNode, which allows fields to have a node as their value. There's also an MFNode, for a field whose value is an array of nodes.

The complete list of VRML 2.0 field types is shown in Table 21.2.

Table 21.2 VRML 2.0 Field Types

VRML Type	Description
SFBool	TRUE or FALSE value
SFInt32	32-bit integer value
SFFloat	Floating-point number
SFString	Character string in double quotes
SFTime	Floating-point number giving the time in seconds
SFVec2f	Two-element vector (used for texture map coordinates)
SFVec3f	Three-element vector (locations, vertices, and more)
SFRotation	Four numbers: a three-element vector plus an angle
SFColor	Three numbers: the red, green, and blue components
SFImage	Bitmapped image
SFNode	A VRML node
MFInt32	Array of 32-bit integers

VRML Type	Description
MFFloat	Array of floating-point numbers
MFString	Array of double-quoted strings
MFVec2f	Array of two-element vectors
MFVec3f	Array of three-element vectors
MFRotation	Array of four-element rotations
MFColor	Array of colors
MFNode	Array of nodes

Translation

Moving a point in space is referred to as *translation*. This is one of the three basic operations you can perform with a `Transform` node; the other two are *scaling* and *rotation*.

Scaling

Scaling means changing the size of an object. Just as you can translate objects along the X, Y, and Z axes, you can also scale them along each of those axes.

Scaling is always represented by three numbers, which are the amount to stretch the object along the X, Y, and Z axes, respectively. A value greater than 1.0 makes the object larger along that axis, and a value less than 1.0 makes it smaller. If you don't want to stretch or shrink an object along a particular axis at all, use a factor of 1.0 (as was done for the Z axis in the previous sphere example).

Rotation

Rotation is more complex than scaling or translation. Rotation always takes place around an axis, but the axis doesn't have to be aligned with one of the axes of the coordinate system. Any arbitrary vector pointing in any direction can be the axis of rotation, and the angle is the amount to rotate the object around that axis. The angle is measured in *radians*. Because there are 3.14159 radians in 180 degrees, you convert degrees to radians by multiplying by 3.14159/180, or about 0.01745.

Transformations

Translation, rotation, and scaling are all *transformations*. VRML stores these transformations in the `Transform` node that was discussed earlier. A single `Transform` can store a translation, a rotation, a scaling operation, or any combination of them. That is, a `Transform` node can scale the nodes below it in the tree, rotate them, translate them, or any combination. The sequence of operations is always the same: the objects in the subtree are first scaled, then rotated, and then translated to their final location. For example, Listing 21.2 shows what a typical `Transform` node might look like.

Part

IV

Ch

21

Listing 21.2   A Typical *Transform* Node

```
Transform
    {
    scale 1 2 3
    rotation 0 1 0 0.7854
    translation 10 0.5 -72.1
    children
        [
        PointLight { }
        Shape { geometry Sphere { } }
        ]
    }
```

This particular `Transform` node has four fields: `scale`, `rotation`, `translation`, and `children`. The `scale` and `translation` fields are vectors (`SFVec3f`), and the `rotation` is an `SFRotation` (consisting of a three-element vector and a floating-point rotation in radians).

Because `Transform` is a grouping node, it has children that are stored in its `children` field. The children are themselves nodes—in this case, a point light source and a shape whose geometry is a sphere (you'll find out more about these things later in this chapter). Both the light and the shape have their location, orientation, and scale set by the fields of the `Transform`. For example, the sphere is scaled by (1 2 3), then rotated by 0.7854 radians around the Y axis (0 1 0). Finally, it's translated 10 meters along X, half a meter along Y, and negative 72.1 meters along Z.

The full `Transform` node is actually more complex than this, because it can specify a center of rotation and an axis for scaling. Those features are beyond the scope of this chapter. There's also a version of `Transform` called `Group`, which simply groups nodes together without performing any transformations on them.

Transformation Hierarchies

Each `Transform` node defines a new coordinate system or frame of reference. The scaling, rotation, and translation are all relative to the parent coordinate system. For example, consider Figure 21.2.

A typical VRML world has a number of different coordinate systems within it. There's the World Coordinate System, of course, but a coordinate system also exists for each `Transform` node in the world. To understand how all this works, take a look at Figure 21.3.

The top-level `Transform` node is used to position the pool table itself in the World Coordinate System. This positioning might involve scaling the table, rotating it to a different orientation, and translating it to a suitable location. Each of the balls on the table has its own `Transform` node for positioning the ball on the table. Each ball, therefore, has its own little coordinate system that is embedded within the coordinate system of the pool table. As the balls move, they move relative to the table's frame of reference. Similarly, the table's coordinate system is embedded within the coordinate system of the room.

FIG. 21.2
Transformations and
coordinate systems are
key ideas in VRML.

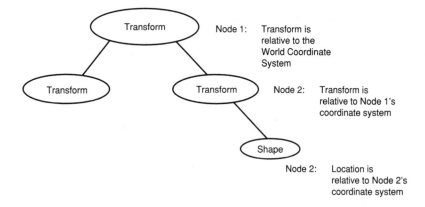

FIG. 21.3
The transformation
hierarchy for a pool
table.

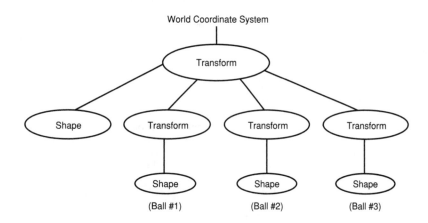

Each of these coordinate systems has its own origin. The coordinate system for each ball
might have its origin at the geometric center of the ball itself. The coordinate system of
the table might have its origin at the geometric center of the table. The coordinate system of
the room might have its origin in the corner near the door. The Transform nodes define the
relationships between these coordinate systems. Listing 21.3 shows this transformation hierarchy as it would appear in a VRML file.

Listing 21.3 A Pool Table and Balls

```
#VRML V2.0 utf8

DirectionalLight { direction -1 -1 -1 }
DirectionalLight { direction 1 1 1 }
```

continues

Listing 21.3   Continued

```
Transform {
    translation 5 1 2   # location of pool table in room
    children [
        Shape {  # Pool table
            appearance Appearance {
                material Material { diffuseColor 0 1 0 }
            }
            geometry Box { size 6 0.1 4 }
        }
        Transform {
            translation 0 0.35 0.75
            children [
                Shape {
                    appearance Appearance {
                        material Material { diffuseColor 1 0 0 }
                    }
                    geometry Sphere { radius 0.3 }
                }
            ]
        }
        Transform {
            translation 1.5 0.35 0
            children [
                Shape {
                    appearance Appearance {
                        material Material { diffuseColor 0 0 1 }
                    }
                    geometry Sphere { radius 0.3 }
                }
            ]
        }
        Transform {
            translation -0.9 0.35 0.45
            children [
                Shape {
                    appearance Appearance {
                        material Material { diffuseColor 1 0 1 }
                    }
                    geometry Sphere { radius 0.3 }
                }
            ]
        }
    ]
}
```

Notice that there are `Transform` nodes in the `children` field of another `Transform` node; this is how the transformation hierarchy is represented.

Understanding how coordinate systems work in VRML is very, very important. When you start animating your VRML world using Java, you'll often be moving and rotating objects by altering the fields of their `Transform` nodes.

Shapes

Among the most common of the leaf nodes is Shape. The Shape node is used to create visible objects. Everything you see in a VRML scene is created with a Shape node.

The Shape node has only two fields: geometry and appearance. The geometry field specifies the geometric description of the object, while the appearance field gives its surface properties. Listing 21.4 shows a typical Shape node:

Listing 21.4   An Example of a *Shape* Node

```
Shape
    {
    geometry Sphere { radius 2 }
    appearance Appearance { material Material { diffuseColor 1 0 0 } }
    }
```

This example creates a red sphere with a radius of two meters. The geometry field has a type of SFNode, and in this case it has a Sphere node as its value. The Sphere has a radius field with a value of 2.0 meters.

The appearance field can take only one type of node as its value: an Appearance node. The Appearance node has several fields, one of which is illustrated here: the material field. The material field can take only a Material node as its value. At first, these appearance Appearance and material Material sequences may seem very odd and redundant, but as you'll see later, these sequences actually turn out to be useful. The other fields of the Appearance node allow us to specify a texture map to use for the shape and information about how the texture map should be scaled, rotated, and translated. You'll learn more about the Appearance node in a later section, under "Appearance."

The Material node specifies only one field in the previous example: the diffuseColor of the sphere. In this case, it has a red component of 1.0 and a value of 0.0 for each of the green and blue components. As you'll see later in this chapter, the Material node can also specify the shininess, transparency, and other surface properties of the shape.

Geometry

There are 10 geometric nodes in VRML. Four of them are straightforward: Sphere, Cone, Cylinder, and Box. There's also a Text node that creates large text in a variety of fonts and styles, an ElevationGrid node that's handy for terrain, and an Extrusion node that allows surfaces of extrusion or revolution to be created. Finally, the PointSet, IndexedLineSet, and IndexedFaceSet nodes let you get right down to the point, line, and polygon level.

Sphere, Cone, Cylinder, and Box   The Sphere node has a radius field that gives the size of the sphere in meters. Remember that this is a radius, not a diameter; the default 1.0 value produces a sphere that's two meters across.

Part
IV

Ch
21

A Cone has a bottomRadius field that gives the radius of the base of the cone. It also has a height and a pair of flags (side and bottom) that indicate whether the sides and/or bottom should be visible.

Like the Cone, the Cylinder node has fields that indicate which parts are visible: bottom, side, and top. This node also has a height and a radius.

The Box node is simple: it has only a size field, which is a three-element vector (an SFVec3f) that gives the X, Y, and Z dimensions of the box. In VRML 1.0, Box was called Cube. That name was misleading, though, because the sides are not necessarily all the same length.

ElevationGrid, Extrusion, and Text   The ElevationGrid node is useful for creating terrain; it stores an array of heights (Y values) that are used to generate a polygonal representation of the landscape. This data is sometimes referred to as a heightfield.

The Extrusion node takes a 2-D cross-section and extrudes it along a path (open or closed) to form a three-dimensional shape.

The Text node creates flat, 2-D text that can be positioned and oriented in the three-dimensional world.

Points, Lines, and Faces   The PointSet node is useful for creating a cloud of individual points, and the IndexedLineSet node is handy for creating geometry that consists entirely of line segments.

However, the most important and widely used geometric node is the IndexedFaceSet. This node allows you to specify any arbitrary shape by listing the vertices of which it's composed and the faces that join the vertices together. Most of the objects you find in a VRML world are IndexedFaceSets, and a large part of any VRML file is made up of long lists of X, Y, and Z coordinates.

Appearance

The Appearance node (which is found only in the appearance field of a Shape node) has three fields. One is used to specify a material for the shape, the second provides a texture map, and the third gives texture transform information.

The example shown in Listing 21.5 will make this clearer.

Listing 21.5   Using the *Appearance* Node

```
#VRML V2.0 utf8

DirectionalLight { direction -1 -1 -1 }
DirectionalLight { direction  1 -1 -1 }
DirectionalLight { direction  0  0 -1 }

Shape {
    geometry Sphere { }
    appearance Appearance {
```

```
        material Material {
            diffuseColor 0 0 0.9
            shininess 0.8
            transparency 0.6
        }
        texture ImageTexture {
            url "brick.bmp"
        }
        textureTransform TextureTransform { scale 5 3 }
    }
}
```

This example creates a blue sphere that is shiny and partially transparent. It applies a brick texture, loaded from a BMP file out on the Web, to the surface of the sphere. The texture coordinates are scaled up, which makes the texture itself smaller. This causes it to get repeated, or *tiled*, across the surface as needed.

In addition to the `diffuseColor`, `shininess`, and `transparency`, a `Material` node can specify the `emissiveColor` (for objects that appear to glow), the `specularColor` (for objects that have a metallic highlight), and an `ambientIntensity` factor (which indicates what fraction of the scene's ambient light should be reflected).

The previous example shows an `ImageTexture`, which loads the texture from an imagemap (in this case, a Windows BMP file). Another alternative would be to use a `MovieTexture` node, which would specify an MPEG file that would produce an animated texture on the surface. You could also use a `PixelTexture` node, in which case you would probably generate the texture map using Java. Generating texture maps is beyond the scope of this chapter.

The `TextureTransform` node allows you to scale the texture coordinates, shift them, and rotate them. This node is like a two-dimensional version of the `Transform` node.

Instancing

VRML files can be pretty big. That means they take a long time to download, and the nodes can take up a lot of memory. Is there some way to reduce this bloat? It turns out that there is. You can reuse parts of the scene by creating additional instances of nodes or complete subtrees.

Earlier on, you saw how it's possible to assign a name to a node using DEF. Once you've done that, you can create another instance of the node by using USE. Listing 21.6 shows an example.

Listing 21.6 An Example of Instancing

```
#VRML V2.0 utf8

DirectionalLight { direction -1 -1 -1 }
DirectionalLight { direction  1 -1 -1 }
```

continues

Listing 21.6   Continued

```
DEF Ball Shape {
    appearance Appearance {
        material Material { diffuseColor 1 0 0 }
    }
    geometry Sphere { }
}

Transform {
    translation -8 0 0
    children [
        USE Ball
    ]
}

Transform {
    translation 8 0 0
    children [
        USE Ball
    ]
}
```

The sphere is created once and then instanced twice—once inside a Transform that shifts it to the left eight meters, and once inside a Transform that shifts it to the right eight meters.

Note that USE does not create a copy of a node; it simply reuses the node in memory. USE does make a difference; if a behavior came along and altered the color of the ball, it would affect all three instances. Figure 21.4 shows this relationship.

FIG. 21.4

Instancing of nodes saves memory.

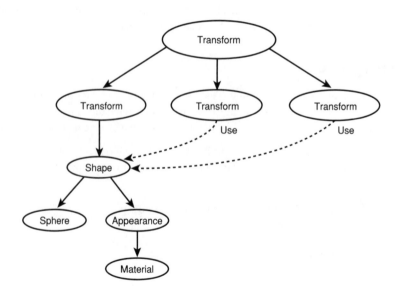

Lights

VRML supports three different types of light sources: `PointLight`, `SpotLight`, and `DirectionalLight`. One important thing to keep in mind is that the more light sources you add to a scene, the more work the computer has to do in order to compute the lighting on each object. You should avoid having more than a few lights turned on at once.

All of the lights have the same basic set of fields: `intensity`, `color`, and `on` (which, not surprisingly, indicates that the light is on). Each light also has an `ambientIntensity`, which indicates how much light it contributes to the ambient illumination in the scene, as well as some `attenuation` factors (which are beyond the scope of this chapter).

PointLight

A `PointLight` has a `location` field that indicates where the light is placed within its parent's coordinate system. `PointLights` radiate equally in all directions.

SpotLight

`SpotLights` are similar to `PointLights`, except they also have a `direction` field that indicates which way they're pointing (again, relative to their parent's coordinate system). `SpotLights` also have some additional information (`beamWidth` and `cutOffAngle`) that describes the cone of light that they produce.

DirectionalLight

Unlike `PointLight` and `SpotLight`, a `DirectionalLight` has no `location`. It appears to come from infinitely far away, and the light it emits travels in a straight line. A `DirectionalLight` puts less of a burden on the rendering engine, which can result in improved performance.

Sound

One of the most important additions to VRML 2.0 is support for sound. Two nodes are used for this purpose: `Sound` and `AudioClip`.

A `Sound` node is a lot like a `SpotLight`, except that it emits sound instead of light. It has a `location`, a `direction` vector, and an `intensity`. It also contains an `AudioClip` node to act as a source for the sound.

An `AudioClip` node gives the URL of the sound source (a WAV file or MIDI data), a human-readable `description` of the sound (for users with no sound capabilities), a `pitch` adjustment, and a flag that indicates whether the sound should `loop`.

Part

IV

Ch

21

Viewpoint

The `Viewpoint` node allows the author of a world to specify a location and orientation from which the scene can be viewed. The `Viewpoint` is part of the transformation hierarchy, and the user is attached to it. In other words, you can move the user around the environment at will by altering the values in the Transform nodes above the Viewpoint.

Other VRML Nodes

There are a number of other nodes in VRML that are beyond the scope of this chapter. They are as follows:

- Fog   Creates fog in the environment.
- Background   Allows you to specify a background image as well as give the colors for the sky and ground.
- NavigationInfo   Lets you control the speed and movement style of the user.
- WorldInfo   Lets you embed arbitrary information (the author's name, copyright, and so forth) in the world in a way that won't get eliminated when comments are stripped out.
- Billboard   A type of Transform that always keeps its local Z axis pointing toward the user. It's useful for geometry that must always be seen head-on.
- Anchor   Allows you to make any object or group of objects in your scene work as a link to other VRML worlds or HTML documents.
- Inline   Lets you bring other VRML worlds into yours (much like the include mechanism in the C programming language).
- Collision   Enables or disables collision detection for its subtrees, allowing you to make some of the shapes solid to prevent the user from passing through them.

There are grouping nodes for automatically switching the level of detail (LOD) or selecting any of several different subtrees (Switch).

The Sensor Nodes

Interactivity is a key element of the VRML 2.0 specification; therefore, a number of nodes are dedicated to detecting various types of events that take place in the virtual environment. These nodes are referred to as *sensors*.

At the moment, there are seven such sensors, as follows:

- CylinderSensor
- PlaneSensor
- ProximitySensor
- SphereSensor
- TimeSensor
- TouchSensor
- VisibilitySensor

Sensors are able to generate *events*, which should be familiar to anyone who's programmed for Windows, the Macintosh, X-Windows, or other windowing environments. An event contains a timestamp (indicating the time at which the event occurred), an indication of the type of event, and event-specific data. All sensors generate events, and they can generate more than one type of event from a single interaction.

A complete description of all the sensors and how they work is beyond the scope of this chapter. However, two sensors in particular are worth a closer look: TouchSensor and TimeSensor.

TouchSensor

A TouchSensor is a node that detects when the user has touched some geometry in the scene. The definition of *touch* is quite open in order to support immersive environments with 3-D pointing devices as well as more conventional desktop metaphors that use a 2-D mouse. "Touching" in a desktop environment is usually done by clicking the object on screen.

The TouchSensor node enables touch detection for all its siblings. In other words, if the TouchSensor is a child of a Transform, it detects touches on any shapes under that same Transform.

Listing 21.7 shows how a TouchSensor would be used.

Listing 21.7 A *TouchSensor* Example

```
#VRML V2.0 utf8
Transform {
    children [
        TouchSensor { }
        Shape { geometry Sphere { } }
        Shape { geometry Box { } }
    ]
}
```

A TouchSensor generates several events, but the two most important ones are isActive and touchTime. The isActive event is an SFBool value that is sent when contact is first made; touchTime is an SFTime value that indicates the time at which contact was made.

A TouchSensor can be used for operating a light switch or a door knob, or for triggering any event that is based on user input.

Clicking either the sphere or the box in the previous example would cause the TouchSensor to send both an isActive event and a touchTime event, as well as several other events that are beyond the scope of this chapter.

TimeSensor

A TimeSensor is unusual in that it's the only sensor that doesn't deal with user input. Instead, it generates events based on the passage of time.

Time is very, very important when doing simulations—especially when it comes to synchronizing events. In VRML, the TimeSensor is the basis for all timing; it's a very flexible and powerful node, but a bit difficult to understand.

The best way to visualize a TimeSensor is to think of it as a kind of clock. It has a startTime and a stopTime. When the current time reaches the startTime, the TimeSensor starts

Part
IV

Ch
21

generating events. It continues until it reaches the stopTime (assuming the stopTime is greater than the startTime). You can enable or disable a TimeSensor by using its enabled field.

Sometimes you want to generate continuous time values. At other times, you want to generate discrete events, say once every five seconds. At still other times, you want to know what fraction of the total time has elapsed. A TimeSensor is able to do all three of these things simultaneously. It does this by generating four different kinds of events, one for each of these three situations and one that indicates when the TimeSensor goes from active to inactive.

The first type of event is simply called time. It gives the system time at which the TimeSensor generated an event.

N O T E   Bear in mind that although time flows continuously in VRML, TimeSensor nodes generate events only sporadically. Most VRML browsers will cause TimeSensors to send events once per rendered frame, but there's no guarantee that this will always be the case. The time value output by a TimeSensor is always correct, but there's no way to be sure you're going to get values at any particular time. ▪

The second type of event is called cycleTime. The TimeSensor has a cycleInterval field, and whenever a cycleInterval has elapsed, the TimeSensor generates a cycleTime event. Again, there are no guarantees that the cycleTime event will be generated at any particular time, only that it will be generated after the cycle has elapsed. The cycleTime is useful for events that have to happen periodically. With loop set to TRUE, the timer will run until it reaches the stopTime, and multiple cycleTime events will be generated. If the stopTime is less than the startTime (it defaults to zero) and loop is TRUE, the timer will run continuously forever and generate a cycleTime event after every cycleInterval.

The third type of event is called fraction_changed. It's a floating-point number between 0.0 and 1.0 that indicates what fraction of the cycleInterval has elapsed. It's generated at the same time as time events.

The final type of event is isActive, which is an SFBool that gets set to TRUE when the TimeSensor starts generating events (such as when the startTime is reached). isActive is set to FALSE when the TimeSensor stops generating events.

Figure 21.5 shows how to conceptualize a TimeSensor node.

FIG. 21.5

The TimeSensor node provides a time base.

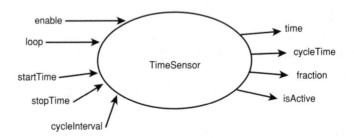

N O T E The TimeSensor is probably the most complex and potentially confusing node in VRML 2.0, and the details of its operation are extremely subtle. Before making extensive use of it, you should read the description in the VRML 2.0 specification. If you still have problems with it, post a message to the **comp.lang.vrml** newsgroup and someone should be able to help. ■

Routes

Now that you're able to generate events from sensors, you need to be able to do something with those events. This is where the ROUTE statement comes in.

A ROUTE is not a node. It's a special statement that tells the VRML browser to connect a field in one node to a field in another node. For example, you could connect a TimeSensor's fraction_changed event output to a light's intensity field, as shown in Listing 21.8.

Listing 21.8   Using a *ROUTE*

```
#VRML V2.0 utf8

Viewpoint { position 0 -1 5 }

DEF Fizzbin TimeSensor { loop TRUE cycleInterval 5 }

DEF Bulb PointLight { location 2 2 2 }

Shape { geometry Sphere { } }

ROUTE Fizzbin.fraction TO Bulb.intensity
```

This example would cause the light intensity to vary continuously, increasing from 0.0 to 1.0 and then jumping back down to zero again.

Note what's happening in this example. The default value for the enabled field of the TimeSensor is TRUE, so the timer is ready to run. Because the default value for startTime is zero and the current time is greater than that, the TimeSensor will be generating events. Because loop is TRUE and the default value for stopTime is zero (which is less than the startTime), the timer will run continuously. The cycleInterval is five seconds, so the fraction_changed value will ramp up from 0.0 to 1.0 over that interval.

The ROUTE statement is what connects the fraction_changed value in the TimeSensor named Fizzbin to the intensity field in the PointLight named Bulb. Note that both ROUTE and TO should be all uppercase.

N O T E Not all fields can be routed to or routed from; for example, the radius field of a Sphere node can't be used as the source or destination of a ROUTE. However, you can change the size of a sphere by altering the scale field of the surrounding Transform node. Check the VRML specification for details. ■

Part
IV

Ch
21

The type of values in the fields referenced in a ROUTE must match. In other words, it's possible to route the TimeSensor's fraction_changed value (an SFFloat) to the PointLight's intensity field (also an SFFloat). However, routing an SFBool (like a TimeSensor's isActive field) to the PointLight's intensity field would have been an error.

Interpolators

There are many times when you want to compute a series of values for some field. For example, you may want to have a flying saucer follow a particular path through space. This is easily accomplished using an *interpolator*.

Every interpolator node in VRML has two arrays: key and keyValue. Each interpolator also has an input, called set_fraction, and an output, called value_changed. If you imagine a 2-D graph with the keys along the horizontal axis and the key values along the vertical axis, you'll have an idea of how an interpolator works (see Figure 21.6).

FIG. 21.6

Linear interpolation computes intermediate values.

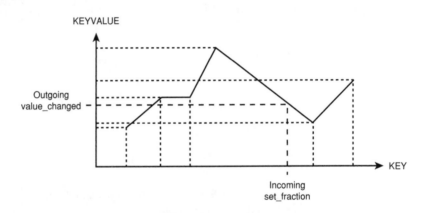

The keys and the key values have a one-to-one relationship. For every key, there's a corresponding keyValue. When an interpolator receives a set_fraction event, the incoming fraction is compared to all of the keys. The two keys on either side of the incoming fraction are found, along with the corresponding key values, and a value is computed that's the same percentage of the way between the key values as the incoming fraction is between the keys. For example, if the incoming fraction value were two-thirds of the way between the 15th and 16th keys, then the output would be two-thirds of the way between the 15th and 16th key values.

There are half a dozen different interpolators in VRML, as follows:

- ColorInterpolator
- CoordinateInterpolator
- NormalInterpolator
- OrientationInterpolator
- PositionInterpolator
- ScalarInterpolator

Each serves a purpose of some kind, but this chapter will use only one—the PositionInterpolator.

In a PositionInterpolator, the key values (and value_changed) are of type SFVec3f—that is, they're 3-D vectors. Listing 21.9 shows an example of a PositionInterpolator at work.

Listing 21.9   A *PositionInterpolator* at Work

```
#VRML V2.0 utf8

DEF Saucer-Transform Transform {
    scale 1 0.25 1
    children [
        Shape {
            geometry Sphere { }
        }
    ]
}

DEF Saucer-Timebase TimeSensor { loop TRUE cycleInterval 5 }

DEF Saucer-Mover
PositionInterpolator {
    key [ 0.0, 0.2, 0.4, 0.6, 0.8, 1.0 ]
    keyValue [ 0 0 0, 0 2 7, -2 2 0, 5 10 -15, 5 5 5, 0 0 0 ]
}

ROUTE Saucer-Timebase.fraction_changed TO Saucer-Mover.set_fraction
ROUTE Saucer-Mover.value_changed TO Saucer-Transform.set_translation
```

The saucer is just a sphere that's been squashed along the Y axis using a scale in the surrounding Transform node. The translation field for the Transform isn't given, so it defaults to (0 0 0). The TimeSensor is just like the one you looked at earlier.

The Saucer-Mover is a PositionInterpolator. It has six keys, going from 0.0 to 1.0 in steps of 0.2. There's no reason why it had to go in fixed-sized steps; any set of values can be used, as long as the values steadily increase.

There are six values that correspond to the six keys. Each one is a three-element vector, giving a particular position value for the saucer.

Once the nodes are defined, you can create the ROUTEs. The first ROUTE connects the TimeSensor's fractional output to the PositionInterpolator's fractional input. As the TimeSensor runs, the input to the PositionInterpolator increases steadily from 0.0 to 1.0, which it reaches after five seconds (the cycleInterval). The second ROUTE connects the value_changed output of the PositionInterpolator to the translation field of the saucer's Transform node; this ROUTE is what lets the interpolator move the saucer. Figure 21.7 shows the relationship between these nodes.

Part
IV

Ch
21

FIG. 21.7
The routes between
nodes for the flying
saucer example.

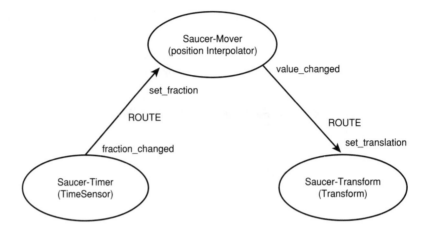

Note that the saucer doesn't jump from one value to another; its location is linearly interpolated
between entries in the PositionInterpolator keyValue field.

Scripts and the Interface to Java

So far, you've seen how to create sensors to detect user input or the passage of time, as well as
how to create interpolators to compute intermediate values for various quantities. You've also
seen how to connect nodes together using a ROUTE. This gives us quite a bit of power, and there
are a number of fun things you can do using nothing more than those basic building blocks.

However, you will eventually want to be able to use the power of the Java programming language in building your VRML worlds. The way you do this is through the Script node.

N O T E   The remainder of this chapter assumes that you are already familiar with programming in
Java. If you aren't, then check out Que's *Special Edition Using Java 1.1* for more details. ▪

The *Script* Node

The Script node is a kind of nexus. Events flow in and out of the node, just as they do for
interpolators or other types of nodes. However, the Script node is special—it allows an actual
program written in Java to process the incoming events and generate the outgoing events.
Figure 21.8 shows the relationship between the Script node in VRML and the Java code that
implements it.

The Script node has only one built-in field that you need to worry about at this stage—url—
which gives the URL of a Java bytecode file somewhere on the Internet. There are a couple of
other fields, but you don't need to worry about them here.

FIG. 21.8

Java accesses VRML through a Script node.

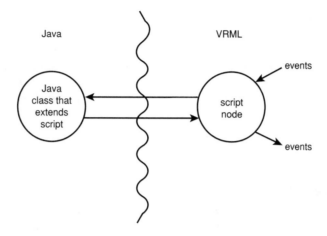

The Script node can also have a number of declarations for incoming and outgoing events, as well as fields that are accessible only by the script. For example, Listing 21.10 shows a Script node that can receive two incoming events (an SFBool and an SFVec3f), and send three outgoing events. It also has two local fields.

Listing 21.10   A *Script* Node

```
#VRML V2.0 utf8
Script {
    url "bigbrain.class"
    eventIn SFBool recomputeEverything
    eventIn SFVec3f spotToBegin
    eventOut SFBool scriptRan
    eventOut MFVec3f computedPositions
    eventOut SFTime lastRanAt
    field SFFloat rateToRunAt 2.5
    field SFInt32 numberOfTimesRun
}
```

The eventIn, eventOut, and field designators are used to identify incoming events, outgoing events, and fields that are private to the Script node.

The Java bytecode file bigbrain.class is loaded in, and the constructor for the class is called. The class should contain a method called initialize(), which will be called before any events are sent to the class. As events arrive at the Script node, they're passed to the processEvent() method of the class. That method looks like this:

```
public void processEvent(Event ev);
```

where ev is an incoming event. An event is defined as follows:

```
class Event {
        public String getName();
        public ConstField getValue();
```

Part

IV

Ch

21

```
        public double getTimeStamp();
}
```

The getName() method returns the name of the incoming event, which is the name the event was given in the Script node in the VRML file. The getTimeStamp() method returns the time at which the event was received at the Script node. The getValue() method returns a ConstField which should then be cast to the actual field type (such as ConstSFBool or ConstMFVec3f).

There are Java classes for each type of VRML field. Each of these classes defines methods for reading (and possibly writing) their values.

A Simple Example

Let's say you want to have a light change to a random intensity whenever the user touches a sphere. VRML itself doesn't have any way to generate random numbers, but Java does (the java.util.Random class). Listing 21.11 shows how you would construct your VRML world.

Listing 21.11   A Simple Random Light

```
#VRML V2.0 utf8

Viewpoint { position 0 -1 5 }

NavigationInfo { headlight FALSE }

DEF RandomBulb DirectionalLight { -1 -1 -1 }

Transform {
    children [
        DEF Touch-me TouchSensor { }
        Shape {
            geometry Sphere { } # something for the light to shine on
        }
    ]
}

DEF Randomizer Script {
     url "RandLight.class"
    eventIn SFBool click
    eventOut SFFloat brightness
}

ROUTE Touch-me.isActive TO Randomizer.click
ROUTE Randomizer.brightness TO RandomBulb.intensity
```

Most of this example should be familiar territory by now. The DirectionalLight is given the name "RandomBulb" using a DEF. A Sphere shape and a TouchSensor are grouped as children of a Transform, which means that touching the Sphere will trigger the TouchSensor.

The Script node is given the name Randomizer, and it has one input (an SFBool called click) and one output (an SFFloat called brightness).

When the RandLight class is first loaded, its constructor is invoked. Next, its initialize() method is called. The initialize() method can do whatever it likes, including send initial events.

Whenever you touch the sphere, the TouchSensor's isActive field is set to TRUE and routed to the script's click eventIn; this in turn causes an event to be sent to the processEvent() method of the RandLight class. The event would have a name of "click," and a value that would be cast to a ConstSFBool. That ConstSFBool would have a value of TRUE, which would be returned by its getValue() method. When you release the button, another event is sent that's identical to the first, but this time with a value of FALSE in the ConstSFBool.

When any of the methods in the RandLight class sets the brightness value (as described later in this chapter), that event gets routed to the intensity field of the PointLight called RandomBulb.

The View from Java Land

Now that you've seen how the VRML end of things works, take a look at it from the Java perspective. You'll return to the random-light project shortly, but first take a little detour through the VRML package.

The VRML package is imported as you would expect:

```
import vrml.*;
import vrml.field.*;
import vrml.node.*;
```

N O T E   The VRML package isn't included in the Java Platform 1.1.3 Core API. ▪

These packages define a number of useful classes. There's a class called Field (derived from Object) that corresponds to a VRML field. From Field there are a number of derived classes, one for each of the basic VRML data types, such as SFBool and SFColor. There are also read-only versions of all those classes; they have a Const prefix, as in ConstSFBool.

The read-only versions of the fields provide a getValue() method that returns a Java data type corresponding to the VRML type. For example, the ConstSFBool class looks like the following:

```
public class ConstSFBool extends Field {
    public boolean getValue();
}
```

The read/write versions of the fields also provide the getValue() method, but in addition they have a setValue() method that takes a parameter (such as a Boolean) and sets it as the value of the field. Doing this causes an event to be sent from the corresponding eventOut of the Script node in the VRML file.

Part
IV

Ch
21

There are, of course, classes that correspond to multiple-valued VRML types such as MFFloat. These classes have the getValue() and setValue() methods, but they also have other methods that let you do things like setting a single element of the array (the set1Value() method). Listing 21.12 shows what the MFVec3f class looks like.

Listing 21.12 The *MFVec3f* Class from the *"vrml.field"* Package

```
public class MFVec3f extends MField
{
    public MFVec3f(float vecs[][]);
    public MFVec3f(float vecs[]);
    public MFVec3f(int size, float vecs[]);

    public void getValue(float vecs[][]);
    public void getValue(float vecs[]);

    public void setValue(float vecs[][]);
    public void setValue(int size, float vecs[]);
    public void setValue(ConstMFVec3f vecs);

    public void get1Value(int index, float vec[]);
    public void get1Value(int index, SFVec3f vec);

    public void set1Value(int index, float x, float y, float z);
    public void set1Value(int index, ConstSFVec3f vec);
    public void set1Value(int index, SFVec3f vec);

    public void addValue(float x, float y, float z);
    public void addValue(ConstSFVec3f vec);
    public void addValue(SFVec3f vec);

    public void insertValue(int index, float x, float y, float z);
    public void insertValue(int index, ConstSFVec3f vec);
    public void insertValue(int index, SFVec3f vec);
}
```

An MFVec3f is an array of three-element vectors (the three elements being the X, Y, and Z components, as you saw earlier). A single entry is a float[], and an MFVec3f is a float[][] type in Java.

Notice that there are three versions of setValue(), one which takes an array of floats, one which takes an array of floats and a count, and one which takes another MFVec3f.

Not only is there a class in the VRML package corresponding to a field in a VRML node, there's also a class for VRML nodes themselves. The Node class provides methods for accessing exposedFields, eventIns, and eventOuts by name. For example, the name of a field in the node is passed to getExposedField(), and it returns a reference to the field. The return value needs to be cast to be of the appropriate type.

There's also a Script class, which is related to Node. When you write Java code to support a Script node, you create a class that's derived from the Script class. The Script class provides a getField() method for accessing a field given its name, and a similar getEventOut() method. It also has an initialize() method, as described earlier, and of course a processEvent() method. There's also a shutdown() method that gets called just before the Script node is discarded, in order to allow the class to clean up after itself.

The Script node also defines two other methods: processEvents() (not to be confused with processEvent()) which is given an array of events and a count so that they may be processed more efficiently than by individual processEvent() calls, and an eventsProcessed() method, which is called after a number of events have been delivered.

And finally, there's a Browser class which provides methods for finding such things as the name and version of the VRML browser that's running, the current frame rate, the URL of the currently loaded world, and so on. You can also add and delete a ROUTE and even load additional VRML code into the world either from a URL or directly from a String.

Back to *RandLight*

Now take a look at some Java code. Listing 21.13 shows the Java source for the RandLight class, which would be stored in a file called RandLight.java.

Listing 21.13   The *RandLight* Class

```
// Code for a VRML Script node to set a light to a random intensity

import vrml.*;
import vrml.field.*;
import vrml.node.*;
import java.util.*;

public class RandLight extends Script {

    Random generator = new Random();

    SFFloat brightness;

    public void initialize() {
        brightness = (SFFloat) getEventOut("brightness");
        brightness.setValue(0.0f);
    }

    public void processEvent(Event ev) {
        if (ev.getName().equals("click")) {
            ConstSFBool value = (ConstSFBool) ev.getValue();
            if ((value.getValue() == false) {  // touch complete
                brightness.setValue(generator.nextFloat());
            }
        }
    }

}
```

The RandLight.java file defines a single class, called RandLight, which extends the Script class defined in the VRML package as described earlier.

The RandLight class contains a random number generator, and it also has an SFFloat called brightness. As described earlier, the Script class has a method called getEventOut(), which retrieves a reference to an eventOut in the Script node in the VRML file using the name of the field (in this case, brightness). Because the type of eventOut (SFBool, SFVec3f, and so on) is unknown, the getEventOut() method simply returns a Field that is then cast to be a field of the appropriate type using (SFFloat). This is then assigned to the variable called brightness, which is of type SFFloat. The variable didn't have to be called brightness, but it's a good idea to keep the field name in the Script node consistent with its corresponding variable in the class that supports that Script node.

Like all read/write classes that correspond to VRML fields, the SFFloat class has a method called setValue(). This method takes a float parameter and stores it as the value of that field. This in turn causes the Script node in VRML to generate an outgoing event, which may be routed somewhere.

Most of the code is straightforward. The initialize() method sets the brightness to zero. The processEvent() method, which gets called when an event arrives at the Script node in VRML, checks for "click" events and sets the brightness to a random value on false clicks (that is, releases of the mouse button). That's all there is to it.

The Towers of Hanoi

Now that you have learned how all the pieces work, it's time to put them together. The remainder of this chapter will take one of the oldest puzzles in recorded history and implement it using the latest in cutting-edge technologies.

The Towers of Hanoi is a very simple puzzle, yet it's intriguing and fun to watch. There are three vertical posts that are standing side by side. On one of the posts is a stack of disks. Each disk has a different diameter. The disks are stacked so that the largest disk is on the bottom, the next largest is on top of it, and so on until the smallest disk is on top.

The goal is to move the entire stack to another post. You can move only one disk at a time, and you are not allowed to place a larger disk on top of a smaller one. Those are the only rules.

If you were moving the stacks by hand, you would start by taking the top-most (smallest) disk from the first post and placing it on the second post. You would then take the next largest disk and place it on the third post. Then you'd take the disk from the second post and place it on the third one. This process would continue until you'd moved all of the disks.

Even though it's fun to watch the stacks being moved, it's a lot less fun to actually do it. (I could watch people work all day!)

Building a VRML/Java application to move the stacks is a multi-stage process. The first step is to build the posts and base, along with some lighting and a nice viewpoint. The disks are added next and, finally, the script that animates them. The process of building this simple world will make use of everything you've learned about in this chapter, including TouchSensors, TimeSensors, PositionInterpolators, Scripts, ROUTE statements, and basic VRML nodes.

The Posts and the Base

The three posts are created using Cylinder nodes, and the base is a Box. The base is positioned first, as shown in Listing 21.14.

Listing 21.14 The Base of the Towers of Hanoi

```
#VRML V2.0 utf8

# Base

Transform {
    translation 0 0.0625 0
    children [
        Shape {
            appearance Appearance {
                material Material { diffuseColor 0.50 0.50 0  }
            }
            geometry Box { size 1.5 0.125 0.5 }
        }
    ]
}
```

The box is 1.5 meters wide (X axis), 0.125 meters high (Y axis), and 0.5 meters deep (Z axis). Because you want it resting on the ground (the X-Z plane), you need to position its lowest point at Y=0. Because the origin of the box is at its geometric center, you need to shift it vertically by half of its height: half of 0.125 is 0.0625, which is why you have a translation of (0 0.0625 0): no translation in X or Z, and a 0.0625 meter translation in Y.

The next step is to add the first post, as shown in Listing 21.15.

Listing 21.15 The Base and One Post

```
# Posts

Transform {
    translation 0 0.375 0
    children DEF Cyl Shape {
        geometry Cylinder { height 0.5 radius 0.035 }
    }
}
```

Part
IV

Ch
21

The first post is a Cylinder that is half a meter high with a radius of 0.035 meters. This shape is assigned the name Cyl, because we'll be making "USE" of it later. You want the bottom of the post to rest on top of the box. Because the origin of the `Cylinder` is at its geometric center, you need to shift it vertically by half of its height (0.25 meters) plus the height of the base (0.125 meters). Because 0.25 plus 0.125 is 0.375, this shape has a translation of (0 0.375 0). Because there's no X or Z translation, the post will be centered over the middle of the box.

Rather than create two more cylinders, let's make use of instancing. Listing 21.16 shows how this works.

Listing 21.16   Two More Posts, Instances of the First

```
Transform {
    translation -0.5 0.375 0
    children USE Cyl
}

Transform {
    translation 0.5 0.375 0
    children USE Cyl
}
```

The `USE Cyl` creates another instance of the post shape that was created earlier. The first `Transform` moves the post to the left (X = –0.5 meters), the second moves the post to the right (X = 0.5 meters), and they both move the posts to the same Y = 0.375 location as the first post.

A `WorldInfo` node is added to store author information and a title for the world, as well as a `NavigationInfo` node to put the user's VRML browser in `FLY` mode and turn off the headlight. A `TouchSensor` is added to the base to give the user a way to start and stop the movement of the disks. Finally, some lights are thrown in. Listing 21.17 shows our world so far.

Listing 21.17   The Complete Base and Posts

```
#VRML V2.0 utf8

WorldInfo {
    title "Towers of Hanoi"
    info "Created by Bernie Roehl (broehl@ece.uwaterloo.ca), July 1996"
}

NavigationInfo { type "FLY" headlight FALSE }

PointLight { location 0.5 0.25 0.5 intensity 6.0 }
PointLight { location -0.5 0.25 0.5 intensity 6.0 }

DirectionalLight { direction -1 -1 -1 intensity 6.0 }

Viewpoint { position 0 0.5 2 }

# Base

Transform {
```

```
            translation 0 0.0625 0
            children [
                DEF TOUCH_SENSOR TouchSensor { }
                Shape {
                    appearance Appearance {
                        material Material { diffuseColor 0.50 0.50 0  }
                    }
                    geometry Box { size 1.5 0.125 0.5 }
                }
            ]
    }

# Posts

Transform {
        translation 0 0.375 0
        children DEF Cyl Shape {
            geometry Cylinder { height 0.5 radius 0.035 }
            }
    }

Transform {
        translation -0.5 0.375 0
        children USE Cyl
    }

Transform {
        translation 0.5 0.375 0
        children USE Cyl
    }
```

The static part of our world is complete. Now it's time to add the moving parts—the disks themselves.

The Disks

For the example, you'll use five disks. The definition of each disk is pretty simple, as shown in Listing 21.18.

Listing 21.18   A Disk

```
DEF Disk1
Transform {
        translation -0.5 0.305 0
        children [
            Shape {
                appearance Appearance {
                    material Material { diffuseColor 0.5 0 0.5 }
                }
                geometry Cylinder { radius 0.12 height 0.04 }
            }
        ]
    }
```

The disks are just cylinders. All of the disks are the same, except for the value of the translation (they're stacked vertically, so the Y component will be different), the value of the radius (each disk is smaller than the one below it), and the diffuseColor of the disk.

There'll be some additional nodes for each disk, but for now let's just stop at the geometry. Now that all of the geometry is in place, it's time to start dealing with behavior.

Adding the Interpolators and TimeSensors

There's going to be a PositionInterpolator for each disk to handle its movement, and it'll be driven by a TimeSensor node. Let's look at the interpolator first. The interpolator for the first disk is shown in Listing 21.19.

Listing 21.19   The *PositionInterpolator* for a Disk

```
DEF Disk1Inter
PositionInterpolator {
     key [ 0, 0.3, 0.6, 1 ]
}
```

There are four keys, spaced roughly 0.3 units apart. Each disk is going to move from its current location to a point immediately above the post it's on. The disk then moves to a point immediately above the post it's moving to, then finally down into position. Four locations, four keys. Notice that no key values are specified; they'll be filled in later by our Java code.

The timer associated with each disk is a TimeSensor, as shown in Listing 21.20.

Listing 21.20   The *TimeSensor* for a Disk

```
DEF Disk1Timer
TimeSensor {
     loop FALSE
     enabled TRUE
     stopTime 1
}
```

The timer is designed to run once each time it's started (which is why its loop field is FALSE). It starts off being enabled. The startTime is not specified; again, this is because it will be filled in from our Java code.

The next step is to connect the TimeSensor to the PositionInterpolator and the PositionInterpolator to the Transform node for the disk. A pair of ROUTE statements does the trick:

```
ROUTE Disk1Timer.fraction_changed TO Disk1Inter.set_fraction
ROUTE Disk1Inter.value_changed TO Disk1.set_translation
```

Our next step is to add a Script node. It will need to be able to update the keyValue field of the PositionInterpolator and the startTime field of the TimeSensor, so let's add a couple of additional ROUTE statements:

```
ROUTE SCRIPT.disk1Start TO Disk1Timer.startTime
ROUTE SCRIPT.disk1Locations TO Disk1Inter.keyValue
```

The Script node called SCRIPT will have a disk1Start field into which it will write the start time for the interpolation. This node will also have a disk1locations field into which it will write the four locations that this disk should move through (current location, above the current post, above the destination post, and final location).

The complete VRML source for a single disk, therefore, looks like Listing 21.21.

Listing 21.21   The Complete VRML Code for a Single Disk

```
DEF Disk1
Transform {
    translation -0.5 0.305 0
    children [
        Shape {
            appearance Appearance {
                material Material { diffuseColor 0.5 0 0.5 }
            }
            geometry Cylinder { radius 0.12 height 0.04 }
        }
    ]
}
DEF Disk1Inter PositionInterpolator { key [ 0, 0.3, 0.6, 1 ] }
DEF Disk1Timer TimeSensor { loop FALSE enabled TRUE stopTime 1 }
ROUTE SCRIPT.disk1Start TO Disk1Timer.startTime
ROUTE Disk1Timer.fraction TO Disk1Inter.set_fraction
ROUTE Disk1Inter.value_changed TO Disk1.set_translation
ROUTE SCRIPT.disk1Locations TO Disk1Inter.keyValue
```

This complete sequence is replicated for each of the five disks. Of course, Disk1 is replaced with Disk2, Disk3, and so on.

Adding the *Script* Node

To keep things simple, there's going to be a single Script node to drive the entire simulation. This node has a large number of inputs and outputs, as shown in Listing 21.22.

Listing 21.22   The *Script* Node for the "Towers of Hanoi"

```
DEF SCRIPT Script {
    url     "Hanoi.class"

    eventIn     SFBool clicked
    eventIn SFTime tick
```

continues

Part
IV

Ch
21

Listing 21.22   Continued

```
    eventOut MFVec3f disk1Locations
    eventOut SFTime disk1Start

    eventOut MFVec3f disk2Locations
    eventOut SFTime disk2Start

    eventOut MFVec3f disk3Locations
    eventOut SFTime disk3Start

    eventOut MFVec3f disk4Locations
    eventOut SFTime disk4Start

    eventOut MFVec3f disk5Locations
    eventOut SFTime disk5Start

}
```

The script is loaded from a file called Hanoi.class, which is the result of compiling Hanoi.java. It's described in excruciating detail later. The clicked eventIn is used to let the Script node know when the user has clicked the base of the posts (to start or stop the simulation). The tick eventIn is used to advance the simulation.

For each disk, there's the set of locations that get routed to the PositionInterpolator's keyValue field as described earlier. There is also a start time that gets routed to the disk's TimeSensor's startTime value.

There's also a ROUTE to connect the TouchSensor on the base to the clicked field of the Script:

```
ROUTE TOUCH_SENSOR.isActive TO SCRIPT.clicked
```

A TimeSensor drives the simulation, as shown in Listing 21.23.

Listing 21.23   The *TimeSensor* which Drives the Simulation

```
DEF TIMEBASE TimeSensor {
    cycleInterval 1.5
    enabled TRUE
    loop TRUE
}
```

This TimeSensor sends a cycleTime event every 1.5 seconds, forever. Each of these cycleTime events triggers the moving of one disk.

And, finally, there's a ROUTE to connect this timer to the Script node's tick field:

```
ROUTE TIMEBASE.cycleTime TO SCRIPT.tick
```

That's it for the VRML end of things. Figure 21.9 shows an overall diagram of how the nodes are connected to each other.

FIG. 21.9
The routing relation-
ships for the Towers of
Hanoi example.

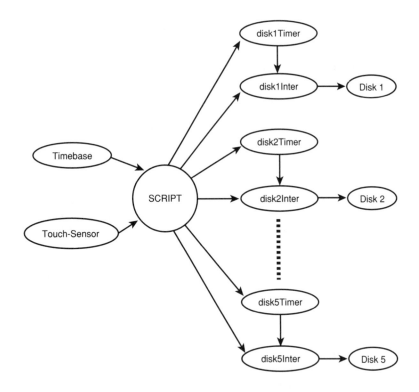

The complete source for HANOI.WRL is found on the CD-ROM that accompanies this book.

Now it's time to create our script in Java.

Hanoi.java

The Towers of Hanoi problem is usually given as an example of the power of *recursion*. An explanation of recursive algorithms is beyond the scope of this chapter, but the basic idea is that a function is able to partition a problem and then call itself to handle each of the two (or more) pieces that result.

The `initialize()` method of our `Hanoi` class will be used to generate the complete sequence of moves and store them in an array. Whenever a message arrives from the `TimeSensor`, the next step in the sequence will be carried out. The `click` message will allow the user to turn us on (or off).

The moves themselves will be stored in three arrays: `disks[]`, `startposts[]`, and `endposts[]`. The `disks[]` array stores the number of the disk (0–4, because there are five disks) that's supposed to be moved. The `startposts[]` and `endposts[]` arrays store the starting and ending post numbers (0 through 2, because there are three posts).

There's also a `postdisks[]` array, which keeps track of the number of disks on each post. It'll be used to compute the height of the top-most disk on each post in order to make the moves.

Part
IV

Ch
21

We'll begin with the standard header and declarations for our data, shown in Listing 21.24.

Listing 21.24 The Beginning of the Hanoi Class

```
import vrml.*;
import vrml.field.*;
import vrml.node.*;

public class Hanoi extends Script {

    // the following three arrays record the moves to be made

    int disks[] = new int[120];       // which disk to move
    int startposts[] = new int[120];  // post to move it from
    int endposts[] = new int[120];    // post to move it to
    int nmoves = 0;          // number of entries used in those three arrays

    int current_move = 0;             // which move you're on now

    boolean forwards = true;          // initially, move from
                                      //   post 0 to post 2

    int postdisks[] = new int[3];     // number of disks on each of the posts
```

Next comes our initialize() method. It just calls a recursive routine called hanoi_r() to do the actual work, then initializes the number of disks on each post. Because all of the disks are on the first post to begin with, and the entries in postdisks[] are all zero initially, this initialization is pretty easy. Listing 21.25 shows how all this works.

Listing 21.25 The *initialize()* Method

```
/***** initialize() builds table of moves *****/

public void initialize() {
   int number_of_disks = 5;
   postdisks[0] = number_of_disks;  // first post has all the disks
   hanoi_r(number_of_disks, 0, 2);  // generate the sequence of moves
}
```

Next, a flag is defined that indicates whether the routine is running. There's also a processEvent() method to handle events coming into the script. These are shown in Listing 21.26.

Listing 21.26 The *processEvent()* Method

```
boolean running = false;  // true if we're running

/***** clicking on the base starts and stops the action *****/
```

```
public void processEvent(Event ev) {
    if (ev.getName().equals("click")) {
        ConstSFBool value = (ConstSFBool) ev.getValue();
        if (value.getValue() == false) {
            running = running ? false : true;   // toggle
        }
        else if (ev.getName().equals("tick"))
        tick(ev.getTimeStamp());
    }
}
```

This code fragment is similar to that from our earlier example. Recall that all readable fields have a getValue() method, which returns a standard Java value. In the case of a ConstSFBool field, the getValue() method returns a Boolean type value. If that value is true, then the user touched the object (by clicking it with the mouse) and if the value is false, the user "untouched" the object (for example, by releasing the mouse). In such a case, the running flag is toggled true or false. If the incoming event is a tick rather than a click, then the next move in the sequence is executed.

When we hit the end of the list of moves, all the disks have been moved to their destination post. At that point, we replay the sequence backwards to return to the original configuration. We then play the sequence forwards again, and so on. This is shown in Listing 21.27.

Listing 21.27 The *tick()* Method

```
/***** at each tick (cycleTime), make the
           next move in the sequence *****/

void tick(double time) {
    if (running == false)
        return;  // do nothing if we're not running
    if (forwards)   // moving from source to destination
        {
        make_move(disks[current_move], startposts[current_move],
                            endposts[current_move], time);
        if (++current_move >= nmoves) {
            current_move = nmoves-1;
            forwards = false;
        }
    }
    else {  // moving in the other direction
        make_move(disks[current_move], endposts[current_move],
                            startposts[current_move], time);
        if (--current_move < 0) {
            current_move = 0;
            forwards = true;
        }
    }
}
```

Part
IV

Ch
21

The `tick()` method does nothing if `running` is `false`. If the sequence is running forward, the `tick()` method makes the move and increments the `current_move` counter. When it hits the last move, it makes the last move into the next one and reverses directions.

If the sequence is running backward, the opposite move is made—from the `endposts[current_move]` post to the `startposts[current_move]` post. The current move is decremented. When the first move is reached, it becomes the next one and again the direction is reversed.

The `make_move()` method is where most of the talking to VRML is done. To start with, some constants are defined for use in array indexing:

```
static final int X = 0, Y = 1, Z = 2;    // elements of an SFVec3f
```

Doing this lets you say (for example) `vector[Y]` to refer to the Y component of the three-element vector, instead of having to say `vector[1]`.

To make a move, it's necesary to fill in the four-element array of locations, each of which is itself an array of three elements (X, Y, and Z). Listing 21.28 shows how the first position for the disk is computed.

Listing 21.28 Finding the Starting Location

```
/**** Routine to make an actual move *****/

void make_move(int disk, int from, int to, double now) {
    float four_steps[][] = { { 0, 0, 0 }, { 0, 0, 0 },
                             { 0, 0, 0 }, { 0, 0, 0 } };

    // compute starting location for disk

    // center post is at x=0, left post is x=-0.5 and
    // right post is x=0.5
    four_steps[0][X] = (from - 1) * 0.5f;

    // vertical position is height of disk (0.04) times
    // number of disks on source post, plus height of base
    four_steps[0][Y] = 0.04f * postdisks[from] + 0.145f;

    // disk is centered on post in Z axis
    four_steps[0][Z] = 0f;
```

Since the center post is at X = 0, the left post is at X = – 0.5, and the right post is at X = 0.5, the expression `(from-1) * 0.5f` gives the X coordinate of the "from" post. Since each disk is 0.04 meters high, and there are `postdisks[from]` disks on the "from" post, and the base is 0.145 units tall, it's easy to compute the current Y component of the disk's location. The Z component is even easier—it's zero, because the disk is centered on the post along that axis.

Computing the destination location is almost exactly the same, as shown in Listing 21.29.

Listing 21.29 Finding the Ending Location

```
// compute ending location for disk

// center post is at x=0, left post is x=-0.5 and
// right post is x=0.5
four_steps[3][X] = (to - 1) * 0.5f;

// vertical position is height of disk (0.04) times
// number of disks on four_steps[0] post, plus height of base
four_steps[3][Y] = 0.04f * postdisks[to] + 0.145f;

// disk is centered on post in Z axis
four_steps[3][Z] = 0f;
```

The intermediate locations are the same, except that the Y coordinates will be one meter up, as shown in Listing 21.30.

Listing 21.30 Finding the Intermediate Locations

```
// now fill in the missing steps

// one meter above the source post
four_steps[1][X] = four_steps[0][0];
four_steps[1][Y] = 1f;
four_steps[1][Z] = 0f;

// one meter above the destination post
four_steps[2][X] = four_steps[3][0];
four_steps[2][Y] = 1f;
four_steps[2][Z] = 0f;
```

The next step is to adjust the count of the number of disks on each post:

```
--postdisks[from];   // one less disk on source post
++postdisks[to];     // one more disk on destination post
```

Finally, the move is made by updating the eventOuts in the Script (which are routed to the disk's PositionInterpolator and TimeSensor). The code to do this is shown in Listing 21.31.

Listing 21.31 Moving the Disk

```
// now move the disk

MFVec3f locations = (MFVec3f) getEventOut("disk"
                              + (disk+1) + "Locations");
locations.setValue(four_steps);
```

continues

Listing 21.31 Continued

```
        SFTime timerStart = (SFTime) getEventOut("disk"
                                      + (disk+1) + "Start");
        timerStart.setValue(now);

    }
```

The name of the eventOut is based on the disk number. Notice that 1 is added to the disk. This is because in the VRML file, the disks were counted starting from 1 instead of 0. The eventOut that is found using getEventOut() is routed to the keyValue field of a PositionInterpolator for the disk in question.

The timer is found in a similar fashion. The value now, which is the timestamp of the event that caused this routine to run, is set as the start time for the timer. This starts the timer going, which drives the interpolator, which moves the disk.

So far so good. All that's needed now is the actual recursive routine for generating the moves. This is shown in Listing 21.32.

Listing 21.32 The Recursive Move-Generator

```
/***** hanoi_r() is a recursive routine for
       generating the moves *****/

// freeposts[starting_post][ending_post] gives which post is unused

static final int[][] freeposts = { { 0, 2, 1 },
                                   { 2, 0, 0 },
                                   { 1, 0, 0 } };

void hanoi_r(int number_of_disks, int starting_post, int goal_post) {
    if (number_of_disks > 0) {  // check for end of recursion
        int free_post = freeposts[starting_post][goal_post];

        hanoi_r(number_of_disks - 1, starting_post, free_post);

        // add this move to the arrays
        disks[nmoves] = number_of_disks - 1;
        startposts[nmoves] = starting_post;
        endposts[nmoves] = goal_post;
        ++nmoves;

        hanoi_r(number_of_disks - 1, free_post, goal_post);
    }
}
```

The freeposts[] array is used to determine which post to use to make the move. If the move is from post 0 to post 2, then post 1 is free. This is represented by freeposts[0][2] having the value 1. Note that the main diagonal of this little matrix (the [0][0], [1][1], and [2][2] elements) will never be used because the `starting_post` and `goal_post` will never be the same.

And that's it—the complete Towers of Hanoi puzzle, solved using Java and VRML. The complete Hanoi.java source code is included on the CD-ROM that comes with this book.

The Bleeding Edge

All of the examples listed in the text of this chapter should work with any final release (not beta) VRML 2.0 browser that supports scripting in Java.

This chapter has barely scratched the surface of VRML. There's lots more to learn about, such as `PROTO` and `EXTERNPROTO`, and there are many other nodes that have only been mentioned in passing. There are also other newer developments on the VRML front such as the External Authoring Interface, using VRML with JavaScript (instead of Java) and the proposed VRMLScript language to allow for lightweight behavioral scripting within a WRL file. VRML promises to be as revolutionary as Java itself, and the combination of the two is very powerful indeed.

From Here...

There is a wealth of VRML Resources on the Internet. You simply need to take some time to browse the Internet. Here is a listing on some helpful resources that you may want to check into.

- **VRMLSite Magazine (http://www.vrmlsite.com/)**   An internet magazine devoted to covering all aspects of VRML.
- **The SDSC VRML Repository (http://www.sdsc.edu/vrml/)**   A very comprehensive site containing links to just about everything you could ever want to know about VRML, including authoring tools, browsers, and documentation.
- **3-D Café (http://www.3dcafe.com)**   One of my favorite sites for getting a hold of object models, cool fonts, and other VRML stuff.
- **SGI's VRML Site (http://vrml.sgi.com)**   Another great VRML resource featuring a weekly animated VRML 2.0 cartoon.
- **comp.lang.vrml**   A newsgroup for general VRML Discussion.
- **sci.virtual-worlds**   A newsgroup for Virtual Reality Information.

Building and Managing a Web

Building a Web

In days of yore (say, 18 months ago), building an entire Web from scratch meant planning out in advance exactly what you wanted to include, then writing each page in succession. Once the pages were done, you'd link them all together through a series of internal hyperlinks. If you wanted graphical unity, you'd have to add the appropriate colors and/or backgrounds to each page.

Advanced planning is still a very good idea, but FrontPage 98 makes it possible to put together a fully functioning Web site, complete with forms programming and graphical themes, by filling in a few dialog boxes. That's because FrontPage 98 offers you, right from the opening screen, a series of wizards for building new Webs. The wizards guide you step by step through some fairly complex designs, and when you've finished you'll have a perfect starting point for developing your Web even further. In other words, the initial drudgery is taken away from you, and as a result, you can concentrate your efforts on developing the site exactly as you want it to appear and function.

Of course, you might already have a Web in place. If so, see Chapter 24, "Working with an Existing Web," for details on importing it into the FrontPage Explorer. The present chapter examines the creation of brand new Webs, taking you through the most complex of the various Web creation wizards. ■

Requirements for Building a Web

To create a Web with FrontPage 98, you must be running a Web server. The server software can reside either on a remote computer accessible over the Internet or on your local computer. FP98 ships with two Web servers, the Microsoft Personal Web Server and the FrontPage Personal Web Server, and either of these is sufficient for developing a site on your local machine. The Microsoft PWS is substantially better, however, so you should install it rather than the older FrontPage PWS. If you have other server software— several good packages are available, many downloadable from the Net— feel free to use it instead. However, this and succeeding chapters assume, for the most part, the existence of the Microsoft PWS.

When you create a Web, you must specify where you want that Web to reside. That is, you must tell it which machine you want your Web served from. Usually this is a remote machine, because a fully accessible Web must be served from a machine that is connected to the Internet on a 24-hour basis and (ideally) at high speed. But if you want to build a local Web, which you do primarily for the sake of testing it out, you can specify the address as **http://localhost**. Addressing is covered later in this chapter.

When you begin the Web creation, FrontPage 98 will automatically start the Personal Web Server to make the Web functional.

Of course, you might have a server in place already. Several server packages are popularly available, including O'Reilly & Associates' WebSite and Netscape's FastTrack. To use all of FrontPage 98's features with these servers, you must install the *server extensions* for them. These installations are handled during the initial FP98 installation process, but if you add a server later you must install the extensions for it manually. The server extensions let the server handle FP98's advanced features, such as forms programming and easy incorporation of ActiveX controls (among other features).

▶ **See** Chapter 1, "Getting Started," **p. 15**

As shipped, FrontPage supports several popular Web servers, including the Netscape Commerce and Communications servers and O'Reilly's WebSite server. As they become available, extensions for most servers will be made available on Microsoft's Web site, at:

http://www.microsoft.com/frontpage/softlib/fs_fp_extensions.htm

If you're running a Web server that isn't supported by a FrontPage extension, you can still make use of FrontPage. Using a machine other than your Web server machine (always a good idea anyway), connect to the Internet and load the FrontPage Personal Web Server, and then create your Web. Once it's completed, you can export it to the Web server machine by using FP98's Publish feature, found in FrontPage Explorer's File menu, or by using the WebPost Wizard that ships with the FrontPage 98 Bonus Pack.

▶ **See** Chapter 27, "Serving Your Web to the World with the Microsoft Personal Web Server," **p. 611**

 T I P   Even if you have a machine with a server supported by FrontPage extensions, you should seriously consider designing, developing, and testing your Webs on a nonpublic machine, using the Microsoft

Personal Web Server that ships with the FrontPage package. This is a much better idea than developing on a live Web server because you can guarantee that nobody will be able to visit it while it's in progress. That way, data is secure, errors and difficulties don't become public, and the final public Web is exactly the one you want people to see.

Starting a New Web Site

To build a Web site, load FrontPage Explorer and select Create a New FrontPage Web from the Getting Started dialog box and click OK. If Explorer was already loaded in memory, choose File, New, FrontPage Web. In both cases, the New FrontPage Web dialog box appears, which you can see in Figure 22.1.

This dialog box gives you several choices, ranging from Empty Web through Corporate Presence Wizard. The difference lies in the relative simplicity or complexity of the possibilities. An empty Web is exactly what its name suggests; you get a Web, but there's nothing in it. Selecting the Corporate Presence Web, on the other hand, launches a wizard that takes you step by step through the initiation of a Web site fully populated by page templates designed specifically for establishing a corporate presence. The choice is yours: Start with nothing or start with a sophisticated template.

Why would anybody forego the templates and start with an empty Web? The answer lies very much in your confidence and creativity, as well as your experience in Web page design. If you've put together a number of Webs and you know exactly how you want to start and what you want to include, a template might very well be a detriment rather than a benefit. But, if you're about to begin your first site or you know very well that you could use a good assistant, by all means, start with a template.

The real problem with templates is that they tend to produce Webs that are very similar to other Webs out there. In fact, as FrontPage becomes more and more popular, there's a very real danger that you'll see all kinds of FrontPage-assisted Web designs that offer nothing distinctive whatsoever. Still, the templates in FrontPage are strong enough that even a moderate amount of tinkering produces something at least worth looking at, which is far better than nothing.

If you select Empty Web, you'll have to create all your Web pages from scratch. This process is covered throughout Part II, "Creating Your Web Pages with FrontPage Editor." For now, adding to an empty Web means choosing Tools, Show FrontPage Editor in Explorer. Once Editor loads, choose File, New Page and proceed from there.

▶ **See** Chapter 4, "Introducing FrontPage Editor," **p. 53**

Using the Wizards for Creating New FrontPage Webs

FrontPage Explorer offers two wizards for creating new Webs: the Corporate Presence Wizard and the Discussion Web Wizard. Both offer an extremely usable system of dialog boxes, and once you've completed them all, you'll have a Web filled with easy-to-alter Web page templates.

To see how these wizards work, you'll now step through the Corporate Presence Wizard, creating a site for an imaginary company called FrontPagers Corporation. In this hypothetical example, you've applied to the InterNIC registry service (**http://rs.internic.net/rs-internic.html**) for the domain name **frontpagers.com**, but you haven't yet received confirmation of ownership. As a result, you'll use the *localhost* feature of Explorer to set the Web site for your local machine, in which case you don't even need to be connected to the Web to create the site (see Step 3 later).

N O T E As of this writing (July 1997), the domain name **frontpagers.com** was still unclaimed, as revealed by a WHOIS search at the InterNIC site. But this book's authors didn't actually buy the name (it costs money), so it might very well be no longer available by the time this book is published. Then again, Microsoft might object if someone *actually* did take it. They can be like that sometimes. ■

Step 1: Load FrontPage Explorer   Start FrontPage Explorer.

Step 2: Start the Corporate Presence Wizard   From the Getting Started dialog box, click the Create a New FrontPage Web option and then OK. If Explorer was already running, you can accomplish the same thing by selecting File, New, FrontPage Web. From the resulting New FrontPage Web dialog box (see Figure 22.1), highlight Corporate Presence Wizard, but don't click OK until after Step 3. The other New Web choices offered by the dialog box are discussed later in this chapter.

FIG. 22.1
The choices shown in the New FrontPage Web dialog box let you begin a new Web easily.

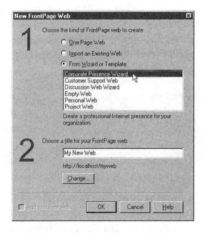

Step 3: Specify a Name and IP Address for Your Web   The bottom third of the New FrontPage Web dialog box is labeled with the large numeral 2. Here, you type a name for your new Web, and you also choose a location where it will reside. First, name the Web, by highlighting the "My New Web" text and typing whatever you want the Web to be called (but you can't use spaces). For the sake of this tutorial, type the word FrontPagers.

The next stage is establishing a location for the Web. This means giving the Web a Uniform Resource Locator (URL) address so that it can be accessed across the Internet. This URL begins with either the IP address for your computer, the domain name that has been assigned to that computer, or the computer's network name, as determined in the Identification area of the Network dialog boxes in Windows 95/NT's Control Panel. (Since the **frontpagers.com** domain name has not actually been assigned to you, you can't use it, but there are other options available.)

One option is to have a Web server on a remote computer already set up to serve your pages. In that case, you would click the <u>C</u>hange button and type the appropriate IP address and directory name. The rest of this tutorial, however, assumes that this is not the case.

▶ **See** Chapter 27, "Serving Your Web to the World with the Microsoft Personal Web Server," **p. 611**

One IP address always available to a Web server, however, is the localhost address of 127.0.0.1 (it's the standard address for a local machine). You may use this IP address to create your Web even if your machine is not currently connected to the Internet. Since FrontPage Explorer lets you copy an entire Web to a different server, the support for localhost means that you can develop the full Web site on an unconnected machine and then transfer it to the server machine later. This is an immensely convenient solution.

To establish a localhost Web, click the <u>C</u>hange button and type 127.0.0.1 in the text box labeled, Please specify the location of the new FrontPage <u>W</u>eb. To the right of that IP address, type the forward-slash character (/) and the letters fp. The full line should now appear 127.0.0.1/fp. This means that you want the Web associated with the localhost address on the server, and placed in a directory called fp. The full URL of the Web will now be http:// 127.0.0.1/fp/ and typing this in your browser will load the file FrontPage will call default.htm. The true full URL, in fact, will be **http://127.0.0.1/fp/default.htm**, which is the same as **http://localhost/fp/default.htm**.

Click OK to return to the New FrontPage Web dialog box. Double-check that everything's in order, including the highlighting of the Corporate Presence Web choice, and then click OK. FrontPage 98 will launch the Corporate Presence Web Wizard.

Step 4: Select the Types of Pages You Want in Your Web   The Corporate Presence Web Wizard walks you through this procedure of creating your Web, beginning with an opening screen that tells you what you're about to do. From this screen, click the <u>N</u>ext button to go to the second stage.

Figure 22.2 shows your first array of choices. You have to create a home page (it's required; thus, the option is grayed out), but you can also include the following types of pages. At this point, you're concerned only with the type of pages you want in your Web. FrontPage creates the pages you decide you need, and they'll all be template pages. After the Web is created, you use FrontPage Editor to change the details on each page, and you use FrontPage Explorer to delete unwanted pages or add new ones.

The page types that you can create from this dialog box are as follows:

- **What's New**   The What's New page, a standard offering on almost all corporate Web sites, gives readers who revisit your site a quick means of determining whether or not you've added information that might be to their benefit. This page is linked from your home page.

- **Products/Services**   The Products/Services page, also very common in business sites, allows you to supply information to your readers about what you're actually selling. This page is linked from your home page.

- **Table of Contents**   Since the Corporate Presence Web is quite extensive, a table of contents page helps your readers find their way around. This page looks like (obviously) a table of contents from a book, with each item linking to the appropriate page.

- **Feedback Form**   The wizard can create a form for users to fill in and comment on the site. You can revise this form in any way you like after it's created.

- **Search Form**   If you have an extensive site, you should provide a search form for users to locate specific information. Note that this isn't a search form for the entire Web (that is, it's not OpenText or AltaVista) but rather to all the pages within your own Web site.

For this example, you'll create all possible pages from this wizard. To do so, click the check boxes for all page types that aren't already checked by default. Click Next to continue.

FIG. 22.2

The more page types you select, the larger your Web site will be.

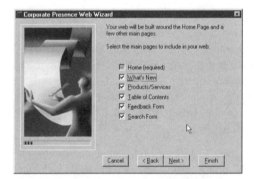

CAUTION

Although this example suggests creating all available pages, in practice you might want to be more selective. Remember that the more pages you create, the more pages you'll need to edit and customize after the Web is in place.

Step 5: Select the Types of Information You Want on Your Home Page   The wizard creates areas on the home page itself for specific kinds of information. The Introduction offers you a place to tell your users what your home page is about. You can also include a Mission Statement about the company and a full Company Profile outlining what the company is like. Finally, the wizard creates Contact Information for users to get in touch with you.

Again, you'll create all possible template areas. Click the check boxes for all types. Click Next to continue.

Step 6: Select Elements for the What's New Page   In the Step 5: Select the Types of Pages You Want in Your Web section, you told the wizard to create a What's New page. Now, you're asked to select the various elements that appear on that page (see Figure 22.3). Web Changes offers an area to tell users what new pages have been added to the Web since their last visit. If your company issues Press Releases (statements designed for magazines and newspapers about your products, services, and corporate activities), mark the appropriate check box. If your company is well served by Articles and Reviews about your products and services or about further research into your product type, include these as well. In this example, mark all of them for the fullest possible What's New page. Click Next to continue.

FIG. 22.3

This dialog box lets you tell your reader exactly what's been going on with your company.

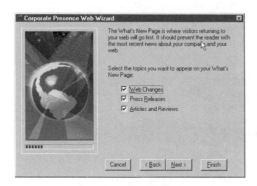

Step 7: Tell the Wizard How Many Products and Services You Want to List   Since you decided in the Step 5: Select the Types of Pages You Want in Your Web section to create a Products/Services page, the dialog box lets you determine how many products and services you want to list. The default is three Products and three Services, but change it to four products and one service. To do so, enter **5** in the Products text box, and enter **1** in the Services text box. Click Next to continue.

Step 8: Enter Information to Be Displayed About the Products and Services   The dialog box shown in Figure 22.4 lets you set the information you want to offer about the products and services included in the Step 7: Tell the Wizard How Many Products and Services You Want to List section. Select Product Image if you have a graphics file with a picture of the product. Pricing Information gives you a place to tell users how much the product costs, while Information Request Form produces a form that potential customers can use to get additional information about the products. For your services, you can offer a list of Capabilities, and you can point to satisfied customers with the Reference Accounts option (but make sure you check with those customers first). A separate Information Request Form lets readers ask for more details about your services.

For this example, check all the items. Click Next to continue.

Step 9: Tell the Wizard How to Construct the Feedback Form   In this step, you specify the fields you want to appear on the feedback form you chose in the Step 5: Select the Types of Pages You Want in Your Web section (see Figure 22.5). The choices are straightforward, and they include Full Name, Job Title, Company Affiliation, Mailing Address, Telephone Number, FAX Number, and E-Mail Address. Keep in mind that the more information you ask users to produce, the less likely it is they'll fill out the form. But for now, since you're after the most complete site possible, mark all of them. Click Next to continue.

FIG. 22.4

Determine in advance how much information you need to provide about each product and service to satisfy your visitors.

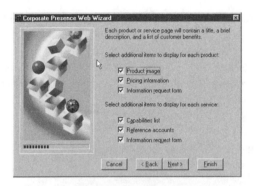

FIG. 22.5

FrontPage creates a feedback form page with all the options you select.

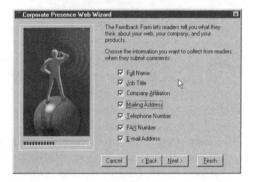

Step 10: Determine Which Format You Want for Forms Information When users fill in the feedback form, the information is stored in one of two ways. You can have it in Web-page format, which is good if you're going to be taking all the information directly from that page. If you want the information to be fed into a spreadsheet or database, however, you can choose tab-delimited format, which is especially useful if you construct a CGI (Common Gateway Interface) script to place it directly into such a package. As your data needs become more extensive, choosing the tab-delimited method becomes important, but for now, mark Web-Page Format to have the information presented as a Web document. You can change this information once you're inside Editor, where you can add multiple methods for receiving the information. Click Next.

Step 11: Set the Options for the Table of Contents Page Keep Page List Up-To-Date Automatically does just what it says; FrontPage monitors your Web, adding pages and links to those pages as you create them. Show Pages Not Linked into Web tells Explorer to display, in its viewing area, pages you've created that you haven't actually linked to the main Web (experimental pages or abandoned pages, for example). Use Bullets for Top-Level Pages puts bullets in the Table of Contents beside the main pages, helping your users navigate through your Web. Select all three, and click Next to continue.

Step 12: Tell the Wizard the Information that Should Be Shown on Each Page Essentially, this dialog box provides a means of adding headers and footers to all the pages in your site (see Figure 22.6). This dialog box lets you specify what elements you want to see on every page in the site, although once the Web is created, you can use Editor to alter or delete these elements on individual pages. If you have a company logo, you might want it to appear on every page, in which case mark Your Company's Logo. The Page Title appears on each page if you want (that is, the HTML title you specify in the document preferences in Editor), and you can include a navigation bar with Links to Your Main Web Pages. At the bottom of the page, you can also offer Links to Your Main Web Pages; you probably don't want this navigation bar both on top and bottom, though, so mark only one. You can also include the E-Mail Address of Your Webmaster (in other words, you), a Copyright Notice that handles the legal thing, and the Date the Page Was Last Modified.

FIG. 22.6
Several options for presentation style are available for global inclusion across your Web.

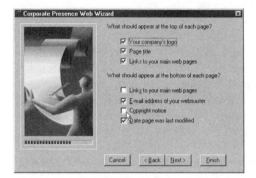

Once again, mark all the boxes, except for the Links to Your Main Web Pages box in the top section of the dialog box (place the navigation bar at the bottom, instead). Click Next to continue.

Step 13: Specify Whether or Not You Want Under Construction Signs on Your Unfinished Pages   One of the most common symbols on the Web is the Under Construction sign. The sign tells you that the page has not yet been completed, but at this stage in the Web's history the sign is so overused that it's practically meaningless. This dialog box lets you decide whether or not you want these signs on your pages. Explorer automatically creates a To Do List of uncompleted pages in your Web, which you can update as you complete them (see Chapter 26, "Managing a Web"). As you do so, the Under Construction sign disappears from these pages. However, some people now find the Under Construction sign a bit objectionable, so you should take a few seconds to decide whether or not you want to include it. If so, choose Yes; if not, choose No. Click Next to continue.

Step 14: Enter the Name and Address of Your Company   The next step is to type the full name, abbreviation, and address of your company. This information appears on your Web pages throughout. The full name of your company goes in the top text box, and the company's street address in the bottom text box. Type "FrontPagers Corporation" in the first, and any address you want in the bottom. In the middle field goes a one-word version of this name, and the obvious choice is, simply, FrontPagers. When you've completed these entries, click the Next button.

Step 15: Complete Your Company Information   In the dialog box following the name and address dialog box, you can enter the Company's Telephone Number and Fax Number, along with the E-Mail Address of Your Webmaster (that is, the individual responsible for maintaining the Web, probably you), and the E-Mail Address for General Info about the company. Typically, the Webmaster's address is webmaster@yourcompany.com, and the information address is info@yourcompany.com, so for this example type in **webmaster@frontpagers.com** and **info@frontpagers.com**, respectively. Keep in mind, however, that the domain name is still not fully registered, so you can't assign e-mail addresses to it. As a result, you might want to enter your own e-mail address instead. When you're done, click Next.

Step 16: Select a Web Theme for Your Site   The next step is to select a theme (optional) for your Web site. A theme establishes common fonts, bullet types, background pattern, and other graphical styles for all the pages in your Web. Every page is created based on the theme you choose, and if you want some pages to appear differently, you can alter them by using the document options in Editor. For this tutorial, click Choose Web Theme and then, when the Choose Theme dialog box loads (see Figure 22.7), select the theme you want from the choices in the left pane (click through them to see the differences). Select the Vivid Colors and Active Graphics options at the bottom left of the dialog box, then click OK. This places you back in the Corporate Presence Web Wizard; click Next to continue to the next stage.

FIG. 22.7

Cycle through the theme choices on the left side. Several will do nicely for your corporate site.

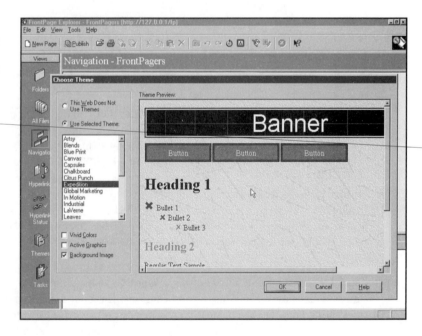

Step 17: Decide Whether or Not to View the To Do List   The last step in the creation of the Corporate Presence Web is to choose if you want the To Do List to appear whenever the Web is loaded into Explorer. It's always a good idea, so mark the check box. This time, though, click

<u>F</u>inish, which has replaced the <u>N</u>ext button, because the wizard has taken you as far as it can go.

Now that you've created the Web, your To Do List appears in the FrontPage Explorer main window. This is the Tasks view, which you can access any time by clicking the Tasks icon in the Views toolbar at the left side of the screen. Here, you are shown the pages you have yet to complete, along with a number of other important details. As explained in detail in Chapter 26, "Managing a Web," you explore how to work with this list, but for now take note of it as an important step in the building of your Web. FrontPage continues to revise this list as you finish some pages and add others. For now, click the Navigation icon in the Views toolbar, and bring this important view to the main window.

▶ **See** Chapter 26, "Managing a Web," **p. 595**

The Navigation View (Figure 22.8) shows what you've been aiming for: a Web in place and ready for action. If you were connected to the Internet, and if you'd assigned this Web to a real IP number instead of the generic localhost number, your site would now be accessible from any computer in the world connected to the Internet. From this point on, all you need to do is modify and alter your new Web, and once it's finished, you can transfer it to a fully operational, 24-hour Web server machine.

FIG. 22.8

Presto! Your new Web is ready for your loving care.

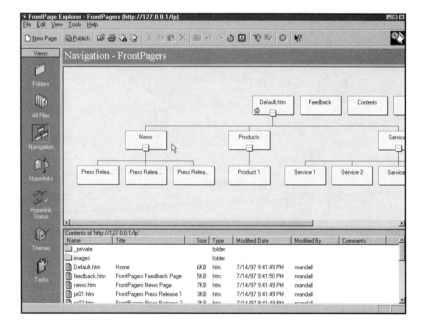

From Here...

In this chapter, you've performed the most fundamental task in FrontPage: creating a Web. Since this is the essential purpose of FrontPage, taking it step by step is an important way to get started, hence the approach taken in this chapter. But, there's far more to building the perfect Web than just running through a wizard, no matter how helpful that wizard may be. First, you'll need to consider which wizard or template is the most suited to your needs, and then you'll have to configure the Web and put it into place. To explore all of these issues and to move beyond them, see the following chapters:

- Chapter 23, "FrontPage's Web Templates and Wizards," examines each of Explorer's templates and wizards in detail.
- Chapter 24, "Working with an Existing Web," shows you how to use FrontPage to develop a Web you've already put in place.
- Chapter 25, "Configuring Your Web," covers the details pertaining to establishing Web permissions and other issues.

FrontPage's Web Templates and Wizards

The Discussion Web Wizard

Create a full chat site and customize it to your liking by using the Discussion Wizard.

Empty Web

If all you want is a starting point, the Empty is for you.

Customer support Web

What does a support Web look like? What should it contain? How should the FrontPage version be altered?

Project Web

How to use Explorer to establish an intranet-like project management site.

Personal Web

Put your resume and your favorite links on the Web with all the necessary trimmings.

In Chapter 22, "Building a Web," you explored the sophistication of FrontPage Explorer's wizard for creating a Corporate Presence Web, and what to do with it once you've stepped through the process. FrontPage also includes several other templates and wizards for Web building, and this chapter explains how to create each of them and what each of them contains. Because these templates have the potential to form the basis of your Webs—even Webs created for larger organizations—knowing what they hold for you is necessary if you want to use FrontPage to its greatest potential.

Once again, there's a downside to all of this. If you let FrontPage create your entire site, and all other FrontPage users decide to do the same, pretty soon your Web site looks almost identical to lots of other sites on the Net. To avoid this problem, let the FrontPage wizards work their magic, but also cast a few of your own design spells to make the Web your own. The whole point about the Web wizards is that they give you something to work with, not that they give you a site that needs no further work. To increase your Web's effectiveness, load each page into the FrontPage Editor and change the wording, the appearance, and even the navigation from page to page. In other words, use the Editor to make your site unique.

After creating a Web, the most effective way of seeing what you've done is to load the Web's home page into a Web browser such as Netscape Navigator or Microsoft Internet Explorer. The Webs created by FrontPage's templates and wizards offer links among the various pages to help you discover what's been built. The home page for each Web is the file named INDEX.HTM within that Web's main directory.

The Discussion Web Wizard

The procedure for creating Webs based on one particular FrontPage wizard, the Corporate Presence Wizard, is covered in Chapter 22, but Explorer offers a second wizard, the Discussion Web Wizard, and it deserves a close look as well. Its purpose and its requirements are considerably different from and significantly more advanced than the Corporate Presence Wizard. The Discussion Web creates an area where readers can participate in a forum on a topic of their choice and, as such, demands some special considerations at the time of creation.

Creating a discussion Web from scratch requires an intimate knowledge of the Discussion Component. This is covered in detail in Chapter 11, "Using FrontPage Components, Forms, and Interactive Page Templates," but its basics are covered here. Essentially, the Discussion Component lets discussion groups come into being in the first place by allowing documents created with FrontPage to cooperate with the Web server in a fully interactive way. The Discussion Web, in fact, demonstrates the practical value of FrontPage, because creating such a Web without FrontPage's Components requires an advanced knowledge of the Common Gateway Interface (CGI). Ultimately, CGI is something you'll want to know, but FrontPage lets you create interactive Web sites of considerable sophistication without some of the most frequently used programming requirements necessary with CGI.

CAUTION

It's important to keep in mind as you build Webs with FrontPage that its CGI capabilities, although immensely useful and time saving, are limited. If you want to develop a full Web site with extensive links to databases and other information sources, you'll need to understand CGI programming. What makes FrontPage so welcome in this regard is that it takes care of the most common CGI elements.

The first step in creating a Discussion Web is to launch your Web server (the Microsoft PWS or another) and choose File, New, FrontPage Web. From the resulting Create New Web dialog box, choose Discussion Web Wizard. This launches the Wizard, which guides you through the creation of this Web much as the Corporate Presence Web Wizard helps you build a Web of that type from scratch. You will need to name your new Web, place it on a server, and inform FrontPage on the initial dialog box whether or not you want to add this Web to the current Web or create an entirely new one.

 To keep easy control over access to your Webs and to help you keep track of HTML files you've added, create new Webs rather than adding them to your existing Web. This places your Web files in a new directory and helps compartmentalize your Web designs.

Types of Pages to Include

The first choices you have to make come from the second screen in the wizard. Here you can choose to include the following pages of information:

- **Submission Form** The submission form is necessary for readers to compose and post articles. You don't have a choice about including this one, but it's the only required element.

- **Table of Contents** This page offers readers an easy-to-navigate area from which to choose whether they want to search or read the discussions, or post a message of their own. If you want, the Discussion Web (on a later dialog box), replaces the current home page of the Web with this table of contents, a recommended procedure if the discussion forum is a primary focus of your Web. You can just as easily offer a link to the contents page from your existing home page (or any other document for that matter), so at this stage it's probably better to say no to that replacement.

- **Search Form** The wizard creates a search form with which your readers can find articles in the Web that have the specified text strings or patterns. If you're planning a site with numerous postings, and especially on a variety of topics, be sure to include this form. Without it, the forum is less useful than it might be.

- **Threaded Replies** Threaded replies are practically a necessity in any kind of discussion forum, especially those with numerous postings. Simply, threads let readers reply to specific articles within a topic, rather than posting only the topic itself. Again, this is a good choice to make, although if your readers don't use threading effectively, you might find that articles tend to be disordered. A well-run discussion forum can make extremely good use of threaded replies, so unless you know why you wouldn't want them, they're always a good idea.

- **Confirmation Page** The confirmation page lets readers know whether or not they've successfully sent their postings to the Web. Without this page, readers' articles are posted without the readers having any way of knowing it. Like the other possible elements, the confirmation page is a good idea, so there's every reason to include it.

Title and Input Fields

After selecting the pages you want to include, you can give your discussion forum a descriptive title. Don't just call it "Discussion"—instead, give it a name that makes its purpose clear to all your readers. This title appears on the top of all pages in the discussion Web, so giving it a bit of thought is worthwhile.

N O T E The name you give to your Web is also the name of the subdirectory FrontPage creates in the main document directory for your Web server. This is normally established at the time of naming your Web, not while giving it the descriptive title described here. Still, you can change the name of this folder to something more meaningful as long as you remember to begin the new name with the underscore character. ■

In the subsequent dialog box, you must decide which input fields you want on the submission form for the Web. At the very least, this form includes a subject field and a comments field. In the subject field, the user enters the topic the posting is about; in the comments field, the user types the actual message. You can determine the possible topics of discussion by including all possibilities in a drop-down menu; this way, you can ensure that all messages are assigned a meaningful topic.

If you want, you can add either a category field or product field to this list. If you have a discussion about a large topic (let's say types of Internet software), you might want to offer categories in addition to subjects. As with subjects, you can specify the available categories through a drop-down menu on the submission form. The product field replaces the category field on the final grouping of input fields, and if you offer several different products to your customers, or if your subjects are product-based rather than category-based, choose the product field instead.

Registration

The most difficult (and perhaps significant) decision you will make when creating a discussion Web is whether or not to insist that your readers register in order to read or post articles. If you choose to do so, you can build a *protected* Web, and all who register will have their user names and passwords built into your Web's permissions area. Your other choice is to leave the Web unprotected, meaning that anyone can post messages.

▶ **See** Chapter 25, "Configuring Your Web." **p. 579**

On the surface of it, an unprotected Web might seem the more desirable choice. After all, the World Wide Web is known as a place of freedom and openness, and offering a discussion group in which users must register might seem inappropriate or even offensive. But, there are a few things to keep in mind about this issue. First, on a purely nice-to-have basis, articles posted within a registered Web automatically include the user's registered names.

More importantly, though, you should consider the purpose of the discussion forum. If you want to offer your readers a place all their own in which to post messages, questions, and suggestions to one another, why not give them a protected area in which to do so? Of course, there's nothing stopping anyone on the Web from registering, so even here the discussion can be considered open. To prevent this, you can build in further password protection to your Web, based on product serial numbers or, possibly, passwords based on the words in a document—or anything else you can devise.

Order of Articles and Home Page

After deciding on registration, you can elect to sort the posted articles from oldest to newest or newest to oldest. They will then appear on the Web's Table of Contents in the chosen order. The former gives a chronological feel to the discussions, and as readers scroll the messages, they can see how the discussion has developed. On the other hand, this means that extended discussions require scrolling at virtually all times, and that could become a bit annoying. Sorting from newest to oldest places the most recent articles at the top of the page, and frequent readers will know what has come before. Generally, newest to oldest is the preferred order.

After making this decision, you're given the option of having the Table of Contents page become the home page for the discussion Web. If you take the option, the Table of Contents page replaces the current home page. This option takes effect only if you have not chosen to add the discussion Web to the current Web when first creating the Web, because if not, the Table of Contents page automatically becomes the home page for a discussion Web on its own.

Search Details

The next dialog box lets you select the criteria by which the search form reports documents a search has located. There are four choices:

Subject

Subject and Size

Subject, Size, and Date

Subject, Size, Date, and Score

All searches reveal the subject of the located article. Adding size gives information about the size of the article in kilobytes. Date adds information about when the article was posted. Score shows the reader a measure of how relevant the article is to the search string entered. A score of 1000 is a direct hit, whereas a score of 100 or less is of lesser relevance.

The choice has to do with how much information you want your server to compute, as well as how much you feel your readers need. For a large discussion forum, the more information you provide, the more useful are the searches. Smaller discussion forums, on the other hand, might very well not need this much information about the search.

Web Theme

As with the Corporate Presence Web shown in Chapter 22, "Building a Web," the wizard for the Discussion Web lets you select the global Web theme for text and link colors, button styles, and the background graphics or color. After selecting the theme, the Discussion Web Wizard carries the design choice one step further by offering a dialog box for the style of a page displaying frames. This dialog box is shown in Figure 23.1.

FIG. 23.1

The Frames dialog box of the Discussion Web Wizard offers four choices.

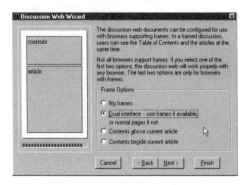

The purpose of this dialog box is to let you display your articles on a Web page that contains frames. Frames, or windows inside a main Web window, were first offered with Netscape Navigator 2.0 but have since become an important design component on the Web in general. All current Web browsers support frames without difficulty, so the hesitation behind designing pages with frames (a hesitation present when they first became possible) should no longer influence your design decisions.

▶ **See** Chapter 11, "Using FrontPage Components, Forms, and Interactive Page Templates." **p. 225**

The Discussion Web Wizard offers to divide the discussion articles page into zero, two, or three frames. If you want to guarantee that all Web users are able to access your articles, choose No Frames. If you want to use frames to their fullest extent, choose either Contents Above Current Article or Contents Beside Current Article (the latter is pictured in Figure 23.1). Both choices create three frames: one showing the page's contents; one, the actual articles; and one, a banner displaying whatever you want. If you want the best of both worlds—an articles page that offers frames to those with frames-capable browsers and an articles page with no frames for those without—choose Dual Interface. The frames in this last case include one showing the contents and another showing the actual text of the articles; the banner frame is not included.

The Self-Registration Form

After making your decision about frames, you've completed the wizard. Clicking Finish starts the actual creation of the Web with all your pages in place. Before the Web is formed, however, the Wizard loads FrontPage Editor with the Web self-registration form loaded (see Figure 23.2). Note that this document is created only if you have chosen the registration option just discussed.

FIG. 23.2

The self-registration form allows your users to register themselves.

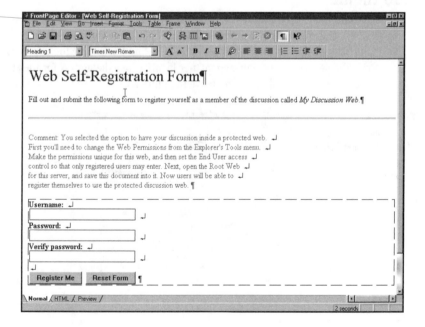

Installing the self-registration form into your Web is a bit complex, and even a bit confusing. Nevertheless, the instructions provided on the template page itself are complete enough to guide you through.

To get the self-registration system working properly, you must first switch from the Editor (don't close it, though) to Explorer, where you'll find the Discussion Web fully created (it's shown in Figure 23.3). Next, you must open the Permissions dialog box in Explorer (from the Tools menu), and choose the option Use Unique Permissions for This Web. Click Apply from that dialog box to set these permissions and click the Users tab to make another change. Here, select the choice Only Registered Users Have Browse Access and click Apply once more. Finally, click OK to close the dialog box. You have now set the permissions in your discussion Web to accommodate registered users.

▶ **See** Chapter 25, "Configuring Your Web." **p. 579**

You probably noticed that in the Users dialog box you can set users manually. What makes the self-registration form particularly useful is that you don't have to do this because the information from the self-registration form is passed to Explorer to create the users automatically. Obviously, this saves you both time and trouble.

Part
V
Ch
23

FIG. 23.3

The completed discussion Web makes a number of pages available for editing.

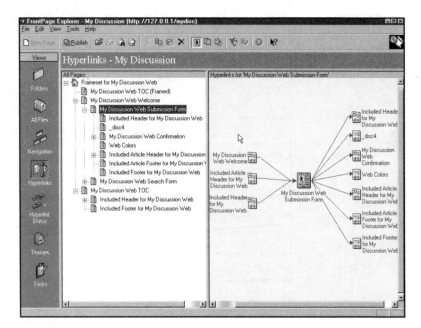

The next step makes the self-registration page available for your readers to add the information necessary to update the Users configuration area.

1. With the Web self-registration form still loaded in FrontPage Editor, return to Explorer.

2. Select File, Open FrontPage Web.

3. From the Getting Started dialog box, click More Webs.

4. From the Open FrontPage Web dialog box, select List Webs (for the current server), then open the root Web of the server.

5. Switch back to Editor.

6. Using the File menu, save the self-registration page into the root Web. Leave the title and file name as suggested by the Save As dialog box.

To assure yourself that the self-registration form is being properly applied to the discussion Web:

1. Click any of the form fields (Username will do) to select it.

2. Right-click in the field and select Form Properties.

3. From the resulting Form Properties dialog box, click Options and you'll see the Options for Registration Form Handler dialog box shown in Figure 23.4. The form should show the same name in the Web name field as you entered when you began building the Web. This ensures that the registrations are applied to that Web alone.

FIG. 23.4

Make sure the correct Web name appears in the Forms Settings dialog box.

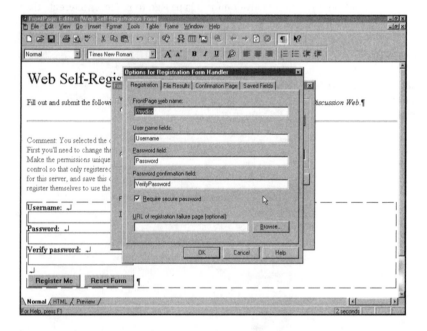

At this point, you should test the self-registration form. With your Web server running, launch a Web browser such as Microsoft Internet Explorer or Netscape Navigator and enter the URL for the file WEBSELF.HTM (that is, the file containing the self-registration form). If you're running the Personal Web Server from the localhost address, for example, enter in the Location Box of your browser the URL **http://localhost/webreg.htm** or **http://127.0.0.1/webreg.htm** (if you changed the name of the file, enter it instead). If you've saved the file to a remote Web server, enter the appropriate IP number or domain name in place of **localhost** or

127.0.0.1. Because the self-registration form was saved to the root Web, you need not enter a path for the file, merely the file name itself. Later, you'll want to link the self-registration file from your home page, so users can access it without typing the file name. The self-registration form is shown in Figure 23.5.

FIG. 23.5

The self-registration form in Internet Explorer 3.02, ready to accept its first registrant.

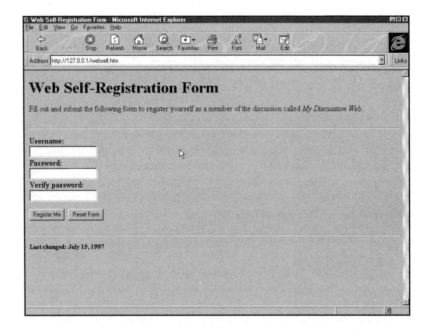

Fill in the username and password fields with whatever names and passwords you want and click the Register Me button. You'll receive a confirmation page showing that the registration has been successful, unless the username is already in the FrontPage database (this happens if you choose your administrator username as a name here, for instance), if your password is shorter than six characters, or if the password doesn't verify because of mistyping.

To see if the user has been registered, open the discussion Web in Explorer and select the Permissions dialog box from the Tools menu. Click the End Users tab and you should see that the registered username now appears in the user area. As more and more users register themselves, this listing increases in size. You may close this dialog box.

Returning to the confirmation page, you'll see that it contains a link to the discussion Web itself. When you click that hyperlink, you'll get a dialog box requiring you to enter a username and password. Choose the newly registered name, and you'll be allowed into the Web. At this stage, you may begin posting messages to the discussion forum, and if you establish more than one username, you can experiment by sending and replying to messages, and then searching them and checking the contents page for results.

Finishing the Discussion Web

With the discussion Web in place, very little remains to put it into place. You'll probably want to edit the registration form and give it a title that clarifies what Web it belongs to, and you'll definitely want to provide a hyperlink from your main home page to both the registration page—to allow users to register—and to the discussion Web's home page—to let them sign in and participate. Assuming you allowed the wizard to establish the table of contents page as the discussion Web's home page, the name of that file will be [WebName]/INDEX.HTM (replace [WebName] with the actual name of the Web, of course). The registration file is in the root Web directory and is named whatever you called it when you saved it to that directory after the completion of the wizard.

Inside the Web, you might want to edit the Contents page and the Welcome page to add some spice to them. Open other pages in Editor and see which ones you want to edit in addition to these. The last change you might want to make is to set password protection for the posting page itself, in order to restrict further who has access to it. This must be done from your Web server's administrator, however, not from within FrontPage.

Posting to a Discussion Web

Once the discussion Web is in place, users can post articles to it. To do so, they need only enter the URL in the Location or Address field of their Web browser (or you can provide a direct link from your home page). Once there, and depending on which frames option you used, they'll see a page that includes existing articles plus hyperlinks to Post a New Article or conduct a Search through the existing articles. If they click an existing article in the Contents frame, they can read that article and then Reply to it or Post a new one. Replies are hierarchically organized (visually threaded) in the Contents frame so that it's clear which reply belongs to which thread.

Deleting Articles from a Discussion Web

Given the ease with which FrontPage's designers let you create a discussion Web, it's surprising they apparently gave no thought to an easy means of managing it. Nobody wants articles to accumulate on these things indefinitely (as many discussions currently on the Web attest), and the Webmaster needs to clean it out once in a while. Posted articles in a FrontPage discussion Web, however, stay there forever and accumulate until the page becomes a nightmare of scrolling. This is something that clearly has to be addressed in future versions.

As it stands, there's only one way to get rid of postings in a discussion Web. First, load the Web into FrontPage Explorer and choose Tools, Web Settings to bring up the FrontPage Web Settings dialog box. Click the Advanced tab and click the option Show Documents in Hidden Directories. Click Apply.

Now enter the Folders view for your discussion Web. Click the subdirectory named _disc$x$ (x may be any number). Inside, you'll see files named with eight digits before the HTM extension. These are the postings. The first posting, for example, will be 00000001.htm, the hundredth posting 00000100.htm, and so on. Deleting the file deletes the posting from the Web.

How do you know which file belongs to which posting? Using your Web browser, enter the discussion Web in your browser and click the posting you want to delete, to bring it up for reading. Call up the properties for that posting (the manner differs for each Web browser), and the resulting box tells you the name of the associated HTM file. Go back to the Folders view in FrontPage Explorer and delete the file. You can also do this in Windows Explorer, if you prefer.

Empty Web and One Page Web

Two of FrontPage's Web templates are designed to offer only minimal help to you as Web designer. The Empty Web template creates, as its name suggests, a Web with nothing in it. Its only purpose is to create the directory (which it takes from your Web's name) into which all documents will be stored, after which it's your task to develop the Web as you want. The One Page Web, available at the top of the New FrontPage Web dialog box as a option button, adds only one element to this: a home page that gives you a place to start. This home page, however, doesn't actually include any text or graphics; it's simply an empty HTML page, waiting for your design decisions.

Customer Support Web

Creating the customer support Web does not require working through a wizard; in fact, there is no corresponding wizard. To create this Web, select Customer Support Web from the New Web dialog box, and FrontPage creates a Web that looks like that shown in Figure 23.6.

FIG. 23.6
The customer support Web features all you need to offer top-notch service.

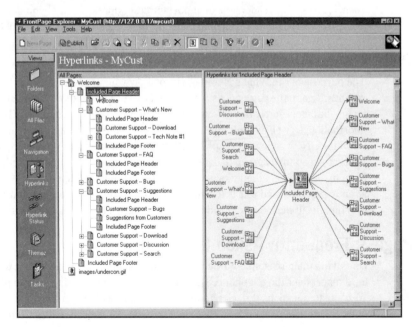

Part
V

Ch
23

This Web is designed to let you provide a full range of services for your clients. Its design, however, replicates the many computer company sites on the Web, and if you have a different kind of product or service, not all the pages will be of use to you. They can be modified, of course, and certainly two or more of the pages will be useful, but expect to do a significant amount of redesign on this Web. If you plan to offer software or hardware products, on the other hand, the Customer Service Web gets you halfway to your goal.

To make the suggested changes to this Web, you'll need to load each individual page into FrontPage Editor, usually by double-clicking the page's icon from Explorer's Link View. To get an idea of what the page looks like, load it into your Web browser by using the appropriate URL with the path /[Support Web Name]/INDEX.HTM.

Page 1: Welcome

The first page in the Customer Service Web (INDEX.HTM) welcomes your users to your site and provides a set of links to all the other pages on the site. This page provides a general welcome, along with parenthesized fields which you are expected to alter to customize the page for your own company. Begin at the top of the file, give a clear company name and add a logo if you have one, and be sure to use the Page and Web Properties features to give your site a color and graphical thematic unity. Be sure to change the copyright information at the bottom of the page as well.

▶ **See** Chapter 5, "Developing the Basic Page: Text, Lists, and Hyperlinks." **p. 71**

The important thing to realize is that this page provides the entry to the entire Web site. As such, it gives your readers an all important first impression, and you don't want to let that get away. Work hard on this Welcome page, perhaps even harder than on all the rest.

Page 2: What's New

The purpose of the What's New page is to show your readers what has been added to the site recently. Again, the page needs a great deal of work to make it consistent with your company's image, but more importantly, you must decide precisely how to display the links to the new information, as well as (and this is crucial) how often to update. In a true customer service site, the What's New page is perhaps the single most important component of the site. If you don't intend to keep the page up to date regularly, get rid of it and erase all links to it. If you do keep it up, make sure that the links point correctly to their corresponding documents. One link is already provided, and this is to a template for a technical document, complete with inline graphic. By all means, use this document as a basis, but if you have your own, use it instead.

Page 3: Frequently Asked Questions

One of the main reasons for offering customer support over the Web is to minimize the need for support over the telephone. The most effective way of doing so is to provide answers on the Web site to questions the telephone support staff receive regularly. The FAQ (Frequently Asked Questions) page of the customer support site is designed as a template to help you put these together. This page offers a set of questions early in the page that contain internal links to answers further down the page. This is a good structure by which to get started, but if questions demand more than a paragraph or two of response, it would be better to link to other, longer documents instead.

Page 4: Bug Report

If your business is to sell software, you'll inevitably run into the problem known as *bugs* or imperfections. The purpose of the Bug Report page in the Customer Service Web is to allow your users to report bugs they find in your product. It's not acceptable for software companies to insist that their product does not contain bugs, because all computer users know differently, and generally accept the fact that bugs exist. This page shows that you're up-front about trying to fix them, rather than suggesting that they're not there in the first place.

The Bug Report page offers a form for readers to fill in and submit. This form is shown in Netscape Navigator in Figure 23.7, and it contains two drop-down selection menus and several fill-in fields. Your primary task, aside from introducing the bug report according to your company policies and redesigning the page according to a consistent color and graphic scheme, is to customize the form to invite the information you need. Spend some time considering exactly that question, because an effective bug report form can optimize the usefulness, and thus the salability, of your product.

FIG. 23.7
The Bug Report form offers several fields for readers to select.

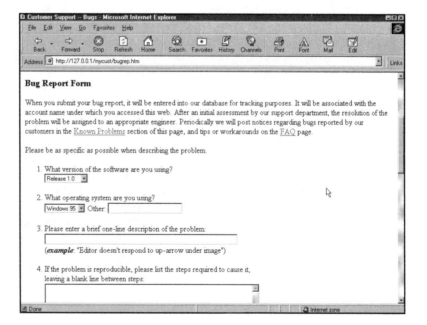

Page 5: Suggestions

If you're genuinely not interested in what your site's visitors think of your Web site or your products, get rid of this page immediately. There's nothing worse than offering a suggestion page that you never pay attention to. Visitors who make suggestions want to feel that they're making a difference. If you are interested in your visitors suggestions, however (and any good service-oriented company should be), customize this page to invite the feedback you need to make your products or services more successful. Of particular importance is customizing the category portion of the form because through this drop-down menu, you encourage readers to speak up about specific topics.

Page 6: Download

It's become a given on the Internet that if you want to sell software, you have to let users download at least a demo version so they can try it out. When people purchase your software, you must also provide downloadable upgrades from your Web site. The Download page lets you provide these services, although to make it work properly, you'll have to customize it significantly. The template page provides a simple suggestion of how to deal with different file formats and multiple download items, but visiting any software or hardware company on the Web will give you much better ideas about how to offer your product.

> **CAUTION**
>
> Failing to test the Download page causes a negative impression from your readers. If a click does not produce the software, your users will be angry or at least disappointed. Be sure to test from more than one machine. Log in to your site through a modem and make sure everything works right.

Page 7: Discussion

The Discussion page on the Customer Service Web offers a place for your readers to discuss your products and services with other users and with company representatives. Note that, although there's no requirement in the Web itself for a company representative to take part, it's extremely important that one be present to avoid the embarrassing possibility of customers saying incorrect or demeaning things about your products. The discussion area resembles one created with the full discussion Web examined earlier in this chapter, and you can customize it to provide as full a discussion forum as you want, including offering user registration.

N O T E   As with the Download page, be absolutely certain the discussion area works well before making it public, and also be sure that you intend to pay attention to the discussion. ■

Page 8: Search

Figure 23.8 shows a portion of the Search page created by the Customer Service Web template. It's simple, but as the description of the query language at the bottom of the page demonstrates, it's not simplistic. You can't possibly know how or even if your readers will make use of this page, but it's a good idea to have one, and it's a good idea also to construct pages that anticipate reader searches, building in common keywords and text strings.

FIG. 23.8
The Search page contains a description of the query language used by FrontPage.

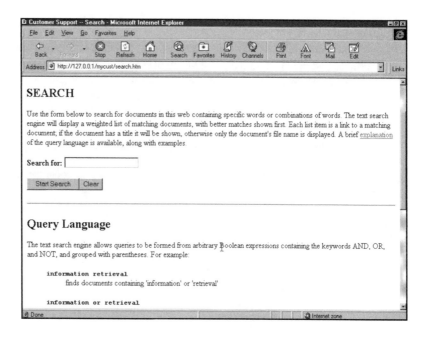

Project Web

The Project Web offers a means for members of a team project to keep in touch with each other, and perhaps more importantly, a place for you to put all information about the project that everyone involved should be able to retrieve. Its primary use is in an *intranet*, which is a Web site that exists within an organization and which typically does not offer access to users outside the organization. For some organizations, the Project Web is sufficient to replace more complex software packages such as Lotus Notes, but even within these organizations, a Project Web might suffice for a small working group collaborating on a specific project or portion of a project.

Page 1: Home

The template home page for the Project Web offers a brief description and a What's New area, as well as a series of links to the other pages in the Web. Because a Project Web is meant primarily as an internal site, there's not as much need for extensive editing to appeal to customers. The design decisions made here should reflect your management goals of professionalism and efficiency, and should be less marketing-driven than the customer support site. Members of the Project Web are usually your co-workers and employees of the same company as yourself, and will expect a certain amount of cutting through the hype. The efficiency will be displayed in providing ease of access to information and by constantly updating the What's New information.

Page 2: Members

The Members page of the Project Web offers an alphabetical listing of those involved in the project, and the links from that list lead to the type of generic profile shown in Figure 23.9. By replacing all the names with real names, the pictures with real pictures, and the e-mail addresses and personal URLs with valid ones, you can create a useful, dynamic page of information that members can share. From this page, members can e-mail one another and visit one another's home page, and the page can act as a team bond. Be absolutely certain, however, that all information is correct, or risk anything from embarrassment to downright anger.

FIG. 23.9

From the Members page, team members can interact with one another.

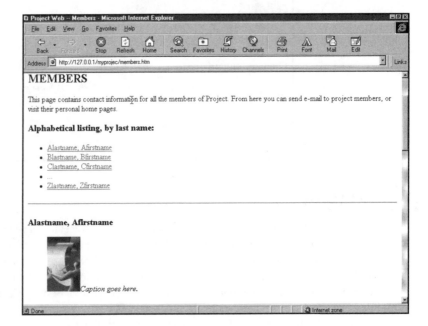

Page 3: Schedule

What's a project without a schedule? Nothing, obviously, so the template creates a schedule page for you. On this page are three main sections: a list of goals and activities in the current and following weeks, a showcase of upcoming events pertaining to the project, and a listing of milestones and deliverables.

The function of the schedule, of course, is to keep all project members aware of progress to date and necessary progress to come. To that end, it's imperative that this page be kept updated constantly. Slip here, and you risk losing the very credibility of the Web site. The best bet is to alter this page as soon as you can to fit the project you're running rather than the one the template suggests and keep returning to it to keep the project team focused.

Page 4: Status

Assuming the project is large and long enough, you'll probably be required to file status reports as the work continues. The Status page offers a place to collect those reports and make them available to members of the project team. The titles of the hyperlinks on the template page assume monthly and quarterly reports for the current year, quarterly and annual reports for last year, and annual reports for previous years of the project. The links on the page don't lead anywhere, and it's your job to supply the actual documents. Clearly, this page is only as useful as your status reports allow, and you might not want it as part of your Web if you have no reports to include. But it can be easily modified to allow weekly reports, subteam reports, and so forth.

Part
V

Ch

23

Page 5: Archive

If your project team has developed a significant number of documents, prototypes, programs, tools, and other demonstrable items, you will want to offer them as a project archive. The Archive page (see Figure 23.10) is designed as a kind of catch-all for this kind of material. Each internal link leads to a description of the item and further links to the documents in a variety of formats. Obviously, it's up to you to provide the materials, and in all likelihood, you'll want to completely revamp the presentation of this page, but it's an excellent suggestion for a page within the Web.

FIG. 23.10

The Archive page offers links to documents in various formats.

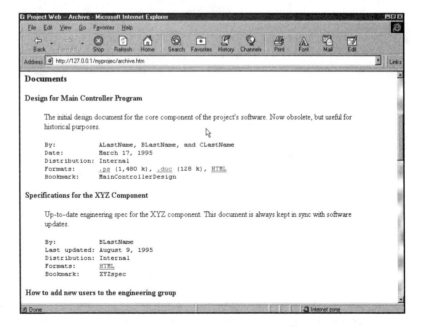

Page 6: Search

The Search page is identical to the one offered in the Customer Support Web previously discussed, and requires only a minor degree of tinkering. Otherwise, just leave it as it stands.

Page 7: Discussions

Page 7 of the Customer Support Web was also a discussion area, but the difference here is that the Discussions page of the Project Web contains two discussion groups already built in. The principle is to provide a separate discussion forum for as many topics as your project members require, and the page describes each forum and invites participation from the appropriate parties. You can add as many discussion groups as you want, but starting with two or three seems the best idea, to keep things under control.

Personal Web

The Personal Web is, essentially, a combination resume and special interest Web. Figure 23.11 shows the generic home page information offered by this page, all of which is in need of customization before this Web becomes public.

FIG. 23.11

The Personal Web is little more than a resume, but a complete one.

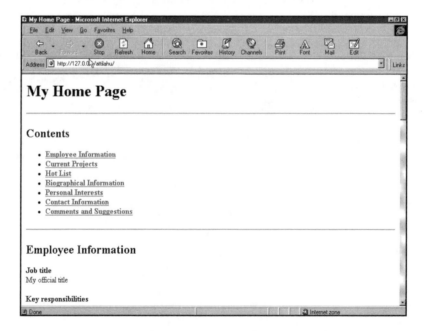

Lower on the page, the template offers a place to insert links to external sites, as well as contact information and even a form for comments from outsiders. There's even an area on this page for links to reports from associates and employees, and obviously you want to make sure these are flattering. In fact, this entire Web template is of questionable value, because a personal site should be handled with very great care depending on its purpose. If you want employers to look at it, be sure to keep that audience in mind. If you want friends or random Web visitors to see it, why include job information? And so on. Consider carefully, and change the site dramatically.

Files Created by FrontPage's New Webs

When you build a Web with the FrontPage New Web feature, several directories and files are created on the machine running the Web server software. Note that these are in addition to the directories and files created by installing the FrontPage server extensions in the first place.

Each Web produces the same directory structure, although individual files differ according to the type of Web (Corporate Presence, Project, and so on) being built. This structure is as follows, and is shown in Figure 23.12 in a Windows 95 Explorer window.

FIG. 23.12
All FrontPage-created Webs share this rather elaborate directory structure.

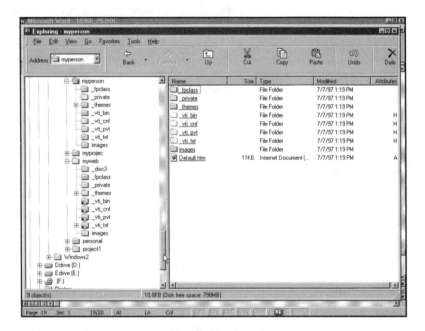

WebName/

The files and directories for the individual Webs you create are stored within a directory that bears the name you gave the Web in the New Web dialog box.

_private/

In general, all directories that begin with the underscore character (_) are hidden from Web visitors. They're also hidden from the view in FrontPage Explorer, unless the option Show Documents in Hidden Directories is toggled within the Advanced portion of the Web Settings dialog box.

The _private/ directory works somewhat differently. It contains files that you want to keep invisible to your Web's visitors, and these files will not show up in a search produced by the Search Component. The directory *is* visible within FrontPage Explorer, because it's one to which you'll want frequent access.

_fp-class/

The _fp-class directory holds the Java classes for the hover buttons and navigation buttons, both of which are Java applets, created through the process of designing your Web. You can also use it to store other Java applets you develop. This directory doesn't exist by default; it is created when FrontPage automatically creates Java items.

images/

The images directory offers a place to store image files (GIF and JPG, for example). This directory makes it easy for FrontPage Editor to locate your images when you use the Insert Image dialog box.

_themes/

The themes directory stores the files necessary to display the Web theme chosen for your Web. Whenever you select a theme, FrontPage automatically uploads the GIF (graphics) and CSS (style sheet) files necessary to ensure that the theme is displayed correctly. These files are stored in a subdirectory that bears that theme's name. Each time you select a different theme for a particular Web, FrontPage replaces that specific theme's subdirectory with one bearing the new theme name, and stores the new theme information. Each Web, therefore, can have only one theme at a time.

_vti_cnf/

Every Web page you create, that is, every HTM file within the Web, has a corresponding file of the same name within the Web's _vti_cnf directory. This private directory holds files that contain name values for the public page, with information such as the last author to edit the page, when the page was edited, and so forth.

_vti_bin/

The private _vti_bin directory contains three executable programs to be used in conjunction with FrontPage Components and administrative functions. _vti_bin itself contains the file SHTML.EXE, which handles all HTML documents in your Web that control some aspect of the browser's behavior (such as FrontPage Components forms). Within _vti_bin there are two subdirectories, _vti_adm and _vti_aut. The first of these contains the ADMIN.EXE file, which handles administrator procedures such as permissions and Web creation. The second contains AUTHOR.EXE, which handles author procedures, including permissions.

_vti_txt/

To make searches possible, each Web contains a _vti_txt directory that contains a text index file. Within each _vti_txt directory is a default.wti/ directory, which contains one set of files for discussion groups created with the Discussion Group Web Wizard (if you've done so for that Web), and another set for all other HTML documents.

TIP If you don't plan to allow searches against your site, consider deleting the _vti_txt directory completely. This reduces the memory needed for the Recalculate Links command.

_vti_pvt/

The _vti_pvt directory contains several private files, including the Web's parameters, the list of sub-Webs (in the root directory only), the To-Do list, and the To-Do list history.

Other Directories

Some Web types created by FrontPage have a subdirectory unique to the functions of that Web. The Project Web, for example, stores information for its Knowledge Base in a directory called _knobas, necessary for user searches against the Knowledge Base. Also in the Project Web is _reqdis, which contains the files for the discussion of requirements among team members. Discussion Webs contain a directory called _disc$x$ (where x represents a single digit), in which posted articles are stored. Customer Support Webs contain the _cusudi directory for the Customer Support discussion.

From Here...

The wizards and templates in FrontPage Explorer's New Web dialog box are immensely useful as a starting point for Web creation. Be careful not to build a generic Web and then let it drop. Among other reasons, if all FrontPage buyers did the same thing, your site would be utterly indistinctive. More importantly, though, the Web site is the way potentially millions of people will see you and your company, or how your employees or fellow project members will get a first-hand look at your work. The templates are great to have, but they're just the beginning of the real work. Now it's time to start that work, by moving on to:

- Chapter 24, "Working with an Existing Web," details how to edit and improve a Web already on your server.
- Chapter 25, "Configuring Your Web," is where you'll learn the techniques behind Web configurations and permissions.
- Part VI, "Using the FrontPage 98 SDK," is where you'll explore the means by which the package's Software Development Kit lets you fully customize your FrontPage environment.

Part
V

Ch
23

## CHAPTER 24

Working with an Existing Web

Creating a Web using FrontPage's templates and wizards is all well and good, but once those procedures are complete, your work has merely begun. You'll have to alter each page in the Web by working closely with FrontPage Editor but, just as important, you must change and enhance the existing Web through the powerful features of FrontPage Explorer. This chapter contains a detailed look at the Explorer windows and menu and demonstrates several shortcuts and advanced features for working with your Webs. ■

Loading a FrontPage Web into Explorer

How to display and work with a FrontPage Web that already exists on your site.

Working with Explorer's views

What are the differences among FrontPage Explorer's various views? How do they work together?

FrontPage Explorer's menus

Learn the effects of all the commands in Explorer's drop-down menus.

Importing Webs

If you have a Web you created before you started using FrontPage, you can easily import it into FrontPage Explorer.

Publishing Webs

How to transfer an entire Web from your test computer to a working Web server.

Loading a FrontPage Web into Explorer

Once you have one or more Webs created with FrontPage 98, you can load them into FrontPage Explorer by choosing File, Open FrontPage Web or by clicking the Open icon on Explorer's toolbar. If you've just loaded FrontPage itself, you can also open a Web by clicking Open an Existing FrontPage Web from the Getting Started beginning screen. Whichever method you choose, the Getting Started dialog box appears with your existing Webs ready to be loaded (see Figure 24.1).

Note that this command is useful only for loading Webs created with FrontPage itself. If you have a Web created outside FrontPage, use the Import Web feature described later in this chapter.

FIG. 24.1

The Getting Started dialog box lists the Webs you've been working on. You can open any one them directly from here.

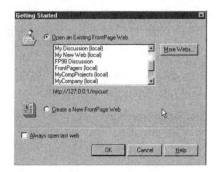

The titles of all the Webs you've been recently working on appear in the window below the Open an Existing FrontPage Web selection. These include Webs that exist on your local server (for instance, those with an URL of http://localhost or http://127.0.0.1), and those you've been working on that are stored on a remote server. Local Webs are indicated as such through the [local] designation; remote Webs show only the Web title.

To launch one of these Webs, double-click the title, or single-click and choose OK. Note that, if you wish, you can tell FrontPage to open the most recently worked-on Web every time it loads, by clicking the Always Open New Web option at the bottom left of the Getting Started dialog box. This is especially useful if you're involved in a long-term Web creation project and have no need to see a choice of other Webs.

If you need to load a Web that does not appear in the small window—perhaps you've been asked to work on a new Web that's already been started on a remote server—click the More Webs button. This action reveals the Open FrontPage Web dialog box (see Figure 24.2), where you can access any Web server you want by clicking in the Select a Web Server or Disk Location field and typing the IP address of the server (for example, **http://www.microsoft.com/**) and then clicking List Webs. Of course, if you don't have permission to enter a server, typing the URL won't do you any good, but go ahead and try anyway. If you do have access to an IP address you type, the Webs on that server will appear in the FrontPage Webs Found At Location window.

Note that selecting a server and listing the Webs is a one-step process if you're dealing with a non-default Web. Just locate the IP address in the Web Server drop-down menu and click it; Explorer automatically selects the List Webs button.

▶ **See** Chapter 22, "Building a Web." **p. 523**

Here's a basic run-through for Web loading. First, determine whether or not you want to connect to the server using Secure Sockets Layer (SSL). This will be the case only if your server supports SSL and if you, in fact, have the necessary authorization on that server to make this kind of connection. Most full-featured servers do support SSL, but you must establish authentication keys before this feature can be used. Check with your server's documentation to determine how to do this (it's beyond this book's scope). If you do want to establish a secure connection in this manner, click the Secure Connection Required toggle on the Open FrontPage Web dialog box.

Now, click the down-arrow on the Select a Web Server drop-down menu and select the server you wish to access. Unless it's the default server (the one displayed when this dialog box first appears), Explorer will locate the server and load the Web titles and display them in the location window. For the default server, you must click the List Webs button. If you're opening a Web from a server on a remote computer, and especially if you're using a modem connection (even 28.8 Kbps), getting a list of the Webs can take several minutes (see Figure 24.2).

> **N O T E**   In most cases, you won't actually click the List Webs button. When the list in the Web Server or File Location field contains more than one entry, and you click the down-arrow to choose an entry different from the entry that appears when the dialog box first opens, the List Webs button is selected automatically by FrontPage Explorer and is thus grayed out. You'll actively select List Webs only if you want to see the Webs on the default entry in the dialog box. ▪

FIG. 24.2
To avoid frustrating yourself with long load times, click the Cancel button to stop the loading process.

Click the Web you want to work with and click the OK button. The remainder of this chapter assumes you'll be working with the Web created in Chapter 22, "Building a Web," called FrontPagers, which was built with the help of the Corporate Presence Web Wizard. When you click OK, a dialog box might appear (depending on the server you're using) that requires a username and password for author permissions, which you established earlier. Once the FrontPagers Web is loaded, you will see the Explorer window shown in Figure 24.3.

FIG. 24.3
The FrontPagers Web is
now loaded and ready
to edit.

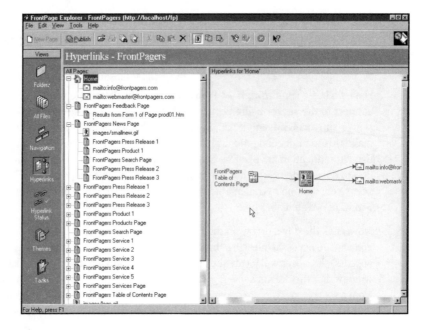

Working with Explorer's Views

When creating a new Web, the Explorer window shows the Navigation View by default. However, each Web you work on will later open in the most recent view you've used. As you use FrontPage, you'll find yourself gaining a favorite view, one that you use most frequently, and quite likely even a different favorite view for each type of Web you create. You'll examine the various views here, although they reappear throughout this section of the book.

Hyperlink View

The Hyperlink View in Figure 24.3 has two parts: All Pages on the left and Hyperlinks for *PageName* on the right (where *PageName* is the title of the currently selected individual page). You'll call this latter view the Individual Pages pane. The purpose of Hyperlink View is to provide both an outline-like perspective and a visual-style perspective of your Web site.

Hyperlink View is accessible through Explorer's View, Hyperlink View command and also by clicking the Hyperlink View icon in Explorer's toolbar.

All Pages

Figure 24.4 shows the All Pages pane expanded by sliding the vertical separator fully to the right edge of the screen. This figure demonstrates how All Pages functions: It's very similar to the outline feature of word processors or personal information managers and shows the various headings and subheadings distinguished from one another by indentation. In this figure, some of the visible headings are fully expanded, as indicated by the minus signs beside the main topic headings. By contrast, other topic headings remain unexpanded (closed), as indicated by the plus signs beside them.

If you click the minus sign beside an expanded topic, you also close all the subordinate topics of that topic. Therefore, if you want to close all topics in the All Pages pane, close the highest topic in the hierarchy (in this case, Customer Support Welcome). If you do, you'll see only one topic with a plus sign beside it. Again, those familiar with a word processor outliner or with the Windows Explorer interface will find all of this quite apparent.

Actually, the division is not topic and subtopic; instead, the All Pages pane shows hierarchical relationships—parent and child—between pages. Pages contain links to other pages, which in turn link to yet other pages.

As you move the pointer up and down the All Pages view, the topic you're currently pointing at is highlighted to show where you are in the view (see Figure 24.4). This helps you orient your way through the hierarchy of topics.

FIG. 24.4

These are the cascaded headings of Explorer's All Pages pane.

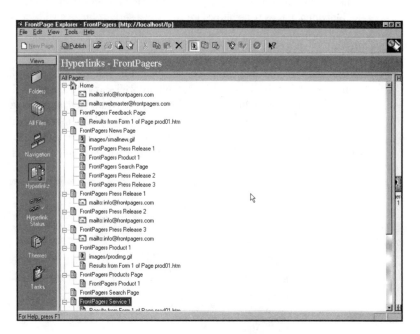

Using the All Pages Pane   By studying the All Pages pane of your Webs, you can maintain a good sense of how the Web is constructed. Combining this view with the Individual Pages pane gives you two different perspectives, and together they make a powerful tool.

The main purpose of the All Pages pane is to help you easily find your way around your Web. You can locate everything in the Individual Pages pane or in Folder View, but it's more cumbersome to do so. Again, there's a similarity here with a word processing outline; a well outlined word processing document is an extremely easy document in which to locate specific headings and sections. This is exactly the case of the All Pages pane in FrontPage Explorer.

You can't actually manipulate the Web—move pages around and rearrange relationships—from the All Pages pane. Instead, it puts you in the position of being able to do so. Clicking any page in the All Pages pane immediately shows that page in the center of the Individual Pages pane, complete with all the links that stem from it. Clicking from subtopic to subtopic changes the display immediately and lets you jump back and forth from one perspective of the Web to the next.

Some icons in Hyperlink View display a plus sign at their top left corner. This indicates that additional documents in the Web are linked to the page represented by the icon. Clicking the plus sign displays the icons for the linked pages and simultaneously changes the plus sign to a minus sign. Clicking the minus sign hides the icons for the linked pages.

Using the Individual Pages Pane   Explorer's Individual Pages pane is where you'll do a considerable amount of your work on your Web, except of course for the actual task of constructing HTML pages, for which you'll use FrontPage Editor. The Individual Pages pane shows the Web from the perspective of the currently selected page in the All Pages pane, but you can maneuver around the Web by using the Individual Pages pane alone. Like the All Pages pane, the Individual Pages pane shows the Web as a series of pages with or without additional links leading from them, and you can expand or contract the links to see a larger portion of that particular part of the Web.

To show how the Individual Pages pane changes as you open an increasing number of pages, examine the following series of figures. Figure 24.5 shows the Individual Pages pane of the FrontPagers Web from the perspective of only the News Page and its direct links. In this case, the Hyperlinks to Images toggle in the View menu has been marked, which is why both panes now show the image links in addition to the normal document links. Notice the plus signs on several of the pages; as in the All Pages pane, these pages can be expanded to reveal their links.

FIG. 24.5

In this figure, you can see the basic Individual Pages pane with hyperlinked images.

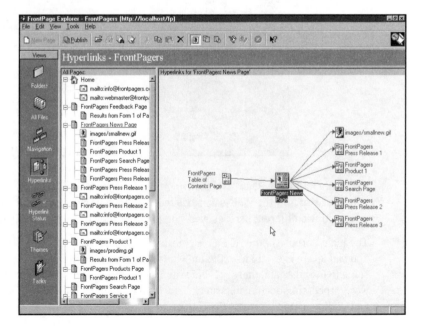

Notice that as you move your mouse pointer over any icon in the Individual Pages pane (or indeed the All Pages pane), a small information box appears giving you the URL for that hyperlink. This box is shown in Figures 24.6 and 24.7, and is extremely useful as a Web management tool.

Folders View

While Hyperlink View gives you a designer-oriented perspective on your Web and offers an outline and a visual representation, Folder View provides a more technically oriented perspective. Folder View exists for Webmasters who want to see the Web as a series of individual files in various folders. In other words, it gives you the Web in computer-ese, which for many is more efficient.

 TIP The term *folder* is instantly recognizable to Windows 95 and Macintosh users. If you're more familiar with UNIX, MS-DOS, or Windows 3.x, think of folders as directories instead. Also, in the Contents frame of Folder View, Name really means file name.

You can access the Folder View either by clicking the Folder View icon on FrontPage Explorer's Views toolbar or by selecting Folder View from FrontPage Explorer's View menu.

As Figure 24.6 shows, Folder View offers two separate panes: All Folders and Contents. "Contents" will be the latter to make its function more apparent. Essentially, the All Folders pane shows the folders for that Web, and these are the folders that FrontPage created when it built the Web you're working with. The Contents page shows the files and subfolders within the folder selected in the All Folders pane.

Part

V

Ch

24

FIG. 24.6

The Folder View for the FrontPagers Web shows the folders on the left and the contents of the folder, including subfolders, on the right.

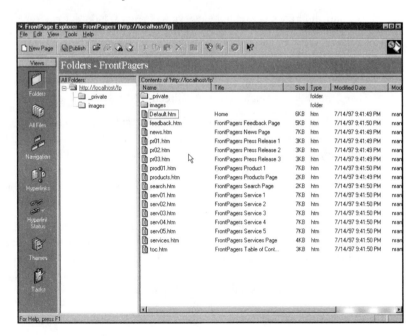

In other words, Folder View is very much like the Windows Explorer file viewer found in Windows 95 and Windows NT 4.0. This is immediately apparent when you look at Figure 24.7, which shows the FrontPagers Web as it appears in the C:\WEBSHARE\WWWROOT\FP directory in Windows Explorer.

FIG. 24.7
Windows Explorer's view of the Web is very similar to FrontPage Explorer's view.

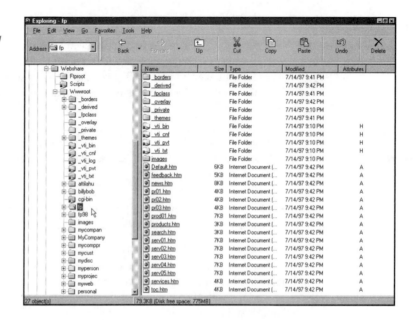

The only difference between the two views is that Windows Explorer shows all hidden directories, whereas FrontPage Explorer shows only the private hidden directory. If you want to see all hidden folders in the FrontPage Explorer Folder view, open the Web Setting dialog box from Explorer's Tools menu and select Show Documents in Hidden Directories from the Advanced tab. Incidentally, it's clear from the name of this command that Microsoft hasn't quite completed the shift in terminology from "directories" to "folders" either.

The All Folders pane is primarily a navigational aid. When you click a folder, the subfolders and files contained within that folder appear in the Contents pane. If you right-click a folder, you can Cut, Copy, Rename, or Delete the folder, or you can view its Properties. The difference between Cut and Delete is that Cut moves the folder to the Clipboard, whereas Delete simply erases it. Use Cut when you want to move the folder and Delete only when you no longer need it. Deleted folders cannot be retrieved.

Be careful, however, when cutting, deleting, or renaming folders. Remember that internal links within your Web use the folder name as part of the hyperlink reference; changing the folder means invalidating those links. Fortunately, FrontPage keeps track of renamed folders and automatically changes the links when you choose Tools, Recalculate Links. Cut or deleted folders appear as broken links in your FrontPage Web.

In the Contents pane, right-clicking a file name offers additional options. You can load the page into FrontPage Editor or another editing program, and you can cut, copy, rename, or delete it or view its properties. Finally, you can Add Task, an action that opens the New Task dialog box for that particular file.

Working with Individual Pages

Once you reach a page in Folder View or any Explorer view that you want to work with, click it to obtain several choices. Double-clicking opens that page in FrontPage Editor, where you can edit it and save it directly back to the Web (even if you're editing it on a remote computer). Depending on which view and which pane you're working in, right-clicking the icon reveals a pop-up menu with some of the following five options:

Part

V

Ch

24

- ■ Move to Center   Centers the Individual Pages pane on that page's icon (Hyperlink View only).

- ■ Show Hyperlinks   Opens the Hyperlink View with the selected page in the center of the display (Folder View only).

- ■ Open   Loads the page into the editor you have specified for that file (for more details, see the section, "FrontPage Explorer Menus," later in this chapter).

- ■ Open With   Loads the page into an editor you select from the resulting Open With dialog box.

- ■ Cut   Removes the page or folder from the display and places it in the Clipboard, making it available for pasting elsewhere. Simultaneously erases links to other pages and restores them when you paste. Use Cut to move files or folders.

- ■ Delete   Permanently erases the page from the Web and simultaneously erases links to other pages.

- ■ Copy   Copies the page or folder to the Clipboard and makes it available for pasting to other locations.

- ■ Rename   Lets you change the name of the file or folder and simultaneously changes names in links to that item.

- ■ Properties   Opens the Properties dialog box (for more details, see the section "FrontPage Explorer Menus" later in this chapter).

- ■ Add Task   Opens the Add Task dialog box for that specific file.

Beyond that, any work you do on individual pages occurs through FrontPage Editor, not Explorer. The point of Explorer is to let you see your Web and keep track of it, not to alter or edit individual pages.

All Files View

Where the Folders View helps you visualize your Web according to the standard directory-file appearance of Windows Explorer, the All Files View provides an immensely useful look at all files in your Web, plus their location and their status. You can see the All Files View by clicking the All Files icon in the Views toolbar or by selecting View, All Files.

As Figure 24.8 shows, All Files View displays the file name in the leftmost column (the Name column), and all associated information about that file in the remaining eight columns. These columns include the file's title within the Web, the folder in which the file can be found, the size and type of the file, when it was last modified, who performed the modifications, and any comments that have been recorded about that file. This information is merely taken from the File Properties box (right-click a file name anywhere in FrontPage and select Properties), but having it all in one place is extremely useful.

FIG. 24.8

This is the complete All Files View, complete with all hidden files and directories showing.

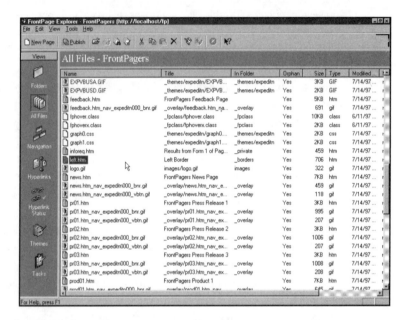

The power of the All Files View comes into play when your Web takes on multiple files across multiple folders. It's extremely easy to lose track of where all your Web's files are located and what their current status is. All Files View gives you this information at a glance and also lets you access any of those files for renaming, cutting, deleting, copying, or loading into FrontPage Editor.

Hyperlink Status View

The Hyperlink Status View gives you a fast and comprehensive glance at all of the hyperlinks in your Web, both internal and external. The URL of the link itself is displayed, as are the file name and the title of the page that contains that hyperlink. Also, and most importantly, this view shows you the status of that hyperlink.

There are three possible status values: OK, Broken, or Unknown. OK indicates that the hyperlink has been checked and verified as in working order (see Figure 24.9). Broken reveals the opposite, that the hyperlink is not functional. Unknown, as the name suggests, tells you that FrontPage has yet to verify that link.

By right-clicking an individual hyperlink, you can call up the Edit Hyperlink dialog box and change the URL for the link, either across the entire Web or in selected pages. A right-click also lets you verify the links, a procedure that sends Explorer out onto the Web to check the validity of the hyperlinks. You can check all the hyperlinks in the Web simultaneously by selecting Tools, Verify Hyperlinks.

▶ **See** Chapter 26, "Managing a Web." **p. 595**

FIG. 24.9

The Edit Hyperlink View lets you choose to change the link in all pages or only in the pages you have selected.

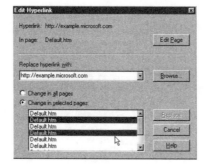

Navigation View

FrontPage 98 has introduced the Navigation View, which quite possibly will emerge as the most popular view. Microsoft obviously thinks so, too, because when you create a Web using a FrontPage wizard or template, the Navigation View opens by default. Clearly, you're *supposed* to use this view.

Navigation View is accessible by clicking the Navigation icon on Explorer's Views toolbar or by selecting Navigation from the View menu. When you do, you'll see a screen resembling Figure 24.10.

As Figure 24.10 shows, Navigation View is divided into two panes. The Contents pane is at the bottom of Explorer and shows the folders and files for the Web, whereas the unnamed primary pane at the top offers a graphical representation of the Web with connections shown by lines between boxes. For the sake of this book, this pane will be called the Representation pane.

In the Representation pane, each box represents a page in the Web. Each box also has a corresponding file name in the Contents pane. The Navigation View lets you structure your Web quickly and easily, simply by dragging and dropping files from the Contents pane or by adding pages directly in the Representation pane and dragging them among the boxes to create your Web's hierarchy. Here, too, you can easily rename your pages.

You can see how this view works by opening your FrontPagers Web and selecting the Navigation View. Doing this gives you a Navigation View showing several boxes in the Presentation pane and several folders and files in the Contents pane. Your screen should look much like Figure 24.11.

Part
V

Ch

24

FIG. 24.10
The Navigation View shows you the structure of your Web in clear and unambiguous detail.

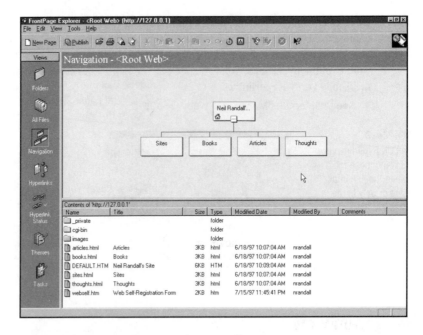

FIG. 24.11
You must scroll horizontally to see all of a large Web in Navigation View.

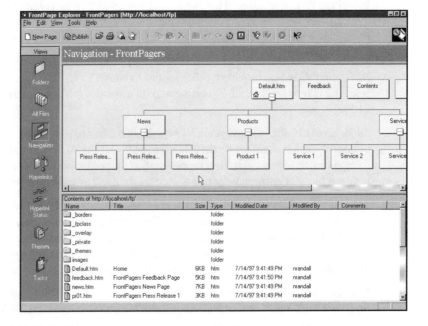

Notice the lines running between the boxes that demonstrate the hierarchy for the Web and shows which pages are subordinate to which other pages. Several pages lead directly from the Home Page—News, Products, and Services are visible in Figure 24.11—and several more lead from that second row into the third. Notice also that pages with subordinate pages also have an expansion toggle (the plus or minus sign). Click the expansion toggle to expand or contract the structure.

First, you rename a few pages. Find the Product 1 box in the third row and click it to select it. After a pause, click it again to highlight the text. (The pause is necessary because clicking twice quickly is read as a double-click, which loads the page into FrontPage Editor.) With the text highlighted, type **Books** and press Enter.

Now you'll add a second product page to the Web. To do so, select the Products page again by single-clicking it and then click the New Page icon in the toolbar. You can do the same thing by right-clicking the Products page and selecting New Page. You'll see a new page called New Page 1 connected to the Products page and right beside the Books page. Rename this new page **Magazines**. Finally, create two pages leading from the Magazines page, one called **Computer** and the other called **Fashion**. Your Navigation View should look like Figure 24.12.

FIG. 24.12
This Web now has three hierarchical levels, but still needs a lot of work before publishing.

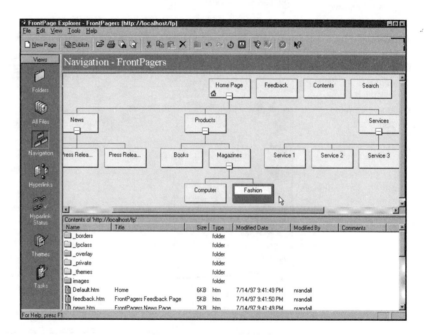

Part
V

Ch
24

You can easily delete a page you've just created. Select the page and either press the Delete key, right-click and choose Delete, or select Delete from the Edit menu. When you do, you'll be presented with the Delete Page dialog box, which allows you to remove the page from only the Navigation View or from the entire Web itself.

At this stage, however, only the first of those choices is available to you, because although you've altered the appearance of your Web in the Presentation pane, you haven't actually created any files. To do so, either change views by clicking a different icon in the Views toolbar or right-click in the Presentation pane and select Apply Changes. When you do, you'll see the new files in the Contents pane, complete with the names you've given them.

To show the complete power of Navigation View, you'll move a child page from one parent to another. Assume that you don't need all four Service pages, but only two. You also need one more Product page and a subordinate page to the Feedback page. Instead of creating new pages, you can just drag the two unneeded Service pages to their new locations.

To do so, click the page called Service 1 and drag it towards the main Products page until the line from the Service 1 page attaches itself to the Products page. Release the mouse button and the page is in its new location. Rename it **Software** to account for the third product in your line. Now drag the Service 2 box to the Feedback box and rename it **Archives**. Apply your changes and you've successfully restructured your Web.

By now, the Web is probably far too wide for the display. To get a different perspective and one that uses a bit less space, you can rotate it 90 degrees. To do so, right-click in the Presentation pane and select Rotate, or choose View, Rotate. To see what you've been working on, scroll down until the Home Page, Feedback page, and Products pages are visible. Your screen should look like Figure 24.13.

FIG. 24.13

The Navigation View lets you rotate the appearance of the Web to give you a different perspective on your Web's structure.

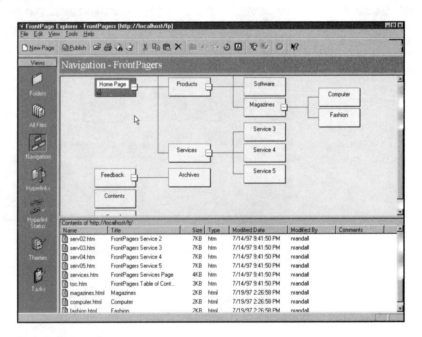

 You can also create new pages in Navigation View by dragging files from the Content pane into the Presentation pane until the line attaches to the parent page you want.

FrontPage Explorer Menus

Explorer offers four main menus through which to complete its tasks. Everything you want to do in the program is accessible through these menus. Here you examine all the menu commands. In the following sections, the menu name is shown first and then the command from that menu.

File, New, Page

Available in Folders, All Files, and Navigation View, this command lets you create a new page in the Web and, thus, a new file on the Web server.

File, New, Task

Available in all views, this command lets you create a new task for inclusion in the Task View.

File, New, Folder

Available only in Folders and Navigation View, this command lets you create a new folder in the Web, and thus a new directory on the Web server.

File, New, FrontPage Web

With the New, FrontPage Web command, available in all views, you begin the process of creating new Webs. Choosing this command opens the New Web dialog box where you can select a wizard or a template to help automate the creation of a Web.

▶ **See** Chapter 22, "Building a Web," **p. 523**

Another option is to add the new Web to the current Web. If you have a Web currently loaded, you can create a new Web and insert it directly into the loaded Web. In this case, you are asked if you want to replace or retain files with duplicate names.

File, Open FrontPage Web and File, Close FrontPage Web

If you have already created Webs, you can load them into Explorer through the Open FrontPage Web command. The resulting Open FrontPage Web dialog box lets you choose the Web server on which the Web resides (in the Web Server or File Location drop-down list box). Once you click the List Webs button, the FrontPage Webs list box displays the Webs that exist on that server. By highlighting the one you want and clicking OK, you load that Web into Explorer.

Choosing the Close FrontPage Web command from the File menu removes the current Web from Explorer. Both commands are available in all views.

File, Publish FrontPage Web

When you complete a Web and you want to store it on another Web server, use the Publish FrontPage Web command from the File menu. When you choose this command, the Publish FrontPage Web dialog box appears. Here you specify the Destination Web Server or File Location with either the IP address or the domain name for the server. You also specify the Name of Destination FrontPage Web on the destination server (it adopts that name in its new location). You can choose to Connect Using SSL if your server is capable of Secure Sockets Layer authorization, and you can elect to Copy Changed Pages Only or Add This Web to an Existing FrontPage Web on the Server.

N O T E The Publish FrontPage Web command isn't the same as the Web Publishing Wizard. FrontPage launches the Web Publishing Wizard automatically if it determines that you are trying to publish your Web to a server that doesn't have the FrontPage Server Extensions. ■

In addition, if you are copying the root Web from your current server, you can tell Explorer to copy the child Webs to the destination as well. The root Web is created automatically by Explorer on your server, and the child Webs are all other Webs you create on that server. By copying the root Web and the child Webs, you are, in effect, copying all Webs from your current server.

File, Delete FrontPage Web

If you no longer need a Web, you can delete it by choosing the Delete command. A warning box appears and explains to you that, once deleted, the Web can't be retrieved.

File, Import

If you have files or folders you want to bring into the current Web from your hard drive, choose Import from the File menu. To import a file, click in the All Pages pane or the Individual Pages pane where you want your file to appear in the Web and choose File, Import. You'll see the Import File to FrontPage Web dialog box, shown in Figure 24.10. Clicking Add File displays the Add File to Import List dialog box, whereas clicking Add Folder yields the Browse for Folder dialog box, also shown in Figure 24.10. You can add multiple files and folders into the Import File box before clicking OK. By clicking Edit URL, you can change the hyperlink reference as well.

When you select the appropriate file and click Open, the Add File to Import dialog box disappears and the file name appears in the Import File to Web dialog box. You can add additional files by clicking the Add File button again, and if you change your mind about importing them, you can remove files from the list box by clicking Remove. You can click any file in the list box and click Edit URL to change the URL of the selected page. When you've made the decisions you want, click Import. As the file is importing, you can click the Stop button, if you change your mind, or simply wait for it to be added.

You can also import files and folders to a Web through drag and drop. With a Web open in FrontPage Explorer, drag files or folders from Windows Explorer into either pane of the

Explorer window and drop them. FrontPage immediately uploads the file to the Web server, even if the server is on a remote machine. Once the files are in place, you can provide links to them or manipulate them as you manipulate other files in your Webs.

If you import files created in Microsoft Office, FrontPage Explorer creates icons for these files that reflect the program of origin. When you double-click these files, instead of loading FrontPage Editor or Image Composer (the two standard editing programs), the file loads into the appropriate Office application instead. But, there's one very important point to keep in mind. Unless your visitors are using Microsoft Internet Explorer 3.0 or Netscape Navigator (with the appropriate Office viewers plugged in) as their browser, they won't be able to view these Office documents. For this reason, importing Office files directly is best reserved for private intranets, in which the choice of browser can be guaranteed.

FrontPage also provides an Import Wizard, which is available only if no Web is currently loaded into FrontPage Explorer. In such a case, selecting File, Import reveals the Import Web Wizard series of dialog boxes, in which you can select individual files or entire folders for import. The wizard can also be selected from the Getting Started with Microsoft FrontPage dialog box.

File, Export

Exporting files copies a Web document or graphics file from the current Web to your hard disk for later use with another Web or for later alteration with an editor. To export, click the desired file in one of the views and choose File, Export. The Export Selected As dialog box appears, which is essentially a Save File dialog box. Choose the directory, name the file, and click Save.

Edit, Cut

The Cut command removes the selected file or folder from the Web and places it in the Clipboard. It is now available to be pasted elsewhere on that Web or another Web. Links to that item are destroyed, then reestablished to where it's pasted.

Edit, Copy

Copy lets you duplicate the selected file or folder elsewhere in the Web or on another Web. Highlight the item, copy it, and paste it wherever you want.

Edit, Paste

If you used the Cut or Copy command, the Paste command is available. Move to the Web and location where you want the item to be placed, and select Paste.

Edit, Delete

Delete permanently removes the currently selected page or graphics file from the current Web. When you choose this command, the Confirm Delete dialog box appears; if more than one file appears in the Files to Delete field, you can elect to delete the current file or all of them at the same time. Links to the item are also eliminated.

Edit, Rename

If you want to change the name of file or folder, use the Rename command. Links will be changed to reflect the name change.

Edit, Open

When you want to edit the HTML elements of a specific page, click that page in Explorer to select it and choose Edit, Open. This command loads the selected page into FrontPage Editor, where you can edit it, save it, and manipulate it. Part II, "Creating Your Web Pages with FrontPage Editor," discusses FrontPage Editor in detail.

Edit, Open With

Using the Tools, Options, Configure Editors command, you can choose specific editors for particular types of files. When you select Edit, Open With, the Open with Editor dialog box appears and offers you the choice of editors in which to load the currently selected file. If you use a specific program to edit graphics files, for example, you can choose that particular editor to manipulate the current file, in which case the Open With command loads that editor and the file inside it. You can even choose to establish additional HTML editors to do specific tasks and then open your Web documents into them.

Edit, Add To Do Task

As you work on building your Web, you may want to add elements that you don't currently have time to complete. The Add To Do Task command lets you add these elements to your To Do List.

▶ **See** Chapter 26, "Managing a Web," **p. 595**

Edit, Properties

A Properties dialog box is common in Windows programs, but FrontPage's page Properties dialog box is unusually powerful. When you select a file and choose Edit, Properties, you'll see the Properties dialog box. There are two tabs in this dialog box: Summary and General.

The General tab shows the type of document and the document's URL, and it offers one editable text box, Page URL. You can edit the document's URL in this field. You can change the document's name or you can change its directory. (The full directory is displayed in the URL text box at the bottom of the General tab.) If you change the directory, Explorer automatically moves the document into that directory of your Web. If you specify a directory that does not exist, Explorer creates the directory and then moves the document into it. This procedure can be extremely useful as you maintain your Web.

The Summary tab shows you when the file was created and last modified and allows you to add comments for your own reference.

View, ...

The View commands allow you to access the various FrontPage views from keyboard commands and the menus.

These commands let you switch among the various Explorer views and are identical to clicking the corresponding button in the Views toolbar.

▶ **See** Chapter 26, "Managing a Web," **p. 595**

View, Hyperlinks to Images

To keep your Web from looking cluttered, the Individual Pages pane and the All Pages pane, by default, don't show links to images (that is, images in your Web pages). If you want a more complete view of your Web, toggle on the Links to Images to have the images display with the image icon. This is available in Hyperlinks View only.

Part
V

Ch
24

View, Repeated Hyperlinks

Often your pages contain multiple links from one page to another. There's usually no reason to see these links more than once in the Individual Pages pane, but for a complete picture, you can toggle on the Repeated Links. This is available in Hyperlinks View only.

View, Hyperlinks Inside Page

When you create pages, you can include a link to another place within that same page. The purpose is to give your readers strong navigational assistance. By default, however, Explorer's Individual Pages pane doesn't show these links because they clutter the display. If you want to see how many of these links you've created, toggle on the Links Inside Page to get a more complete view. This is available in Hyperlinks View only.

View, Refresh

Because several people can be working a Web at the same time, it's entirely possible for new pages and new links to be added without your knowledge. To ensure that you have the most complete Web showing in Explorer, choose View, Refresh to make the entire Web visible, complete with all current changes.

View, Expand All

Available in Navigation View only, this command toggles full expansion of all parent pages.

View, Rotate

Available in Navigation View only, this command rotates the appearance of the Web in the Presentation pane for easier viewing and a different perspective.

View, Size to Fit

Available in Navigation View only, this command compresses the page boxes so that they all fit inside the Presentation pane. The titles might be unreadable as a result, but you can locate individual pages by right-clicking the file name in the Contents pane and selecting Find in Navigation. This highlights that page in the Presentation pane.

View, Show All Hyperlinks

By default, Hyperlink Status View displays only links with a Broken or Unknown status to keep the view from getting cluttered. To show all hyperlinks in your Web, choose this command.

Tools, Spelling, Find, Replace

This collection of three separate commands are all tasks for Web managers. As such, they are covered in full in Chapter 26, "Managing a Web."

Tools, Verify Hyperlinks and Recalculate Hyperlinks

The Verify Hyperlinks command lets you verify the validity of all hyperlinks in your Web. The Recalculate Hyperlinks command performs several important maintenance functions. Both commands are covered in Chapter 26, "Managing a Web."

Tools, Show FrontPage Editor

Choosing Tools, Show FrontPage Editor opens the FrontPage Editor with no Web documents loaded into it for editing. If FrontPage Editor is already open, this command switches to it. Note that this command does not display a specific page in Editor, even if you've selected that page in Explorer. That task is reserved for the Open command (see Edit menu commands earlier in this chapter).

Tools, Show To Do List

If you want to see the To Do List for the current Web, select this command. The To Do List opens, or if it is already open, the To Do List command switches to it. The menu shows how many tasks remain on the To Do list.

Tools, Show Image Editor

This command opens the editor you've assigned to edit graphics files. If you've installed Microsoft Image Composer from the Bonus Pack CD-ROM, it automatically establishes as the program to open with the Show Image Editor command.

Tools, Web Settings, Permissions, Change Password

These three separate commands are all tasks for Web administrators. They are covered in full in Chapter 25, "Configuring Your Web."

Tools, Options

Three tabs are available from Tools, Options. Chapter 25, "Configuring Your Web," covers Proxies. General contains three items. You can elect to have the Getting Started dialog box display whenever you use FrontPage, you can tell FrontPage to warn you when the included FrontPage Components are out of date because of changes you've made, and you can also specify that you want to be warned when your Text Indexes, (which are created by Search Bots), are out of date. These latter two are covered in Chapter 26, "Managing a Web."

The final tab lets you configure editors to let you edit various types of files. Many of these are already set up for you, but you can change them by using the Modify button or add new ones by clicking the Add button. The principle, as with Windows Explorer, is that specific file types are associated with specific programs. The Modify Editor Association box shows the File Type, the Editor Name, and the Command that opens that editor. You can change the editor and the command so that a different editor handles these files.

Part
V

Ch
24

From Here...

Although you'll use FrontPage Explorer initially to create new Webs, eventually your main task will be to update and edit existing Webs. Explorer makes this relatively easy by giving you full access to and control over your Webs, and the Explorer menu items let you perform all necessary tasks.

- Chapter 25, "Configuring Your Web," discusses how to set permissions and passwords for your Webs.
- Chapter 26, "Managing a Web," teaches you about the details and issues surrounding managing people and documents with the help of the To Do List.
- Chapter 27, "Serving Your Web to the World with the Microsoft Personal Web Server," teaches you how to deal with the intricacies of server administration.

## CHAPTER 25

Configuring Your Web

To get your Web working correctly, you need to set its configurations; to make sure the right people are adding and altering material, you need to set permissions; and to establish the appropriate editors and programs for performing various functions that FrontPage doesn't handle, you need to establish when these programs will open. All of these settings and configurations are handled through the Tools menu of FrontPage Explorer, and you'll learn about them in this chapter. ■

Establishing parameters, configurations, and advanced settings

How should you fill out the various sections of the Web Settings dialog boxes?

Setting administrator, author, and user permissions

How do you guarantee that only authorized persons are changing and accessing your Web site?

Changing passwords

Passwords can be changed regularly by administrators and authors alike.

Proxy servers

Setting FrontPage to work from behind your organization's security firewalls.

Configure editors

FrontPage will launch the program of your choice to edit documents of various types.

T I P Explorer is not used for the purpose of configuring the Web server and the root Web—that's the role of the server administrator.

Establishing Parameters, Configurations, Advanced Settings, and Language Options

The major settings for the currently loaded Web can be set through the Web Settings command in FrontPage Explorer's Tools menu. For the most part, only the Web administrator can change these settings, but because you're probably already that person (having established that during program setup), you'll continue as if that's a given. If not, you'll need to contact your Web administrator if you want to alter any settings.

Choosing Tools, Web Settings opens the Web Settings dialog box (see Figure 25.1).

FIG. 25.1

The Parameters, Configuration, Advanced, and Language tabs comprise the Front Page Web Settings dialog box.

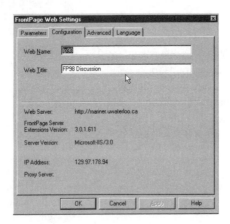

Parameters

Initially, the Parameters tab is probably the most confusing of the three tab choices available from the Web Settings dialog box, mainly because it's not at all obvious what this tab is supposed to accomplish. Clicking the Help button helps a bit, but even here the purpose is a bit obscure. Once you go through the procedure of establishing even one parameter on your own, however, it's all crystal clear (well, more or less).

To fully understand what these parameters are all about, you have to know what *Substitution Components* do. These Components (automated procedures) are covered in Chapter 11, "Using FrontPage Components, Forms, and Interactive Page Templates," which discusses FrontPage Editor. When you create a Web page in Editor, you can create a component that tells the Web browser to substitute the text in the component for text stored in the parameters, or configuration variables, established through the Parameters dialog box.

In other words, it's like entering a variable time and date stamp in a word processing docu-ment—when the file loads into the word processor, the time and date are automatically changed by the software itself, without any action on your part. In your Web, you might want to show the reader who developed that page, but the information might change or you might want to have the exact current URL for the page, instead of a fixed URL. You also might want your company's phone and fax numbers to appear throughout the Web. To do so, you create a Substitution Component to take care of the substitution, thereby letting FrontPage, instead of yourself, make the changes.

This is especially useful if you want that information to appear on multiple pages in your Web. Instead of having to type the information on individual pages, you need only include the Substi-tution Component on each applicable page, and whenever that page is loaded in a visitor's browser, the component locates the information on the server and performs the substitution. The major benefit is that, if the information changes, only the Value item in the Parameters area of Web Settings needs to be altered.

Even though you use FrontPage Editor to program these components, the configuration vari-ables that they rely upon are stored in Explorer, not Editor. They are established primarily in the FrontPage Explorer's Properties dialog box, which you can access by right-clicking a page in an Explorer view and choosing Properties.

The two tabs of the Properties dialog box are shown in Figures 25.2 and 25.3. Figure 25.2 shows the page URL and the title of the document (you can change the title in Editor or Ex-plorer), whereas Figure 25.3 shows the date the page was created and modified, as well as who did the creating and who did the modifying. The Substitution Component takes the information primarily from these tabs.

Part
V

Ch
25

 T I P To see your new configuration variables in action, load a page from your Web into Editor, and choose Insert/FrontPage Component. Choose Substitution Component from the resulting dialog box and click the arrow to the right of the Substitute With drop-down list box.

FIG. 25.2

Several information items are available from the General tab of the Properties dialog box.

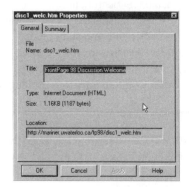

FIG. 25.3

Only a comments field is accessible from the Summary tab of the Properties dialog box.

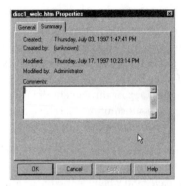

Even though the Substitution Component is designed to capture information from the configuration variables (Author, Modified By, Description, and Page URL) in these dialog boxes, it's not restricted to that information. The Web Wizards create some of them. Furthermore, you can set additional configuration variables by adding them through the Parameters tab of the Web Settings dialog box. To do so, from the Web Settings dialog box's Parameters tab, click the A̲dd button. The Add Name and Value dialog box appears (see Figure 25.4).

FIG. 25.4

In this dialog box, you can add the Name and Value of the parameter.

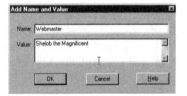

In the Name text box, add the name of the configuration variable you want to be available to the Substitution Component. This can be any name you want; in Figure 25.4, the text box shows Department, but that's only one possibility. The value of the Name text box is whatever you want to appear on the Web page when the Substitution Component is used. Because this is the public display of information, you'll want to make sure it's appropriate. Here the example is Public Relations. What this means is that, when the Web author engages a Substitution Component, one of the items available will now be Department, and if chosen, the Web page displays Public Relations. For the Web author, the substitution parameters are available by choosing I̲nsert, FrontP̲age Component, and then Substitution from the resulting window.

When you've finished specifying the name and value of the name, click OK and the new configuration variable (which is a combination of the Name and Value fields) appears in the Parameters tab. From here you can click OK or A̲pply to place it into the Web and thus make it available as a Substitution Component item. You can also modify or remove it, but when you do, remember to click OK or A̲pply to actually place it in the Web.

Configuration

In the Configuration tab (see Figure 25.5) of the Web Settings dialog box, you have the following information:

- **Web Name** The name of the Web as it appears in the Open Web dialog box and as it appears as a directory in your Web Server software. You can change that name if you are the authorized administrator of the root Web and if your server, such as Personal Web Server, supports the changing of Web names. The name of the Web is the same as the name of the directory on the server in which that Web is stored, so the Web name must be permissible as a directory name on the server.

- **Web Title** By default, the title of the Web is the same as the Web Name, but you can change it here. The Web title appears in the title bar of the Explorer window, as it is significant for that purpose only.

- **Web Server** This is the URL of the Web server. If your server does not have a domain name, this URL is the same as the IP Address information shown in this tab. You can't change the Web Server information; this was set when you created the Web.

- **Server Version** This gives you information about the version of your Web server. This cannot be altered, unless of course you upgrade your server, in which case the change is automatic.

- **IP Address** The IP address of your server, always expressed in numerical format (for example, 129.97.48.53). This is the actual number Web browsers look for; the domain name is simply a more easily remembered alias for the IP address, and is subject to the Internet's Domain Name System and the ability of DNS servers to locate it.

- **FrontPage Server Extensions Version** FrontPage installs software in your server software to allow the two to work together. These are known as server extensions. This link shows you the version of those extensions and cannot be altered except automatically through software upgrade.

- **Proxy Server** This line shows the URL of the proxy server, the server connected to your internal network that acts as a firewall or buffer between the internal network and the external Internet. You set this information with Explorer's Tools, Proxies.

FIG. 25.5

The Configuration tab provides several items of important information.

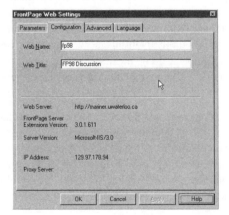

Part

V

Ch

25

Advanced

The Advanced tab (see Figure 25.6) on the Web Settings dialog box gives you access to four items: imagemaps, validation scripts, hidden directories, and recalculate status.

FIG. 25.6

The Advanced tab is extremely important if you plan to include imagemaps in your Web.

The Image Maps section lets you configure your Web to accept one of several different types of imagemaps. *Imagemaps* are single graphics on your Web page that contain multiple hyperlinks and can be created with FrontPage Editor (see Part II, "Creating Your Web Pages with FrontPage Editor," for details). Imagemaps are of several types so you must tell FrontPage which type you want to use. The Advanced tab of the Web Settings dialog box allows you to set the type (or style) of the imagemap you prefer.

The five imagemap types are FrontPage, NCSA, CERN, Netscape, and None. CERN imagemaps were the first type available to Web designers, and NCSA imagemaps came next. Netscape and FrontPage imagemaps are recent additions to the list. Each type handles resolution of imagemap hyperlinks differently, including the formatting of the file which contains the coordinate and hyperlink information.

Essentially, the type of imagemap you choose depends on the type of Web server on which you're placing your Web. If you're using the Personal Web Server that comes with the FrontPage package, use FrontPage imagemaps. If your server uses NCSA or CERN imagemaps, choose either of those types instead (in which case imagemaps are handled by entirely separate programs on the server). Netscape servers have their own type of map, but they also handle NCSA maps. Choosing None means, in effect, that your server doesn't handle imagemaps, in which case you should probably find a new server because imagemaps are extremely popular.

If you select FrontPage maps, the Prefix text box of the Web Settings dialog box remains grayed out; you can't change it. It isn't necessary to do so because FrontPage handles map directories automatically. If you choose NCSA, CERN, or Netscape maps, you must specify the directory where those maps are found on the Web server. These are given a default directory where the server software typically sets up its maps, but if the server administrator changed those directories, you must specify them here as well.

N O T E   NCSA map files are generally found in the **/cgi-bin/imagemap/...** directory.
CERN map files are generally found in the **/cgi-bin/htimage/...** directory.

The final choice in the Image Maps section of the Advanced tab is whether or not you want FrontPage to generate HTML code for client-side imagemaps. If you do not, FrontPage generates only server-side imagemaps. The difference is that *server-side maps* have their coordinate information stored on the server, whereas *client-side maps* send the coordinate information to the user's Web browser and thus are somewhat faster. In practical terms, the user sees the difference when passing the cursor over the map: The browser's status bar shows x/y coordinates for server-side maps, whereas for client-side maps, the status bar shows the URLs for the individual links. Not all browsers support client-side maps, but recent ones certainly do. For the most part, client-side imagemaps are far more common today than the server-side versions, because they're faster and more informative to the user.

N O T E   Not sure if your readers' browsers support client-side imagemaps? You can include client-side and server-side information in the same file. Given that browsers ignore HTML information they can't process, a server-side imagemap browser will use that code; client-side imagemap browsers will use the local data.

▶ **See** Chapter 6, "Enhancing Pages with Themes, Graphics, and Multimedia," for more on imagemaps. **p. 123**

If you want full compatibility across all browsers and have no interest whatsoever in providing imagemaps, leave the Generate Client-Side Image Maps check box empty. Otherwise, fill in the check box by clicking it.

Part
V

Ch
25

CAUTION

Don't simply guess at what kind of imagemap your server uses—check with your server's software manual or with your system administrator. Otherwise, you'll end up with imagemaps that almost certainly will not work.

The Options section of the Advanced tab also contains the option to Show Documents in Hidden Directories. As explained in Chapter 23, "FrontPage's Web Templates and Wizards," FrontPage 98 installs some directories as hidden directories. If you want to display these in FrontPage Explorer's views, you must specify this on the Web Settings dialog box. All hidden directories and files will be included in the Explorer views, but not in the Web itself. Unless you have a specific reason for working with these directories, it's best to leave them hidden. If you want full control over all directories, however, or even if you only want to see every single file that FrontPage generates, by all means unhide them.

When you select to show the hidden directories, FrontPage 98 recalculates the links. If this recalculation takes place on a remote server, it could take several minutes. If you subsequently uncheck this option in order to remove the hidden directories from view, FrontPage 98 will take a minute or two to refresh the Web.

The final section on the Web Settings dialog box is to specify the Recalculation Status of the Web currently loaded into FrontPage Explorer. As you add links and pages to your Web, the text index needs to be regenerated, as well as the page dependencies on which these new links rely. The Web Settings dialog box tells you that these are out of date by placing a check mark next to the out-of-date item. In this case, you should use the Tools menu to Verify Hyperlinks and Recalculate Hyperlinks. When you do so, reopening the Web Settings dialog box no longer shows those check marks.

Language

Through the Language tab of the FrontPage Web Settings dialog box, you can change the default Web language and HTML coding.

The Default Web Language refers to the human language in which error messages are displayed in your visitors' browsers. If your audience is primarily English, leave this setting as the default. You can also return error messages in French, German, Italian, Japanese, and Spanish, and you should keep this in mind if developing pages for audiences whose primary language is one of those.

The Default HTML Encoding refers to the character set that will be used across your Web. By default, the character set is US/Western European, but many others are available, including Korean, Greek, Baltic, Cyrillic, and several flavors of Japanese. When you choose a default encoding, all pages you create are saved with this encoding. You can alter this for individual pages with the Page Properties dialog box in FrontPage Editor.

Giving Permission to Administer, Author, and Browse Your Webs

Your Webs are important primarily because they show off your company or your personal preferences to the world, or because they offer important information to members of your company or organization. Because of this, you don't want just anybody putting information on your site. In fact, you need strict control over who can make changes, add documents, and alter the Web's contents or appearance. If FrontPage didn't offer a system for setting permissions, anyone on the Internet could make changes to your Web, and you'd wake up every morning wondering exactly how your public image had been modified. Although that would certainly be exciting, it would obviously be unacceptable.

FrontPage lets you set permissions for users to administer, author, and browse your Webs. Each of these are explored in detail in this section.

Basically, the differences are as follows:

- *Browse permissions* are given to people who are permitted to visit your Web by using a Web browser such as Netscape Navigator. They can read your pages, but they cannot alter them in any way, nor can they add, delete, or otherwise manage your Webs. Their only access to your Web site is through a browser, not through FrontPage Editor or FrontPage Explorer.

- *Author permissions* are given to people who are permitted to create and edit content in the Web, but they cannot add or delete Webs, or manage them in any other way. In other words, they can use FrontPage Editor in conjunction with a particular Web (and only that Web), but they can use FrontPage Explorer only as a viewing tool, or as a means of invoking FrontPage Editor or Image Composer. Those with Author permissions automatically have Browse permissions.

- *Administer permissions* are given to people whom you want to have full access to Web administration. They can add and delete Webs, and they can set Web permissions and configurations. Note, however, that only you can restrict administrators to individual Webs, with only one administrator having full access to the root Web. Those with Administer permissions automatically have Author and Browse permissions.

In other words, people with Administer permissions on a Web have unlimited access to that particular Web, whereas those with Author permissions have less access, and those with Browse permissions, the least complete access of all.

Using the Server Administration dialog boxes (see Chapter 26, "Managing a Web"), you can set the permissions for the root Web, which is the Web that FrontPage creates as the primary Web for your server. If you want, you can have all your Webs contain the same permissions. Using the Web Permissions dialog box, however, you can set unique permissions for each Web on your server. This allows you maximum flexibility for determining who will work on your Webs. This might, in fact, be your most important administrative task as Webmaster.

Establishing the Main Settings

Figure 25.7 shows the Settings tab of the Web Permissions dialog box. You have two choices in this area. You can have the currently loaded Web use the same permissions as the root Web, or you can establish unique permissions for this Web. If you mark the Use Same Permissions as Root Web option button, you can set no other permissions in this dialog box; everything, instead, must be set using the Server Administration dialog boxes. By marking the Use Unique Permissions for This Web option button, you can establish specific permissions for the current Web, although this Web automatically inherits the root Web settings as well.

Setting Permissions: People versus Computers

FrontPage offers two ways of setting browse, author, and administer permissions. You can give these permissions to people via the Users tab, giving each user a name and a password, which is the most common way (see Figure 25.8). But, you can also restrict access by the IP (Internet Protocol) address of computers themselves, through the Computers tab. You can restrict access to individual computers, or to computers who share portions of an IP address.

FIG. 25.7

For the greatest possible flexibility, establish unique permissions for each Web.

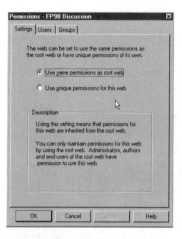

FIG. 25.8

Adding Users requires that you specify a name and a password for the person, as well as the level of permissions you're granting.

Why would you choose the Computers option? The most obvious choice would be to restrict browse permissions to groups of computers in a single organization. For example, you might be creating a Web that contains important company information, and designed to be seen only by employees of that company (an intranet, in other words). Each machine in that company has an IP address, for example, 139.205.104.72, and all machines on the company network are likely to have IP addresses that are identical for the first 3–6 numbers (139.205). In this case, to prevent outsiders from seeing the information, you can tell FrontPage 97 to restrict browse access to computers with an IP address of 139.205.*.* (the asterisks are called wildcards). This means that when anyone tries to access the Web, the server checks the IP address, and if the address is not within that restricted range, the server won't serve any information. This process is called setting an IP *mask*.

By default, all Webs give administer, author, and browse permissions to *all* computers on the Internet (IP *.*.*.*), but to *no* users other than the root Web administrator. This means that only the users you set up can get into your Web (with whatever level of permissions you grant them), but that they can do so from any computer on the Net. By carefully combining User and Computer restrictions, you can specify exactly who gets to do what on your Web.

Setting Administer Permissions

Administrators play an important role in creating Webs. They have permission to create Webs and individual Web documents, to delete these pages and Webs, and to establish permissions for authors and users. In other words, administrators control exactly who gets to work on the Web and, in fact, who gets to see it. Administrators are also automatically registered as end users and authors.

Through the Users and Computers tabs of the Web Permissions dialog box, the administrator of the root Web can give administer permissions on individual Webs to users or computers. The process is simple, but it's extremely important.

> **CAUTION**
>
> When you first create a Web, especially if you're not a large company, your first inclination might be to give administer positions to just about anyone. However, give careful thought to this decision; administrators have a lot of power over the Web.

When you click the Add button, the Add User dialog box appears. The username and password are entirely up to you, but be sure to remember the password so that the new administrator can access the site. Select the option User Can Administer, Author, and Browse This Web, and click OK. The new name appears in the Permissions dialog box.

When you have finished adding users, click Apply. If there's a problem, FrontPage 98 gives you an error message. If you've made an error, or want to change permissions, you can try to edit the entry by clicking the Edit button, but usually it's easier to just Remove it and try adding it without committing the same error.

 Don't let each administrator set their own password. Only one person should be the chief administrator of the Web, and that person should establish all access. Set that as a policy as soon as you install FrontPage.

To further assure controlled permissions in your Webs, you can click the Computers tab and restrict administer permissions to specific IP addresses or address masks. IP address masks are ranges of IP addresses; you can specify a full IP address, or you can use the wildcard asterisk character to specify IP addresses within a certain range.

For example, if you want to restrict access so that administrators can access the Web only from one specific machine, you can enter the full IP address of that machine. Click Add and fill in the machine's IP number in the resulting New IP Address dialog box. The IP address looks something like 135.201.123.91—always a four-part number.

More likely, you'll want to restrict access to an IP address range. Because users with dialup connections are usually given a dynamic IP address, that is, one that changes with each new logon—specifying a full IP restriction means that dial-up administration is next to impossible. Instead, you can use the wildcard asterisk character in place of some of the IP numbers. In the

Part
V

Ch
25

previous example, the first two numbers (135.201) specify the high level of the domain, so a restriction to that portion of the address means that users have to be logged on to that overall domain, which means a specific organization such as your company, to perform administrative tasks. For this example, click the Add button and type **135.201.*.*** in the New IP Mask dialog box.

TROUBLESHOOTING

I restricted access to a domain mask, but my administrators can still get in from anywhere they like. What happened? All administrators listed in the Administrators tab share the same restrictions. You can't restrict one administrator to access from one IP range and a second from a different IP range. Because of this, if you're going to restrict ranges at all, be sure to remove the default IP address mask (*.*.*.*). This mask allows access from anywhere, which is exactly what you don't want.

When you've set your administrators and IP address masks, click <u>A</u>pply to save them to the Web. Remember that they apply to the current Web only; you must set individual restrictions for each Web you administer.

Setting Author Permissions

In addition to establishing administrative authority for each Web, you can also set authoring authority. Authors can create and delete individual Web pages from the specific Web for which they're authorized. They cannot create or delete the Webs themselves, and they can't establish authorial permission for other authors.

Setting author permissions is identical to the process described in the previous "Setting Administer Permissions" section. From the Users tab, click Add, provide a name and password, and select User Can <u>A</u>uthor and Browse This Web and click Apply. From the Computers tab, restrict Author permissions according to IP number or IP mask for added security.

TROUBLESHOOTING

I try to add myself as an author, and it tells me my name already exists with administrator permissions. Does this mean I can't author pages in my own Web? Not at all. All administrators automatically have authoring permissions for that Web, even though their names do not appear in the Authors tab.

Establishing author permissions is one area in which Web management becomes just that— Web management. As chief administrator, you have the sole authority to authorize administrators for each Web, but each of those administrators, in turn, can establish as many new authors as they want. It's extremely important to set firm guidelines about who has permission to author, and this has to be done through frequent communication with your administrators.

Setting Browse Permissions

One of the most important security tasks of Web administrators is to establish who may visit your Web. Doing so restricts who gets to look at your Web, and this can be useful for any number of reasons. When you're first constructing a Web, for example, you don't want the world to see it, and once it's established, you might want it to be accessible only to users you choose to register.

Establishing Browse permissions with the User or Computer tabs is identical to establishing Administer and Author permissions, except that, after providing a name and password, you select User Can Browse This Web. If you've set your Web so that everyone has browse access (on the Permissions dialog box), restricting by IP number or IP mask comes into play if you want to control access anyway. If you've established that everyone has browse access and that all computers have access, then setting user browse permissions effectively does nothing at all.

Restricting user access by name can be valuable if you want to set up a Web whereby purchasers of your service or product, for example, are given a common username and password that allows them to access a special Web just for them. The only way they can know the username and password is to buy the service or product (perhaps you include it in the packaging), so you can establish all customers as registered users with one username and one password.

N O T E This one may sound better than it actually plays out. Software distributors are still trying to find ways to restrict usage to those who are authorized users (for example, purchasers). Passwords, special code sheets, and secret decoder rings haven't stopped the determined yet. Everyone seems to have a friend with password, code, or a copy of the sheet who'll pass the information on. ▨

Part
V

Ch
25

Creating User Registration Forms   Obviously, this process is tedious if you're attempting to establish a Web where all individual users have their own unique usernames and passwords, as is the case in many Web sites on the World Wide Web. To allow users to register themselves and to provide you with valuable information for your database, use FrontPage's Registration Component. You can initiate this Component while authoring a page or from the Discussion Web Wizard.

▶ **See** Chapter 11, "Using FrontPage Components, Forms, and Interactive Page Templates," **p. 225**, and Chapter 23, "FrontPage's Web Templates and Wizards," **p. 535**, for more information about these topics.

With the Registration Component, you create a registration form that you can specify as belonging to the precise Web you want. When users fill in this form and submit it to your server, their usernames and passwords (which they supply) are automatically added to the end user permissions of that Web. The following steps describe this process:

1. Specify the current Web as being accessible to Registered Users Only. This is accomplished through the End User tab of the Web Permissions dialog box.

2. Open the root Web of your server.

3. Open FrontPage Editor and choose File, New and select User Registration.

4. Edit the page that appears by clicking inside any form field (such as the Make Up a Username field) and choosing Edit, Properties. The Text Box Properties dialog box appears.

5. Select Form from this dialog box and choose Settings in the dialog box.

6. Select the name of the Web for which you want to register users (that is, the Web that you've just established end user permissions for) in the Registration tab.

7. Copy the form from the current page onto the home page for the root Web, or place a link from the root Web's home page to the new page that contains the form. Once that's done, your end users can start registering themselves, and the results appear in the End Users tab of the Web Permissions dialog box. As you'll discover, this is an extremely powerful system.

Changing Passwords

As with most network-based programs, you can change your password to prevent unwanted access. In fact, as long as the root Web administrator agrees, you should change it frequently. To do so, choose Tools, Change Password. You'll be presented with the Change Password for ... (user name) dialog box, in which you type the current password, the new password, and the new password a second time (to make sure you don't accidentally type something you'll never remember).

Any users with administer or author permissions can change their own passwords. You should set policy on password changes if you're the main administrator for your organization's Webs, and instruct those with administer or author permissions when and if they can make such changes. This is a significant issue in managing your Web site because you'll want full control over who gets to access it for the sake of adding, editing, and deleting Webs and files, and you should clarify password procedures immediately.

Setting General Options for the Web

Three options are available for each Web through the Tools, Options dialog box. The first is to show the Getting Started dialog box when you load FrontPage 98; this dialog box is shown in Chapter 22, "Building a Web." Next, you can have FrontPage 98 warn you when FrontPage Components included in your Web are out of date. Similarly, you can be warned if the text index is out of date. If your Web depends on up-to-date information, be sure to toggle these warnings on.

Establishing Proxy Servers

If you're using FrontPage 98 over a local area network (LAN) in your company or organization, there is a good possibility that you are operating behind a proxy server, which acts as a buffer between your company's LAN and the unruly Internet outside.

Proxies operate from behind *firewalls* on the organization's network; firewalls are software systems designed to prevent machines inside the organization from accessing outside computers directly. Instead, any requests for information on a machine outside the organization are sent to the proxy server, and then forwarded out to the server on the Internet. When the requested information is received, the proxy server decides, based on various criteria, whether or not to pass it through to the internal computer.

Contact your system administrator to get proxy information and enter this information in the Proxies dialog box, accessible by choosing Tools, Options, and click the Proxies tab.

The HTTP Proxy name appears as a full URL, probably with a port assignment added to the end, for example, **http://mycompany.com:2522**. The List of Hosts Without Proxy list box, which accepts anything you type, gives you a place to include servers within your LAN that you know you must connect to. Again, your system administrator provides this information if you don't know it. If you need proxy information but you don't have it, none of your Webs will be accessible from the outside Internet.

Configuring Editors

As you work in FrontPage 98, you realize that the package does a great deal—but not everything. The Bonus Pack includes the Image Composer graphics package, for example, but you might have a favorite image editor you'd also like to use. FrontPage also doesn't have a tool for editing sound or video files. To compensate, FrontPage lets you configure editors to handle specific types of documents.

To establish the editors, choose Tools, Options and click the Configure Editors tab. The Configure Editors dialog box appears. Here, the file extension is shown in the Type column, although the editor you want to use for viewing that kind of file is displayed in the Editor column.

When you click the Add button, the Add Editor Association dialog box appears. This dialog box allows you to specify a file type, the editor name, and the location of that program on your hard disk. In this example, sound files with the WAV extension are edited by a sound-editing program called GoldWave, which exists on the hard drive in the path C:\GOLDWAVE\ GOLDWAVE.EXE. If you don't know the exact path, click the Browse button to locate it.

Once the editors are established, you can invoke them by clicking that file type anywhere in a FrontPage Explorer view and choosing Edit, Open. The appropriate editor automatically opens with the specified file loaded into it and ready for viewing or editing.

From Here...

In this chapter, you've examined the ins and outs of configuring a server created with FrontPage 98—everything from setting passwords to establishing permissions for administrators, authors, and end users. Even though you're technically ready to show your Web to the

Part
V

Ch
25

world, it's nowhere near complete. You have to determine who will develop each Web page, and you must set the Web server software itself in place. Then it's on to the much larger task of editing and creating the Web documents themselves.

- Chapter 26, "Managing a Web," examines the management of people, machines, and software and also the usefulness of FrontPage's To Do List.

- Chapter 27, "Serving Your Web to the World with the Microsoft Personal Web Server," looks at the requirements for making your work available on the World Wide Web itself.

- Part II, "Creating Your Web Pages with FrontPage Editor," is all about the actual Web pages themselves.

## CHAPTER 26

Managing a Web

Creating Web sites is a fascinating exercise, but managing them from initial conception through frequent updates is a challenging task that FrontPage 98 can help you with. Working with the various views of the Web, Explorer's automatic link updating, as well as the mini-project management capabilities of the Tasks View, you can have some control over your Web as you work on it. ■

Managing people, information, and machines

What resources do you need to manage when building a sophisticated Web site?

FrontPage's Tasks View

Using the Tasks View for your basic project management tasks.

Tasks View Columns and buttons

Getting a handle on the inner workings of the Tasks View dialog box.

Adding and removing tasks

How to note new tasks to be completed, and how to show that tasks are completed.

Managing through Explorer's views

How do the three views from Explorer work together to help you manage and manipulate your site?

Web Site Management

One of the primary reasons to work with Microsoft FrontPage 98 is that it can help you create Web sites and manage them. It's exciting and enjoyable to create a new site from scratch, especially using FrontPage's wizards and templates that get you started. The first few Web documents are thoroughly enjoyable to design and develop, especially for anyone who's authored Web documents using raw HTML codes. If you've been stumped or simply bored with CGI scripting and developing such advanced items as discussion sites, working with FrontPage provides enjoyable alternatives to brute-force or boring coding.

But creating Webs isn't the greater part of a Webmaster's work. Instead, that dubious honor falls to maintaining and updating Webs. In fact, from start to finish, managing a Web site is every bit as important as creating one, even though the glory clearly goes to the people who design and develop the pages that everyone sees. Once a Web is in place, however, it remains of interest to users only if it is frequently updated, with new information and new reasons for visiting constantly being built in. Your job as Webmaster is to make sure that everything gets done, and that the new and replacement elements are placed in the Web so that they work right from the start.

Managing People

You might be in the position of using FrontPage 98 to create and manage a Web alone. In this case, the only person you'll need to manage is yourself. Assuming that you can be relied on to listen to yourself, FrontPage offers all you need to do the job. But if, like a growing number of Webmasters, you're creating and developing a Web site in conjunction with others, the management of people becomes quite probably the most difficult task of any you'll face. It's one thing to force a computer to do what you want it to do—it's quite another to get a group of people, no matter how small, to work together on a top-notch creative effort like a Web site. Workgroup dynamics, thankfully, are far beyond the scope of this book.

One of FrontPage 98's greatest strengths is its ease of use. What this means, from a manager's perspective, is that you have a far greater choice when hiring potential Web authors. In the past, you needed to find someone who knew HTML and probably CGI if you wanted to get anything done with reasonable speed, and those skills were hard to find. With a graphical package like FrontPage 98, you can begin to focus your recruitment on people with an eye to design rather than those who can code or program. This isn't to suggest that you no longer need people with programming experience, but FrontPage makes it much easier to share tasks among contributors with differing talents.

Here you'll take a look at the tools within FrontPage that will at least partly ease the assignment of tasks to authors and co-administrators. These tools—the Permissions dialog boxes of the Explorer Configuration menus and the Tasks View with its limited but effective tracking mechanism—are by no means extensive, but they're better than nothing by a long shot.

Managing Information

After managing people, the hardest thing about creating a Web site is managing all the information. Information itself changes constantly but, more importantly, so do the needs and the expectations of its users. If you want your Web site to be effective—which translates into many users visiting many times and finding many rewards for doing so—you have to change the information and its presentation regularly. You also need to change the ways in which your readers interact with that information and, as a result, you'll frequently have to reconsider the interface your Web offers to its users.

With the advent of intranets, a new kind of information has appeared in Webs. This information—which consists of everything from procedures documents, meeting and event schedules, project milestones, and even financial details—is restricted to viewing by members of the organization to which it belongs. As a manager of an intranet site as opposed to an Internet site, your attention to information will be different but at least as important. The organization's information must be complete, readily accessible, and secure. Changes to some intranet information might be less frequent than for an Internet site, but that doesn't make it less demanding.

While information management is an organizational issue and hardly something one person can be responsible for, FrontPage offers a few tools that make such management a bit easier. First, the close link between FrontPage Editor and FrontPage Explorer makes on-the-fly editing and adding of Web pages easier than ever before. Second, Explorer's built-in links management system helps you keep your pages properly connected to one another, solving the problem of hyperlinks that lead nowhere or to the wrong page entirely. Finally, Explorer's multiple views let you see the way the information is presented, thereby negating the need for flow diagrams or such niceties as index cards. Your information is easier to manage because you can visualize it easily.

Part
V

Ch
26

Managing Computers

At this point in the Web's history, there's still nothing easy about setting up a Web server and making all connected computers work with it happily and without incident. Simply put, managing a Web is still very much about managing computers.

This is one area in which FrontPage does as good a job as anything out there. The facts are that most Web servers exist on UNIX or Windows NT machines and most would-be Web designers work with computers running Windows 3.x or Windows 95, although certainly this is changing with the increasing popularity of NT Workstation. Through its server extensions, and hence its ability to let you work directly with the Webs on your server, FrontPage makes setting up a Web site relatively transparent. Similarly, by incorporating into the authoring software many of the tasks normally given over to the Common Gateway Interface (CGI), FrontPage lets you take command of the server in a way that most nonprogrammers could barely even dream of.

None of this is to suggest that using FrontPage replaces an intimate knowledge of UNIX, networking, or the workings of an HTTP server. What FrontPage does, however, is to render computer management something apart from those highly technical concerns. Suddenly it's up to the technical professionals to try to make the machines do what you want them to do. As long as the server owner cooperates, FrontPage gives you a considerable amount of power when it comes to managing computers.

FrontPage 98's Tasks View

The single most useful piece of direct Web management available through FrontPage is the Tasks View. Although it's certainly no replacement for sophisticated project management software, it is nevertheless a surprisingly powerful assistant. From the Tasks View, you can launch and work on every one of the outstanding projects, and you can get an entire history of who did what and when during the building of your site.

FrontPage automatically creates a Tasks View for each Web you create. The principle behind the Tasks View is this: all pages are incomplete (under construction) on a newly created Web. They will show in the Web as being under construction and will bear the Under Construction icon. As you work on individual pages, you can load them into FrontPage Editor from the Tasks View. If you change anything on that page and then save it to the Web, FrontPage will, if you want, automatically mark the task as completed within the Tasks View. You can add new tasks in the Tasks View from within the Tasks View itself, or you can add them from the Explorer and Editor programs as well. To use the Tasks View, you must have the Web currently open in FrontPage Explorer.

Tasks View Columns

Figure 26.1 shows the Tasks View. Along the top of the list are the following column headings: Status, Task, Assigned To, Priority, Linked To, Modified Date, and Description. Most of these are created through the Task Details or Add To Task dialog boxes, discussed later. The exceptions are Modified Date and Linked To, and their appearance is also discussed later.

Status   The Status column shows the status of each task in your Web. Only two statuses are available: Not Started and Completed. Not Started covers everything from the time the task is established on the Web to the time when you specify it as being Completed.

When you finish a task, you tell FrontPage by right-clicking that task and choosing Mark Complete (or selecting Edit, Mark Task Complete). This changes the icon in the Status bar for that task to a green light, and the status to Completed. Completed tasks disappear from the Task View, and if you wish to see them, you need to show the Task History. When the Task View is showing, the View menu changes to show the Task History command. Toggling this on shows Tasks that have been marked as completed, as well as those still in process.

You can sort the Tasks View according to any of the columns by clicking the column heading itself. Figure 26.2, for example, shows the same Tasks View as seen in Figure 26.1—this time sorted by the Assigned To column. It also can be useful to sort a much longer list in the pictured Tasks View by page linked to, person assigned to, or priority.

FIG. 26.1
The Tasks View contains enough information to keep track of a Web's planned progress.

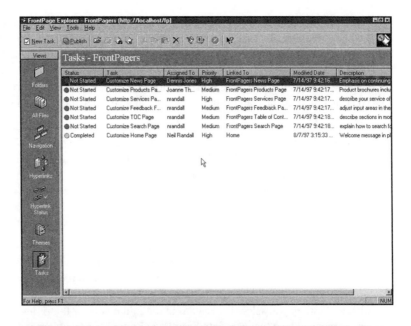

FIG. 26.2
By sorting the Tasks View, you can get a different perspective on the tasks at hand.

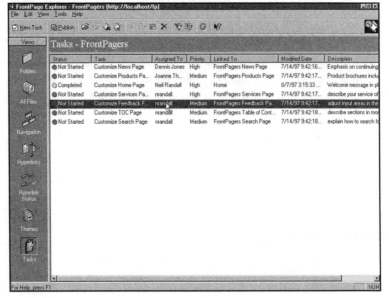

Part
V

Ch
26

Task   The Task column simply lists the name of the Task itself. FrontPage adds a name automatically when you use a wizard to create a Web, but when you add a task manually, you can give it whatever name you wish (up to 256 characters long). You can edit the name of manually created tasks at any time by right-clicking the Task and selecting Edit Task (or Edit, Properties). You cannot edit the name of a task created by a FrontPage wizard.

Assigned To   All tasks contain an Assigned To field. You can type whatever you like in this field, but the idea is to assign each Web task to a member of your authoring team. FrontPage does no internal checking for names or user IDs; however, this field is entirely free-form. By default, the Web administrator's name appears in this field, but you can edit the field by right-clicking the task and selecting Edit Task (or Edit, Properties). If you create a task manually, you can assign the task at the same time as you give it a name. You can sort the Task View by assignments to help you manage your team.

Priority   Whenever you create or edit a task, you assign it a priority. There are three priority levels: High, Medium, and Low. You can change priority by right-clicking the task and selecting Edit Task (or Edit, Properties). Assigning a priority in FrontPage doesn't actually do anything to the task, because FrontPage doesn't check due dates or alert you to unfinished tasks (as a Personal Information Manager such as Microsoft Outlook or Lotus Organizer does). You can, however, sort by priority as a means of helping you organize your team's work.

Linked To   The Linked To field shows the title of the page in the FrontPage Web that the task actually belongs to. This field appears only when you create a link through FrontPage Editor (see the following instructions on doing so), at which point the task takes the title of the page you're working on as its "link." The link performs the central function of telling FrontPage what to do when you select Do Task from the Edit menu (or the right-click menu). Do Task simply means, "load this page into FrontPage Editor." If a task does not have a link, Do Task is not an available command.

You cannot add a link to a task manually created in FrontPage Explorer.

Modified Date   The Modified Date column shows the date and time the task was last modified. It shows when the linked page was last changed and saved, or when the task was marked as Completed. This field cannot be manually modified.

Description   As its name suggests, this column is simply a description of that task. FrontPage offers its own generic descriptions of tasks it creates through wizards, but you can (and should for clarity's sake) change the description at any time through the Edit Task command. The description field of the Edit Task dialog box is completely free-form, so feel free to be as explanatory as you wish. In fact, you can use it for simple checklists for the task, milestones, due dates, and so forth.

Tasks View Commands

When you choose a Task and right-click it, you get a shortcut menu showing four commands: Edit Task, Do Task, Mark Complete, and Delete. These can also be accessed by selecting the task and accessing the Edit menu, and selecting (correspondingly) Properties, Do Task, Mark Task Complete, and Delete.

Do Task   Although simple in concept, this is an extremely powerful tool. When you select a task in the Tasks View and click Do Task, the file associated with the task opens into its appropriate editor. HTML files will open by default inside the FrontPage Editor, while graphics files will load inside the associated graphics editor. You establish these editors and their associations in the Configure Editors dialog box, which is available with the Tools, Options command in Explorer.

Edit Task/Edit Properties   When you select a task and select Edit Task from the shortcut menu, or Properties from the Edit menu, the Task Details dialog box appears. As Figure 26.3 shows, this dialog box contains several fields; some of these are alterable but five of them are not.

FIG. 26.3

The Task Details dialog box gives you control over responsibilities and specifications.

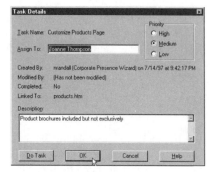

The first item in the dialog box is the Task Name. This name is created either by the FrontPage Wizard that created the Web, or by the person who added the task to the Tasks View. You cannot change this name.

The Assign To text box lets you specify who should complete the task. This box is wide open, meaning that its contents aren't checked against the list of authors or administrators for the Web (an option to do so would be helpful, in fact). You can enter any name you want in here, but it's a good idea to keep your naming scheme consistent.

To the top-right of the dialog box are the Priority option buttons. You can set the selected task as High, Medium, or Low priority, and the choice appears in the Priority column of the Tasks View. While it's tempting to set everything at high priority, as a Web manager you'll want to set only the most truly important tasks as such.

The Description list box is another free-form field. Type in anything that might be helpful here, including specific suggestions to the person to whom the task has been assigned. The first few characters of this description appear in the Description column of the Tasks View.

The other four fields are determined by FrontPage itself, and cannot be altered except by working on the task. Created By shows which author established the task in the first place, including the time and date of its creation and the wizard through which it was created (if any). Modified By displays the author responsible for the modification. The Completed field is either Yes or No, and simply refers to whether or not the task has been set as Completed in the Tasks View. Linked To displays the file to which the Task item is linked, and this appears in the Linked To column of the Tasks View. This can be changed only by altering the link within FrontPage Editor or Explorer.

Part
V

Ch
26

Mark Complete   When a task in the Tasks View has been finished to your satisfaction, select Mark Complete from the shortcut menu (or Edit, Mark Task Complete). The task will be shown on the Task View with a green icon and with the status of Completed.

Delete   The Delete command erases the task from the Task View but the document to which it refers is unaffected. Notice that there's a difference between deleting a task and marking it completed. If you want to keep track of what's been done, use Mark Completed; if you have no interest in the history of your Web's tasks, simply use Delete.

Adding Tasks   The Add command—available through New Task on the shortcut menu when you right-click in the Tasks View—lets you enter an entirely new task into the Tasks View. The dialog box is identical to the Task Details dialog box shown in Figure 26.3 except that the Task Name and Description text boxes are not filled in, and the Linked To field shows Is not Linked. Because the task hasn't originated from FrontPage Explorer or Editor, the task is not associated with a file in your Web, and thus you cannot open it automatically into an editor. In fact, selecting a task added this way results in the Do Task button being grayed out and thus unavailable.

As a Web manager, you can use this button to add tasks to the list that aren't actually Web creation tasks. For example, you might need several graphics created for a page or series of pages, or you might need pictures or documents scanned for presentation in a document. For that matter, you can use the Add button to schedule meetings if it helps to get your assistant's attention. But this method of adding tasks is less effective than adding them from FrontPage's main programs because they can't be completed as part of FrontPage activity itself.

Adding to the Tasks View from FrontPage Editor

Often, when working on a page in FrontPage Editor, you'll realize that something needs to be completed on the page that you don't have time or resources for at that particular time. Instead of jotting down a note to yourself in a text file or a word processor, you can add a task to the Tasks View directly from within Editor itself. The following is an example of this extremely useful process.

With the FrontPagers Web open (originally begun in Chapter 22, "Building a Web"), the Webmaster has decided to add a new page showing an employee directory. FrontPage Editor has been opened, and the Employee Directory template has been selected.

At this point, the Webmaster decides that it would be a nice idea to add a photograph of each employee. Knowing that it will take a few days to get these photographs together and to get permission to use them, she decides to add a task to remind her of this and assigns the task to an assistant, Marty. She chooses Add Task from the Edit menu. This yields the New Task dialog box (see Figure 26.4), where she can specify the name of the task, the person assigned the task, the priority of the task, and a description of the task.

FIG. 26.4

The description box will be seen by the Webmaster only.

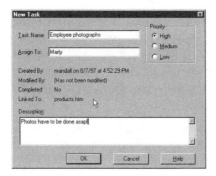

An important element of this dialog box is the Linked To field. The file being edited was saved as **EMPLOYEE.HTM**, and this now appears in that field. This means that clicking the Do Task button in the Tasks View loads the EMPLOYEE.HTM file into FrontPage Editor.

The Task Name is "Employee photographs," and the task is assigned to Marty. This is given medium priority, and the description (which is meant to be seen by the Webmaster, not the assistant), explains what is to be done. Clicking OK sets this task into the Tasks View, as the highlighted line of Figure 26.5 demonstrates.

FIG. 26.5

The new task is ready for action in the FrontPage Tasks View.

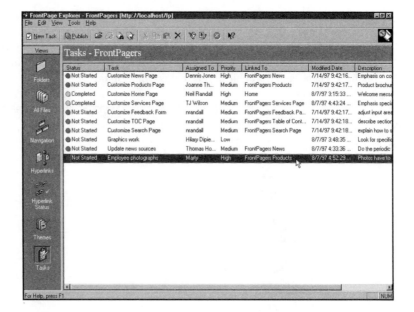

Adding to the Tasks View from FrontPage Explorer

If you're working in Explorer's Folders, All Files, Navigation, or Hyperlinks views, and you want to add a task to the Tasks View, the procedure is almost identical to the procedure for adding from Editor. With the View visible, click the page to which you want to associate the To Do task. Now, with the page highlighted, choose Edit, Add To Do Task. Basically, anywhere you can select a single page, you can add a task.

The Add To Do Task dialog box appears, with the selected page appearing in the Linked To field. After you fill in the appropriate information, the task appears in the Tasks View, ready for action.

Managing Through Explorer's Views

Throughout Part V, "Building and Managing a Web," you've seen examples of the graphical Hyperlinks View or Navigation View in FrontPage Explorer. So far, the suggestion has been that these views help you create a Web site and develop all the associated pages. That's true, but if your role is that of site manager rather than (or in addition to) page creator, these views will help you here as well. In fact, two other views, Folder View and All Files View, are especially useful in this regard.

Hyperlinks View

Figure 26.6 shows a Customer Support Web as created by Explorer. The view, which you've seen throughout these chapters, is the Hyperlinks View, with a textual hierarchy of hyperlinks in the left pane, and a graphical view of these links in the right.

FIG. 26.6

The Hyperlinks View for a Customer Service Web.

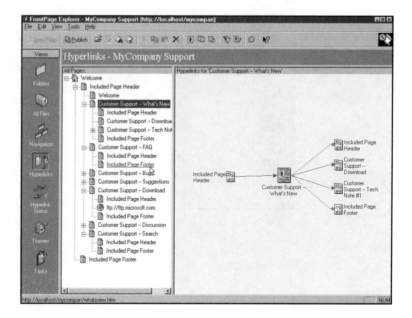

The All Pages pane offers one possible assistant for Web management. Using this pane, you can quickly get a top-level hierarchical look at your Web by keeping all the headings compressed, or you can look in detail at any particular heading and its components by selectively expanding them. As you expand headings by clicking the plus signs (+) to the left of the items, you get a sense of the size and scope of your Web, and you can move quickly to an individual component for editing or assigning.

The right pane of the Hyperlink View shows you the Web in a graphical format. With this view, you can tell exactly which pages link to which pages and how the links fit together to form the overall Web. The strength of the Hyperlink view lies in its ability to show you exactly what needs to be added or completed, rather than simply presenting it, like the Tasks View, as yet another item in a list. The weakness of the Hyperlink view, however, is that it can show you only a portion of the Web at any one time. Obviously a 21-inch monitor set to ultra-high resolution can display a larger portion than a 14-inch monitor and low resolution, but on such a display, the Hyperlink view can become unwieldy. From a management perspective, the graphical Hyperlink view is best as a means of assessing and detailing specific portions of the Web, while the hierarchical All Hyperlinks view gives you a sense of scope and overall shape.

Folders View

In Figure 26.7, you see the same Web as in Figure 26.6, but this time the Hyperlinks View has been replaced by the Folders View, which is similar to the file view of Windows Explorer: folders in the left pane, and subfolders and files in the right. Accessing the Folders View is simply a matter of choosing View/Folders View, or clicking the Folders icon in the Views toolbar. Obviously, the Folders View is text-based rather than graphical, and as such it doesn't provide the same kind of information the Hyperlinks View offers. What it does provide, however, is a short summary of all the details pertaining to the files in your Web site.

Part
V

Ch
26

FIG. 26.7
The Folders View shows you exactly which files make up your Web.

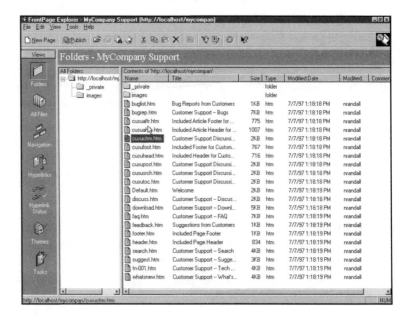

The columns in the Folders View display the following data:

- **Name**   This is the actual file name of the folder or file. Web documents will almost always end in HTM or HTML (note that Windows 95 and Windows NT accept extensions of more than three characters); graphics will end in JPG or PCX. You can use the file name information, for example, if you want to edit the file directly by using a different editor, or even a text editor such as Windows' Notepad.

- **Title**   The title of the Web file, as set during the creation of the page. You can change the title using the Page Properties dialog box of FrontPage Editor. In the case of images, the Title column shows the path and file name instead of a title.

- **Size**   The Size column shows the size of the file in bytes. Files smaller than 1K (1,024 bytes) are shown with their actual byte count, while files greater than 1K are displayed in kilobytes and rounded to the nearest kilobyte. Files larger than 1M (1,024K) are displayed in megabytes, rounded to the nearest megabyte.

TIP   It's entirely possible that files greater than one gigabyte (1,024M) appear in number of gigabytes, but it was not tested on a large enough hard drive. Besides, if you have a file that large in your Web, you should get rid of it if you don't want hordes of angry modem users storming your house.

- **Type**   The file type simply repeats the extension shown in the file name, unless your operating system doesn't use file extensions in file names. In that case, Type is the only place to find the actual file type.

- **Modified Date**   This column shows the last date and time the file was modified.

- **Modified By**   This column shows who did the modifications for that page or file.

- **Comments**   The Comments column shows the comments about the document as entered through the Properties dialog box.

Together, these columns can provide a wealth of information. You can sort the Folders View according to any of these columns by clicking the column heading showing you precise details ordered as you need them. For example, sorting by Modified Date lets you instantly see which pages haven't been updated recently enough to suit the site's needs, as established during planning. With large Webs, it's extremely easy to overlook one or two pages that need updating, especially pages that are less frequently accessed, and this column can help keep your attention focused on that strategy.

The Title, File Name, and Type columns can help you locate specific pages, and here another useful element of the Folders View comes into play. When you find the item you need in the Folder view, you can right-click it and select Show Hyperlinks, which opens the Hyperlink view centered on that file.

All Files View

Like the Folders View, the All Files View offers a file-oriented approach to Web management. This time, though, the focus is away from the folders and on the files themselves. As Figure 26.8 shows, the All Files View gives you the name of each file, plus detailed information about that file in the context of the entire Web.

FIG. 26.8

The All Files View lets you see each file, its size and location, and details such as its status as an orphan.

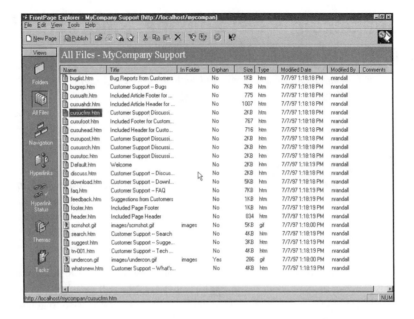

The difference between using the All Files View and the Folders View is simple but important. In the Folders View, you are shown your Web as if it were in Windows Explorer: you see each folder, and you can locate the files inside the folders in order to work with them. In the All Files View, by contrast, you see a complete listing of all the files in the Web, and the rest of the columns display what folder they can be found in plus additional information. In other words, the All Files View gives you a complete look at the specific files and recognizes that the actual folder location is often of little consequence.

The All Files View contains two columns that do not appear in the Folders View:

- **In Folder**   This column shows the folder in which the file resides on the Web server. If nothing is displayed, then the folder is the root folder for that Web.

- **Orphan**   This column shows the orphan status of a file. A file is orphaned if it is not linked to another file in the Web.

Navigation View

The Navigation View of FrontPage Explorer gives you a rich graphical look at your Web. From a Web creation standpoint, Navigation View is indispensable. From a management standpoint, for instance, working with a Web once it's in place, it offers an extremely convenient means of reorganizing a Web and adding to it. The Navigation View is covered primarily in Chapter 24, "Working with an Existing Web."

Part
V

Ch
26

Management Tools: Spelling, Find, Verify Hyperlinks, and Recalculate Hyperlinks

FrontPage 98 offers four important tools specifically designed to help Webmasters manage their Webs. These tools tackle four simple but crucial tasks: Global Spell-Checking, Global Find and Replace, and two means of checking a Web's links: Verify Hyperlinks and Recalculate Hyperlinks.

Global Spell-Checking

One of the problems every Webmaster encounters is the difficulty of ensuring accurate spelling across the entire site. Authors can check their work on individual documents in FrontPage Editor, but when all the documents are linked together in a Web, it's essential that spelling be checked for errors and for lack of standardization. Almost nothing can reduce the professional appearance of a site more quickly than a measly little spelling mistake. It simply looks bad.

To invoke global spell-checking, choose Spelling from the Tools menu of FrontPage Explorer. This can be done from any of Explorer's views. You will be asked if you want to check all pages or only the pages you've selected, and whether or not you wish to add a new task to the Tasks View for any pages that contain misspellings. Since FrontPage's spelling tool cannot actually correct the spelling (as a word processor can), adding to the Tasks View is a good idea. If you wish, however, you can choose to Edit pages directly from the results of the spell check, so the Tasks View addition might not be necessary, especially in the case of a relatively small Web site.

N O T E   Unfortunately, FrontPage does not offer a global thesaurus to match the global spelling checker. Thesaurus activities are available only within FrontPage Editor and, thus, can be done only one document at a time. ▪

Global Find and Replace

Sometimes, several documents in a Web contain a piece of information that needs to be located or changed. The names of products might change, or the names of corporate contacts, the prices of services, or any other type of repeated information might need to be found and possibly altered. In a large Web, changing repeated data is extremely tedious, requiring the Webmaster to load each page individually and edit the material. FrontPage 98 makes this considerably more convenient by providing a global Find feature and a separate global Replace feature.

To perform a global Find, select Find from FrontPage Explorer's Tools menu. You will be asked first to save any pages from the current Web that are open in FrontPage Editor. You'll then type the text string you wish to find and whether or not you wish to match the whole word or the upper- or lowercase of the word as typed. You'll also be asked if you want to find the string in all pages in the Web, or only in the pages you've highlighted.

The results of your search appear in a Find occurrences of... dialog box. This box shows the pages on which the search string has been found. By clicking a page and choosing Edit Page, you can load the selected page into Editor, or by clicking Add Task, you can place the page in the Tasks View.

Performing a global Replace is almost identical. Select Replace from the Tools menu of FrontPage Explorer and type the text strings in the respective Find What and Replace With fields on the Replace in FrontPage Web dialog box. You'll also be asked, as with Find, to specify case and whole word matches, and whether to replace the string across the Web or only in selected pages.

The results of the Replace command appear in the Find occurrences box shown in Figure 26.9. You'll see the titles of the pages on which the string is found, as well as the number of times it occurs on each page. You're also informed, in the information line below the box, that FrontPage is ready to make the replacements.

FIG. 26.9

You can add each document to the Tasks View to edit later, or you can edit directly from here.

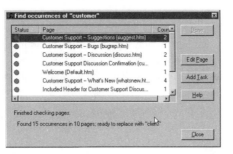

By highlighting a page and clicking Edit Page, you load the document into FrontPage Editor and are immediately presented with the Replace dialog box, complete with the Find and Replace fields already filled in. In other words, you haven't actually replaced anything yet, and you have to perform the replacement operations from there.

If you add the document to the Tasks View by clicking Add Task instead, you will be presented with the same Replace dialog box when you edit the page from within the Tasks View.

Verify and Recalculate Hyperlinks

Another of a Webmaster's crucial but tedious tasks is to check the hyperlinks that point inside and outside a Web. This task is crucial because broken links will frustrate users of the Web, and tedious because a heavily linked site (as most Webs are) contains any number of potential erroneous hyperlinks.

FrontPage 98 offers two ways of checking hyperlinks across the Web, both of which are accessible from the Tools menu. Verify Hyperlinks determines whether or not hyperlinks internal and external to the pages in your site are valid. Recalculate Hyperlinks updates the views of your Webs in FrontPage Explorer and also updates various components of your Webs. Both ways require that you first be online.

Part
V

Ch
26

Selecting Verify Hyperlinks causes FrontPage to ensure the validity of hyperlinks internal to your Web. It then displays the Verify Hyperlinks dialog box, which displays the URLs it has checked. It displays a green bullet for valid hyperlinks, a yellow bullet for links that have been changed since the last verification or that aren't yet verified, and a red bullet for broken hyperlinks.

From this dialog box, you can edit the page or add the page to the Tasks View and you can perform one other essential task. By clicking Verify, you tell FrontPage to check the external URLs to which your Web pages point. These take time, which is why they're not checked in the first place, so while the process is going on, the Verify button changes to a Stop button, allowing you to halt the process whenever you wish.

Recalculate Hyperlinks performs several important updating functions. It updates the views of the Web in FrontPage Explorer, which is extremely important if you've edited hyperlinks or added or deleted pages. It also updates the text indexes that are produced by any Search component you have in your Web. Search components create indexes of all searchable pages, and as you add or delete pages, these indexes become incomplete. In addition, Recalculate Hyperlinks regenerates all the Include components in your Web. These components are, in a sense, empty containers with pointers to fields in your Webs containing specific information. When a visitor calls up the page, the components retrieve the most current version of that information. Recalculate Hyperlinks updates all the Web content that depends on these components.

You should run the Recalculate and Verify Hyperlinks commands frequently, certainly after any significant changes to your Web.

From Here...

From a Web management perspective, the two Web views and the Tasks View are important. When you begin to create Webs, you're almost certain to be captivated by the Hyperlink view and its colorful graphical view of your Web, but from the standpoint of simply getting the work done, you'll quickly find the Folder View and the Tasks View your everyday assistants. Outline View, meanwhile, will always be the focus during Web design sessions, and the Hyperlink View offers a convenient way to show people responsible for specific portions of the Web precisely what needs to be changed or added. Even if you're creating a Web purely on your own, the views and the Tasks View are helpful, but as soon as you start working with a team of people, these views can become indispensable.

You've almost completed your examination of FrontPage Explorer. At this point, you're ready to move on to:

- Chapter 27, "Serving Your Web to the World with the Microsoft Personal Web Server," provides a detailed look at FrontPage's server administrator and server extensions.
- Chapter 30, "Setting Up an Intranet with FrontPage," takes you through the basics of the important task of building intranets with the FrontPage package.
- Part VI, "Using the FrontPage 98 SDK," helps you use the Software Development Kit to customize your FrontPage environment even further.

Serving Your Web to the World with the Microsoft Personal Web Server

Using the Personal Web Server

This effective server lets you see your work before posting it to the Web.

Running the TCP/IP tests

How can I make use of the FrontPage TCP/IP Test? What does it tell me?

Using the server adminstrator

Control server extensions and other variables with the multipart administrator.

Install FrontPage server extensions

How to configure FrontPage to work with your Web server by installing the proper extensions.

Building a Web with FrontPage 98 is always fascinating. Certainly the program's tools make Web creation as easy as—or easier than—any other products on the market and, unlike many of those other packages, the time you spend with FrontPage almost always translates directly into a more effective, more impressive Web. If you've tried to build a Web from scratch in the past, far too often you spent your time simply trying to get things working. FrontPage doesn't spare you from all such necessities, but certainly from the bulk of them.

A fully constructed Web is, however, of no use whatsoever if nobody can see it. To make it a part of the World Wide Web or a part of your organization's intranet, you have to place your Web on a server. A *server* is a computer that (ideally) contains Web server software and a full-time, high-speed connection to the Internet. This computer can be on a machine running any flavor of Microsoft Windows (3.x, 95, NT Workstation, or NT Server), a Macintosh, a UNIX machine such as a Sun, Silicon Graphics, or DEC Alpha (and many others), or any other computer for which Web server software is available.

FrontPage 98 contains not just one, but two pieces of server software. The more basic of the two is the FrontPage Personal Web Server, while the more advanced is the Microsoft Personal Web Server (yes, the similarity of the names is confusing). This chapter includes both of them, but it focuses on the Microsoft PWS because of its greater capabilities.

▶ **See** Part VIII, "Using Other Servers with FrontPage 98," **p. 765**, for information on other Web server software. ■

How a Web Gets Served

To serve your information to the World Wide Web, you need a computer with (ideally) Web server software and a full-time, high-speed connection to the Internet. The hardware and software combination together is called a *Web server*. You can run a server entirely on your own, or you may be assigned it as part of your organization's local area network (LAN).

Increasingly, Webs servers are owned by companies who exist precisely to provide such services (they're known as *presence providers*), and it's entirely likely that your Internet service provider (ISP) offers some free Web space for its subscribers. Check the Web page for your ISP and see if they offer this service. If not, and if you need a small Web, switch to another provider.

If such a service exists, you won't need Web server software at all, nor will you need a full-time connection to the Internet. Anyone with an account with the provider, a modem, and a copy of a Web creation tool such as FrontPage can develop sophisticated Webs and then transfer them to the server. In such a case, however, be sure that your provider is willing to allow the Front-Page extensions for its server; if not, you will be restricted to using only certain features of the FrontPage package. As this chapter proceeds, you'll see what server extensions allow you to do.

It's not actually necessary to have a full-time, high-speed connection to the Internet to serve a Web. By using FrontPage's Personal Web Server, you can create a Web and run it whenever you log on to your ISP. The problems with doing so are threefold: first, your readers can access your Web only when you're online; second, the connection is slow; third, most ISPs give you a different Internet Protocol (IP) address every time you log on, so you won't be able to provide permanent hyperlinks to your site from anywhere else on the Web. The only way this works is if you have a Web designed for private use by you and a few friends or colleagues, and you can supply them with the IP number every time you're up and running.

On the other hand, your ISP might be willing to provide you (at significant cost) with a 24-hour modem connection and a fixed IP address, in which case you can leave the modem on all the time. This, however, requires a second phone line in your house, and the whole scheme is usually more expensive than renting server space from the same ISP. Several megabytes of server space is typically available for anywhere from $50 to $250 per month.

Web server software is available for practically all types of computers, but the most common serving platforms are UNIX (by far the most prevalent), Windows NT, the Macintosh, and more recently, Windows 95 and Windows 3.x. This software exists solely to serve files; that is, it waits for incoming requests from the Internet and then sends the requested file to the requesting machine. Primarily, this is handled through the protocol known as *HyperText Transport Protocol* (*HTTP*). All requests from Web browser software begin with a protocol statement. This is usually http://, but it can also be one of several others. The most common protocols besides http are the following:

- **mailto://** Sends an e-mail message to the specified address.
- **ftp://** Requests a document via File Transfer Protocol.
- **https://** Requests a document using SSL (Secure Sockets Layer) security technology.
- **gopher://** Requests a document from a Gopher server (much less common today).

CAUTION

In browsers such as Netscape Navigator and Microsoft Internet Explorer, it's no longer necessary for users to type the protocol itself in the Location or Go To field. To reach the Microsoft site, for example, users need only type **www.microsoft.com**, not **http://www.microsoft.com**; and to download from the Netscape FTP site, they need only type **ftp.netscape.com**, not **ftp://ftp.netscape.com**. Be sure to include the full address, complete with protocol, in the links you create in your Web documents, or they won't work.

In effect, the server acts as a communications assistant between the user's machine and the machine on which the Web is stored. When the browser registers a click from the user, the server software initiates the transfer of the HTML file and all its included subfiles, such as graphics, imagemaps, and Java scripts.

FrontPage 98's Two Personal Web Servers

FrontPage ships with two server packages. The most capable is the Microsoft Personal Web Server 3.0, which is essentially a stripped-down version of Internet Information Server 3.0, which ships with Windows NT Server 4.0. Microsoft Personal Web Server is abbreviated as MS-PWS. The second server package in FrontPage 98 is the FrontPage Personal Web Server. This is a fully capable piece of server software, but it's called "Personal" because of its built-in limitations. Simply put, if you plan to run a business across the Web and you're trying for a large number of hits to your server, you'll need a more powerful server—one that can handle more simultaneous accesses and is more configurable—than the FrontPage PWS. With FrontPage 98, Microsoft no longer supports the FrontPage PWS, and includes the software only for the sake of backwards compatibility with earlier FrontPage versions.

Chapter 29 is devoted to the Microsoft Personal Web Server (MS-PWS), which answers the limitations of the FrontPage PWS. For now, you'll look at how Microsoft PWS installs, and then at server administration and server extensions.

Microsoft PWS's primary function is to let you build Webs on your local computer, and test them thoroughly before placing them on the main server. When you're developing a Web on a main server, the only way to keep external users out is to protect the Web directory by assigning a username and password to that directory; this is a reasonable solution, but it's safer still

Part
V

Ch
27

to have the developing Web on a different machine entirely. Microsoft PWS lets you do so, and then FrontPage Explorer or the Web Publishing Wizard lets you copy the entire Web over to your main server.

If you're running a Windows 95 machine, FrontPage 98's setup program offers to install MS-PWS before installing FrontPage itself. If you choose to do so, MS-PWS is automatically configured to run on port 80. The TCP port is the network port that the server uses to listen for incoming requests from Web browsers. As a general rule, ports with numbers lower than 1024 (except for 80 itself, which is the standard HTTP port) are used for Internet services such as FTP, e-mail, and news. Port 80 is the normal port on which servers operate, but if you serve more than one root Web from the same computer, MS-PWS automatically chooses a second port. By default, it chooses port 8080, which is the standard port for experimental servers.

The benefit to having your main Web server configured to port 80 is that Web access is simpler. Typing the URL **http://www.microsoft.com/**, for instance, assumes that the server software uses port 80. If the server uses a different port, the number must be included in the URL. If a second server at Microsoft Corporation also served documents, for example, and that server used port 8080, you would have to type **http://www.microsoft.com:8080/**, as you would for all other documents within that Web.

Of course, there's a very good chance that you're installing FrontPage 98 on a machine that is already running server software such as Netscape FastTrack or O'Reilly WebSite. If so, FrontPage will recognize the server during installation, and will automatically configure itself—that is, it will install the appropriate server extensions to the correct port—at that time. But, if you're not currently running a server, and especially if you're installing to a machine on which you'll build and test your Webs, MS-PWS (or FrontPage PWS) will be necessary.

If your server is working properly, there's no reason to change your port number. You can do so, however, by using the Server Administrator, which is described in the next section "Server Administration and Server Extensions." Note, however, that except for the FrontPage PWS, the port number for the server is set in the server software's configuration system, not through FrontPage itself. A sample process of changing port numbers and uninstalling server extensions is also described in "Server Administration and Server Extensions."

Server Administration and Server Extensions

Even though FrontPage ships with fully functional Web server software, FrontPage's Server Administration tools do not actually control the Personal Web Server; instead, they provide an interface to whatever Web server software you happen to be running. If you're running O'Reilly's WebSite, the Netscape Commerce Server, or the NCSA UNIX server, you can still use Server Administration, although you will do so in conjunction with the Server Administration tools provided by that server.

What does FrontPage Server Administration do? Primarily, it exists as a means of installing FrontPage's server extensions so that FrontPage's features work smoothly with your existing server. All Web servers ship with server administration tools, but in all cases these tools let you configure only that particular server. FrontPage Server Administrator, on the other hand, works hand in hand with a wide number of popular servers, with more to be added by Microsoft as the product matures. FrontPage accomplishes this task through the use of *server extensions*, which (as their name suggests) extend FrontPage's capabilities to other Web server software.

The Web servers supported by FrontPage are listed in Table 27.1 Note that these servers are the ones currently available for FrontPage 97. At the time of writing, FrontPage 98 is in beta and Microsoft has published no support information for FrontPage 98. They can be found at **http://www.microsoft.com/frontpage/softlib/current.htm**.

Table 27.1   Web Servers Supported by FrontPage Extensions

Operating System	Web Servers
Microsoft Windows 95	WebSite (O'Reilly & Associates), Microsoft Personal Web Server, Netscape FastTrack Server, FrontPage Web Server.
Microsoft Windows NT Workstation	WebSite, FrontPage Personal Web Server, Netscape Commerce Server, Netscape Communications Server, Netscape FastTrack Server, Netscape Enterprise Server, NT Peer Web Services.
Microsoft Windows NT Server	As for NT Workstation, plus Microsoft Internet Information Server.
HP/UX 9.03, 10.01 (Hewlett Packard)	Apache, NCSA, CERN, Netscape Commerce Server, Netscape Communications Server, Netscape Enterprise Server.
IRIX 5.3, 6.2 (Silicon Graphics)	Same as HP/UX
Solaris 2.4, 2.5 (SPARCstations)	Same as HP/UX
SunOS 4.1.3, 4.1.4 (SPARCstations)	Same as HP/UX
BSD/OS 2.1 (BSDI UNIX on Intel)	Same as HP/UX
Digital UNIX 3.2c, 4.0 (Alpha)	Same as HP/UX
Linux 3.0.3 (Red Hat)	Same as HP/UX

Part
V

Ch
27

Note that if you're using FrontPage 1.1, you must disable the SSL (Secure Sockets Layer) security of your Web server before installing the FrontPage extensions because 1.1 doesn't support SSL. FrontPage 97 and 98, however, includes support for SSL.

How Server Extensions Work

As previously mentioned, FrontPage's server extensions are designed to work in conjunction with existing Web servers, such as those available from O'Reilly & Associates, Netscape Communications, the National Center for Supercomputing Applications, and Microsoft. If you have a server for which a FrontPage extension does not currently exist, you will especially want to know the principles under which the server extensions operate. With this information, you can use FrontPage to develop your Web pages despite having an unsupported server.

Generally, the server extensions communicate with the Web server through the *Common Gateway Interface (CGI)*. This is the interface mechanism by which servers themselves communicate with databases and other nonWeb functions (CGI controls many fill-in forms, for instance), and the server extensions are designed to use CGI exactly as each specific server demands. CGI passes user-configured variables and environment specifics to the server, and CGI returns the requested information in one file format or another, typically HTML. The FrontPage server extensions use this generalized process to communicate with the different servers.

At times, it's necessary for the server extensions to communicate directly with the server. This happens in the instance of setting server configuration and for establishing permissions for administrators, users, and authors. Most Web servers have their own idiosyncratic way of managing this information, and the task of the server extension is to interact appropriately with the type of server being run. In addition, newer servers have their own rich interfaces for setting these details (O'Reilly, OpenMarket, and Netscape servers for example), and often the configurations must be set using the server's software before FrontPage's Server Administrator can deal with them.

FrontPage Server Administrator

While the majority of the administration for your individual Webs is handled through the configuration dialog boxes of FrontPage Explorer (see Chapter 25, "Configuring Your Web"), and administration of the Web server itself is through the interfaces to the various Web servers, FrontPage Server Administrator administers the extensions themselves and provides some basic security features.. When you load the Server Administrator, the FrontPage Server Administration dialog box appears (see Figure 27.1).

Note that FrontPage 98 has no separate icon in the FrontPage programs folder for running the Server Administrator. In fact, to get to the Server Administrator, you have to go through the rather annoying process of using Windows Explorer to enter the directory where you installed FrontPage 98 (C:\PROGRAM FILES\MICROSOFT FRONTPAGE by default) and locate the shortcut for FrontPage Server Administrator. If you prefer, you can use the command line version of the Server Administrator, which is accessible by double-clicking the FPSRVADM.EXE file.

FIG. 27.1
All major server configurations result from working with this dialog box.

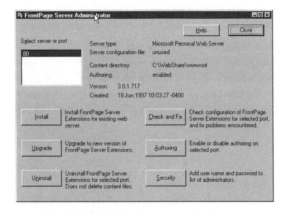

Server Administrator Information Area

In the example shown in Figure 27.1, the port number (8080) is shown in the Select Port Number box, while the text beside the Select Port Number box displays the current server information. This information consists of the following four parts:

- **Server type** The server type reflects the server corresponding to the port number. It also reflects the server extensions that you have installed. You can have several server extensions installed simultaneously. In Figure 27.1, the Microsoft PWS and the FrontPage PWS are both installed.

- **Server configuration file** Some server software has a corresponding configuration file. The Microsoft PWS does not, but the FrontPage PWS's configuration file is HTTPD.CNF, found in C:\FRONTPAGE\SERVER\CONF\. This file, shown in the printout under the Install section, can be found in the path C:\FRONTPAGE WEBS\SERVER\CONF, assuming you allowed FrontPage 98 to install into its default directories.

- **Content directory** This item shows the folder in which the Web's actual content files can be located. By default, the FrontPage PWS installs these in the C:\FRONTPAGE WEBS\CONTENT folder, while the Microsoft PWS places them in C:\WEBSHARE\WWWROOT. O'Reilly WebSite, as another example, places content by default in C:\WEBSITE\HTDOCS.

- **Authoring** You can enable or disable authoring permissions on the selected port. By default, authoring is enabled. If you want full security, or if the Web on that port needs no further authoring, you can disable it. This action is explained in the next section, "Server Administrator Configuration Buttons."

Part
V

Ch

27

Server Administrator Configuration Buttons

The six configuration buttons in the bottom half of the Server Administration dialog box let you install and configure your server extensions. Clicking some of these buttons result in very simple dialog boxes or even none at all (that is, FrontPage just performs an action instead), but the functions *are* important.

Install: Installing FrontPage Server Extensions   No matter what Web server software you use, you'll need to install the server extensions for that particular server if you want to use all of FrontPage 98's features in conjunction with your server. Table 27.1 lists the servers for which Microsoft has supplied server extensions (which includes the most popular ones), and if yours is not included, you should either contact the FrontPage team and request it, or consider changing servers.

Before trying to install the server extensions, keep in mind that the server software itself must be installed and working properly. Moreover, installing server software is rarely easy and automatic, so plan to spend an entire evening, maybe an entire week, putting your server software and Microsoft FrontPage into place. Given the potential importance of a Web server to your organization, this is one area in which speed definitely isn't in order.

 T I P   The easiest way to set up the extensions for your server is to do so when you install the FrontPage 98 software in the first place. If you have server software on your system, FrontPage will find it and offer to install the extensions. Especially if this is the only server software you'll be using, by all means say yes.

Installing Server Extensions for MS-PWS and FrontPage PWS   The example here will demonstrate how to install the server extensions for the FrontPage PWS onto port 8080 and the Microsoft PWS onto the default http port 80. That will allow us to use both: FrontPage PWS as a quick and dirty testing server, and Microsoft PWS as the main server.

In all cases, the procedure for installing server extensions begins by clicking the Install button. When you do, you'll see the Configure Server Type dialog box (see Figure 27.2). By default, this box displays the FrontPage Personal Web Server, but clicking the down-arrow will reveal others.

FIG. 27.2

The Configure Server Type dialog box contains existing built-in extensions.

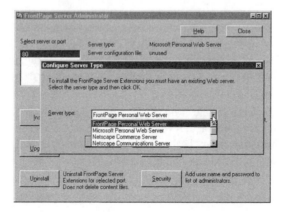

Click OK to continue with the installation of the FrontPage PWS. This yields the Server Configuration dialog box in which you browse for the name of the file that contains the httpd (http daemon, i.e. server) information for the PWS. By default, this file is a text file called HTTPD.CNF, and is found in the C:\FRONTPAGE\SERVER\CONF\ directory. But before you select this file, you have to edit it to change the port number to which it is assigned. Remember, you want the FrontPage PWS on port 8080, and the Microsoft PWS on port 80.

Here is a listing showing part of the HTTPD.CNF file as it ships with FrontPage 98:

```
# -FrontPage- version=2.0
#-------------------------------------------------------------------
#
#   HTTPD.CNF
#
# Main server configuration for the FrontPage Personal Web Server
#
# This is the main server configuration file. It is best to
# leave the directives in this file in the order they are in, or
# things may not go the way you'd like.
#
# ServerRoot: The directory the server's config, error, and log files
# are kept in. This should be specified on the startup command line.
#
# Format: ServerRoot <path>
#
ServerRoot c:/frontpage\ webs/server/

# Port: The port the standalone listens to. 80 is the network standard.
#
Port 80

# ServerName allows you to set a host name which is sent back to clients for
# your server if it's different than the one the program would get (i.e. use
# "www" instead of the host's real name). Make sure your DNS is set up to
# alias the name to your system!
#
# Format: ServerName <domain name>
#
# no default
```

The important area of concern right now is the Port #, highlighted in the middle of this listing. By default, this port number shows as 80, but you should now change it to 8080. Make a copy of the HTTPD.CNF file within the same directory, give it a different name (in case you want to get it back in its default form) and load HTTPD.CNF into Notepad or another ASCII editor and change the line Port 80 to read Port 8080. Now you're ready to install the server extensions.

1. Select the HTTPD file (it might show without its CNF extension, depending on how you have Windows 95 configured). The Server Configuration dialog box appears.

2. Click OK to get an information box displaying the choices you've just made.

3. Click OK again to open the Administrator Setup box.

4. Enter your FrontPage Webs administrator name and password. If you have an administration name and password already established for your server, use these here.

5. Click OK to receive the message Install completed successfully.

6. The port number and server information will appear on the FrontPage Server Adminis-trator dialog box.

Now install the Microsoft PWS server extensions. Before starting, make sure that you've in-stalled the Microsoft PWS from the FrontPage CD-ROM.

1. On the FrontPage Server Administrator dialog box, click Install.

2. From Configure Server Type, choose Microsoft Personal Web Server (it's immediately below the FrontPage Personal Web Server default choice).

3. Click OK.

4. If you have the Microsoft PWS running, you'll get a Confirmation dialog box, in which case click OK and carry on.

If you don't have the Microsoft PWS running, you'll be told: In order for FrontPage to work, the WWW Service of the Personal Web Server must be started. At this point:

1. Go to the Win95 Control Panel, double-click the Personal Web Server icon, click the Startup tab, and click Start.

2. The Web Server State area will read The server is running, and the server's icon will appear in the Taskbar tray.

3. Close Control Panel and return to the FrontPage Server Administrator dialog box.

4. Start the Install process again until you see the Confirmation Dialog box and click OK.

Now let's install the Microsoft PWS server extensions. Again, make sure that you've installed the Microsoft PWS from the FrontPage CD-ROM. On the FrontPage Server Administrator dialog box, click Install. From Configure Server Type, choose Microsoft Personal Web Server (it's immediately below the FrontPage Personal Web Server default choice).

Click OK, and you'll receive one of two responses. If you have the Microsoft PWS running, you'll get a Confirmation dialog box, in which case click OK and carry on. If you don't have the Microsoft PWS running, you'll be told: In order for FrontPage to work, the WWW Service of the Personal Web Server must be started. Go to the Win95 Control Panel, double-click the Personal Web Server icon, click the Startup tab, and click Start. The Web Server State area will read The server is running, and the server's icon will appear in the Taskbar tray. Close Control Panel and return to the FrontPage Server Administrator dialog box. Start the Install process again until you see the Confirmation Dialog box and click OK.

Next, enter the account name you'll use when administering and authoring your Webs. This will probably coincide with the user name you use for your system, but it need not. Click OK, and the installation will proceed. A Server Administrator box will tell you that the WWW Ser-vice of the Microsoft PWS must be restarted, and clicking Yes lets that happen automatically. Next you'll see: Install completed successfully, and the server will appear on port 80 on the FrontPage Server Administrator dialog box.

Now you're ready to roll.

By this point, if you've been authoring Webs from earlier chapters, you've established several different passwords for your Web. It's a good idea to start a word processing, spreadsheet, or database file to store these usernames and passwords, but be sure to give the file an innocuous name or to password-protect it using your software. Just don't forget this password!

Upgrade   Once the server extensions are installed, you can upgrade them easily. When you receive new versions of the server extensions, either directly from the Web server publisher or from the Microsoft Web or FTP site, you can upgrade the relationship between FrontPage and the server by clicking the appropriate port number, then on the Upgrade button. The upgrade software must be placed within the SERVSUPP\ directory of the main FrontPage area on your hard drive.

The only thing that happens when you click Upgrade is that you see a small dialog box saying that FrontPage will perform the upgrade, and a second dialog box saying that the upgrade has been done successfully.

Uninstall   If you want to remove the server extensions, highlight the port you no longer want in the Select Port Number list box and click Uninstall.

As the Warning box tells you, only the server extensions for that port will be uninstalled. Nothing will happen to the content files of the Web, so your HTML files, graphics files, and everything else will remain in place. In fact, the uninstall action doesn't actually remove the extension files themselves. All it does, in essence, is to disconnect FrontPage from direct contact with the server. You can no longer perform, for that server software, all the actions available in FrontPage itself. See the section "Using FrontPage Without Server Extensions" later in this chapter for the effect this action will have.

So why do you bother uninstalling extensions? For the most part, you don't. But if you upgrade your server software, you might find that the extensions no longer work properly, so uninstalling them and then reinstalling them might be the only solution. Furthermore, you might need to change a port number to which FrontPage links through your server software. In this case, you have to uninstall the server extensions, set the port number through your server's configuration system, and then reinstall the extensions so that FrontPage can read the appropriate port.

 Uninstalling extensions is a painless process, and you can reinstall as soon as you've uninstalled them. If you're having difficulty with any aspect of the communication between FrontPage and your server, try uninstalling and then reinstalling as a means of getting past the trouble.

Check and Fix   Clicking the Check and Fix button causes FrontPage to determine whether or not the server extensions are configured properly for the currently selected port. If anything is wrong, you receive an appropriate error message. Otherwise, you are told that the check was performed okay.

Authoring   By default, the authoring option is enabled. To disable it, click the Authoring button; or, if the option is already disabled, click the Authoring button to enable it again. When

Part
V

Ch
27

authoring is disabled, FrontPage Explorer and FrontPage Editor are not able to access that particular Web. You might want this to happen if there is no more work to be done on the Web, or for any number of other administrative reasons.

Security The final button on the FrontPage Server Administrator dialog box is called Security. Clicking this yields the Administrator Name and Password dialog box.

N O T E To change the security, your machine must be set to "User-level access control." From the Control Panel, select Network, then the Access Control tab, then User-level access control. ■

In the Web Name text box, you can type the Web for which you want to change or create administrator information. By default, the root Web is selected, but you can type in whatever Web Name you want to change. In the Name password, enter an administrator name and that name will be added as a valid administrator for that particular Web.

If you are using a Web server other than the MS-PWS or NT's Internet Information Server (IIS), you will see a Name box and a Password box. If the administrator name already exists for your server (that is, you specified that name when you installed the extensions previously), this action replaces the existing password for that name with the password you now enter. If the administrator name is a new one, it is now created and applied to that Web.

If you're not using MS-PWS or IIS, the Administrator Name and Password dialog box will include an Advanced button. You can specify the exact IP address from which the administrator can access the Web, or a partial address specifying a range of IP addresses. An exact IP address takes a four-part form, such as 129.88.125.37, while a restriction to the first portion of that address (hence, an organization rather than an exact workstation, for example) reads 129.88.*.* (the wildcard asterisk character allows any number, while the first two parts of the address remain fixed). The default address is *.*.*.*, which means that the administrator can access the Web from anywhere on the Internet, as long as the username and password are entered correctly.

Using FrontPage Without Server Extensions

Server extensions do not exist for all Web server software, but that doesn't mean you can't make use of FrontPage's Web creation and page creation features. You won't be able to use all of them, but it will still be an extremely useful program for building Webs. The following sections provide some items to keep in mind when dealing with a server without FrontPage extensions.

Copying Webs

Copying Webs from your computer to a server without FrontPage extensions requires the following considerations:

■ Don't use the Publish Web feature found in FrontPage Explorer. Instead, transfer files via FTP from your machine to the appropriate directory on the server. Alternatively, use the Web Publishing Wizard that comes with the FrontPage Bonus Pack, and which when installed, appears in START/PROGRAMS/ACCESSORIES/INTERNET TOOLS.

■ Don't transfer directories beginning with _VTI_. These directories are proprietary to FrontPage's extensions system.

■ Don't transfer files that contain access control information, such as author and administer permissions. These access controls will not work on a server that does not support FrontPage extensions.

Server Differences

Web server software packages differ in the way they treat files and documents. The following points must be considered when building Webs for a server without FrontPage extensions:

■ Web servers vary in what file types they recognize. UNIX servers, for example, typically recognize only files with an HTML extension as Web documents, while FrontPage for Windows generates these files with an HTM extension. You might need to change the extension on all files either before or after you FTP them to the destination server. Other file incompatibilities might occur as well, depending on the operating system and the server software on the destination machine.

■ Access control differs from server to server. Even FrontPage's server extensions don't solve all the possible access control problems. In general, try to avoid extensive access restrictions on your Web.

■ Find out what the destination server needs as the name for its default document, that is, the document that appears when users enter your domain name but don't specify an actual document name. Some servers recognize INDEX.HTML as this name, but others use other names (such as WELCOME.HTML). You'll need to know this before transferring your Web to the server.

FrontPage Component Interactions

FrontPage's Components are extremely powerful, but they won't work with a Web server for which FrontPage server extensions do not exist. The following are two points that must be considered if building Webs for such a server:

■ Don't use FrontPage imagemaps. Instead, set them as appropriate for your server when you create them.

■ Some of FrontPage's Components depend on the existence of server extensions for correct operations. These include the Search Components, Registration Components, Discussion Components, Save Results Components, and Confirmation Components. Avoid building these into your documents.

Part
V

Ch
27

FrontPage TCP/IP Test

A surprisingly useful utility within the FrontPage 98 package is the TCP/IP Test (see Figure 27.3). TCP/IP Test is found in the FrontPage Explorer's Help menu. Click Help, choose About Microsoft FrontPage Explorer and click the Network Test button. This will yield the FrontPage TCP/IP Test box, where you'll see a Start Test button. By clicking this button, you get useful information about the behavior of your TCP/IP network connection.

FIG. 27.3

FrontPage's TCP/IP Test after clicking Explain Results.

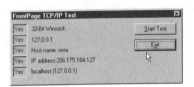

The TCP/IP protocol is the protocol under which the Internet operates. To be on the Internet, in fact, a computer must be running the TCP/IP protocol. Without it, you can be on all kinds of other networks but not on the Internet. Computers connected to LANs sometimes share the TCP/IP stacks necessary to connect to the Internet, but the protocol is still there even if the individual machine doesn't know it.

N O T E   If you are connecting to the Internet through a dynamic IP address system, as is usually the case with modem connections to an Internet Service Provider, you and your readers can access your site only by typing the actual IP number (for example, **http://129.97.38.164/**). This is because your IP address does not actually have a domain name associated with it. Domain names are available through fixed IP addresses only. ▦

From Here...

Server administration is simplified considerably through FrontPage's tools, but it still demands constant attention. This is especially true if your Web server resides on a remote machine and uses a different operating system from your own, and if that server software is upgraded at any time. Microsoft promises fast action on creating and upgrading server extensions, so keep visiting the FrontPage Web site at **http://www.microsoft.com/frontpage**, but in the case of upgrades, you can expect a few days' or weeks' delay.

With your server extensions installed and FrontPage working comfortably in conjunction with it, and with the ins and outs of FrontPage Explorer fully under your control, the creative part of Web design begins. The next several chapters take you directly into FrontPage Editor, the powerful tool for authoring the actual pages that will populate your Webs. You'll learn the ins and outs of Web page creation from start to finish, and when you've finished, you'll have built a complete and functional Web site.

- Chapter 30, "Setting Up an Intranet with FrontPage," demonstrates the capabilities of FrontPage in creating and managing private intranets.
- Part VI, "Using the FrontPage 98 SDK," explains how to make use of the Software Development Kit to customize FrontPage to your needs.

Part
V

Ch
27

## CHAPTER 28

Defining Your Web as a Channel

Until just recently, the Web has been based on *pull technology*: Web sites needed to pull visitors in by appearing in searches, or by advertising themselves on TV, in print, or in Web banners. With the explosion of information on the Web, it's impractical to expect visitors to be pulled in by these rather hit-or-miss methods.

Enter *push technology*. Push automatically sends content from a site or server to the visitor, now a more passive consumer of information. Push operates somewhat like newsletters—the reader signs up for the newsletter and waits for the content to arrive from the publisher. The publisher determines the newsletter's content; if the reader doesn't like the content, he or she can cancel delivery of the newsletter.

In the Web's world, a channel is the delivery mechanism of push content. Channels still have a pull component, as readers must *subscribe* to a channel in order to automatically receive content. Once subscribed, however, channels push the requested information to the reader.

Microsoft's version of channel technology uses CDF, or Channel Definition Format, to define how the site displays and pushes its content selections. FrontPage 98 includes the Channel Definition Wizard to help you create channels with your Web content. ◼

Understanding push technology

Instead of waiting for users to request information from your Web, you can send it to them directly.

Understanding channel concepts

Explore the basic channel concepts: the CDF file and the channel items, which include the primary page plus the subpages and their content.

Creating channel definition files

Use the FrontPage Channel Definition Wizard to organize channel items and deliver them according to a schedule.

Track channel usage

Use optional target logs to find out how and when users are accessing your channel.

Push Technology and Channels

During 1997, push technology emerged as an extremely important factor in the future of the World Wide Web. The principle behind push technology is simple: you can no longer expect Web users to come to you, so you have to go to them instead. The Web has grown far too large for any user to keep tabs on, and because of this, there's almost no chance a user might accidentally find your site; and even if they do, there's only a small chance they'll remember to return to it.

For this reason, the concept of push was developed. Push, of course, is the opposite of pull, and the reference here is to the way in which Web users get information. In the classic Web browsing scenario, users pull pages into their browsers. In fact, the HTTP protocol calls this activity a *request*, and that request has to come from the client software—the browser—rather than from the server. Servers just serve; clients request. The problem with this approach is simple: if users don't find you, they can't request anything from you and even if they reach your site, you have no way of controlling what information they'll ask for. That's why the Web offers such a feeling of freedom to users, but it's also why companies are leery about throwing big bucks into site development. If nobody's going to look at what they offer, why have it there in the first place?

Push reverses the paradigm. Instead of waiting for users to request information, Web developers can send it to them directly. This can be done through e-mail, as is the case with many push solutions in 1997-98, or through more transparent means as screen savers or *channels*. The screen saver approach has been in existence since late 1995 with Pointcast, a news service that delivers information to your desktop at regular intervals and displays the information on a specially designed screen saver.

Channels and the CDF

The channel concept is newer (late 1996). The word *channel* had been bandied about for several months before that, but it first started appearing in force with the introduction of Marimba Castanet (**http://www.marimba.com/**) software that enables you to design and serve Java-based information via push technology. Channel quickly became the accepted term for all such activity, and Microsoft made it official by proposing the Channel Definition Format (CDF) to the W3 Organization (**http://www.w3.org/**) in early 1997.

The CDF has been implemented in Microsoft Internet Explorer 4.0 and Netscape Communicator 4.0 (with its add-on called Netcaster). IE 4 actually merges CDF with Microsoft's own Active Channel Format in order to display channels as push buttons on the IE 4.0 desktop, but the core of the channel design is through the CDF specification. Check out *Special Edition Using Netscape Communicator 4* and *Special Edition Using Internet Explorer 4* from Que for more information about Netscape Communicator 4 and Internet Explorer 4, respectively. CDF is actually a subset of XML (Extensible Markup Language), which is being considered as the successor to HTML as the next main Web language, primarily because unlike HTML, it is easily tailored and configured (for instance, extensible). XML's goal is to eliminate the need for proprietary HTML tags, which both Netscape and Microsoft have implemented numerous times. Web coding language is supposed to be universal, and XML is exactly that. CDF is just one possible XML extension.

What Makes Up a Channel?

A channel consists of a primary Web document plus a series of *channel items*, also called subpages. You may have any number of items in your channel, just as you may have any number of documents in your Web site. The primary Web document could be an already existing page on your site, or you could create an entirely new page to act as the opening document (like a home page) for your channel.

In IE 4.0's Channel Bar, all items in the channel appear when the users click the channel logo. Users can select whichever item they want to view. As a Web designer, you control which items are shown in that list, but the most important point of the channel is that users don't search for it, it appears on their desktop. Furthermore, the channel and all its items can be updated according to a schedule established either by your users; or by you, as channel designer, for those with 24-hour connections. The way this normally works is that the users go to work in the morning, sit down in front of their computers, click the Channel Bar, and see the new information or they look at it in their screen savers, or a message appears in their e-mail inbox.

All channels consist of two major components: the channel items and the CDF file. The channel items include the primary page plus the subpages, and anything that can be displayed on the Web itself can be included in the subpages. This includes:

- Java applets
- ActiveX controls
- Special effects using Dynamic HTML
- All manner of graphics and multimedia.

The CDF file sets the organization of these pages as well as the schedule for delivery.

 TIP If you want your channels to be readable when your users are offline, don't include elements that require connection to the server. This includes most Java and ActiveX components and many types of multimedia files.

FrontPage's Channel Definition Wizard

Developing channels from scratch isn't overly difficult; all it requires is the ability to create a small CDF file to organize your channel items and deliver them according to a set schedule. FrontPage 98 cuts through even those steps by offering the *Channel Definition Wizard* (CDF Wizard). The wizard is a multistep process that begins when you select Define Channel from the Tools menu. By the time you've worked your way through the wizard, you'll have a channel ready to serve to users who subscribe to it.

Part
V

Ch
28

The best way to explain the CDF Wizard is to step through its operation and look at each step. That's what we'll do here.

1. Launch FrontPage Explorer and open an existing Web and start the CDF Wizard by selecting Tools, Define Channel. You'll see the Welcome dialog box shown in Figure 28.1. Here you can either Create a new channel or Open an existing one. For this example, we'll create a new one.

FIG. 28.1

If you choose to open an existing channel, the subsequent dialog boxes are identical to creating a new one.

2. Click the Next button to show the Channel modifiable except for Last Modified dialog box. All these fields are seen by your users, so take special care with them. Give your channel a title (a memorable one is a good idea), and type a description in the Abstract field. The abstract will appear in the browser when your users rest the mouse pointer over the channel's title. The CDF Wizard needs the URL for your Introduction Page (the primary Web page), which the users will see first. This field will offer the default value of the default page for the currently opened FrontPage Web. See Figure 28.2.

FIG. 28.2

If you create a new image for your logo and icon, remember to use FrontPage Explorer to import it into your Web.

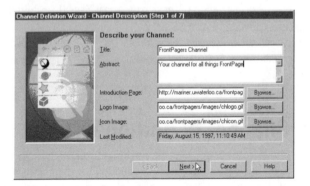

The logo image is displayed on the Channel Bar of Internet Explorer 4.0 and Netscape Navigator 4.0. Users click this image to open the channel. To be consistent with the Channel Bar standard, this image should be a small image of 80×32 pixels. If you don't include this image, the browser will display a default logo that applies generically to all channels. It's therefore best to develop one, even if it's extremely simple (you can do this with FrontPage Editor's image tools or through Image Composer). The Icon image identifies each of your pages as being in your channel, and should be 16×16 pixels in size and GIF in format. This will be displayed on each of your channel's items, and if not included, the browser will display a generic icon instead. Again, it's best to have one.

The Last Modified field displays when the Channel was created or last modified.

3. Click Next when you've finished these selections. You'll be taken to the Choose Source Folder (step 2 of 7) dialog box. Here you can type the location of the source folder from which your channel will draw its Web pages. The default is the home page for the currently opened Web. If your channel will be using pages from the source's subfolders, toggle Include Subfolders. Click Next when you've made your choices.

4. Make selections in the Edit Page List dialog box (step 3 of 7). This is crucial because the pages you select here will be those that will be part of the channel. Actually, it's the pages you choose *not* to select that figure into this dialog box, rather than the other way around. By default, all pages in the currently opened Web will be included in the channel. Your task is to decide if you wish to exclude any files (pages), select each, and click the Exclude button. The selected file will disappear from the list. If you make a mistake, click the Restore button and all excluded files will reappear. In Figure 28.3, the SEARCH.HTM file is about to be excluded, but as you'll see in Figure 28.4 (further along), many other pages are being excluded as well.

FIG. 28.3

It's a good idea not to overwhelm your channel subscribers, so be very selective about which pages to include.

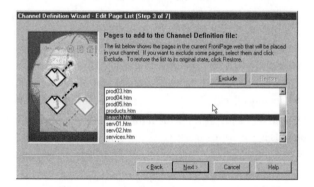

Actually, you get another chance to decide what gets included in the channel. The next dialog box is Channel Items Properties (step 4 of 7), which essentially determines how your channel will operate (Figure 28.4).

5. Select each page from the Channel Items list on the left and apply a variety of options to it. Notice that you make these decisions for *each* channel item, not for the channel as a whole.

Part
V

Ch
28

FIG. 28.4

This step is crucial to the way in which your users will receive your information.

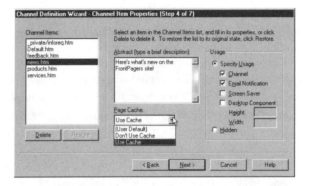

6. Include an abstract, a usage instruction, and caching instruction for each channel item, if you want. The defaults are no abstract, channel usage, and User Default caching. This is fine, but your channel can be more useful both to you and your users if you take the time to establish the behavior of each item.

7. Click the item in the Channel Items window and click Delete (as with step 3) if you choose to remove channel items from the channel. Click Restore to bring all deleted items back into the window.

You can type whatever you want in the Abstract field, but the idea is to offer a short, informative lead-in to the channel item. The abstract appears in the user's browser when the mouse pointer rests over the page's icon or title.

8. Decide whether or not you want the channel item to be stored (cached) on the user's machine so that they can view them offline with no need to connect to your server. The Page Cache area offers three choices.

   - Use Cache automatically stores the item, overriding the caching options specified in the user's browser. For pages that are graphics heavy but which rarely change, you should select this option so that the user has ready and fast access to it.

   - Don't Use Cache prevents the item from being cached, again overriding the options in the user's browser. Select this if an item is updated regularly and you want to force the user to see the latest version of that page.

   - User Default lets the user decide, and the item acts according to the caching options the user has turned on or off in the browser. This is the default and is the best because it lets the user decide. Otherwise, you risk the danger of angering them—nobody likes to lose control of what's being stored on their hard disks.

9. Choose the methods by which you want the channel item to be pushed to the user in the Specify Usage area. Each item can have from zero to all four of the options chosen. The default is Channel, which means that it will be sent with the channel as a whole. If you want a specific page to be automatically sent to the user via e-mail whenever it changes, select Email Notification. Screen Saver serves the page as a screen saver on the user's machine (but remember, users can easily override this by choosing a different screen saver).

10. Specify the Height and Width of the component as it will appear on the user's desktop if you select Desktop Component. Desktop Component pushes the item to the user's Internet Explorer 4.0-based machine as a desktop component, a small area of the screen that shows channel information. This could be a special message that pops up, a list of new prices, or new product details—anything that might be of use to the subscriber. Don't make it too big, or the user will simply get rid of it.

11. Select <u>H</u>idden if you want the channel item available for use but not seen by default. An example of this might be a page that is linked from a nonhidden item, but which you don't want the user to access unless they specifically request it by clicking the hyperlink.

12. Click Next after you've made these decisions. This will yield the Channel Scheduling (step 5 of 7) dialog box, shown in Figure 28.5. Indicate how often you want the user's browser to check your server for updated information and download the new or changed channel items. You begin by establishing the dates over which the channel is to operate. These dates are expressed in the format chosen in your Date/Time utility in Control Panel, typically mm/dd/yy. The defaults are to serve the channel between (now) and (forever), or in other words, with no date restrictions.

13. Specify how often you want your users' browsers to institute an automatic check for channel updates. The default is a manual operation, where the user must click the channel in their browser and elect to download new information. If you want, however, you can change this to automatic updates every *n* days, hours, or even minutes.

14. Type the desired number in the first subfield beside <u>C</u>heck Every and click the drop-down arrow to select days, hours, or minutes. In Figure 28.5, the channel will be automatically checked every three days.

N O T E You have no absolute control over how often a browser checks your channel. These settings can be overridden by each user by altering their browser's channel options. ▪

FIG. 28.5
Be careful in choosing check times. If you push your channel to your subscribers too often, you might tie up their Internet connection.

The final stage in scheduling is designed to help you, not the user. Automatic connections from user browsers begin at midnight in the users' individual time zones. If you have a popular channel and a subscriber base physically located in one or two time zones, this might mean a huge server load during those automatic checks.

Part
V

Ch
28

15. Set the channel to delay those checks randomly to minimize this load. For instance, you can specify that you'll Delay Checks between 1 and 6 hours, which means user browsers will randomly launch the checking procedure over that span of time, rather than all at once.

16. Click Next to proceed to the Log Target (step 6 of 7) dialog box. This is an optional step, and you need consider it only if you want to keep tabs on how users are accessing your channel, either offline or online. The information will be captured on the users' machines when they use their browsers. It is sent to a file on your server (the file must be a programmed form) whenever the user logs on to their Internet accounts. Type the Log Target URL of the programmed form (form handler) in the box and click Next.

17. Specify the file name for your new CDF file (Figure 28.6 in the Finish CDF Wizard (step 7 of 7). By default, this is CHANNEL.CDF, and it's a good idea to simply use the defaults. If you already have a CHANNEL.CDF file, and you wish to create another CDF file for that Web, the next one will automatically be named CHANNEL1.CDF, then CHANNEL2.CDF, and so forth. Remember to include the CDF extension.

FIG. 28.6

The last stage means saving your channel to your Web server for implementation.

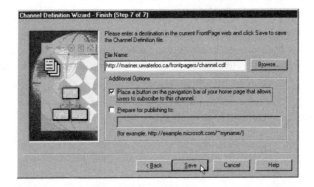

You then have two more options. The first is to Place a button on the navigation bar of your home page that allows users to subscribe to this channel. This is toggled on by default, and it's a good idea to leave it that way. Without it, users won't know the channel exists, or how to subscribe. If you elect not to place a button on the page, you must offer a hyperlink to the CDF file that allows users to subscribe.

The other option (and you can select both) is to Prepare for publishing to a Web server. If FrontPage Explorer is already connected to your server, this is obviously less useful, but it's an extremely powerful feature if you're developing your site locally and you want only the channel to appear on another server. It's also a means of mirroring channels on multiple servers.

18. Click Save to store the CDF file on the server and you're finished. Now, any users loading your home page will see a Subscribe button, and if they select it, they'll be provided with information at scheduled times.

N O T E　Don't worry if you don't like your initial choices. You can change any and all parts of your
channel definition by restarting the CDF Wizard and select Open an Existing Channel
Definition file. If you know what you're doing, you can also edit the .cdf file directly. ▨

　T I P　Make sure your channel is worth subscribing to. Change the information constantly, or your users will
simply ignore it or unsubscribe.

From Here...

Channels are leading-edge technology, and it may be a while before you're using them on a
regular basis. In the meantime, you may want to finish up this section on Web construction and
management, and perhaps go on to explore methods of tweaking FrontPage itself. These topics
are covered in:

- Chapter 29, "Using Microsoft Personal Web Server and FrontPage Personal Web
  Server," which explores the details of using the server software that ships with
  FrontPage 98.

- Chapter 30, "Setting Up an Intranet with FrontPage," which demonstrates the capabilities
  of FrontPage in creating and managing private intranets.

- Chapter 31, "Extending and Customizing FrontPage with the SDK," where you learn to
  modify FrontPage to suit your specific needs.

Part
V

Ch
28

## CHAPTER 29

Using Microsoft Personal Web Server and FrontPage Personal Web Server

As Chapter 27, "Serving Your Web to the World with the Microsoft Personal Web Server," makes clear, FrontPage 98 ships with two servers, the FrontPage Personal Web Server, included for the sake of backwards compatability, and the Microsoft Personal Web Server (MS-PWS), by far the more powerful of the two. This chapter examines the MS-PWS in detail, a necessity given its greater number of features (remote administration, FTP service) and its greater range of configuration choices. ■

Establish Microsoft personal Web server as your main web server

You can have MS-PWS load with Windows itself, so you're ready to serve your Webs online or to test those you're building.

Setting MS-PWS as an FTP server

Web serving isn't the only thing this server is good for. It also operates as a server for file transfer, including anonymous FTP.

Administering MS-PWS for Web and FTP services

The server contains a sophisticated administration tool that operates as a set of local Web pages in your favorite browser.

The server configuration files

Configuring your server to serve up new file types and advanced configuration settings.

Getting Started with Microsoft PWS

This chapter assumes that you've already installed the Microsoft Personal Web Server. If you haven't, do so now by doing the following:

1. Insert your FrontPage 98 CD-ROM in your CD-ROM drive.
2. Use Start/Run/Browse or Windows Explorer and locate the PWS directory on the CD-ROM.
3. Open the PWS directory and double-click the Setup program.
4. Restart Win95 when instructed.

For this chapter, it will also be assumed that you're running Microsoft PWS as your localhost server. You can test this by doing the following:

■ Open your Web browser and type **http://localhost** in the location box. Press Enter. At the bottom of the page is the phrase: "Brought to you by the Personal Web Server from Microsoft." If this is the case, ignore the next two bullet points.

■ To make the change in localhost servers, load the FrontPage Server Administrator (see Chapter 27 for instructions), and change the port number for the FrontPage PWS to **8080**. Now install the Microsoft PWS server extensions on port 80. Localhost (which is IP 127.0.0.1) requires port 80 to function.

N O T E   When you have TCP/IP configured on your computer, the IP address 127.0.0.1 automatically becomes the local loopback address. You can use this loopback address to "ping" the server, or check that the TCP/IP connection functions correctly. The 127.0.0.1 address by default is named "localhost." ■

■ Return to your Web server and try http://localhost again. You should get the bland but proper home page. This will also work if you type **http://COMPUTERNAME**, using the name of your computer as you've established it in Windows networking. That's because MS-PWS operates as an intranet server as well as an Internet server.

None of this is necessary if you've already established the MS-PWS as a server on your system under another IP address or domain name. If so, skip ahead to the details about properties and administration.

Setting the Microsoft PWS Properties

After installing MS-PWS, you can set properties or administer it from two different locations. You can go into Control Panel and double-click Personal Web Server to open the Properties dialog box. If you've restarted Windows 95 or NT, the MS-PWS icon will appear in the taskbar tray at the bottom right of your screen (unless of course you've moved the taskbar). Double-clicking this icon reveals the tabbed dialog box shown in Figure 29.1. On the other hand, right-clicking the PWS taskbar icon will yield three choices. Administer takes you to the

HTML-based administration pages. Home Page opens your browser with the DEFAULT.HTM page showing. Properties opens the same Properties dialog box (see Figure 29.1) you can get to from Control Panel, or from double-clicking the PWS taskbar icon.

FIG. 29.1

The Personal Web Servers Properties dialog box lets you control all aspects of the MS-PWS.

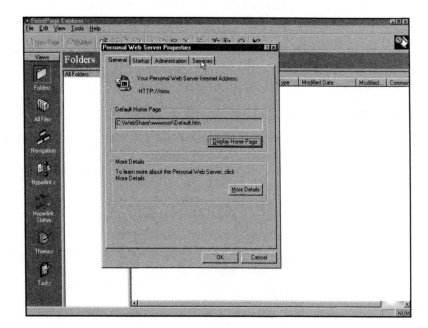

There are four tabs on this dialog box: General, Startup, Administration, and Services, as follows:

General Offers two points of information (refer to Figure 29.1). The first is the location of the default home page for your server (clicking Home Page from the taskbar icon does the same thing). Note that this is the default home page for the root Web of the server, not for any other Webs you create with FrontPage (each contains its own home page). If you wish to change this default home page, you can do so through the Services button (covered in last item). The second button, More Details, takes you to the documentation for the server that's stored in a set of Web files on your hard drive. The docs will appear in your browser, and they're extremely useful.

Startup Lets you start or stop the server whenever you wish. Simply click the Start or Stop button to change its current state. From here you can also specify whether or not you want MS-PWS to load whenever you boot Windows (Yes by default), and whether or not you want the server icon to appear in the taskbar tray (Yes by default). If you don't elect to have the icon appear, you must access properties through the Windows Control Panel.

Administer Offers only one button. Clicking it takes you to the Administration pages in your browser, which we'll cover next. This is the same as what happens when you select Administer from the taskbar icon.

Services Lets you establish how you want the Web (HTTP) or FTP services to behave. You can change the FTP root directory from here, and you can also specify whether or not the FTP service will start automatically whenever Windows loads. By clicking HTTP Service and selecting Properties, you can change the root Web of the server, and also determine whether or not the Web service should start automatically. Notice that this is different from the Startup tab, which simply lets you load the Web server when Windows loads. Just because the server is loaded into memory doesn't mean it's actually started and available to serve a Web. It has to be started first.

Administering Microsoft PWS

Clicking the Administration button from the Administration tab of Properties dialog box, or selecting Administer from the MS-PWS taskbar icon, opens the Server Administration pages in your Web browser. You can also get to these pages by loading your browser and typing **http://localhost/htmla/HTMLA.HTM** in the location box. Either way, you'll see a screen (see Figure 29.2) where you can specify how your server will operate as a Web server and as an FTP server, and how you will grant access to local users.

FIG. 29.2
The MS-PWS Server Administrator pages give you access to WWW, FTP, and Local User administration.

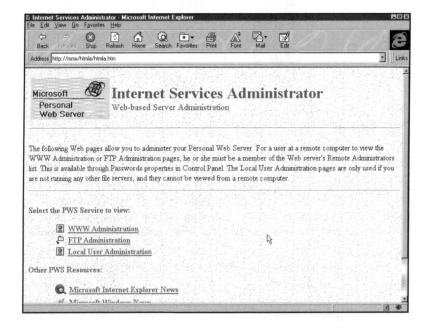

Web Administration

When you click WWW Administration, you'll see a Web page with three tabs and several fields. The tabs offer you the following options:

Service   You can specify here how long in seconds it will take a connection to time out if nothing happens. Set it low if you want to kick users out quickly or high if you want to give them additional time to connect. You can also restrict the maximum number of simultaneous connections. By default this is set at 300, but if you have a slow connection, you'll want to limit this considerably. Also available from the Service tab is the system of password authentication you wish to use. If you're running a public Web, you can allow anonymous connections (the standard). Basic password authentication offers no secure encoding of passwords but is sufficient in many cases. Windows NT Challenge/Response authorization provides fully encrypted password security, but you require at least one Windows NT machine on the network for it to work.

N O T E   When setting the maximum connections value, keep this rule of thumb in mind: divide network connection speed by number of users to get the effective connection speed per user. Two users on a 28.8 connection share it at 14.4 each; three users share the connection at 9600 each. Anything below 9600 is likely to be perceived as unacceptably slow. If you're running a small intranet on a nondedicated machine, any more than three or four users will slow the network to unusable speeds. ▪

Directories   This tab takes you to a page that lets you specify the directories on your machine that will be accessible to Web visitors. By default, these are limited to the C:\webshare\wwwroot\ directory and its subdirectories, as well as C:\Program Files\WebSrv\ (where MS-PWS is located) and its subdirectories. As you add FrontPage Webs to this directory, these subdirectories will show up here as well. You can, however, add accessible directories directly from this page and edit or delete existing directories. You can also specify the default home page from here, and you can specify whether or not you want to allow your users to browse these directories. By default, this feature is on, but you can turn it off without anything important happening except a bit more security.

Logging   If you want MS-PWS to log its activity, you can do so from the Logging tab. You can also specify how often a new log will be started (a busy server might want a daily log), and where you want the log file to be placed. The log file is called INETSERVER_EVENT.LOG, and can be read with a text editor such as Notepad. If you intend to use log analysis software (available from a number of third-party providers) to keep specific track of your site's activities, be sure to have logging turned on, and if your server is a busy one, set logging to Daily to capture the fullest possible range of statistics.

FTP Administration

Often you'll design a Web that allows visitors to download files. This is true, for example, of Webs created with the Customer Support Web Wizard in FrontPage Explorer, which assumes you'll have programs and documents available for download. Or, you might simply want FTP access for yourself and your colleagues to transfer files from your home machine to the machine at work running the MS-PWS. Whatever the reason, you can easily establish MS-PWS as an FTP server as well as a Web server.

You'll first need to start the FTP service. To do so, go to the MS-PWS Properties dialog box, click Services, FTP Service, and Start. Now return to your browser and from the Administration contents page, click FTP Service.

You'll see four tabs. The Logging tab is identical to the Logging tab for MS-PWS. The Directories tab is also similar, but far fewer directories will be available. Since the purpose of this FTP server is simply to provide Web visitors with the ability to download files through anonymous FTP (that is, they can click an ftp:// link and the file downloads automatically), the MS-PWS is not a full-featured FTP server. It's extremely difficult, for example, to restrict certain users to certain directories, as more powerful FTP servers do (Windows NT's IIS and Peer Web Services are far more capable in this regard). For now, the best idea is to establish a directory and/or subdirectories in which you'll place files and allow FTP logins to those directories alone.

The Service tab lets you specify how quickly the connection times out if nothing happens, and the maximum number of simultaneous connections (16 by default, and it's best to keep it small). You can also specify that you want to allow anonymous connections (the standard for downloading from the Web). Remember that this isn't a full FTP server, it's primarily a server to help you put together a full-featured Web site. The Service tab also lets you see who's currently connected, and by clicking here you can disconnect specific users or even all of them. You might want to do this if users have been taking too long, or if you have to stop the FTP service for any reason whatsoever.

From the Messages tab, you can specify a message that will welcome your visitors, another that will display when they exit your server, and a third that will be shown if they attempt an FTP when the maximum number of connections has been reached. These messages aren't really important, but an appropriate message can help your overall image.

Administering Local Users

If you're running an intranet, you'll want to establish specific users who can access your files. This is accomplished through the Local User system, which is also part of the MS-PWS Administration pages.

From the Users tab, you can add new users, remove users, or view the properties of existing users. The Properties dialog box holds the username and the user password; you can change the password by typing the new password into the User Password and Confirm Password fields and clicking Change Password. If that user belongs to a group, this information will appear at the bottom of the User properties page.

N O T E   Before you can work with users, you'll need to set up the appropriate access levels. From the Control Panel, select Network, then click the File and Print Sharing button. Turn off all the access options. ▨

The Groups tab lets you create groups, which are essentially collections of usernames. Click New Group, enter the name of the group, and press OK. Now, by clicking the User/Group tab, you can add users to groups. Match the username in the User List box with the group name in the Group List box and press Add User to Group. Now when you return to the Groups tab, the Properties button will show which users are in that group.

It's important to note that, since MS-PWS is designed to run under Windows 95, you will never achieve the same kind of user access security that you will with a Windows NT or UNIX server. NT and UNIX offer highly specific user access rights and privileges, and user profiles form an important part of the Web server configuration. Windows 95 allows specific user profiles—and Windows 98 with Internet Explorer 4 even better ones—but Windows 95 is not, by its nature, a system focused on multiple users with specific user configurations.

The Microsoft PWS Configuration Entries

All settings for the MS-PWS are stored in Win95's registry. To access these settings, open the registry by clicking Start/Run, typing **regedit** and clicking OK. This will yield the Registry Editor, where you can find details about your system and your programs.

> **CAUTION**
>
> Do *not*, under any circumstances, edit Registry entries unless you know exactly what you're doing. It's extremely easy to change something seemingly innocent and then discover that Win95 no longer starts. Take a look at things, but don't change anything without first consulting either your favorite Win95 guru or a book that contains details about how to handle registry changes.

To see the MS-PWS settings, click the plus sign (+) in the left pane beside HKEY_LOCAL_MACHINE, to expand that entry. You'll see several other collapsed keys (entries). Now expand the sub-key System, and within System, the sub-key W3Svc. Here you'll find two additional sub-keys, Parameters and Users. Expand Parameters to reveal its sub-keys and click Parameters to see the contents in the right pane. Regedit should look like Figure 29.3.

The basic rule of thumb about working with Registry items is this: If you're absolutely sure you know what the name of the item and its corresponding data values mean, feel free to work with them.

 TIP If you intend to edit the Registry, first back up the Registry file by choosing Export Registry File from the Registry directory and saving to a safe location (floppy drive, second hard drive, and so on). That way, if Win95 doesn't operate correctly on re-boot, you can open Regedit, select Registry, Import Registry File, load the old registry file, and reboot once more.

FIG. 29.3
The Win95 registry shows extensive details about the MS-PWS configuration.

One easy possible change, for example, is the Registry entry called AccessDeniedMessage. By default, the value for this entry is "Access to this resource has been denied." If you want your users to see a different message, right-click the entry name, select <u>M</u>odify, and type in a different message. Close Regedit, and that message will now read as you changed it.

There is no need to change any of these values from within Regedit, however. Everything can be altered using FrontPage's administration and configuration dialog boxes.

The FrontPage PWS Server Configuration Files

The PWS is descended from the original NCSA httpd Web server, as are almost all Web servers. The configuration settings for this original server were stored in the HTTPD.CNF, SRM.CNF, ACCESS.CNF and MIME.TYP files and those files still exist with the Personal Web Server. By default, they are stored in the \FrontPage Webs\server\conf\ folder, which exists only if you choose to install the FrontPage Web Server. The in-depth documentation for these files can be found at the NCSA httpd Web site, **http://hoohoo.ncsa.uiuc.edu**. We'll briefly cover each of the files and what they contain, but it is highly recommended that you read all of the NCSA documentation before you change things in these files.

HTTPD.CNF

This is the main server configuration file. This file contains settings for the following:

- **ServerRoot** The directory the server's config, error, and log files are kept in.
- **Port** The port the standalone listens to. The network standard is 80.

- **Timeout**   The timeout applied to all network operations. It's the maximum time for a network send or receive, and the maximum time that a CGI script is allowed to take. The default is 20 minutes (1200 seconds).
- **ServerAdmin**   Your address, where problems with the server should be e-mailed.
- **ErrorLog**   The location of the error log file. If this does not start with / or a drive spec (recommended!), ServerRoot is prepended to it.
- **TransferLog**   The location of the transfer log file. If this does not start with / or a drive spec (recommended!), ServerRoot is prepended to it.
- **ServerName**   Allows you to set a host name which is sent back to clients for your server if it's different than the one the program would get (for example, use "www" instead of the host's real name).

SRM.CNF

This file is responsible for controlling how files are mapped out for users of your Web site. It provides for aliasing and redirection, as well as setting default document directories. Some of the information in this file includes:

- **DocumentRoot**   The directory out of which you will serve your documents. By default, all requests are taken from this directory, but aliases may be used to point to other locations.
- **Aliases**   You can have up to 20 aliases in the format Alias, fakename, realname.
- **Automatic Directory Indexing**   Allows you to specify how the server generates a directory index if there is no file in the directory whose name matches DirectoryIndex.

ACCESS.CNF

This file is the global access configuration file. It is not a good idea to mess around with this file.

MIME.TYP

This file is a little different than the other three. They were all server configuration information dealing with how the server worked. This file has to do with the content the server sends. A browser knows how to display a file by means of a MIME type, which is a piece of information sent by the server indicating the type of file that is being sent. The MIME.TYP file is where you can add new types and modify existing ones. A MIME type declaration is simple. Here is what a portion of the file looks like:

```
audio/basic      au snd
audio/x-aiff     aif aiff aifc
audio/wav        wav
image/gif        gif
image/ief        ief
```

image/jpeg   jpeg jpg jpe

image/tiff   tiff tif

As you can see, there is the MIME type listed on the left (for example, audio/wav) and the file extensions that should be designated by that type on the right (for example, wav). That is all that needs to be there for a new MIME type to be served up by the PWS.

From Here...

You now know just about everything there is to know about your FrontPage package. From this point on, you'll be embellishing and expanding that knowledge, encountering some detailed technical information in the process. Next comes:

- Part VI, "Using the FrontPage 98 SDK," which gives you the details behind creating your own wizards, templates, and other customizations of FrontPage.

- Part VII, "Integrating Microsoft FrontPage 98 and Microsoft Office," demonstrates the ways in which FrontPage works in conjunction with the programs in MS's famous suite of applications.

- Chapters 35-37 cover the creativity possible with the Microsoft Internet Assistants for each of the Office apps.

## CHAPTER 30

Setting Up an Intranet with FrontPage

This chapter covers using FrontPage to develop intranet applications. While intranet technology may be new to the Web, its importance is understood to be as great as the Internet itself. The intranet is quickly invading the corporate desktop and becoming seamlessly integrated with existing applications.

The intranet is now in a position to overtake traditional groupware solutions through its ease of use and cost effectiveness. A network environment once dominated by Lotus Notes and Groupwise is now embracing intranet technology.

Imagine that you own a company with 50 employees on a Windows NT network. Using a client/server application such as Lotus Notes would cost approximately $5,000 for the software alone, not to mention time spent developing the content and testing functionality. An intranet solution could quite easily reduce costs while adding additional benefits. The same 50 employees could be using Internet Explorer for the client software and the Microsoft Internet Information Server as the server portion. Total cost? Beyond the initial cost of the NT Server software itself, the answer is zero. Zilch. Nothing. Nada.

Build an intranet

Learn how to leverage existing Internet technology into an internal network solution.

Plan out your intranet for optimum results

Planning your intranet correctly is just as important as the content itself.

Incorporate office documents

Utilize existing documents for file-sharing capabilities on the intranet.

Reduce costs associated with networking

Build a cross-platform network application with virtually no associated costs.

N O T E Microsoft provides the Internet Information Server as a free add-on to the NT Server that adds extended Web features to Windows NT. ▪

Rise of the Intranet

Simply defined, an *intranet* is an internal network using TCP/IP technology. Generally, businesses already have networked computers using protocols such as NetBEUI (Microsoft Windows-based networks) and IPX/SPX (Novell NetWare). The idea of another network protocol to monitor and maintain may sound scary, but the cost justification is overwhelming.

One fantastic advantage of using an intranet over existing network products is that employees only have to learn one interface. This amounts to reduced training time, reduced support costs, and easy migration to new client/server technologies. You may be asking yourself: My employees use Word, Excel, and Access, so why switch? Good question. The truth is, you don't have to stop using your existing tools. Think about using intranet technologies to embrace and extend your existing operations base.

With the release of FrontPage 98 and Internet Explorer 3.0 and now 4.0, Microsoft has handed over the tools to incorporate many Microsoft Office features into a FrontPage-developed intranet. Through the use of OLE technology, or ActiveX as we are growing to know it, desktop applications are migrating into Web applications.

Key Advantages of an Intranet

There are a number of advantages to building an intranet, including a reduction in operating expenses and an increase in resource usability (because of the familiarity of the browser interface to most employees). Typical IS (Information Services) departments are constantly looking for new ways to increase productivity and reduce costs at the same time. Developing an intranet is clearly the way to take care of both goals simultaneously.

Reduce Publishing Costs

A typical mid-sized company has a Human Resources department that twice a year publishes an employee directory. If the company has 500 employees and prints a directory consisting of 100 pages, the company can expect to pay anywhere from one to three dollars per book, which includes typesetting, printing, and binding. Printing that kind of information twice a year can lead to costs of over $3,000 annually. Using an intranet, the same employee directory could be deployed across the network virtually free of charge. If an employee needed to take a portion of the directory home, he could save it to disk or print the pages desired.

Now, imagine all of a company's documents available electronically. Quarterly reports, financial statements, employee memos, and lunchroom menus could all be put into a Web interface, saving the company hundreds or thousands of dollars per year. Of course, you probably wouldn't want all your employees to see sensitive financial documents. Such access can be limited through security steps described later in this chapter.

Sales Support

Many companies have salesmen traveling constantly. Keeping up with pricing changes, product availability, and contact information can be a headache for a salesperson on the go. An intranet solution is much needed here.

Quite a few companies have dedicated modems and special software for their sales force to dial into remotely. While this can provide up-to-the-minute information for the salesperson, it can hold a tremendous cost weight for the employer. An intranet solution would allow a salesperson to dial into a national Internet service provider, log on to the network, and access such mission-critical documents. Of course, the site would have to be secure to retain its effectiveness, but this is a small price to pay for reducing costs while making information readily available.

Part

V

Ch

30

Reduce Training Time

One of the largest costs resulting from a new hire is time spent training the employee on existing systems and software. The employee may have to learn a word processor, a spreadsheet application, and the structure of the internal network all at once. This can be quite overwhelming, both for the new employee and the employer. Integrating an intranet into your existing network structure can help lift the weight off both persons.

Imagine sitting down with the employee on her first day and explaining to her that her main work window will be a Web browser. Furthermore, you explain that all internal company information and documents as well as internal correspondence will be accessed from one interface. You might have to explain what a bookmark file is for, or what a Reload button does, but it's a far cry from trying to show the employee why help in one program is accessed differently from in another. The key to an intranet is consistency—and consistency leads to better productivity.

Reduce Software Costs

Many of today's proprietary client/server software solutions are expensive to keep up with. Most software is now updated on a yearly schedule, resulting in outlandish registration fees for the company trying to keep up with technology. Another problem with proprietary solutions is that they can only be used one way, with one specific client program.

An intranet can be viewed from any Web browser—unless specific tags are used to render the site platform specific. There are many free Web browsers on the Internet available for downloading, including Microsoft's Internet Explorer, which runs on all Windows platforms, Macintosh, and UNIX in the near future. There are also quite a few Web servers available for free, such as the Internet Information Server by Microsoft, Apache, EMWAC, and Win-HTTPD.

Technical support for network software can also be quite costly, not to mention the time and money spent on long distance charges while waiting on hold for a technician. Most documentation for intranet-related programs is already on the Web. Forums such as FAQs and discussion groups via UseNet are free to use and can be a real time-saver when you need support quickly.

Creating an Intranet with FrontPage

Although most Web authors like to jump right into development, it's important to remember that a little organization and planning can go a long way. Effective intranets take weeks or months to develop while constantly changing to fit the needs of the company and the promise of technology.

Authoring a functional intranet consists of five main steps:

- Planning the Content   Good planning leads to good results.
- Building a Foundation   The intranet must be structured and organized.
- Adding Components   These incorporate the pieces that glue the framework together.
- Final Touches   Use this to add graphics and other elements.
- Deployment   This is the final phase of Web site development.

Planning the Intranet

The first step to the development cycle of a good intranet is strategic planning. Although you may be able to build a site one page at a time, it's often more useful to create the foundation of a site first and fill in the gaps as you come to them. Begin your development by mapping out, by hand, the different areas that you plan to incorporate into your site. For our sample Web, we will have five different departments: accounting, human resources, support, announcements, and feedback.

It is recommended that you begin your Web site development by sketching out the rough flow of the pages on paper. Once the ideas are carefully laid out (including additional components like databases and custom scripts), it's time to create a storyboard. The storyboard is a great tool for instant visual feedback. There will be no question about how the site will flow if you can look at its physical form before you design the actual Web pages. The storyboards do not have to be anything complex. In fact, they can be built on one sheet of paper with boxes drawn for each of the Web pages. Don't worry if you're not an artist—most Web authors are not. The purpose of the storyboard is just to give you an idea of the layout at a quick glance.

Erecting the Framework

Now that the initial site is mapped out, it's time to create the base on which our intranet will be built. You must have a strong foundation on which to develop an intranet application. Many Web authors feel that creating empty pages with text-based links as placeholders help speed up the overall development process. In this section, you will lay out the basis of your intranet, including all of the main sections and pages within. You will also incorporate some existing Microsoft Office documents into your pages to gain an understanding how integrating legacy applications fits into FrontPage.

Begin by opening the FrontPage Explorer and making sure that your Web server is up and running. Take the following steps:

1. Create a new Normal Web on the server of your choice in the FrontPage Explorer (http://localhost is fine) called Intranet. In Hyperlinks View, double-click the Home Page icon to load it into FrontPage Editor.

2. In the blank Editor document type: **Accounting | Human Resources | Support | Announcements | Feedback**. Click within the line of text and choose the center button from the toolbar.

3. Create new pages for the first four sections of your intranet by highlighting the heading for each individual department and choosing the Hyperlink button from the toolbar. For each one, click the Create a Page icon (the last of the four icons beside the URL field). When prompted, select Normal Page for each one. Save each page with a Title and file name the same as the desired link on the Home Page. Return to the Home Page window in Editor after each one to select the next and save the Home Page each time.

4. Click within the word Feedback and choose the Hyperlink button. Create a New Page called FEEDBACK.HTM and choose Feedback Form from the list.

You should now have five hyperlinks on your first page, each leading to a new page within your intranet. Although you may be anxious to enhance your site with graphics and bullets, it's easier to set up the foundation and fill in the rest later, especially if there are going to be multiple authors working on the Web site.

In the FrontPage Explorer, your new intranet Web will look like Figure 30.1.

Part
V

Ch

30

FIG. 30.1

A solid foundation to your corporate intranet leads to a reliable final application.

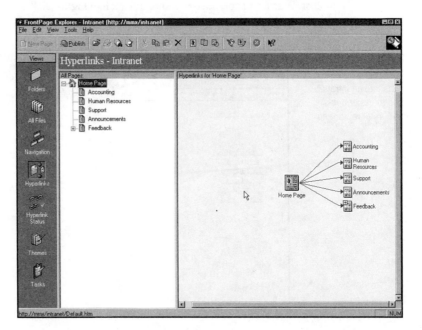

Adding Components

Now that the foundation is laid out, it's time to add content to your intranet. Any existing document can be linked into your intranet, allowing legacy applications to continue to be utilized in the workplace. Adding components is done through building upon the base site and growing it from there much like a tree sprouts new branches.

The Accounting Page   The Accounting department has asked for six spreadsheets to be made easily accessible to everyone on the network. Your task is to incorporate the Excel files seamlessly into your intranet. Take the following steps:

1. Double-click the Accounting page to open it for editing.

2. Type **Accounting Spreadsheets** and hit Enter. Type **Spreadsheet 1** and highlight your text.

3. Click the Hyperlink button on the toolbar. On the URL line of the Create Hyperlink dialog box, click the folder icon. This will eventually anchor the Excel file to your hyperlink.

4. Locate an Excel file to insert (this assumes you have one; if not, create a test file). When you have finished choosing your file, click OK.

5. Repeat the process for spreadsheets 2 to 6.

6. Highlight all six of the spreadsheet links and choose the Bulleted List button from the toolbar. Your list of spreadsheets should look like Figure 30.2.

7. Save your page.

FIG. 30.2
Incorporating spreadsheets into an intranet leads to easier document retrieval for end users.

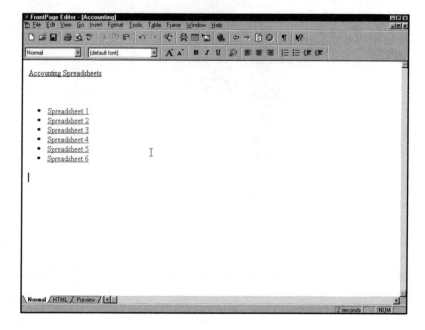

If you open this page in Internet Explorer and click one of the spreadsheet links, Excel will open inside Internet Explorer, allowing the page to be viewed and printed. In other browsers, the user is prompted to save the file to disk or to configure a helper application. By associating Excel with this file type, the program file will launch, allowing instant information at the employee's fingertips.

The Human Resources Page   The Human Resources department has greater needs than that of Accounting. You have been asked to incorporate an Employee Directory, Open Positions, Employee Handbook, and Meeting Schedule into the Human Resources portion of the intranet. Take the following steps:

1. Double-click the Human Resources page in the FrontPage Explorer to open it in FrontPage Editor.

2. Type **Employee Directory | Open Positions | Employee Handbook | Meeting Schedule** into the page. Click within the entire line and center the text in the page.

3. Highlight Employee Directory and choose Hyperlink from the toolbar. Create a new page called EMPLOYEE.HTM and choose OK. When prompted, choose Employee Directory from the New Page templates listing.

   The Employee Directory page that you've just created will be edited later. For now, we are just setting up the framework.

4. Highlight Open Positions and choose the Hyperlink button. Create a new page called OPENPOS.HTM and choose OK. When prompted, choose Employee Opportunities from the list of templates.

5. Import the file into FrontPage because the Employee Handbook is already formatted in the form of a Word document.

   Highlight Employee Handbook and choose Hyperlink from the toolbar. Click the World Wide Web tab and choose file://. Click Browse to locate the Word document and click OK to complete the link.

6. Highlight Meeting Schedule and create a hyperlink to a new page called MEETING.HTM. Choose Meeting Agenda from the templates menu and click OK.

While the Meeting Agenda template was meant for one specific meeting, it serves our purpose here. You could have just as easily created a new blank page for the Meeting Schedule page and inserted a number of Meeting Agenda pages.

Your addition to the FrontPage intranet project should look like Figure 30.3 when you return to FrontPage Explorer.

Your intranet is beginning to take shape. You have already created the basis of the Accounting and Human Resources departments and have only three more sections to go.

The Technical Support Page   The manager of your company's Technical Support department has approached you about putting a detailed list of Frequently Asked Questions into your intranet application. He feels that providing help online for your coworkers will help their department free up time spent on tedious problems. Take the following steps:

Part

V

Ch

30

1. Double-click the Support page in the FrontPage Explorer and give it a title of **Technical Support**.

2. Type **Frequently Asked Questions** in the body of the page and click within the text. Choose Hyperlink from the toolbar and choose New Page. Save the new page as FAQ.HTM and choose Frequently Asked Questions from the template menu. Click OK to continue.

FIG. 30.3
Organizing intranet content by a departmental basis leads to easier navigation.

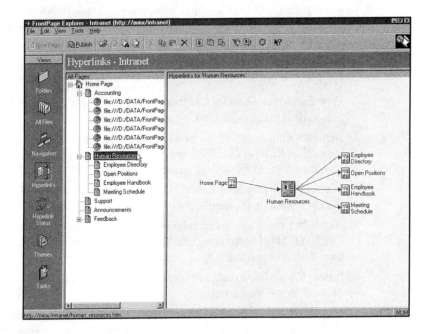

For now, we will leave the new FAQ page as is. It can be completed and then updated at any time.

The Announcements Page Your company's Executive Secretary has asked that you incorporate an announcements page into your intranet so that employees are kept abreast of new happenings, and she doesn't have to keep stuffing everyone's mailboxes with memos every day. The company has announcements often, and she would like people to be able to view the announcements on a monthly basis, with the daily announcement benefiting from a little pizzazz. Take the following steps:

1. Double-click the Announcements page in the FrontPage Explorer. The blank page will open in FrontPage Editor, eagerly awaiting your commands.

2. Choose Insert, Active Elements, Marquee from the menu. Type **Today's Big Announcement** in the Text field. Click OK.

3. Click the new marquee once to highlight it and choose the Center button on the toolbar.

4. Add the line **Previous Announcements** under the marquee. This is where you would normally retype the previous day's marquee and date the entry.

At a later time, you could add a link on the Announcements page pointing to older announcements. This could be done weekly or monthly, depending on the length of the content.

The Feedback Page Management wants to know what the employees are thinking about and, more important, how the company can grow to be more profitable. They have requested a Feedback page that will report its comments to a text file that management can review at board meetings. The feedback form is already in working order, although it will need some formatting to reach management's expectations. Take the following steps:

1. Double-click the Feedback page in the FrontPage Explorer.

2. In the FrontPage Editor, highlight all of the form components, beginning with "What kind of comment would you like to send down" to the end of the last text line "Please contact me...." Hit the Delete key to remove this portion of the form.

3. With your cursor at the beginning of the form, choose Insert, Form Field, Scrolling Text Box from the menu. Click the box and resize it (by dragging on the corner handle) to the width of the Submit and Clear buttons and about eight lines tall. Click to the right of the text box.

4. Press Enter to drop down one line. Type **Name:** and choose Insert, Form Field, One-Line Text Box. Stretch the text box so that it is even with the rest of your form.

5. Right-click within the border of the form and choose Form Properties from the menu. Pay special attention to the location where your text file will be saved (in Send To, Filename).

The results of the form submission will write to a text file called FEEDBACK.HTM that resides in a directory called _private. This directory is one that FrontPage created when you created your initial intranet Web. Only the Web Administrator can read this file. No employee without permission will be able to access this file from within the intranet.

The last step to completing your feedback page is to format the text that asks the visitor for his or her comments. Anything that management will approve of is fine. When you view the page in a Web browser, it should look like Figure 30.4.

Final Touches

In just a short time, you've seen how to piece together the framework of an intranet. Although it's a simple process, it's far from complete. Graphics can be incorporated into your Web site without much worry about file sizes. The only bandwidth that you are consuming is on your internal network, where speeds are probably much greater than your Internet access. You don't have the usual limitations against incorporating huge graphics or other multimedia elements that would normally take a long time to load in a Web browser.

Your intranet might start with only text-based links, but can soon develop into a beautiful site navigated by imagemaps and colorful buttons. Music can be added on the Announcements page to liven things up, or a video excerpt on the main page to provide a true cutting-edge feel.

Part
V

Ch
30

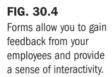

FIG. 30.4

Forms allow you to gain feedback from your employees and provide a sense of interactivity.

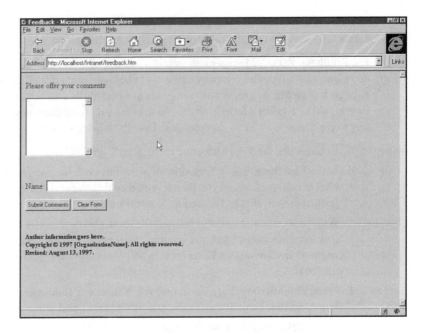

An intranet can also be much more involved than simply linking internal documents and providing feedback forums. In Chapter 17, "Using ActiveX Controls," you learned about incorporating ActiveX controls into your FrontPage Webs. Advanced ActiveX controls will help make your intranet communicate its purpose through multimedia-rich elements like Real Audio streamed files and VDO's streamed video segments. Training videos and vocal announcements can be utilized in your intranet for a more personal feel, while still keeping costs down by reducing equipment needs.

Deployment

Actually implementing your intranet is the last step in the creation process. You must decide where your Web will be housed and what type of server will serve the Web pages. Keep in mind that you also want your intranet secure. Most of the security features for your Web site will be implemented on the server side to restrict access. Many people, however, forget that an unattended Web server is just as open to malicious acts as a Web site published on the Internet with no security at all.

The Personal Web Server by Microsoft is a fine choice for a small company ranging from 10 to 15 people. This Web server is not as robust as other large ones, but it is totally free and it installs with very few modifications. The Personal Web Server can be downloaded from **ftp://ftp.microsoft.com/msdownload/frontpage/enu/pwssetup.exe**.

Windows NT 4.0 incorporates Peer Web Services into the operating system. Peer Web Services is actually a scaled-down version of the Microsoft Internet Information Server found in Windows NT Server. FrontPage extensions can be installed into the Web server just as if it were the complete Internet Information Server. Different departments within your company can actually author and house their own content for the intranet, allowing you to link the content together into navigable form.

The Microsoft Internet Information Server, which currently runs only on Windows NT Server, is a free product that holds robust Web serving capabilities and is easy to install and maintain. The Internet Information Server depends only on your computer's hardware configuration for the amount of simultaneous connections possible. The Internet Information Server can also utilize the Microsoft Index Server for cross-referencing Web pages and providing detailed search features.

Part
V

Ch
30

The Web server that you choose to host your intranet can actually be any Web server, but you must find one that works with FrontPage extensions in order to gain the maximum impact from your FrontPage-authored site.

From Here...

The development of the intranet is still in its infancy, although its importance is as great as the Internet itself. The intranet gives System Administrators the freedom to create content once, as if every computer on the network ran the same operating system. The intranet technology itself is easy to understand and far less complicated than a multitude of existing network tools. For more information about protecting your new intranet, refer to the following chapter:

Chapter 29, "Using Microsoft Personal Web Server and FrontPage Personal Web Server," covers the intricacies of installing and administering the new Microsoft Web server created especially for Windows 95.

Using the FrontPage 98 SDK

Extending and Customizing FrontPage with the SDK

For the majority of users, FrontPage provides them with everything they need to create great Web sites. However, there are those of you out there who look at just about any program and think to yourselves, "You know what this thing needs? More power! (insert grunts here)." Well, Microsoft has been kind enough to provide you with a means to tweak FrontPage to your heart's delight, including the capability to use FrontPage as a component in our own applications for you programmers out there. It's the FrontPage SDK (Software Developer's Kit) and it's the focus of this and the next two chapters.

What exactly is a Software Developer's Kit? In a nutshell, an *SDK* normally consists of documentation of a program's underlying behavior and information on how to modify or add to that behavior. It may also contain header files for programmers who would like to add the capabilities of a piece of software to their own programs, and possibly even sample code to show, by example, how to use the SDK. All of these things are part of the FrontPage SDK. Now, you may be saying to yourself, "Hey, I'm not a computer programmer. When would I ever use the SDK?" The answer to that is: maybe never. Still, even you non-programmers might want to learn about it to Add a menu item to the FrontPage editor that starts up the great new

Overview of the SDK
Learn about how the SDK allows you to extend the capabilities of FrontPage.

Customizing FrontPage menu items
Learn how to add your own commands to the Explorer and Editor menus.

Designer HTML
Incorporate the newest HTML tags into the FrontPage editor with Designer HTML.

Creating custom page templates
Create your own templates to eliminate redoing tedious, repetitive sections of documents.

Creating custom Web templates
Make a skeleton Web site that you can use to start your own Webs.

Creating custom framesets
Frames are a pain. Create your own frameset templates to save yourself some work.

Creating custom wizards
Write your own programs in Visual Basic or Visual C++ to step users through complicated processes.

graphics program you just bought to edit your images, create your own custom templates, or even extend the HTML capabilities of FrontPage.

That's right. You are not limited to the templates or menu choices that Microsoft has chosen to give you. You can modify FrontPage to work the way you work, and if you do happen to be a Windows programmer, the SDK will also tell you how to add FrontPage to your application and program it through OLE automation, as well as how to create your own Wizards and FrontPage Components.

The SDK is a powerful part of FrontPage, and it will let you get under the hood and make the program work the way you want it to. Some of these topics are discussed in depth in the next two chapters. ■

Overview of the SDK

At the time this book went to press, Microsoft had not yet released the SDK for FrontPage 98. Although we have been assured that the things that worked with FrontPage 97 will continue to work with FrontPage 98, there will likely be changes and additions to the SDK.

The FrontPage SDK consists of a set of files on your FrontPage CD-ROM in the \FRONTPG\FPSDK30\ directory. These files include documentation in Word format, templates, wizards, some utility programs, CGI scripts, Designer HTML, and some custom FrontPage Components. As was mentioned in the introduction to this chapter, these files give you the capability to extend and customize FrontPage.

FrontPage can be extended and customized in many ways by programmers and nonprogrammers alike. Why is it important to be able to extend FrontPage? Well, the computer world—especially the Internet—changes rapidly. New extensions get added to HTML; new programming languages and ways of making your pages interactive and exciting keep popping up. You just might want to be able to keep working with the piece of software you've bought and learned and still be able to do the new stuff. With the SDK, you can. There are other reasons to extend FrontPage. For instance, maybe you are just used to a certain text editor, or you have a special graphics program and you want to make it work with FrontPage. Great! What if you find that the templates included with FrontPage just don't really suit your needs? No problem. The SDK will show you how to create new ones. As you can see, the FrontPage SDK is where you can personalize FrontPage and make it work the way you want (or need) it to.

FrontPage can be extended in many useful ways with no programming experience whatsoever, and with some HTML knowledge you can do even more. In this chapter, you'll start with the easier stuff and then move on to the more advanced things.

Depending on what you want to do with the SDK, you will need the following:

■ A text editor (such as Notepad)

■ Some knowledge of HTML

- For custom wizards, a Windows programming language such as Visual C++ or Visual Basic

- For custom FrontPage Components, knowledge of CGI programming using either a Windows development tool such as Visual C++ or Visual Basic, and/or programming with another Web language such as Java, PERL, JScript, or VBScript.

Customizing FrontPage Menus

The concept of extending and customizing menus is fairly simple. You can add your own menu commands and your own menus to the FrontPage Editor or Explorer. These commands can be used to provide links to other applications you use regularly, to insert the contents of other files into your pages, or even just to insert commonly used text when a menu item is chosen. They work just like the menu items that come with FrontPage. You call the shots, and all it requires is a little planning and the addition of some items to the Windows Registry. In this section, you will be walked through the addition of a custom menu and a couple of custom menu items.

Part
VI

Ch
31

How It Works

In Windows 95 and NT, there is a database file in Windows called the Registry. This is the place where applications store information about themselves when they are installed and running. FrontPage reads the Registry when it boots up and looks for Registry keys that extend its menus. When you add new items to the Registry, you can extend the menus of FrontPage. This may seem like a lot to do, but the process is actually fairly straightforward. But first, a little about the Windows Registry and the Registry Editor (REGEDIT.EXE).

The Windows Registry Editor

The *Windows Registry* is a system database filled with keys and values. If you are at your computer, you can bring up the Windows Registry editor by doing the following:

1. Click the Start Button.
2. Choose Run…
3. Type: **regedit**.

You should get a window that looks something like Figure 31.1.

The items on the left are keys, and they define the behavior of various aspects of your system and applications. Clicking the plus sign (+) to the left of a key will expend that key. Feel free to explore in here, but don't start changing values just for the fun of it. Most of the changes made to the Registry are done by applications themselves. Most Windows 95 books include large sections on the Registry, but this chapter only covers enough to know how to create Registry entries. For more information on the Windows Registry, check out *Special Edition Using the Windows 95 Registry* from Que Publishing.

FIG. 31.1

The Windows 95
Registry Editor.

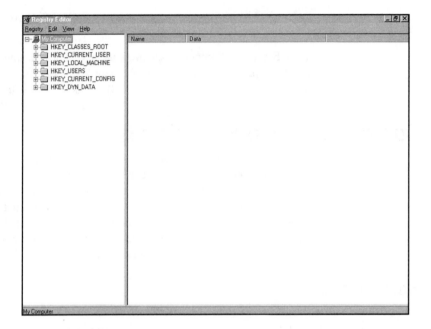

When you select a key, you might see values set over on the right side. There are two columns, Name and Data. These columns are where the settings for the keys are stored. Each key can have many named values. In order to change a value, do the following (as illustrated in Figure 31.2):

1. Right-click the Name of the value you wish to change.
2. Choose Modify from the pop-up menu.
3. Change the value name or data in the box that pops up.
4. Click OK.

That's all there is to changing a key. To add a new key, do the following:

1. Choose Edit.
2. Select New from the Edit menu.
3. Choose Key.

FIG. 31.2
Modifying Registry
data.

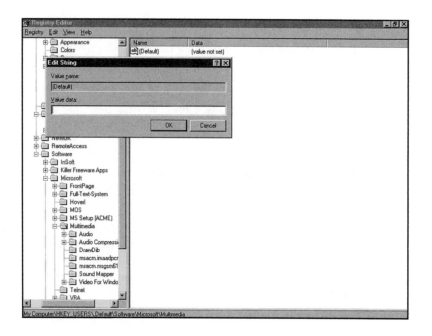

The Registry Editor will insert a new key value. The name will be highlighted so that you can change it. In order to add a new value to an existing key, do the following:

1. Choose Edit.
2. Select New from the Edit menu.
3. Choose either String value, Binary value, or DWORD value, depending on the type of value you wish to add.

In order to extend the menus of FrontPage, you will be adding only String values.

Adding New Menus

Now that you know how to start up the Registry Editor and are familiar with the basics of working with it, let's do something with it. As mentioned before, in order to extend the menus for FrontPage, you will be adding values to Registry keys. In FrontPage, both the Explorer and the Editor can be extended, but the process is a little bit different for each. We will start with the Explorer.

Adding New Menus to FrontPage Explorer   The custom menus for the FrontPage Explorer are all stored in the same place in the Registry. This place in the Registry can be referred to by a path name, just like a file on a disk. The path name to this Registry key is:

`HKEY_CURRENT_USER\Software\Microsoft\FrontPage\Explorer\Init Menus`

Now you can add a custom menu called MyMenu to the FrontPage Explorer, and then you can look at what you did.

First, start up the Registry Editor and do the following:

1. Click the plus sign (+) next to the key HKEY_CURRENT_USER.
2. Click the plus sign next to the key Software, under HKEY_CURRENT_USER.
3. Click the plus sign next to the key Microsoft, under Software.
4. Click the plus sign next to the key FrontPage.
5. Click the plus sign next to Explorer.
6. Click the key Init Menus.

This will take you to the place in the Registry just mentioned. When you first install FrontPage, there should be no values on the right side except one named (Default) with a value of (value not set).

Now you need to add a new value by selecting Edit, New, String Value. This command will add a new value named New Value #1 to the list on the right. The text should be highlighted, so change the name to **menu1**. You can name the values anything you wish, as long as the name is unique. Now, right-click your new menu1, choose Modify from the menu, and type the following into the Value box:

```
2, , 1, M&yMenu, Tools
```

Then click OK and close the Registry Editor. Congratulations! You've just added a menu item to the FrontPage Explorer. The next time FrontPage starts, you will see the menu MyMenu added to the FrontPage Explorer. Take a look at Figure 31.3 to see what it should look like. You will also find that there are no menu items underneath that menu, just the heading. This is where the next section, "Adding Custom Commands" will come in, but for the time being take a look at what you have. What does the value you typed in mean?

The extended menus in FrontPage are a series of values with the following syntax:

```
first_version, last_version, menu_bar_num, menu_name, menu_position
```

Table 31.1   Custom Menu Arguments

Argument	Description
first_version	The number of the earliest version of FrontPage which should add this new top-level menu command. Values less than 2 are treated as 2 (since that is the first version of FrontPage to support custom menus). Values greater than the current running version of FrontPage tell FrontPage not to create this menu.
last_version	The number of the last version of FrontPage which should add this new top-level menu command. Values less than the current running version of FrontPage tell FrontPage not to create this menu. If omitted, this argument is treated as being higher than the current running version of FrontPage.

Argument	Description
menu_bar_num	Number of the built-in menu bar to which you want to add the menu. This field is ignored because there is currently only one set of menus in the Explorer, but the field value should be set to 1 to allow for future expansion.
menu_name	Name of the new menu. The ampersand (&) is the character that places an underscore in your menu name and works with the ALT key to select your menu from the keyboard. Therefore, M&yMenu will show up as MyMenu and be accessible with ALT+Y. If you wish to include an ampersand in your menu name, simply put two ampersands in a row.
menu_position	Position of the new menu on the menu bar. This may be the name of the menu before which you want to place the new menu, or a number indicating the menu's position from the left end of the menu bar (1-based). If the number or name does not exist, or the argument is omitted, the new menu is placed to the right of the Tools menu. When comparing this string against menu names, any accelerators present in the menu names are ignored.

Part

VI

Ch

31

FIG. 31.3

The FrontPage Explorer shows your new menu.

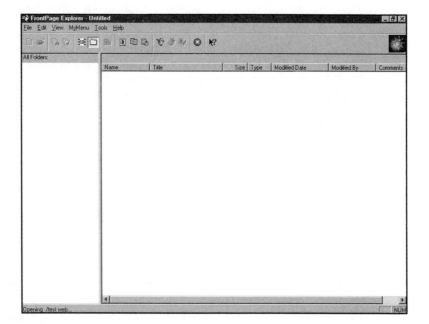

So the string you added said the following:

2 Don't show this menu if the version of FrontPage running is less than 2.

<no value> There is no limit on how high the version number can be.

1 Show this on Menu Bar number 1.

M&yMenu The menu should be shown as MyMenu.

Tools Show this menu to the left of the Tools menu.

That's it. Any custom menu you need can be created by adding more values to this section in the Registry.

Adding New Menus to FrontPage Editor Adding new menus to the FrontPage Editor is identical to adding them to the Explorer, with exception of the location in the Registry where the commands are added. To add menus to the Editor, simply go to HKEY_CURRENT_USER\SOFTWARE\MICROSOFT\FRONTPAGE\EDITOR\INIT MENUS in the Registry and follow the same instructions as for the Explorer. There is one more difference. In the Explorer, there is currently only one menu, so the menu_bar_num value will always be 1. In the Editor, there are two menu bars: the empty document menu (0) and the active document menu (1), and you will need to specify which one you want your menu to appear on.

Adding Custom Commands

But, you may ask, what good are menus without commands under them? Let's now see how to add commands to new and existing menus. The process is a bit different for the Editor and the Explorer, so we'll start with the Explorer.

Adding Custom Commands to FrontPage Explorer Now you are going to add a custom command to our MyMenu menu in the FrontPage Explorer. The syntax for adding a new command is a little bit more complicated than the syntax for adding a menu, and we will now go through it by adding a command that starts the Windows Registry Editor from within FrontPage.

As you might expect, the process starts in the Windows Registry again, so open the Windows Registry Editor, and this time find the following key:

```
HKEY_CURRENT_USER\Software\Microsoft\FrontPage\Explorer\Init Commands
```

Add a new value to the key by choosing Edit, New, String Value. A new value will be added to the list on the right. You can change the name of the value to anything you wish, as long as it is not the name of an existing custom command. You might just want to name it **MyCommand1**. Now, right-click your new MyCommand1 and choose Modify. In the Values box, type the following (note that you will need to specify the location of your Windows directory if it is something other than C:\WINDOWS):

```
2,,1,MyMenu, &Registry Editor, C:\WINDOWS\REGEDIT.EXE, , 0, Launches the Windows
Registry Editor.,
```

Now click OK and close the Registry Editor. The next time you start FrontPage, you will see something like Figure 31.4.

Now, what do all of those values mean? The following is the syntax for custom commands (direct from the SDK documentation):

```
first_version, last_version, menu_bar_num, menu_name, command_name, command_line,
command_position, macro_key, status_text, help_reference
```

FIG. 31.4

The FrontPage Explorer with your new menu command.

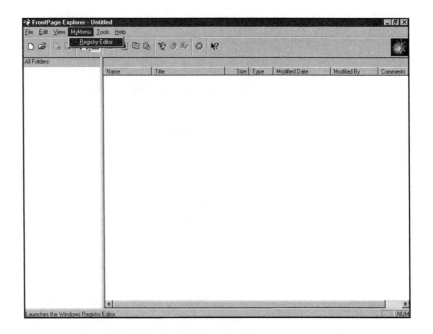

Table 31.2 Custom Command Arguments

Argument	Description
first_version	The number of the earliest version of FrontPage which should add this new command to the menus. Values less than 2 are treated as 2. Values greater than the current running version of FrontPage tell FrontPage not to create this command. This is exactly the same as when creating a menu.
last_version	The number of the last version of FrontPage which should add this new command to the menus. Values less than the current running version of FrontPage tell FrontPage not to create this command. If omitted, this argument is treated as being higher than the current running version of FrontPage. Combined with first_version, this argument allows you to create add-ins which are tailored to work only with specific versions of FrontPage. This is also the same as when creating a menu.
menu_bar_num	Number of the built-in menu bar to which you want to add the menu. This field is ignored because there is currently only one set of menus in the Explorer, but the field value should be set to 1 to allow for future expansion.
menu_name	Name or number (1-based) of the menu on which to insert the new command. If the number or name does not exist or the argument is omitted, then the new command is placed on the Tools menu.

continues

Part
VI

Ch
31

Table 31.2 Continued

Argument	Description
command_name	Name of the new command. If a separator is to be added, then the command name is a single dash character "–". If a separator is added, the only remaining argument after command name that is significant is the command position argument; the other arguments are ignored. The menu accelerator is indicated by an ampersand character preceding the accelerator key, for example, "My &Addin."
command_line	Fully specified file name and path to the executable file that should be run when the user chooses this command in the FrontPage Explorer.
command_position	Position of the command on the menu. This may be the name of the command before which you want to place the new command, or a 1-based number indicating the command's position on the menu, counting from the top of the menu (separators are counted). If the name or position does not exist or the argument is omitted, the command appears at the end of the menu.
insert_flag	Determines whether to insert the file pointed to by command line or to execute it. For the Explorer, the command_line is always executed and the value of this field must be 0.
status_text	Message to be displayed in the status bar when the command is selected.
help_reference	File name and topic number for a custom Help topic for the command, separated by an exclamation point.

The string we entered reads as follows:

2 Don't show this if the version of FrontPage is less than 2.0.

<no value> Any version above 2.0 can show this command.

1 Put this choice on the main menu bar.

MyMenu Put this command under menu MyMenu.

&Registry Editor Show command as Registry Editor.

C:\WINDOWS\REGEDIT.EXE The command line to launch when this command is chosen.

<no value> Placed at the end of the menu, a number would indicate the menu placement.

0 This number doesn't really mean anything for the Explorer, only for the Editor, but it has to be 0.

Launches the Windows Registry Editor Displays this message on the status bar when this item is highlighted.

<no value> There is actually one more parameter that can be specified that we did not do. It is indicated by the comma on the end with no value after it. This one has to do with Windows Help and which help file and help topic should be used to obtain help on this item.

If you would like to add a separator line to the menu for the sake of organization, simply add a menu item with a name "-." This will create a separator line.

That's all there is to adding custom commands to the Explorer. FrontPage Editor is a little different, as you shall see.

Adding Custom Commands to FrontPage Editor As you may have guessed, the process is the same with a few exceptions. The first is the location of the Registry keys for the Editor. You will need to go to HKEY_CURRENT_USER\SOFTWARE\MICROSOFT\FRONTPAGE\EDITOR\INIT COMMANDS to add commands to the Editor menus.

The syntax for adding commands to menus in the Editor is identical to adding them to the Explorer, except the Editor will use some settings that are ignored (and required to be a fixed value) by the Explorer. One was mentioned when the Explorer menu command was added—the `insert_flag`. In Explorer, it is meaningless, but in the Editor, it allows you to create different types of commands. The other one is the `menu_bar_num`. In Explorer, there is only one menu bar, but in the Editor this can be 0, empty document menu, or 1, active document menu.

The `insert_flag` value demonstrates a very significant difference between custom commands for the Explorer and those for the Editor. This flag can only be used to execute a `command-line` argument in the Explorer, but it can be used to insert text in the Editor. The flag can mean one of the following:

    0 Execute the `command_line` argument as an EXE program file (this is the only one that is allowed for Explorer).

    1 Insert the file pointed to by the `command_line` argument as HTML text. The file will be inserted in the current document with paragraph breaks before and after.

    2 Insert the literal text contained in the `command_line` argument as HTML. The actual text of the `command_line` argument will be inserted inline without paragraph breaks before or after.

You have already seen how option 0 behaves for this parameter. This is the way you added a command to start the Registry Editor. However, what about 1 and 2? The process for creating these commands is exactly the same, but the results are different. In the case of 1, the file listed in the `command_line` parameter is not executed, but inserted with a paragraph break before and after it. This is useful if you have a section of preformatted HTML code that you use regularly, such as a copyright notice or contact information, that you would like to be able to insert quickly and easily into pages as you work on your Web. Parameter number 2 also inserts text, but inserts the actual text placed in the `command_line` parameter inline with no paragraph breaks before or after. How is this useful? One possible use would be to allow for insertion of HTML tags that are not currently available in FrontPage. In order to create a new tag `foo`, you could simply put `<foo></foo>` as your `command_line` parameter.

Part

VI

Ch

31

Custom menus are a very powerful way of customizing the FrontPage working environment and allow you to extend FrontPage to work the way you do.

Designer HTML

This is a powerful feature of FrontPage—and a very important one for a quickly changing Internet world, where there are new things showing up every time you turn around. Designer HTML is what Microsoft calls the extensions added to its FrontPage Components HTML pseudo-tag. Since I have probably already lost you, I'll explain a little about the pseudo-tag and how it's used, and then touch on some possible uses of this nifty little capability.

The FrontPage Components Pseudo-Tag

Basically, the FrontPage Components pseudo-tag is an HTML tag that has been created to work with FrontPage. Why is it a pseudo-tag? This is because the FrontPage Components tag takes place inside an HTML comment, and thus is never seen by a Web browser. It exists for the sole purpose of interacting with FrontPage, either with the development environment at design time, or with FrontPage Components and the FrontPage Server Extensions at runtime. The tag looks like the following:

```
<!--WEBBOT bot="HTMLMarkup" ALT= "<Font Size=+3><I>Foobar ISV Feature Place-
holder</I></FONT>" StartSpan -->

[## A bunch of text goes here, maybe preprocessor directives or a new HTML tag]

<!--WEBBOT bot="HTMLMarkup" EndSpan -->
```

Had this been a normal FrontPage Component—TimeStamp, for example—you would have seen the tag bot="TimeStamp", but in the case of Designer HTML, it will always be "HTMLMarkup." Also note the use of the StartSpan and EndSpan attributes to indicate the start and end of your block of unknown HTML. These always have to be used.

To let the user specify the display characteristics of a block of unknown HTML in the FrontPage Editor, there are two new attributes on the FrontPage Components pseudo-tag. These attributes are as follows:

U-SRC=filename Points to an image file to use to display the unknown HTML block in the FrontPage Editor. If the image is a file (URL on the local machine), it will be automatically included into the Web and the URL adjusted to point to the version contained in the Web.

Only image files are allowed for the U-SRC tag. Included HTML is not allowed. If text is needed for display, either it should be encoded into the image or the ALT attribute should be used instead of the U-SRC attribute.

ALT=text Limited HTML text to show inside a rectangle in the FrontPage Editor as the display for the unknown HTML block. If both U-SRC and ALT are specified, then U-SRC is used in preference to ALT. Typically, however, only one or the other would be specified.

These attributes allow for an alternate display in the WYSIWYG editor of your Designer HTML, either in the form of text or a graphic. When this tag is inserted into your document, it will either appear as the image, or the text and the standard FrontPage Components cursor will appear whenever you move the mouse over it.

Using Designer HTML

Once you have created your Designer HTML document, you will no doubt want to use it in a document. There are three ways to get this new Designer HTML into your document:

- Copy and paste the HTML (described in the next section).
- Insert file.
- Drag and drop.

FrontPage applies what Microsoft calls IntelliSense when a user pastes regular text into the Editor. FrontPage will do an autodetection pass through the content before pasting it and will determine if the text is valid HTML. If it is, it will automatically parse it as HTML and merge the content with the rest of the existing page.

Drag-and-drop operations work just like their copy and paste equivalents. FrontPage allows you to drop in text itself, or text and HTML files. Just drop the files you create onto the Web page, and they are automatically handled.

If you combined this capability with a custom menu, you would be able to create a menu command that inserted your own custom HTML that FrontPage didn't even recognize when you bought it, and have that HTML formatted on your WYSIWYG display however you wanted it to display—all without any computer programming. Pretty neat, huh?

Part
VI

Ch
31

Creating Custom Web and Page Templates

Custom menu items allow you to tailor your work environment to fit your needs, but I know they were not the first thing I wanted to do when I first worked with FrontPage. My first thought was the ability to define my own templates so that I could simplify the creation of the Web pages and site layouts that I used regularly. Fortunately, FrontPage allows you to do just that. We aren't going to discuss this in great detail here because custom templates are covered in greater depth in Chapter 32, "Creating Templates," but we will just state that you can do it. If you're just dying to do it right now, head on over to Chapter 32 to find out more.

N O T E In addition to custom pages and sites, you also have the ability to create your own custom framesets. We will also cover those in depth in Chapter 32, "Creating Templates."

N O T E So far, everything we have covered can be done without any real programming except for a little HTML. Things start to change when you begin to create custom wizards, which require some programming ability. The process of creating wizards, as well as some samples, will be outlined in Chapter 33, "Creating Wizards."

Creating Custom Components

This is one of the more advanced parts of the SDK and is not going to get coverage in its own chapter. We won't discuss it in gruesome detail here either, since it really goes beyond the scope of this book. However, we will go under the cover on FrontPage components a little—what they really are, how they work, and how you can go about creating them.

FrontPage Components: What Are They?

Components are a concept peculiar to Microsoft FrontPage, and had me puzzled a little at first. They are a way to put interactive content in a page for the average end user without any programming knowledge. For the typical user who bought FrontPage because he didn't want to learn HTML, this is great. No CGI programming, just FrontPage components. So what exactly are these components?

FrontPage components are built-in code pieces that run when you save the page, or when a user accesses the page. Components generally create some HTML code that then carries out that component's specific function.

Each component has three main parts:

- A property editing user interface to interact with users in FrontPage
- A presentation to show in the WYSIWYG editor
- A server-side program that delivers the actual interactivity

Components are similar to CGI programs, but the additional pieces—the property editor and the WYSIWYG presentation—make them easier for end users to add to their pages. We are not going to cover the actual creation of a custom component in this book, since that requires extensive programming knowledge in a Windows programming language like C++ or Visual Basic. For those of you who are programmers and would like to create your own components, the SDK contains extensive documentation, and I will cover the basics on how they work here.

How Do Components Work?

When an end user chooses to insert a component in his Web page, a dialog box comes up that gets the properties for the component from the end user and then saves that information in the page inside an HTML comment field. When the HTML file is processed, the component information is read, processed, and then expanded into the actual HTML that the end user expects to see in his browser.

A component becomes active at the following times:

- When a page is saved by the FrontPage editor
- When a page is regenerated by the FrontPage Server Extensions due to a dependency which required updating
- When a page is the target of an HTTP POST request, such as when the browser submits the form
- When a page is fetched through the SmartHTML interpreter by an HTTP GET request

When the component is activated, it can perform whatever actions you would like, based on the current values of its properties, CGI environment variables, or form data that a user may have submitted. The types of things you might have it do could be to insert generated HTML into the component's location in the HTML file, to handle a form that was submitted to the page, or even to generate a completely new page.

Automating FrontPage Using OLE

For those of you developing your own applications with Visual Basic or Visual C++, or any other Windows programming language that allows you to do OLE automation, you can use FrontPage as a component in your application. This gives you the ability to include an HTML editor in a company application or to extend your current client/server applications to include publishing on the Web. This provides a tremendous resource and saves you a lot of work. How might you go about doing this? Let's cover the basic process in Visual Basic.

Part
VI

Ch
31

The FrontPage Objects

FrontPage exposes three main interfaces for OLE automation: the Explorer interface, the Editor interface, and the To Do List interface. Each one of these interfaces can be automated through OLE automation, and they all include a large set of methods that are documented in the SDK. Let's cover the three objects briefly, as follows:

FrontPage Explorer Interface   Just as this is the main interface to the program, it is also the main interface for OLE automation. The Explorer interface operates on Web-level objects and can currently be used to create a Web, delete a Web, move documents from a local file system to a Web server and vice versa, remove documents from a Web, set and get Web meta-info variables, get page meta-info variables, retrieve a list of files or images in the current Web, launch the To Do List, and get the URL and title of the current Web.

FrontPage Editor Interface   The FrontPage Editor is the Web page editing part of FrontPage. The FrontPage Editor can open, edit, and save HTML files in the current Web being viewed by the FrontPage Explorer, or in the local file system. This can be used to create a new empty page, open a page from the current Web or local file system, or determine if a named page is currently being edited. You can also insert files, images, or HTML into the current page at the insertion point.

FrontPage To Do List Interface   The FrontPage To Do List is exactly what it sounds like: a grid object that manages and displays a list of tasks to be performed on the Web currently opened by the FrontPage Explorer. These tasks are removed from the To Do List as they are completed. Operations exposed to OLE in this interface include the ability to add, remove, and edit items in the list.

All right, so there are three OLE interfaces to FrontPage. You might be wondering how you would use them to create your own applications. The basic OLE process works like this. There is an OLE client (your application) and an OLE server (in this case, FrontPage). The server provides the functionality, and the client uses it. The process in codes starts by creating an object variable of the correct type. In VB, you would do the following:

```
Dim explorer as Object
Set explorer = CreateObject("FrontPage.Explorer.2.0")
```

or in Visual C++:

```
Iwebber explorer
explorer.CreateDispatch("FrontPage.Explorer.2.0");
```

The preceding code would start up the FrontPage Explorer and allow you to use it in your code just like any other object. Once you have the object, there are quite a few things you can do with it, as the following partial list of the available methods will show you.

Some of the OLE Automation Methods for FrontPage.Explorer.2.0.

- vtiCreateWeb   Creates a new Web
- vtiRefreshWeb   Refreshes current Web
- vtiRemoveWeb   Removes the specified Web from the server
- vtiEditWebPage   Opens a page in the Editor
- vtiGetPageList   Lists pages in current Web

Some of the OLE Automation Methods for FrontPage.Editor

- vtiOpenWebPage   Opens an HTML document for editing
- vtiNewWebPage   Starts a new document
- vtiInsertHTML   Inserts HTML in the document

Some of the OLE Automation Methods for FrontPage.ToDoList

- vtiAddTask   Adds a new task to the To-Do list
- vtiGetActiveCount   Gets the number of active tasks in the To-Do List
- vtiCompletedTaskByUrl   Marks a task completed

To put this all together, here is some sample code in Visual Basic and also in Visual C++ that creates a FrontPage Explorer object and refreshes the contents of the Web from the server.

Visual Basic:

```
Function btnSomeEvent_Click()
{
Dim explorer as Object

    Set explorer = CreateObject("FrontPage.Explorer.2.0")
    explorer.vtiRefreshWebFromServer
    Set explorer = Nothing
    ' NOTE: it is important to set the OLE object variable
    ' to Nothing so that the OLE connection is released
}
```

Visual C++:

```
#include "webber.h"
```

```
void OnSomeEvent()
{
IWebber explorer;
COleException error;

    if(!explorer.CreateDispatch("FrontPage.Explorer.2.0",&error))
    {
        AfxMessageBox("Error connecting to FrontPage Explorer.");
        return;
    }
    explorer.vtiRefreshWebFromServer();
    explorer.ReleaseDispatch();
}
```

If you do have an application that can benefit from the capabilities that FrontPage has to offer or you want to customize FrontPage to fit some very specific Web publishing application, all of the power you need is right here.

From Here...

Now that you've examined the essentials of the FrontPage SDK, you'll likely want to go on to more detail about using the package. Alternatively, you might prefer to explore the relationship between FrontPage 98 and Office 97. The following chapters will take you in either direction.

- Chapter 32, "Creating Templates," which teaches you how to use the SDK to set up and save Web templates for your particular needs.
- Chapter 33, "Creating Wizards," which explores the basics of wizards according to the SDK, and gives you a start on creating them in Visual Basic or C++.
- Chapter 34, "FrontPage 98 and Office 97," which shows you how to integrate Office 97 applications and documents into Webs produced with FrontPage 98.

Part
VI

Ch
31

## CHAPTER 32

Creating Templates

In the previous chapter, several powerful ways were discussed to extend and customize FrontPage ranging in scope from adding a new menu command that didn't previously exist, to extending the HTML that FrontPage displays, and even to full-fledged programming of FrontPage through OLE automation. Most of these things have their applications, but the place where most of us will customize FrontPage the most is custom templates. When you create a Web or a page in FrontPage, you likely use templates to get a headstart on your work. After all, often the general layout of all the pages on a site is identical—it is just the content of the pages that changes. ▨

What templates are

Page templates, Web templates. What are they and what can they do for you?

Page templates

Creating your own page templates is easy, you'll learn how.

Web template creation by using Web template maker

FrontPage can help you create your own Web templates with this utility.

Manual Web template creation

The Do-It-Yourselfer's guide to creating a Web template.

Frameset templates

Frameset templates let you quickly create great frame layouts by using the Frameset wizard.

What Are Templates?

At press time, Microsoft had not yet published the SDK, so some things may have changed since FrontPage 97, although Microsoft said that the things that work with 97 will work with 98.

A template is a special directory on a user's local disk that contains prototype Web content (Web pages, text files, images, and so on). This prototype content can be used to start a new Web or page and then edited and managed using FrontPage. There are three kinds of templates in FrontPage:

- **Page** Single page templates stored in C:\PROGRAM FILES\MICROSOFT FRONTPAGE\PAGES.
- **Web** Templates consisting of several interconnected pages stored in C:\PROGRAM FILES\MICROSOFT FRONTPAGE\PAGES.
- **Framesets** A special kind of template that is used only by the Frameset wizard.

The simplest type of template is a Page template. Page templates can be easily created by end-users while in the FrontPage Editor by choosing Save As from the File menu, and then clicking the As Template button. Fill in the information, press OK, and a complete page template automatically creates. Since these templates are so easy to create, it is likely that you will want to create them frequently for the page styles that you use regularly.

To remove a template once you have created it, you simply need to delete the file you created. In the Windows Explorer, go to C:\PROGRAM FILES\MICROSOFT FRONTPAGE\PAGES and find the directory by the name of your template with the extension TEM. Delete that directory and your template is gone. If you want to modify an existing template, first start the FrontPage Editor and select File, Open and click the Other Location tab in the dialog box that appears. Select From File and click browse. Go to the C:\PROGRAM FILES\MICROSOFT FRONTPAGE\PAGES directory and find the TEM directory that contains the template you want to modify. In that directory, you should find an HTML file for the template you want to modify. Open it, make the changes you want to make, and save it. Any documents you create with that template will contain the modifications you made.

If you want to create an entire site in a basic style, what you really need is a Web template, complete with linked documents and images. There are two ways to create these and they both are covered in the next section.

Creating Web Templates

While the ability to save a Page as a template is a useful feature of FrontPage, if you want to create an entire Web in the style of your choice, you will need to create a Web template. FrontPage contains a Visual Basic program called Web Template Maker that automates the process of creating a Web template.

N O T E This program requires that you have the Visual Basic 4.0 runtime DLL in your WINDOWS\SYSTEM directory. This file is called VB40032.DLL and if you do not have it installed, you can get it from the Microsoft Web site, **http://www.microsoft.com/**. ▪

To use the Web Template Maker (assuming you have the support DLL installed), follow these steps:

1. Launch the Web Template Maker (WEBTMPL.EXE in the FRONTPG\FPSKD30\ UTILITY\WEBTMPL folder on the CD-ROM). You see the dialog box shown in Figure 32.1.

2. Select from the Available Webs list.

3. Enter the New Web Template information.

4. Click the Make Web Template button.

FIG. 32.1

The Web Template Maker utility.

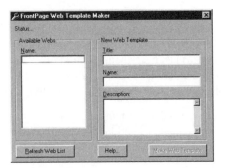

Everything that the Web template maker does can be done by hand. It creates a copy of an existing site to use as a building block for a new site. If you cannot get the Web Template Utility to work for you, you must create the template by hand. This isn't as hard as you might think. Let's go through the process:

1. Create a Web to make your template from, by using the FrontPage Explorer on your local Web server, or copy a Web from a remote server to a local Web server.

2. Use the Windows Explorer to locate the folder containing the Web's content. By default, this is a folder under C:\FRONTPAGE WEBS\CONTENT. For example, if your Web is called Test, then the Web content is located in C:\FRONTPAGEWEBS\CONTENT\TEST.

3. Use the Windows Explorer to create a folder by the name you wish to refer to your new template by, for example MYTEMPLATE.TEM under the Webs folder of where the FrontPage client is installed. By default this would be the C:\PROGRAM FILES\MICROSOFT FRONTPAGE\WEBS folder.

4. Copy the Web's IMAGES folder into SAMPLE.TEM. For example, if the Web is called Test, copy C:\FRONTPAGE WEBS\CONTENT\TEST\IMAGES into your new directory,

MYTEMPLATE.TEM. If you are using the Windows Explorer, be sure to hold down the CTRL key when doing the copy, or else the folder will be moved, not copied.

5. Copy the Web's pages in the main Web directory (C:\FRONTPAGE WEBS\CONTENT\ TEST) into MYTEMPLATE.TEM. Do not copy access control files, such as #HACCESS.CTL. Don't forget that MYTEMPLATE.TEM is a folder, not a file.

6. Use NotePad to create a file called MYTEMPLATE.INF, in the MYTEMPLATE.TEM folder. This is the template information file.

7. Create an [info] section in MYTEMPLATE.INF with appropriate title and description keys. For example, type the title "Sample Web" and the description "Create a sample Web from a template." Add any tasks or Web meta info variables in their appropriate sections. See later in this chapter for more about the INF file.

8. Repeat the steps previously mentioned if you have any content in Web subfolders (such as _PRIVATE), and copy the pages to the same subfolder (_PRIVATE) in the Web template.

9. Create a CGI-BIN folder inside your template folder if you have any scripts or programs in your Web's CGI-BIN folder, and copy the programs into it (CGI-BIN).

10. Create a [FileList] section, as just described, in the MYTEMPLATE.INF file, if your Web includes any content in subfolders (IMAGES, CGI-BIN, or _PRIVATE), in order to make sure those files get uploaded properly by the FrontPage Explorer.

That's all there is to it. You have created a new template. Now, what about this INF file and the different sections? Well, an INF file looks something like this:

```
[info]
title=Customer Support Web
description=Create a web to improve your customer support services, particularly
for software companies.
[FileList]
bugrep.htm=
cusuaftr.htm=
cusuahdr.htm=
images\scrnshot.gif=images/scrnshot.gif
images\undercon.gif=images/undercon.gif
index.htm=
search.htm=
suggest.htm=
tn-001.htm=
[MetaInfo]
CompanyName=Microsoft
CompanyAddress=One Microsoft Way, Redmond Washington
```

N O T E It is important to have a meaningful title and description for a page or Web template, since a list of wizards and templates could be quite large. As you can see, this information is kept in an INF file inside the template directory in the [info] section. The base name of this file must match the base name of the template directory. For example, you would create SAMPLE.INF inside the SAMPLE.TEM directory. ■

The INF file is in the same format as a Windows INI file. The INF file can have several named sections, each surrounded by angle brackets like this: [Section Name]. Underneath each section are name-value pairs, one on each line. An attribute name (also called a *key*) and its value are separated by an equal sign (=).

The Info Section

FrontPage reads the [info] section of the INF file when it presents a list of wizards and templates to a user. If the INF file is not found, or if the [info] section does not exist, FrontPage displays the base name of the template directory (such as sample), otherwise the dialog boxes display the values of the title and description keys found in the [info] section.

Web templates can also specify three optional sections that are used by the FrontPage Explorer when loading Web templates: [FileList], [MetaInfo], and [TaskList].

The FileList Section

The [FileList] section allows explicit mappings between the file names inside the template directory and the Web-relative URLs where they will be uploaded. It also allows you to upload files from subdirectories of the Web template. Each line has the form filename=URL. This gives you control over which files in your template go where when a Web is created, and even if certain files should be copied at all.

When you do not provide a [FileList] section, the FrontPage Explorer scans the template directory and uploads all available files except those in subdirectories. All file names are converted to lowercase, and the URLs are set to be the same as the file names. Also, all file names with the image extensions GIF, JPG, and JPEG are uploaded to the IMAGES directory in the Web.

When you provide a [FileList], however, only the files mentioned in the section are uploaded. FrontPage will not change the case on these URLs either. Your files will contain the exact upper-lower case you specified.

If you look at the previous sample, you will notice that many of the files are referred to only by their file name and an equals sign with no further data. When you do this, you simply tell FrontPage to use that file as part of your template, retaining its current name.

You may refer to files in template subdirectories when creating a [FileList] section, however, only valid Web URL subdirectories can be used. The valid Web subdirectories are IMAGES, _PRIVATE, and CGI-BIN. You must use forward slashes when specifying these directories in URLs. These Web directories, and a few others, are created by the FrontPage Server Extensions when you make a new Web using the FrontPage Explorer.

The MetaInfo Section

This section is for meta-info variables. You are probably shaking your head and wondering, what are they? *Meta-info variables* are a set of name-value pairs stored inside each Web. They allow you to use labels to refer to certain values that might be subject to change, or need to be inserted commonly throughout every site created with your new template. For instance, let's say your template includes company name info throughout the site. If you created a template that just contained this information in every place you wanted to use it, changing it would be difficult. You would have to change the value in every file in which it occurred. However, if you use a meta-info variable section such as

```
[MetaInfo]
    CompanyName=Microsoft
    CompanyAddress=One Microsoft Way, Redmond Washington
```

you could then use the meta-info value in order to insert the actual value of the variable. These variables can be used to store configuration information about the Web, or when used in conjunction with the Substitution Component, to replace instances of certain strings in all your Web pages. You may define a number of these variables in the optional [MetaInfo] section. Keys are case insensitive. Names beginning with vti_ are reserved for Web administration.

The TaskList Section

You can upload some tasks for the FrontPage To Do List using items in the optional [TaskList] section. A task consists of six attributes:

- **TaskName**   A short phrase, typically three or four words, telling the user what to do.
- **Priority (1 to 3)**   An integer, where 1=High, 2=Medium, and 3=Low.
- **CreatedBy**   The name of the template creating the task.
- **URL**   The page or image the task refers to, such as NEWS.HTM or LOGO.GIF.
- **Cookie**   An additional identifier for a point within the target URL; currently limited to HTML bookmarks, specified as #bookmark. Basically, this allows you to pinpoint an area that needs work even more specifically than just naming the HTML file. You can point to a specific section within the file.
- **Comment**   A short sentence describing in detail what needs to be done; cannot contain any new-line characters.

These attributes are encoded in each line of the [TaskInfo] section as follows:

TaskNum=TaskName|Priority|CreatedBy|URL|Cookie|Comment

TaskNum is a unique key, such as t01, t02, and the Task attributes are separated by vertical bar characters ([|]).

This is useful if you have things that you want to make sure are consistently done to every new Web created in the style of this template.

Frameset Templates

You might think that since framesets are actually just another type of HTML document, that you would be able to create an HTML frames page and use it as a template and be done with it. That is not the case, however. FrontPage has a Frames wizard that is used for creating and editing HTML frameset pages and you will need to create a FRM file containing the information that the Frames Wizard needs. It is similar to the INF file you would use to strore information about a Web Template only with different sections and keys. The creation of framesets is covered in the next section.

What Is a Frameset?

A frameset page divides up a page into independent scrollable regions that can each contain a separate Web page. Authors can cause documents to be loaded into individual frames regions by using a special TARGET attribute that can be attached to most kinds of links. Whenever you find yourself at a Web page with separate regions of the page that can change independently of each other, you are looking at frames.

A *Frameset* is the HTML code that defines how a frames page should look. Some HTML code for a frameset page that created a 65 pixel top frame, a 65 pixel bottom frame, and gave the rest of the room to the middle frame would look like this:

```
<HTML>
<FRAMESET ROWS="65, *, 65">
     <FRAME SRC="doc1.html">
     <FRAME SRC="doc2.html">
     <FRAME SRC="doc3.html">
</FRAMESET>
</HTML>
```

As you can see, framesets are just HTML. Why, can't you just create an HTML frameset and make it into a template? This is where the Frames Wizard comes in.

The Frames Wizard

The Frames Wizard automates the creation of a Frameset and the pages that fill the frames. It offers an option to create an entire frameset, including its component pages, from one of several templates. These templates are stored in the Frames Wizard directory, which is underneath the FrontPage PAGES directory. (C:\PROGRAM FILES\MICROSOFT FRONTPAGE\PAGES\FRAMEWIZ.WIZ BY DEFAULT.)

Frameset templates are stored differently from the Web and page template structure just described. Each frameset template is kept in its own file, with the extension FRM. The FRM files are kept in INI format so they are easily read by the Frames Wizard. Each FRM file has the following structure:

```
[info]
title=name of frameset as it will appear in the wizard
description=long description of the purpose of the wizard
noframesURL=ignored; alternate page is assigned by wizard
layout=specification of frameset geometry using compact notation

[frame name 1...N]
title=name of frame as it will appear in the page title
description=long description of what the frame should contain
URL=ignored; page URL for frame is assigned dynamically by wizard
```

Part
VI

Ch
32

```
marginWidth=width of margin; default is 1
marginHeight=height of margin; default is 1
scrolling=how scrollbars are displayed; default is 'auto'
noresize=turns off scrolling; default is 'False'
target=name of default target frame for this page
```

The first section, [info], describes the main frameset page. Subsequent sections each describe a component frame page. The section names must match the frame names, which are derived from the frameset layout specification in the [info] section. The frameset layout specification is where the frameset geometry is defined. The notation used to define a frameset takes a little getting used to. For example, look at the following sample frameset layout specification:

layout=[R(15%,85%)F("banner",[C(35%,65%)F("contents","main")])]

This layout is describing a frame that looks like Figure 32.2.

FIG. 32.2

The sample frameset.

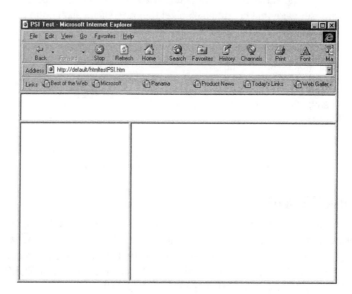

In standard HTML format, the frameset would be defined:

```
<HTML>
<FRAMESET ROWS="15%, 85%">
    <FRAME NAME="banner">
    <FRAMESET COLS="35%,65%"
        <FRAME NAME="contents">
        <FRAME NAME="main">
    </FRAMESET>
</FRAMESET>
</HTML>
```

The condensed notation works like this. Each frameset, including the topmost frameset, is surrounded by square brackets [like these]. Inside the frameset is a row and/or column specification followed by a list of frames. A row specification is an "R" followed by a comma-separated list of row sizes in parentheses (like these), where each entry is expressed as a percentage of the total available height (unlike HTML frameset definitions, you cannot specify exact pixel measurements). The column specification is the same format as the row specification, but with an initial "C." The frame list is an "F" followed by a comma-separated list, where each item is either a frame name (inside double quotes) or a full frameset specification (inside square brackets).

This sample layout string can be decoded as follows. The frameset consists of two rows, a short one at 15% of the window height and a long one at 85% of the height. A frame called "banner" is assigned to the short row. The long row contains another frameset, this one divided into two columns of 1/3 and 2/3 of the window width. This interior frameset is composed of two frames, the first called "contents" (which is assigned to the leftmost third) and the second called "main" (which is assigned to the rightmost two-thirds).

The Frames Wizard reads the frameset information for any files in its directory with the extension FRM. It uses the layout string to display a preview graphic with the frame names alongside the frameset's title and description strings. When a frameset template is chosen, the wizard reads the information for each named frame by looking up a section with the same name in the FRM file. For this reason, the section names must match the frame names.

Finally, the wizard generates the frameset page and its component pages and loads them into the current Web or the FrontPage Editor, as appropriate. The wizard will place a FrontPage Component Annotation on each page describing its purpose, the frameset it belongs to, what the default target is (if any), and how the page can be edited.

Part
VI

Ch
32

From Here...

At this point you may want to continue with the next chapter to complete your exploration of the SDK, or you may prefer to skip ahead to work with Office 97 and Office 95 applications in the context of FrontPage 98. These chapters give you your choice:

■ Chapter 33, "Creating Wizards," which explores the basics of wizards, and gives you a start on creating them in Visual Basic or Visual C++.

■ Chapter 34, "FrontPage 98 and Office 97," which shows you how to integrate Office 97 applications and documents into Webs produced with FrontPage 98.

■ Chapter 35, "Using the Internet Assistant for PowerPoint 95," which shows you how (or whether) to prepare PowerPoint 95 slideshow presentations that you can integrate into a FrontPage Web.

Creating Wizards

▬ If you have worked with FrontPage for any amount of time, it is likely that you have used a wizard or two to create either a page or a Web or both. Wizards are actually external programs that take you step by step through a process, whether that is creating a new Web, page, or frameset. You can write your own wizards in any programming language you want, as long as they behave the way FrontPage expects them to. This chapter discusses how wizards work and shows you a wizard written in Visual Basic (VB) to illustrate how wizards need to work. You don't need to write your wizards in VB, any Windows development platform will do; but, because of its common usage, VB is used in this chapter. ▬

Wizards: What They Are and How They Work

At press time for this book, Microsoft had not released the SDK for FrontPage 98. Therefore, the information in this chapter actually applies to FrontPage 97. Microsoft claims that things that worked with the 97 SDK will also work with the 98 SDK, so this shouldn't be a big issue.

First, let's cover what wizards are and how they work. In Chapter 31, "Extending and Customizing FrontPage with the SDK," we discussed using FrontPage's OLE automation interfaces. The Explorer, Editor, and To Do List in FrontPage are all programmable via OLE, and by using a third-party development tool, can be automated in just about any way you would like. This is what a *wizard* is, an independent executable program that usually collects input from a user in a series of dialog boxes and places OLE automation calls to drive FrontPage by remote control to create the new Webs or Web pages.

To get a little better feel for how wizards actually work, let's step through the process of what happens in FrontPage when you use a wizard. Say you decide to start the Corporate Presence Wizard from the FrontPage Explorer. What happens behind the scenes? FrontPage starts up the executable file VTIPRES.EXE located in the directory [FRONTPAGE ROOT]\WEBS\ VTIPRES.WIZ. Just like a template, a wizard is contained in a special directory on a user's local disk. A wizard directory must be called *.WIZ, and in order to be recognized by FrontPage, this directory must be placed in either the FrontPage Webs or pages directory, depending on what kind of content it holds.

Once the program begins, a series of dialog boxes are presented, prompting the user for all sorts of information about his or her company as well as prompting for information like background and text colors and style of Web design. Most wizards look something like the one shown in Figure 33.1.

FIG. 33.1

The Corporate
Presence Wizard.

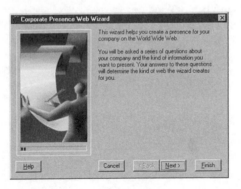

As you can see, the wizard has navigation buttons along the bottom to step through the process: Next, Back, Finish, Cancel, and Help. There is nothing in the world that says that your wizards have to look like the wizards that come with FrontPage, but consistency usually is a good thing for end-users. After having collected all of the information it needs, the wizard uses OLE Automation to make FrontPage create the file or files it needs and then closes, leaving you with FrontPage and your new site or page.

N O T E There really is no enforced difference between a Web wizard and a page wizard other than where they are stored on the disk and from which part of FrontPage they launch. You can write a program that does just about anything, even connecting to a corporate database or getting information from the Internet. It is up to you to logically label your wizards as Web or page wizards, and to make sure that the user interface is easy for your end-users to use. There are some sample VB and VC++ projects in the SDK that can help get you going in the right direction. ■

So now that you know that wizards are nothing more than external programs that launch from and interact with FrontPage, you can take a deeper look at what your program should do to be a wizard.

Writing Wizards

As we mentioned before, wizards need to live in one of two directories. Either the C:\PROGRAM FILES\MICROSOFT FRONTPAGE\WEBS directory or the C:\PROGRAM FILES\MICROSOFT FRONTPAGE\PAGES directory. When you install your wizard on an end-users machine, one of the first things you will have to do is put your EXE in the right place. You can find out where by checking the settings in the FRONTPG.INI file installed in a user's Windows directory, which will look something like this:

```
[Ports]
Port 80=
[FrontPage 2.0]
FrontPageRoot=C:\Program Files\Microsoft FrontPage
PWSRoot=C:\FrontPage Webs
FrontPageLangID=0x0409
FrontPageLexicon=C:\Microsoft FrontPage\bin\mssp2_en.lex
FrontPageSpellEngine=C:\Microsoft FrontPage\bin\mssp232.dll
CheckedHostName=arbus
[Port 80]
servertype=frontpage
serverconfig=C:\FrontPage Webs\Server\conf\httpd.cnf
authoring=enabled
frontpageroot=C:\Program Files\Microsoft FrontPage
```

N O T E In version 1.0, the INI file was called VERMEER.INI. The section was called "FrontPage", and it contained keys for FrontPageRoot, FrontPageBin, WebWizardsDir, and PageWizardsDir. As of version 1.1, the only required key is `FrontPageRoot`. If you set one of these keys, the change will take effect the next time the FrontPage Explorer or FrontPage Editor are run. ■

Once you have determined where FrontPage is, you will also need to create a WIZ subdirectory for your wizard where the base name of the wizard executable program matches the base name of the wizard directory, for example, SAMPLE.WIZ\SAMPLE.EXE. If you want your wizard to be listed as a Web wizard, put it in the Webs subdirectory and list it in the Pages subdirectory if you wish it to appear as a page wizard. Then create a subdirectory of the same name as your EXE file, but with a WIZ extension. Here's an example.

Let's say you have two wizards you have written and want to install, MYWEBWIZARD.EXE and MYPAGEWIZARD.EXE. You would place the first in C:\PROGRAM FILES\MICROSOFT FRONTPAGE\WEBS\MYWEBWIZARD.WIZ and the second in C:\PROGRAM FILES\MICROSOFT FRONTPAGE\PAGES\MYPAGEWIZARD.WIZ.

So you've installed the program in the right place. Is it now a wizard? Not quite. Your wizard needs to tell FrontPage about itself and you will use an INF file to accomplish that task. The INF file is in the exact format as a Windows INI file and contains an [info] section that contains title and description keys. Place this file in the same directory as your wizard and give it the same name as the EXE file. It can also contain a key called `exename` giving the name of the wizard program, if it does not match the name of the wizard directory as just described. If a page wizard can function as an editor in addition to a generator, the INF file should contain the line `editor=1`.

This is the INF file for the Corporate Presence wizard mentioned previously:

```
[info]
title=Corporate Presence Wizard
description=Create a professional Internet presence for your organization.
```

Web and page wizards have no inherent restrictions imposed on them. A page wizard could create a Web and vice-versa. However, when looking at your wizard, you will want to categorize it as one or the other. How? Well, generally, a page wizard creates a single page, while a Web wizard creates several interconnected pages. These criteria can help you decide what type of wizard you either have or need. Another thing to keep in mind is the fact that page wizards are always run from the FrontPage Editor, while Web wizards are always run from the FrontPage Explorer. Where you install your wizard can depend as much on where you want users to start it from as what it does.

A Wizard Is Born: How FrontPage Launches Your Wizard

Now you know where to put your program and what it should do in general. Now you'll learn a little more about what FrontPage does when it starts a wizard. All wizards are launched with a single argument: the path to a temporary file in INI format containing name-value pairs. If a wizard is run without any arguments, because the user started it from the Windows File Manager or Windows Explorer, it should behave as similar wizards do. It is up to you as the programmer to determine how your wizard will run if started like this, but typically a page wizard should load a page into the FrontPage Editor, and a Web wizard should load pages into the current Web.

The format of the parameter file is as follows:

```
[Input]
arg1=value1
arg2=value2
[Environment]
var1=value1
var2=value2
[Output]
```

The Input section contains all required and optional wizard parameters. The Environment section contains a snapshot of the parent's environment variables. The Output section is initially empty—this is where the wizard can write variables that get sent back to the calling process under certain circumstances.

All wizards receive the following built-in arguments when they are run:

```
Dir=absolute path to wizard directory
Inf=absolute path to wizard's INF file
Blocking=0 or 1 (1 if caller is blocked)
Editing=0 or 1 (1 if wizard is being invoked as an editor)
```

As was mentioned before, a page wizard's INF file should contain the key/value editor=1 if it can be launched as an editor; otherwise the Editing key will always be set to 0. The Blocking variable has to do with whether or not the wizard will be returning some values to FrontPage in the [Output] section. If that is the case, Blocking will be set to 1 and the launching program will take care of deleting the parameter file when the wizard exits. If your program will not be sending any output back to FrontPage, your program should also delete the temporary parameter file.

A few additional parameters have special meaning to a page wizard:

```
Destination=editor ¦ web ¦ disk
PageURL=web-relative URL where page should be saved
PageTitle=title for new web page
PageFile=path to file being edited (only set if Editing=1)
```

Each page wizard has a notion of its default destination. This is usually the FrontPage Editor; but if a wizard generates content that cannot be edited by the FrontPage Editor, the wizard should load it to the current Web instead. If you use Destination=editor, the generated file should be loaded directly into the FrontPage Editor via OLE automation. If you use Destination=web, the generated file should be loaded directly to the current Web via OLE automation. If you use Destination=disk, the wizard should generate its output into temp files and return a list of filename/URL pairs via the Output section.

PageURL is the Web-relative path to the page being created (such as INDEX.HTM). PageTitle is the title of the page being created (such as "My Home Page"). PageFile is an absolute path to the file being edited, which has typically just been downloaded by the Explorer.

N O T E For backward compatibilty, the following arguments are still passed to wizards by the FrontPage Explorer when it runs a Web wizard: WebName, ServerName, Proxy, User. ▨

If Blocking=1, then page wizards should return some values via the parameter file's Output section. Those key values that you need to return are:

- ▨ ExitStatus   This key should be set to either error, cancel, or ok. If ExitStatus is not present, the launching program will assume that an error occurred in the wizard.

- ▨ FileCount   If Destination=disk, the wizard should write a FileCount key and a list of keys from File1 to FileN and Url1 to UrlN. The values of these keys should be set to the absolute paths and target URLs of each file generated by the wizard.

Part

VI

Ch

33

For example, a wizard that generated two files might create an Output section like this:

```
[Output]
ExitStatus=ok
FileCount=2
File1=c:\temp\wiz01.tmp
Url1=index.htm
File2=c:\temp\wiz02.tmp
Url2 = test.htm
```

It is assumed that File1 will be the main HTML file created by a page wizard.

The FrontPage SDK includes Visual Basic code to do some of these common tasks for you. They have included WIZUTIL.BAS, HTMLGEN.BAS, and BOTGEN.BAS in the FRONTPG\ FPSDK20\WIZARDS\VB directory on the CD-ROM. These three files contain many generic utility functions for creating wizards, including generating HTML. There are functions to read the information the FrontPage passes your wizards ready-made for you. For example, the following is a Form_Load event that executes at the startup of a wizard that simply gets all of the parameter info that the wizard requires:

```
Private Sub Form_Load()

    GetFrontPageInfo
    GetWizardInfo

    Exit Sub

End Sub
```

Of course, you will probably have more happening than this in your start-up event for your wizard, but it illustrates how easy it is for you to get all of these parameters into your program.

Designing Your Wizard

A wizard should look like a dialog box but should have the following buttons to step through the dialog pages: Back, Next/Finish, and Cancel. Most wizards should be self-explanatory, but some may require a Help button. These buttons should always be visible and accessible at the bottom of the wizard's dialog box. If necessary, an image or graphical output area appears to the left of the dialog pages but above the main navigation buttons. The FrontPage SDK contains some sample wizards written in Visual Basic that you can use for templates to get you going. One of them, the Real Estate Wizard, is shown in Figure 33.2.

As you can see in Figure 33.2, the wizard has been created using one main Visual Basic form that contains panels for each step in the wizard process and one set of wizard controls of the same style as the ones that come with FrontPage. In the VB code, the panels are simply moved into place as each step in the process is created. This is a good model for creating your wizard in VB.

Much of the behavior that your wizard needs to exhibit has been discussed, but there are a few more things you need to know. If you wish to store any settings for your wizard in a permanent state, you will need to use your wizard's INI file, which is stored in the Data subdirectory of the

FrontPage installation directory. The name of each INI file should be the same as the base name of the wizard executable program but with an INI extension. The INI file is separated from the program so that the wizard directory can be mounted on a read-only disk drive, such as in a local area network or with a CD-ROM. This is also why all wizards place their generated files into the FrontPage Temp directory.

FIG. 33.2
The Real Estate Wizard in the VB development environment.

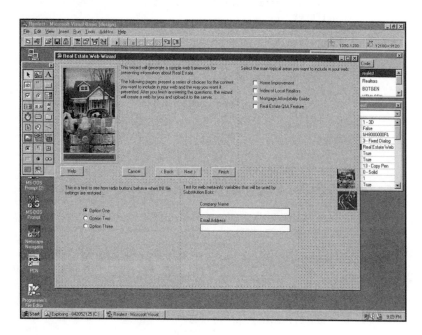

Putting It All Together: A Sample Wizard

Now that you know everything a wizard needs to do, take a look at one that does it. The FrontPage SDK contains a sample wizard for creation of a Real Estate Web site. Figure 33.2 shows the main form in the development environment, but take a look at the underlying code.

When the wizard loads up, it gets the information that it needs from FrontPage and then arranges all of the panels on the form so that they will appear in sequence. The following is the Form_Load code that accomplishes this:

```
Private Sub Form_Load()

    Dim titleH As Integer
    Dim i As Integer
    Dim msg As String
    Dim obj As String

    GetFrontPageInfo
    GetWizardInfo
```

```
                    ' IMPORTANT: have to set the highest page number index manually
                    PageMax = 3

                    ' fetch any previous settings from INI file
                    LoadSettings

                    ' set any initial values on pages
                    InitPages

                    ' shrink-wrap form around controls
                    ' (allows form to be much larger in design mode);
                    ' this part will vary depending on your control
                    ' names and layout
                    titleH = Me.Height - Me.ScaleHeight   ' with and without border
                    Me.Width = pg(0).Left + pg(0).Width + pnlLeft.Left
                    Me.Height = titleH + btnHelp.Top + btnHelp.Height + pnlLeft.Left

                    ' since a wizard is supposed to work like a dialog,
                    ' make it centered like a dialog
                    CenterFormOnScreen Me

                    ' initialize page meter control
                    meter.value = 0
                    meter.Min = 0
                    meter.Max = PageMax

                    ' set all pages to be same size and location
                    ' (allows them to be spread all over large form in design mode)
                    For i = 0 To PageMax
                        pg(i).Left = pg(0).Left
                        pg(i).Top = pg(0).Top
                        pg(i).Width = pg(0).Width
                        pg(i).Height = pg(0).Height
                    Next i

                    ' set initial conditions and show first page
                    PageNum = -1
                    GoToPage 0

                    Exit Sub

            End Sub
```

After this code executes, the wizard displays the first page in a series. The overall operation of the wizard is actually pretty simple. When you click the Next or Back button, the code makes a call to a function called `GoToPage`, which validates the contents of the current page, hides it, and displays either the next or previous page. It also determines which buttons should be enabled and if the Next button should actually read Finish because of the completion of the wizard. Here is what that looks like:

```
Private Sub GoToPage(num As Integer)

    If num >= 0 And num <= PageMax Then
        ' validate and then take down previous page (if any)
```

```
      If PageNum >= 0 And PageNum <= PageMax Then
          ' check for valid input on the current page
          If Not ValidatePage(PageNum) Then Exit Sub
          pg(PageNum).Visible = False
      End If
      PageNum = num
      ChangePicture PageNum
      pg(PageNum).Visible = True
      If PageNum = 0 Then
          btnBack.Enabled = False
      Else
          btnBack.Enabled = True
      End If
      If PageNum = PageMax Then
          btnNext.Enabled = False
      Else
          btnNext.Enabled = True
      End If
      meter.value = PageNum
      SetFinishState ' see if Finish button can be enabled
  End If

End Sub
```

The ValidatePage function checks to make sure that all of the controls have been filled out properly and that will vary from page to page. This is the basic technique for gathering information throughout the whole wizard. The last thing the wizard needs to do is create the Web (or page) and tell FrontPage what it's been up to. For this wizard, that is done when the Finish button is clicked in the GenerateWeb procedure shown here:

```
Private Sub GenerateWeb()

    ' replace this routine with your own version;
    ' it should generate the HTML pages one-by-one
    ' in the system-dependent temp directory
    ' and upload the files to the web server

    Dim i As Integer
    Dim tempfile As String
    Dim curfile As String
    Dim retval As Long
    Dim wizname As String
    Dim wizversion As String
    Dim tmp As String
    Dim done As Integer
    Dim FileList As String
    Dim URLList As String
    Dim webURL As String

    ' put up the hourglass
    Screen.MousePointer = 11

    Set webber = CreateObject(FrontPageExplorerID)
```

Part

VI

Ch

33

```
webURL = webber.vtiGetWebURL
If Len(webURL) = 0 Then
    MsgBox "The FrontPage Explorer does not have a web open.", vbExclamation
    Set webber = Nothing
    Exit Sub
End If

Set todo = CreateObject(FrontPageToDoListID)

' set tool name for document upload
wizname = "Real Estate Web Wizard"
wizversion = "0.1"

InitFiles     ' establish a clean slate for upload list
InitMetaVars  ' establish a clean slate for meta-info variables

' ----------
' construct list of required meta-info vars
' ----------
AddMetaVar "CompanyName", CStr(txtCompanyName.text)
AddMetaVar "EmailAddress", CStr(txtEmailAddress.text)

' ----------
' construct list of files to be uploaded
' ----------
' (AddFile takes name of file as first arg,
'  and whether or not file is generated dynamically
'  as second arg)

' first add any pre-existing files (such as images)
AddFile "masthead.gif", False, "masthead image"
' then add any INCLUDED files (for IncludeBots)
' *BEFORE* the files which will "include" them
AddFile "inc.htm", True, "page footer"
' finally any files that must be generated
AddFile "index.htm", True, "home page"  ' default home page is *REQUIRED*
If chkImprove.value Then AddFile "improve.htm", True, "home improvement
guide"
    If chkRealtors.value Then AddFile "realtors.htm", True, "index of Realtors"
    If chkMortgage.value Then AddFile "mortgage.htm", True, "mortgage guide"
    If chkQuestions.value Then AddFile "question.htm", True, "answers to common
questions"

done = nFiles - 1

' ----------
' upload any web meta-info variables
' ----------

tmp = PackMetaInfoVars()
If tmp <> "" Then
    retval = webber.vtiPutWebMetaInfo(tmp)
    If retval <> 1 Then
        ' failure
        Set webber = Nothing
```

```
          Set todo = Nothing
          MsgBox "Warning: " & Chr$(10) & "Wizard failed PutWebMetaInfo call."
          Exit Sub
       End If
End If

' ----------
' loop through list of files, generating files and creating upload lists
' ----------

FileList = ""
URLList = ""

For i = 0 To done

    If Files(i).IsNew Then

        ' create temp file where output will go
        Files(i).path = TempFileName()

        If Not GenerateFile(Files(i).Name, Files(i).path) Then
            MsgBox "Couldn't generate file: '" & Files(i).Name & "'."
            Files(i).path = ""   ' couldn't create file
        End If

    Else

        ' generate full path to file
        Files(i).path = App.path & "\" & Files(i).Name

    End If

    If Files(i).path <> "" Then
        ' TODO: images should go in /images web dir
        FileList = FileList & Files(i).path
        URLList = URLList & Files(i).Name
        ' item separator is newline char
        FileList = FileList & Chr$(10)
        URLList = URLList & Chr$(10)
    End If

Next i

' perform upload

retval = webber.vtiPutDocuments(FileList, URLList)

If retval = 0 Then          ' failed
    MsgBox "Unable to load documents into web."
End If

' ----------
' refresh Explorer's views
' ----------
```

Part

VI

Ch

33

```
    webber.vtiRefreshWebFromServer

    ' ..........
    ' add any items for To Do List
    ' ..........

    todo.vtiAddTask "Customize home page", 1, wizname, "index.htm", "", "Add
local content to reinforce unique identity."

    ' ..........
    ' remove any temp files
    ' ..........

    For i = 0 To done
        If Files(i).IsNew And Files(i).path <> "" Then
            Kill Files(i).path
        End If
    Next i

    ' ..........
    ' all done
    ' ..........

    Set webber = Nothing
    Set todo = Nothing

    ' take down the hourglass
    Screen.MousePointer = 0

    ' all done
    Unload Me

End Sub
```

Now look at what this procedure is doing. After declaring some variables, an OLE automation object is created for both the FrontPage Explorer and the To-Do List. The wizard then creates lists of files to be uploaded and meta-info variables to be added to the Web and goes through the lists adding meta-info variables and files to the Web using OLE automation methods. After finishing with this, the wizard refreshes the Web from the server and adds items to the To-Do list, removes its temp files, sets the OLE objects to "nothing," and quits.

As you can see, wizards are fairly simple programs and the behavior your wizard needs to exhibit is well illustrated by the samples included.

From Here...

Having completed your examination of the SDK, you can go on to learn about using FrontPage 98 Webs with Office 97 or Office 95 applications. These chapters give you the details of how this is done:

- Chapter 34, "FrontPage 98 and Office 97," which shows you how to integrate features of Office 97 applications and documents into Webs produced with FrontPage 98.

- Chapter 35, "Using the Internet Assistant for PowerPoint 95," which shows you how (or whether) to prepare PowerPoint 95 slideshow presentations that you can integrate into a FrontPage Web.

- Chapter 36, "Using the Internet Assistants for Excel 95 and Word 95," where you learn to use Word 95 as a rudimentary HTML editor, and to export Excel 95 spreadsheet data to HTML files.

Part

VI

Ch

33

Integrating Microsoft FrontPage 98 and Microsoft Office

## CHAPTER 34

FrontPage 98 and Office 97

Since the release of Office 95, Microsoft has gradually moved toward a tighter coupling of its Office applications with Web technology—HTTP, HTML documents, and so on. Internet Assistants, which are add-ins for Office 95 applications, have been available for some time. They enable the user to save, for example, an Excel table in HTML format, to include a mailto in a document, or to insert a hyperlink from a Word document to an HTML file.

Non-HTML documents that have been created with Office 95 applications can also be imported into FrontPage Webs. For example, you might create a hyperlink from a standard Web page to an Excel workbook that contains financial information, or to a Word document that contains boilerplate text and images. If the user has access to the document's native application or viewer, invoking the hyperlink causes the document's native application to start up and display the document. The user can then view or edit the document.

Word 97's Web tools

Word 97 has a new hyperlink capability that functions both inside and outside the context of a Web. You can also use hyperlinks as cross-references and save documents in the HTML format.

Excel 97's Web tools

Excel 97 has a hyperlink capability similar to Word's, as well as a hyperlink worksheet function. You can save worksheets in HTML format and design forms for user input.

PowerPoint 97's Web tools

Creating a Web-based slideshow is a snap with PowerPoint's Web Wizard and FrontPage Explorer's Import command.

Access 97's Web tools

The Web Publishing Wizard makes exporting Access 97 data to HTML format fast and easy.

Office 97 has taken these capabilities to a new level of sophistication, chiefly by integrating the Internet Assistant tools into the various Office 97 applications and extending their power. If you have Office 97, you no longer have to download the Internet Assistants (IAs) and then install them to their matching applications. In fact, the IAs will not install to Office 97 at all—they are for use only with Office 95 programs. However, to fully use Office 97's Web capabilities, you must install the Web Page Authoring component when you install Office 97. You'll have to use a Custom install to do this because the Web Page Authoring component is not part of the default installation.

This chapter describes the use of Office 97 Web capabilities and how you can integrate Office 97 documents with FrontPage. If you have not obtained Office 97, you can still provide much of the same functionality by using Office 95 applications in conjunction with their respective Internet Assistants. These topics are covered in Chapter 35, "Using the Internet Assistant for PowerPoint 95;" Chapter 36, "Using the Internet Assistants for Excel 95 and Word 95 ;" and Chapter 37, "Using the Internet Assistants for Schedule+ and Access." ▓

Using Word 97's Web Tools

If you're an experienced user of Microsoft Word 97, you might find it more convenient to construct Web pages by using that application than by means of an HTML editor. Word 97 does not give you the degree of control over the HTML formatting that you would get with FrontPage Editor, but it can give you a head start.

Furthermore, if you have Word documents that you would like to convert to HTML format, doing so from Word is likely the most efficient approach.

The Web features new in Word 97 are the Web toolbar, the insertion of hyperlinks, saving a Word document as an HTML file, the Web Page Wizard, and several tools specifically oriented to editing Web pages.

> **CAUTION**
>
> When Word 97 saves a file as an HTML file, it defaults to adding the four character extension HTML (not HTM, as you might expect) to the file name. FrontPage Editor, of course, defaults to providing the HTM extension. There is no apparent reason for this inconsistency, so to keep your file extensions uniform, you may want to manually add the HTM extension to Word 97 files saved as HTML.

N O T E   For the following procedures to work, you must have installed the Web Page Authoring component when you installed Office 97. If you didn't do so, rerun the Office 97 Setup program and install the component before proceeding. ▓

Using the Web Toolbar

The Web toolbar is available in Excel 97, Access 97, PowerPoint 97, and Access 97, but for convenience we'll discuss it in the context of Word.

To turn on the toolbar, if it is not visible, you choose View, Toolbars, and then click Web in the popup menu to toggle the toolbar on. The toolbar is actually a simple browser toolbar, with (from left to right) the following buttons:

- *Back*   Moves back one page.
- *Forward*   Moves forward one page.
- *Stop*   Stops the current network operation.
- *Refresh Current Page*   Reloads the page now displayed.
- *Start Page*   Opens the default start page of the system's default browser.
- *Search the Web*   Opens the default search page of the system's default browser.
- *Favorites*   Opens the system's Favorites folder.
- *Go*   Allows navigation, plus user selection of start and search pages.
- *Show Only Web Toolbar*   Removes all toolbars but the Web toolbar (see Figure 34.1).

FIG. 34.1
The Web toolbar in Office 97 applications offers the functions of a simple browser.

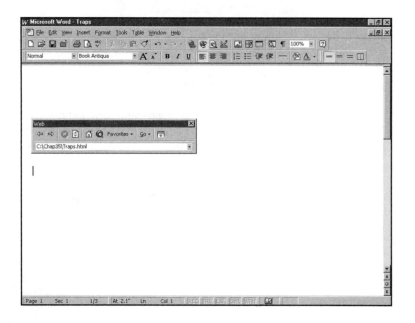

Inserting Hyperlinks

Suppose that you have written a Word document, TRAPS.DOC, that discusses some problems with Excel worksheet functions, and you've saved it on the Windows Desktop. You are at present writing a guide, GUIDE.DOC, to using Office 97 as deployed at your firm. You would like to insert a hyperlink in the GUIDE.DOC that points to TRAPS.DOC. To do so, take the following steps:

Part
VII

Ch
34

TIP Before inserting hyperlinks into Office documents, save both the document with the hyperlink and the destination document.

1. Open GUIDE.DOC in Word. Just as you've done in FrontPage, select the text or image that you want to use as the link. (If you don't select something, Word inserts the full file name of the destination document as the text of the hyperlink.) Choose Insert, Hyperlink and the Insert Hyperlink dialog box appears (see Figure 34.2).

FIG. 34.2

You choose the destination for the Word hyperlink by using the Insert Hyperlink dialog box.

2. Choose the Browse button in the upper-right corner of the dialog box. The Link to File dialog box appears (see Figure 34.3). Use this dialog box to locate and select the destination document of the hyperlink, which in the example is TRAPS.DOC. When you've selected the destination file, choose OK.

FIG. 34.3

It's usually easier to browse to a destination file than to type its path name or URL.

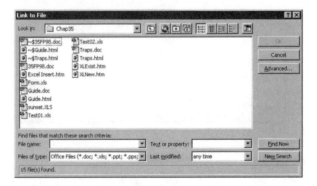

3. Choose OK when the Insert Hyperlink dialog box reappears. The dialog box closes, and if you selected some text for the link, you'll see that it's now in blue and underlined (see Figure 34.4). Images serving as hyperlinks aren't changed in appearance.

FIG. 34.4

You can use a hyperlink to any file, as long as the destination file has an accessible application associated with its extension.

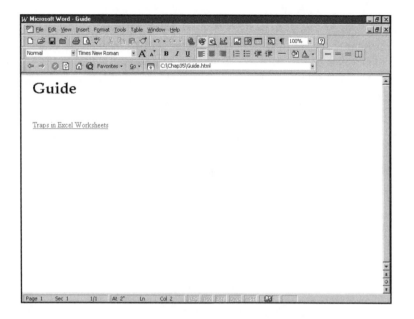

N O T E If you're familiar with Office applications, you know about OLE links. These links behave differently from a hyperlink, and you edit them by choosing Edit, Links. The Edit, Links command has nothing to do with hyperlinks, despite the confusing similarity of nomenclature. ■

You can now save both the hyperlinked document and the destination document as Word files or HTML files. To save them in Word format, just choose File, Save for each. To save them as HTML, choose File, Save As for each and choose HTML Document from the Save as Type drop-down list. Now, if you want, you can import the HTML files into a FrontPage Web.

In Word documents, (that is, documents in native Word format, not in HTML) hyperlinks are inserted as field codes. You can switch back and forth between viewing the hyperlink itself and viewing it as a field code. Right-click the hyperlink and choose Toggle Field Codes from the shortcut menu.

Part
VII

Ch
34

CAUTION

Saving a Word file as an HTML file doesn't change the destination file names of the hyperlinks. So, if you create and link the files as Word documents, and then save them as HTML files for importing to a Web, be sure you edit the hyperlinks in the newly created HTML files to make sure they point to the proper destinations. In other words, if a destination file started life as a DOC file, then was saved as an HTML file, the hyperlink pointing to it will have to be changed.

Linking to Destinations Within Documents

If the destination document is a long one, and the point of interest in it isn't close to the beginning, you'll probably want to link to a *named location* in the file. This corresponds to the *named anchor* tag of HTML. To insert such a link, do this:

1. Open the destination document in Word. Locate the position you want to jump to and select some text to be the named location.

2. Choose Insert, Bookmark. The Bookmark dialog box appears (see Figure 34.5).

FIG. 34.5
Use the Bookmark dialog box to insert named locations into documents.

3. Type a name for the book mark into the Bookmark Name text box and choose Add. The dialog box vanishes and the bookmark is assigned the name you specified.

4. Open the Word document that is to have the hyperlink in it. As you did earlier, select text or an image to be the link and choose Insert, Hyperlink. The Insert Hyperlink dialog box appears.

5. Use the upper-right Browse button in the dialog box to locate and select the destination file; that is, the one where you just placed the bookmark. Make sure the file name appears correctly in the Link to File or URL text box.

6. Choose the lower-right Browse button. This opens the Bookmark dialog box, which now shows all the bookmarks located in the destination document (see Figure 34.6).

7. Select the bookmark you want the hyperlink to jump to and choose OK to return to the Insert Hyperlink dialog box. Both text boxes in the dialog box now have entries (see Figure 34.7). Choose OK again to close the dialog box and install the link. When you use the link, the bookmarked location appears in the document window.

You can, of course, work with either Word 97 documents or HTML documents to do this. However, if you create and link the documents as Word 97 files, remember that when you save them as HTML files, you will need to edit the hyperlinks to point to the correct destinations. Actually, if you have a lot of links to set up, you might prefer to complete and save all the files as HTML documents before you begin creating the hyperlinks.

FIG. 34.6
The Bookmark dialog box shows all the bookmarks entered into a Word document.

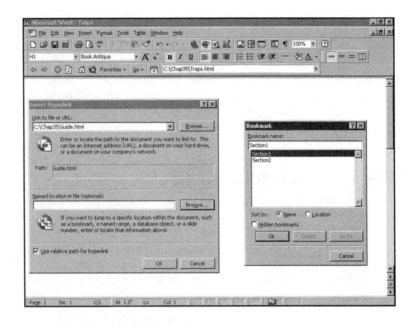

FIG. 34.7
Two text boxes need to be filled in for a named location hyperlink to work properly.

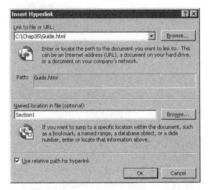

 TIP When you create an Office document that will be the destination of a hyperlink in your Web, do not save the destination document with an embedded blank in the file name—for example, NEW CHART.XLS. The resulting URL will not be evaluated properly, because it is interpreted as ending with the "w" in "New."

Part
VII

Ch
34

Using the Paste as Hyperlink Command with Word Documents

This is a very useful shortcut method, and is by far the best way to create links between documents in different applications.

In the destination document, select some item (usually text) that will be the target of the link. This selected text actually functions as a named location, but because Word creates its own special code for this named location, you don't need to fuss around with bookmarks.

When you've selected the text, choose Edit, Copy. Open the document where the link is to reside and place the insertion point where you want the link to appear. Choose Edit, Paste as Hyperlink. If you selected text as the named location in the destination page, this text will appear also as the hyperlink; you can edit it, if you need to. If you chose an image as the named location, the image itself is placed in the origination page to serve as the hyperlink.

Editing and Deleting Hyperlinks

To edit and delete hyperlinks, open the document with the hyperlink—it can be either a native Word 97 document, or an HTML document—and right-click the hyperlink. From the shortcut menu, choose Hyperlink, Edit Hyperlink. This opens the Edit Hyperlink dialog box. This dialog box, except for its title and the presence of a Remove Link button, is identical to the Insert Hyperlink dialog box you saw in Figure 34.2. Make the changes you want in the appropriate text boxes and choose OK. To remove the link entirely, choose Remove Link and the text or image loses its hyperlink properties.

If you want to change the wording of a textual link, right-click the link and choose Hyperlink, Select Hyperlink from the shortcut menu. With the link selected, type the new text to replace the old text. If you don't want to use the shortcut menu, just drag across the link text to select it and type the new text.

Modifying Link Colors

In Word, the appearance of the hyperlink is governed by your choice of hyperlink style. The default appearance for a hyperlink uses the standard blue underlined font, and a followed hyperlink uses the standard violet underlined font. If consistency of appearance is not an issue, you can change the defaults by taking these steps:

1. Open a document that you have saved in HTML format.
2. Choose Format, Style and select Hyperlink from the Styles list box.
3. Choose Modify, and in the Modify Style dialog box choose Format. Choose Font from the shortcut menu. In the Font dialog box, you can choose from different fonts, font styles and font sizes, underline types, colors, and effects.
4. Repeat Steps 2 and 3 for the Followed Hyperlink style.

After you have resaved the HTML document, your browser displays hyperlinks in the styles you selected.

Viewing HTML Source Code

If you want to directly edit the HTML of the page, you can do so by choosing View, HTML Source. This changes the view of the page from a near-WYSIWYG appearance to straight-forward HTML code. You can edit this code to get the effects you want on the page. When you've finished the edit, save the file and choose the Exit HTML Source button on the toolbar. The modified page appears in the Word workspace. Note that no syntax checking is done.

Using the Web Page Wizard

FrontPage 98, as you already know, comes with a selection of page templates. If none of these quite suits your needs, you might try using the Web Page Wizard to create a more suitable specimen. Here's how to do it:

1. Choose File, New to open the New dialog box; from the New dialog box, choose the Web Pages tab to open the Web Pages sheet.

2. Double-click the Web Page Wizard icon to open the Wizard opening dialog box (see Figure 34.8). Choose from several choices—the example uses Two-Column Layout—and choose Next. To assist you, the different templates appear behind the Wizard dialog box as you select among the choices.

FIG. 34.8
The Web Page Wizard assists you in creating a standard-layout Web page.

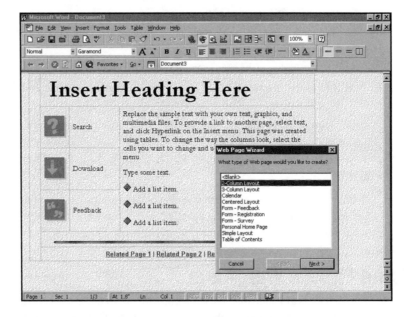

3. In the next dialog box of the Wizard, choose the overall appearance of the page from a list of eight possibilities. Click the "flavor" that seems best to serve your needs and then choose Finish.

4. Edit the page to add your own information, images, and to modify the layout, if necessary. Save the page (it defaults to saving as HTML unless you specify a different format). Now you can import it into your FrontPage Web.

Part
VII

Ch

34

Using Word 97's Other Web Tools

Word, even though it doesn't have the rich capabilities of FrontPage Editor, does have some further basic tools for Web page creation. If the page you're editing is an HTML file, you'll have some extra menu commands with which you can:

- ▪ *Add horizontal lines*   Choose Insert, Horizontal Line and choose from a selection of weights and appearances.
- ▪ *Add a page background color*   Choose Format, Background and select from a number of colors.
- ▪ *Add scrolling text (also known as a marquee)*   Choose Insert, Scrolling text and use the dialog box to create the text and set scroll direction and speed.
- ▪ *Add tables*   Choose Table, Insert Table and select the number of columns and rows from the popup.
- ▪ *Add a video*   Choose Insert, Video and use the dialog box to set the source file and properties of the video clip.
- ▪ *Add picture bullets*   Choose Format, Bullets and Numbering and choose any of several different bullet images.
- ▪ *Add an Image*   Choose Insert, Picture and choose from clip art, image files, or charts.
- ▪ *Add background sound*   Choose Insert, Background Sound and select the sound file and its properties.

Note, however, that whenever the inserted items are files—video clips, images, sounds, and so on—these items should also be imported into the FrontPage Web that hosts the page where they reside. If you import the page's HTML file only, the links to these various elements are broken.

Note also that graphical elements that don't start out as files, like bullets and lines, are saved as GIF files in the current Word documents folder when you insert the element into the page; you'll find them in that folder when you get around to importing them into the Web.

Using Excel's Web Tools

The Web tools available to you in Excel are similar to those available in Word. You can save an Excel worksheet in HTML table format, insert hyperlinks, and view the Web toolbar.

There are also some significant differences between Excel's Web capabilities and those in Word. For example, Excel offers a method to build a Web form and includes a new HYPERLINK() worksheet function. These differences are discussed in this section.

Saving Excel 97 Worksheet Data to an Existing HTML Page

Note that to save Excel 97 worksheet data in HTML table format, you need to have included the Web Page Authoring component when you installed Office 97. Assuming this has been done, you have two possibilities: one is where the existing page is already in a FrontPage Web; the other, if the page has not yet been imported into a FrontPage Web.

If the Existing HTML Page Is Already in a FrontPage Web You must begin by hand-editing the HTML file that is to contain the table of Excel 97 data. Open the file in FrontPage Editor, click the HTML tab to go to the HTML editing mode, and place the insertion point where you want the table's top margin to go. Next, type the following line into the page:

<!--##Table##-->

N O T E Alternatively, you can use the HTML insertion bot to add the line as indicated. (Choose Insert, FrontPage Component, Insert HTML). ▉

Save the page (you'll see the yellow question mark icon indicating inserted HTML). Close it and follow the next procedure:

1. Start the FrontPage Web server, if it isn't already running. Start FrontPage Explorer and open the Web that contains the page you want.

2. Open the Excel 97 spreadsheet and select the range of cells you want to convert to HTML.

3. Choose File, Save as HTML. This opens the Internet Assistant Wizard (see Figure 34.9). Edit the data ranges if necessary, and then choose Next.

FIG. 34.9

The opening dialog box of the Internet Assistant Wizard lets you edit the ranges selected for the conversion.

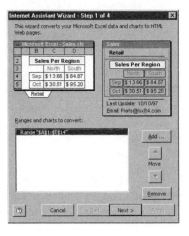

Part
VII

Ch

34

4. Click the lower option button in the next Wizard dialog box to specify that you want the data inserted as a table into an existing HTML page.

5. Choose Next. The third Wizard dialog box allows you to open the page where the Excel data is to be inserted. Mark the Open the File from My FrontPage Web option button and choose Browse. This opens a Pages Available dialog box that displays the file names of the pages in the open Web (see Figure 34.10). Select the file you want and choose OK to close the dialog box. Now, in the Wizard dialog box, choose Next.

CAUTION

The Pages Available dialog box displays only files that have an HTM extension. If they have an HTML extension, they won't appear. If you need a file with this extension, you'll have to type the URL of the page in the URL Address text box of the Wizard dialog box.

FIG. 34.10

You use the third dialog box of the Wizard to identify the Web page for the tabular Excel data.

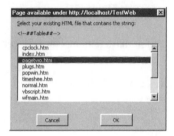

6. Mark the option button labeled Add the Result to my FrontPage Web in the final dialog box of the Wizard. The URL Address text box may not display the name of the file you selected in the previous dialog box. Assuming you still want this to be the save file for the Excel data, use Browse to open the Pages Available dialog box again and select that file. Choose OK and then Finish. A dialog box appears asking if you want to replace the existing file.

7. Choose Yes to insert the Excel tabular data into the page (despite the somewhat ambiguous dialog box, information already on the page will not be changed).

8. Open the modified page in FrontPage Editor to see the results of your work. The table of Excel data will be there, along with several question mark HTML Markup icons above and below it. If you want to delete these icons, go ahead—they just represent some commenting that you can see if you switch to HTML mode.

If the Existing HTML Page Is Not in a FrontPage Web   If you're adding Excel data to a page you haven't yet imported into a FrontPage Web, begin by opening the page in an ASCII text editor, such as Windows Notepad. Place the insertion point where you want the table, then type this line:

<!--##Table##-->

Save and close the page and then follow these steps:

1. Open the Excel 97 spreadsheet and select the range of cells you want to convert to HTML.

2. Choose File, Save as HTML. This opens the Internet Assistant Wizard, as in the previous procedure (refer to Figure 34.9). Edit the data ranges if necessary and choose Next.

3. Mark the lower option button in the next Wizard dialog box to specify that you want the data inserted as a table into an existing HTML page. Choose Next.

4. Mark the Open the File Directly option button in the third Wizard dialog box. Choose Browse to open the Select Your HTML File dialog box (see Figure 34.11). In this dialog box, locate and select the file and choose Open to return to the Wizard. You should now see the file's path name in the text box labeled Path of the Existing File.

FIG. 34.11
Use this dialog box to locate the file where the Excel tabular data will be inserted.

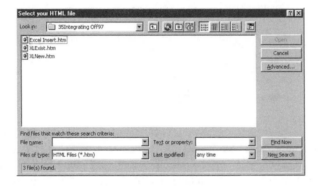

5. Choose Next. The final dialog box appears.

6. Mark the Save the Result as an HTML File option button. Choose Browse to open the Save Your HTML Document As dialog box. Locate and select the file you want to receive the Excel data and choose Save to return to the Wizard.

7. Choose Finish. When asked if you want to replace the existing file, choose Yes. Open the HTML file in a browser or in Word to see the results of your work.

Creating Web Pages from Excel 97 Worksheet Data

In some cases, you don't want to place an Excel-derived table in an existing HTML page, but in one of its own. Excel 97's Internet Assistant Wizard provides an efficient way to do this.

1. Open the Excel 97 spreadsheet and select the range of cells you want to convert to HTML.

2. Choose File, Save as HTML. This opens the Internet Assistant Wizard, as in the previous procedures (refer to Figure 34.9). Edit the data ranges if necessary and choose Next.

3. Mark the upper option button in the dialog box to specify that you want to create a new HTML document and choose Next.

4. Enter a Title that will appear in the title bar of a browser window, a header to be the first line on the page, a description, and horizontal lines in the dialog box (see Figure 34.12). Add the items you want and choose Next.

Part
VII

Ch
34

FIG. 34.12
Customize the appearance of your HTML table page by adding headers, descriptions, and lines.

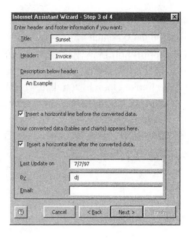

5. Mark the <u>S</u>ave the Result as an HTML File option button in the dialog box. Choose <u>B</u>rowse to open the Save Your HTML Document As dialog box. In this dialog box, supply the path and file name for the new file and choose <u>S</u>ave to return to the Wizard dialog box. Note that Excel-created file names default to an HTM extension, unlike Word 97, which uses an HTML extension.

6. Choose Finish. The new page will be created and stored, ready for importing into a FrontPage Web.

 The page formatting as supplied by the Wizard is pretty dull. Once you've got it in a FrontPage Web, you'll want to liven it up with FrontPage Editor.

Inserting Hyperlinks into Excel 97 Worksheets

Putting a hyperlink into an Excel worksheet is simply a matter of selecting the cell where you want the hyperlink, and choosing <u>I</u>nsert, Hyper<u>l</u>ink. The Insert Hyperlink dialog box appears, with the same functionality as Word's Insert Hyperlink dialog box (refer to Figure 34.2).

As you did earlier, fill in the text box labeled <u>L</u>ink to File or URL. If you want to link to a named location, choose the lower Browse button next to the Named Location in File text box. This opens the dialog box shown in Figure 34.13.

FIG. 34.13
Select sheet names and cell references, or Defined Names, to be the named location for a hyperlink destination.

If you have already defined a name for the cell or the range, mark the Defined Name option button, select the Defined name from the list box, and choose OK to return to the Insert Hyperlink dialog box. Choose OK to close the dialog box. When executed, the hyperlink takes the user to that range and highlights it. Alternatively, you can simply specify a worksheet and cell reference.

You can also use the Copy/Paste as Hyperlink method (discussed in the Word section earlier) to insert hyperlinks within worksheets, across worksheets in the same workbook, or across workbooks.

 To select a cell containing a hyperlink, use the arrow keys to move the selection box to the cell. Clicking the cell, as you would do with an non-linked cell, activates the hyperlink. To edit the text of the hyperlink, select the cell and type the next text into the formula bar.

Using Excel 97's *HYPERLINK()* Function

You can also create a hyperlink with Excel 97's new HYPERLINK() function. The syntax of this function is:

```
=HYPERLINK(link location, friendly name)
```

where *link location* is a reference to the destination file (including its path), and *friendly name* is the text that's displayed in the cell containing the function. So, entering this function in cell A1:

```
=HYPERLINK("C:\My Documents\Background.doc","Show Explanation")
```

would appear as Show Explanation in cell A1, and clicking it would open the Word file BACKGROUND.DOC.

You can combine the HYPERLINK() function with other worksheet functions. Suppose that you want to display a hyperlink in cell C1, but only if the user has entered an invalid equation in cell A1—otherwise, you want nothing to appear in C1. Enter this formula in C1:

```
=IF(ISERROR(A1),HYPERLINK("C:\My Documents\HelpUser.doc","Click here for
help"),"")
```

Now, if the user enters something like =10/0 in cell A1, which returns the #DIV/0! error value, the IF() function calls the HYPERLINK() function that's nested within it. The HYPERLINK() function then displays the Click here for help message in cell C1, and if the user clicks it, the hyperlink opens the Word file named HELPUSER.DOC.

Otherwise, if there's no error value in A1, the IF() function displays the empty text "".

Building a Web Form

Another Web-related add-in for Excel is the Web Form Wizard. This wizard guides you through setting up a form in your Web for users to return information to you. When a user accesses the form from a browser, it appears in an Excel worksheet. The limitation of this is that the user must have a copy of Excel installed on their machine to use the form (just the viewer won't do) so it's a less useful form tool than the ones available with FrontPage.

Begin by opening a new workbook and enter labels for the data that the user will provide—for example, name, address, age, and so on. If you want to include controls such as option buttons and check boxes, choose View, Toolbars and activate the Forms toolbar.

TIP   It's important to use the Forms toolbar rather than the Control Toolbox toolbar. Both give you access to controls, but the Web Form Wizard does not recognize controls placed on the worksheet from the Controls toolbar.

To complete the Web Form Wizard, you must first open the Web that will contain the form. Open it by using FrontPage Explorer and switch back to Excel.

Choose Tools, Wizard and click Web Form in the cascading menu. Step 1 of the Web Form appears, as shown in Figure 34.14.

FIG. 34.14

Create the layout of your Excel worksheet as suggested in the Web Form Wizard's first step.

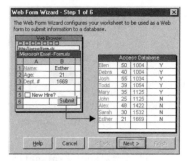

There is no information for you to enter in Step 1. Click Next. Step 2 of the wizard appears, as in Figure 34.15.

FIG. 34.15

You specify controls and information cells in the second step of the Form Wizard.

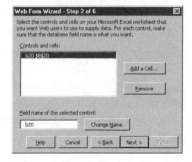

Any controls that you have included in the worksheet with the Controls toolbar are shown in the Controls and Cells list box. You can add to the list box cells where you want the user to supply information. Click Add a Cell, select one of the data entry cells, and click OK in the Add a Cell dialog box. You can associate a name with each cell and each control by selecting them in the Controls and Cells list box, and clicking the Change Name button.

When you have finished selecting the necessary cells and controls, click Next. Step 3 appears, as in Figure 34.16.

FIG. 34.16
Choose Common Gateway Interface to supply the form to your FrontPage Web.

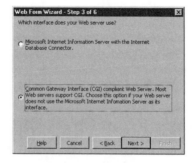

Unless you're also using the Microsoft Internet Information Server, you should choose the CGI interface server in Step 3. Click Next to reach Step 4 (see Figure 34.17).

FIG. 34.17
You may want to save your form both as an Excel file and to your Web.

You should save the form as an Excel file if you have not finished designing it. If you're ready to add it to your Web, verify the URL and change it if necessary, and then choose Add the Results to Your FrontPage Web. Click Next to display Step 5, shown in Figure 34.18.

Part
VII

Ch
34

FIG. 34.18
The Web Form Wizard automatically generates the requisite Perl script.

In Step 5, you can modify the nature of the message back to the user. When you click Next, the wizard adds your form, including the Perl script and message data, to your Web. Step 6 appears and provides you with some standard instructions about submitting the files to the Web administrator. There is no input for you to supply and there are no options to select. Click Finish to end the wizard.

Web forms and databases are complicated animals. If you run into trouble getting Excel forms to work with the server hosting your FrontPage Web, you will likely save yourself time and aggravation if you get help from your system administrator.

Using PowerPoint 97 with FrontPage 98

In PowerPoint 97, you have a Wizard to help you create a slideshow, which you can then import into a FrontPage 98 Web. Begin by opening (or creating and saving) the PowerPoint presentation you want in the Web and then:

1. Choose File, Save as HTML to start the Save as HTML Wizard in PowerPoint (see Figure 34.19). In the first Wizard dialog box, you don't do anything, so choose Next.

FIG. 34.19

Use the PowerPoint Save as HTML Wizard to create a set of files that FrontPage can use as a slideshow.

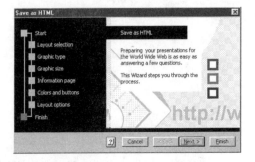

2. Mark the New Layout option button in the dialog box unless you have a saved layout you want to use. Choose Next.

3. Mark the Standard option button in the dialog box unless you want a framed setup for the slideshow. Choose Next.

4. Select whether you want the graphics converted to GIF or JPEG in the dialog box, or whether you're using a PowerPoint animation. (You may never need to use the animation selection, because FrontPage 98 will let you insert an animation file directly, using the Insert, Active Elements, PowerPoint Animation command.) Choose Next.

5. Specify the monitor resolution your viewers are most likely to be using, and the width of screen the presentation is to occupy in the dialog box. Choose Next.

6. Create the information page options in the next dialog box. Choose Next.

7. Specify custom colors if you want them, otherwise mark the Use Browser Colors option button in the dialog box. Choose Next.

8. Specify button style and layout styles, respectively, in the next two dialog boxes. Then choose Next to move to the next dialog box. Here you specify the folder where the PowerPoint HTML file will be saved. Provide a folder name and choose Next to move to the next dialog box. Choose Finish and PowerPoint readies to create the HTML slideshow.

9. Save the layout options you've developed in the preceding steps in the last dialog box. If you want to do this, provide a name for the saved layout; otherwise choose Don't Save. When that step is complete, the conversion process begins. When it completes successfully, you'll see a message stating that.

Now you must get the slideshow presentation into the FrontPage 98 Web. Switch to FrontPage Editor, open the target Web, and choose File, Import. Choose Add Folder to open the Browse for Folder dialog box. Locate the folder you named in Step 8. Select it and choose OK.

Now all the files in that folder display in the list box of the Import File to FrontPage Web dialog box. Choose OK. This creates a folder in the Web with the name you gave it in Step 8, and the files are imported into it. If you inspect the folder, you'll see a file named INDEX.HTM. Open this in FrontPage Editor and preview it. You'll see something resembling the display in Figure 34.20, which was made up in a plain-vanilla way with PowerPoint 97's Financial Performance template.

FIG. 34.20
The first page (INDEX.HTM) of an HTML-based PowerPoint presentation provides a TOC.

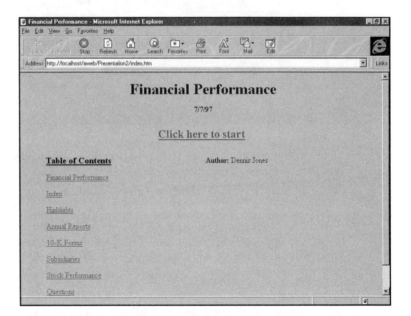

Using Access 97's Web Tools with FrontPage 98

True database integration with FrontPage Webs requires the use of FrontPage Editor's Database Region Wizard, as described in Part IX, "Advanced Database Connectivity." However, if you simply need to extract information from an existing database, and put it into HTML form so a Web can display it, Access 97 has a Save As HTML command that will help you do this.

In the example that follows, you'll use the sample Northwind database that ships with Office 97. Begin by starting Access 97 and opening this database, which if installed during setup will be in C:\Program Files\Microsoft Office\Office\Samples. If it's not there, you'll have to use Office 97 Setup to locate and install it.

Now do this:

1. Choose File, Save as HTML. This opens the Publish To the Web Wizard. You won't need to provide any information in this dialog box, so choose Next.

2. In the second dialog box, select which elements of the database you want to place in the Web page. To keep the example simple, click the Tables tab and mark the Suppliers check box (see Figure 34.21). Choose Next.

FIG. 34.21

You can select a wide range of information from the database to publish to a Web page.

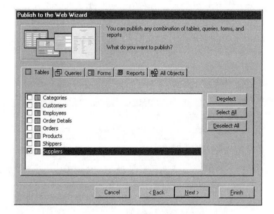

3. Select a document template, if you have one, in the dialog box. For this example, assume you have no template, and choose Next.

4. Make the Static HTML option button if it isn't already marked in the next dialog box. Choose Next.

5. Choose the destination folder for the HTML output in the dialog box. Because FrontPage is happier if it does its own file importing, select a suitable non-FrontPage folder by typing it into the upper text box, or using the Browse button. Choose Next.

6. Clear the check box labeled Yes I want to Create a Home Page in the next dialog box and choose Next.

7. Decide whether to save the selection and layout information you've provided so far, to make a publication profile. If this profile is one you'll use often, mark the check box to save the profile and choose Finish. Once the Wizard closes, inspect the save folder, and you'll see the Web page file or files (and any required associated ones needed, such as graphics) there. Note that the page files have the extension HTML, not HTM.

8. Close Access and import the file into the FrontPage Web. You may want to change the page file extensions to HTM, depending on the type of system where they are to reside. You can see an example of the results in Figure 34.22. The file has already been imported into a FrontPage Web and is being viewed with the Preview in Browser command.

FIG. 34.22

Access 97's Save as HTML command makes it easy to prepare database information, such as this example, for use in a FrontPage Web.

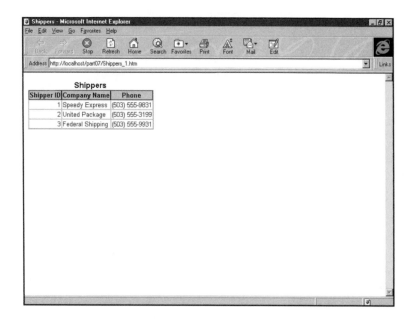

From Here...

Because not everyone has migrated to Office 97 from Office 95, there will still be many people who can use the Internet Assistants that Microsoft provides for Office 95 applications. If you fall into this category, you may want to go to:

- Chapter 35, "Using the Internet Assistant for PowerPoint 95," which shows you how (or whether) to prepare PowerPoint 95 slideshow presentations that you can integrate into a FrontPage Web.

- Chapter 36, "Using the Internet Assistants for Excel 95 and Word 95," where you learn to use Word 95 as a rudimentary HTML editor and to export Excel 95 spreadsheet data to HTML files.

- Chapter 37, "Using the Internet Assistants for Schedule+ and Access," in which you can find out techniques of getting Schedule+ and Access 95 information into a FrontPage 98 Web.

Part
VII

Ch
34

Using the Internet Assistant for PowerPoint 95

Even if you don't have Powerpoint 97 with its built-in HTML conversion and Web tools, you can get much the same functionality with the combination of PowerPoint 95 and its Internet Assistant. Like Powerpoint 97, PowerPoint 95 is a software package that enables you to design and present slide shows on your computer. It offers a variety of capabilities and special effects that you can use to display any sort of topic, from a sales presentation to a meeting guide to a training session.

The drawback is that the people who view or guide the presentation must have access to the file that contains the slide show. By using PowerPoint 95's Internet Assistant (IA), you can convert the presentation's individual slides to files that use HTML and graphic formats. By making the files available to the Web or to an intranet, your presentation becomes accessible to anyone with a browser and the proper connection. ◼

Use Some of PowerPoint 95's Basic Tools

Although this is not a primer on PowerPoint, it discusses several of the capabilities that work differently (or that don't work at all) in the exported version of a PowerPoint slide show.

Assess PowerPoint's Usefulness

What do you do if you've produced a PowerPoint presentation that you want to distribute more broadly? Apply simple principles to decide whether to use PowerPoint's IA on a presentation.

Install PowerPoint's IA

Identify and use the necessary files to put the IA functionality into PowerPoint.

Manage the Exported Files

Understand which files are created when you use the IA on a PowerPoint presentation, what they contain, and how to use them.

Understanding PowerPoint 95

PowerPoint 95 is a presentation manager. Using PowerPoint, you can:

- Design a series of slides, each of which might contain graphics and text. The graphic and text elements can be created by and linked to other Office applications.

- Apply special effects to elements in the slide. For example, you might use flying text to cause individual bullet points to appear on the slide sequentially, instead of simultaneously.

- Present the slides as a full screen show, so that PowerPoint's menus and toolbars are hidden from view. Buttons or other objects in a slide enable the user to move through the slides consecutively, or to jump directly to a particular slide.

- Edit various aspects of the slides, such as their order in the presentation.

PowerPoint comes with several templates that contain preformatted presentations. These templates have been designed to cover the important aspects of different kinds of presentations.

For example, the template for selling a product or idea provides a slide to describe:

- The objective for the presentation
- The customer's requirements
- How the product meets those requirements
- A cost analysis
- The vendor's strengths
- Key product benefits
- The next steps to take

You might not regard each of these as necessary for a sales or marketing presentation, but it's a good framework to build on.

Starting with a template, such as this one, frees you from initial outline and formatting concerns so that you can concentrate on content. Figure 35.1 gives an example of one slide from the sales template.

Figure 35.2 shows how you might modify the slide for a particular sales presentation.

After you have finished designing the presentation and modifying the template's slides to communicate your content, display the slides in full-screen mode by choosing View, Slide Show from the PowerPoint menu. Click your mouse button or press Enter to advance manually through the slides.

FIG. 35.1
PowerPoint's templates give you good starting points to develop many different kinds of presentations.

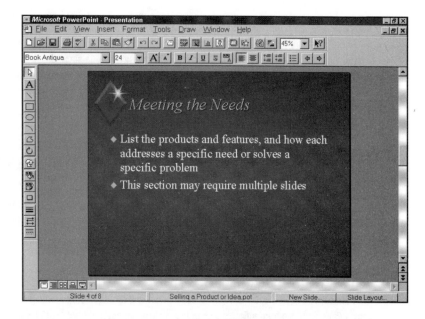

FIG. 35.2
All the contents of this slide are included in the exported graphics image.

Graphic —
Background —

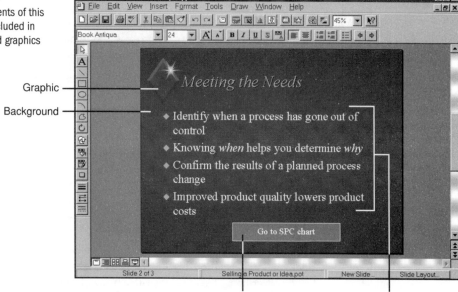

Transition to Another Slide

Text

T I P Another way to move among slides in a slide show is with a Pop-up button. Choose Tools, Options, select the View tab, and ensure that the Show Pop-up Menu button check box is checked. This places control buttons in the lower-left corner of each slide during the slide show. Clicking the buttons moves you from slide to slide. The buttons become visible when you move the mouse pointer across the slide. This becomes particularly important when you are using the IA: see "Running PowerPoint's IA," later in this chapter.

Deciding to Use PowerPoint's Internet Assistant

The Web has been used largely as a marketing medium, and you might want to use it to publish a sales presentation, or to distribute descriptive information about your products. You might have developed a training presentation that you want to make available to employees with access to your company's intranet.

N O T E   Some users of PowerPoint's IA put presentations on the Web because they think it's more convenient to view it that way at a client's site. Keep in mind, though, that your client's data communications equipment is unlikely to operate faster than 28,800 bps. On the other hand, you can copy a PowerPoint file from a floppy disk to the client's computer at fractional T1 speeds. PowerPoint comes with a small viewer application that you can take with you. ▓

PowerPoint's IA is a convenient way to accomplish this; you just install the IA and run it. Unlike the IAs for other Office applications, almost the entire process is automated. Other IAs, however, give you more choices about the characteristics of the resulting files.

You can, of course, use a text editor to modify the tags in the HTML files that PowerPoint's IA creates. However, the IA saves your slides' appearance in a series of JPG or GIF files, one file per slide. These files are static. That is, they do not retain certain special effects that you might have specified for the slide. For example, in PowerPoint:

- Choose Tools, Slide Transition. In the Slide Transition dialog box, choose Cover Left from the Effect drop-down list. This causes the slide to appear from the right side of the screen during the slide show, and to move left to cover the prior slide.
- Choose Tools, Build Slide Text and click Fly From Left in the cascading menu. When you view the slide show, any text on the slide is hidden until you press Enter or click the mouse button. After clicking, the bullets and their attached text fly in from the left side of the screen, one per mouse click. This is a useful way to keep your audience's attention on the current bullet point. (You've probably attended meetings where the presenter emulates this effect by covering up bullet points with a piece of paper and reveals them one by one.)

These effects can be functionally useful and cosmetically attractive but you can't retain them in files created by PowerPoint's IA. The absence of such capabilities might not cause you to decide against converting a presentation to HTML, but you shouldn't expect the resulting files to retain all their PowerPoint features.

One feature that you can retain is the ability to jump to a specific slide. Suppose that on the presentation's 10th slide, you want to allow the user to quickly jump back to the fifth slide, which is named *Benefits*. With the 10th slide active, take these steps:

1. Select a shape, such as a rectangle or oval from PowerPoint's Drawing toolbar. Drag in the slide to establish a new object.

2. Choose Edit, Edit Text Object after the new object is selected. Type an instruction, such as "Go to Benefits," inside the object.

3. Choose Tools, Interactive Settings with the new object still selected. In the Interactive Settings dialog box, choose the Go to option button and select Slide from the associated drop-down list (see Figure 35.3).

4. Choose the Benefits slide from the Slides list box in the Go To Slide dialog box. Click OK to return to the Interactive Settings dialog box and click OK again to return to the active slide.

FIG. 35.3
Including interactive settings makes it easier for a user to navigate among the exported version of your slides.

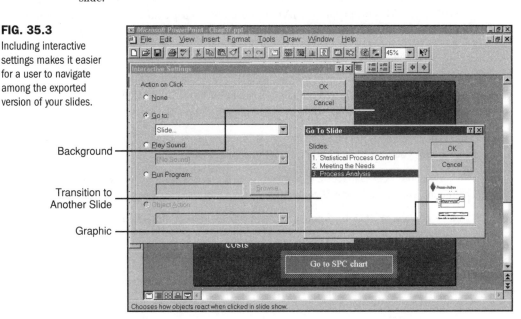

Now, during a slide show, clicking the drawing object displays the Benefits slide.

PowerPoint's IA maintains this functionality. A user who is viewing the exported files with a browser is able to click the object and go to its destination file. (Remember that the IA converts each PowerPoint slide to a different file.)

Part
VII

Ch
35

If you are willing to live without PowerPoint's animation effects, you can convert your PowerPoint slide presentation to HTML and graphic format for users to browse. Your presentation maintains any special navigation capabilities that you have built into it.

Installing the Internet Assistant for PowerPoint

All the IAs for Office applications are available via download from the Web at **www.microsoft.com/msdownload/**. It is compressed into an executable file named PPTIA.EXE. From the Windows Explorer, double-click PPTIA.EXE to extract its contents.

N O T E   You must be running PowerPoint for Windows 95 to use the IA. PowerPoint versions 4.0 and earlier are incompatible with the IA, and PowerPoint 97 does not need it. ■

Among those contents is another executable file, which at the time of this writing was named IA4PPT95.EXE. This file installs the IA in PowerPoint. To perform the installation, follow these steps:

1. Exit the application if you have PowerPoint running.
2. Double-click IA4PPT95.EXE from the Windows Explorer.
3. Respond Yes to the Install Internet Assistant for PowerPoint? query.
4. Click OK in response to the Successful Installation message.

If the installation does not complete successfully, try moving IA4PPT95.EXE into the same folder where you have stored the PowerPoint application file.

The installation process places a new menu item, Export as HTML, in PowerPoint's File menu. The menu item is visible only if you open a presentation.

To uninstall PowerPoint's IA, remove these files from PowerPoint's folder:

■ PPT2HTML.PPA
■ PPT2HTML.DLL
■ SLIDEDMP.EXE
■ PP2HINTL.DLL
■ IMAGE.TPL
■ TEXT.TPL

Another file that you find when the initial extraction process is complete is IA4PPT95.DOC. This is a Word document that contains additional documentation and recent changes to information about running PowerPoint's IA.

Running PowerPoint's IA

To convert a PowerPoint presentation to HTML and graphic files, open the presentation in PowerPoint and choose File, Export as HTML. The dialog box shown in Figure 35.4 appears.

FIG. 35.4
Compared to the GIF format, JPEG bitmaps can save file space, but very small JPEG files tend to have poor image quality.

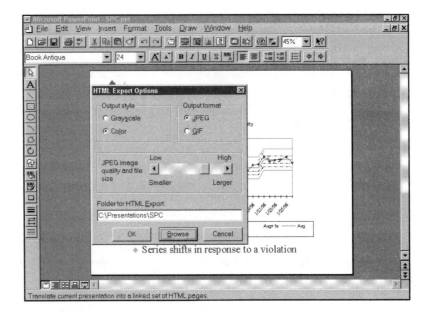

Use the HTML Export Options dialog box to specify:

- Whether the graphics files should be saved in black and white (Grayscale) or Color.
- Whether you want the graphics files saved in the JPEG or GIF format.
- The size and image quality that the JPG file is to maintain (if you select JPEG).
- The location to store the converted files on your working disk. Type the path in the Folder for HTML Export edit box or use the Browse button to navigate to your preferred location.

PowerPoint's IA automatically creates a new folder at the end of the path. The new folder is where the IA stores the converted files. The folder's default name is the same as that of the presentation. That is, if the active presentation is named Training.ppt, the default folder is named Training.

When you are satisfied with your choices in the HTML Export Options dialog box, choose OK. The IA converts your slides to HTML and graphic format.

During the conversion process, you may see a window with the contents of any folders that you have open, or another active application, appear on top of the PowerPoint window. This is normal behavior.

You next see a window appear in the upper-left quadrant of your screen. This window displays your slide show, slide by slide. PowerPoint's IA takes pictures of the show and saves them in either JPG or GIF format.

Because of the way that the IA captures your slides in this slide show window, you should take a few steps prior to beginning the export process:

Part
VII

Ch
35

- Close any floating toolbars that may occupy the upper-left quadrant of the PowerPoint screen. (For this reason, you might want to close any applications other than PowerPoint.)

- Close any dialog boxes or Help files whose Always on Top property has been set and that appear in the upper-left quadrant.

- Choose Tools, Options, select the View tab, and clear the Show Popup Menu Button check box. If you leave it checked, and if you move your mouse pointer during the export process, the pop-up menu buttons might appear and be captured in the exported graphic files.

Of course, you need sufficient space on your working disk to store the exported files. Typically, you should budget for around 20K for each graphic file. However, the export process itself requires considerably more space. Try to have at least 5M free on your working disk before beginning the export.

 If you have text in any grouped objects in a PowerPoint slide, ungroup them via Draw, Ungroup prior to the export process. Grouped text is not added to the text-only versions of your slides.

Understanding the Converted Files

After PowerPoint's IA completes its export of your slides, you will find several types of files in the destination folder:

- An INDEX.HTM file containing the presentation's name, your name, your company name, and hyperlinks to each slide in the presentation.

- Files with the GIF extension that contain Next, Previous, First Page, and Text View buttons. These display on each slide when viewed with a browser.

- Files with the JPG or GIF extension, depending on which format you selected in the HTML Export Options dialog box. These files contain the graphic representation of each slide.

- Files with the HTM extension, and those that begin with Sld001, Sld002, and so on. These contain the conventional HTML tags for each slide.

- Files with the HTM extension, and those that begin with Tsld001, Tsld002, and so on. These are text-only versions of your slides, for users who still have an antediluvian browser that can't handle graphics—or, for quicker browsing.

It's time to take a look at these files. Figure 35.5 shows a slide as PowerPoint displays it.

 It's easy to put an object from another Office application into a PowerPoint slide. Select the object, such as an Excel chart, within its native application. Choose Edit, Copy. Switch to PowerPoint and choose Edit, Paste. More options are available if you choose Edit, Paste Special.

FIG. 35.5
PowerPoint is a useful way to provide commentary about a chart created in Excel.

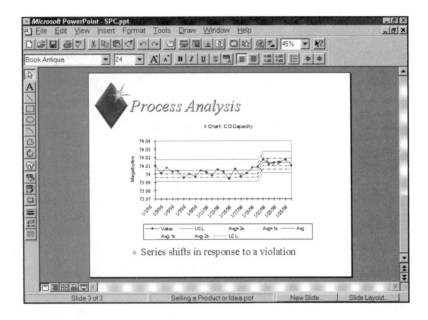

Figure 35.6 shows a graphic version of the same slide after it's been exported. Notice the navigation buttons that PowerPoint's IA added. There's a Back shortcut, a Forward shortcut, a shortcut that takes the user to INDEX.HTM, and a shortcut that switches to the text-only version.

FIG. 35.6
The graphic version of the slide is identical to that displayed by the PowerPoint slide show.

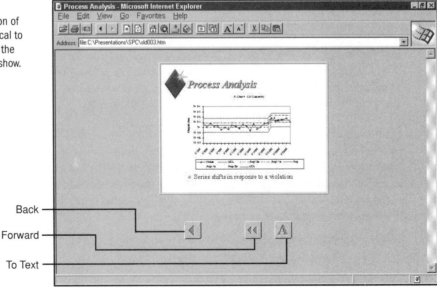

Back

Forward

To Text

The text-only version of the slide is shown in Figure 35.7.

FIG. 35.7

The graphic version's navigation buttons are replaced by hyperlinked text in the text-only version.

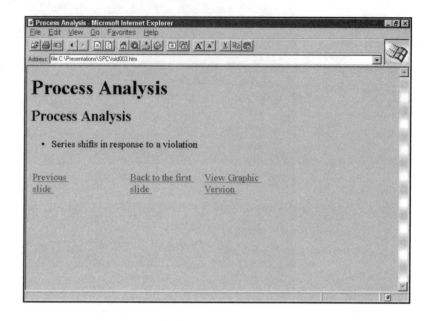

Notice that, compared to the graphic version of the slide, the text-only version is uninformative. If you anticipate that many users will choose to view the text-only version, if only to accelerate their browsing, you should probably add enough textual material to each slide so that users are able to infer their current location in the show.

N O T E PowerPoint's IA treats any hidden slides in your presentation as normal slides—that is, it converts them to HTML and graphic files. (To hide a slide in PowerPoint, choose Tools, Hide Slide. This prevents its display during a slide show.) If you don't want the browser to display these slides, save the presentation with a new name and delete the hidden slides. ■

PowerPoint offers a way for you to keep speaker's notes for each slide. These notes are text material that's associated with each slide. As you are developing a presentation, you can make notes to yourself: these might be reminders to bring up a topic that's not shown in the slides, or information about your audience, or the name and location of another document that you want to display temporarily. It is virtually anything that you, as the presenter, would want to see and that you do not want the audience to see.

To attach speaker's notes to a slide while you're running PowerPoint, choose View, Notes Pages. The slide changes and appears as shown in Figure 35.8.

Type whatever notes you wish in the Notes window. When you finish designing your presentation, choose File, Print. In the Print dialog box, choose Notes Pages from the Print what drop-down list. You now have a copy of your notes to refer to as you're delivering the presentation.

PowerPoint's IA exports these notes to the HTML version, as shown in Figure 35.9.

FIG. 35.8

Speaker notes are visible only via View, Notes Pages—they do not appear in a slide show.

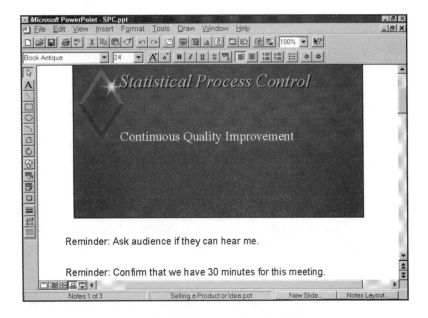

FIG. 35.9

Be careful to remove unnecessary or irrelevant speaker's notes from the exported presentation.

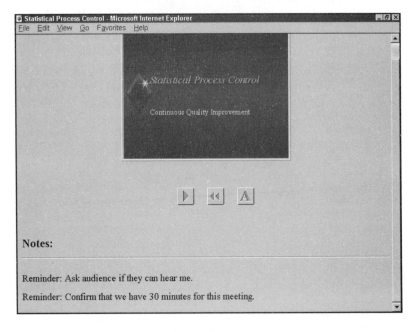

You can, of course, construct these notes to provide additional information to a user who views the presentation with a browser. But if you want to suppress the notes without deleting them from the PowerPoint presentation, modify the HTML code. Open the associated HTML file with your text editor and delete these lines (which, in this case, correspond to the notes shown in Figure 35.9):

```
<Font size=4> <STRONG> Notes:</FONT></STRONG>
<HR  SIZE=3>
<P> </P>
<P>Reminder: Ask audience if they can hear me.</P>
<P></P>
<P></P>
<P></P>
<P>Reminder: Confirm that we have 30 minutes for this meeting.</P>
<P> </P>
```

Save the modified HTML code with its original name. Now, when the presentation is viewed, the notes are suppressed in both the graphic and text-only versions.

From Here...

The PowerPoint 95 Internet Assistant is just one of several IAs you can use with Office 95 applications. To examine the rest of them, or to go on to exploring server technology, continue with:

- Chapter 36, "Using the Internet Assistants for Excel 95 and Word 95" where you learn to use Word 95 as rudimentary HTML editor, and to export Excel 95 spreadsheet data to HTML files.

- Chapter 37, "Using the Internet Assistants for Schedule+ and Access," in which you can find out techniques of getting Schedule+ and Access 95 information into a FrontPage 98 Web.

- Chapter 38, "Using FrontPage with Microsoft Internet Information Server," which looks at the details of the highly regarded Microsoft Internet Information Server and the details behind using FrontPage 98 with this server.

Using the Internet Assistants for Excel 95 and Word 95

The Internet Assistants for Word 95 and Excel 95 do not resemble one another.

In Word, the Internet Assistant (IA) provides a reasonably rich set of formatting options. You create an HTML document in Word by means of different menu items and toolbars. Most permissible HTML elements are supported.

In contrast, Excel's IA is a wizard—a sequential series of dialog boxes where you select among various options. It provides an abbreviated set of HTML formatting elements, limited to data tables, horizontal rules, headers, footers, and e-mail addressing.

However, the Word and Excel applications combine beautifully by means of object linking and embedding (OLE). By using them and their associated IAs judiciously, you can create some very sophisticated HTML documents. ■

Installation and operation of the Word and Excel IAs

Learn how to make the IAs available to their respective applications, and invoke them to create HTML documents.

Integration of Excel data with Word documents

Bring Excel worksheet ranges into Word documents for subsequent HTML formatting, and link the information so as to keep it current in both locations.

Creation of pivot tables in Excel

Special capabilities of pivot tables can extend your presentation options and make data summaries more flexible.

Installing and Running the Internet Assistants

Both the IA for Excel and the IA for Word are add-ins. Add-ins are programs that modify the way Excel and Word work: For example, they typically add capabilities via new options in the applications' menus. Add-ins must be made available to the application that uses them, and you do this with an installation process. You can install and uninstall both the Word and the Excel IA anytime.

Installing Excel's Internet Assistant

Use the Windows Explorer, if necessary, to determine where Excel IA is stored. (Excel's IA is named HTML.XLA.) To install Excel's IA, take the following steps:

1. Start Excel and choose Tools, Add-Ins. The dialog box shown in Figure 36.1 appears.

2. If you stored HTML.XLA somewhere other than Excel's Library folder, use the Browse button to navigate to its location. When you reach the correct folder, select HTML.XLA and click OK. A new item, Internet Assistant Wizard, appears in the Add-Ins list box.

3. Fill the Internet Assistant Wizard check box and choose OK.

FIG. 36.1

It's easiest to locate Excel add-ins if you put them all in the Excel Library folder.

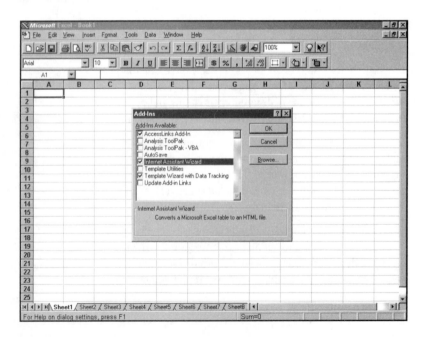

After the Assistant installs, an Internet Assistant Wizard item appears in the Tools menu. Selecting this menu item starts the wizard.

To uninstall the IA, choose Tools, Add-Ins and clear the Assistant's check box.

Installing the Internet Assistant for Word

Word's IA is also an add-in. When you obtain the Word IA, it's usually in an executable file. Double-clicking the file from the Windows Explorer causes several new files to extract. The extraction routine stores one of these files, WIAHTM32.WLL, in Word's Startup folder.

After you next start Word, the Glasses button appears in Word's toolbar area. Clicking the button changes the view to Web Browse, and the button changes to depict a pencil. Click the Pencil button to return to Edit view. See Figure 36.2.

FIG. 36.2
Word's menus and toolbars change, depending on whether you are in Edit view or Web view.

Pencil button

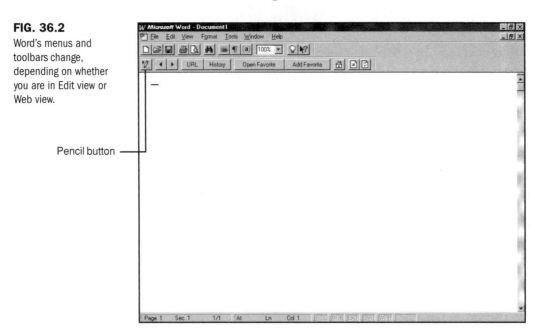

If you see neither of these buttons, choose File, Templates. In the Global Templates and Add-ins box, make sure that WIAHTM32.WLL is checked and then choose OK.

To uninstall Word's IA, clear the WIAHTM32.WLL check box.

Using the Internet Assistants in Excel and Word

Using Excel's IA is easy—it is a five-step wizard, and the choices it offers are quite restricted. Word's IA is more complex, and it's necessary to become familiar with its different menu items and toolbars to use it to the best advantage.

Running the Internet Assistant Wizard in Excel

To use Excel's IA, click to highlight the range of data that you want to convert to HTML format and follow these steps:

1. Choose Tools, Internet Assistant Wizard. Step 1 of the wizard appears, as shown in Figure 36.3. Use this step to adjust the selected range, if necessary, and click Next.

FIG. 36.3

Use the Reference Edit box in Step 1 if you want to extend or reduce your worksheet selection.

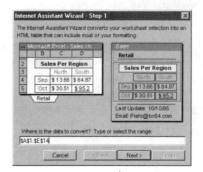

2. Choose (in Step 2 of the wizard) to create an HTML page with header, table, and footer or to insert the table into an existing HTML document (see Figure 36.4). Because inserting the table requires that you first open and edit a target document, it's recommended that you choose to create a full HTML document. Click Next.

FIG. 36.4

Choosing to create an HTML page results in an HTML document that can be viewed with a browser.

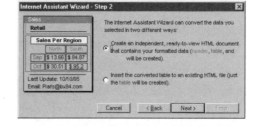

3. Step 3 appears, as in Figure 36.5. Provide whatever title, header, description, update, and name you choose, and insert an e-mail address if you wish. (This works for viewers only if an e-mail application is available to them.) Click Next.

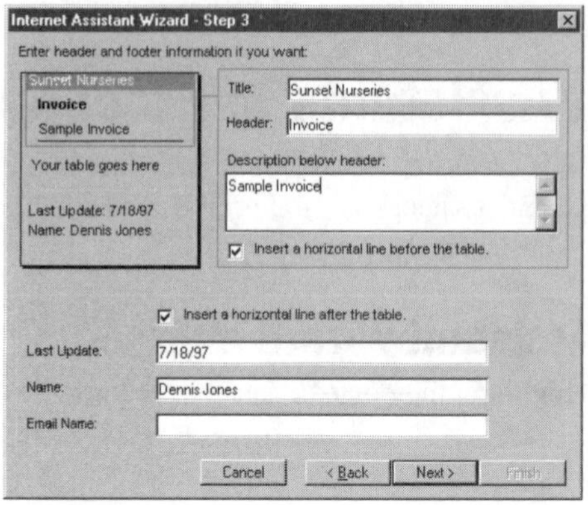

FIG. 36.5

Customize the appearance of the HTML document in Step 3 of the wizard.

4. In Step 4, choose to convert as much formatting as possible to HTML or choose to convert the data only. Click Next.

5. In Step 5, indicate a document path and name for the HTML document. Click Finish.

You now have a ready-to-view HTML document saved in the path you specified.

Using the Internet Assistant in Word

Word's IA gives you considerably more control over HTML formatting than does Excel's IA. It is more than just a matter of running a simple wizard: There are menu choices, toolbars, and formatting styles to set.

To see the menu items and toolbars that are available with Word's IA, click the Glasses button to switch to Web Browse view. This action also gives you access to Help files that are specific to Word's IA.

The typical tasks that you might need to accomplish are discussed in the following sections.

Creating an HTML Document   From Word's File menu, choose New and click the HTML.DOT document template. In the new document, enter whatever information you want, including text, graphics, tables, and hyperlinks. You could also begin by opening an existing Word or text document.

To apply a particular style to an element in the document, select the element and click the Style box drop-down arrow to see the available styles (see Figure 36.6).

FIG. 36.6
You can select an HTML style from the Style box as shown, or by choosing Format, Style.

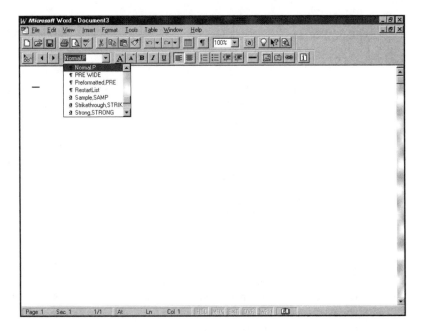

Click a style from the Style box drop-down list to apply it. After you finish applying the HTML formats to the elements in your document, choose File, Save As. In the Save As dialog box, choose HTML Document from the Save File As Type list box.

Establishing a Hyperlink to a Local File or to an URL Type the text or insert the graphic that you want to display as the hyperlink's hotspot and save the active document.

Select the text or graphic and choose Insert, HyperLink. The Hyperlink dialog box appears, as shown in Figure 36.7.

FIG. 36.7

If you began by selecting a graphic, the Text to Display edit box is unavailable.

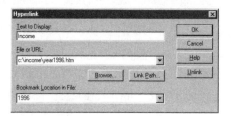

If you began by selecting text, you can change the text that displays in the Text to Display edit box. Either type the path and name of the destination file in the File or URL box, or use the Browse button to navigate to the file on your computer or your LAN; you can also enter a Web URL.

Click Link Path to convert a relative link path to a fixed file location or a fixed location to a relative path.

You can also specify a target location in the destination file with the Bookmark Location in the File drop-down list. If the destination file is a Word document, you could specify a bookmark that it contains.

Inserting a Form Word's IA supports forms with text edit boxes, drop-down lists, and check boxes. To insert these form fields into your document, choose Insert, Form Field. The dialog box shown in Figure 36.8 appears.

It's easiest to insert these fields into your document by using the Forms toolbar. Click one of the toolbar's buttons to insert a form field and then drag in your document to establish a location and size for the form field.

When you have finished inserting fields, supply a Submit button in the document for the user to click when the fields have been completed. To prepare it for data entry by its user, click the Protect Form button on the toolbar.

N O T E The IA does not support scripting: that is, you cannot use the IA to write a script that enables the retrieval and storage of information that users supply to your form. Use VBScript or JavaScript for this purpose (see Chapter 18, "Scripting with VBScript" and Chapter 19, "Scripting with JavaScript"), or use FrontPage's scripting capabilities. Otherwise, you should check with your system administrator to find out how you can enable data retrieval. ▪

FIG. 36.8
Including a Reset button enables the user to abandon the current entries and begin again.

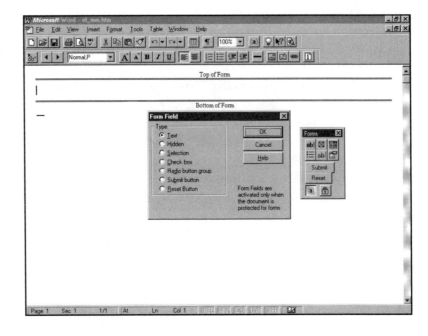

Integrating Excel's IA with Word's IA

The options provided in Excel's IA are quite limited. As you have seen, you can use it to do the following:

- Display cell values in a table
- Insert horizontal rules
- Include a header and footer
- Include an e-mail field

But, in addition to tables, rules, headers, and footers, you can use Word's IA to format elements. Some of these include:

- Hyperlinks and cross-references
- Form fields
- Marquees
- Directory lists

Integrating Excel with Word gives you the best of both applications: Excel's ease of creating tables of values, and the extra capabilities of Word's IA.

Embedding Excel Data into Word

Once you have established a range of data in an Excel worksheet, you're in a position to copy the data from the worksheet into a Word document. Follow these steps:

1. Start Word. If you have already created a Word document to contain the Excel data, open it.

2. Start Excel and open the workbook that contains the data that you want to convert to HTML format.

3. Select the range of worksheet cells that you want to convert by dragging across them with the mouse pointer.

4. Choose Copy from Excel's Edit menu.

5. Switch to Word. Click in the Word document where you want the Excel data to appear.

6. Choose Paste Special from Word's Edit menu. The dialog box shown in Figure 36.9 appears.

FIG. 36.9

Paste Special gives you greater control over the way Word treats the pasted object.

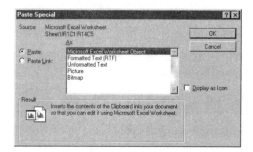

The Paste Special dialog box gives you several options for the format of the data that you paste. In most cases, you will want to choose Microsoft Excel Worksheet Object. If you choose this option, you can later edit the data with Excel's tools by double-clicking the worksheet object.

Another option is Formatted Text. This option means that the object appears in your target document with most of the formatting (fonts, borders, and so on) from the source document. This option is different from the Unformatted Text option in which the text takes on the default format of the target document.

Once you paste the Excel data into the Word document, you can use the capabilities of Word's IA to add any HTML formatting elements.

Linking Excel Data into Word

Another option to consider when you paste Excel data into a Word document is the Paste Link option in the Paste Special dialog box (refer to Figure 36.9). This option is particularly useful if you expect the Excel data to change.

For example, you might place an income statement in HTML format on your intranet. As long as the company is making transactions, its income statement's numbers change from time to time. You would want any changes to Excel's income statement to be reflected in the Word document.

You can arrange for this direct, live linkage between the Word and Excel documents by choosing the Paste Link option. You need to update the HTML document manually because HTML documents created by an IA are not live; they're static. But, at least by linking the files you can save the effort of moving data from Excel to Word.

To create the linkage, follow these steps:

1. Choose Paste Link instead of Paste in the Paste Special dialog box. Choose OK.
2. Choose Tools, Options and select the General tab. Ensure that the Update Automatic Links at Open check box is checked.
3. Select the Print tab while you still have the Options dialog box open and make sure the Update Links check box is checked. Choose OK.
4. Choose Edit, Links. Select the Automatic option and choose OK.

Now, whenever you open the Word document, it links to the Excel workbook and automatically updates to show the most recent information. You need only resave the Word document as an HTML file to ensure that the current data is seen by those who view it.

Creating Pivot Tables in Excel

The principal function of Excel's IA is to convert a range of data in an Excel worksheet to HTML format. If you're not yet familiar with Excel pivot tables, you're missing out on one of Excel's most powerful and flexible capabilities. Without it, the HTML representation of the data will not be as useful as it could be.

A pivot table is a way to summarize long, detailed lists of data. Figure 36.10 contains an example of a pivot table and its underlying data.

FIG. 36.10

Identical values in the Date column are combined in the pivot table.

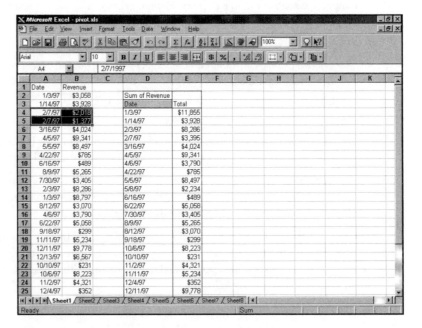

Notice in Figure 36.10 that the list, in columns A and B, contains the dates on which a company earned its revenue. In the pivot table, the revenue is totalled for each month. Also, notice that multiple entries in the list are combined into one entry in the pivot table: for example, the entries for 2/7/97. To create this pivot table, follow these steps:

1. Select any cell in the list.
2. Select Data, Pivot Table. The Pivot Table Wizard starts.
3. Confirm, in Step 1, that the data source is a Microsoft Excel list or database. Click Next.
4. Confirm or edit, in Step 2, the address of the worksheet range that contains the list. Click Next.
5. Drag the Date button, in Step 3, into the Row area and drag the Revenue button into the Data area.
6. Double-click the Revenue button in the Data area. While you are still in Step 3, click Number in the Pivot Table Field dialog box. Choose a currency format and choose OK. Click OK to exit the Pivot Table field dialog box and click Next.
7. Enter, in Step 4, the address of the cell in the Pivot Table Starting Cell edit box where you want the pivot table to begin. Click Finish.

The pivot table appears, as shown in Figure 36.11.

Once you have created a pivot table, you can modify its characteristics very easily. For example, if you decide that you want the different dates to occupy columns instead of rows, you click and drag the Date button on the pivot table to the right. When you release the mouse button, the pivot table reorients.

Another very useful aspect of pivot tables is the ability to group their control variable (in this example, the control variable is Date). Suppose that you wanted to show total revenue for each month rather than each day in the underlying list. Follow these steps:

1. Select any cell containing a date in the pivot table's Date column.
2. Choose Data, Group and Outline. Select Group from the cascading menu to open the Grouping dialog box.
3. Choose Month in the By list box and choose OK.

The pivot table's Date field changes to show the revenue total for each month, rather than for each day. You could also choose, for example, Month *and* Quarter in the By list box. This causes the pivot table to employ two control variables: Quarter and Month within Quarter.

To convert the pivot table to HTML format, drag across the table with the mouse pointer to select it and choose Tools, Internet Assistant Wizard. You can also select and copy the pivot table and paste it into a Word document to use Word's IA.

As noted at the beginning of this section, pivot tables are extremely powerful. Many choices are involved in structuring them—too many to describe here. To become more familiar with the capabilities of pivot tables, you'll need to experiment with them. A few possibilities you might consider include the following:

- Add another control variable as a pivot table column. Extending the present example, you might include Region to show total revenue by both region and date.

- Show the data field (here, Revenue) as a percent of total. In the Pivot Table Field dialog box, click Options. Select Percent of Total in the Show Data As drop-down list.

- Show the data field with some other subtotal function, such as Count or Average. Or, drag the data field's button into the Data area twice to show the data two different ways in the same pivot table.

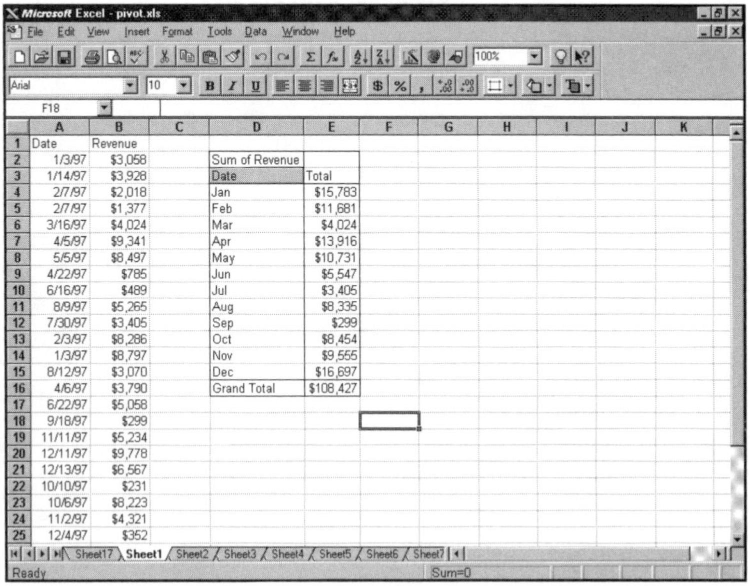

FIG. 36.11
In HTML documents, brief summaries are usually more informative than lengthy, detailed lists.

From Here...

At this point, several possibilities present themselves:

- In Part VIII, "Using Other Servers with FrontPage 98," you can learn about the Microsoft Internet Information Server (IIS) as well as other servers you might want to use with FrontPage 98.

- If that's familiar to you, or if you don't want to explore the subject of servers just now, you might prefer to go to Part IX, "Advanced Database Connectivity."

- Or you might like to take a break and enjoy yourself (if you haven't already) with the new version of Image Composer, as described in Part III, "Creating and Adapting Graphics with Image Composer."

Part
VII

Ch
36

## CHAPTER 37

Using the Internet Assistants for Schedule+ and Access

Schedule+ enables you to set different permission levels as to the availability of your Schedule+ files. You can, for example, enable an assistant to maintain your schedule on your behalf, or a colleague to view your schedule without the ability to modify it. Although convenient, Schedule+ permissions assume that these coworkers have the necessary connectivity to the location of your Schedule+ files. By exporting your Appointment Book in HTML format and posting it to a Web server, you can broaden the availability of your schedule.

Access 95 also supports different permission levels for different users; but, Access databases (particularly in a corporation), are likely to contain sensitive, proprietary information that must be kept inaccessible to prying eyes, both inside and outside the company. By using the Access IA, you can publish any information on a Web server—for example, product lists or the current standings in sales contests—that is fit for public consumption, and still keep some information hidden safe in the Access database. ■

Installation procedures

You learn how to install the IAs for Schedule+ and Access 95 and to identify and understand the purpose of files that accompany the IAs.

Running the Schedule+ IA

The Schedule+ IA enables you to create HTML files that display your Schedule+ Appointment Book. Maintaining your privacy is important when you publish your appointments on a Web server, and you learn the privacy implications of different choices you make when you run the Schedule+ IA.

Running the Access 95 IA

You can convert Access tables, queries, forms, and reports to HTML format with the Access IA. It's useful to understand how to use the different HTML templates that accompany the Access IA, and important to know how to avoid problems when you create the HTML versions of Access Forms.

Specifying Access output

The HTML pages generated by the IA will differ depending on the type of database object you choose, and the way you dictate its formatting.

Installing the Schedule+ IA

The Schedule+ IA is packaged in a file named SCHIA.EXE. To install the IA, install the Schedule+ application on your computer, but close Schedule+ if it is running. From the Explorer, double-click the SCHIA.EXE file. There are no questions for you to answer or options for you to choose. When SCHIA.EXE finishes, the IA for Schedule+ is installed.

N O T E The IAs for Access and Schedule+ are available via download from the Web at **www.microsoft.com/msdownload/**. ▪

A text file, SCHPOST.TXT, is placed in your Windows folder. This file, which you can read with any text editor or word processor, contains recent information about the IA. The Beta 2 IA does not offer complete functionality. In particular, there is a Post to Web function that's intended to enable you to post the output HTML file (SCHEDULE.HTM) to a Web server. Although the installation process places the associated menu item in the Schedule+ menu, the capability is not implemented in Beta 2.

N O T E Microsoft does not appear intent on updating the beta IA for Schedule+, and the IA available on the Microsoft download site was still in beta form as of August 1997. This is because Schedule+ has been superseded by Microsoft Outlook in Office 97. ▪

To uninstall the Schedule+ IA, use Add/Remove Programs in the Control Panel. Click the Windows Taskbar Start button, choose Settings, and select Control Panel from the cascading menu. In the Control Panel window, double-click Add/Remove Programs. Select Microsoft Schedule+ Internet Assistant (Remove Only) from the list box and choose Add/Remove.

Installing the Access IA

Installing the Access IA is only slightly more complicated than installing the Schedule+ IA. Have Access installed, but not running, when you double-click the Access IA's installation program (IA95.EXE).

The installation process starts the familiar Setup routine. You are asked to confirm that you want to install the Access IA, and that you accept the terms and conditions of the end user license agreement. A Setup message box appears with an Install button. After you click the button, the required files are made available to Access. Now you only need to start Access.

To uninstall the Access IA, follow the same Add/Remove Programs procedure as for the Schedule+ IA (see the prior section, Installing the Schedule+ IA).

Running the Schedule+ IA

After the Schedule+ IA installs, a new item, Internet Assistant, appears in the Schedule+ File menu. When you choose File, Internet Assistant, the dialog box shown in Figure 37.1 appears.

FIG. 37.1
When you choose to publish *times and descriptions*, the Include Private appointments check box becomes enabled.

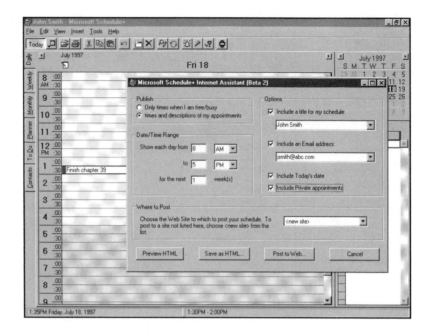

The dialog box, as shown in Figure 37.1, includes all the options that are available to you in the Schedule+ IA. These options have the effects that are described next.

Publishing Schedule+ Items

In the Schedule+ IA dialog box, you can choose to display whether you are free or busy at each date and time, or display the appointment descriptions for each date and time. If you choose Only times when I am free/busy, the resulting HTML shows the word Busy for any day and time that you are unavailable. Otherwise, the HTML shows that day and time as blank. Figure 37.2 displays the result of choosing this option.

You would, of course, choose the times only option if you wanted to keep some information from appearing in the HTML file—all it shows is that you're busy.

If you choose times and descriptions of my appointments, the HTML shows the appointment description. The description shown is the one that's entered in the Appointment Book, not the description that's in the associated To-Do entry. Figure 37.3 illustrates this distinction.

Notice in Figure 37.3 that the To-Do list's description for October 11 shows an appointment with a doctor. The Appointment Book merely indicates that the user is off-site from 10:00 A.M. until noon, and it is this description that appears in the HTML file.

Specifying a Date/Time Range

Use the Date/Time group box in the Schedule+ IA's dialog box (refer to Figure 37.1) to specify which hours of each day are displayed in the HTML file, and how many weeks ahead to display. The more hours you choose, the longer the file—there is one table row for each hour. And, of course, the more weeks you specify, the longer the file.

FIG. 37.2

Choosing to publish times only suppresses details that you might want to keep private in the HTML output.

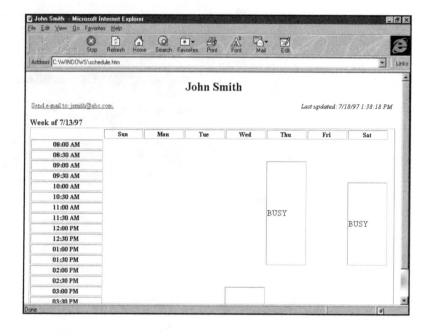

FIG. 37.3

The HTML shows Off site, not Doctor's appointment.

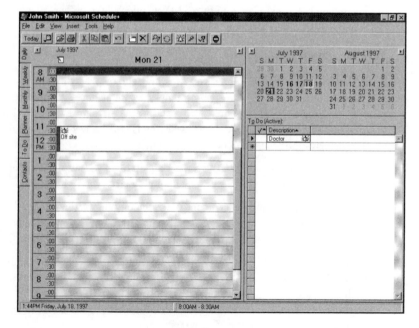

TIP On occasion, you might see this error message: Error updating file C:\Windows\Schedule.htm! You may need to reinstall. If you do, before you reinstall the IA, make sure that you have entered a valid range of times of day. In Beta 2, you would receive this message if you specify, for example, 8 A.M. as both a "from" time and a "to" time.

Figure 37.4 shows how the HTML file appears if you display 8:00 A.M. to 10:00 A.M., and how it appears if you display 8:00 A.M. to 12:00 P.M.

FIG. 37.4
Choosing 10:00 A.M. as an ending time displays appointments beginning through 9:30 A.M.

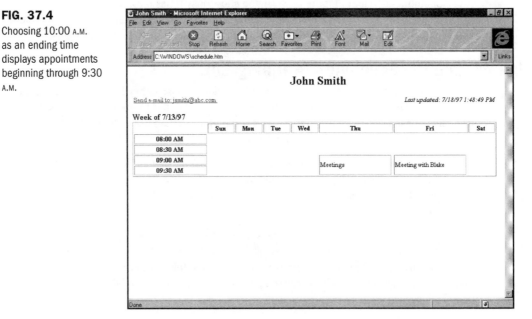

 TIP Keep in mind that Schedule+ and its IA both treat 12:00 P.M. as noon, and 12:00 A.M. as midnight.

Setting Other Options

Fill the Include a Title for My Schedule check box if you want the HTML file to have a title. This is a convenient way to display your name in the file, so users who are browsing it can easily determine whose schedule it is.

If your e-mail address makes your identity self-evident, you could save a small amount of file space and a useful amount of screen space by omitting the title. Fill the Include an Email Address check box to put a mailto tag in the HTML file.

The Beta 2 version of the Schedule+ IA associates no functionality with the Include Today's date check box.

Clearing the Include Private Appointments check box is a useful way to suppress the details of any appointments that you might have flagged as Private. To make an appointment Private, select the appointment and choose Edit, Private; or, press Ctrl+Shift+P.

If you have cleared the Include Private Appointments check box, any private appointments display as Busy in the HTML file. This is a good way to display the appointment description for most appointments.

Recall that you can choose to show either the times that you are busy, or a description of a given appointment (refer to Figure 37.3). If you show busy times only, no appointment descriptions are given. If you choose to show appointment descriptions, you can still clear the Include Private Appointments check box to suppress the descriptions of private appointments.

Completing the Schedule+ IA Dialog Box

When you have made your choices in the IA dialog box, choose either Preview HTML or Save as HTML. As noted at the beginning of this chapter, Beta 2 of the IA does not enable you automatically to post a schedule directly to a Web server. Rather than using the Post to Web button, it's necessary to post the schedule manually.

Choose the Preview HTML button to save the HTML in a file named SCHEDULE.HTM. Beta 2 of the IA saves the file in your Windows folder. The IA then invokes your Web Browser so that you can view the output file. This means, of course, that you must have a Web browser installed on your computer.

After previewing the output, make any changes you want to the options you have chosen. Choose the Save as HTML button to save the output HTML file. A standard Save As dialog box appears, to enable you to name the file and navigate to the folder where you want to save it. After saving the file, provide it to your Web administrator so that it can be posted to the appropriate Web server.

Running the Access IA

After you install the IA for Access, invoke it by choosing Tools, Add-Ins and choose Internet Assistant from the cascading menu. You need to have a database open before the Add-Ins menu item is available. This section demonstrates the use of the IA by means of the Northwind Traders sample database that accompanies Access.

The Access IA works by means of a four-step wizard—a sequence of dialog boxes to specify options. The steps you take to complete the wizard are the same regardless of the type of information to output.

When you choose Tools, Add-Ins, Internet Assistant, a welcome screen identifying the IA appears. No input is required, so choose Next. The next step appears as shown in Figure 37.5.

FIG. 37.5
The <u>N</u>ext and <u>F</u>inish buttons become available after you choose at least one <u>O</u>bject Name.

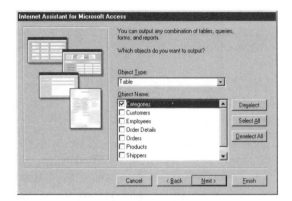

The step shown in Figure 37.5 is how you specify the information to output to HTML format. It is a complex step, and this chapter covers it in greater detail in the next section, "Specifying the Access Output." For now, notice two aspects of the dialog box:

■ **The Object <u>T</u>ype drop-down list box** Table is the currently selected object type, but the drop-down list box also enables you to select Query, Form, Report, and All. They are not mutually exclusive choices so you can decide to output both queries and forms during the same instance of the IA.

■ **The <u>O</u>bject Name list box** Because Table is the currently selected object type, the names of the tables defined for the database appear in the list box. If *Query* is the selected object type, the names of all defined queries appear in the <u>O</u>bject Name list box.

Any tables, queries, forms, or reports that you create in the database are accessible by means of the combination of the Object <u>T</u>ype drop-down list box and the <u>O</u>bject Name list box.

After you select an object name, click <u>N</u>ext. (You could also click <u>F</u>inish to accept the defaults for remaining options and complete the wizard.) The next step appears as shown in Figure 37.6.

FIG. 37.6
In this step, you can choose an existing template or elect to use no template.

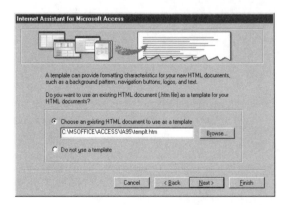

The Access IA comes with several templates. The default template, named TEMPLT.HTM, adds little more than a title and a logo to the database information that the IA outputs. Other templates, such as STONES.HTM and SKY.HTM, provide different background patterns for the HTML output files.

Each template that accompanies the Access IA has another version, identified by an underscore and the letter "r" (for *report*): an example is TEMPLT_R.HTM. These report templates provide linked hypertext to enable the user to go to the Next, Previous, First, and Final pages.

Each template also places the Access logo (MSACCESS.JPG, and supplied with the IA) at the bottom of each HTML page. If you want to display a different logo on the HTML output, change the reference to MSACCESS.JPG in the templates to the name of some other graphic file. Store that graphic file in the same folder that contains the templates.

If, in the wizard's second step, you choose the Report Object Type, the IA automatically uses a report template with the linked hypertext. Suppose that you decide to output both a table and a report, and specify TEMPLT.HTM as the template. The IA uses TEMPLT.HTM for the table output, and TEMPLT_R.HTM for the report output. When a report template is used, the HTML file includes the linked hypertext to navigate from page to page even if the IA creates only one page.

When you have made your template choice in this step, click Next. The final step, shown in Figure 37.7, appears.

FIG. 37.7
All you need do in this step is specify a location for the output HTML files.

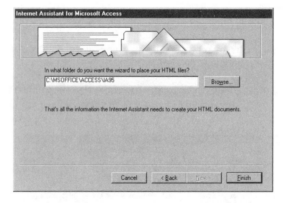

If you click the Browse button, the HTML documents folder dialog box enables you to navigate to the site where you want to store the output. Once you have identified a site for the HTML files, click Finish.

If you decide to save the HTML files in a different location than is proposed by the IA, be sure to put a JPEG-format file named MSACCESS.JPG in the destination folder. Otherwise, the HTML output displays a missing file placeholder instead of the logo.

When you click Finish, a message box appears and keeps you posted on the IA's progress if your output contains multiple pages. A counter shows which output page is being built. This is a convenient way to tell how many pages each HTML file contains. There is at least one file for each object type that you selected, and an object type that contains page breaks results in multiple files—one per page.

NOTE If you create, in the same folder, more than one file based on the same object name, the Access IA gives the files an incremental index. For example, three HTML files based on the Employees table would be named EMPLOYEES.HTM, EMPLOYEES1.HTM, and EMPLOYEES2.HTM. ■

Part VII

Ch 37

Specifying the Access Output

Here's a closer look at how the Access IA wizard's second step works. In the second step, you choose the type of database object—table, query, form, or report—as the basis for the HTML files. The resulting HTML files differ according to the choice you made in the wizard's second step.

Selecting a Table for Output

Suppose that you choose to output the contents of a database table, and the table you want is the Northwind database's Customers table. In the second step, you would select Table from the Object Type drop-down list box, and you would fill the Customers check box in the Object Name list box. Figure 37.8 shows a portion of the resulting HTML file.

FIG. 37.8
The Access IA presents the information from an Access table in a simple table format.

Customers - Microsoft Internet Explorer

Address C:\MSOffice\Access\IA95\Customers.htm

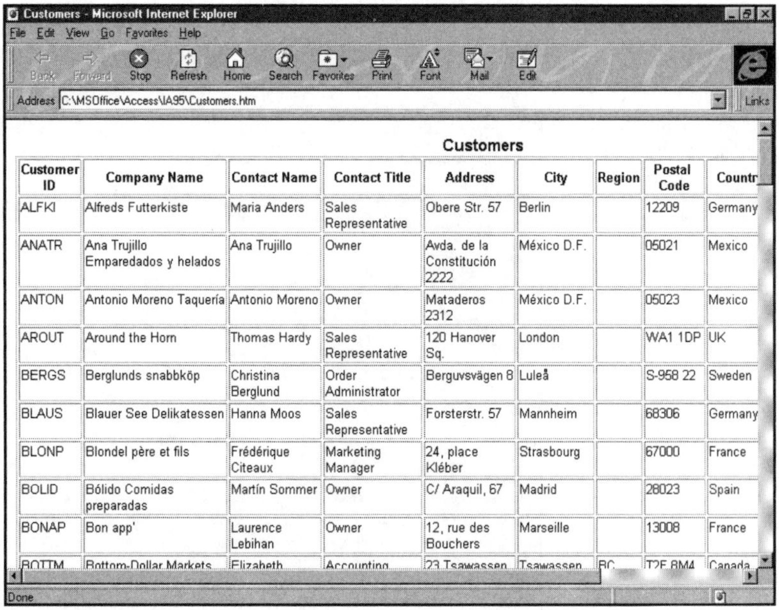

Customers

Customer ID	Company Name	Contact Name	Contact Title	Address	City	Region	Postal Code	Countr
ALFKI	Alfreds Futterkiste	Maria Anders	Sales Representative	Obere Str. 57	Berlin		12209	Germany
ANATR	Ana Trujillo Emparedados y helados	Ana Trujillo	Owner	Avda. de la Constitución 2222	México D.F.		05021	Mexico
ANTON	Antonio Moreno Taquería	Antonio Moreno	Owner	Mataderos 2312	México D.F.		05023	Mexico
AROUT	Around the Horn	Thomas Hardy	Sales Representative	120 Hanover Sq.	London		WA1 1DP	UK
BERGS	Berglunds snabbköp	Christina Berglund	Order Administrator	Berguvsvägen 8	Luleå		S-958 22	Sweden
BLAUS	Blauer See Delikatessen	Hanna Moos	Sales Representative	Forsterstr. 57	Mannheim		68306	Germany
BLONP	Blondel père et fils	Frédérique Citeaux	Marketing Manager	24, place Kléber	Strasbourg		67000	France
BOLID	Bólido Comidas preparadas	Martín Sommer	Owner	C/ Araquil, 67	Madrid		28023	Spain
BONAP	Bon app'	Laurence Lebihan	Owner	12, rue des Bouchers	Marseille		13008	France
BOTTM	Bottom-Dollar Markets	Elizabeth	Accounting	23 Tsawassen	Tsawassen	BC	T2F 8M4	Canada

Done

Because the default template, TEMPLT.HTM, was used in Figure 37.8, the HTML file contains no hyperlinks—just the table itself and the Access logo.

Selecting a Query for Output

Now, suppose that you filled the check box for the Customers table, and then selected Query from the Object Type drop-down list box and Quarterly Orders by Product from the Object Name list box (see Figure 37.9).

FIG. 37.9

Choosing to output a Query often invokes the relational database's table-linking capability.

When you click Finish, the Access IA outputs the two files that you specified: one for the Customers table, and one for the crosstab query Quarterly Orders by Product. A portion of the Query output is shown in Figure 37.10.

FIG. 37.10

HTML output is most useful when it provides summaries of the underlying details.

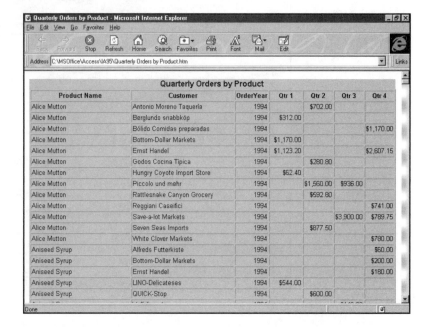

Quarterly Orders by Product

Product Name	Customer	OrderYear	Qtr 1	Qtr 2	Qtr 3	Qtr 4
Alice Mutton	Antonio Moreno Taquería	1994		$702.00		
Alice Mutton	Berglunds snabbköp	1994	$312.00			
Alice Mutton	Bólido Comidas preparadas	1994				$1,170.00
Alice Mutton	Bottom-Dollar Markets	1994	$1,170.00			
Alice Mutton	Ernst Handel	1994	$1,123.20			$2,607.15
Alice Mutton	Godos Cocina Típica	1994		$280.80		
Alice Mutton	Hungry Coyote Import Store	1994	$62.40			
Alice Mutton	Piccolo und mehr	1994		$1,560.00	$936.00	
Alice Mutton	Rattlesnake Canyon Grocery	1994		$592.80		
Alice Mutton	Reggiani Caseifici	1994				$741.00
Alice Mutton	Save-a-lot Markets	1994			$3,900.00	$789.75
Alice Mutton	Seven Seas Imports	1994		$877.50		
Alice Mutton	White Clover Markets	1994				$780.00
Aniseed Syrup	Alfreds Futterkiste	1994				$60.00
Aniseed Syrup	Bottom-Dollar Markets	1994				$200.00
Aniseed Syrup	Ernst Handel	1994				$180.00
Aniseed Syrup	LINO-Delicateses	1994	$544.00			
Aniseed Syrup	QUICK-Stop	1994		$600.00		

Notice in Figure 37.10 that the conditions set up by the query are maintained in the HTML output. For example, this domain aggregate function:

```
ProductAmount: Sum(CCur([Order Details].[UnitPrice]*[Quantity]*(1-[Discount]))/
100)*100)
```

is used in the Quarterly Orders by Product query to calculate the order value of each record in the Order Details table. The resulting values are then summarized, in crosstab fashion, by Product, by Customer, by Year, and by Quarter.

Selecting a Report for Output

If you were to choose Report in the Object Type drop-down list, and Employee Sales by Country in the Object Name list box, you would observe two differences in the IA's behavior:

- When the output process begins, you see two input boxes: one for you to enter a beginning date, and one to enter an ending date. These are in response to the requirements of the Employee Sales by Country report's design. This report uses a dialog box form to request that the user specify the date criteria that the report should use to select the desired records.

- The report design calls for page headers and footers. When the report generates a new page, the IA closes the current HTML file and begins another. You see a progress report on your screen as each new file is created.Because the Object Type is a report, the IA uses a report template. Report templates add hyperlink text to the HTML files so that the user can navigate through the pages (see Figure 37.11).

FIG. 37.11
Consider replacing the Microsoft Access logo with one that represents your own firm.

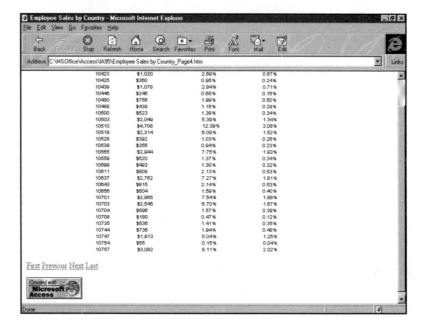

If you find it inconvenient to move back and forth between the Object Type drop-down list and the Object Name list box, begin by choosing All from the Object Type drop-down list. The Object Name list box now includes each of the tables, queries, forms, and reports available in the database. Fill in the check boxes associated with each object that you want to export to an HTML file.

The most visually complex HTML output usually results from exporting a report object type. Notice the special formatting in Figure 37.12 that illustrates the output of the Invoice report in the Northwind sample database. The HTML file employs the fonts and patterns that the designer used to create the report.

FIG. 37.12
Use Access reports to create visually interesting formats, such as italic and font colors.

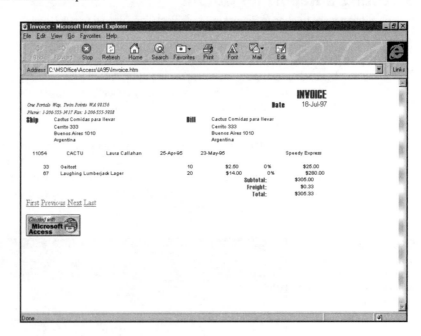

Although the Access IA can handle a report's fonts and patterns, it does not output certain special elements—lines and control borders, for example, or charts and pivot tables created in Excel—that you might have included in your database design and contents.

For example, the Northwind database includes bitmap pictures of the company employees. Although HTML output based on a database element that includes the picture field contains a placeholder for the picture, the pictures themselves are not output. You can, however, modify the resulting HTML to reference the associated bitmap files.

Selecting a Form for Output

Some care is needed when you decide to convert an Access Form to HTML format. Some of the forms contain no information, and the resulting HTML files therefore include nothing of value.

The Northwind sample database includes, among others, forms named Customer Labels dialog box, Sales by Year dialog box, and Sales Reports dialog box. If you choose to convert any of these to HTML format, the IA reports successful completion. If you open the HTML file, however, you find nothing of interest. This is because these forms are used by other elements in the database that *do* contain information.

For example, to use the Sales by Year dialog box, you must be previewing or printing the Sales by Year Report. You are alerted to this if you run the Sales by Year dialog box in Access—but not if you are attempting to output the Sales by Year dialog box with the Access IA.

Similarly, if you attempt to output the Sales Analysis form, you obtain an HTML page with nothing but the logo shown. The Sales Analysis form is an Excel pivot table, and, as just noted, the Access IA cannot output pivot tables. (In this case, you would use the Excel IA to obtain HTML output of the pivot table.)

If you try to create HTML files from Access forms, be sure that you know what's in the form. Using the Access IA to create HTML output willy-nilly is liable to create meaningless files.

From Here...

As the end of the book approaches, you can:

- Go on to the next chapter, which covers the Microsoft Internet Information Server, as well as other servers that can be used with FrontPage 98.
- Skip ahead to Part IX, "Advanced Database Connectivity," to learn about making databases communicate with FrontPage Webs.
- Use the appendixes, where you'll find useful information about FrontPage resources on the World Wide Web, plus references for HTML, VBScript, and JavaScript.

Using Other Servers with FrontPage 98

## CHAPTER 38

Using FrontPage with Microsoft Internet Information Server

For larger-scale Web implementations, Microsoft's Internet Information Server, combined with Windows NT Server, provides a comprehensive Web server solution. Combined with FrontPage, IIS allows you excellent content creation and management abilities. ■

The Microsoft Internet Information Server

The Microsoft Internet Information Server is compatible with FrontPage through server-side extensions.

Download the Internet Information Server

Download the right version for your machine.

Install the FrontPage extensions

Server extensions extend the ability of your FrontPage Webs to utilize FrontPage Components on a robust server.

Administer the Internet Information Server

Configure IIS to work the way you need it to.

Control IIS remotely via the WWW

Adjust Web settings and monitor activity in the Internet Service Manager across the Internet.

Up and Running with the Internet Information Server

The Personal Web Server included with FrontPage is great for serving out a few documents a day to the world or your friends. But what if you needed to serve hundreds of thousands of requests a day while still retaining all of your FrontPage-specific features like the FrontPage Components? Enter the Microsoft Internet Information Server.

In early 1996, Microsoft announced the release of the Internet Information Sever 1.0. What caught the world by surprise was the fact that the new Web server would be absolutely free and available for downloading from the Internet. The Internet Information Server promised ease of use, advanced security features, and scalability between multiple servers and across a network. While the server software runs only in Windows NT Server, and thus requires a copy of that operating system to run, it provides a cheaper alternative to other Web server software ranging from $500.00 to $5,000.00.

On the face of it, Microsoft has gone to great lengths to become a leader in the field of Web servers, and IIS 3.0 and 4.0 are indeed highly advanced server solutions. By making IIS free, and additionally a fully featured and powerful piece of software, the company has raised the level on which Web server expectations are created. Bundling the Internet Information Server with NT 4.0, Server and Workstation puts a complete Web serving solution in the hands of everyone who can author one line of HTML.

Of course, skepticism in this regard is only natural, since it's hard to figure out why Microsoft is giving this product away. The answer, obviously, is to compete with their rival, Netscape, whose main business is server software. You also have to take a hard look at the actual cost of an IIS-based Web server machine, since it's necessary to license NT Server—not the less expensive NT Workstation—to use IIS in the first place. But still, a freebie is a freebie, and a powerful freebie is even better. Maybe it's just not wise to look a relative gift horse in the mouth, even when that mouth happens to belong to the richest man in the U.S.

N O T E Don't confuse NT Server and IIS Web server. NT Server is a flavor of Microsoft's Windows NT operating system. NT Server is a richly endowed operating system and, as such, carries a richly endowed price tag. IIS is Microsoft's major Web server, which runs on NT. As with Internet Explorer, Microsoft provides Internet Information free of charge, hoping to gain the lion's share of the Internet browser and server markets. ■

Obtaining and Installing the Server

To obtain the Internet Information Server (IIS), go to **http://www.microsoft.com/iis/ default.htm** and follow the links to the download area. You'll typically find a release version (3.0 as of this writing) and an in-progress beta version (4.0 as of this version). The beta version is always the most advanced product, but it's also unfinished (which is what *beta* means in software-speak), so it's not reliable. If you want to experiment with the newest technologies, use the in-progress beta, but if you want the highest degree of stability, go with the release version.

Once you download the software, you should return to the Microsoft site regularly, to see if any upgrades have been posted. Often these are in the form of *service packs*, which is a nice term for bug fixes and the addition of features that should have been there in the first place.

Whether beta or not, IIS can be downloaded at no cost, although you'll probably be asked to fill in a series of truly annoying forms. See, there isn't actually any such thing as a free lunch (or server, in this case). You have to provide Microsoft with what, for them, is valuable marketing information.

Internet Information Server, like FrontPage itself, is built into the Windows NT Server operating system (starting with version 4.0). You will find the option to install the server software when you install Windows NT onto your system, or by adding the component under Network in Control Panel. When the program is finished installing, you will have a new group set up called Internet Information Server where you can access the Internet Service Manager and product documentation.

 T I P A special note to Windows NT Workstation 4.0 users: The Internet Information Server is also integrated into NT Workstation. Microsoft refers to the server as Peer Web Services and gears the product toward corporate intranets, or anywhere that information needs to be served from in a small-scale environment. All of the functionality of the Internet Information Server is included with Peer Web Services, although it is not as optimized for file throughput as machines running NT Server. In fact, even advanced features such as Web-based administration and remote use of the Internet Service Manager through Windows 95 are included.

Installing the FrontPage Extensions

Microsoft created the Internet Information Server with extensibility in mind. The server can easily be upgraded to host other Internet servers such as FTP, Gopher, and the new suite of add-on servers such as the Microsoft Commerce. One of the first add-on releases for the Internet Information Server was the FrontPage Web bot extensions (now called FrontPage Components). These extensions allow for all of FrontPage's components to be scaled to the IIS server and retain all of their functionality. FrontPage's extensions also allow for remote uploading of Web content to a secure NT Server. A FrontPage author must have Administrator permissions on the NT Server before the files can be uploaded. Once the user submits his username and password, the authentication process checks the user's identity against the User Manager and will reject any user that does not have a valid account.

You must have both FrontPage and its IIS extensions installed onto the Web server to make full use of IIS. Fortunately, the FrontPage installation program makes this easy by recognizing the IIS server automatically and installing the extensions accordingly. If for any reason you need to install the server extensions afterwards, or to update them, load the Server Administrator (the shortcut can be found by default in C:\Program Files\Microsoft FrontPage\) and click the Install or the Upgrade button.

If you are installing only the FrontPage extensions, the installation process will be very brief. Once installed, the Server Administrator will start, displaying the installed ports that the

FrontPage extensions reside in, as well as giving you options for setting up security for authoring and adding extensions to new FrontPage Webs (see Figure 38.1).

 T I P When you install or upgrade the server extensions, FrontPage temporarily shuts down NT's Web service. This means that visitors to your Web will not be able to access it. If you have a busy Web, therefore, restrict the installation or upgrade to off-peak hours.

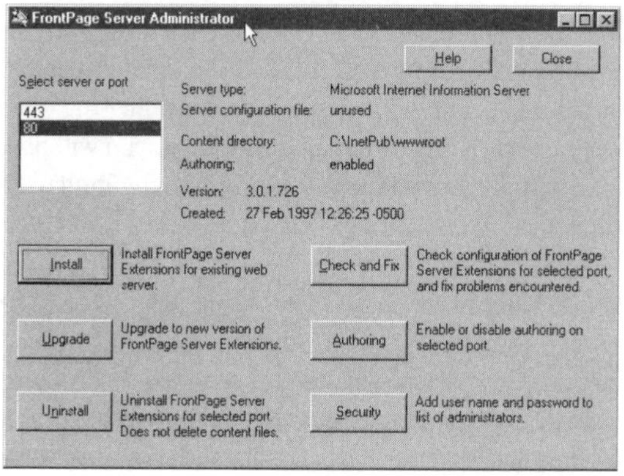

FIG. 38.1
The FrontPage Server Administrator allows you to control the FrontPage extensions on your Web server and set security permissions.

The Server Administrator will always show Port 80 as your default Web address. This essentially means that the base IP address for your machine has the FrontPage extensions loaded on the Web server found at Port 80. If the machine has multiple IP addresses assigned to the Network card, you will see additional addresses below Port 80. Additional IP addresses can be added to your server in Network which is found in Control Panel. By default, Windows NT can hold up to five separate IP addresses and bind them to one card. In actuality, hundreds of IP addresses can be bound to the network card through editing of the System Registry. Documentation for adding IP addresses to the System Registry can be found in Microsoft's Knowledge Base at **http://www.microsoft.com/kb/bussys/winnt/q149426.htm**. Do not change any System Registry settings unless you know exactly what you are doing. One minor change to the Registry can cause a system to fail to start when rebooted.

When the server extensions are installed, FrontPage adds several hidden folders (their names begin with an underscore) to the root folder of your Web. It is recommended that you do not modify this directory structure, or any of the files contained within it. These directories and their respective files are used for the FrontPage extensions and for security settings. If any of these files or directories are modified, it can lead to server instability.

Configuring the Internet Information Server

The Internet Information Server is configured through the Internet Service Manager. The Internet Service Manager holds all of the Microsoft Internet server components, including WWW, FTP, and Gopher (see Figure 38.2). This centralized way of containing the different servers provides a uniform way of running services, monitoring servers, and configuring the different options.

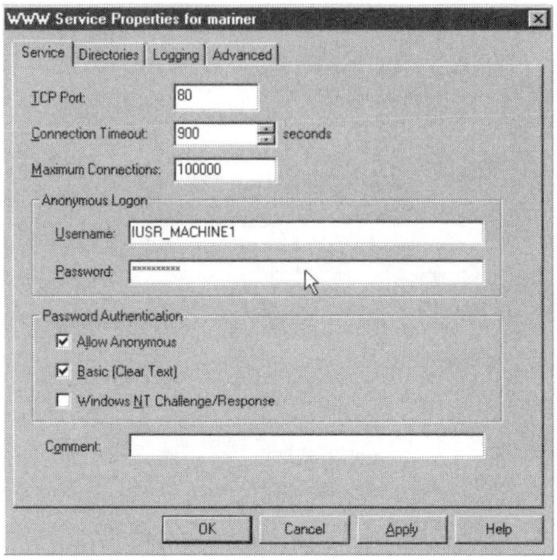

FIG. 38.2

The Internet Service Manager controls every aspect of the Internet servers installed on your local machine and across the network.

All of your Internet services should be currently running. If not, highlight the server that you want to start and click the Start Service button on the toolbar at the top of the Internet Service Manager.

To administer the WWW server component, begin by double-clicking the WWW Service. The WWW Service Properties for your machine will open, allowing you to administer changes on your Web server.

The Service Properties window contains tabs for each of the configuration screens: Service, Directories, Login, and Advanced. Examining each of these screens in more detail will help you gain a better understanding of the customizable functions.

You can also install the Internet Services Manager to operate through your Web browser (see Figure 38.3). This offers a somewhat more attractive interface, but the functionality is identical. It is your choice.

The Service Window

The Service window is made up of two main components: connection settings and access authentication. The connection settings determine which port the Web server is running on, as well as limits for connection times and maximum connections. The access authentication settings allow you to specify which system account will be used for anonymous access and which type of authentication schemes to use.

Connection Settings The TCP Port is normally set to Port 80, the standard Port for HTTP. You can change the port number, although standard settings are generally fine. You will have to restart your server after modifying port changes.

FIG. 38.3

The Internet Service Manager controls every aspect of the Internet servers installed on your local machine and across the network.

Connection Timeout refers to the amount of time that the server will wait until it disconnects a connected user with no activity. Although the HTTP protocol generally closes the TCP/IP connection after the requested document is served, the connection timeout ensures that all clients will be disconnected if the protocol fails to close properly.

Maximum connections places a limit on the number of connections that the Web server will try to serve simultaneously. If you have a high volume Web site, placing limits on maximum connections can help to stabilize the server in case it encounters too many requests for information. Monitoring the memory and processor usage with the Performance Monitor will help you judge the number of simultaneous users your Web server can handle.

Access Authentication   By default, the Anonymous user uses an account set up in the User Manager called IUSR_computername. This account was generated with a random password upon installation; make changes to the password in the User Manager as well as in the Internet Service Manager. If you choose to restrict access to your Web server, you do so by adding a different account into the Anonymous Logon region. Note that if you restrict access, it restricts users globally, and only those users who know the Username and Password of the WWW account will be allowed access. Restricting access to only a portion of your Web site is obtained through the FrontPage Explorer's Security features, or by changing the access rights for a directory in Explorer or File Manager. Note that, in this way, FrontPage 98 is integrated directly with both IIS and NT 4.0 security features.

Choose the correct authentication process under Password Authentication. If you allow anonymous users, there will be no authentication. Basic authentication can be used by most browsers and should be implemented when you want to restrict access other than by NT's built-in security mechanisms. Windows NT Challenge/Response should be used when directories of

files from the Web site have been restricted to accounts in the NT Domain. All NT Challenge/
Response logons are encrypted and, therefore, kept protected from hackers. You must choose
at least one type of Authentication to allow users to log onto your Web site.

The Comments line allows you to enter a description of your Web server that will appear next
to the service's name within the Internet Service Manager.

The Directories Window

The Directories Window contains settings for mapping directories to the Web, setting directory permissions, and general Web server properties (see Figure 38.4).

FIG. 38.4

The Directories Window
maps out file system
directories that will be
accessed by Internet
visitors.

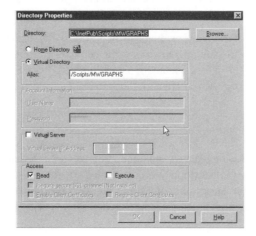

Part
VIII

Ch
38

The Directory Listing Box   In the Directory listing box, a mapped directory is shown next to
its Web alias. For example, if you had an area on your Web called Technical Support, you could
map a directory called c:\techsup to an alias called /techsup. This would make it possible for a
user to type in the name of your Web server followed by the Web alias and reach the Technical
Support area (**http://www.yourserver/techsup/**).

To install a new Web alias, begin by clicking the Add button.

1. Choose the Browse button to search your file system for the correct directory that you
   want to alias. Click OK to make your selection.

2. Choose Virtual Directory to enter an alias.

3. Determine whether the directory needs executable access for CGI scripts and make the
   appropriate choice.

4. Choose OK to complete the aliasing process.

It is also possible to map a directory to a virtual IP address. This is useful when you want to
host multiple domains on your Web server instead of a dedicated server for each Web site. If
you have more than one IP address bound to your network card, choosing Home directory will
allow you to map the alias of an IP address by specifying it within the Directory Properties.

This allows you to give the IP address a name in your Domain Name Server such as **http://Web2.domain.com** and have it answer as if it were a stand-alone server.

To remove a mapped Web directory, simply highlight the specific directory and choose the Remove button. All traces of the original alias are gone and cannot be restored unless you enter all of the information again.

Default Documents and Directory Browsing   The Default Document refers to the document name that the Web site needs to contain to open up to a Web page correctly when the machine's address is entered into a Web browser. The default document name is default.htm. This means that if your URL is **http://www.domain.com**, you must have a document titled default.htm in your root Web directory or the user will be returned the HTTP 404 error message stating that the document is not found.

Directory browsing is useful when providing lists of downloadable files from the Web. Placing a check mark in the box will allow anyone to view the contents of a directory that does not contain a document with the default document name. For safety's sake, it's best to leave Directory browsing unchecked unless you are sure that you want a user to see all of the contents of your directories.

The Logging Window

The Logging window allows the Web site administrator access to the advanced logging features built into the Internet Information Server. Log files are important for spotting trends in Web site access, calculating the number of visitors, and effectiveness of different Web site areas (see Figure 38.5). A straight log file is written in a comma-delimited format which can be easily imported into your favorite database.

FIG. 38.5

Logging WWW activity can produce informative feedback about your Web site such as which pages are most effective, and how many visitors your Web site serves out documents to.

There are two major ways of logging activity. You can configure the server to write to a text-based log file, or directly to a SQL/ODBC-compliant database.

Logging to a File   Log files can be written in two different formats: NCSA and Standard. The NCSA log file is considered to be the standard among Web servers around the world. Many programs have been written to interpret NCSA log file results, providing detailed statistics and graphs. The Standard log file format is Microsoft's standard way of writing log files in Windows NT. Both types of log files are easily imported into databases or interpreted by simple parsing tools.

The Internet Information Server can log files daily, weekly, monthly, or to a specific file size. For a high-traffic site, these files can easily be 10 megabytes a day. When setting up file logging, it's important to remember that parsing programs and databases can choke on very large files. It's probably best to generate log files on a daily or weekly basis for the best performance.

The default location that Windows NT uses for all of its log files is C:\WINNT\System32\LogFiles. Grouping all system log files together ensures that you will not have to hunt around the entire Web server to find the information you are looking for. The WWW log files are identified by the prefix INyymmww, where yy is years, mm is months, and ww is weeks. If you choose daily reports, the file will begin with the prefix Inmmwwdd where dd is the day of the week.

Logging to a Database   If you choose to log directly to a SQL/ODBC database, you'll be happy to know that you can use any ODBC-compliant database you want. Databases ranging in scale from Access to SQL Server can all be used easily. The database must be registered with the ODBC component in the Control Panel.

To begin logging Web site access directly to a database:

1. Enter the ODBC Data Source Name (DSN). This must be the DSN that is registered to the database you want to use in the ODBC section of the Control Panel.

2. Enter the name of the table you want to log to under Table. This must be the exact name of the database table. For integrity's sake, use a case-sensitive format.

3. Enter the Username and Password of the account set up to access the database. The WWW log file will not be allowed to write to the database table unless it is granted permission through authentication.

Once the log file is captured to a database, the raw data can be easily formatted into Queries for information retrieval.

The Advanced Window

The Advanced Window gives you the option of restricting access to specific IP addresses on the Internet. This is useful for blocking suspicious Web addresses from the Web server completely, or publishing an intranet on the Internet and keeping visitors out (see Figure 38.6).

To block users from accessing your site:

1. Click the Add button to access the security controls.

2. Enter the IP address of the machine that you want to deny access to.

3. Click OK to deny access.

FIG. 38.6
Blocking access through
IP address will secure
your site from unwanted
visitors.

For blocking access to a range of machines:

1. Enter the block of IP addresses that you want to block in the following format:
   `127.0.0.*`

2. Enter the Subnet Mask of the range of IP addresses like the following:
   `255.255.255.0`

3. Click OK to finish the restricting process.

If you want the default Web server function to deny access to all computers except those that you specify, click the Deny Access button. By choosing this feature, you will have to manually enter individual or groups of IP address that can access the Web site. This would be useful in an intranet situation where you might want remote salespersons to have the ability to reach online company resources.

Finally, by placing a check in the Limit Network Use box, you can place a limit on the amount of network activity generated by Internet services on your machine. This is best utilized when your internal network will route for the Internet server and you want to reduce the overall amount of Internet network traffic.

Integrating FrontPage and IIS

Using the Internet Information Server as the back end for your FrontPage Webs is a robust solution for scalable Web-serving needs. The Internet Information Server provides a set of high-performance, secure, comprehensive HTTP services.

To create a site using FrontPage on the Internet Information Server, follow these steps:

1. Create a directory on your server where you want the Web site housed.

2. Open the Internet Service Manager, double-click the server you want to modify, and choose the Directories Tab.

3. Click Add to access the Directory Properties.

4. Click the Browse button and locate the desired directory. Choose OK.

5. Enter the name of the Virtual Directory. Click OK to finish.

If you want to create a virtual Web server:

1. Open Network in Control Panel and assign a new IP address to your server. You will have to know the Subnet Mast to complete the addressing successfully.

2. Restart the server for the new IP address to be bound to your server.

3. Once the server is restarted, access Directory Properties within the Internet Service Manager for the machine you want to modify.

4. Click Add to access the Directory Properties.

5. Click the Browse button and locate the desired directory. Choose OK.

6. Click the Home Directory option box to create a mapped root directory to your new Web site.

7. Place a check in Virtual Server and enter the new IP address for the Web site. Click OK to close the Directory Properties. Choose OK again to close the Internet Service Manager Properties.

8. Open the FrontPage Server Administrator. Choose the Install button to install the FrontPage extensions on the new IP address.

9. Choose Microsoft Internet Information Server from the drop-down menu. Click OK.

10. Enter the new IP address in the Multi-Homed section. Click OK. When the confirmation window appears, verify the information and choose Install.

The FrontPage Server Administrator will take a few minutes to install the extensions for your new Web site. Once completed, you will be able to log in to the new virtual server as you would any other.

HTML Administration

Both of the 4.0 versions of NT Server and NT Workstation come with a feature for remote Web server administration from a Web browser. The browser does not have to be Internet Explorer or Netscape Navigator. Any HTML-compliant Web browser with the ability to authenticate users can be used for administration.

The default URL for administering the Internet Information Server is **http:// www.domain.com/iisadmin/default.htm**.

To administer to Web server, simply click the WWW button and enter your Username and Password. Note that you must log on with an account that has Administrator privileges. Any other account will not grant you access.

All of the functionality of administering your Web server is contained within these Web pages, with the exception of starting and stopping Internet services. You now have the ability to remotely alias Web directories and create new Web sites, without laying a finger on the keyboard of the server.

Part VIII
Ch
38

From Here...

In this chapter, you learned how to utilize Microsoft's Internet Information Server for robust serving of your FrontPage Webs. Microsoft's IIS, in conjunction with the FrontPage server extensions, creates a powerful Web-serving environment with advanced security functions and logging capabilities. To learn more about advanced serving environments and added database functions, read the following:

- Chapter 39, "Using NonMicrosoft Servers," describes how to use FrontPage server extensions with other popular Web servers, such as Website by O'Reilly and the Fast Track series by Netscape.

- Chapter 40, "Custom Database Query Scripts," examines further database integration within FrontPage.

Using NonMicrosoft Servers

Microsoft includes two servers with the FrontPage 98 package, and FrontPage 98 is designed expressly to work well with the company's major Web server, the Internet Information Server (covered in Chapter 38, "Using FrontPage with Microsoft Internet Information Server"). But, you don't have to use the server that Microsoft provides. A wide variety of additional servers is available for use, and some are extremely popular among Webmasters. A number of them will be covered here. ■

Server Basics

Web server software is a software package that, when installed on a computer (the host system), lets the computer operate as a World Wide Web site or intranet Web server. What this means is that the computer will now support HTTP, officially known as Hypertext Transport Protocol. This protocol effects the connection between the client software (usually a browser) and the server software, allowing a connection, request, response, and close. Server software and the network on which it operates can handle only a limited number of requests, so large companies will have several machines operating as Web servers simultaneously.

Like all software, Web server packages come in many shapes and sizes. Server software exists across operating system platforms including UNIX, OS/2, NetWare, Windows (NT, 95, and/or 3.x), and Macintosh. The most recent ones boast speed of response, support for security such as Secure Sockets Layer (SSL) and Secure HTTP, and the ability to handle Java, JavaScript, ActiveX, advanced database connectivity, and many other features. Server software is advancing as quickly as browser software, albeit much more quietly since very few people realize it even exists.

While prices have come down on server software, especially in 1997, the price range in U.S. dollars still can be anywhere from free to several thousand dollars. Functionality, robustness, and capability are three factors that impact the price of server software. As a result, unless you are extremely familiar with server software, it is highly recommended that you complete a thorough investigation of the available software before using a new or another Web server. Some Web sites exist today that help you do this and they provide resources in helping assist you make a decision. One such site is Webcompare at **http://www.wecompare.internet. com/** and another is ServerWatch at **http://serverwatch.internet.com/**. You should also take advantage of the Microsoft FrontPage Web site at **http://www.microsoft.com/ frontpage/support/**.

Any computer on the Internet that contains TCP/IP networking software and has its own Internet Protocol (IP) address, even temporarily, can act as a Web server. That means dedicated machines with an ultra-fast T3 connection, right down to a lowly 486 PC running on a 28,800-Kbps modem. But to be efficient, a Web server should be connected to the Internet on a 24-hour basis at a speed high enough to enable file transfers that won't bore and frustrate users unduly. That means, practically, an ISDN connection at the very least (even a 33.6-Kbps modem won't cut it), and preferably something even faster, such as an Ethernet connection through a company local area network (LAN) that is sharing a T1 or T3 line with the rest of the organization's computers. The server will ideally possess its own Internet domain name as well, because then it can easily be assigned memorable addresses. This last suggestion, however, isn't really necessary, since virtual domain names (for instance, aliases) are possible.

Of the many different server packages available, some support Web features that others don't, such as server-side scripting, security, and Java. Some come bundled with HTML tools and browsers; others leave the choice of editing and viewing tools up to you. They can offer varying security levels, which are sometimes dependent on the host machine's operating system;

for example, Microsoft's Internet Information Server runs under Windows NT and uses the NT security features. In short, to run a Web site, you have to have a Web server installed on the computer.

All Web servers support the CGI standard, and many support Perl, a scripting language used for creating simple Web applications such as forms. Increasingly, servers are differentiated according to whether or not they support such advanced features as digital signature security, various key-level security, and the newest in programmability.

Installing Servers

Often, the installation of server software is as simple as slipping a CD-ROM or a few floppies into the host machine, running the setup program, and responding to a series of prompts about passwords and defaults. This is what you did when you installed FrontPage 98; you may have hardly noticed that you were installing a Web server. However, the Personal Web Server is just that—a personal Web server. Microsoft says it can handle up to 64 simultaneous connections. Heavy-duty Web server software, intended to run large or multiple Webs and deal with large numbers of access requests at the same time, are considerably more complex, although their installation may be almost as simple.

What's All This About the FrontPage Server Extensions?

When you installed FrontPage 98, you installed not only the Personal Web Server software, but software "extensions" that run in complement with the Personal Web Server itself. The extensions are intended to:

- Add to the server some specialized functions that are needed by the *FrontPage client*. This client is simply the package comprised of FrontPage Explorer, FrontPage Editor, and the To Do List.

- Make it possible for different types of servers to operate properly with the functions that FrontPage offers. This is necessary because different servers handle some common tools, such as image maps, in different ways.

- Make it possible for FrontPage-generated Webs to be fully interactive with their visitors, providing facilities for registrations, searches, and forms submission.

FrontPage has built-in extensions for Windows 95 and Windows NT 4. This means that you don't have to worry about extensions at all, if you create and operate your Web site on a Windows-based PC with FrontPage installed on it. However, if you decide to base your Web on your ISP's site, the ISP administrator will have to install FrontPage extensions that have been designed for whatever server software is running on the ISP host machine. FrontPage 98 comes with extensions for O'Reilly WebSite 1.1 for Windows 95 and for Netscape FastTrack

Windows NT. Other extensions can be downloaded free from the Microsoft site at **http://www.microsoft.com/frontpage/**. The FrontPage 98 extensions currently available on the Web are for Apache 1.1.3, and 2.0; CERN 3.0; NCSA 1.5.2 (note: not 1.5a or 1.5.1); Netscape Commerce Server 1.12; Netscape Communications Server 1.12; Netscape Enterprise Server 2.0, 3.0; and Netscape FastTrack 2.0. More will doubtless be added as the demand for FrontPage-based Web sites grows.

Server Extension Compatibility

Microsoft has made the old server extensions in FrontPage 98 backward compatible. What this means is that the extensions supported in FrontPage 97 will still be supported by FrontPage 98. However, if the server you are using has only FrontPage 97 extensions and you are attempting to use a brand-new FrontPage 98 server extension that was not in FrontPage 97, it most likely will not be available or produce unexpected results. Some of those extensions included support for new features such as Shared Borders, Themes, and Navigation view.

The Major Servers

These are the servers most commonly in use at the moment, although there are plenty of others. You'll find an excellent site for server information at **http://www.webcompare.internet.com/**.

O'Reilly WebSite and WebSite Pro (O'Reilly)

WebSite is a 32-bit multithreaded World Wide Web server for Windows NT and Windows 95. The server supports access control, desktop directory indexing, multi-homing, and server-side includes. You can also do custom CGI programming to process data from spreadsheet, database, and word processing applications. Site management is handled with a graphical display of documents and links on the server. The software also provides for searching and indexing (it has an integrated search engine). Setup and maintenance are GUI-based and remote maintenance is permitted. WebSite supports the Windows CGI interface. WebSite Pro supports advanced security mechanisms, plus Java and all the latest goodies, and includes a package that allows for relatively easy but powerful database connectivity.

The package comes with several bundled applications, notably the Spyglass Mosaic browser, Sausage Software's HotDog Standard HTML editor, and WebView printing, which lets users print out a view of what's in their Web. O'Reilly will be releasing version 2.0 of their server in the fall of 1997.

Commerce Builder (Internet Factory)

Running under Windows NT or Windows 95, this server from the Internet Factory offers Secure Sockets Layer (SSL) 2 technology and Public Key encryption technology. In the security area, you can prohibit access by both domain name and IP address, and parts of documents can be hidden according to security rules. One useful feature is that you can change the user access control list without a server restart. Setup and maintenance are GUI-based and remote maintenance is permitted. There is no search engine included, but the server does support chat and a newsgroup system. It can be used as an HTTP proxy server, and as a proxy server it will do caching. One interesting feature is its online store software.

Netscape FastTrack Server (Netscape)

This Windows NT or UNIX server is designed for lower-end World Wide Web or intranet sites that do not have extremely heavy traffic. It comes with an installation wizard to automatically detect system configuration and uses Netscape Navigator as its administrative interface. Also with the package is Netscape Composer, a WYSIWYG Web page editor that supports forms. Remote management of the server is supported, and it provides statistics like total site hits, unique users hitting the site, and most frequently served documents. For security, document access can be granted to user name/password pairs, groups, IP addresses, host names, or domain names. The security layer itself is Secure Sockets Layer 3.0.

For development work and CGI interfacing, the server supports Java and JavaScript, as well as C and Perl. In addition, developers using Visual Basic can communicate with the server through Windows CGI support. An optional add-on, LiveWire, converts popular image file formats such as BMP and WMF, provides conversion for document file formats like Microsoft Word and provides a compiler to compile applications that include JavaScript, images, and HTML. LiveWire also does external link checking and carries out automatic link reorganization when part of a site is changed.

Part
VIII
Ch
39

Netscape Enterprise Server (Netscape)

This UNIX and Windows NT package is a high-end server designed for sites with large amounts of traffic. It has or extends all the features of the Netscape FasTrack Server and adds integrated full-text search (the Verity search engine), multiple version control (the MKS Integrity Engine), and server-parsed HTML, which allows system administrators to replace HTML tags with dynamic content. Security is also upgraded, with read/write access control for individual files and directories and authentication based on public-key certificates. The LiveWire package is included with the server, instead of being an option, as with FastTrack.

Purveyor (Process Software Corporation)

This server runs under Windows NT and Windows 95 and is compatible with Novell Netware. It includes a data wizard to create HTML forms that allow users to execute database queries. There is also a special API, intended as an alternative to CGI scripting. There are proxy services to screen HTTP, gopher, and FTP functions, in support of firewalls. Further security is provided by SSL 2 and user names/passwords can reside in external databases. Search engines (Verity and WAIS) are provided, and a link viewer helps with the location and correction of broken links. Maintenance and setup are GUI-based, and the server can be remotely maintained.

SPRY Web Server (Spry)

This is a Windows NT server that lets you publish Web documents over an internal network and on the World Wide Web. Typical applications, according to Spry, might include sales force updates, customer database access, and online policy and procedure manuals. It has a built-in scripting language called BGI and built-in image map handling, but it doesn't support the Windows CGI interface. There is password support and access prohibition by domain name or IP address but no support for SSL security. You can configure user groups, but to change the access control list you must restart the server. GUI-based setup and maintenance are provided, as well as remote maintenance. It can act as a proxy server, and in this mode provides caching.

SPRY Safety Web Server (Spry)

This is the secure version of the Spry Web Server just described, with the additional security provided by SSL 2 technology. GUI-based installation and maintenance are provided, as well as remote maintenance. Included is a Web search engine and the HoTMetaL Pro HTML editor. The server is targeted to organizations with financial security needs, for conducting transactions over the Internet or over an intranet. Suggested applications are subscription-based access to financial records and electronic retailing through online order forms.

NCSA HTTP (NCSA)

Running under UNIX, this is among the longest lived servers around and has the virtue of being small, fast, and free. It lets users create HTML directory indexes and allows them to access publishing tools on the Web. ISP administrators can customize CGI scripts for searches and form handling, and the server also supports image map files without requiring an external CGI application. There is no built-in scripting language, however. Security is provided by password and by access prohibition by domain name or IP address, but SSL is not supported. However, Kerberos and MD5 provide extra security tools. It has an internal search engine and WAIS support. Installation is GUI-based, but maintenance is not. Additionally, remote maintenance is not allowed.

Apache (Apache Group)

Apache is based on the NCSA server and runs under UNIX only. It's the most common Web server around because it's happy with most UNIX variants and is fast and efficient. It doesn't have GUI-based installation or maintenance, but it does allow remote maintenance. There is no built-in scripting language. Image map support has been improved in version 1.1 with better handling of default, base, and relative URLs and with support for creating nongraphical menus. Access protection is based on passwords, domain name, and IP address prohibition and, most recently, by URL-based security. Version 1.1 can be used as a proxy server, with caching. Filetype-based script actions permit the running of CGI scripts whenever a particular type of file is requested. Anonymous HTTP logons are now supported.

Open Market Secure WebServer (Open Market)

This high-performance server runs under UNIX. With its multiprocessor capabilities, it can (in an appropriate configuration) support up to 5,000 simultaneous connections, according to the vendor. It supports FastCGI, a new open-architecture programming interface that reduces the performance penalty of standard CGI. In addition to FastCGI, it offers the scripting language TCl (Tool Control Language). It also provides tools for interfacing existing code from the user's choice of programming languages.

Security is extensive, with support for Secure Hypertext Transfer Protocol (S-HTTP), SSL 2, and Microsoft's new Private Communications Technology (PCT). This flexibility lets developers write applications that work with all secure browsers.

It has elaborate methods of logging user access. In combination with Open Market's WebReporter utility, system administrators can track individual users' movements through a site, log the most frequent browsers and machine types, report the most frequent referring URLs, and determine the most used entry and exit points for a site. The WebReporter output, which has several preconfigured report formats, can be in HTML, postscript, or text documents. Installation and setup are GUI-based, and remote maintenance is permitted.

From Here...

We're close to the end of the book now, and have just two places left to go: databases and the appendix. So now it's off to:

- Chapter 40, "Custom Database Query Scripts," which introduces database connectivity in the context of FrontPage 98.
- Appendix A, "FrontPage on the Net," where you can find out about the best World Wide Web sites dedicated to FrontPage.
- Appendixes B, C, and D, for command references to HTML, VBScript, and JavaScript.

Custom Database Query Scripts

Using the World Wide Web to access databases can save your organization tremendous amounts of time. The task may seem daunting at first, but any effort on your part to integrate your existing database with the Web is well worth the effort.

No matter how much information the Web site for your organization might contain, a great deal more information is undoubtedly available on the computer databases that the organization has been building over the years. These databases will contain everything from employee information through detailed customer profiles, product and service information, prices, items in inventory, and any number of other important details. If you're creating a company intranet, you'll find yourself face to face with the problem of allowing access to some of the information stored in these databases, and if you're creating an Internet Web site where users are asked to provide or request information, you'll need to access these databases as well.

FrontPage 98 offers sophisticated database connectivity. In fact, it's one of the leading additions to the upgraded FrontPage package. Furthermore, FrontPage offers a Database Connector Wizard to make this difficult process as user-friendly as possible. Connecting your Web site with your databases is still anything but a walk in the park, and it helps a great deal to know how it's done before starting to use the wizard, but FrontPage eases the burden to a considerable degree. ■

Database Connectivity Using the Database Connector

Connecting an organization's Web to its databases has become one of the most important considerations of all for Webmasters. So much information already resides on databases that it makes no sense whatsoever reproducing it so that Web visitors—whether intranet or Internet users—can make use of it. Whether that data has to do with internal company information such as policies, procedures, employee statistics, sales figures, client profiles, or contact details, or with externally important data such as products, services, programs, and pricing, the point is that if it already exists in a form that's being regularly updated, why not make use of it?

Let's say, in a very simple example, that you're using your Web site to market a line of shirts. You have T-shirts and sweatshirts in various sizes and colors, and each with a picture of one (of five) dangerous snakes (hey, it's an example, okay?). You're not allowing them to actually buy the shirts over the Web, but you want them to be able to fill in a form that will show them a picture of the particular shirt they want. You also want to use the form to collect information about the visitors to your site, and you'll invite them to subscribe to a mailing list and to get a product brochure via snail-mail. So you use FrontPage 98 to design a form that lets them request information about precisely the shirt they want, and which also gives you the information you need for your business.

Here's what you need on your form:

- Customer's Name
- Customer's E-Mail
- Customer's Street Address
- Customer's City
- Customer's State or Province
- Customer's City
- Customer's Country
- Customer's ZIP or Postal Code
- Type of Shirt (choice: T-shirt, Sweatshirt)
- Size of Shirt (choice: Small, Medium, Large)
- Color of Shirt (choice: White, Black, Red, Green)
- Dangerous Snake (choice: Python, Anaconda, Cobra, Viper, Rattler)
- Get information by E-Mail? (choice: yes or no)
- Receive Product Brochure by Mail? (choice: yes or no)

You finish the form, and it looks great—drop-down lists, option buttons, whatever. The only problem is: What exactly is it supposed to do? Where will it get the information about the shirts, and where will it store the information about the customers and their choices?

To make this form work properly, you'll need to build a database of information (or tap into one you already have). Your database should have fields for type of shirt, color of shirt, and type of snake, and a means of querying those items so that a request returns a picture of that particular shirt and a price for that shirt. You might even need data on shipping costs to various locations—and it doesn't stop there. Your database (or another related database) must be able to accept data from the Web form, collecting the customer's name and address information into the appropriate fields.

Obviously, this is way beyond basic HTML. In fact, it requires database programming knowledge. Fortunately, FrontPage 98 ships with tools to help you do some of this programming, although certainly nothing that takes programming away from you completely. FrontPage's database connectivity features, which come to life in the Database Connector Wizard, helps your data make the transition from your databases to your Web pages, and from your Web forms into your databases. In effect, it lets you use your Web to query your databases and to add records to them as well.

The Database Connector Wizard helps you with the process of producing an Internet Database Connector or IDC file. This file includes the information necessary to interact with a database that is compliant with the ODBC (Open Database Connectivity) standards and that is currently running on a Web server. It interacts by allowing requests that conform to the Structured Query Language (SQL) for data retrieval, data additions, and data changes.

N O T E *Structured Query Language (SQL)* is a language which provides a user interface to relational database management systems (RDBMS). Originally developed by IBM in the 1970s, SQL is the de facto standard for storing and retrieving information for relational databases, as well as being an ISO and ANSI standard. The current standard is SQL2 with SQL3 being planned for release in 1998.

The purpose of SQL is to provide a language, easily understandable by humans, which interfaces with relational databases. ■

The information contained in the IDC file tells the database connector how to connect with the database and what queries and operations to conduct. In addition, the wizard lets you point to a file known as a query results file, which will have an HTX extension in the file name and which will cooperate with the IDC file. This results file, which in effect is a different type of Web document, holds information such as database record values, parameters for a variety of operations, if…then programming choices, and so on. The Edit menu of FrontPage Editor lets you add and modify the information in this HTX file.

The whole point of creating these files is to let your Web forms make use of them. You do so by calling up the Form Properties dialog box from within FrontPage Editor and choosing Database Connector in the Form Handler field. If the form shares field names with the IDC file, the

HTX file can run the queries and return the results right in the Web browser, where the user can see them.

Using the Database Connectivity Wizard

Once you've created your form which will allow the visitor to place an order, you will want to use the FrontPage Database Connectivity Wizard to create the IDC file which will process the visitor's order.

If you haven't already done so, at the top of the FrontPage editor, click File and then click New. This will display a listing of different types of templates and wizards that can be used to help you create a new FrontPage document (see Figure 40.1).

FIG. 40.1

The Database Connector Wizard will take you through a step-by-step process which will help you create an IDC file.

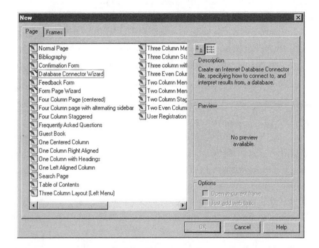

Once the window appears on your screen, click the Database Connector Wizard and select OK. The wizard will open and allow you to specify an ODBC data source (see Figure 40.2). This field is required because it tells the Wizard (and your IDC file) which database it will retrieve or store your visitor's information in. The ODBC (Open Database Connectivity) data source should be a data source already specified through the use of the ODBC32 icon on your system's Control Panel.

Next, set the username and password required to access your database, if required (not all databases require the use of a username and password; most SQL servers do, though).

Specify the name of the HTX file (required) that will be used to display information that the user entered, and information collected from the database (if any). If you haven't created the HTX file already, you will have to do so before allowing visitors to your site to fill out your form.

You will notice the Advanced Options button which allows you to set options (see Figure 40.3) for your ODBC driver, including information on how, or if, the database is supposed to cache information retrieved, set timeouts, translations, and additional information.

FIG. 40.2

The wizard will allow you to specify the ODBC data source and the HTX file.

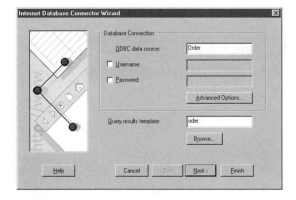

FIG. 40.3

The Advanced Options Dialog box will allow you to control various aspects of your ODBC driver.

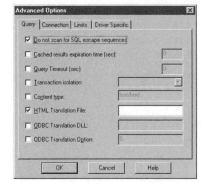

Part

IX

Ch

40

Once you have finished entering the ODBC data source, the HTX filename, and additional information for your ODBC driver, click Next. The wizard will provide you with another dialog box that will allow you to enter one or more database queries, which will be placed in the IDC file required to process the information entered in your form. In the example, information is taken from the visitor and placed into the database, which can be later retrieved by the appropriate personnel, who will then process the customer's order.

As you can see in Figure 40.4, the wizard only makes entering a query a little easier. You will still have to know how to query the database, deciding what information you want to store, and how that information will be stored.

The Insert Parameter button helps you enter information into the query by allowing you to enter the name of a field from the form, and insert that information into the actual query in the proper format. For example, if you clicked Insert Parameter, a dialog box will appear asking for the name of the field from the form. If you were to enter **name**, the dialog box would place the string, *%name%* into the query box.

FIG. 40.4

Using the Internet Database Connector Wizard, enter a query that will enter, retrieve, or change information in the database.

Since our query will simply enter the information provided by the visitor, the following query is placed into the Query Dialog Box:

```
INSERT name,email,street,city,state,country,zip,
type,size,color,snake,list,brochure
INTO orderinfo
VALUES ('%name%', '%email%', '%street%', '%city%', '%state%', '%country%',
'%zip%',
'%type%', '%size%', '%color%', '%snake%', '%list%', '%brochure%')
```

Once you are finished entering your query, click Next. The Wizard will then allow you to enter additional parameters as shown in Figure 40.5.

FIG. 40.5

The Internet Database Connector Wizard will allow you to enter additional parameters which can be used by the database.

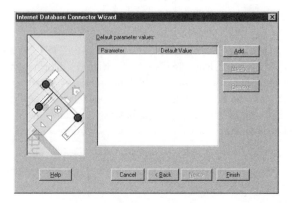

Along with the Datasource, Template, and SQLStatement directives, which are placed in the IDC file by the Database Connector Wizard, additional directives are available. These directives are not required, but add a bit of flexibility when dealing with the database connector. The rest of this section examines each of these directives and explains how you can use them.

The *DefaultParameters* Directive

You can use the DefaultParameters directive to specify the default parameters to use if the visitor doesn't fill out the form completely. For example, you can set the following default in case a visitor fails to enter a name:

```
DefaultParameters: name=%John Doe%
```

You can specify more than one parameter, but you must separate each with a comma.

The *RequiredParameters* Directive

The RequiredParameters directive enables you to specify which items the visitor must fill. If you want to ensure that the visitor enters a name and address, for example, you specify the following:

```
RequiredParameters: name, street, city, state, zip
```

The *MaxFieldSize* Directive

With the MaxFieldSize directive, you can specify a record's maximum length. If you don't specify the MaxFieldSize, the default value is 8,192 bytes.

The *MaxRecords* Directive

You can use the MaxRecords directive to set the maximum amount of records that a query returns. If you don't set the MaxRecords directive, the IDC allows the return of all records that match the query. This default setting isn't a problem with smaller databases, but can be with larger ones. Set this directive to a reasonable number of records, based on the kind of information that you are retrieving.

Part
IX

Ch
40

The *Expires* Directive

If you don't set the Expires directive, the database is accessed each time for information. If you do set this directive, the query returns to the user from a cache instead of accessing the database again. This can help reduce the system's load and return information to the visitor more quickly. Using the Expires directive, you specify the amount of seconds before the cache is refreshed.

For our example, we don't require any additional parameters, so we will then click Finish. The wizard will disappear, and the IDC file is then created, storing the information we entered. Listing 40.1 shows you what our IDC file looks like.

> **Listing 40.1   order.idc—The IDC File Specifies Which Data Source to Use, and the Query Information Which Will Process the Information Entered by the Visitor**

```
Datasource: Order
Template: order.htx
```

continues

Listing 40.1 Continued

```
SQLStatement: INSERT name,email,street,city,state,country,zip,
+type,size,color,snake,list,brochure
+INTO orderinfo
+VALUES ('%name%', '%email%', '%street%', '%city%', '%state%',
+'%country%', '%zip%', '%type%', '%size%', '%color%', '%snake%',
+'%list%', '%brochure%');
```

HTML Extensions

Now all you need to do is create an HTX file that creates the HTML document that you return to the visitor. The Database Connector Wizard can help you with the HTX file. Using the FrontPage editor, click Edit, and then click Database. A list of options will be shown. These options are:

- Database Column Value
- IDC Parameter Value
- Detail Section
- If...Then Conditional Statement
- Else Conditional Statement
- Remove Database Directive

As with the IDC file, the HTX file uses special directives that help format the HTML document. Here you are introduced to each of these directives, and you'll create an HTX file which will process some of the information entered by the visitor when they ordered one of our very special snake T-shirts.

Database Column Values

This item allows you to insert a value from the database into your HTX file. If you have the columns, name, e-mail, and phone in the database, you can enter these into the dialog box (one at a time please), and they will be placed in your HTC file as:

`<%name%>, <%email%>, and <%phone%>` respectively.

These tags will be replaced by the actual information stored in each column when the database has been queried.

IDC Parameter Values

After a visitor enters fields within an HTML form, you can pass them directly to the HTX file by adding the *idc.* prefix. For example, if you want to return information to the visitor that entered it, you could use the following code line:

```
Hello %idc.name%. How is the weather in %idc.city%,
➡ %idc.state%?<BR>
```

The *Detail* Directives

If a visitor to your site wants to query the database, the <%begindetail%> and <%enddetail%> directives store the returned information. For example, suppose that a visitor perusing your company product catalog enters a query to search for shirts, and that your database includes a field called shirt. You can format the HTX file to report each instance that matches the field:

```
<table>
<%begindetail%>
<tr><td><%shirt%><td><%price%></td></tr>
<%enddetail%>
</table>
```

This code opens the <TABLE> tag. For each instance of a match, the file creates a row with the shirt (which could simply be a name) and the price. The <%enddetail%> directive specifies he end of a section. You then use the <\TABLE> tag to close the table. If no records are found, this section is skipped.

An option not provided by the menu, but used often, is the CurrentRecord directive. The CurrentRecord directive counts the number of times that records are processed. You can use this directive to check whether the query generated any results and then inform the visitor of any results.

Soon you'll see how to use the CurrentRecord directive, but first you need to examine another directive that enables you to check information and return results based on conditions.

Conditional Operators *If...Then* and *Else*

Within the HTX file, you can use the following simple conditional operators: <%if%>, <%else%>, and <%endif%>. Using these operator directives, you can check whether certain conditions are met. For example, you can check whether any records were returned, and if not, you can inform the visitor:

```
<table>
<%begindetail%>
<tr><td><%shirt%><td><%price%></td></tr>
<%enddetail%>
</table>
<%if CurrentRecord EQ 0 %>
I'm sorry, but there isn't anything in the database
➥ that matches your query.
<center>
<a href="tshirt.htm">[Product Database]</a>
</center>
```

The <%if%> directive uses four conditional words that you can use to check information.

EQ checks whether a value is equal to the test, as in the following example:

```
<%if snake EQ "Viper" %>
Viper T-Shirt
<%endif%>
```

GT enables you to check whether one value is greater than another, as in the following example:

```
<%if price GT 500 %>
```

LT checks whether a value is less than another value, as in the following example:

```
<%elseif price LT 10 %>
<%endif%>
```

CONTAINS enables you to check whether a value is anywhere within another value, as in the following example:

```
<%if snake CONTAINS "Cobra" %>
Cobra
<%endif%>
```

The MaxRecords variable contains the value of the MaxRecords directive that the IDC file specifies, as in the following example:

```
<%if CurrentRecord EQ MaxRecords %>
Results have been abridged
<%endif%>
```

You can also use HTTP variables within HTX files. To do so, select the HTTP variable. The variable will be displayed in the HTX file within the <% %> delimiters, as in the following example:

```
You are using, <%HTTP_USER_AGENT%>
```

Continuing with Our Example

To continue with the order-entry example, you should simply thank the visitor for entering the order and let the visitor know that you have processed their order, storing it in the database. Listing 40.2 shows the process.

Listing 40.2   Thanking the Visitor for the Order

```
<!DOCTYPE HTML PUBLIC "-//IETF//DTD HTML//EN">
<html>

<head>
<meta http-equiv="Content-Type"
content="text/html; charset=iso-8859-1">
<meta name="GENERATOR" content="Microsoft FrontPage 2.0">
<title>Thank you!</title>
</head>

<body bgcolor="#FFFFFF">
<div align="center"><center>

<table border="0" width="580">
    <tr>
        <td><img src="cobra5.jpg" width="320" height="240"></td>
        <td align="center"><h1>Thank you for your order!</h1>
        </td>
```

```
    </tr>
</table>
</center></div>

<p> </p>

<hr>

<h2>Thank you, <%idc.name%>.</h2>

<p>You ordered:<br>
Type of shirt: <%idc.type%><br>
Size: <%idc.size%><br>
Color: <%idc.color%><br>
Type of snake: %idc.snake% <%if% idc.list EQ "No">
<%else%></p>

<p>You have been placed on our mailing list <%if% idc.brochure EQ "No">
<%else%> </p>

<p>Also a brochure will be send to you at the following address:</p>

<pre>
<%idc.name%>
<%idc.street%>
<%idc.city%>
<%idc.state%>
<%idc.country%>
<%idc.zip%>
<hr></pre>
</body>
</html>
```

The HTX file produces a page similar to that shown in Figure 40.6.

Using the Database Region Wizard

For those using Microsoft's Internet Information Server, Active Server Protocols (ASP) have been added to FrontPage. By using ASPs, you can create scripts that are executed on the fly giving you some of the functionality that Unix Web servers provide when using CGI scripts. This functionality is provided with the FrontPage Database Region Wizard.

The Database Region Wizard can be used to add database connectivity within existing Web documents and save them as ASP files.

To use the Database Region Wizard, use the Insert drop-down window and select Database. Another window will appear where you will need to select the Database Region Wizard. A dialog box will appear asking for the ODBC Data Source Name (DSN) and username and password (shown in Figure 40.7). Once the DSN and username and password information have been entered, select Next.

Part
IX

Ch
40

FIG. 40.6
By using the .HTX file, you can embed a database's information into the final HTML document.

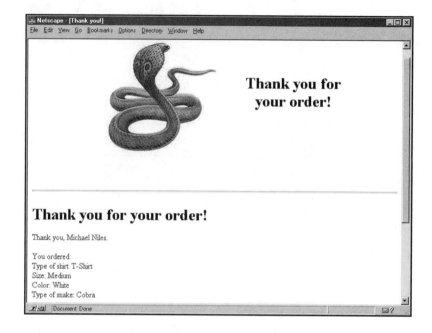

FIG. 40.7
Using the Database Resource Wizard, you can easily add database information within your Web document.

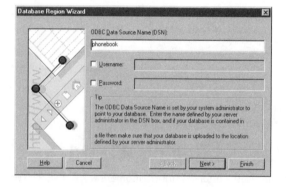

Now you will have to enter an SQL statement that is used to query the database. A simple query to grab all the information from the Contacts table within the phonebook database is provided in Figure 40.8.

By clicking the Insert Form Field Parameter, you can link parameters from your HTML form to an SQL query.

Optionally, you can enter the query field names within the Database resource wizard. This will allow you to customize each query further.

Once all the needed information has been entered, click Finish. This will place the query into your FrontPage document. If you take a look at Figure 40.9, you can see what this entails.

FIG. 40.8
Any valid query used to access an ODBC compliant database can be used to get information from the database.

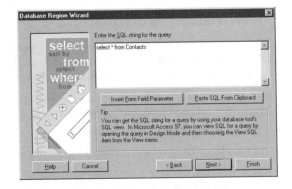

FIG. 40.9
To save you time, all code for each query is automatically generated and placed within your document.

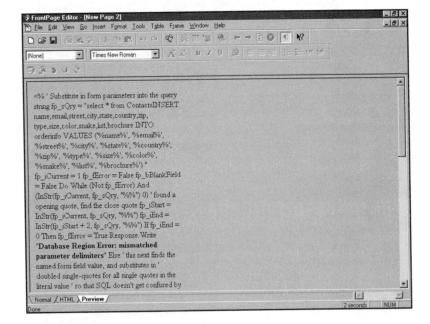

At this point, information is simply loaded and ready for use. To actually use this information within your forms, you have to select Insert, highlight Database, and click Column Value. By doing so, you can place any information from the database anywhere within your document, including within HTML forms.

N O T E Using the Database Resource Wizard is especially useful with Microsoft's new databinding technology. Using Databinding (available only with Internet Explorer 4.0), you can make queries within a Web document without needing to repeatedly access the database.

For additional information on databinding see:

http://www.microsoft.com/ie/ie40/demos/arcadia/

Understanding Database Design

How you go about designing your database depends on the tools you currently have, what type of information you need to store, and what you're willing to purchase. The nice thing is that there are different methods to save and retrieve information, no matter what your budget.

The most difficult and daunting task is how to design your database to store information, and to retrieve that information. What would happen if you wanted to upgrade your database, or if you needed to add on to your database?

Figure 40.10 shows you how information flows from the point in which someone on the Web requests a page that needs information from your database. When requesting information that derives from a database, quite a few steps are involved to complete that request. Your Web server receives the request from the visitor to your site and sends that information on to your CGI script. The CGI script acts as the main gateway tying two very different systems together. The CGI script performs the actual query, receives the results from the database, formulates a proper reply, and sends it off to the Web server, which in turn sends it to the person visiting your site.

FIG. 40.10

This diagram shows the information flow between those on the Web and your database.

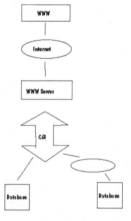

As you can see, there's quite a few steps involved in this process. Your goal is to tie all this together in such a way that it is totally transparent to the person visiting your site.

Why Access a Database?

Most likely your organization already has an existing database in which they have stored information about their products, their customers, and other aspects of business life. Some of this information you might want to allow your customers to see, or you might even want to make the information in the database available to your workers stationed away from the office. If so, you would have to create HTML documents that contain all this information all over again, which, if you're part of a large organization, can be a tedious task. Integrating the Web with your databases can save you tremendous amounts of time in the long run, especially when it comes to maintaining that information. As the database changes, your Web pages change.

Another good reason to use the World Wide Web to access your database is that any Web browser that supports forms can access information from the database—no matter which platform is being used.

Database Access Limitations

Although the limitations in accessing databases have decreased in the last few months as database companies have scrambled to ensure that their product easily integrates with existing Web applications, there are still a few left you will want to look out for.

There is a lack of an official standard which you can use to connect to a database. If you were to create a script to access one type of database, there is no guarantee that the same script would work on a different database—even if the query used was the same. (People are working on this, though). Because of this, you will be required to learn a good deal about each database application that you come across.

Also, the browser and the server are stateless in relation to each other. The browser makes a request, the server processes the query, sends the result back to the browser, and the connection is closed. This creates a problem with databases, because a connection to a database is usually constant. Someone, through a normal method, would access the database, which keeps a connection open, locking a record if any editing is performed (when accessing a ODBC-compliant database through FrontPage, this is automatically done), and closes the connection only when the person is finished. Accessing a database doesn't work exactly the same way when doing so from the Web.

Consider the following events:

1. Person one accesses the database for editing.
2. Person two comes along and does the same thing.
3. Person one makes his changes, and saves that information to the database.
4. Person two saves his information as well, possibly writing over what person one just saved.
5. A short time later, person one is wondering where his data went.

There are two ways to go about handling this. The first method involves keeping track of all entries with a timestamp. This will allow both entries to be maintained by the database, without the possibility of either person's entries being overwritten.

Another way is to only provide information from the database, and not allow someone on the Web to edit, remove, or insert information to the database. While this limits some of the possibilities for having the database on the Web, it also alleviates some of the security problems.

Security Issues

The major problem with having those on the Web accessing your database is that your CGI script is trusted by your database program. That is to say, your database has to accept commands from your CGI script, and your CGI script needs to perform queries based upon what you want to provide to those on the Web. This can lead to problems if someone with ill intentions gains access to a script that has the capability to edit your database.

Also, most databases require the use of a password. Since your CGI script stores user information to the database, as well as retrieving information from the database, your script requires the password to access your database. You need to ensure that your script cannot be read by others both within your organization and outside your organization.

Relational Databases

Most relational database servers consist of a set of programs which manage large amounts of data, offering a rich set of query commands that help manage the power behind the database server. These programs control the storage, retrieval, and organization of the information within the database. This information within the database can be changed, updated, or removed, once the support programs or scripts are in place.

They provide a field in which information can be matched and the results of which can be sent back to the person performing the query as if the database was organized that way.

Relational databases store information in tables. Tables are similar to a smaller database that sits inside the main database. Each table usually can be linked with the information in other tables to provide a result to a query. Take a look at Figure 40.11 which shows how this information could be tied together.

FIG. 40.11
A relational database stores certain information in various parts of the database, which can later be called with one query.

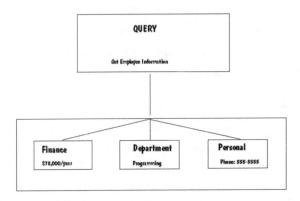

To get a complete response, information is retrieved from three different tables, each of which store only parts of the information requested. In the figure, information about the person's pay rate is retrieved, while Departmental information and Personal information is retrieved from other tables. Working together, this can produce a complete query response, producing an abundant amount of information on an individual.

Each table consists of columns and rows. The columns identify the data by a name, while the rows store information relevant to that name. Take a look at the following example:

Name	Number	E-Mail
Fred Flinstone	01–43	ff@bedrock.com
Barney Rubble	01–44	br@bedrock.com

The column heads give a name to each item below it. Information within a table is stored in much the same way.

Now if you add more tables to the database, you could have something that looks like the following:

Name	PayRate
Fred Flintstone	$34/month
Barney Rubble	$29/month

And, you could have department information as well.

Name	Department	Tardy Record
Fred Flintstone	Dino-Digger	17
Barney Rubble	Pebble Pusher	3

With this information, you can perform a query to get a complete picture of an individual.

```
Select * from personal,department,finance where Name="Fred Flintstone
```

This would pull up all information on Fred Flintstone, from all three records. You could even be more specific, pulling only certain parts from each table:

```
select Name.finance,Name.finance where Tardy > 5
```

With this information, I think Fred would be in serious trouble—but you should have an idea of how relational databases work.

Existing Databases

In this section, you'll take a quick look at the most commonly used databases on the Web and where you can look for further information and support.

Oracle

Oracle is the largest database developer in the World. Microsoft exceeds them only in the software arena. Oracle provides databases for Windows NT and various UNIX flavors. Oracle has created their own set of tools (mainly PL/SQL) which, coupled with the Oracle Webserver,

Part
IX

Ch
40

allows you to create Web pages with little effort from information from the database. PL/SQL allows you to form stored procedures, which help speed up the database query. The Oracle database engine is a good choice for large businesses that handle large amounts of information but of course, you're going to pay for that. Today's price range for Oracle 7 and the Oracle Webserver together is over $5,000.

ON THE WEB

http://dozer.us.oracle.com/   For more information on Oracle and how you can use Oracle with the World Wide Web, visit their Web page online.

Sybase

Sybase System 11 is a SQL database product that has many tools that can be used to produce dynamic Web pages from the information data in your database. A new product by Powersoft, the NetImpact Studio, integrates with Sybase providing a rich set of tools to help anyone create dynamic HTML documents. The NetImpact Studio consists of an HTML Browser/Editor accompanied by a Personal Web Server. These allow you to create pages using a WYSIWYG or "What You See Is What You Get" interface. The Studio also comes with a Web database, support for JavaScript (which they see as the future of CGI scripting), and support for connecting to application servers.

NetImpact can be used in conjunction with PowerBuilder, an application which is used to create plug-ins and ActiveX components. It also can be used to complement Optima++, which is used to create plug-ins and will support the creation of Java applets.

Sybase also can be used with web.sql to create CGI and NSAPI (Netscape Server Application Programming Interface) applications that access the Sybase database server using Perl. Sybase is available for Windows NT, and Unix.

ON THE WEB

http://www.sybase.com/   For more information on Sybase, web.sql, and other Sybase-related API's, visit the Sybase home page.

mSQL

mSQL is a middle-sized SQL database server for Unix that has been ported to Windows95/NT as well as OS/2. Written by David Hughes, it was created to allow users to experiment with SQL and SQL databases. It is free for noncommercial use (nonprofit, schools, and research organizations)—although for individual and commercial use, the price is quite fair, at about $170.

ON THE WEB

http://Hughes.com.au/product/msql/   This site provides additional information on mSQL, along with documentation, and a vast array of user-contributed software.

Informix Workgroup/Workstation Server

Informix provides two solutions in which you can use their database solutions with the World Wide Web. The Informix Workgroup Server allows your organization to allow those on the Web to access your company's database. Useful for both Internet and intranet applications, the Informix Workstation is available for single users, allowing an individual to access his or her database via the Web—no matter where they are located. Using DSA (or Dynamic Scalable Architecture) queries from either server are returned at amazing speeds. The servers use a GUI (Graphical User Interface) which helps with setting up a database, making it more intuitive.

ON THE WEB

http://www.informix.com/   This site contains detailed information on the Informix Workgroup Server; along with additional information on how you can use the Workgroup server with your Web-based applications.

Microsoft SQL

Microsoft released their own SQL database server as a part of their back office suite. Microsoft is trying heavily to compete with Oracle and Sybase. They have released the server for $999 but you also must buy the SQL Server Internet Connector which costs $2,995. These two products allow you to provide unlimited access to the server from the Web.

ON THE WEB

http://www.microsoft.com/sql/   This site will provide additional information on Microsoft's SQL server and how you can use Microsoft's SQL server in conjunction with the World Wide Web.

Part
IX

Ch
40

Ingres

Ingres (Interactive Graphics Retrieval System) comes in both a commercial and public domain version. The University of California at Berkeley originally developed this retrieval system, but Berkeley no longer supports the public domain version. You can still find it on the University's Web site.

Ingres uses the QUEL query language as well as SQL. QUEL is a superset of the original SQL language, making Ingres more powerful. Ingres was developed to work with graphics in a database environment. The public domain version is available for UNIX systems.

ON THE WEB

ftp://s2k-ftp.cs.berkeley.edu/pub/ingres/   Visit this site to download the public domain version of Ingres.

Computer Associates owns the commercial version of Ingres. This version is quite robust and capable of managing virtually any database application. The commercial version is available for UNIX, VMS, and Windows NT.

ON THE WEB

http://www.cai.com/products/ingr.htm   Visit this site to find out more information on the commercial version of Ingres.

ON THE WEB

http://www.naiua.org/   For information about both the commercial and public domain versions of Ingres, visit the North American Ingres Users Association.

FoxPro

Microsoft's Visual FoxPro has been a favorite for Web programmers, mostly because of its long-time standing in the database community as well as its third party support. Foxpro is an Xbase database system that is widely used for smaller business and personal database applications.

ON THE WEB

http://www.microsoft.com/catalog/products/visfoxp/   Visit the FoxPro home page on Microsoft's Web site for more information on FoxPro and visit Neil's Foxpro database page at

http://adams.patriot.net/~johnson/html/neil/fox/foxaol.htm

Microsoft Access

Microsoft Access is a relational database management system that is part of the Microsoft Office suite. Microsoft Access can be used to create HTML documents based on the information stored in the Access database with the help of Microsoft's Internet Assistant. Microsoft's Internet Assistant is an add-on that is available free of charge for Access users. Microsoft Access can also support ActiveX controls which makes Access even more powerful when used with the Microsoft Internet explorer.

A Job forum page was created to allow you to see how Access can be used in conjunction with the World Wide Web.

For more information on Microsoft Access and the Job forum, see:

ON THE WEB

http://www.microsoft.com/accessdev/DefOff.htm   This site will provide you with details on Microsoft Access and how you can use Access with your Web based applications. Additionally, you can test the Job Forum as well as look at the code used to create this application.

From Here...

Now that you've reached the end of the book, you may want to return to earlier sections for review. The key parts are:

■ Part II, "Creating Your Pages with FrontPage Editor," which examines in detail the rich tool set provided by FrontPage Editor for creating Web pages.

■ Part IV, "Integrating Active Content into Your Web," which explores the use of ActiveX, scripts, plug-ins, and VRML.

■ Part V, "Building and Managing a Web," where you learn the details of constructing and maintaining FrontPage Webs.

Part
IX

Ch
40

Appendixes

FrontPage on the Net

Hopefully, you won't need a great deal more information than this book provides about producing excellent Web sites with FrontPage 98. However, you should keep in touch with the FrontPage resources available on the Internet. Upgrades, free software, add-ons, discussion groups, and Web providers can be found very easily, and these will provide you with even more grist for your Web-designing mill. In this appendix, some of the growing collection of resources are listed. ■

What Resources Are Available on the Web

The Web contains many resources for FrontPage users. Some of these resources are specific to FrontPage and others are specific to technologies used with FrontPage. All of them can be useful for creating better Web sites.

What's on the Microsoft Site?

Microsoft's FrontPage area is the obvious starting place, and here you'll find information and assistance.

Web Presence Providers that Support FrontPage Extensions

You want to make full use of FrontPage 98, so why not get an account with a presence provider that supports it fully?

FrontPage Resources on the Web and the Net

Since FrontPage 98 exists to let you produce Web sites, it only makes sense that you can find information about the package on the Web itself; and, because FrontPage is constantly increasing in popularity, you can rest assured that an increasing number of sites will become available in the near future, especially since the program is open ended enough to invite input from its users. In fact, you might want to start your own FrontPage site, complete with hints, tips, pointers, technical help, and maybe even some nicely designed templates or wizards. A couple of such sites are:

- **http://www.gkweb.com/spider/frontpage.html**   This link introduces you to WebSpider, which helps promote your Web pages by submitting them to over 250 search engines. WebSpider can also be used on Web sites created without FrontPage.

- **http://www.frontpage97.com/frontpage98/**   This page, which is contained on a Web site dedicated to FrontPage 97, discusses issues about the FrontPage 98 beta. It is not clear how it will be used in relation to the final release of FrontPage 98.

N O T E Web sites that discuss and promote FrontPage 98 may be scarce immediately after the final version is released, but should steadily increase as more people begin to use it. Use a search engine like Yahoo! (www.yahoo.com) or AltaVista (altavista.digital.com) to locate sites dedicated to FrontPage 98. ▪

The other areas dedicated to FrontPage beginning to spring up are discussion groups on UseNet. Currently, only Microsoft itself offers FrontPage-specific newsgroups, but these, too, will begin to appear on news servers in a short while. Again, feel free to start your own such group.

If you're a FrontPage user with no access to a Web server that supports the FrontPage extensions, the Web will help you here as well. The number of *Web presence providers* (companies who give you a place to put your Web) that support FrontPage is growing constantly as the package becomes widely accepted among designers, and as of this writing, these providers number close to a hundred. If you need a place to put your Web, you should consider spending a few dollars a month to give yourself the opportunity.

Note that this appendix, however, is about FrontPage resources only. There is also a nearly infinite number of resources available about Web design in general, including collections of Java applets and ActiveX controls, HTML style guides, tutorials and assistants, and software to assist your Web building.

Parts of this book cover more than just FrontPage. Here's a quick list to give you somewhere to start looking for information on these other topics:

- Gamelan (**http://www.gamelan.com**)

  This is the most important place to surf to if you are interested in any and all things Java. There are tons of resources and lots of applets to play with.

- Javasoft (**http://www.javasoft.com**)

  This is the official Sun Java site and a good place to find breaking Java news and, of course, to get your hands on the latest Java releases.

- ActiveX.COM (**http://www.activex.com**)

  A huge archive of ActiveX controls and information.

- Microsoft's ActiveX Resource Center (**http://www.microsoft.com/activex/**)

  The official ActiveX center of the Universe, at the Redmond company's own site.

- Yahoo!, World Wide Web Section (**http://www.yahoo.com/ Computers_and_Internet/Internet/World_Wide_Web/**)

  For lots of resources on HTML, VRML, and so on, this is a great place to start your search.

FrontPage Resources on the Microsoft Web Site

Okay, so maybe the company that produces a product isn't the most unbiased when it comes to presenting it. Still, if you're looking for the latest news about your software or hardware, or the latest upgrades, patches, drivers, and so forth, it's a fact that heading for that company's Web site is the right place to go. For FrontPage users, that's certainly the case. Here, we'll look at what you'll find on that site as a FrontPage user.

The URL for the site is **http://www.microsoft.com/frontpage/**. This takes you to the FrontPage section of the Microsoft Web site. No pictures are shown of it because it changes frequently. As of this writing, text links were available to the following pages:

- The download area for FrontPage 98 (**http://www.microsoft.com/frontpage/ download/**).

  This link takes you to a page with a link to the actual download site and a link to a form for ordering a CD-ROM of the software. While this link is normally used to download beta versions of FrontPage, it might also be used to obtain additional FrontPage-related software, such as updates, templates, or wizards.

- Online Multimedia Demo (**http://198.107.140.10/frontpage/demo/default.asp**).

  This online demo shows the features of FrontPage 98, including all of the new features. Macromedia Shockwave technology is used to enhance this demo, but you can view the demo without Shockwave.

N O T E   The links that are provided within the text of the FrontPage Web site's home page may also be contained in the graphical links that appear on the page. ■

- FrontPage 98 Tips and Tricks (**http://www.microsoft.com/frontpage/tips/**).

  This page provides links to pages that help you create great-looking Web pages by using FrontPage 98. The features covered on these pages include:

Authoring Resources—HTML conversion tools, background image libraries, ActiveX applications and Microsoft Office viewers, Web servers and Web utilities, and Microsoft Internet applications.

Applying a Theme to Your Web—FrontPage Themes help you develop appealing Web sites using more than 50 professionally designed graphical themes. Themes make your Web site look more professional by giving all of your pages a consistent look and feel.

Creating a Channel with the Channel Definition Wizard—Push technology is made easy with this wizard that lets you broadcast information to users of Internet Explorer 4.0 and Netscape Netcaster.

Using the Navigation View and Shared Borders to Make Navigation Bars—Learn how to easily create site navigation tools. FrontPage 98 automatically updates these elements when you make changes to your Web site.

Creating Images for Hover Buttons—Use buttons that change when users move or click their mouse over them.

Integrate FrontPage 98 with Your Browser—FrontPage 98 can be used to edit documents while browsing. You must use Internet Explorer or Netscape Communicator to take advantage of this feature.

■ FrontPage 98 Beta: Support Options (**http://www.microsoft.com/frontpage/ support.htm**).

As FrontPage 98 moves from beta to its final release, this page will provide support information for FrontPage 98. This page contains links that are used to obtain FrontPage server extensions.

■ Questions about FrontPage 98? (**http://www.microsoft.com/frontpage/productinfo/ faqs.htm**). This page provides answers to the most frequently asked questions about FrontPage 98. It is an excellent starting place for finding information on compatibility issues and new features.

In addition, graphical links were available to the following areas:

■ Product Info (**http://www.microsoft.com/frontpage/productinfo/**)

Here, you'll find a brief overview of FrontPage 98 that touches on many of its important features. In addition, links are provided to pages that discuss how to create and manage FrontPage Web sites.

■ What's New (**http://www.microsoft.com/frontpage/work.htm**)

This page is basically a list of links that provide information on using FrontPage effectively. Links to the top 10 features and improvements are also located on this page.

■ Demo (**http://198.107.140.10/frontpage/demo/default.asp**)

This online demo shows the features of FrontPage 98, including all of the new features. Macromedia Shockwave technology is used to enhance this demo, but you can view the demo without Shockwave.

■ News and Reviews (**http://www.microsoft.com/frontpage/productinfo/news/**)

This page provides links to news stories and reviews that were published on the Web. Use these links to review information about FrontPage and its capabilities.

■ Hosting Your Site (**http://www.microsoft.com/frontpage/hosting.htm**)

Use this page to learn about Web Presence Providers (WPP) and FrontPage extensions. Not all WPPs use the FrontPage extensions. If you plan to use the extensions in your Web site, you want to make sure that they are supported by your WPP. The complete list of providers is located at **http://microsoft.saltmine.com/frontpage/wpp/list/**.

■ FrontPage 97 and Mac (**http://www.microsoft.com/frontpage/FP97_Mac/**)

Although they are normally viewed as Apple's biggest enemy, Microsoft is the second leading producer of software for the Mac. While Office products account for the majority of this, FrontPage is also available for the Mac. This page provides information about FrontPage and the Mac.

■ Web Administrators (**http://www.microsoft.com/frontpage/wpp/**)

Web site administrators can use this page to learn how to support FrontPage Extensions on their servers. This page also provides information on how to join the FrontPage Web Presence Provider Program.

As with anywhere else on the Web, any of these links can change or disappear at any time, but it's worth checking sites once every week or so to see what's been added. Dig down into sites to extract the most from them. Microsoft's Web site contains a substantial amount of valuable information that no FrontPage user should be without.

▶ These are covered in much more detail in Chapter 23, "FrontPage's Web Templates and Wizards."

FrontPage Web Presence Providers

A growing number of presence providers are offering space on their servers to host FrontPage Webs. What this means is that their servers will fully support the FrontPage extensions so that programmable elements such as FrontPage Componenets for forms and database connectivity will function properly when served to the Web. Without support for the FrontPage extensions, these features would not work at all and would need to be redesigned using much more complex programming methods.

Table A.1 shows a partial listing of providers that advertised support specifically for FrontPage 98 at the time of this writing. Rates vary widely, but in general they are from $15-$300 per month. These are the standard rates only—additional traffic and disk space add significantly to the totals. Initial setup costs also increase this amount. In addition, you might want to set up your own domain name, which costs anywhere from $150 to $300 extra. In general, there are rates in each provider's offerings for personal sites and varying levels of business sites.

Table A.1   FrontPage Web Presence Providers

Name	URL
FrontPage Today	http://www.fptoday.com/
1800Access	http://1800access.net/frontpage.htm
A1 TeraBit	http://www.terabit.net/frontpage.htm
ACS	http://www.acserve.com/frontpag.htm
BeeNet	http://www.bee.net/frontpage/
BitShop	http://www.bitshop.com/webhosting/oldpage.html
Computer Peripherals Plus	http://www.cpplus.com/frontpage/default.htm
Computer Routines	http://criweb.com/FrontPage/
Digital Marketplace	http://www.digital-marketplace.net/frontpag.htm
Digital Publishing Resources	http://www.digipub.com/frontpage.html
FrontPage Today	http://www.fptoday.com/
GBS	http://www.gbso.net/host/
Happy To Serve You	http://www.storehouses.com/HTSY/FP_Hosting.htm
NCN Prime	http://www.ncnprime.com/frontpage/
PacificWest	http://www.pacificocean.com/msfp.htm
Paragon Computer Solutions	http://www.fp-webs.com/
PowerNet	http://www.powr.net/frontpag.htm
Realacom	http://www.realacom.com/
Sioux Soft	http://www.midearthbbs.com/frontpage.htm
The Site Shop	http://www.site-shop.com/frontpage.htm
Web Presence	http://www.awebpresence.com/default.htm
DeZines Web Hosting	http://dezines.com/fpbasic.html

From Here...

At this point, you're probably eager to get your Web site underway and find a server where you can post it to the world. There are a couple important issues to resolve first, though, about graphics creation and building interactivity into your site. From this point, head for the following:

- Part III, "Creating and Adapting Graphics with Image Composer," where you'll discover the rich resources of this excellent package.

- Part IV, "Integrating Active Content into Your Web," which introduces you to the ins and outs of database integration and adding Java applets, ActiveX controls, Netscape plug-ins, and JavaScript and VBScript applets to your pages.

- Part V, "Building and Managing a Web," which takes you through the Web creation and management features of FrontPage Explorer and its integration with servers.

HTML 4.0 Quick Reference

Interest in and use of the World Wide Web has been expanding at a phenomenal rate. As the Web grows, so must its vehicle of communication, HTML. The HTML 2.0 specification is dated November 1995. Since then, the HTML 3.0 draft specification expired on September 28, 1995, without reaching recommendation status, and HTML 3.2 became a W3C (World Wide Web Consortium) Recommendation on January 14, 1997. Now, we have the public draft for HTML 4.0, announced on July 8, 1997. This draft is almost certain to undergo changes before being accepted by the W3C as a Proposed Recommendation—if it does, indeed, ever make it to the recommendation state.

In addition to this official work on HTML, the browsers have been making their own additions to HTML. Some changes were eventually adopted into W3C HTML Recommendations; others remain proprietary coding aspects that only the individual browsers recognize. The browsers' versions of HTML changed, too, in a game of marketing and programming one-upmanship, hoping to lock Web developers into using one browser or the other exclusively.

Designing for the Web can be a confusing activity, indeed. ■

What's Different in HTML 4.0

In order to keep up with (or try to) the rapidly changing world of HTML authoring, we present here the changes between HTML 3.2 and HTML 4.0. HTML 4.0 introduces eight new elements, deprecates 10 (more about deprecation in a bit), and made obsolete three more. Frames, formerly only found in the browsers' versions of HTML, join the official fold. Tables provide better tabular presentation, forms more readily respond to the needs of the disabled, style sheets provide for better formatting and presentation, and multimedia, scripting, and printing are improved. And, if that weren't enough, HTML 4.0 uses a different character-encoding format that expands the number of alphabets and languages able to implement Web documents.

Let's start with the changes to single tags first and then move on to the topics, like tables, that encompass more than an individual tag.

New Tags in HTML 4.0

The W3C document, "Changes between HTML 3.2 and HTML 4.0," lists eight new tags in HTML 4.0. A brief description of these tags follows.

<Q>...</Q>   The `<Q>...</Q>` tag acts much the same as the `<BLOCKQUOTE>` tag, but applies to shorter quoted sections—ones that don't need paragraph breaks.

Example:

```
According to the W3C, <Q>BLOCKQUOTE is for long quotations and Q is intended for
short quotations that don't require paragraph breaks.</Q>
```

HTML 4.0 requires both the start tag and the end tag for `<Q>`.

<ACRONYM>...</ACRONYM>   The `<ACRONYM>...</ACRONYM>` tag indicates an acronym in the text. `<ACRONYM>` is a *phrasal* tag, meaning that it helps define the structure of a text phrase. Make sure to use `<ACRONYM>` for the acronym itself, not the title that the letters stand for. `<ACRONYM>` behaves like `<EM>`, `<STRONG>`, and `<CODE>`.

Example:

```
Working with the World Wide Web requires a good head for acronyms.
<ACRONYM>HTML</ACRONYM>, <ACRONYM>WWW</ACRONYM>, and <ACRONYM>HTTP</ACRONYM> are
but a few of the acronyms found around the Web.
```

HTML 4.0 requires both the start tag and the end tag for `<ACRONYM>`.

<INS>...</INS> and <DEL>...</DEL>   Use `<INS>...</INS>` to mark parts of a document that have been added since the document's last version. `<DEL>...</DEL>`, similarly, marks document text that has been deleted since a previous version.

Example:

```
Welcome to our on-line personnel policy guide.<INS>In the spirit of relaxed
living, our dress code now requires only that you meet TV's decency standard.</
INS> <DEL>In the spirit of conservative virtues, we require every employee to
wear a suit to word every day.</DEL>
```

HTML 4.0 requires both the start tag and the end tag for both <INS> and <DEL>.

<COLGROUP>...</COLGROUP>   <COLGROUP>...</COLGROUP> allows you finer control over the formatting of tables by specifying groups of columns that share width and alignment properties. Every table must have at least one <COLGROUP>; without any specific <COLGROUP> definition, HTML 4.0 assumes the table consists of a single column group that contains all the columns of the table.

If you wanted, for example, to create a table that had a single, wide description column, followed by a series of small check boxes, you would code:

```
<TABLE>
<COLGROUP span="10" width="30">
<COLGROUP span="1" width="0*">
<THEAD>
<TR>
...
</TABLE>
```

This way, the first <COLGROUP> tag formats all 10 check boxes; much nicer than typing in 10 identical specifications—for each row!

The start tag for <COLGROUP> is required; the end tag is optional.

<FIELDSET>...</FIELDSET>   With the <FIELDSET>...</FIELDSET> tag, you can group related form fields, making your form easier to read and use. Human brains like to be able to classify information, and <FIELDSET> helps do just that.

When you enclose a group of form elements in the <FIELDSET> tags, the browser will group the elements so that you can easily tell they belong together. HTML 4.0 requires both the start tag and the end tag for <FIELDSET>.

```
<HTML>
<HEAD>
<TITLE>Work preferences</TITLE>
</HEAD>
<BODY>
We'd like you to help us design your new personnel policies. Please give us your
preferences for the areas below.

<FORM action="..." method="post">
   <FIELDSET>
      <LEGEND align="top">Work week preferences</LEGEND>

      Number of days in work week:
      <SELECT NAME="WorkWeek" SIZE="5">
      <OPTION VALUE="3day">3
      <OPTION VALUE="4day">4
      <OPTION VALUE="5day">5
      <OPTION VALUE="6day">6
      <OPTION VALUE="7day">7</SELECT>

      Number of hours in work day:
      <SELECT NAME="WorkDay" SIZE="5">
```

```
        <OPTION VALUE="3day">5
        <OPTION VALUE="4day">6
        <OPTION VALUE="5day">7
        <OPTION VALUE="6day">8
        <OPTION VALUE="7day">9</SELECT>
    </FIELDSET>
<P>
    <FIELDSET>
        <LEGEND>Boss preferences</LEGEND>
        I want a boss who is:
        <INPUT NAME="BossValues" TYPE="checkbox" VALUE="Fair">Fair</INPUT>
        <INPUT NAME="BossValues" TYPE="checkbox" VALUE="Generous">Generous</INPUT>
        <INPUT NAME="BossValues" TYPE="checkbox" VALUE="Easygoing">Easygoing</
INPUT>
    </FIELDSET>
</FORM>
</BODY>
</HTML>
```

<LABEL>...</LABEL>   If you looked at the code for the <FIELDSET> example, you saw the <LABEL>...</LABEL> tags in action. Use <LABEL> with <FIELDSET> to attach a label to the form grouping. In this example, the first <LABEL> has been removed. HTML 4.0 requires both the start tag and the end tag for <LEGEND>.

<BUTTON>...</BUTTON>   The <BUTTON>...</BUTTON> tag, another addition to forms, allows you to have push buttons on forms that more closely resemble push buttons available in Windows and other applications. Many aspects of <BUTTON> are similar to those of the submit and reset <INPUT> elements, but <BUTTON>, in the words of the W3C, "allows richer presentational possibilities."

One example of a richer presentational possibility is the fact that a <BUTTON> has beveled, shadowed edges, looking 3-D rather than flat, and moves when clicked, giving the impression of being pushed in, then released. The code shows buttons at work.

Example:

```
<HTML>
<HEAD>
<TITLE> Moccasin Day </TITLE>

</HEAD>
<BODY>

<FORM action="http://somesite.com/prog/adduser" method="post">
Do you want to celebrate Wear Your Moccasins to Work Day?

<P>
        <INPUT type="radio" name="vote" value="Yes"> Yes<BR>
        <INPUT type="radio" name="vote" value="No"> No<BR>
        <P>
        <BUTTON name="submit" value="submit" type="submit">
        Send</BUTTON>
        <BUTTON name="reset" type="reset">
```

```
        Reset</BUTTON>
    </FORM>

</BODY>
</HTML>
```

HTML 4.0 requires both the start tag and the end tag for `<BUTTON>`.

Deprecated Tags in HTML 4.0

Deprecated tags and attributes are those that have been replaced by other, newer, HTML constructs. Deprecated tags are still included in the HTML draft or recommendation, but are clearly marked as deprecated. Once deprecated, tags may well become obsolete. The draft strongly urges the nonuse of deprecated tags.

<ISINDEX>...</ISINDEX> `<ISINDEX>` allowed a form to contain a simple string search. This action should be replaced by an `<INPUT>` form element.

<APPLET>...</APPLET> The `<APPLET>...</APPLET>` tag enabled the running of a Java applet. This tag has been replaced by the more encompassing `<OBJECT>...</OBJECT>` tag.

<CENTER>...</CENTER> The `<CENTER>...</CENTER>` tag, oddly enough, centered text or graphics. `<CENTER>` is deprecated in favor of `<DIV>` tag with the align attribute set to center.

<FONT>...</FONT> `<FONT>...</FONT>` allowed the specification of font sizes, colors, and faces. Style sheets, rather than HTML code proper, have taken over character formatting duties.

N O T E   Based as it is on SGML, HTML purists have never been happy using *markup*—the description of a document's structure—to define presentation, or how a document appears. With the formal (pending) adoption of style sheets, character formatting can be taken out of HTML code. ■

<BASEFONT>...</BASEFONT> `<BASEFONT>...</BASEFONT>` set a base font size that could then be referenced for size increases or decreases. Use style sheets instead to set and reference relative font sizes.

<STRIKE>...</STRIKE> and <S>...</S> Both `<STRIKE>...</STRIKE>` and `<S>...</S>` created strikethrough characters. Replace these tags with style sheets.

<U>...</U> `<U>...</U>` created underlined characters. As with the tags just mentioned, use style sheets to create underlines.

<DIR>...</DIR> Moving away from fonts, we have the `<DIR>...</DIR>` tag. `<DIR>` describes a directory list. While originally designed to output elements in horizontal columns like UNIX directory listings, browsers formatted `<DIR>` lists like unordered lists. As there is no difference between the two, use a `<UL>...</UL>` list instead of a `<DIR>...</DIR>` list.

<MENU>...</MENU> `<MENU>...</MENU>` lists have also fallen by the wayside. The `<MENU>` tag described single column menu lists. As with `<DIR>` lists, browsers made no distinction between `<MENU>` and `<UL>` lists. Use `<UL>...</UL>` lists instead of `<MENU>` ones.

Obsolete Tags in HTML 4.0

Obsolete tags have been removed from the HTML specification. While browsers may still support obsolete tags, there is no guarantee that this support will continue.

The three tags that become obsolete in HTML 4.0 are <XMP>, <PLAINTEXT>, and <LISTING>. In all cases, replace these tags with <PRE>.

N O T E   Despite the fact that the HTML 4.0 draft doesn't specifically mention frames as new and despite the fact that you may have seen them in use for some time now, frames are new to the official HTML specification.

Internationalization

Despite its name, the World Wide Web has had some difficulty reaching out past the Western languages and alphabets. In general, character representation in HTML was largely confined to the use of the ISO 8859-1 (Latin-1) character set. This character set contains letters for English, French, Spanish, German, and the Scandinavian languages, but no Greek, Hebrew, Arabic, or Cyrillic characters, among others, and few scientific and mathematical symbols. The Latin-1 character set also contains no provisions for marking reading direction.

Part of the problem with Latin-1 is that it simply doesn't have room to handle all the alphabets and languages of the world. It is an 8-bit, single-byte coded graphic character set and, as such, can represent only up to 256 characters.

Enter Unicode. Unicode is a character-encoding standard that uses a 16-bit set, thereby increasing the number of encoded characters to more than 65,000 characters.

HTML 4.0 uses the Universal Character Set (UCS) as its character set. UCS is a character-by-character equivalent to Unicode 2.0.

VBScript Command Reference

To quote Microsoft, VBScript is a lightweight subset of Visual Basic. Don't confuse lightweight with wimpy, however. VBScript is not wimpy. You can create remarkably complex, dynamic Web pages with VBScript, and instantly distribute those Web pages to millions of users around the world. Try that with Visual Basic.

Although VBScript is a subset of Visual Basic, you'll find a lot of differences between the two. That won't keep Visual Basic programmers from quickly getting up to speed, as long as they understand these differences. If you're a Visual Basic programmer, you'll find an overview of the differences in this appendix, as well as a list of Visual Basic keywords available in VBScript and a list of Visual Basic keywords omitted from VBScript. ■

Key Differences Between VB and VBScript

You didn't run out to the computer store and buy a copy of VBScript. You didn't install a VBScript disk on your computer, either. All you did was install the Internet Explorer browser, which supports VBScript, on your computer—just like millions of other folks. Everyone of them has the VBScript engine on their computer, and everyone of them has the ability to create Web pages with VBScript.

So where's the integrated development environment that you're used to using in Visual Basic? Keep looking, because there isn't one. All you have is your favorite text editor, the ActiveX Control Pad, and a Web browser. That in itself is the single largest difference between Visual Basic and VBScript. It leads to some specific differences, too. Here's what they are:

- ■ Debugging   VBScript doesn't have a debugger like Visual Basic. You'll resort to using lots of message boxes, instead.

- ■ Event-handlers   You don't have an editor in which you select an object and event to edit an event-procedure. You have to name event-procedures in your scripts so that the scripting engine can find the appropriate handler when an object fires an event.

- ■ Forms   VBScript doesn't have a forms editor. It doesn't need one, because you can't display forms anyway. You put forms and controls on the Web page, instead. You can use the ActiveX Control pad to insert all those nasty <OBJECT> tags in your Web page, however.

You don't compile a VBScript program into an EXE file like you do with a Visual Basic program. You distribute your scripts as plain, old text embedded in HTML files. Everyone and his uncle can read your scripts. The script engine interprets this text into intermediate code when it loads the Web page. It also creates a symbol table so that it can quickly look up things such as event-procedures and variable names. The scripting engine uses the ActiveX Scripting technology to interact with the browser.

N O T E   You'll find a plethora of nit-picky differences between Visual Basic and VBScript, too. You have to use the `value` property to query an objects value, for example. Thus, instead of reading a text box's value using `form.text`, you have to read it using `form.text.value`. These subtle differences are too numerous to document in this appendix. Go to Microsoft's Web site (**www.microsoft.com**) and their knowledge base for further explanation of these differences. ■

Another significant difference between Visual Basic and VBScript is the keywords that Microsoft omitted from VBScript. You'll learn more about the keywords included in VBScript in the next section. You'll learn about the keywords that Microsoft omitted from VBScript in "Visual Basic Keywords Omitted from VBScript," later in this appendix.

Visual Basic Keywords Included in VBScript

VBScript includes all the keywords and features that you need to activate a Web page. You can't read or write files, as you'll learn later in this appendix, but you can handle any event that an object fires. You can also handle just about any type of data that you'll find on a Web page and manipulate the Web page in anyway you want.

Table C.1 describes each keyword or feature available in VBScript. I've divided this table into broad categories, with each entry under a category describing a single feature. I've used the same categories that Microsoft uses so that you can keep this information straight as you bounce back and forth between Microsoft's Web site and this book. If you don't find a feature that you expect to see, check out Table C.2 to see if that feature is in the list of Visual Basic features omitted from VBScript.

You can find more information about VBScript's features at Microsoft's VBScript Web site: **http://www.microsoft.com/vbscript.**

Table C.1   VBScript Keywords

Keyword/Feature	Description
Array handling	
IsArray	Returns True if a variable is an array
Erase	Reinitializes a fixed-size array
LBound	Returns the lower bound of an array
UBound	Returns the upper bound of an array
Assignments	
=	Assigns a value to a variable
Let	Assigns a value to a variable
Set	Assigns an object to a variable
Comments	
'	Includes inline comments in your script
Rem	Includes comments in your script
Constants/Literals	
Empty	Indicates an uninitialized variable
Nothing	Disassociates a variable with an object
Null	Indicates a variable with no data
True	Boolean True
False	Boolean False

App

C

continues

Table C.1   Continued

Keyword/Feature	Description
Control flow	
Do...Loop	Repeats a block of statements
For...Next	Repeats a block of statements
For Each...Next	Repeats a block of statements
If...Then...Else	Conditionally executes statements
Select Case	Conditionally executes statements
While...Wend	Repeats a block of statements
Conversions	
Abs	Returns absolute value of a number
Asc	Returns the ASCII code of a character
AscB	Returns the ASCII code of a character
AscW	Returns the ASCII code of a character
Chr	Returns a character from an ASCII code
ChrB	Returns a character from an ASCII code
ChrW	Returns a character from an ASCII code
CBool	Converts a variant to a boolean
CByte	Converts a variant to a byte
CDate	Converts a variant to a date
CDbl	Converts a variant to a double
Cint	Converts a variant to an integer
CLng	Converts a variant to a long
CSng	Converts a variant to a single
CStr	Converts a variant to a string
DateSerial	Converts a variant to a date
DateValue	Converts a variant to a date
Hex	Converts a variant to a hex string
Oct	Converts a variant to an octal string
Fix	Converts a variant to a fixed string
Int	Converts a variant to an integer string

Keyword/Feature	Description
Conversions	
Sgn	Converts a variant to a single string
TimeSerial	Converts a variant to a time
TimeValue	Converts a variant to a time
Dates/Times	
Date	Returns the current date
Time	Returns the current time
DateSerial	Returns a date from its parts
DateValue	Returns a date from its value
Day	Returns day from a date
Month	Returns month from a date
Weekday	Returns weekday from a date
Year	Returns year from a date
Hour	Returns hour from a time
Minute	Returns minute from a time
Second	Returns seconds from a time
Now	Returns current date and time
TimeSerial	Returns a time from its parts
TimeValue	Returns a time from its value
Declarations	
Dim	Declares a variable
Private	Declares script-level private variable
Public	Declares public-level public variable
ReDim	Reallocates an array
Function	Declares a function
Sub	Declares a subprocedure
Error Handling	
On Error	Enables error handling
Err	Contains information about last error

continues

App
C

Table C.1 Continued

Keyword/Feature	Description
Input/Output	
InputBox	Prompts the user for input
MsgBox	Displays a message to the user
Math	
Atn	Returns the Arctangent of a number
Cos	Returns the cosine of a number
Sin	Returns the sine of a number
Tan	Returns the tangent of a number
Exp	Returns the exponent of a number
Log	Returns the logarithm of a number
Sqr	Returns the square root of a number
Randomize	Reseeds the randomizer
Rnd	Returns a random number
Operators	
+	Addition
−	Subtraction
^	Exponentiation
Mod	Modulus arithmetic
*	Multiplication
/	Division
\	Integer Division
−	Negation
&	String concatenation
=	Equality
<>	Inequality
<	Less Than
<=	Less Than or Equal To
>	Greater Than
>=	Greater Than or Equal To

Keyword/Feature	Description
Operators	
Is	Compares expressions
And	Compares expressions
Or	Compares expressions
Xor	Compares expressions
Eqv	Compares expressions
Imp	Compares expressions
Objects	
CreateObject	Creates reference to an OLE object
IsObject	Returns True if object is valid
Options	
Option Explicit	Forces explicit variable declaration
Procedures	
Call	Invokes a subprocedure
Function	Declares a function
Sub	Declares a subprocedure
Strings	
Instr	Returns index of a string in another
InStrB	Returns index of a string in another
Len	Returns the length of a string
LenB	Returns the length of a string
Lcase	Converts a string to lowercase
Ucase	Converts a string to uppercase
Left	Returns the left portion of a string
LeftB	Returns the left portion of a string
Mid	Returns the mid portion of a string
MidB	Returns the mid portion of a string
Right	Returns the right portion of a string
RightB	Returns the right portion of a string
Space	Pads a string with spaces

App
C

continues

Table C.1 Continued

Keyword/Feature	Description
Strings	
StrComp	Compares two strings
String	Pads a string with a character
Ltrim	Removes leading spaces from a string
Rtrim	Removes trailing spaces from a string
Trim	Removes leading and trailing spaces
Variants	
IsArray	Returns True if variable is an array
IsDate	Returns True if variable is a date
IsEmpty	Returns True if variable is empty
IsNull	Returns True if variable is null.
IsNumeric	Returns True if variable is a number
IsObject	Returns True if variable is an object
VarType	Indicates a variable's type

Visual Basic Keywords Omitted from VBScript

VBScript leaves out a bunch of Visual Basic keywords such as DoEvents, Print, and Shell. You can't read or write files, either, and you can't do much graphical programming. This won't stop you from creating great Web pages with VBScript, though, because VBScript provides every feature you need to do just about anything you want on the Web page. For example, you can dynamically change the contents of the Web page itself and you can interact with every object on the Web page.

Don't look at the list of omitted keywords and features yet. You need to understand why Microsoft didn't include them so that you'll understand why each feature is on this list. Take a look:

- Portability   Microsoft intends to make VBScript available on a variety of platforms including Windows, Mac, UNIX, and so on. They've wisely removed keywords and features that make VBScript less portable to these platforms.
- Performance   You've heard it before: speed or features—pick one. Microsoft removed many nonessential features from VBScript so scripts load and run faster.
- Safety   You should be concerned with security on the Internet. You don't want to open a Web page and discover that it contains a script which crashes your drive, do you?

Microsoft removed any Visual Basic feature that might cause a security problem with scripts such as file I/O. You can still get access to these features, however, if you create an ActiveX object which you control with VBScript.

Table C.1 describes each keyword or feature available in Visual Basic but omitted from VBScript. I've divided this table into broad categories, with each entry under a category describing a single feature. I've used Microsoft's categories so that you can keep the list on Microsoft's Web site in sync with this list.

N O T E The Internet Explorer Script Error dialog box tells you that it found a statement in your script which couldn't interpret. I'm sure that you've seen error messages such as "Expected while or until" or `nested comments` that just don't make any sense. When VBScript encounters a keyword it doesn't recognize, it spews out all sorts of garbage like the previous example. It usually points to the offending keyword, however, by placing a caret (^) directly underneath it. The next time you get one of these unexplained errors, look up the keyword in Table C.2 to see if Microsoft omitted it from VBScript. ▪

App
C

Table C.2 Visual Basic Keywords Not in VBScript

Keyword/Feature	Description
Array Handling	
Option Base	Declares default lower bound
Arrays with lower bound <> 0	All arrays must have 0 lower bound
Clipboard	
Clipboard object	Provides access to the clipboard
Clear	Clears the contents of the clipboard
GetFormat	Determines format of clipboard object
GetData	Returns data from the clipboard
SetData	Stores data in the clipboard
GetText	Returns text from the clipboard
SetText	Stores text in the clipboard
Collection	
Add	Adds an item to a collection
Count	Returns number of items in collection
Item	Returns an item from a collection

continues

Table C.2 Continued

Keyword/Feature	Description
Collection	
Remove	Removes an item from a collection
Access collections using ! character	Accesses a collection with !
Conditional Compilation	
#Const	Defines a compiler constant
#If...Then... #Else	Conditional compilation
Constants/Literals	
Const	Defines a constant
All intrinsic	Predefined constants such as vbOK constants
exponent-based	Real numbers using exponents real number
Trailing data type characters	Defines data types implicitly
Control Flow	
DoEvents	Yields execution to Windows
GoSub...Return	Branches to a label in a procedure
GoTo	Goes to a label in a procedure
On Error GoTo	Goes to a label on an error
On...GoSub	Branches to a label on an index
On...GoTo	Goes to a label on an index
Line numbers	Line numbers
Line labels	Labels define GoTo/GoSub targets
With...End With	Provides easy access to an object
Conversion	
Chr$	Returns a character from an ASCII code
Hex$	Returns string hex from a number
Oct$	Returns string octal from a number
Ccur	Converts expression to currency

Keyword/Feature	Description
Conversion	
Cvar	Converts expression to a variant
CVDate	Converts an expression to a date
Format	Formats a string
Format$	Formats a string
Str	Returns a string form of a number
Str$	Returns a string form of a number
Val	Returns a number from a string
Data Types	
All intrinsic data types except variant	Data types such as Date
Type...End Type	Defines user-defined data type
Date/Time	
Date statement	Returns the current date
Time statement	Returns the current time
Date$	Returns the current date
Time$	Returns the current time
Timer	Returns seconds elapsed since midnight
DDE	
LinkExecute	Sends command during DDE conversation
LinkPoke	Sends data during a DDE conversation
LinkRequest	Receives data during DDE conversation
LinkSend	Sends data during a DDE conversation
Debugging	
Debug.Print	Prints to the debugging window
End	Shuts down the application
Stop	Stops the application
Declaration	
Declare	Declares a DLL
Property Get	Defines a user-defined class

App

C

continues

Table C.2 Continued

Keyword/Feature	Description
Declaration	
Property Let	Defines a user-defined class
Property Set	Defines a user-defined class
Public	Declares a public variable
Private	Declares a private variable
ParamArray	Accepts a variable number of arguments
Optional	Specifies an optional argument
New	Creates a new object
Error Handling	
Erl	Returns the line number of an error
Error	Returns an error message
Error$	Returns an error message
On Error...Resume	Enables error handling
Resume	Resumes after an error
Resume Next	Resumes after an error
File Input/Output	
All	Opens, reads, writes, and closes files
Financial	
All financial	Financial function such as Rate functions.
Graphics	
Cls	Clears the screen
Circle	Draws a circle
Line	Draws a line
Point	Draws a point
Pset	Changes a point's color
Scale	Defines the coordinate system
Print	Prints to a file
Spc	Position output using Print

Keyword/Feature	Description
Graphics	
Tab	Inserts a tab character
TextHeight	Returns height of a text string
TextWidth	Returns width of a text string
LoadPicture	Loads a picture from disk
SavePicture	Saves a picture to disk
QBColor	Returns an RGB color code
RGB	Combines RGB color codes
Manipulating Objects	
Arrange	Arranges windows
Zorder	Changes z-order of windows
SetFocus	Sets focus to a window
InputBox$	Prompts the user for a string
Drag	Begins a drag-and-drop operation
Hide	Hides a form
Show	Shows a form
Load	Loads a form
Unload	Unloads a form
Move	Moves a form
PrintForm	Prints a form
Refresh	Repaints a form
AddItem	Adds item to list box
RemoveItem	Removes item from a list box
Miscellaneous	
Environ	Returns the user's environment
Environ$	Returns the user's environment
SendKeys	Sends keystrokes to a window
Command	Returns the command line parameters
Command$	Returns the command line parameters
AppActivate	Activates an application's window

App

C

continues

Table C.2   Continued

Keyword/Feature	Description
Miscellaneous	
Shell	Launches another program
Beep	Beeps the speaker
Object Manipulation	
GetObject	Returns an OLE object from a file
TypeOf	Returns the type of an object
Operators	
Like	Compares to strings
Options	
def *type*	Sets default data type for variables
Option Base	Sets default lower bound for arrays
Option Compare	Defines default comparison method
Option Private	Defines default scope Module
Printing	
TextHeight	Returns height of a text string
TextWidth	Returns width of a text string
EndDoc	Terminates a print operation
NewPage	Ejects the current page
PrintForm	Prints a form
Strings	
All fixed-length	Strings with a fixed length
LCase$	Converts a string to lowercase
UCase$	Converts a string to uppercase
Lset	Left aligns a string
Rset	Right aligns a string
Space$	Pads a string with spaces
String$	Pads a string with a character
Format	Formats a string
Format$	Formats a string

Keyword/Feature	Description
Strings	
Left$	Returns left portion of a string
Mid$	Returns mid portion of a string
Right$	Returns right portion of a string
Mid Statement	Replaces a portion of a string
Trim$	Removes leading and trailing spaces
LTrim$	Removes leading spaces from a string
RTrim$	Removes trailing spaces from a string
StrConv	Performs various conversions
Using Classes	
TypeName	Defines a user-defined class
Optional Arguments	
IsMissing	Indicates missing optional argument

App

C

JavaScript Command Reference

Terms

While not necessarily JavaScript objects or keywords, the following items can help in your understanding of JavaScript and how it works. These are the general terms that are used in most discussions about JavaScript and its implementation.

Cookie   A special object containing state/status information about the client that can be accessed by the server. Included in that state object is a description of the range of URLs for which that state is valid. Future HTTP requests from the client falling within a range of URLs described within the state object will include transmission of the current value of the state object from the client back to the server.

This simple form of data storage allows the server to provide personalized service to the client. Online merchants can store information about items currently in an electronic shopping basket, services can post registration information and automate functions such as typing a user ID, and user preferences can be saved on the client and retrieved by the server when the site is contacted. For limited-use information, such as shopping services, it is also possible to set a time limit on the life of the cookie information.

CGI scripts are typically used to set and retrieve cookie values. To generate the cookie requires sending an HTTP header in the following format:

```
Set-Cookie: NAME=Value; [EXPIRES=date;] [PATH=pathname;] [DOMAIN=domainname;]
[SECURE]
```

When a request for cookie information is made, the list of cookie information is searched for all URLs which match the current URL. Any matches are returned in this format:

```
cookie: NAME1=string1; NAME2=string2; ...
```

Cookie was an arbitrarily assigned name. For more information about the cookie and its function, see **http://home.netscape.com/newsref/std/cookie_spec.html**.

Event Handler   Attributes of HTML tags embedded in documents. The attribute assigns a JavaScript command or function to execute when the event happens.

Function   A user-defined or built-in set of statements that perform a task. It can also return a value when used with the `return` statement.

Hierarchy   Navigator objects exist in a set relation to each other that reflects the structure of an HTML page. This is referred to as *instance hierarchy* because it only works with specific instances of objects, rather than general classes.

The `window` object is the parent of all other Navigator objects. Underneath `window`, `location`, `history`, and `document` all share precedence. `Document` includes forms, links, and anchors.

Each object is a descendant of the higher object. A form called `orderForm` is an object, but is also a property of `document`. As such, it is referred to as `document.orderForm`.

Java   An object-oriented, platform-independent programming language developed by Sun Microsystems and used to add additional functionality to Web pages. Programming in Java requires a Java Development Kit with compiler and core classes.

Although Java started out as a language intended for writing Web applets, more and more stand-alone Java applications are being created.

JavaScript   A scripting language developed by Netscape for HTML documents. Scripts are performed after specific user-triggered events. Creating JavaScript Web documents requires a text editor and compatible browser.

Literal   An absolute value not assigned to a variable. Examples include `1`, `3.1415927`, `"Bob"`, `true`.

Method   A function assigned to an object. For example, `bigString.toUpperCase()` returns an uppercase version of the string contained in `bigString`.

Object   A construct with properties that are JavaScript variables or other objects. Functions associated with an object are known as the *object's methods*. You access the properties of an object with a simple notation:

```
objectName.propertyName
```

Both object and property names are case sensitive.

Operator   Performs a function on one or more operands or variables. Operators are divided into two classes: binary and unary. Binary operators need two operands, and unary operands can operate on a single operand.

For example, addition is a binary operand:

```
sum = 1 + 1
```

Unary operands are often used to update counters. The following example increases the variable by 1:

```
counter++
```

Property   Used to describe an object. A property is defined by assigning it a value. There are several properties in JavaScript that contain *constants:* values that never change.

Script   One or more JavaScript commands enclosed with a `<script>` tag.

Objects

JavaScript is an object-oriented language, so at its heart are a predefined set of objects which relate to the various components of an HTML page and their relation to each other. To view or manipulate the state of an object requires the use of properties and methods, which are also covered in this appendix. If an object is also used as a property of another object, that relationship is listed following the definition. Related properties, methods, and event handlers for each object are listed following the definition.

anchors   A piece of text that can be the target of a hypertext link. This is a read-only object which is set in HTML with `<A>` tags. To determine how many anchors are included in a document, use the `length` property.

App
D

`document.anchors.length`

Unless the anchor name is an integer, the value of `document.anchor[index]` will return null.

Property of `document`. See `link` OBJECT; see `anchor` METHOD.

button   An object that is a form element and must be defined within a `<form>` tag and can be used to perform an action.

Property of `form`.

See OBJECTS `reset` and `submit`; see PROPERTIES `name` and `value`; see `click` METHOD; see `onClick` EVENT HANDLER.

checkbox   A form element that the user sets to `on` or `off` by clicking and that must be defined in a `<form>` tag. Using the `checkbox` object, you can see if the box is checked and review the name and value.

Property of `form`. See `radio` OBJECT; see PROPERTIES `checked`, `defaultChecked`, `name`, `value`; see `click` METHOD; see `onClick` EVENT HANDLER.

Date   Replaces a normal date type. Although it does not have any properties, it is equipped with a wide range of methods. In its current release, `Date` does not work with dates prior to 1/1/70.

Methods for getting and setting time and date information are divided into four classes: `set`, `get`, `to`, and `parse`/`UTC`.

Except for the date, all numerical representation of date components begin with zero. This should not present a problem except with months, which are represented by zero (January) through 11 (December).

The standard date syntax is `"Thu, 11 Jan 1996 06:20:00 GMT"`. US time zone abbreviations are also understood; but for universal use, specify the time zone offset. For example, `"Thu, 11 Jan 1996 06:20:00 GMT+0530"` is a place five hours and 30 minutes west of the Greenwich meridian.

See METHODS `getDate`, `getDay`, `getHours`, `getMinutes`, `getMonth`, `getSeconds`, `getTime`, `getTimezoneOffset`, `getYear`, `parse`, `setDate`, `setHours`, `setMinutes`, `setMonth`, `setSeconds`, `setTime`, `setYear`, `toGMTString`, `toLocaleString`, `toString`.

document   An object created by Navigator when a page is loaded, containing information on the current document, such as title, background color, and forms. These properties are defined within `<body>` tags. It also provides methods for displaying HTML text to the user.

You can reference the anchors, forms, and links of a document by using the `anchors`, `forms`, and `links` arrays of the `document` object. These arrays contain an entry for each `anchor`, `form`, or `link` in a document.

Property of `window`. See `frame` OBJECT; see PROPERTIES `alinkColor`, `anchors`, `bgColor`, `cookie`, `fgColor`, `forms`, `lastModified`, `linkColor`, `links`, `location`, `referrer`, `title`, vlinkColor; see METHODS `clear`, `close`, `open`, `write`, `writeln`; see `onLoad` and `onUnload` EVENT HANDLERS.

elements   An array of `form` elements in source order, including buttons, check boxes, radio buttons, text and text area objects. The elements can be referred to by their index:

```
formName.elements[index]
```

Elements can also be referenced by the element name. For example, a password element called newPassword is the second form element on an HTML page. It's value is accessed in three ways:

```
formName.elements[1].value
formName.elements["newPassword"].value
formName.newPassword.value
```

Values can not be set or changed using the read-only `elements` array.

Property of `form`. See `length` PROPERTY.

form   A property of the `document` object. Each form in a document is a separate and distinct object that can be referenced using the `form` object. The `form` object is an array created as forms are defined through HTML tags. If the first `form` in a document is named `orderForm`, then it could be referenced as `document.orderForm` or `document.forms[0]`.

Property of `document`. See hidden OBJECT; see PROPERTIES `action`, `elements`, `encoding`, `forms`, `method`, `name`, `target`; see `submit` METHOD; see `onSubmit` EVENT HANDLER.

frame   A window that contains HTML subdocuments that are independently, although not necessarily, scrollable. `Frames` can point to different URLs and be targeted by other frames—all in the same window. Each `frame` is a `window` object defined using the `<frameset>` tag to define the layout that makes up the page. The page is defined from a parent HTML document. All subdocuments are children of the parent.

If a `frame` contains definitions for `SRC` and `NAME` attributes, then the `frame` can be identified from a sibling by using the `parent` object as `parent.frameName` or `parent.frames[index]`.

Property of `window`. See `document` and `window` OBJECTS; see PROPERTIES `defaultStatus`, `frames`, `parent`, `self`, `status`, `top`, `window`; see METHODS `setTimeout` and `clearTimeout`.

hidden   A text object suppressed from appearing on an HTML form. `Hidden` objects can be used in addition to `cookies` to pass name/value pairs for client/server communication.

Property of `form`. See PROPERTIES `cookie`, `defaultValue`, `name`, `value`.

history   This object is derived from the Go menu and contains URL link information for previously visited pages.

Property of `document`. See `location` OBJECT; see `length` PROPERTY; see METHODS `back`, `forward`, `go`.

App

D

link   A `location` object. In addition to providing information about existing hypertext links, the `link` object can also be used to define new links.

Property of `document`. See anchor OBJECT; see PROPERTIES `hash`, `host`, `hostname`, `href`, `length`, `pathname`, `port`, `protocol`, `search`, `target`; see `link` METHOD; see `onClick` and `onMouseOver` EVENT HANDLERS.

location   Contains complete URL information for the current document, while each property of `location` contains a different portion of the URL.

Property of `document`. See `history` OBJECT; see PROPERTIES `hash`, `host`, `hostname`, `href`, `location`, `pathname`, `port`, `protocol`, `search`, `target`.

Math   Includes properties for mathematical constants and methods for functions. For example, to access the value of pi in an equation, use:

`Math.PI`

Standard trigonometric, logarithmic, and exponential functions are also included. All arguments in trigonometric functions use radians.

See PROPERTIES `E`, `LN10`, `LN2`, `PI`, `SQRT1_2`, `SQRT2`; see METHODS `abs`, `acos`, `asin`, `atan`, `ceil`, `cos`, `exp`, `floor`, `log`, `max`, `min`, `pow`, `random`, `round`, `sin`, `sqrt`, `tan`.

navigator   Contains information on the current version of Navigator used by the client.

See OBJECTS `link` and `anchors`; see PROPERTIES `appName`, `appCodeName`, `appVersion`, `userAgent`.

option   Objects created within HTML `<form>` tags and represent option buttons. A set of option buttons enables the user to select one item from a list. When it is created, it takes the form of `document.formName.radioName[index]`, where the index is a number representing each button beginning with zero.

Property of `form`. See OBJECTS `checkbox`, `select`; see PROPERTIES `checked`, `defaultChecked`, `index`, `length`, `name`, `value`; see `click` METHOD; see `onClick` EVENT HANDLER.

password   Created by HTML password text fields, and are masked when entered by the user. It must be defined with an HTML `<form>` tag.

Property of `form`. See text OBJECT; see PROPERTIES `defaultValue`, `name`, `value`; see METHODS `focus`, `blur`, `select`.

reset   Correlates with an HTML reset button, which resets all `form` objects to their default values. A reset object must be created within a `<form>` tag.

Property of `form`. See OBJECTS `button` and `submit`; see PROPERTIES `name` and `value`; see `click` METHOD; see `onClick` EVENT HANDLER.

select   A selection list or scrolling list on an HTML form. A selection list enables the user to choose one item from a list, while a scrolling list enables the choice of one or more items from a list.

Property of form. See radio OBJECT; see PROPERTIES length, name, options, selectedIndex; see METHODS blur and focus; see EVENT HANDLERS onBlur, onChange, onFocus.

For the options PROPERTY of select, see defaultSelected, index, selected, text, value.

string A series of characters defined by double or single quotes. For example:

```
myDog = "Brittany Spaniel"
```

returns a string object called myDog with the value "Brittany Spaniel". Quotation marks are not a part of the string's value—they are only used to delimit the string. The object's value is manipulated using methods that return a variation on the string, for example myDog.toUpperCase() returns "BRITTANY SPANIEL". It also includes methods that return HTML versions of the string, such as bold and italics.

See text and text area OBJECTS; see length PROPERTY; see METHODS anchor, big, blink, bold, charAt, fixed, fontcolor, fontsize, indexOf, italics, lastIndexOf, link, small, strike, sub, substring, sup, toLowerCase, toUpperCase.

submit Causes the form to be submitted to the program specified by the action property. It is created within an HTML <form> tag. It always loads a new page, which may be the same as the current page if an action isn't specified.

Property of form. See OBJECTS button and reset; see PROPERTIES name and value; see METHOD click; see EVENT HANDLER onClick.

text A one-line input field on an HTML form that accepts characters or numbers. Text objects can be updated by assigning new contents to its value.

Property of form. See OBJECTS password, string, textarea; see PROPERTIES defaultValue, name, value; see METHODS focus, blur, select; see EVENT HANDLERS onBlur, onChange, onFocus, onSelect.

textarea Similar to a text object, with the addition of multiple lines. A textarea object can also be updated by assigning new contents to its value.

Property of form. See OBJECTS password, string, text; see PROPERTIES defaultValue, name, value; see METHODS focus, blur, select; see EVENT HANDLERS onBlur, onChange, onFocus, onSelect.

window Created by Navigator when a page is loaded containing properties that apply to the whole window. It is the top-level object for each document, location, and history object. Because its existence is assumed, you do not have to reference the name of the window when referring to its objects, properties, or methods. For example, the following two lines have the same result (printing a message to the status line):

```
status("Go away from here.")
window.status("Go away from here.")
```

A new window is created using the open method:

```
aNewWindow = window.open("URL","Window_Name",["windowFeatures"])
```

App
D

The variable name is used to refer to the window's properties and methods. The window name is used in the target argument of a form or `anchor` tag.

See OBJECTS `document` and `frame`; see PROPERTIES `defaultStatus`, `frames`, `parent`, `self`, `status`, `top`, `window`; see METHODS `alert`, `close`, `confirm`, `open`, `prompt`, `setTimeout`, `clearTimeout`; see EVENT HANDLERS `onLoad` and `onUnload`.

Properties

Properties are used to view or set the values of objects. An object is simply a vague generality until a property is used to define the values which make it specific.

action   The `action` property is a reflection of the `action` attribute in an HTML `<form>` tag, consisting of a destination URL for the submitted data. This value can be set or changed before or after the document has been loaded and formatted.

In this example, the `action` for a form called `outlineForm` is set to the URL contained in the variable `outlineURL`.

```
outlineForm.action=outlineURL
```

Property of `form`. See PROPERTIES `encoding`, `method`, `target`.

alinkColor   The color of a link after the mouse button is depressed—but before it's released—and expressed as a hexadecimal RGB triplet or string literal. It cannot be changed after the HTML source is processed. Both of these examples set the color to alice blue.

```
document.alinkColor="aliceblue"
document.alinkColor="F0F8FF"
```

Property of `document`. See PROPERTIES `bgColor`, `fgColor`, `linkColor`, `vlinkColor`.

anchors   An array of all defined anchors in the current document. If the length of an anchor array in a document is 5, then the anchors array is represented as `document.anchors[0]` through `document.anchors[4]`.

Property of `document`. See anchor OBJECT; see PROPERTIES `length` and `links`.

appCodeName   Returns a read-only string with the code name of the browser.

```
document.write("The code name of your browser is " + navigator.appCodeName)
```

For most Netscape Navigator 2.0, this returns:

```
The code name of your browser is Mozilla
```

Property of `navigator`. See PROPERTIES `appName`, `appVersion`, `userAgent`.

appName   Returns a read-only string with the name of the browser.

Property of `navigator`. See PROPERTIES `appCodeName`, `appVersion`, `userAgent`.

appVersion Returns a string with the version information of the browser in the format "releaseNumber (platform; country)." For a release of Netscape 2.0:

```
document.write(navigator.appVersion)
```

returns

```
2.0 (Win95; I)
```

This specifies Navigator 2.0 running on Windows 95 with an international release. The U country code specifies a US release, while an I indicates an international release.

Property of `navigator`. See PROPERTIES `appName`, `appCodeName`, `userAgent`.

bgColor The document background color expressed as a hexadecimal RGB triplet or string literal. It can be reset at any time. Both of these examples set the background to alice blue.

```
document.bgColor = "aliceblue"
document.bgColor = "F0F8FF"
```

Property of `document`. See PROPERTIES `alinkColor`, `fgColor`, `linkColor`, `vlinkColor`.

checked A Boolean value (`true` or `false`), indicating whether a check box or radio button is selected. The value is updated immediately when an item is checked. It's used in the following form:

```
formName.checkboxName.checked
formName.radioButtonName[index].checked
```

Property of `checkbox` and `radio`. See `defaultChecked` PROPERTY.

cookie String value of a small piece of information stored by Navigator in a client-side COOKIES.TXT file. The value stored in the `cookie` is found using substring `charAt`, `IndexOf`, and `lastIndexOf`.

For more information, see the discussion under TERMS.

Property of `document`. See `hidden` OBJECT.

defaultChecked A Boolean value (`true` or `false`) indicating whether a check box or radio button is checked by default. Setting a value to `defaultChecked` can override the checked attribute of a form element. The following section of code will reset a group of radio buttons to its original state by finding and setting the default button:

```
for (var i in menuForm.choices) {
   if (menuForm.choices[i].defaultChecked) {
      menuForm.choice[i].defaultChecked = true
   }
}
```

Property of `checkbox` and `radio`. See `form` OBJECT; see `checked` PROPERTY.

defaultSelected A Boolean value (`true` or `false`) representing the default state of an item in a form select element. Setting a value with this property can override the selected attribute of an <option> tag. The syntax is identical to `defaultChecked`.

Property of `options`. See PROPERTIES `index`, `selected`, `selectedIndex`.

defaultStatus The default message displayed in the status bar at the bottom of a Navigator window when nothing else is displayed. This is preempted by a priority or transient message, such as a `mouseOver` event with an `anchor`. For example:

```
window.defaultStatus = "Welcome to my home page"
```

displays the welcome message while the mouse is not over a link, or Netscape is not performing an action that it needs to notify the user about.

Property of `window`. See `status` PROPERTY.

defaultValue The initial contents of `hidden`, `password`, `text`, `textarea`, and `string` form elements. For password elements, it is initially set to null for security reasons, regardless of any set `value`.

Property of `hidden`, `password`, `text`, `textarea`. See `value` PROPERTY.

E The base of natural logarithms, also known as Euler's constant. The value is approximately 2.7182818285...

Property of `Math`. See PROPERTIES `LN2`, `LN10`, `LOG2E`, `LOG10E`, `PI`, `SQRT1_2`, `SQRT2`.

elements An array of objects containing form elements in HTML source order. The array index begins with zero and ends with the number of `form` elements –1.

Property of `form`. See `elements` OBJECT.

encoding Returns a string reflecting the Mime encoding type, which is set in the `enctype` attribute of an HTML `<form>` tag.

Property of `form`. See PROPERTIES `action`, `method`, `target`.

fgColor The color of foreground text represented as a hexadecimal RGB triplet or a string literal. This value cannot be changed after a document is processed. It can take two forms:

```
document.fgColor="aliceblue"
document.fgColor="F0F8FF"
```

Property of `document`. See PROPERTIES `alinkColor`, `bgColor`, `linkColor`, `vlinkColor`; see `fontcolor` METHODS.

forms An array of objects corresponding to named forms in HTML source order and containing an entry for each `form` object in a document.

Property of `document`. See `form` OBJECT; see `length` PROPERTY.

frames An array of objects corresponding to child frame windows created using the `<frameset>` tag. To obtain the number of child frames in a window, use the `length` property.

Property of `window`. See `frame` OBJECT; see `length` PROPERTY.

hash   Returns a string with the portion of a URL beginning with a hash mark (#), which denotes an `anchor` name fragment. It can be used to set a `hash` property, although it is safest to set the entire URL as a `href` property. An error is returned if the `hash` isn't found in the current location.

Property of `link` and `location`. See anchor OBJECT; see PROPERTIES `host`, `hostname`, `href`, `pathname`, `port`, `protocol`, `search` `properties`.

host   Returns a string formed by combining the `hostname` and `port` properties of a URL and provides a method for changing it.

```
location.host = "www.montna.com:80"
```

Property of `link` and `location`. See PROPERTIES `hash`, `hostname`, `href`, `pathname`, `port`, `protocol`, `search`.

hostname   Returns or changes a string with the domain name or IP address of a URL.

Property of `link` and `location`. See PROPERTIES `hash`, `host`, `href`, `pathname`, `port`, `protocol`, `search`.

href   Returns a string with the entire URL. All other `location` and `link` properties are substrings of `href`, which can be changed at any time.

Property of `link` and `location`. See PROPERTIES `hash`, `host`, `hostname`, `pathname`, `port`, `protocol`, `search`.

index   Returns the index of an option in a select element with zero being the first item.

Property of `options`. See PROPERTIES `defaultSelected`, `selected`, `selectedIndex`.

lastModified   A read-only string containing the date that the current document was last changed, based on the file attributes. The string is formatted in the standard form used by JavaScript (see `Date` object). A common usage is:

```
document.write("This page last modified on " + document.lastModified)
```

Property of `document`.

length   An integer reflecting a length- or size-related property of an object.

Object	Property Measured
history	Length of the history list
string	Integer length of the string; zero for a null string
radio	Number of radio buttons
anchors, forms, frames, links, options	Number of elements in the array

Property of `anchors`, `elements`, `forms`, `frame`, `frames`, `history`, `links`, `options`, `radio`, `string`, `window`.

App
D

linkColor The hyperlink color displayed in the document, expressed as a hexadecimal RGB triplet or as a string literal. It corresponds to the `link` attribute in the HTML `<body>` tag, and cannot be changed after the document is processed.

Property of `document`. See PROPERTIES `alinkColor`, `bgColor`, `fgColor`, `vlinkColor`.

links An array representing `link` objects defined in HTML using `<a href=URL>` tags with the first `link` identified as `document.links[0]`.

See `link` object. See PROPERTIES `anchors` and `length`.

LN2 A constant representing the natural logarithm of 2 (approximately 0.693).

Property of `Math`. See PROPERTIES `E`, `LN10`, `LOG2E`, `LOG10E`, `PI`, `SQRT1_2`, `SQRT2`.

LN10 A constant representing the natural logarithm of 10 (approximately 2.302).

Property of `Math`. See PROPERTIES `E`, `LN2`, `LOG2E`, `LOG10E`, `PI`, `SQRT1_2`, `SQRT2`.

location Returns a string with the URL of the current document. This read-only property (`document.location`) is different from the location `objects` properties (`window.location.propertyName`), which can be changed.

Property of `document`. See `location` OBJECT.

LOG2E A constant representing the base 2 logarithm of `e` (approximately 1.442).

Property of `Math`. See PROPERTIES `E`, `LN2`, `LN10`, `LOG10E`, `PI`, `SQRT1_2`, `SQRT2`.

LOG10E A constant representing the base 10 logarithm of `e` (approximately .434).

Property of `Math`. See PROPERTIES `E`, `LN2`, `LN10`, `LOG2E`, `SQRT1_2`, `SQRT2`.

method Reflects the `method` attribute of an HTML `<form>` tag: either `<GET>` or `<POST>`. It can be set at any time. The first function returns the current value of the form object, while the second function sets the method to the contents of `newMethod`.

```
function getMethod(formObj) {
   return formObj.method
}
function setMethod(formObj,newMethod) {
   formObj.method = newMethod
}
```

Property of `form`. See PROPERTIES `action`, `encoding`, `target`.

name Returns a string with the `name` attribute of the object. This is the internal name for `button`, `reset` and `submit` objects, not the on-screen label.

For example, after opening a new window with `indexOutline = window.open("http://www.wossamatta.com/outline.html","MenuPage")` and issuing the command `document.write(indexOutline.name)`, JavaScript returns `MenuPage`, which was specified as the name attribute.

Property of `button`, `checkbox`, `frame`, `password`, `radio`, `reset`, `select`, `submit`, `text`, `textarea`, `window`. See `value` PROPERTY.

options   An array of `option` objects created by a `select` form element. The first option's index is zero, the second is 1, and so on.

See `select` OBJECT.

parent   Refers to the calling document in the current frame created by a `<frameset>` tag. Using `parent` allows access to other frames created by the same `<FRAMESET>` tag. For example, two frames invoked are called index and contents. The index frame can write to the contents frame using the syntax:

```
parent.contents.document.write("Kilroy was here.")
```

Property of `frame` and `window`.

pathname   Returns the path portion from a URL. Although the `pathname` can be changed at any time, it is always safer to change the entire URL at once using the `href` property.

Property of `link` and `location`. See PROPERTIES `hash`, `host`, `hostname`, `href`, `port`, `protocol`, `search`.

PI   Returns the value of pi (approximately 3.1415927). This is the ratio of the circumference of a circle to its diameter.

Property of `Math`. See PROPERTIES `E`, `LN2`, `LN10`, `LOG2E`, `LOG10E`, `SQRT1_2`, `SQRT2`.

port   Returns the port number of a URL address, which is a substring of the `host` property in `href`.

Property of `link` and `location`. See PROPERTIES `hash`, `host`, `hostname`, `href`, `pathname`, `protocol`, `search`.

protocol   Returns a string with the initial portion of the URL, up to and including the colon, which indicates the access method (`http`, `ftp`, `mailto`, and so on).

Property of `link` and `location`.

See PROPERTIES `hash`, `host`, `hostname`, `href`, `pathname`, `port`, `search`.

referrer   Returns a read-only URL of the document that called the current document. In conjunction with a CGI script, it can be used to keep track of how users are linked to a page.

```
document.write("You came here from a page at " + document.referrer)
```

Property of `document`.

search   Returns a string containing any query information appended to a URL.

Property of `link` and `location`. See PROPERTIES `hash`, `host`, `hostname`, `href`, `pathname`, `port`, `protocol`.

App
D

selected   Returns a Boolean value (`true` or `false`) indicating the current state of an option in a `select` object. The selected property can be changed at any time, and the display will immediately update to reflect the new value. The selected property is useful for `select` elements that are created by using the `multiple` attribute. Using this property, you can view or change the value of any element in an `options` array without changing the value of any other element in the array.

Property of `options`. See PROPERTIES `defaultSelected`, `index`, `selectedIndex`.

selectedIndex   Returns an integer specifying the index of a selected item. The `selectedIndex` property is useful for `select` elements that are created without using the `multiple` attribute. If `selectedIndex` is evaluated when the `multiple` option is selected, the property returns the index of the first option only. Setting the property clears any other options that are selected in the element.

Property of `select`, `options`. See PROPERTIES `defaultSelected`, `index`, `selected`.

self   Refers to the current window or form, and is useful for removing ambiguity when dealing with `window` and `form` properties with the same name.

Property of `frame` and `window`. See `window` PROPERTY.

SQRT1_2   The square root of 1/2, also expressed as the inverse of the square root of 2 (approximately 0.707).

Property of `Math`. See PROPERTIES `E`, `LN2`, `LN10`, `LOG2E`, `LOG10E`, `PI`, `SQRT2`.

SQRT2   The square root of 2 (approximately 1.414).

Property of `Math`. See properties `E`, `LN2`, `LN10`, `LOG2E`, `LOG10E`, `PI`, `SQRT1_2`.

status   Specifies a priority or transient message to display in the status bar at the bottom of the window, usually triggered by a `mouseOver` event from an `anchor`. To display when the mouse pointer is placed over a link, the usage is:

```
<A anchor definition onMouseOver="window.dstatus='Your message.'; return
true">link</A>
```

Note the use of nested quotes and the required `return true` required for operation.

Property of `window`. See `defaultStatus` PROPERTY.

target   A string specifying the name of a window for responses to be posted to after a form is submitted. For a link, `target` returns a string specifying the name of the window that displays the content of a selected hypertext link.

```
homePage.target = "http://www.wossamatta.com/"
```

A literal must be used to set the `target` property. JavaScript expressions and variables are invalid entries.

Property of `form`, `link`, `location`. See PROPERTIES `action`, `encoding`, `method`.

text Returns the value of text following the `<option>` tag in a `select` object. It can also be used to change the value of the option, with an important limitation: while the value is changed, its appearance on screen is not.

Property of `options`.

title Returns the read-only value set within HTML `<title>` tags. If a document doesn't include a title, the value is `null`.

Property of `document`.

top The topmost window, called an ancestor or Web browser window, that contains `frames` or nested `framesets`.

Property of `window`.

userAgent Header sent as part of HTTP protocol from client to server to identify the type of client. The syntax of the returned value is the same as `appVersion`.

Property of `navigator`. See PROPERTIES `appName`, `appVersion`, `appCodeName`.

value The value of an object depends on the type of object it is applied to.

Object	Value Attribute
button, reset, submit	Value attribute that appears on screen, not the button name
checkbox	On if item is selected, off if not
radio	String reflection of value
hidden, text, textarea	Contents of the field
select	Reflection of option value
password	Return a valid default value, but an encrypted version if modified by the user

Changing the value of a `text` or `textarea` object results in an immediate update to the screen. All other `form` objects are not graphically updated when changed.

Property of `button`, `checkbox`, `hidden`, `options`, `password`, `radio`, `reset`, `submit`, `text`, `textarea`.

For `password`, `text`, and `textarea`, see `defaultValue` PROPERTY.

For `button`, `reset`, and `submit`, see `name` PROPERTY.

For `options`, see PROPERTIES `defaultSelected`, `selected`, `selectedIndex`, `text`.

For `checkbox` and `radio`, see PROPERTIES `checked` and `defaultChecked`.

App
D

vlinkColor   Returns or sets the color of visited links using hexadecimal RGB triplets or a string literal. The property cannot be set after the document has been formatted. To override the browser defaults, color settings are used with the `onLoad` event handler in the `<BODY>` tag:

```
<BODY onLoad="document.vlinkColor='aliceblue'">
```

Property of `document`. See PROPERTIES `alinkColor`, `bgColor`, `fgColor`, `linkColor`.

window   A synonym for the current window to remove ambiguity between a `window` and `form` object of the same name. While it also applies to the current frame, it is less ambiguous to use the `self` property.

Property of `frame` and `window`. See `self` PROPERTY.

Methods

Methods are functions and procedures used to perform an operation on an object, variable, or constant. With the exception of built-in functions, methods must be used with an object:

```
object.method()
```

Even if the method does not require any arguments, the parentheses are still required.

The object which utilizes the method is listed after the definition as "Method of *object*," followed by any cross-references to other methods. Standalone functions that are not used with objects are indicated with an asterisk (*).

abs   Returns the absolute (unsigned) value of its argument.

```
document.write(Math.abs(-10));
document.write(Math.abs(12))
```

These examples return 10 and 12, respectively.

Method of `Math`.

acos   Returns the arc cosine (from zero to pi radians) of its argument. The argument should be a number between –1 and 1. If the value is outside the valid range, a zero is returned.

Method of `Math`. See METHODS `asin`, `atan`, `cos`, `sin`, `tan`.

alert   Displays a JavaScript Alert dialog box with an OK button and a user-defined message. Before the user can continue, they must press the OK button.

Method of `window`. See METHODS `confirm` and `prompt`.

anchor   Used with `write` or `writeln` methods, anchor creates and displays an HTML hypertext target. The syntax is:

```
textString.anchor(anchorName)
```

where `textString` is what the user sees, and `anchorName` is equivalent to the `name` attribute of an HTML `<anchor>` tag.

Method of `string`. See `link` METHOD.

asin Returns the arc sine (between –pi/2 and pi/2 radians) of a number between –1 and 1. If the number is outside the range, a zero is returned.

Method of `Math`. See METHODS `acos`, `atan`, `cos`, `sin`, `tan`.

atan Returns the arc tangent (between –pi/2 and pi/2 radians) of a number between –1 and 1. If the number is outside the range, a zero is returned.

Method of `Math`. See METHODS `acos`, `asin`, `cos`, `sin`, `tan`.

back Recalls the previous URL from the history list. This method is the same as `history.go(-1)`.

Method of `history`. See METHODS `forward` and `go`.

big Formats a string object as a big font by encasing it with HTML `<big>` tags. Both of the following examples result in the same output—displaying the message "Welcome to my home page" in a big font:

```
var welcomeMessage = "Welcome to my home page."
document.write(welcomeMessage.big())
```

```
<BIG> Welcome to my home page.</BIG>
```

Method of `string`. See METHODS `fontsize`, `small`.

blink Formats a `string` object as a blinking line by encasing it with HTML `<blink>` tags. Both of the following examples produce a flashing line that says `Notice`:

```
var attentionMessage = "Notice"
document.write(attentionMessage.blink())
```

```
<BLINK>Notice</BLINK>
```

Method of `string`. See METHODS `bold`, `italics`, `strike`.

blur Removes focus from the specified `form` element. For example, the following line removes focus from `feedback`:

```
feedback.blur()
```

assuming that `feedback` is defined as:

```
<input type="text" name="feedback">
```

Method of `password`, `select`, `text`, `textarea`. See METHODS `focus` and `select`.

bold Formats a `string` object in bold text by encasing it with HTML `<b>` tags.

Method of `string`. See METHODS `blink`, `italics`, `strike`.

ceil Returns the smallest integer greater than, or equal to, its argument. For example:

```
Math.ceil(1.01)
```

returns a 2.

Method of Math. See floor METHOD.

charAt   Returns the character from a string at the specified index. The first character is at position zero and the last at length –1.

```
var userName = "Bobba Louie"
document.write(userName.charAt(4)
```

returns an a.

Method of string. See METHODS indexOf and lastIndexOf.

clear   Clears the contents of a window, regardless of how the window was filled.

Method of document. See METHODS close, open, write, writeln.

clearTimeout   Cancels a timeout set with the setTimeout method. A timeout is set using a unique timeout ID, which must be used to clear it:

```
clearTimeout(waitTime)
```

Method of frame and window. See setTimeout METHOD.

click   Simulates a mouse click on the calling form element with the effect dependent on the type of element.

Form Element	Action
Button, Reset, and submit	Same as clicking button.
Radio	Selects option button.
Checkbox	Marks check box and sets value to on.

Method of button, checkbox, radio, reset, submit.

close   For a document object, closes the current stream of output and forces its display. It also stops the browser winsock animation and displays Document: Done in the status bar.

For a window object, closes the current window. As with all window commands, the window object is assumed. For example:

```
window.close()
close()
self.close()
```

all close the current window.

Method of document and window. See METHODS clear, open, write, writeln.

confirm   Displays a JavaScript confirmation dialog box with a message and buttons for OK and Cancel. Confirm returns a true if the user selects OK and false for Cancel. The following example closes and loads a new window if the user presses OK:

```
if (confirm("Are you sure you want to enter.") {
    tourWindow = window.open("http:\\www.haunted.com\","hauntedhouse")
}
```

Method of `window`. See METHODS `alert` and `prompt`.

cos   Returns the cosine of the argument. The angle's size must be expressed in radians.

Method of `Math`. See METHODS `acos`, `asin`, `atan`, `sin`, `tan`.

escape*   Returns ASCII code of its argument based on the ISO Latin-1 character set in the form %xx, where xx is the ASCII code. It is not associated with any other object, but is actually part of the JavaScript language.

See `unescape` METHOD.

eval*   This built-in function takes a string or numeric expression as its argument. If a string, it attempts to convert it to a numeric expression. `Eval` then evaluates the expression and returns the value.

```
var x = 10
var y = 20
document.write(eval("x + y"))
```

This method can also be used to perform JavaScript commands included as part of a string.

```
var doThis = "if (x==10) { alert("Your maximum has been reached") }
function checkMax () {
    x++;
    eval(doThis)
}
```

This can be useful when converting a date from a form (always a string) into a numerical expression or number.

exp   Returns `e` (Euler's constant) to the power of the argument to compute a natural logarithm.

Method of `Math`. See METHODS `log` and `pow`.

Formats the calling string into a fixed-pitch font by encasing it in HTML `<tt>` tags.

Method of `string`.

floor   Returns the integer less than, or equal to, its argument. For example:

```
Math.floor(2.99)
```

returns a 2.

Method of `Math`. See `ceil` METHOD.

focus   Navigates to a specific `form` element and gives it focus. From that point, a value can be entered by JavaScript commands or the user can complete the entry.

Method of `password`, `select`, `text`, `textarea`. See METHODS `blur` and `select`.

App

D

fontcolor   Formats the string object to a specific color expressed as a hexadecimal RGB triplet or a string literal, similar to using `<font color=color>`.

Method of `string`.

fontsize   Formats the string object to a specific font size: one of the seven defined sizes using an integer through the `<fontsize=size>` tag. If a string is passed, the size is changed relative to the value set in the `<basefont>` tag.

Method of `string`. See METHODS `big` and `small`.

forward   Loads the next document on the URL history list. This method is the same as `history.go(1)`.

Method of `history`. See methods `back` and `go`.

getDate   Returns the day of the month as an integer between 1 and 31.

Method of `Date`.

See `setDate` method.

getDay   Returns the day of the week as an integer from zero (Sunday) to six (Saturday). There is not a corresponding `setDay` command because the day is automatically computed when the date value is assigned.

Method of `Date`.

getHours   Returns the hour of the day in 24-hour format, from zero (midnight) to 23 (11 PM).

Method of `Date`. See `setHours` METHOD.

getMinutes   Returns the minutes with an integer from zero to 59.

Method of `Date`. See `setMinutes` METHOD.

getMonth   Returns the month of the year as an integer between zero (January) and 11 (December).

Method of `Date`. See `setMonth` METHOD.

getSeconds   Returns the seconds in an integer from zero to 59.

Method of `Date`. See `setSeconds` METHOD.

getTime   Returns an integer representing the current value of the date object. The value is the number of milliseconds since midnight, January 1, 1970. This value can be used to compare the length of time between two date values.

For functions involving computation of dates, it is useful to define variables defining the minutes, hours, and days in milliseconds:

```
var dayMillisec = 1000 * 60 * 60 * 24 //1,000 milliseconds x 60 sec x 60 min x 24 hrs
```

```
var hourMillisec = 1000 * 60 * 60 //1,000 milliseconds x 60 sec x 60 min
var minuteMillisec = 1000 * 60 //1,000 milliseconds x 60 sec
```

Method of Date. See setTime METHOD.

getTimezoneOffset   Returns the difference in minutes between the client machine and Greenwich mean time. This value is a constant except for daylight savings time.

Method of Date.

getYear   Returns the year of the date object minus 1900. For example, 1996 is returned as 96.

Method of Date. See setYear METHOD.

go   Loads a document specified in the history list by its URL or relative to the current position on the list. If the URL is incomplete, the closest match is used. The search is not case sensitive.

Method of history. See METHODS back and forward.

indexOf   Returns the location of a specific character or string, starting the search from a specific location. The first character of the string is specified as zero and the last is the string's length-1. The syntax is:

```
stringName.indexOf([character¦string], [startingPoint])
```

The startingPoint is zero by default.

Method of string. See METHODS charAt and lastIndexof.

isNaN*   For UNIX platforms only, this standalone function returns true if the argument is not a number. On all platforms except Windows, the parseFloat and parseInt return NaN when the argument is not a number.

See METHODS parseFloat and parseInt.

italics   Formats a string object into italics by encasing it an HTML <I> tag.

Method of string. See METHODS blink, bold, strike.

lastIndexOf   Returns the index of a character or string in a string object by looking backwards from the end of the string or a user-specified index.

Method of string. See METHODS charAt and indexOf.

link   Creates a hypertext link to another URL by defining the <href> attribute and the text representing the link to the user.

Method of string. See anchor METHOD.

log   Returns the natural logarithm (base e) of a positive numeric expression greater than zero. An out-of-range number always returns $-1.797693134862316e+308$.

Method of Math. See METHODS exp and pow.

App

D

max   Returns the greater of its two arguments. For example:

```
Math.max(1,100)
```

returns `100`.

Method of `Math`. See `min` METHOD.

min   Returns the lesser of its two arguments.

Method of `Math`. See `max` METHOD.

open   For a document, opens a stream to collect the output of `write` or `writeln` methods. If a document already exists in the target window, then the open method clears it. The stream is ended by using the `document.close()` method.

For a window, it opens a new browser window in a similar fashion to choosing File, New Web Browser from the Netscape menu. Using the URL argument, it loads a document into the new window; otherwise, the new window is blank. When used as part of an event handler, the form must include the window object; otherwise, the document is assumed. Window features are defined by a comma-separated list of options with `=1` or `=yes` to enable and `=0` or `=no` to disable. Window features include toolbar, location, directories, status, menubar, scrollbars, resizable, copyhistory, width and height.

Method of `document` and `window`. See METHODS `clear`, `close`, `write`, `writeln`.

parse   Takes a date string, such as `Jan 11, 1996`, and returns the number of milliseconds since midnight, Jan. 1, 1970. This function can be used to set date values based on string values. When passed a string with a time, it returns the time value.

Because `parse` is a static function of Date, it is always used as `Date.parse()` rather than as a method of a created `date` object.

Method of `Date`. See `UTC` METHOD.

parseFloat*   Parses a string argument and returns a floating-point number if the first character is a plus sign, minus sign, decimal point, exponent, or a numeral. If it encounters a character other than one of the valid choices after that point, it returns the value up to that location and ignores all succeeding characters. If the first character is not a valid character, `parseFloat` returns one of two values based on the platform:

Windows	`0`
NonWindows	`NaN`

See `isNaN` METHOD.

parseInt*   Parses a `string` argument and returns an integer based on a specified radix or base. A radix of 10 converts the value to a decimal, while eight converts to octal, and 16 to hexadecimal. Values greater than 10 for bases above 10 are represented with letters (A through F) in place of numbers.

Floating-point values are converted to integers. The rules for evaluating the string are identical to `parseFloat`.

See `isNaN` and `parseFloat` METHODS.

pow Returns a base raised to an exponent.

Method of `Math`. See `exp` and `log` METHODS.

prompt Displays a prompt dialog box that accepts user input. If an initial value is not specified for `inputDefault`, the dialog box displays the value `<undefined>`.

Method of `window`. See `alert` and `confirm` METHODS.

random On UNIX machines only, returns a pseudo-random number between zero and 1.

Method of `Math`.

round Returns the value of a floating-point argument rounded to the next highest integer if the decimal portion is greater than, or equal to, .5, or the next lowest integer is less than .5.

Method of `Math`.

select Selects the input area of a specified form element. Used in conjunction with the `focus` method, JavaScript can highlight a field and position the cursor for user input.

Method of `password`, `text`, `textarea`. See METHODS `blur` and `focus`.

setDate Sets the day of the month.

Method of `Date`. See `getDate` METHOD.

setHours Sets the hour for the current time.

Method of `Date`. See `getHours` METHOD.

setMinutes Sets the minutes for the current time.

Method of `Date`. See `getMinutes` METHOD.

setMonth Sets the month with an integer from zero (January) to 11 (December).

Method of `Date`. See `getMonth` METHOD.

setSeconds Sets the seconds for the current time.

Method of `Date`. See `getSeconds` METHOD.

setTime Sets the value of a `date` object.

Method of `Date`. See `getTime` METHOD.

setTimeout Evaluates an expression after a specified amount of time, expressed in milliseconds. This is not repeated indefinitely. For example, setting a timeout to three seconds will evaluate the expression once after three seconds—not every three seconds. To call `setTimeout` recursively, reset the timeout as part of the function invoked by the method. Calling the function `startclock` in the following example sets a loop in motion that clears the timeout, displays the current time, and sets the timeout to redisplay the time in one second.

```
var timerID = null;
var timerRunning = false;
function stopclock () {
  if(timerRunning) cleartimeout(timerID);
  timerRunning=false;
}
function startclock () {
  stopclock();
  showtime();
}
function showtime () {
  var now = new Date();
  ...
  document.clock.face.value =   timeValue;
  timerID = setTimeout("showtime()",1000);
  timerRunning = true;
}
```

Method of `window`. See `clearTimeout` METHOD.

setYear   Sets the year in the current date by using an integer representing the year minus 1900.

Method of `Date`. See `getYear` METHOD.

sin   Returns the sine of an argument. The argument is the size of an angle expressed in radians, and the returned value is from –1 to 1.

Method of `Math`. See METHODS `acos`, `asin`, `atan`, `cos`, `tan`.

small   Formats a `string` object into a small font by using the HTML `<small>` tags.

Method of `string`. See METHODS `big` and `fontsize`.

sqrt   Returns the square root of a positive numeric expression. If the argument's value is outside the range, the returned value is zero.

strike   Formats a string object as strikeout text by using the HTML `<strike>` tags.

Method of `string`. See METHODS `blink`, `bold`, `italics`.

sub   Formats a string object into subscript text by using the HTML `<sub>` tags.

Method of `string`. See `sup` METHOD.

submit   Performs the same action as clicking a submit button.

Method of `form`. See `submit` OBJECT; see `onSubmit` EVENT HANDLER.

substring   Returns a subset of a string object based on two indexes. If the indexes are equal, an empty string is returned. Regardless of order, the substring is built from the smallest index to the largest.

Method of `string`.

sup   Formats a string object into superscript text by using the HTML `<sup>` tags.

Method of `string`. See `sub` METHOD.

tan   Returns the tangent of an argument. The argument is the size of an angle expressed in radians.

Method of `Math`. See METHODS `acos`, `asin`, `atan`, `cos`, `sin`.

toGMTString   Converts a date object to a string by using Internet Greenwich mean time (GMT) conventions. For example, if `today` is a `date` object:

```
today.toGMTString()
```

then the string `Mon, 18 Dec 1995 17:28:35 GMT` is returned. Actual formatting may vary from platform to platform. The time and date is based on the client machine.

Method of `Date`. See `toLocaleString` METHOD.

toLocaleString   Converts a `date` object to a string by using the local conventions, such as *mm / dd/yy hh:mm:ss*.

Method of `Date`. See `toGMTString` METHOD.

toLowerCase   Converts all characters in a string to lowercase.

Method of `string`. See `toUpperCase` METHOD.

toString   Converts a `date` or `location` object to a string.

Method of `Date`, `location`.

toUpperCase   Converts all characters in a string to uppercase.

Method of `string`.

See `toLowerCase` method.

unEscape*   Returns a character based on its ASCII value expressed as a string in the format %xxx where xxx is a decimal number between zero and 255, or 0x0 to 0xFF in hex.

See `escape` METHOD.

UTC   Returns the number of milliseconds for a date in Universal Coordinated Time (UTC) since midnight, January 1, 1970.

UTC is a constant, and is always used as `Date.UTC()`, not with a created `date` object.

Method of `Date`. See `parse` METHOD.

write   Writes one or more lines to a document window, and can include HTML tags and JavaScript expressions, including numeric, string, and logical values. The `write` method does not add a new line (`<br>` or `/n`) character to the end of the output. If called from an event handler, the current document is cleared if a new window is not created for the output.

Method of `document`. See METHODS `close`, `clear`, `open`, `writeln`.

writeln   Writes one or more lines to a document window followed by a new line character, and can include HTML tags and JavaScript expressions, including numeric, string, and logical values. If called from an event handler, the current document is cleared if a new window is not created for the output.

Method of `document`. See methods `close`, `clear`, `open`, `write`.

Event Handlers

Event handlers are where JavaScript gets its power. By looking for specific user actions, JavaScript can confirm or act on input immediately, without waiting for server introduction, since user activity within an HTML page is limited to mouse movement and input on form elements.

onBlur   Blurs occur when a `select`, `text` or `textarea` field on a form loses focus.

Event handler of `select`, `text`, `textarea`. See EVENT HANDLERS `onChange` and `onFocus`.

onChange   A change event happens when a `select`, `text`, or `textarea` element on a form is modified before losing focus.

Event handler of `select`, `text`, `textarea`. See EVENT HANDLERS `onBlur`, `onFocus`.

onClick   Occurs when an object, such as a button or check box, is clicked.

Event handler of `button`, `checkbox`, `radio`, `link`, `reset`, `submit`.

onFocus   A form element receives focus by tabbing to or clicking the input area with the mouse. Selecting within a field results in a `select` event.

Event handler of `select`, `text`, `textarea`. See EVENT HANDLERS `onBlur` and `onChange`.

onLoad   A load event is created when Navigator finishes loading a window or all frames within a `<frameset>` tag.

Event handler of `window`. See `onUnload` EVENT HANDLER.

onMouseOver   Occurs when the mouse pointer is placed over a `link` object. To function with the `status` or `defaultStatus` properties, the event handler must return `true`.

Event handler of `link`.

onSelect   A select event is triggered by selecting some or all of the text in a `text` or `textarea` field.

Event handler of `text`, `textarea`.

onSubmit   Triggered by the user submitting a form. The event handler must return `true` to allow the form to be submitted to the server. Conversely, it returns `false` to block the form's submission.

Event handler of `form`. See `submit` OBJECT and METHOD.

onUnload   Occurs when exiting a document. For proper operation, place the `onUnload` handler in the `<body>` or `<frameset>` tags.

Event handler of `window`. See `onLoad` EVENT HANDLER.

Last Words

On June 26, 1997, a language standard for Internet scripting was announced by ECMA, "an international, Europe-based industry association founded in 1961 and dedicated to the standardization of information and communication systems" (from the ECMA site, which seemed reluctant to divulge just what ECMA stands for). The standard will be known as ECMA-262, or ECMA Script. ECMA Script was derived from Netscape's JavaScript specification.

JavaScript is on its way to standardization. ●

App

D

What's on the CD-ROM

The CD-ROM included with this book is filled with valuable programs, utilities, and other information. This appendix gives you a brief overview of the contents of the CD. For a more detailed look at any of these parts, open the "loadme.htm" file in your browser ("file>open file" from your browser menu).The navigation bar at the top will contain the following categories: ■

Code

The source code listings and other significant portions of code used in the book are included on the CD-ROM. You can access this content from the /code directory.

Docs

Important documentation relating to Web page construction is listed here. The following documents are included:

- Admin Guide to Cracking 101
- GIF 87a Specification
- GIF 89a Specification
- HTML 2.0 Specification
- HTML 3.0 Specification
- HTML 3.2 Reference Specification
- VRML Specification
- Latest HTML information from the World Wide Web Consortium

Que Books

The CD contains nine complete books from Que Publishing in easy-to-follow HTML format. After selecting "Que Books" from the navigation bar, you will see the covers for the following books. Just click the cover to access the wealth of information inside.

- *Special Edition Using VBScript*
- *Working With Active Server Pages*
- *Special Edition Using HTML 4*
- *Internet Explorer Plug-In and ActiveX Companion*
- *Special Edition Using JScript*
- *Special Edition Using Microsoft Visual InterDev*
- *Wild Web Graphics with Microsoft Image Composer*
- *Special Edition Using JavaScript*
- *Special Edition Using Java 1.1*

Software

You will find plenty of helpful software on the CD to aid with all aspects of developing and implementing Web pages. From the "Software" button on the navigation bar, the following software categories can be accessed:

- HTML
- Java
- VRML
- Security
- Browsers
- Multimedia
- Compression
- Web Tools

Plus, there is an additional section containing over 30 valuable programs from Que's *Microsoft FrontPage Web Publishing Resource Kit.*

Resources

In addition to software, the CD provides many useful resources to help construct the ultimate Web page. This section provides ready-to-use buttons, bullets, graphics, animations, sounds and much more. Lists of online resources are also provided to give you access to the most current developments in Web page construction and management. ●

App

E

Index

Complete and Return This Card
for a *FREE* Computer Book Catalog

Thank you for purchasing this book! You have purchased a superior computer book written expressly for your needs. To continue to provide the kind of up-to-date, pertinent coverage you've come to expect from us, we need to hear from you. Please take a minute to complete and return this self-addressed, postage-paid form. In return, we'll send you a free catalog of all our computer books on topics ranging from word processing to programming and the Internet.

r. ☐   Mrs. ☐   Ms. ☐   Dr. ☐

me (first) ☐☐☐☐☐☐☐☐☐   (M.I.) ☐   (last) ☐☐☐☐☐☐☐☐☐☐☐☐☐☐☐☐☐☐

dress ☐☐☐☐☐☐☐☐☐☐☐☐☐☐☐☐☐☐☐☐☐☐☐☐☐☐☐☐☐☐☐☐☐

☐☐☐☐☐☐☐☐☐☐☐☐☐☐☐☐☐☐☐☐☐☐☐☐☐☐☐☐☐☐☐☐☐

ty ☐☐☐☐☐☐☐☐☐☐☐☐☐☐☐☐   State ☐☐   Zip ☐☐☐☐☐ ☐☐☐☐

one ☐☐☐ ☐☐☐ ☐☐☐☐   Fax ☐☐☐ ☐☐☐ ☐☐☐☐

mpany Name ☐☐☐☐☐☐☐☐☐☐☐☐☐☐☐☐☐☐☐☐☐☐☐☐☐☐☐☐☐☐☐☐☐

mail address ☐☐☐☐☐☐☐☐☐☐☐☐☐☐☐☐☐☐☐☐☐☐☐☐☐☐☐☐☐☐☐☐☐

Please check at least three (3) influencing factors for purchasing this book.

ont or back cover information on book .... ☐
ecial approach to the content .... ☐
mpleteness of content .... ☐
thor's reputation .... ☐
blisher's reputation .... ☐
ok cover design or layout .... ☐
dex or table of contents of book .... ☐
ce of book .... ☐
ecial effects, graphics, illustrations .... ☐
her (Please specify): _____ ☐

How did you first learn about this book?

w in Macmillan Computer Publishing catalog .... ☐
commended by store personnel .... ☐
w the book on bookshelf at store .... ☐
commended by a friend .... ☐
ceived advertisement in the mail .... ☐
w an advertisement in: _____ ☐
ad book review in: _____ ☐
her (Please specify): _____ ☐

How many computer books have you purchased in the last six months?

is book only .... ☐   3 to 5 books .... ☐
ooks .... ☐   More than 5 .... ☐

4. Where did you purchase this book?

Bookstore .... ☐
Computer Store .... ☐
Consumer Electronics Store .... ☐
Department Store .... ☐
Office Club .... ☐
Warehouse Club .... ☐
Mail Order .... ☐
Direct from Publisher .... ☐
Internet site .... ☐
Other (Please specify): _____ ☐

5. How long have you been using a computer?

☐ Less than 6 months   ☐ 6 months to a year
☐ 1 to 3 years   ☐ More than 3 years

6. What is your level of experience with personal computers and with the subject of this book?

	With PCs	With subject of book
New	☐	☐
Casual	☐	☐
Accomplished	☐	☐
Expert	☐	☐

Source Code ISBN: 0-7897-1343-8

7. Which of the following best describes your job title?

Administrative Assistant ☐
Coordinator ☐
Manager/Supervisor ☐
Director ☐
Vice President ☐
President/CEO/COO ☐
Lawyer/Doctor/Medical Professional ☐
Teacher/Educator/Trainer ☐
Engineer/Technician ☐
Consultant ☐
Not employed/Student/Retired ☐
Other (Please specify): _____ ☐

8. Which of the following best describes the area of the company your job title falls under?

Accounting ☐
Engineering ☐
Manufacturing ☐
Operations ☐
Marketing ☐
Sales ☐
Other (Please specify): _____ ☐

9. What is your age?

Under 20 ☐
21-29 ☐
30-39 ☐
40-49 ☐
50-59 ☐
60-over ☐

10. Are you:

Male ☐
Female ☐

11. Which computer publications do you read regularly? (Please list)

_____
_____
_____
_____
_____
_____
_____
_____
_____

Comments: _____
_____
_____

Fold here and scotch-tape to ma

Check out Que® Books on the World Wide Web
http://www.quecorp.com

As the biggest software release in computer history, Windows 95 continues to redefine the computer industry. Click here for the latest info on our Windows 95 books

Make computing quick and easy with these products designed exclusively for new and casual users

Examine the latest releases in word processing, spreadsheets, operating systems, and suites

The Internet, The World Wide Web, CompuServe®, America Online®, Prodigy®—it's a world of ever-changing information. Don't get left behind!

Find out about new additions to our site, new bestsellers, and hot topics

In-depth information on high-end topics: find the best reference books for databases, programming, networking, and client/server technologies

A recent addition to Que, Ziff-Davis Press publishes the highly successful *How It Works* and *How to Use* series of books, as well as *PC Learning Labs Teaches* and *PC Magazine* series of book/disc packages

Stay on the cutting edge of Macintosh® technologies and visual communications

Find out which titles are making headlines

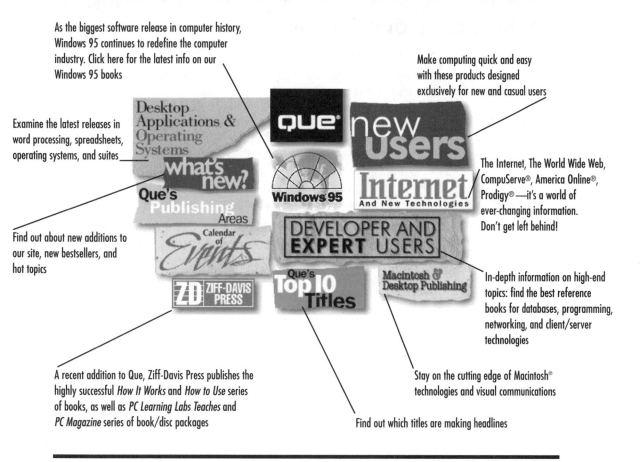

With six separate publishing groups, Que develops products for many specific market segments and areas of computer technology. Explore our Web Site and you'll find information on best-selling titles, newly published titles, upcoming products, authors, and much more.

- Stay informed on the latest industry trends and products available
- Visit our online bookstore for the latest information and editions
- Download software from Que's library of the best shareware and freeware

Before using any of the software on this disc, you need to install the software you plan to use. See Appendix E, "What's on the CD-ROM?" for directions. If you have problems with this CD-ROM, please contact Macmillan Technical Support at (317) 581-3833. We can be reached by e-mail at **support@mcp.com**.

Read This Before Opening Software

By opening this package, you are agreeing to be bound by the following:

This software is copyrighted and all rights are reserved by the publisher and its licensers. You are licensed to use this software on a single computer. You may copy the software for backup or archival purposes only. Making copies of the software for any other purpose is a violation of United States copyright laws. THIS SOFTWARE IS SOLD AS IS, WITHOUT WARRANTY OF ANY KIND, EITHER EXPRESSED OR IMPLIED, INCLUDING BUT NOT LIMITED TO THE IMPLIED WARRANTIES OF MERCHANTABILITY AND FITNESS FOR A PARTICULAR PURPOSE. Neither the publisher nor its dealers and distributors nor its licensers assume any liability for any alleged or actual damages arising from the use of this software. (Some states do not allow exclusion of implied warranties, so the exclusion may not apply to you.)

The entire contents of this disc and the compilation of the software are copyrighted and protected by United States copyright laws. The individual programs on the disc are copyrighted by the authors or owners of each program. Each program has its own use permissions and limitations. To use each program, you must follow the individual requirements and restrictions detailed for each. Do not use a program if you do not agree to follow its licensing agreement.